SHURLEY ENGLISH

HOMESCHOOL MADE EASY

LEVEL 5

Teacher's Edition

By

Brenda Shurley

Shurley Instructional Materials, Inc., Cabot, Arkansas

In Loving Memory of
Gilbert Edwin Strackbein
(Gil)

Dedication

This book is gratefully dedicated to my husband, Billy Shurley, for his love, support, and encouragement during this momentous undertaking.

Acknowledgements

We gratefully thank the following people for their help and support in the preparation of this book:

Rachel Andrews	Janice Graham	Shurley Method Staff
Ardean Coffman	Stacey See	Andrea Turkia
Keith Covington	Billy Ray Shurley, Jr.	Jani-Petri Rainer Turkia
Jamie Geneva	Kim Shurley	Bob Wilson, Ph.D

Homeschool Edition
ISBN 1-58561-032-1 (Level 5 Teacher's Manual)

TABLE OF CONTENTS

TABLE OF CONTENTS

Level 5 Homeschool Teacher's Manual

TABLE OF CONTENTS

TABLE OF CONTENTS

TABLE OF CONTENTS

CHAPTER 1   LESSON 1

New objectives: Long-term goals and short-term goals.

STUDY SKILLS TIME

TEACHING SCRIPT FOR SETTING GOALS

Good management skills come from good organizational skills, and organizational skills are the foundation for good study skills. You must learn to manage your time, your materials, and your work environment. Good study skills do not just happen. It takes time, determination, and the practice of certain guidelines to get organized. The study skills chapter will concentrate on the guidelines you need for success in developing good study habits. Follow them carefully until they become habits that will help you for a lifetime.

Everyone has the same 24 hours, but everyone does not use his/her 24 hours in the same way. In order to get the most for your time, it is important to set goals. Goals will keep you pointed in the direction you want to go, will focus your time, and will keep you on track. With a list of goals, you can check your progress. Long-term goals are what you want to accomplish in life, usually concentrating on your education and your career. Short-term goals will help you plan things to do this school year, and guidelines will give you specific things to do each day to help you achieve your goals. Listen to examples of long-term and short-term goals as I read them. (_Read the examples below or write them on the board._)

Examples of goals for a person interested in business:

Long-term Goals	**Short-term Goals**
1. Get an academic scholarship for college.	1. Make a daily schedule to plan my time.
2. Earn a degree in business management.	2. Make good grades in 5th grade.
3. Own and manage a restaurant chain.	3. Set aside at least 1 hour per night for study time.
	4. Earn spending money by doing odd jobs.
	5. Spend 30 minutes per day studying concepts of successful business management.

Examples of goals for a person interested in sports:

Long-term goals	**Short-term Goals**
1. Get a track and field scholarship for college.	1. Make a daily schedule to plan my time.
2. Earn a degree in physical education.	2. Make good grades in 5th grade.
3. Be a track and field coach in a school.	3. Set aside at least 1 hour per night for study time.
	4. Earn spending money by helping at a parks and recreation center.
	5. Spend 30 minutes per day at home practicing track and field skills.

Notice that getting organized and setting aside study time are always important short-term goals because they help you achieve your other goals. You will now write down your own long-term and short-term goals. Write two or three long-term goals and four or five short-term goals. You can add more as you think of them. (_Give students time to write down their long-term and short-term goals. You may want to discuss what kind of goals were written. Have students make English folders and put their goals in the folders._)

(End of lesson.)

CHAPTER 1   LESSON 2

New objectives: Beginning setup plan for homeschool.

STUDY SKILLS TIME

TEACHING SCRIPT FOR STUDY PLANS

We have learned that goals are important because they are a constant reminder of what you want in your future. If you make a commitment now to work toward your goals, you will be prepared in the future to take advantage of situations that will help you meet those goals. To make the most of your goals, you should take time to evaluate your goals at the end of every month to see if there are any adjustments you wish to make. Goals change as your needs change and as your abilities increase.

Remember, goals are your destination. A schedule is your road map. You may take a few detours, but you still know the direction you are headed in and how to get there. (*Have discussion time with your students at the beginning of each month to evaluate goals and schedules. Help students make any necessary adjustments. This is a worthwhile learning activity that is done nine times for the whole school year. It should be a meaningful experience for your students.*)

I will introduce the first step in good organization: learning how to make and follow a daily schedule, or routine. Turn to page 9 and look at Reference 1. Follow along as I read the guidelines that will help you establish a daily schedule to follow during study time and school time. (*These guidelines will help you get organized with the least amount of wasted effort.*) (*Read and discuss the plan reproduced below with your students.*)

Reference 1: Beginning Setup Plan for Homeschool

You should use this plan to keep things in order!

1. Have separate color-coded pocket folders for each subject.
2. Put unfinished work in the right-hand side and finished work in the left-hand side of each subject folder.
3. Put notes to study, graded tests, and study guides in the brads so you will have them to study for scheduled tests.
4. Have a paper folder to store extra clean sheets of paper. Keep it full at all times.
5. Have an assignment folder to be reviewed every day.

Things to keep in your assignment folder:

A. Keep a monthly calendar of assignments, test dates, report-due dates, project-due dates, extra activities, dates and times, review dates, etc.

B. Keep a grade sheet to record the grades received in each subject. (*You might also consider keeping your grades on the inside cover of each subject folder. You also have a student progress chart on pages 113-114 in your Student Book. However you keep your grades, just remember to record them accurately. Your grades are your business, so keep up with them! Grades help you know which areas need attention.*)

C. Make a list every day of the things you want to do so you can keep track of what you finish and what you do not finish. Move the unfinished items to your new list the next day. (*Yes, making this list takes time, but it's your road map to success. You will always know at a glance what you set out to accomplish and what still needs to be done.*)

6. Keep all necessary school supplies in a handy, heavy-duty Ziploc bag or a pencil bag.

CHAPTER 1 LESSON 3

New objectives: Skills (synonyms, antonyms), Six-Step Vocabulary Plan, and Vocabulary #1.

 VOCABULARY TIME

TEACHING SCRIPT FOR SYNONYMS AND ANTONYMS

Words are your tools for the future. Having a strong command of different vocabulary words can help you express exactly what is on your mind, and it will also help others to fully understand your thoughts and ideas. The ability to communicate is more effective when you do not use the same words over and over again. That is why it is necessary to learn a wide variety of vocabulary words. Think of it as having a large bank account from which you can draw just the right words to best express your thoughts.

Today, we will learn about synonyms and antonyms and how to mark them. Turn to page 9 in the Reference Section of your book and look at Reference 2. (*The first part of Reference 2 is reproduced below*.) This format will be used for identifying vocabulary words as synonyms or antonyms.

Reference 2: Synonyms, Antonyms, and Six-Step Vocabulary Plan
Part 1: Synonyms and Antonyms
Definitions: Synonyms are words that have similar or almost the same meanings.
Antonyms are words that have opposite meanings.
Directions: Identify each pair of words as synonyms or antonyms by putting parentheses ( ) around *syn* or *ant*.

1. brisk, swift	**(syn)** ant	2. dusk, nightfall	**(syn)** ant	3. gentle, callous	syn **(ant)**

Listen carefully as I read the definition for synonyms and antonyms. **Synonyms** are words that have similar or almost the same meanings. **Antonyms** are words that have opposite meanings. Look at the words *brisk* and *swift* beside number 1. What are the meanings of the words **brisk** and **swift?** (*Have students use the dictionary if they do not know the meanings of the words **brisk** and **swift**. Discuss the meanings of the two words*.) Do the words *brisk* and *swift* have almost the same meanings, or do they have opposite meanings? (*almost the same meanings*) Since they have almost the same meanings, are they synonyms or antonyms? (*synonyms*) How do we indicate that they are synonyms? (*By putting parentheses around the **syn**.*) (*For number 1, have students examine the parentheses around the **syn** in their practice box*.)

Look at number 2. Let's discuss the meanings of the words **dusk** and **nightfall**. (*Have students use the dictionary if they do not know the meanings of the words **dusk** and **nightfall**. Discuss the meanings of the two words*.) Do these words have almost the same meanings, or do they have opposite meanings? (*almost the same meanings*) Since they have almost the same meanings, are they synonyms or antonyms? (*synonyms*) How do we indicate that they are synonyms? (*By putting parentheses around the **syn**.*) (*For number 2, have students examine the parentheses around the **syn** in their practice box*.) Remember, synonyms may not have exact meanings, but their meanings will be similar. That is why they are called synonyms.

Look at number 3. Let's discuss the meanings of the words **gentle** and **callous**. (*Have students use the dictionary if they do not know the meanings of the words **gentle** and **callous**. Discuss the meanings of the two words*.) Do these words have almost the same meanings, or do they have opposite meanings? (*opposite meanings*) Since they have opposite meanings, are they synonyms or antonyms? (*antonyms*) How do we indicate that they are antonyms? (*By putting parentheses around the **ant**.*) (*For number 3, have students examine the parentheses around the **ant** in their practice box*.) Remember, antonyms have different meanings because they are opposite words. They do not mean the same. That is why they are called antonyms.

CHAPTER 1 LESSON 3 CONTINUED

If the thought of learning new words is overwhelming, think about what you have available. You have two valuable tools to help you in this task: the dictionary and thesaurus. The nice thing about these tools is that you alone, at any time, can use the dictionary or thesaurus (*for free*) to learn more words with which to express yourself.

Today, you will begin building your "bank account" of words. You will advance your vocabulary by learning synonyms and antonyms. Remember that synonyms are words that have almost the same meanings, and antonyms are words that have opposite meanings. Now that we have discussed several synonym and antonym words, I want you to name two pairs of words and identify one pair as synonyms and one pair as antonyms. (*Allow students to use a dictionary or a thesaurus to look up each pair of words if they need it. Check students' identification of the words for accuracy*).

Since we will be learning or reviewing synonyms and antonyms in almost every chapter, we will call this time **Vocabulary Time**. The purpose of Vocabulary Time is to learn new words; so, you will keep a Vocabulary notebook. During Vocabulary Time, you will always follow the Six-Step Vocabulary Plan. You will find this plan in the second part of Reference 2 on page 9 in your book. You will use this plan every time you enter vocabulary words in your notebook. (*Have students follow along as you read and discuss the vocabulary plan with them.*)

Reference 2: Synonyms, Antonyms, and Six-Step Vocabulary Plan, Continued
Part 2: Six-Step Vocabulary Plan
(1) Write a title for the vocabulary words in each chapter.   Example: **Chapter 1, Vocabulary Words** (2) Write each vocabulary word in your vocabulary notebook. (3) Look up each vocabulary word in a dictionary or thesaurus. (4) Write the meaning beside each vocabulary word. (5) Write a sentence that helps you remember how each vocabulary word is used. (6) Write and identify a pair of synonym words and a pair of antonym words.

You will have a list of synonyms and antonyms to define in two lessons of each chapter. These words are listed on pages 7-8 in the Reference Section of your workbook. (*Have students turn to page 7 and look at the eight words listed for Chapter 1.*)

I will tell you the words you will define during Vocabulary Time. Today, you will define and write sentences for four words. Any of the words you learn during Vocabulary Time could be in the Vocabulary section of your test. You may also use your vocabulary notebook to record any vocabulary word you wish to define for future reference.

 VOCABULARY TIME

Assign Chapter 1, Vocabulary Words **#1** on page 7 in the Reference Section for students to define in their Vocabulary notebooks. Tell students they are to use a dictionary or thesaurus to look up the meanings of the vocabulary words. After they write each word and its meaning, students are to write a sentence using the vocabulary word.

Chapter 1, Vocabulary Words #1
(construction, dilapidation, prodigy, genius)

(End of lesson.)

CHAPTER 1   LESSON 4
New objectives: Writing (journal) and Vocabulary #2.

 **WRITING TIME**

TEACHER INSTRUCTIONS

Have your students turn to Reference 3 on page 10 in the Reference Section of their books and follow along as you read the information on journal writing to them. (*The journal-writing information that you read to your class is reproduced below.*)

Reference 3: What is Journal Writing?

Journal Writing is a written record of your personal thoughts and feelings about things or people that are important to you. Recording your thoughts in a journal is a good way to remember how you felt about what was happening in your life at a particular time. You can record your dreams, memories, feelings, and experiences. You can ask questions and answer some of them. It is fun to go back later and read what you have written because it shows how you have changed in different areas of your life. A journal can also be an excellent place to look for future writing topics, creative stories, poems, etc. Writing in a journal is an easy and enjoyable way to practice your writing skills without worrying about a writing grade.

What do I write about?

Journals are personal, but sometimes it helps to have ideas to get you started. Remember, in a journal, you do not have to stick to one topic. Write about someone or something you like. Write about what you did last weekend or on vacation. Write about what you hope to do this week or on your next vacation. Write about home, school, friends, hobbies, special talents (yours or someone else's), present and future hopes and fears. Write about what is wrong in your world and what you would do to "fix" it. Write about the good things and the bad things in your world. If you think about a past event and want to write an opinion about it now, put it in your journal. If you want to give your opinion about a present or future event that could have an impact on your life or the way you see things, put it in your journal. If something bothers you, record it in your journal. If something interests you, record it. If you just want to record something that doesn't seem important at all, write it in your journal. After all, it is your journal!

How do I get started writing in my personal journal?

You need to put the day's date on the title line of your paper: **Month, Day, Year.** Skip the next line and begin your entry. You might write one or two sentences, a paragraph, a whole page, or several pages. Except for the journal date, no particular organizational style is required for journal writing. You decide how best to organize and express your thoughts. Feel free to include sketches, diagrams, lists, etc., if they will help you remember your thoughts about a topic or an event. You will also need a spiral notebook, a pen, a quiet place, and at least 5-10 minutes of uninterrupted writing time.

Note: Use a pen if possible. Pencils have lead points that break and erasers, both of which slow down your thoughts. Any
      drawings you might include do not have to be masterpieces—stick figures will do nicely.

CHAPTER 1 LESSON 4 CONTINUED

Use the review points below to review what your students should know about journal writing.

Review Points:

1. You may write personal thoughts, personal feelings, poems, stories, events, topics you might develop later, or keep a record of your activities at school, at home, and in your community in your journal.

2. Each journal entry needs the day's date on the title line of your paper.

3. You should write in your journals for at least 5 - 10 minutes. You may finish your entries during your free time if necessary.

4. Recording personal thoughts in a journal is a habit that becomes more important to you as you grow older. Develop a system to label and organize your personal journals by the year. All notebooks used for journal writing should have the appropriate year written on the cover for easy reference. Journals can also be typed on a personal computer.

 WRITING TIME

Have students write the title *My Personal Journal for the Year* ____ indicating the current year on the front covers of their journal notebooks or folders. Students should use their journal notebooks for their journal writing assignments.

Have students make the first entry in their journals at this time.

Teacher's Notes about Journal Writing: Journal writing helps students express themselves in written form, helps students feel comfortable with writing, and gives students an opportunity to practice what they are learning. Check to make sure students are making their entries. Make it a writing routine to have a five-to-ten minute journal-writing time whenever it is assigned. If students finish early, have them go back and read earlier entries. Keeping a journal should develop into a life-long habit.

 VOCABULARY TIME

Assign Chapter 1, Vocabulary Words **#2** on page 7 in the Reference Section for students to define in their Vocabulary notebooks. Tell students they are to use a dictionary or thesaurus to look up the meanings of the vocabulary words. After they write each word and its meaning, students are to write a sentence using the vocabulary word.

Chapter 1, Vocabulary Words #2
(audacious, timid, abolish, destroy)

(End of lesson.)

Level 5 Homeschool Teacher's Manual

CHAPTER 1   LESSON 5
New objectives: Test and Writing (revising, editing).

STUDY TIME

Have students study the vocabulary words in their vocabulary notebooks. Remind students that any vocabulary word in their notebook could be on their test.

TEST TIME

Have students turn to page 53 in the Practice Section of their book and find Chapter 1, Lesson 5, Practice. Tell them that grammar is not tested yet; so, they will have only the vocabulary words for their assignment. Go over the directions to make sure they understand what to do. Assign Chapter 1, Lesson 5, Practice. (*Chapter 1, Lesson 5, Practice key is given below.*)

Chapter 1, Lesson 5, Practice					
Exercise 1: Identify each pair of words as synonyms or antonyms by putting parentheses ( ) around *syn* or *ant*. For number 5, write two synonym words and identify them with *syn*. For number 6, write two antonym words and identify them with *ant*.					
1. prodigy, genius	**(syn)** ant	3. construction, dilapidation	syn **(ant)**	5.	*(Answers will vary.)*
2. timid, audacious	syn **(ant)**	4. destroy, abolish	**(syn)** ant	6.	*(Answers will vary.)*

CHECK TIME

After students have finished, check and discuss their Practice assignment. Make sure they understand why their answers are right or wrong. (*For total points, count each required answer as a point.*)

CHAPTER 1 LESSON 5 CONTINUED

 WRITING TIME

TEACHING SCRIPT FOR REVISING AND EDITING

Before you start your writing assignments in another chapter, there are a few basic things I want you to know. First, writing is a process. You usually do not have a finished product the first time you write. When you write, you start out by writing a rough draft. A rough draft is a rough copy of your writing. It is not a finished piece of writing. In fact, you do not have to worry about errors as you write your rough draft. It usually needs changing to make it better. Today, we will learn the different terminology used as you go through the process of changing your writing to make it better.

Listen to the words, **revise** and **edit**. Both revising and editing make your writing better. It's usually called revising when you find ways to make the content better. Look at Reference 4 on page 11 in your book. Let's read some of the things you need to know about revision. (*Read and discuss only the Revision Checklist on the next page.*)

After you have made revisions in your writing content, your next step is to check your paper for mistakes in spelling, grammar, usage, and punctuation. This is called editing. It begins with careful proofreading. Look at the second part of Reference 4. It is called a Beginning Editing Checklist because it only contains some of the first skills necessary for you to know as you edit.

The editing list will continue to grow as more skills are introduced. We will go through the skills listed under "More Editing Skills" in later chapters. (*Teaching scripts for these additional skills will also be given to the teacher in later chapters.*) Eventually, you will have a regular editing checklist that will have most of the skills added. We will discuss only the beginning editing skills to make sure you understand each of them at this point. (*Read and discuss the Beginning Editing Checklist on the next page.*)

We will now study four paragraphs. Look at the four paragraphs in Reference 5. (*Your copy of Reference 5 is located on page 10 of this chapter.*) Nothing has been done to the first paragraph. It is a rough draft. Notice that the second paragraph has been revised, and the third paragraph has been edited. (*Read and discuss the differences in the first three paragraphs.*) Once you have revised and edited your rough draft, you will make a final copy of your work. Look at the third checklist. It is called "Final Paper Checklist." This will tell you what to expect as you write your final paper. (*Read and discuss the Final Paper Checklist on the next page.*) The last paragraph has gone through the "Final Paper Checklist" and is ready for publishing.

Let's review the procedure you should use for each writing assignment. This procedure is called the "Writing Process Checklist." Look at the last section of Reference 4. You will refer to this section to help you remember the writing procedures used in your writing assignments. (*Read and discuss the Writing Process Checklist on the next page.*)

Listen carefully as I repeat the writing process again. It is too important to forget. First, you gather information. Next, you write a rough draft. Then, you revise and edit the rough draft. Finally, you rewrite the rough draft and turn in a final paper. If your writing assignment takes more than one session, you will finish it in your free time. Make sure you refer to Reference 4 anytime you forget what to do.

CHAPTER 1 LESSON 5 CONTINUED

Reference 4: Checklists
Revision Checklist

1. Eliminate unnecessary or needlessly repeated words or ideas.
2. Combine or reorder sentences.
3. Change word choices for clarity and expression.
4. Know the purpose: to explain, to describe, to entertain, or to persuade.
5. Know the audience: the reader(s) of the writing.

Beginning Editing Checklist

1. Did you indent the paragraph?
2. Did you capitalize the first word and put an end mark at the end of every sentence?
3. Did you spell words correctly?

More Editing Skills

4. Did you follow the writing guidelines? (*located in Reference 13 on student page 13*)
5. Did you list the topic and three points on separate lines at the top of the paper?
6. Did you follow the three-point paragraph pattern?
7. Did you write in the point of view assigned? (*first or third person*)
8. Did you use the correct homonyms?
9. Did you follow all other capitalization and punctuation rules?
10. Did you follow the three-paragraph essay pattern?

Final Paper Checklist

1. Have you written the correct heading on your paper?
2. Have you written your final paper in ink?
3. Have you single-spaced your final paper?
4. Have you written your final paper neatly?
5. Have you stapled the final paper to the rough draft and handed them in to your teacher?

Writing Process Checklist

1. Gather information.
2. Write a rough draft.
3. Revise the rough draft.
4. Edit the rough draft.
5. Write a final paper.

CHAPTER 1 LESSON 5 CONTINUED

Reference 5:
Rough Draft
When Melissa arrived, at the airport last weak, the people was so thick that she could hardly move. Melissa quickly moved through the airports crowded hallways, because she was already late. She arrived at the right terminial just in time to bored her flight. Melissa was out of breath and her hart was beating hard too. When she reached her seat on the plain, she was tired. Before she fell asleep she promised to allow extra time for the large crowds.
Revision of Draft
When Melissa arrived, at the airport last weak, the people was so thick she could **barely** move. **Because she was already late, Melissa rushed through the airports crowded corridors.** She arrived at the **correct** terminial just in time to bored her flight. Melissa was out of breath and **her hart was pounding rapidly from her mad dash through the airport**. When she finally reached her seat on the plain, she was **exhausted**. Before she fell asleep she promised to allow extra time for the **enormous** crowds **at the airport**.
Edit Draft
When Melissa arrived [**delete comma**] at the airport last week, [*week, not weak*] the people were [*were, not was*] so thick she could barely move. Because she was already late, Melissa rushed through the airport's [**apostrophe added**] crowded corridors. She arrived at the correct terminal [*terminal, not terminial*] just in time to board [*board, not bored*] her flight. Melissa was out of breath, [**comma inserted**] and her heart [*heart, not hart*] was pounding rapidly from her mad dash through the airport. When she finally reached her seat on the plane, [*plane, not plain*] she was exhausted. Before she fell asleep, [**comma inserted**] she promised to allow extra time for the enormous crowds at the airport.
Final Paragraph
When Melissa arrived at the airport last week, the people were so thick she could barely move. Because she was already late, Melissa rushed through the airport's crowded corridors. She arrived at the correct terminal just in time to board her flight. Melissa was out of breath, and her heart was pounding rapidly from her mad dash through the airport. When she finally reached her seat on the plane, she was exhausted. Before she fell asleep, she promised to allow extra time for the enormous crowds at the airport.

 **WRITING TIME**

Have students make an entry in their journals.

(End of lesson.)

CHAPTER 2 LESSON 1

New objectives: How to Get Started, Jingles (noun, verb, sentence), Grammar (noun, verb), Activity, and Vocabulary #1.

HOW TO GET STARTED

1. The word *students* will be used throughout the text in reference to the child/children you are teaching. The adult teaching this program will be referred to as *teacher*.

2. Stay one lesson ahead of your students. Study the entire lesson thoroughly before you present it. Then, read each lesson like you read a storybook: word-for-word. Your teacher's manual will give you teaching scripts to read out loud to your students. It will give you teacher's notes, and it will tell you when your students are to participate with you. Do not skip anything, and do not jump ahead. In just a few days, you will be in a comfortable routine that will help your students develop a love of learning.

3. All jingles and references are found in the **Jingle Section** and **Reference Section** in the front of the student book. A **Practice Section** is located after the Jingle and Reference Sections to give students practice on skills taught. A **Test Section** is located after the Practice Section to test students on the skills taught.

4. The lessons in this book are divided into chapters. Each lesson takes approximately twenty to fifty minutes to complete. For best results, you should do one lesson everyday.

5. A Shurley kit contains a teacher's manual, a student workbook, and an audio CD, which demonstrates the Jingles and the Question and Answer Flows for the Introductory Sentences.

Read the six *Jingle Guidelines* below before you teach jingles to your students. These guidelines will give you ideas and help you establish procedures for the oral recitation of jingles.

Jingle Guidelines

1. **Jingles are used** to learn English definitions. Jingle Time should be fun as well as educational.

2. **Knowing English definitions** makes learning English concepts easier because children can use the definitions to remember how to classify words used in sentences.

3. **Approach Jingle Time** as a learning time. Most of the jingles are presented as choral chants with enough rhythm to make them easy to remember, but you can also sing, rap, or just read them. Learning definitions in jingle form makes this necessary practice more fun. Listen to the CD for a suggested example of one way the jingles can be done.

4. **Jingles are more fun** if you make up motions for each jingle. Motions use the kinesthetic learning style of students and help them learn faster. Motions should be incorporated for several of the jingles. Relax and have fun. Have your children help make up motions they enjoy.

5. **You only need** to spend a short time on jingles (five to ten minutes) because you will be working with the jingles every day.

6. **Demonstrate each new jingle** for your students and then lead them in reciting the jingles. Let your students lead the jingles as soon as they are ready.

CHAPTER 2 LESSON 1 CONTINUED

 JINGLE TIME

Have students turn to page 2 in the Jingle Section of their books. The teacher will lead the students in reciting the new jingles (*Noun, Verb, and Sentence*) below. Practice the jingles several times until students can recite the jingles smoothly. Emphasize reciting with a rhythm. Students and teacher should be together! (*Do not try to explain the jingles at this time. Just have fun reciting them. Add motions for more fun and laughter.*)

Jingle 1: Noun Jingle

Yo! Ho! It's the NOUN we know!
A noun names a person;
A noun names a place;
A noun names a person, place, or thing,
And sometimes an idea!
Person, Place, Thing, Idea.

Finding nouns is a game.
Listen now to the nouns we name:
Head, shoulders, knees, and toes,
Girls, boys, shoes, and clothes.

Yo! Ho! It's the NOUN we know!
Yo! Ho! It's the NOUN we know!
Person, Place, Thing, Idea.
Person, Place, Thing, Idea.
Now, it's time to say Yo! Whoa!

Jingle 2: Verb Jingle

A verb, a verb. What is a verb?
Haven't you heard?
There are two kinds of verbs:
The action verb and the linking verb.

The action verb shows a state of action,
Like **stand** and **sit** and **smile**.
The action verb is always doing
Because it tells what the subject does.
We **stand**! We **sit**! We **smile**!

The linking verb is a state of being,
Like **am, is, are, was**, and **were**,
Look, become, grows, and **feels**.
A linking verb shows no action
Because it tells what the subject is.
He **is** *a clown. He* **looks** *funny.*

Jingle 3: Sentence Jingle

A sentence, sentence, sentence
Is complete, complete, complete
When 5 simple rules
It meets, meets, meets.

It has a subject, subject, subject
And a verb, verb, verb.
It makes sense, sense, sense
With every word, word, word.

Add a capital letter, letter
And an end mark, mark.
Now, we're finished, and aren't we smart!
Now, our sentence has all its parts!

REMEMBER
Subject, Verb, Com-plete sense,
Capital letter, and an end mark, too.
That's what a sentence is all about!

CHAPTER 2 LESSON 1 CONTINUED

GRAMMAR TIME

TEACHING SCRIPT FOR THE NOUN AND VERB

Good communication tools are necessary in all areas of life. When you study math, you must learn math terms to help you become effective in computation and problem-solving. When you study English, you must learn English terms that will help you become effective in speaking and writing. When you study a subject, it is like building a house. First, you build the foundation and make it strong. Next, you build the frame and roof and make them solid. Then, you take your time as you work on the inside of the house, filling each room with the special things you have learned over the years. Learning English is like building a house. It does not happen overnight. We will now begin our study of English.

The noun jingle that you learned today says a **noun** names a person, place, thing, or idea. The noun is also known as a naming word. Words like **boy** and **Sarah** name people. Can you tell me two more nouns that name people? (*Give students time to respond.*) Words like **kitten** and **mouse** name animals. Can you tell me two more nouns that name animals? (*Give students time to respond.*) Words like **barn** and **store** name places, and words like **shoes** and **desk** name things. Can you tell me two more nouns that name places and things? (*Give students time to respond.*) (*Then, give students time to identify several nouns in the room.*) We use the abbreviation **N** for the word **noun** when we do not spell it out.

You have already learned several things about the verb from the verb jingle. A word that shows action is a **verb**. The **verb** tells what a person or thing does. Words like **skip** and **jump** tell what children do. Can you tell me two more verbs that tell what children do? (*Give students time to respond.*) We use the abbreviation **V** for the word **verb** when we do not spell it out.

ACTIVITY / ASSIGNMENT TIME

For independent practice, have students take out a sheet of paper. Tell students that they are going to name a noun for each letter in their name (*first, middle, and last names*). They are also allowed to use the dictionary or thesaurus if necessary. To add a higher level of complexity, have students categorize the nouns by writing one of the following labels beside each noun: person, place, or thing. (*Check and discuss students' noun lists after they have finished.*)

VOCABULARY TIME

Assign Chapter 2, Vocabulary Words **#1** on page 7 in the Reference Section for students to define in their Vocabulary notebooks. Tell students they are to use a dictionary or thesaurus to look up the meanings of the vocabulary words. After they write each word and its meaning, students are to write a sentence using the vocabulary word.

Chapter 2, Vocabulary Words #1
(authentic, false, acknowledge, admit)

(End of lesson.)

CHAPTER 2   LESSON 2

New objectives: Grammar (Introductory Sentences, Question & Answer Flow, classifying, labeling, subject noun, verb), Skills (five parts of a complete sentence, the four kinds of sentences), and an Activity.

 **JINGLE TIME**

Have students recite the noun, verb, and sentence jingles with you. (*These jingles are located on page 2 in the Jingle Section of their books*).

Teacher's Notes: Do not spend a large amount of time practicing the new jingles. Students learn the jingles best by spending a small amount of time consistently, **every** day. The teacher should concentrate on the following areas while students are reciting the new jingles: togetherness, smoothness, volume, and enthusiasm. (*Lead your students as they jiggle, wiggle, and jingle! Everyone should enjoy Jingle Time.*)

 GRAMMAR TIME

Put the introductory sentences from the box below on the board. Use these sentences as you go through the new concepts covered in your teaching scripts. For the greatest benefit, students must participate orally with the teacher. (*You might put the introductory sentences on notebook paper if you are doing one-on-one instruction with your students.*)

Chapter 2, Introductory Sentences for Lesson 2
1. Spiders dangled. 2. Lady glanced. 3. Demonstrators screamed!

TEACHING SCRIPT FOR THE QUESTION & ANSWER FLOW

Understanding how all the parts of a sentence work together makes writing sentences easier and more interesting. Learning how to ask the right questions to get answers will help you identify the parts of a sentence. The questions you ask and the answers you get are called a **Question and Answer Flow**.

You will use a Question and Answer Flow to find what each word in a sentence is called. This method is called **classifying** because you classify, or tell, what each word is called in a sentence. Then, you will write the abbreviation above each word identified. This is called **labeling** because you identify the words by writing abbreviation letters above them.

CHAPTER 2 LESSON 2 CONTINUED

TEACHING SCRIPT FOR SUBJECT NOUN AND VERB IN A SENTENCE

I am going to show you how to use the noun and verb definitions and the Question and Answer Flow to find the subject noun and verb in a sentence. The subject of a sentence tells who or what a sentence is about. Since a noun names a person, place, or thing, a subject noun tells who or what a sentence is about. **The abbreviation _SN_ is used for the words _subject noun_ when we do not spell them out.** We ask a subject question to find the noun that works as the subject in a sentence. The subject questions are **who** or **what**. We ask _who_ if the sentence is **about people**. We ask _what_ if the sentence is **not about people,** but about an animal, a place, or a thing.

Look at Sentence 1: Spiders dangled.
What dangled? spiders - subject noun (_Write SN above spiders._)
Since the word _spiders_ is a thing, we ask the subject question _what_.
The subject noun _spiders_ tells _what_ the sentence is about.

Now, let's learn the Question and Answer Flow to find the verb. The verb definition says the verb shows action. The verb tells what the subject is doing. To find the verb, ask **what is being said about** the subject. Let's say **what is being said about** five times. Go. (_Have your students recite "what is being said about" with you at least five times. This will help them remember this important verb question._)

What is being said about spiders? spiders dangled - verb (_Write V above dangled._)

Remember, the questions you ask and the answers you get are called a Question and Answer Flow. I will classify Sentence 1 again, but this time you will classify the sentence with me. We will work on getting the Question and Answer Flow smooth so we can see how all the parts of a sentence work together. After we finish Sentence 1, we will practice the Question and Answer Flows again as we classify Sentences 2 and 3 together.

Teacher's Notes: Make sure students say the questions and answers orally for each sentence. Be sure to lead them so they will say the Question and Answer Flows correctly.

Question and Answer Flow for Sentence 1: Spiders dangled.

1. What dangled? spiders - subject noun (Trace over the SN above _spiders._)
2. What is being said about spiders? spiders dangled - verb (Trace over the V above _dangled._)

Classified Sentence:

        SN   V
    Spiders dangled.

Question and Answer Flow for Sentence 2: Lady glanced.

1. Who glanced? lady - subject noun (Write SN above _lady._)
   (Since _lady_ is a person, we begin the subject question with _who_.
   The subject noun _lady_ tells _who_ the sentence is about.)
2. What is being said about lady? lady glanced - verb (Write V above _glanced._)

Classified Sentence:

        SN   V
    Lady glanced.

CHAPTER 2 LESSON 2 CONTINUED

Question and Answer Flow for Sentence 3: Demonstrators screamed!

1. Who screamed? demonstrators - subject noun (Write SN above *demonstrators*.)
   (Since *demonstrators* are people, we begin the subject question with *who*.
   The subject noun *demonstrators* tells *who* the sentence is about.)
2. What is being said about demonstrators? demonstrators screamed - verb (Write V above *screamed*.)

Classified Sentence: SN   V
                    Demonstrators screamed!

TEACHER INSTRUCTIONS

Have students recite the Question and Answer Flows for the first two sentences with you again, but this time they are to trace the labels on their desks with the first three fingers of their writing hand as they classify. This is excellent practice to develop dexterity and to learn at a faster pace.

Have students write the third sentence on a piece of paper. Then, students should go through the Question and Answer Flow with you again, but this time they are to write the labels above the words they classify. This will give them practice writing the labels before they are tested on them.

The key to success is to keep students constantly saying the Question and Answer Flow until they know it automatically. Follow the suggestions below for your students to get the greatest benefits from the grammar lessons.

1. Be sure to have the students read each sentence with you, in unison, before classifying it.
2. Make sure students are saying the **questions** and the **answers** with you as each Question and Answer Flow is recited.

 SKILL TIME

TEACHING SCRIPT FOR THE 5 PARTS OF THE COMPLETE SENTENCE

Let's recite just the sentence jingle again. As you recite the sentence jingle, listen for the five parts that make a complete sentence. (*Recite the sentence jingle.*) Did you hear the five parts that make a complete sentence when we recited the sentence jingle? Of course, you did. Listen carefully as I go over the definition and the crucial parts of a complete sentence.

A **complete sentence** is a group of words that has a subject, a verb, and expresses a complete thought. A complete sentence should also begin with a capital letter and end with an end mark. Since you will be required to know the five parts of a sentence on a definition test later, you will learn the five parts of a sentence the easy way: by reciting the sentence jingle during Jingle Time. Now, listen for the five parts of a sentence as we recite the sentence jingle one more time. (*Recite the sentence jingle again.*)

CHAPTER 2 LESSON 2 CONTINUED

TEACHING SCRIPT FOR THE FOUR KINDS OF SENTENCES

There are four kinds of sentences. They are declarative, interrogative, imperative, and exclamatory. These sentences have four purposes: to tell, to ask, to request, or to show strong feeling. Now, you will learn more about the four kinds of sentences. Look at Reference 6 on page 10 in the Reference Section of your book. (*Read and discuss the information in the reference box below to your students.*)

Reference 6: The Four Kinds of Sentences and the End Mark Flow	
1. A **declarative** sentence makes a statement. It is labeled with a *D*. Example: Sarah played tennis today. (Period, statement, declarative sentence)	3. An **interrogative** sentence asks a question. It is labeled with an *Int*. Example: Did you see the new teacher? (Question mark, question, interrogative sentence)
2. An **imperative** sentence gives a command. It is labeled with an *Imp*. Example: Put your shoes in your closet. (Period, command, imperative sentence)	4. An **exclamatory** sentence expresses strong feeling. It is labeled with an *E*. Example: The spider is on Jamie! (Exclamation point, strong feeling, exclamatory sentence)

Examples: Read each sentence, recite the End Mark Flow in parentheses, and put the end mark and the abbreviation for the sentence type in the blank at the end of each sentence.

1. Jerry cooked his supper **. D**
   (*Period, statement, declarative sentence*)

2. The snake slithered toward me **! E**
   (*Exclamation point, strong feeling, exclamatory sentence*)

3. Put your homework on the desk **. Imp**
   (*Period, command, imperative sentence*)

4. Are they going to the movies **? Int**
   (*Question mark, question, interrogative sentence*)

Go to the examples listed at the bottom of your reference box and follow along as I identify each sentence by reciting the end-mark flow. Remember, the end-mark flow identifies the punctuation mark, the kind of sentence, and the name of that type of sentence. (*Read the examples with your students and supply the end-mark flow that is provided in parenthesis.*)

 ACTIVITY / ASSIGNMENT TIME

(*Your students will need a white poster board for this activity.*) You will position your poster with the long side on top. After you write this title, *Four Kinds of Sentences*, across the top of your poster, you may color the title to make it look attractive. Next, you will divide the poster board into four equal sections and label each section with one of the four kinds of sentences: declarative, imperative, interrogative, and exclamatory. Under the proper labels, you will write two declarative sentences, two imperative sentences, two interrogative sentences, and two exclamatory sentences. Make sure you put the correct end mark and the abbreviation of that end mark at the end of each sentence.

Illustrate your sentences and color the illustrations after you have finished. Then, you will ask various family members and friends to write the four kinds of sentences under the proper labels. You may need to coach them because they may not be familiar with the abbreviations you are using. (*Discuss the different sentences after students have finished the project.*)

(End of lesson.)

CHAPTER 2   LESSON 3

New objectives: Jingles (adverb, adjective), Grammar (Introductory Sentences, adverb, adjective, modify, article adjectives), Skills (indefinite articles, definite articles), Activity, Practice sheet, and Vocabulary #2.

JINGLE TIME

Have students turn to the Jingle Section in their books and recite the previously-taught jingles. Then, lead students in reciting the new jingles (*Adverb and Adjective*) below. Practice the new jingles several times until students can recite them smoothly. Emphasize reciting with a rhythm. Students and teacher should be together! (*Do not try to explain the jingles at this time. Just have fun reciting them. Remember, add motions for more fun and laughter.*)

Teacher's Note: Again, do not spend a large amount of time practicing the new jingles. Students learn the jingles best by spending a small amount of time consistently, **every** day. The teacher should concentrate on the following areas while students are reciting the new jingles: togetherness, smoothness, volume, and enthusiasm.

Jingle 4: Adverb Jingle
An adverb modifies a verb, adjective, or another adverb.
An adverb asks *How? When? Where?*
To find an adverb: **Go, Ask, Get**.
Where do I **go**? To a verb, adjective, or another adverb.
What do I **ask**? How? When? Where?
What do I **get**? An ADVERB! (Clap) That's what!

Jingle 5: Adjective Jingle
An adjective modifies a noun or pronoun.
An adjective asks *What kind? Which one? How many?*
To find an adjective: **Go, Ask, Get**.
Where do I **go**? To a noun or pronoun.
What do I **ask**? What kind? Which one? How many?
What do I **get**? An ADJECTIVE! (Clap) That's what!

GRAMMAR TIME

Put the introductory sentences from the box below on the board. Use these sentences as you go through the new concepts covered in your teaching scripts. For the greatest benefit, students must participate orally with the teacher. (*You might put the introductory sentences on notebook paper if you are doing one-on-one instruction with your students.*)

Chapter 2, Introductory Sentences for Lesson 3
1. The two spiders dangled effortlessly overhead.
2. The important lady glanced nervously around.
3. Several noisy demonstrators screamed angrily!

CHAPTER 2 LESSON 3 CONTINUED

<u>*TEACHING SCRIPT FOR THE ADVERB & ADJECTIVE*</u>

You are learning that jingles give you a lot of information fast and easily. I will review several things about the adverb. Listen carefully. **The Adverb Definition:** An adverb modifies a verb, adjective, or another adverb. **The Adverb Questions:** How? When? Where? **The Adverb Label:** *Adv*.

I will review several things about the adjective. **The Adjective Definition:** An adjective modifies a noun or pronoun. **The Adjective Questions:** What kind? Which one? How many? **The Adjective Label:** *Adj*.

The adjective and adverb definitions use the word *modifies*. The word ***modify*** means to describe. When the adverb definition says that an adverb modifies a verb, it means that an adverb describes a verb. When the adjective definition says that an adjective modifies a noun, it means that an adjective describes a noun.

You will now learn how to use the adjective and adverb definitions and the Question and Answer Flow to find the adverbs and adjectives in sentences. But first, we will classify the subject and verb before we find the adjective and adverb.

Classify Sentence 1: The two spiders dangled effortlessly above. *over head*
What dangled effortlessly above? spiders - subject noun (*Write SN above spiders.*)
What is being said about spiders? spiders dangled - verb (*Write V above dangled.*)

The adverb jingle tells you the adverb definition and the adverb questions. Look at the adverb jingle in the Jingle Section on page 2 and repeat the adverb jingle with me. (*Repeat the adverb jingle with your students again.*)

I am going to ask you some questions that will show you how to use the adverb jingle to find adverbs. I want you to see that knowing the adverb jingle and knowing how to ask the adverb questions will help you know where to go and what to say when you are finding adverbs. You may look at the adverb jingle in your book so you can answer my questions about adverbs.

1. Where do you go to find an adverb? (*to the verb, adjective, or another adverb*)
2. Where do you go **first** to find an adverb? (*to the verb*)
3. What is the verb in Sentence 1? (*dangled*)
4. What do you ask after you go to the verb *dangled*?
   (*one of the adverb questions: how? when? where?*)
5. How do you know which adverb question to ask?
   (*Look at the words around the verb: (effortlessly and above). Those words will guide you.*)
6. Which adverb question would you use to find an adverb in this sentence? (*how*)

This is how you would ask an adverb question and give the adverb answer in the Question and Answer Flow: **Dangled how? effortlessly - adverb** (*Write Adv above the word **effortlessly.***)

CHAPTER 2 LESSON 3 CONTINUED

Look at the sentence again. As you can see, there is another word that needs to be classified. In order to classify this word, you must again ask the questions that you have learned. You will continue this question-and-answer procedure until all words in the sentence have been identified. That is why we call it the Question-and-Answer Flow.

Let's go back to the verb and do the Question and Answer Flow for another adverb:
Dangled where? above - adverb (*Write Adv above the word **above**.*)
overhead

We will use the same procedure to find the adjective. The adjective jingle tells you the adjective definition and the adjective questions. Look at the adjective jingle in the Jingle Section on page 2 and repeat the adjective jingle with me. (*Repeat the adjective jingle with your students again.*)

I am going to ask you some questions that will show you how to use the adjective jingle to find adjectives. I want you to see that knowing the adjective jingle and knowing how to ask the adjective questions will help you know where to go and what to say when you are finding adjectives. You may look at the adjective jingle in your book so you can answer my questions about adjectives.

1. Where do you go to find an adjective? (*to the noun or pronoun*)
2. Where do you go **first** to find an adjective? (*to the subject noun*)
3. What is the subject noun in Sentence 1? (*spiders*)
4. What do you ask after you go to the subject noun *spiders*?
   (*one of the adjective questions: what kind? which one? how many?*)
5. How do you know which adjective question to ask?
   (*Look at the word or words around the noun: (two) (That word will guide you.)*)
6. Which adjective question would you use to find an adjective in this sentence? (*How many?*)

This is how you would ask an adjective question and give the adjective answer in the Adjective Question and Answer Flow: **How many spiders? two - adjective** (*Write Adj above the word **two**.*)

TEACHING SCRIPT FOR THE ARTICLE ADJECTIVE

We are ready for the article adjectives. **Article Adjectives** are the three most commonly-used adjectives: *a, an,* and *the.* They are sometimes called noun markers because they tell that a noun is close by. These article adjectives must be memorized because there are no questions in the Question and Answer Flow to find the article adjectives. Article adjectives are labeled with an **A.**

This is how you would identify an article adjective in the Question and Answer Flow: **The - article adjective** (*Write A above the word **The**.*)

I will classify Sentence 1 again, but this time you will classify it with me. I will lead you as we follow the series of questions and answers that I have just demonstrated. Then, we will classify Sentences 2-3 together to practice the Question and Answer Flows.

CHAPTER 2 LESSON 3 CONTINUED

Question and Answer Flow for Sentence 1: The two spiders dangled effortlessly overhead.

1. What dangled effortlessly overhead? spiders - subject noun (Trace over the SN above *spiders*.)
2. What is being said about spiders? spiders dangled - verb (Trace over the V above *dangled*.)
3. Dangled how? effortlessly - adverb (Trace over the Adv above *effortlessly*.)
4. Dangled where? overhead - adverb (Trace over the Adv above overhead.)
5. How many spiders? two - adjective (Trace over the Adj above *two*.)
6. The - article adjective (Trace over the A above *The.)*

Classified Sentence:

A   Adj   SN   V   Adv   Adv
The two spiders dangled effortlessly overhead.

Question and Answer Flow for Sentence 2: The important lady glanced nervously around.

1. Who glanced nervously around? lady - subject noun (Trace over the SN above *lady*.)
2. What is being said about lady? lady glanced - verb (Trace over the V above *glanced*.)
3. Glanced how? nervously - adverb (Trace over the Adv above *nervously*.)
4. Glanced where? around - adverb (Trace over the Adv above *around*.)
5. What kind of lady? important - adjective (Trace over the Adj above *important*.)
6. The - article adjective (Trace over the A above *The.)*

Classified Sentence:

A   Adj   SN   V   Adv   Adv
The important lady glanced nervously around.

Question and Answer Flow for Sentence 3: Several noisy demonstrators screamed angrily!

1. Who screamed angrily? demonstrators - subject noun (*SN*)
2. What is being said about demonstrators? demonstrators screamed - verb (*V*)
3. Screamed how? angrily - adverb (*Adv*)
4. What kind of demonstrators? noisy - adjective (*Adj*)
5. How many demonstrators? several - adjective (*Adj*)

Classified Sentence:

Adj   Adj   SN   V   Adv
Several noisy demonstrators screamed angrily!

SKILL TIME

TEACHING SCRIPT FOR ARTICLE ADJECTIVE SKILLS

You have seen how the article is used in the Question and Answer Flows to classify sentences. Now, I will give you more information about article adjectives. Turn to Reference 7 on page 11 in the Reference Section of your book. (*Have students follow along as you read the information in the reference box on the next page.*)

CHAPTER 2 LESSON 3 CONTINUED

Reference 7: Additional Article Adjective Information

1. *A/An* are called <u>indefinite</u> articles, meaning one of several.
    (Examples: **a** candy cane—**an** apron.)

2. *The* is called a <u>definite</u> article, meaning the only one there is.
    (Examples: **the** candy cane—**the** apron.)

3. The article *The* has two pronunciations:

    a. As a long **e** (*where the article precedes a word that begins with a vowel sound: the elephant, the iguana*)

    b. As a short **u** (*where the article precedes a word that begins with a consonant sound: the party, the dress*)

ACTIVITY / ASSIGNMENT TIME

On a sheet of paper, write five nouns that begin with a vowel sound. Write the letter **(e)** in parenthesis after each word to indicate that the article would be pronounced with the long e sound. Next, write ten nouns that begin with a consonant sound. Write the letter **(u)** in parentheses after each word to indicate that the article would be pronounced with the short **u** sound. After you have finished, we will say the words aloud with the proper pronunciation of the article **the** in front of each word. (*After students have finished, listen to them as they pronounce the article correctly for each word they have written on their paper.*)

PRACTICE TIME

Have students turn to pages 53 and 54 in the Practice Section of their book and find the skills under Chapter 2, Lesson 3, Practice (*1-4*). Tell them the practice is not hard, but they must pay attention and think about what they are doing. Go over the directions to make sure they understand what to do. <u>Allow students to use the Jingle and Reference Sections in their books if needed</u>. Check and discuss the Practice after students have finished. (*Chapter 2, Lesson 3, Practice keys are below and on the next page.*)

Chapter 2, Lesson 3, Practice 1: Put the end mark and the abbreviation for each kind of sentence in the blanks below.

1. Check your homework carefully   **. Imp** _____

2. Did you clean your room   **? Int** _____

3. The firemen are on their way   **! E** _____

4. I have already packed my suitcase for our trip   **. D** _____

CHAPTER 2 LESSON 3 CONTINUED

Chapter 2, Lesson 3, Practice 2: On a separate piece of paper, write a sentence to demonstrate each of these four kinds of sentences: (1) Declarative (2) Interrogative (3) Exclamatory (4) Imperative. Write the correct punctuation and the abbreviation that identifies it at the end. Use these abbreviations: D, Int, E, Imp.

Chapter 2, Lesson 3, Practice 3: Match the definitions. Write the correct letter beside each numbered concept.

G	1. exclamatory sentence	A.	verb, adjective, or adverb
H	2. a/an are also called	B.	who
I	3. adjective modifies	C.	what is being said about
C	4. verb question	D.	person, place, thing
J	5. a definite article	E.	what
E	6. subject-noun question (thing)	F.	period
K	7. article adjective can be called	G.	shows strong feeling
L	8. makes a request or gives a command	H.	indefinite articles
D	9. noun	I.	noun or pronoun
B	10. subject-noun question (person)	J.	the
F	11. punctuation for declarative	K.	noun marker
A	12. adverb modifies	L.	imperative sentence

Chapter 2, Lesson 3, Practice 4: Fill in the blank: Write the answer for each question.

1. What are the three article adjectives? _a, an, the_

2. What word tells what the subject does? _verb_

 VOCABULARY TIME

Assign Chapter 2, Vocabulary Words **#2** on page 7 in the Reference Section for students to define in their Vocabulary notebooks. Tell students they are to use a dictionary or thesaurus to look up the meanings of the vocabulary words. After they write each word and its meaning, students are to write a sentence using the vocabulary word.

Chapter 2, Vocabulary Words #2
(withhold, bequeath, pardon, amnesty)

(End of lesson.)

CHAPTER 2   LESSON 4

New objectives: Jingle (article adjective), Grammar (Practice Sentences), and a Test.

 **JINGLE TIME**

Have students turn to the Jingle Section in their books and recite the previously-taught jingles. Then, lead students in reciting the new jingle (*Article Adjective*) below. Practice the new jingle several times until students can recite it smoothly. Emphasize reciting with a rhythm. Students and teacher should be together! (*Have fun reciting the jingles. Remember, add motions for more fun and laughter.*)

Jingle 6: Article Adjective

We are the article adjectives,
Teeny, tiny adjectives:
A, AN, THE - A, AN, THE.

We are called article adjectives and noun markers;
We are memorized and used every day.
So, if you spot us, you can mark us
With the label A.

We are the article adjectives,
Teeny, tiny adjectives:
A, AN, THE - A, AN, THE.

 GRAMMAR TIME

Put the Practice Sentences from the box below on the board. Use these sentences as you practice the concepts that have been taught. For the greatest benefit, students must participate orally with the teacher. (*You might put the Practice Sentences on notebook paper if you are doing one-on-one instruction with your students.*)

Chapter 2, Practice Sentences for Lesson 4

1. The victorious hockey players skated around triumphantly.
2. The elderly gentleman walked gingerly.
3. Two poisonous snakes hissed loudly!

TEACHING SCRIPT FOR CLASSIFYING PRACTICE SENTENCES

We will now classify three different sentences to practice the Question and Answer Flows. We will classify the sentences together. Begin.

CHAPTER 2 LESSON 4 CONTINUED

Teacher's Notes: At this time, your manual will no longer write out the entire name for each part of speech used in the Question and Answer Flow. Instead of writing out *adverb*, your manual will write *Adv*. You will continue to say *adverb* even though you see only the abbreviation *Adv*.

These abbreviations are the same abbreviations that you write above each word as you teach your students the Question and Answer Flow. Always say *subject noun* whenever you see the abbreviation *SN*. Always say *verb* whenever you see the abbreviation *V*, etc. Make sure students are reciting the Question and Answer Flows orally, with you. Oral recitation helps students learn the concepts faster and retain them longer.

Question and Answer Flow for Sentence 1: The victorious hockey players skated around triumphantly.

1. Who skated around triumphantly? players - SN
2. What is being said about players? players skated - V
3. Skated where? around - Adv
4. Skated how? triumphantly – Adv
5. What kind of players? hockey - Adj
6. What kind of players? victorious - Adj
7. The - A (Article adjective)

Classified Sentence:

| A | Adj | Adj | SN | V | Adv | Adv |

The victorious hockey players skated around triumphantly.

Question and Answer Flow for Sentence 2: The elderly gentleman walked gingerly.

1. Who walked gingerly? gentleman - SN
2. What is being said about gentleman? gentleman walked - V
3. Walked how? gingerly – Adv
4. What kind of gentleman? elderly - Adj
5. The - A (Article adjective)

Classified Sentence:

| A | Adj | SN | V | Adv |

The elderly gentleman walked gingerly.

Question and Answer Flow for Sentence 3: Two poisonous snakes hissed loudly!

1. What hissed loudly? snakes - SN
2. What is being said about snakes? snakes hissed - V
3. Hissed how? loudly – Adv
4. What kind of snakes? poisonous - Adj
5. How many snakes? two - Adj

Classified Sentence:

| Adj | Adj | SN | V | Adv |

Two poisonous snakes hissed loudly!

Teacher's Notes: Options for Practice Sentences: (1) If this is your students' first year in Shurley English, the program should stay teacher-oriented. Have students classify all *introductory, practice,* and *test* sentences orally with you to reinforce the concepts they are learning. This recommendation is listed as Option 1 for first-year students. As you progress through the program and see that your students are experiencing no difficulty, you might go to Option 2 for more student independence.

(2) Option 2 is recommended for second-year students or for strong first-year students. In this option, students will classify the Practice Sentences independently on paper. You can check students' Practice Sentences from the Practice Sentences provided in your teacher's manual, or, if you have the CDs for the Practice Sentences, you can have your students check their Practice Sentences with the CDs. (*Practice Sentence CDs are not included in the kit and must be purchased separately because they are supplementary items. A Practice Booklet, with all the Practice Sentences enlarged for the students, is also available.*)

CHAPTER 2 LESSON 4 CONTINUED

Now, I want you to look at Reference 8 on page 12 in the Reference Section of your book. You are given one of the Question and Answer Flows as an example, so it will be easy for you to study. Let's read it together in unison. Remember, we always begin by reading the sentence. (*Read and discuss the Question and Answer Flow in the reference box below with your students.*)

Reference 8: Question and Answer Flow Sentence

Question and Answer Flow Sentence: The determined competitors swam feverishly.

1. Who swam feverishly? competitors - SN
2. What is being said about competitors? competitors swam - V
3. Swam how? feverishly - Adv
4. What kind of competitors? determined - Adj
5. The - A

Classified Sentence: A   Adj   SN   V   Adv
                      The determined competitors swam feverishly.

Teacher's Notes: Adverbs are usually classified in the order they appear after the verb because it is more concrete and easier for the students. Only when an adverb modifies another adverb does the order change. Your teacher's manual will always tell you how to make the change.
Example: Daniel walked very quietly. Walked how? quietly - Adv; How quietly? very - Adv.

STUDY TIME

Have students study the vocabulary words in their vocabulary notebooks. Remind students that any vocabulary word in their notebooks could be on their test. Also, have students study any of the skills in the Practice Section that they need to review.

TEST TIME

Have students turn to page 83 in the Test Section of their books and find the Chapter 2 Test section. Remind them that grammar is not tested yet; so, they are only tested on what they have already practiced. Remind them to pay attention and think about what they are doing. Go over the directions to make sure they understand what to do. (*Chapter 2 Test key is on the next page.*)

CHECK TIME

After students have finished, check and discuss their test papers. Make sure they understand why their answers are right or wrong. (*A handy way to mark errors is by highlighting with a yellow magic marker. For total points, count each required answer as a point.*)

(End of lesson.)

Chapter 2 Test
(STUDENT PAGE 83)

Exercise 1: Put the end marks and the abbreviations for each kind of sentence in the blanks below.

1. Did you sing in the choir   **? Int**

2. My sister started a new job   **. D**

3. The lion ran toward the little girl   **! E**

4. Wash the dishes in the sink   **. Imp**

5. Did Keith meet the president   **? Int**

6. I ran the marathon with my friends   **. D**

7. Dust the top shelf   **. Imp**

8. I won the trip to Europe   **! E**

Exercise 2: On a separate sheet of paper, write a sentence to demonstrate each of these four kinds of sentences: (1) Declarative (2) Interrogative (3) Exclamatory (4) Imperative. Write the correct punctuation and the abbreviation that identifies it at the end. Use these abbreviations: D, Int, E, Imp. (Answers will vary.)

Exercise 3: Match the definitions. Write the correct letter beside each numbered concept.

K	1. tells what the subject does		A.	verb, adjective, or adverb
E	2. a/an are also called		B.	what?
I	3. adjective modifies		C.	what is being said about?
C	4. verb question		D.	person, place, or thing
J	5. a definite article		E.	indefinite articles
B	6. subject-noun question (thing)		F.	period
G	7. article adjective can be called		G.	noun marker
L	8. makes a request or gives a command		H.	who?
D	9. noun		I.	noun or pronoun
H	10. subject-noun question (person)		J.	the
F	11. punctuation for declarative		K.	verb
A	12. adverb modifies		L.	imperative sentence

Exercise 4: Identify each pair of words as synonyms or antonyms by putting parentheses ( ) around *syn* or *ant*.

1. bequeath, withhold	syn **(ant)**	3. false, authentic	syn **(ant)**
2. pardon, amnesty	**(syn)** ant	4. acknowledge, admit	**(syn)** ant

Exercise 5: Write a pair of synonyms beside number 1. Write a pair of antonyms beside number 2.

1. _____

2. _____

Exercise 6: In your journal, write a paragraph summarizing what you have learned this week.

CHAPTER 2   LESSON 5

New objectives: Grammar (Introductory Sentences, Pattern 1 Sentences, complete subject, complete predicate, end punctuation), and Skills (Skill Builder Checks, Noun Checks).

GRAMMAR TIME

Put the introductory sentences from the box below on the board. Use these sentences as you go through the new concepts covered in your teaching scripts. For the greatest benefit, students must participate orally with the teacher. (*You might put the introductory sentences on notebook paper if you are doing one-on-one instruction with your students.*)

Chapter 2, Introductory Sentences for Lesson 5
1. _____ The perspiring marathon runners panted heavily today.
2. _____ The two mighty lions roared very ferociously!
3. _____ The exceptionally tired youth slumbered ~~deeply~~. soundly

---

TEACHING SCRIPT FOR PATTERN 1, COMPLETE SUBJECT/COMPLETE PREDICATE, AND END PUNCTUATION

We will now classify Sentence 1. This time, there will be more information added to the Question and Answer Flow. You will classify the sentence with me until we get to the new part in the Question and Answer Flow. Then, I will show you how to add the new part to the Question and Answer Flow.

Sentence 1: The perspiring marathon runners panted heavily today.
Who panted heavily today? runners - SN
What is being said about runners? runners panted - V
Panted how? heavily - Adv
Panted when? today - Adv
What kind of runners? marathon - Adj
What kind of runners? perspiring - Adj
The – A

I will explain the new parts and show you how to add them to the Question and Answer Flow. I will say all three of the new parts in the Question and Answer Flow, and then I will explain the new parts to you. Listen carefully as I repeat the three new parts.

1. Subject Noun Verb Pattern 1 Check. (*Write SN V P1 in the blank beside the sentence. Be sure to say **check**. You will use the check to identify any new skill that is added to the Question and Answer Flow.*)
2. Period, statement, declarative sentence. (*Write a D at the end of the sentence.*)
3. Go back to the verb - divide the complete subject from the complete predicate.
   (*As you say **divide**, put a slash mark before your verb.*)

Note: Your sentence should look like this:

		A	Adj	Adj	SN	V	Adv	Adv	
SN V	___	The perspiring marathon runners / panted heavily today.							**D**
P1									

CHAPTER 2 LESSON 5 CONTINUED

I will explain each new part, one at a time. Listen to the definition for a Pattern 1 sentence. The pattern of a sentence is the **order of the main parts** in that sentence. **Pattern 1** has only two main parts: the subject and the verb. Adjectives and adverbs add information to sentences, but they are not part of a sentence pattern. A **Pattern 1** sentence is labeled **SN V P1.** (*Put the SN V P1 on the board for your students to see.*) When you see or write the **SN V P1** labels, you will say, "Subject Noun, Verb, Pattern 1."

When you say *Subject Noun, Verb, Pattern 1, Check,* you are classifying the pattern of the sentence and checking for any additional skills to be identified. Remember, the pattern of a sentence is <u>the order of its main parts</u>. <u>The subject and the verb are the main parts of a Pattern 1 sentence.</u>

Adjectives and adverbs are extra words that are not considered essential parts of a sentence pattern because they are used freely with all sentence patterns. To identify Pattern 1 sentences, you will write *SN V P1* on the line in front of any Pattern 1 sentence.

When you say *period, statement, declarative sentence,* you are classifying the end mark, the kind of sentence, and the name of that sentence. To identify the sentence as a declarative sentence, you will write a *D* after the period, but you will always say, "Period, statement, declarative sentence."

When you say *Go back to the verb - divide the complete subject from the complete predicate,* you are identifying all the subject parts and all the predicate parts.

I will now give you more information about the complete subject and the complete predicate. Listen carefully. The **complete subject** is the subject and all the words that modify the subject. The complete subject usually starts at the beginning of the sentence and includes every word up to the verb of the sentence. A vertical line in front of the verb shows where the subject parts are divided from the predicate parts in the sentence.

The **complete predicate** is the verb and all the words that modify the verb. The complete predicate usually starts with the verb and includes every word after the verb. A vertical line in front of the verb shows where the predicate parts are divided from the subject parts in the sentence.

I will classify Sentence 1 again, and you will classify it with me this time. Then, we will classify Sentences 2-3 together.

Teacher's Notes: Make sure students are reciting each Question and Answer Flow orally, with you. They learn the concepts so much faster and retain them longer if they say the Question and Answer Flows orally!

Question and Answer Flow for Sentence 1: The perspiring marathon runners panted heavily today.

1. Who panted heavily today? runners - SN
2. What is being said about runners?
   runners panted - V
3. Panted how? heavily - Adv
4. Panted when? today - Adv
5. What kind of runners? marathon - Adj
6. What kind of runners? perspiring - Adj
7. The - A (article adjective)

8. SN V P1 Check
   (Say: Subject noun, Verb, Pattern 1 Check)
   (Write *SN V P1* in the blank beside the sentence.)
9. Period, statement, declarative sentence
   (Write *D* at the end of the sentence.)
10. Go back to the verb - divide the complete subject
    from the complete predicate.
    (As you say <u>divide</u>, put a slash mark before the verb.)

Classified Sentence:

		A	Adj	Adj	SN	V	Adv	Adv
SN	V	The	perspiring	marathon	runners /	panted	heavily	today. D
	P1							

CHAPTER 2 LESSON 5 CONTINUED

Question and Answer Flow for Sentence 2: The two mighty lions roared very ferociously!

1. What roared very ferociously? lions - SN
2. What is being said about lions? lions roared - V
3. Roared how? ferociously - Adv
4. How ferociously? very - Adv

Note: "very" is an adverb that modifies another adverb in the complete predicate.

5. What kind of lions? mighty - Adj

6. How many lions? two - Adj
7. The - A
8. SN V P1 Check (Say: Subject noun, Verb, Pattern 1 Check)
9. Exclamation point, strong feeling, exclamatory sentence (Write *E* at the end of the sentence.)
10. Go back to the verb - divide the complete subject from the complete predicate. (As you say <u>divide</u>, put a slash mark before the verb.)

Classified Sentence:

	A	Adj	Adj	SN	V	Adv	Adv
SN V	The	two	mighty	lions /	roared	very	ferociously! **E**
P1							

Question and Answer Flow for Sentence 3: The exceptionally tired youth slumbered soundly.

1. Who slumbered soundly? youth - SN
2. What is being said about youth? youth slumbered - V
3. Slumbered how? soundly - Adv
4. What kind of youth? tired - Adj
5. How tired? exceptionally - Adv

Note: "Exceptionally" is an adverb that modifies an adjective in the complete subject. It is part of the complete subject.

6. The - A
7. SN V P1 Check (Say: Subject noun, Verb, Pattern 1 Check)
8. Period, statement, declarative sentence (Write *D* at the end of the sentence.)
9. Go back to the verb - divide the complete subject from the complete predicate. (As you say <u>divide</u>, put a slash mark before the verb.)

Classified Sentence:

	A	Adv	Adj	SN	V	Adv
SN V	The	exceptionally	tired	youth /	slumbered	soundly. **D**
P1						

Teacher's Note: If this is the first year in the program, you might want to reinforce the new concepts by classifying the sentences a second time with students labeling or tracing over the teacher's labels. Check for any problems during this second classifying. Grammar is tested in the next chapter.

I want you to look at Reference 9 on page 12 in the Reference Section of your book. You are given another Question and Answer Flow as an example so it will be easy for you to study. Let's read it together in unison. Remember, we always begin by reading the sentence. (*Read and discuss the Question and Answer Flow in the reference box on the next page with your students.*)

CHAPTER 2 LESSON 5 CONTINUED

Reference 9: Question and Answer Flow Sentence	
Question and Answer Flow for Sentence 1: The exquisite diamond sparkled brightly.	
1. What sparkled brightly? diamond - SN	6. SN V P1 Check *(Say: Subject Noun, Verb, Pattern 1, Check.)*
2. What is being said about diamond? diamond sparkled - V	7. Period, statement, declarative sentence
3. Sparkled how? brightly - Adv	8. Go back to the verb - divide the complete subject from the complete predicate.
4. What kind of diamond? exquisite - Adj	
5. The - A	

Classified Sentence:

                  A   Adj   SN   V   Adv

<u>SN V</u>   The exquisite diamond **/** sparkled brightly. **D**
P1

SKILL TIME

TEACHING SCRIPT FOR INTRODUCING SKILL BUILDER CHECKS AND NOUN CHECKS

Now that we have classified all three sentences, I am going to use them to do a Skill Builder Check. **A Skill Builder Check** is an oral review of certain skills. Skill Builder Checks are designed to make sure you keep basic skills sharp and automatic. The first skill that will be covered by the Skill Builder Check is the **Noun Check**. Even though a noun is only one part of speech, a noun can do many jobs or perform many functions in a sentence. The first noun job you have learned is that a noun can function as the subject of a sentence.

Look at Sentences 1-3. In a Noun Check, we will identify the nouns in all three sentences by drawing circles around them. It will be easy today because we have only one noun job at this point. I will use Sentence 1 to demonstrate the four things that you say: **Number 1** (*You say the sentence number.*) **Subject Noun:** *runners* (*You say the noun job and the noun used for the noun job.*) **Yes** (*You say the word yes to verify that the word **runners** is a noun, not a pronoun.*) So it will not be confusing, I will repeat number 1 again. We will say, "Number 1: subject noun *runners*, yes," and I will circle *runners* because we have identified it as a noun.

Let's start with number 1 again and do a Noun Check. Begin. (*Circle the nouns for all three sentences as your students recite the Noun Check with you: Number 1: subject noun **runners**, yes. Number 2: subject noun **lions**, yes. Number 3: subject noun **youth**, yes.*)

WRITING TIME

Have students make an entry in their journals.

(End of lesson.)

CHAPTER 3 LESSON 1

New objectives: Grammar (Practice Sentences), Skills (singular nouns, plural nouns, common nouns, proper nouns, simple subject, simple predicate), Practice sheet, and Vocabulary #1.

JINGLE TIME

Have students turn to the Jingle Section of their books. The teacher will lead the students in reciting the previously-taught jingles.

GRAMMAR TIME

First-Year Option: Put the Practice Sentences from the box below on the board or notebook paper. Use these sentences as you practice the concepts that have been taught. For the greatest benefit, students must participate orally with the teacher. **Second-Year Option:** Have students classify the Practice Sentences independently on paper. Check students' sentences with the answers provided below. (*If you have the CDs for Practice Sentences, have students check their sentences with the CDs.*)

Chapter 3, Practice Sentences for Lesson 1

1. _____ The boastful salesman spoke rather arrogantly.
2. _____ The small foals pranced happily nearby.
3. _____ The enormous rat ran away quickly!

TEACHING SCRIPT FOR PRACTICING PATTERN 1 SENTENCES

We will classify three different sentences to practice the Question and Answer Flows. We will classify the sentences together. Begin. (*You might have students write the labels above the sentences at this time.*)

Question and Answer Flow for Sentence 1: The boastful salesman spoke rather arrogantly.

1. Who spoke rather arrogantly? salesman - SN
2. What is being said about salesman?
   salesman spoke - V
3. Spoke how? arrogantly - Adv
4. How arrogantly? rather - Adv
5. What kind of salesman? boastful - Adj

6. The - A
7. Subject Noun Verb Pattern 1 Check
8. Period, statement, declarative sentence
9. Go back to the verb - divide the complete subject from the complete predicate.

Classified Sentence:

	A	Adj	SN	V	Adv	Adv
SN V	The boastful salesman **/** spoke rather arrogantly. **D**
P1	

CHAPTER 3 LESSON 1 CONTINUED

Question and Answer Flow for Sentence 2: The small foals pranced happily nearby.

1. What pranced happily nearby? foals - SN
2. What is being said about foals? foals pranced - V
3. Pranced how? happily - Adv
4. Pranced where? nearby - Adv
5. What kind of foals? small - Adj
6. The - A
7. SN V P1 Check
8. Period, statement, declarative sentence
9. Go back to the verb - divide the complete subject from the complete predicate.

Classified Sentence:

```
              A   Adj  SN      V    Adv   Adv
    SN V     The small foals / pranced happily nearby.  D
    ─────
     P1
```

Question and Answer Flow for Sentence 3: The enormous rat ran away quickly!

1. What ran away quickly? rat - SN
2. What is being said about rat? rat ran - V
3. Ran where? away - Adv
4. Ran how? quickly - Adv
5. What kind of rat? enormous - Adj
6. The - A
7. SN V P1 Check
8. Exclamation point, strong feeling, exclamatory sentence
9. Go back to the verb - divide the complete subject from the complete predicate.

Classified Sentence:

```
              A    Adj    SN   V   Adv   Adv
    SN V     The enormous rat / ran away quickly!  E
    ─────
     P1
```

SKILL TIME

TEACHING SCRIPT FOR REVIEWING A NOUN CHECK

Now that we have classified all three sentences, I am going to use them to do a Skill Builder Check. As you have learned, a **Skill Builder Check** is an oral check of certain skills. First, we will do a Noun Check since we have already had that skill. In a Noun Check, we identify the nouns in all three sentences by drawing circles around them.

Remember, you say four things: the sentence number, the noun job, the noun used for the noun job, and the word *yes* to verify that it is a noun, not a pronoun. I will circle the nouns as we identify them. Begin. *(Circle the nouns for all three sentences as your students recite the Noun Check with you: Number 1: subject noun* **salesman**, *yes. Number 2: subject noun* **foals**, *yes. Number 3: subject noun* **rat**, *yes.)*

We will now discuss several definitions that we will discuss in detail during Skill Builder Checks. Look at Reference 10 on page 13 in the Reference Section of your book. *(Reference 10 is located on the next page. Read the definitions with your students. You will discuss each one in the teaching scripts throughout this lesson.)*

CHAPTER 3 LESSON 1 CONTINUED

Reference 10: Definitions for a Skill Builder Check
1. A **noun** names a person, place, thing, or idea.
2. A **singular noun** usually does not end in an *s* or *es* and means only one. (*truck, pencil, plane*) Exception: Some nouns end in s and are singular and mean only one. (*glass-glasses, dress-dresses*)
3. A **plural noun** usually ends in an *s* or *es* and means more than one. (*trucks, pencils, planes*) Exception: Some nouns are made plural by changing their spelling. (*man-men, child- children*)
4. A **common noun** names ANY person, place, or thing. A common noun is not capitalized because it does not name a specific person, place, or thing. (*tiger, yard*)
5. A **proper noun** is a noun that names a specific, or particular, person, place, or thing. Proper nouns are always capitalized no matter where they are located in the sentence. (*Keith, Alaska*)
6. A **simple subject** is another name for the subject noun or subject pronoun.
7. A **simple predicate** is another name for the verb.

TEACHING SCRIPT FOR IDENTIFYING NOUNS AS SINGULAR OR PLURAL

The next skill in our Skill Builder Check is identifying nouns as singular or plural. This is an easy skill, but you would be surprised at the number of people who have trouble with it. We must first learn the general definitions for singular and plural.

A **singular noun** usually does not end in an *s* or *es* and means only one. (*truck, pencil, plane*) There are a few exceptions: Some nouns end in s and are singular and mean only one. (*glass-glasses, dress-dresses*)

A **plural noun** usually ends in an *s* or *es* and means more than one. (*trucks, pencils, planes*) There are a few exceptions: Some nouns are made plural by changing their spelling. (*man-men, child- children*)

We will identify each circled noun in Sentences 1-3 as singular or plural. I will write *S* for singular or *P* for plural above each noun as we identify it. We will say "salesman - singular," and I will write an S above *salesman*. Begin. (*salesman – singular, foals – plural, rat – singular. Mark the nouns with the letter "S" or "P" in all three sentences.*)

TEACHING SCRIPT FOR IDENTIFYING NOUNS AS COMMON OR PROPER

Next, you will learn about common and proper nouns. A **common noun** is a noun that names ANY person, place, or thing. A common noun is not capitalized because it does not name a specific person, place, or thing. A **proper noun** is a noun that names a specific, or particular, person, place, or thing. Proper nouns are always capitalized no matter where they are located in the sentence.

We will look at the nouns that are circled in the three sentences and tell whether they are common or proper. How do we recognize a proper noun? (*It begins with a capital letter no matter where it is located in the sentence.*) Do we have any proper nouns in our sentences? (*No.*) How do you know? (*None of the nouns that are circled begin with a capital letter.*) Since we do not have a proper noun in the three sentences that we have just classified, I want you to think of a proper noun. (*Get several responses and discuss why the nouns named are proper nouns.*) Do we have any common nouns in our sentences? (*Yes.*) Are all the nouns common? (*Yes.*) How do you know? (*All the nouns that are circled begin with a small letter.*)

CHAPTER 3 LESSON 1 CONTINUED

TEACHING SCRIPT FOR IDENTIFYING THE SIMPLE SUBJECT AND THE SIMPLE PREDICATE

We have already discussed the **complete subject** and the **complete predicate**, but I will review them again. The **complete subject** is the subject and all the words that modify the subject. The complete subject usually starts at the beginning of the sentence and includes every word up to the verb of the sentence. I want you to tell me the complete subject for Sentence 1, and I will underline it once. What is the complete subject? (*The boastful salesman*)

The **complete predicate** is the verb and all the words that modify the verb. The complete predicate usually starts with the verb and includes every word after the verb. I want you to tell me the complete predicate, and I will underline it twice. What is the complete predicate? (*spoke rather arrogantly*) (*Mark the answers for Sentences 2-3 in the same way. The small foals pranced happily nearby. The enormously fury rat ran around quickly*!)

We will now learn about the simple subject and the simple predicate. The **simple subject** is another name for the subject noun or subject pronoun. The simple subject is just the subject; it does not include the other words in the complete subject. The **simple predicate** is another name for the verb. The simple predicate is just the verb; it does not include the other words in the complete predicate.

Look at Sentence 1 again. I will draw one line under the simple subject and two lines under the simple predicate as you identify them in the sentence. To identify the simple subject, make sure you respond with the words "the subject noun" before you name the subject noun. **What is the simple subject? (*the subject noun, salesman*)** I will bold, or highlight, the line under the simple subject **salesman** so you can tell the difference between the simple subject and the complete subject.

To identify the simple predicate, make sure you say "the verb" before you name the verb. **What is the simple predicate? (*the verb, spoke*)** I will bold, or highlight, the line under the simple predicate *spoke* so you can tell the difference between the simple predicate and the complete predicate. (*Mark the answers for Sentences 2-3 in the same way. The small foals pranced happily nearby. The enormously fury rat ran around quickly.*)

Look at Reference 11 on page 13 in your book to see how to use the skills you have just learned in a classified sentence. This example is set up in the same format as it will appear on your test. (*Read the directions to your students and then go through the sentence, showing them how to find the answers for the noun job chart. Reference 11 is located below.*)

Reference 11: Noun Job Chart					
Directions: Look at the classified sentence below and underline the complete subject once and the complete predicate twice. Then, complete the table.					
1. SN V P1 A Adj SN V Adv Adv The angry teenager / stormed loudly upstairs. D					
List the Noun Used	List the Noun Job	Singular or Plural	Common or Proper	Simple Subject	Simple Predicate
teenager	SN	S	C	teenager	stormed

CHAPTER 3 LESSON 1 CONTINUED

Teacher's Notes: During a Skill Builder Check, the teacher will ask a series of questions designed to teach and reinforce basic or advanced skills on a regular basis. This exercise helps students identify sentence parts and types of nouns easily and also provides effective vocabulary work as it is added. A Skill Builder Check will enhance students' knowledge and understanding of concepts on a regular basis.

 PRACTICE TIME

Have students turn to page 54 in the Practice Section of their book and find the skill under Chapter 3, Lesson 1, Practice. They will do an independent practice exercise on completing a noun job table. Tell them this practice is not hard, but they must pay attention and think about what they are doing. Go over the directions to make sure they understand what to do. Check and discuss the Practice after students have finished. (*Chapter 3, Lesson 1, Practice key is given below.*)

Chapter 3, Lesson 1, Practice: Look at the classified sentence below and underline the complete subject once and the complete predicate twice. Then, complete the table below.

```
            A     Adj      SN      V     Adv     Adv
SN  V    An enormous elephant / stomped angrily around!  E
P1
```

List the Noun Used	List the Noun Job	Singular or Plural	Common or Proper	Simple Subject	Simple Predicate
elephant	SN	S	C	elephant	stomped

 VOCABULARY TIME

Assign Chapter 3, Vocabulary Words #1 on page 7 in the Reference Section for students to define in their Vocabulary notebooks. Tell students they are to use a dictionary or thesaurus to look up the meanings of the vocabulary words. After they write each word and its meaning, students are to write a sentence using the vocabulary word.

Chapter 3, Vocabulary Words #1
(conceal, exhume, mimic, imitate)

(End of lesson.)

CHAPTER 3   LESSON 2
New objectives: Grammar (Introductory Sentences, adverb exception), Skills (parts of speech), Practice sheet, and Vocabulary #2.

 JINGLE TIME

Have students turn to the Jingle Section of their books. The teacher will lead the students in reciting the previously-taught jingles.

 GRAMMAR TIME

Put the introductory sentences from the box below on the board. Use these sentences as you go through each new concept covered in your teaching script. For the greatest benefit, students must participate orally with the teacher. (*You might put the introductory sentences on notebook paper if you are doing one-on-one instruction with your students.*)

Chapter 3, Introductory Sentences for Lesson 2
1. _____ The young musician often played too loudly.
2. _____ The wild dogs growled viciously today!
3. _____ The roaring engine quickly steamed away.

TEACHING SCRIPT FOR AN ADVERB EXCEPTION

In this lesson, we are going to add another new part to the Question and Answer Flow. This new part is an **adverb exception**. Turn to page 13 in the Reference Section of your book and look at Reference 12 as I explain an **adverb exception**.

Since the verb usually begins the predicate, an **adverb exception** occurs when you have an adverb immediately <u>before</u> the verb that starts the predicate. To add the **adverb exception** to the Question and Answer Flow, you will say, "*Is there an adverb exception?*" If there is not an adverb before the verb, you say, "*No.*" If there is an adverb before the verb, you will say, "*Yes - change the line.*" To show the adverb exception, simply erase your slash mark and put it in front of the adverb that is immediately before the verb. (*Have students follow along as you read and discuss the adverb exception in the example box below.*)

Reference 12: Adverb Exception
(The famous actor **<u>suddenly</u>** / ***collapsed***.) To show the adverb exception: (The famous actor / **<u>suddenly collapsed</u>**.)
To add the adverb exception to the Question and Answer Flow, say, "*Is there an adverb exception?*" If there is not an adverb before the verb you say, "*No.*" If there is an adverb before the verb, you say, "*Yes - change the line.*"

As we classify Sentences 1-3, we will add the adverb exception to the Question and Answer Flows. Remember, the adverb exception question will be added to the end of the Q & A Flow. Begin.

CHAPTER 3 LESSON 2 CONTINUED

Teacher's Notes: Make sure students say the questions and answers orally for each sentence. Be sure to lead them so they will say the Question and Answer Flows correctly.

Question and Answer Flow for Sentence 1: The young musician often played too loudly.

1. Who played too loudly? musician - SN
2. What is being said about musician? musician played - V
3. Played how? loudly - Adv
4. How loudly? too - Adv
5. Played when? often - Adv
6. What kind of musician? young - Adj
7. The - A
8. SN V P1 Check
9. Period, statement, declarative sentence
10. Go back to the verb - divide the complete subject from the complete predicate.
11. Is there an adverb exception? Yes - change the line.

Classified Sentence:

```
                        A   Adj   SN      Adv   V   Adv Adv
         SN  V         The young musician / often played too loudly.  D
         P1
```

Question and Answer Flow for Sentence 2: The wild dogs growled viciously today!

1. What growled viciously today? dogs - SN
2. What is being said about dogs? dogs growled - V
3. Growled how? viciously - Adv
4. Growled when? today - Adv
5. What kind of dogs? wild - Adj
6. The - A
7. SN V P1 Check
8. Exclamation point, strong feeling, exclamatory sentence
9. Go back to the verb - divide the complete subject from the complete predicate.
10. Is there an adverb exception? No.

Classified Sentence:

```
                      A  Adj  SN       V    Adv    Adv
         SN  V       The wild dogs / growled viciously today!  E
         P1
```

Question and Answer Flow for Sentence 3: The roaring engine quickly steamed away.

1. What steamed away? engine - SN
2. What is being said about engine? engine steamed - V
3. Steamed where? away - Adv
4. Steamed how? quickly - Adv
5. What kind of engine? roaring - Adj
6. The - A
7. SN V P1 Check
8. Period, statement, declarative sentence
9. Go back to the verb - divide the complete subject from the complete predicate.
10. Is there an adverb exception? Yes - change the line.

Classified Sentence:

```
                      A   Adj    SN      Adv    V     Adv
         SN  V       The roaring engine / quickly steamed away.  D
         P1
```

CHAPTER 3 LESSON 2 CONTINUED

TEACHER INSTRUCTIONS

Use Sentences 1-3 that you just classified with your students to do an Oral Skill Builder Check. From this time forward, the skills for an Oral Skill Builder Check and a short explanation will be listed in a Skill Builder box. As more skills are covered, they will be added to the skill box. These guidelines will help you know the skills you have covered.

Pg. 33

Oral Skill Builder Check	
1. Noun check. (Say the job and then say the noun. Circle each noun.)	**4. Identify the complete subject and the complete predicate.** (Underline the complete subject once and the complete predicate twice.)
2. Identify the nouns as singular or plural. (Write S or P above each noun.)	**5. Identify the simple subject and simple predicate.** (Underline the simple subject once and the simple predicate twice. Bold, or highlight, the lines to distinguish them from the complete subject and complete predicate.)
3. Identify the nouns as common or proper. (Follow established procedure for oral identification.)	

SKILL TIME

TEACHING SCRIPT FOR THE PARTS OF SPEECH

To have a keen understanding of different subject areas, you must understand the vocabulary used to communicate in any given area. English is no different. In fact, there are several areas in English where vocabulary is important. Knowing the vocabulary for grammar, mechanics, and usage will make it easier to communicate in writing and editing.

First, we must know why it is so important to have an excellent command of grammar. It is important to learn grammar well because it is the vocabulary for the sentences used in writing. We can talk to each other about writing and editing when we know how to talk about the sentences we write and how we put them together in paragraphs.

Second, we must gain mastery in the areas of grammar, mechanics, and usage to have a command of editing. Your study of English this year will help you in all these areas.

We will now discuss the eight parts of speech. Do you know that all words in the English language have been put into eight groups called the **Parts of Speech**? How a word is used in a sentence determines its part of speech. The sentences you have been classifying are made from four parts of speech. Do you know the names of these four parts of speech? *(noun, verb, adjective,* and *adverb)*

These first four parts of speech are easy to remember because you are using them every day. Make sure you remember them because you will also have them on your test. You will learn the other parts of speech later. *(Have students repeat the four parts of speech four or five times together, orally, and in a rhythmic fashion.)*

CHAPTER 3 LESSON 2 CONTINUED

TEACHING SCRIPT FOR ONLY ONE PART OF SPEECH IN A SENTENCE

(Note: Have the example below on the board or on a sheet of paper.)

Adjective(s): 1. The two hungry bears raced swiftly forward!

I am going to show you the steps to use whenever you need to identify only one part of speech in a sentence. First, no matter what part of speech you are looking for, always identify the subject and verb. This will give you the foundation from which to work. In the example on the board, we are looking for only one part of speech: the adjective.

1. Is Sentence 1 about a person, animal, place, or thing? animal
2. What is the sentence about? bears *(Write **SN** above bears.)*
3. What is being said about bears? bears raced *(Write **V** above raced.)*
4. What part of speech is listed to be identified? adjective
5. Where do we go to find adjectives? to nouns or pronouns
6. What is the noun in the sentence? bears
7. Are there any adjectives modifying the noun *bears*? yes
8. What are they? the, two, and hungry
9. We will do an adjective check to verify the adjectives:

> What kind of bears? hungry - adjective (underline the adjective *hungry*)
> How many bears? two - adjective (underline the adjective *two*)
> The - article adjective (underline the adjective *the*)

Your finished sentence should look like this:

SN   V

Adjective(s): 1. The two hungry bears raced swiftly forward!

If you follow this procedure, you should have no trouble finding a specific part of speech without having to classify the whole sentence. But if you are ever in doubt, classify the whole sentence to be sure of your answers.

You will now practice not only this skill, but you will also practice classifying a sentence and completing a noun job table.

CHAPTER 3 LESSON 2 CONTINUED

 PRACTICE TIME

Have students turn to page 54 in the Practice Section of their books and find the skill under Chapter 3, Lesson 2, Practice. They will complete a noun job table and find only one part of speech from a group of sentences. Tell them this practice is not hard, but they must pay attention and think about what they are doing. Go over the directions to make sure they understand what to do. Check and discuss the Lesson 2, Practice after students have finished. (*Chapter 3, Lesson 2, Practice key is given below.*)

Chapter 3, Lesson 2, Practice: Classify the sentence below. Underline the complete subject once and the complete predicate twice. Then, complete the table.

	A Adj Adj SN V Adv Adv
SN V	The beautiful wild horses / raced swiftly away. D
P1	

List the Noun Used	List the Noun Job	Singular or Plural	Common or Proper	Simple Subject	Simple Predicate
horses	SN	P	C	horses	raced

Finding One Part of Speech: For each sentence, write *SN* above the simple subject and *V* above the simple predicate. Underline the word(s) for the part of speech listed to the left of each sentence.

Adjective(s):   1. The <u>crisp,</u> <u>brown</u> leaves wave loudly every autumn.

Adverb(s):   2. The flustered young man <u>finally</u> walked <u>very</u> <u>quickly</u> <u>away</u>.

Noun(s):   3. Several frightened green <u>frogs</u> leaped hurriedly away.

Adjective(s):   4. <u>The</u> dog slowly limped away.

Verb(s):   5. The actors <u>preformed</u> extremely well.

 VOCABULARY TIME

Assign Chapter 3, Vocabulary Words **#2** on page 7 in the Reference section for students to define in their Vocabulary notebooks. Tell students they are to use a dictionary or thesaurus to look up the meanings of the vocabulary words. After they write each word and its meaning, students are to write a sentence using the vocabulary word.

Chapter 3, Vocabulary Words #2
(fact, hypothesis, debate, argue)

(End of lesson.)

CHAPTER 3   LESSON 3

New objectives: Grammar (Practice Sentences), Skills (Adding Vocabulary Check to Skill Builder Time), and a Practice sheet.

JINGLE TIME

Have students turn to the Jingle Section of their books. The teacher will lead the students in reciting the previously-taught jingles.

GRAMMAR TIME

First-Year Option: Put the Practice Sentences from the box below on the board or notebook paper. Use these sentences as you practice the concepts that have been taught. For the greatest benefit, students must participate orally with the teacher. **Second-Year Option:** Have students classify the Practice Sentences independently on paper. Check students' sentences with the answers provided below. (*If you have the CDs for Practice Sentences, have students check their sentences with the CDs.*)

Chapter 3, Practice Sentences for Lesson 3
1. _____ The large, frightened crowd dispersed quickly.
2. _____ The talented young ballerina danced amazingly well.
3. _____ The exhausted traveler finally flew home!

TEACHING SCRIPT FOR PRACTICING PATTERN 1 SENTENCES

We will classify three different sentences to practice the Question and Answer Flows for Pattern 1 sentences. We will classify the sentences together. Begin. (*You might have your students write the labels above the sentences at this time.*)

Teacher's Notes: Make sure students say the questions and answers orally for each sentence. Be sure to lead them so they will say the Question and Answer Flows correctly.

Question and Answer Flow for Sentence 1: The large, frightened crowd dispersed quickly.

1. Who dispersed quickly? crowd – SN
2. What is being said about crowd? crowd dispersed – V
3. Dispersed how? quickly – Adv
4. What kind of crowd? frightened – Adj
5. What kind of crowd? large – Adj
6. The – A

7. SN V P1 Check
8. Period, statement, declarative sentence
9. Go back to the verb – divide the complete subject from the complete predicate.
10. Is there an adverb exception? No.

Classified Sentence:

```
                      A   Adj    Adj   SN     V     Adv
           SN  V     The large, frightened crowd / dispersed quickly.  D
           ────
           P1
```

CHAPTER 3 LESSON 3 CONTINUED

Question and Answer Flow for Sentence 2: The talented young ballerina danced amazingly well.

1. Who danced amazingly well? ballerina – SN
2. What is being said about ballerina? ballerina danced – V
3. Danced how? well – Adv
4. How well? amazingly – Adv
5. What kind of ballerina? young – Adj
6. What kind of ballerina? talented – Adj

7. The – A
8. SN V P1 Check
9. Period, statement, declarative sentence
10. Go back to the verb – divide the complete subject from the complete predicate.
11. Is there an adverb exception? No.

Classified Sentence:

		A	Adj	Adj	SN	V	Adv	Adv
SN V		The talented young ballerina / danced amazingly well. **D**
P1		

Question and Answer Flow for Sentence 3: The exhausted traveler finally flew home!

1. Who finally flew home? traveler – SN
2. What is being said about traveler? traveler flew – V
3. Flew where? home – Adv
4. Flew when? finally – Adv
5. What kind of traveler? exhausted – Adj
6. The – A

7. SN V P1 Check
8. Exclamation point, strong feeling, exclamatory sentence
9. Go back to the verb – divide the complete subject from the complete predicate.
10. Is there an adverb exception? Yes – change the line.

Classified Sentence:

		A	Adj	SN	Adv	V	Adv
SN V		The exhausted traveler / finally flew home! **E**
P1		

TEACHER INSTRUCTIONS

Use Sentences 1-3 that you just classified with your students to do an Oral Skill Builder Check. Use the guidelines below.

Oral Skill Builder Check

1. **Noun check.**
   (Say the job and then say the noun. Circle each noun.)
2. **Identify the nouns as singular or plural.**
   (Write S or P above each noun.)
3. **Identify the nouns as common or proper.**
   (Follow established procedure for oral identification.)

4. **Identify the complete subject and the complete predicate.** (Underline the complete subject once and the complete predicate twice.)
5. **Identify the simple subject and simple predicate.**
   (Underline the simple subject once and the simple predicate twice. Bold, or highlight, the lines to distinguish them from the complete subject and complete predicate.)

SKILL TIME

TEACHING SCRIPT FOR ADDING A VOCABULARY CHECK TO SKILL BUILDER TIME

Look at Sentence 1 that we just classified. We will use this sentence to learn a new Skill Builder. We will add a vocabulary check to the Oral Skill Builder Check time. The vocabulary check will give me an opportunity to expand your vocabulary. I will select different words from the three sentences that we classify together in class for a vocabulary check. We will define the words, use them in new sentences, and name synonyms and antonyms for them.

CHAPTER 3 LESSON 3 CONTINUED

TEACHER INSTRUCTIONS

Look over the words in the classified sentences. Select any words you think your students may not understand or words for which you want students to develop a broader understanding. Use the guidelines below for a Vocabulary Check. (*You might use all the guidelines below for the word **dispersed**. Then, you might ask only for synonyms and antonyms for the words **frightened**, **crowd**, and **quickly**. Talk about how synonym and antonym changes can even affect the meaning of the original sentence. Show your students that synonyms and antonyms are powerful writing tools, and they must learn to use them well.*)

Guidelines for a Vocabulary Check

1. Give a definition for the word.
2. Use the word correctly in a sentence.
3. Think of a synonym for the word.
4. Think of an antonym for the word.

Teacher's Note: A Vocabulary Check is an excellent way to enrich your students' writing vocabulary. There will be times when you may just ask for a synonym and an antonym for different words in the three sentences. This will give students a better command of the options they have when making word choices as they write sentences. Remind students of the power of words and give them plenty of practice as you utilize the three sentences they have classified.

 PRACTICE TIME

Have students turn to page 55 in the Practice Section of their book and find Chapter 3, Lesson 3, Practice. Go over the directions to make sure they understand what to do. Check and discuss the Practice after students have finished. (*Chapter 3, Lesson 3, Practice key is given below.*)

Chapter 3, Lesson 3, Practice: Put this 3-part assignment on notebook paper: (1) Write the four parts of speech that you have studied so far (in any order). (2) Write out the Question and Answer Flow in exact order for the sentence listed. (3) Classify the sentence.

1. noun	2. verb	3. adjective	4. adverb

Practice Sentence: The large frightened crowd dispersed quickly.

Question and Answer Flow Key for Practice Sentence: The large frightened crowd dispersed quickly.

1. Who dispersed quickly? crowd - SN
2. What is being said about crowd? crowd dispersed - V
3. Dispersed how? quickly - Adv
4. What kind of crowd? frightened - Adj
5. What kind of crowd? large - Adj
6. The - A

7. SN V P1 Check
8. Period, statement, declarative sentence
9. Go back to the verb - divide the complete subject from the complete predicate.
10. Is there an adverb exception? No.

Classified Sentence:

```
          A   Adj     Adj     SN      V     Adv
SN V ____ The large frightened crowd / dispersed quickly.  D
P1
```

(End of lesson.)

CHAPTER 3   LESSON 4

New objectives: Test and an Activity.

 JINGLE TIME

Have students turn to the Jingle Section of their books. The teacher will lead the students in reciting the previously-taught jingles.

 STUDY TIME

Have students study the vocabulary words in their vocabulary notebooks. Remind students that any vocabulary word in their notebooks could be on their test. Also, have students study any of the skills in the Practice Section that they need to review.

 TEST TIME

Have students turn to page 84 in the Test Section of their books and find Chapter 3 Test. Remind them to pay attention and to think about what they are doing. Go over the directions to make sure they understand what to do. (*Chapter 3 Test key is on the next page.*)

 CHECK TIME

After students have finished, check and discuss their test papers. Make sure they understand why their answers are right or wrong. (*For total points, count each required answer as a point.*)

 ACTIVITY / ASSIGNMENT TIME

Make a list of ten people in your family (and/or extended family). Write each family member's name on an index card. On the back of each index card, write a descriptive sentence about the person listed on the front. Be sure to include as many adjectives and adverbs as possible. Finally, play a guessing game with different members of your family. Read aloud or hold up the side of the card with the description and let family members guess whose name is written on the other side. Discuss the family members that were the hardest and easiest to guess. Also, discuss the family members that were the hardest and easiest to describe.

(End of lesson.)

Chapter 3 Test
(Student Page 84)

Exercise 1: Classify each sentence.

```
                A    Adj    Adj     SN    V     Adv
1. SN  V        The tired, hungry campers / hiked wearily. D
   ‾‾‾‾
   P1
                A    Adj    Adj     SN    Adv   V     Adv
2. SN  V        The three frightened deer / quickly ran away. D
   ‾‾‾‾
   P1
                A    Adj    Adj     SN    V     Adv    Adv
3. SN  V        The brave young soldier / turned swiftly around. D
   ‾‾‾‾
   P1
```

Exercise 2: Use Sentence 3 to underline the complete subject once and the complete predicate twice and to complete the table below.

List the Noun Used	List the Noun Job	Singular or Plural	Common or Proper	Simple Subject	Simple Predicate
1. soldier	2. SN	3. S	4. C	5. soldier	6. turned

Exercise 3: Name the four parts of speech that you have studied so far. *(Accept answers in any order.)*

1. noun   2. verb   3. adjective   4. adverb

Exercise 4: Finding One Part of Speech. For each sentence, write *SN* above the simple subject and *V* above the simple predicate. Underline the word(s) for the part of speech listed to the left of each sentence.

```
                       SN        V
Adjective(s):   1. The old couple slowly strolled along.
                        SN          V
Adverb(s):      2. The children merrily played outside yesterday.
                         SN     V
Noun(s):        3. The small toddler toppled over.
                       SN        V
Adjective(s):   4. The chickens clucked loudly.
                      SN    V
Verb(s):        5. The hero acted very bravely.
                         SN      V
Adverb(s):      6. The bright balloons sagged sadly today.
```

Exercise 5: Identify each pair of words as synonyms or antonyms by putting parentheses ( ) around *syn* or *ant*.

1. argue, debate	(syn) ant	5. destroy, abolish	(syn) ant	9. acknowledge, admit	(syn) ant
2. authentic, false	syn (ant)	6. timid, audacious	syn (ant)	10. conceal, exhume	syn (ant)
3. prodigy, genius	(syn) ant	7. pardon, amnesty	(syn) ant	11. construction, dilapidation	syn (ant)
4. fact, hypothesis	syn (ant)	8. mimic, imitate	(syn) ant	12. withhold, bequeath	syn (ant)

Exercise 6: In your journal, write a paragraph summarizing what you have learned this week.

CHAPTER 3 LESSON 4 CONTINUED

TEACHER INSTRUCTIONS

Use the Question and Answer Flows below for the sentences on Chapter 3 Test.

Question and Answer Flow for Sentence 1: The tired hungry campers hiked wearily.

1. Who hiked wearily? campers - SN
2. What is being said about campers? campers hiked - V
3. Hiked how? wearily - Adv
4. What kind of campers? hungry - Adj
5. What kind of campers? tired - Adj
6. The - A

7. SN V P1 Check
8. Period, statement, declarative sentence
9. Go back to the verb - divide the complete subject from the complete predicate.
10. Is there an adverb exception? No.

Classified Sentence:

<pre>
                        A   Adj   Adj   SN   V   Adv
           SN V   The tired hungry campers / hiked wearily. D
           ‾‾‾‾‾‾
            P1
</pre>

Question and Answer Flow for Sentence 2: The three frightened deer quickly ran away.

1. What ran away? deer - SN
2. What is being said about deer? deer ran - V
3. Ran where? away - Adv
4. Ran how? quickly - Adv
5. What kind of deer? frightened - Adj
6. How many deer? three - Adj
7. The - A

8. SN V P1 Check
9. Period, statement, declarative sentence
10. Go back to the verb - divide the complete subject from the complete predicate.
11. Is there an adverb exception? Yes - change the line.

Classified Sentence:

<pre>
                        A   Adj   Adj   SN   Adv   V   Adv
           SN V   The three frightened deer / quickly ran away. D
           ‾‾‾‾‾‾
            P1
</pre>

Question and Answer Flow for Sentence 3: The brave young soldier turned swiftly around.

1. Who turned swiftly around? soldier - SN
2. What is being said about soldier? soldier turned - V
3. Turned how? swiftly - Adv
4. Turned where? around - Adv
5. What kind of soldier? young - Adj
6. What kind of soldier? brave - Adj

7. The - A
8. SN V P1 Check
9. Period, statement, declarative sentence
10. Go back to the verb - divide the complete subject from the complete predicate.
11. Is there an adverb exception? No.

Classified Sentence:

<pre>
                        A   Adj   Adj   SN   V   Adv   Adv
           SN V   The brave young soldier / turned swiftly around. D
           ‾‾‾‾‾‾
            P1
</pre>

(End of lesson.)

CHAPTER 3   LESSON 5

New objectives: Writing (expository) and Writing Assignment #1.

 WRITING TIME

Teacher's Notes:

As students write their three-point paragraphs, it is very important that they follow the exact writing pattern that this lesson teaches. If this is done consistently, the students will learn to organize their writing by learning how to do these things: write a topic sentence for any given topic, write sentences that support the topic, and write a concluding sentence that summarizes their paragraph.

Teaching students how to write a three-point paragraph gives students several advantages:

1. It gives students a definite, concrete pattern to follow when asked to write a paragraph.
2. It gives students the practice they need in organizing their writing.
3. It gives students a chance to greatly improve their self-confidence because, as they advance in the program, they become stronger and more independent in all areas of their grammar and writing skills.

TEACHER INSTRUCTIONS

Put the following writing definitions on the board

> 1. **Paragraph** - a group of sentences that is written about one particular subject or topic.
> 2. **Topic** - the subject of the paragraph; the topic tells what the paragraph is about.
> 3. **Expository writing** - the discussion or telling of ideas by giving facts, directions, explanations, definitions, and examples.

TEACHING SCRIPT FOR INTRODUCING EXPOSITORY WRITING AND WRITING DEFINITIONS

As a fifth grade student, you want to be prepared to be a good writer. As a part of that preparation, today, we are going to learn about expository writing and how to organize your writing by writing a three-point paragraph. First, let's look at some key definitions to be sure that we know what we are talking about.

Look at the first two definitions. A **paragraph** is a group of sentences that is written about one particular subject or topic. A **topic** is the subject of the paragraph; the topic tells what the paragraph is about.

Now, let's look at the last definition: **expository writing**. I want you to say "expository writing" with me so we can feel this type of writing on our tongues: **Expository writing**! Expository writing is the discussion or telling of ideas by giving facts, directions, explanations, definitions, and examples.

CHAPTER 3 LESSON 5 CONTINUED

In other words, expository writing is informational. Its purpose is to inform, to give facts, to give directions, to explain, or to define something. Remember that expository writing is informational because it gives some type of information.

Since expository writing deals with information of some kind, it is very important to focus on making the meaning clear and understandable. The reader must be able to understand exactly what the writer means.

Now that we know what expository writing is, we must learn more about it because the first type of paragraph that we learn to write is an EXPOSITORY paragraph. What makes any type of writing easy is knowing exactly what to do when you are given a writing assignment. And the first thing you learn to do is organize your writing.

Expository writing may be organized in different ways. One of the most common ways to write an expository paragraph is by using a **three-point paragraph format.** The three-point paragraph format is a way of organizing the sentences in your expository paragraph that will help make your meaning clear and understandable.

Now, you will learn how to write a three-point expository paragraph. I am going to give you a topic about which you are to write your paragraph. Remember that a topic tells what the paragraph is about; it is the subject of the paragraph. In order to make sure you understand, we are going to write a three-point expository paragraph together, following specific steps.

TEACHING SCRIPT FOR SELECTING THE THREE POINTS OF THE PARAGRAPH

The first thing we learn is how to select and list the points that we are going to write about. Let's begin with our topic. Remember that a topic is a subject. The topic about which we are going to write our paragraph is "Favorite foods." I will write this on the board under "Topic." (_Demonstrate by writing on the board._)

Topic: Favorite foods

Do you have some favorite foods about which you could write? (_Discuss some favorite foods._) Now, let's see how we are going to write this paragraph. Remember that I told you this paragraph is called a three-point paragraph. First, we are going to look at our topic, "Favorite foods," and see if we can list three favorite foods about which we can write.

Teacher's Note:
Even though students have named their favorite foods, the teaching example will use pizza, hamburgers, and ice cream.

CHAPTER 3 LESSON 5 CONTINUED

Pizza, hamburgers, and ice cream: These are three good favorite foods. I will list these three foods on the board under "3 points about the topic." They will be the three points for our three-point expository paragraph. (*Demonstrate by writing on the board.*)

3 points about the topic

1. _____pizza_____ 2. _____hamburgers_____ 3. _____ice cream_____

Now, let's set them aside for a minute and begin our paragraph. We are going to use these three items shortly.

Teacher's Notes: The simplified outline below will give you a quick view of what you will be covering with your students in your discussion of the three-point expository paragraph. Write each part on the board only as it is being discussed so that your students will not be overwhelmed by the amount of written work that they see on the board.

The Three-Point Expository Paragraph Outline

Topic
3 points about the topic
Sentence #1: Topic sentence
Sentence #2: A three-point sentence
Sentence #3: A **first**-point sentence
Sentence #4: A **supporting** sentence for the first point
Sentence #5: A **second**-point sentence
Sentence #6: A **supporting** sentence for the second point
Sentence #7: A **third**-point sentence
Sentence #8: A **supporting** sentence for the third point
Sentence #9: A concluding sentence

Teacher's Notes: As you work through the steps, be sure to show students how the sentences are divided into three categories: the introduction (*topic and three-point sentence*), the body (*the three main points and their supporting sentences*), and the conclusion (*the concluding sentence*).

TEACHING SCRIPT FOR WRITING THE TOPIC SENTENCE

First, we must write what is called a topic sentence. A topic sentence is very important because it tells the main idea of our paragraph. We are going to let the topic sentence be the first sentence in our paragraph because it tells everyone what our paragraph is going to be about. In many paragraphs, it is not the first sentence. Later, we can learn to put the topic sentence in other places in the paragraph, but, for now, it is important that we make it the first sentence in our three-point paragraph.

CHAPTER 3 LESSON 5 CONTINUED

The topic sentence for a three-point paragraph needs three things:

1. It needs to tell the main idea of the paragraph.
2. It needs to be general because the other sentences in the paragraph must tell about the topic sentence.
3. It needs to tell the number of points that will be discussed in the paragraph.

When you write a topic sentence for a three-point paragraph, follow these two easy steps:

1. You will use all or some of the words in the topic.
2. You will tell the number of points, or ideas, you will discuss in your paragraph.

Now, we are going to write a topic sentence by following the two easy steps we have just discussed. Look at our topic, "My Favorite Foods." Without actually listing the three specific points -- pizza, hamburgers, and ice cream -- let's write a sentence that makes a general statement about the main idea of our topic and tells the number of points we will list later.

How about "I have three favorite foods?" I will write this on the board under "Sentence #1: Topic sentence." (*Demonstrate by writing on the board. Read the sentence to the students.*)

Sentence #1. Topic sentence: I have three favorite foods.

Look at the topic sentence on the board. Notice that in this sentence, we have mentioned our topic, "My Favorite Foods," and we have stated that there are three of these foods; we will tell what the three are in the three-point sentence that follows.

Also, notice that we did not say, "I am going to tell you about my three favorite foods." We do not need to tell the reader we are going to tell him/her something; we simply do it. To say "I am going to tell you" is called "writing about your writing," and it is not effective writing. Do not "Write about your writing."

TEACHING SCRIPT FOR WRITING THE THREE-POINT SENTENCE

Now that we have our topic sentence, our next sentence will list the three specific points our paragraph will discuss. Our next sentence could be, "These foods are pizza, hamburgers, and ice cream." I will write this on the board under "Sentence #2: A three-point sentence." (*Demonstrate by writing the information below on the board. Read the sentence to the students.*)

Sentence #2. A three-point sentence: These foods are pizza, hamburgers, and ice cream.

Look at the order in which I have listed the three foods. You must always be aware of the order in which you put your points because that will be the order in which you discuss these points in your paragraph.

I have chosen to place these in this order: pizza, hamburgers, and ice cream. I chose to put "ice cream" last because it is usually thought of as a dessert. I did not have any particular reason for placing pizza before hamburgers. Depending upon your three points as well as your purpose in writing, you will select the order of your three points.

CHAPTER 3 LESSON 5 CONTINUED

Notice three things we have done here:

1. We have put our three items in the order we have chosen, remembering that we will be discussing these points in this order later in our paragraph. (*pizza, hamburgers, and ice cream*)

2. We have written our first sentence, and our first sentence tells us the number of points that will be discussed in the rest of the paragraph. (*I have three favorite foods.*)

3. We have started our listing sentence with words that helped us connect it to our first sentence. (*These foods are **pizza, hamburgers, and ice cream**.*)

Notice how we have used repetition to link our two sentences. Our first sentence mentions **"favorite foods"** by stating **"I have three favorite foods."** Sentence number two, **"These foods are pizza, hamburgers, and ice cream,"** refers to sentence number one by stating **"These foods,"** meaning the favorite foods just mentioned in sentence number one. Although you will not want to use repetition in every sentence to link sentences, repetition is a good device for making your paragraph flow smoothly.

TEACHING SCRIPT FOR DEVELOPING AND SUPPORTING THE POINTS OF THE PARAGRAPH

After you have stated the general topic sentence and then followed it by the more specific three-point sentence, you will begin to discuss each of the three points, one at a time. DO NOT FORGET: You are going to discuss them in the order in which you listed them in sentence number two. You will begin your third sentence by stating, "My first favorite food is pizza." This is your first listed point. I will write this on the board under "Sentence #3: A first point sentence." (*Demonstrate by writing the information below on the board. Read the sentence to the students.*)

Sentence #3. A first-point sentence: My first favorite food is pizza.

Next, you will write one sentence about pizza. It can be a descriptive sentence about pizza. It can be a reason why you like pizza, but it must be about pizza's being your favorite food. This is called a supporting sentence. I will now write a supporting sentence on the board under "Sentence #4: A supporting sentence for the first point." You can use this sentence or make up your own: "I like pizza because of its great Italian taste." (*Demonstrate by writing the information below on the board. Read the sentence to the students.*)

Sentence #4. A supporting sentence for the first point: I like pizza because of its great Italian taste.

When you keep your writing targeted to the topic you are assigned, your paragraph will have what we call "unity," or will be a "unified" paragraph. In a unified paragraph, all sentences work together to form one idea about the subject, or topic.

As you get more skilled at three-point writing, you may write two or more sentences about each of your listed points, but, for now, stay with one sentence for each point. Each of the sentences that you write following your points should support what you have stated in that point. Use only ideas that support. Discard non-supporting ideas.

CHAPTER 3 LESSON 5 CONTINUED

So far, we have introduced our topic and listed our three specific points. We have begun to discuss our three points and have completed the first point along with a sentence that supports the first point. So far, we have four sentences.

Your fifth sentence will introduce the second point of the three-point paragraph. Your second point is "hamburgers." Since "hamburgers" is the second item you listed, your fifth sentence should state, "My second favorite food is hamburgers." I will write this on the board under "Sentence #5: A second point sentence." (*Demonstrate by writing the information below on the board. Read the sentence to the students.*)

Sentence #5. A second-point sentence: My second favorite food is hamburgers.

Just as you wrote the sentence supporting the statement of your first point, so now you must write a sentence supporting your statement about hamburger's being your second favorite food. I will write the next supporting sentence on the board under "Sentence #6: A supporting sentence for the second point." (*Demonstrate by writing the information below on the board. Read the sentence to the students.*)

Sentence #6. A supporting sentence for the second point: To me, the best kind is the hamburger that has all the trimmings, even onions.

By now, you can begin to see a pattern to your paragraph. However, you still have another point about which to write. So far, you have written six sentences in your paragraph. Your seventh sentence will list your third favorite food, ice cream. I will write this sentence on the board under "Sentence #7: A third-point sentence." (*Demonstrate by writing the information below on the board. Read the sentence to the students.*)

Sentence #7. A third-point sentence: My third favorite food is ice cream.

Following this sentence, your eighth sentence should make a supporting statement about ice cream's being your third favorite food. I will write this supporting sentence on the board under "Sentence #8: A supporting sentence for the third point." (*Demonstrate by writing the information below on the board. Read the sentence to the students.*)

Sentence #8. A supporting sentence for the third point: I love ice cream because I love sweet, creamy things to eat.

TEACHING SCRIPT FOR WRITING THE CONCLUSION OF THE PARAGRAPH

We have now introduced our topic, or subject, listed each of our three points, and made one supporting statement about each point. Now, we need to complete our paragraph, leaving the reader with the impression that he/she has read a finished product. In order to complete our paragraph, we need a conclusion, or final sentence.

There are different ways to write a concluding sentence, but one of the best and simplest is the summary statement. This means that the main points of the paragraph are stated again, briefly, in one sentence.

When you write a concluding sentence, follow these two easy steps:

1. You will use some of the words in your topic sentence.
2. You will add an extra, or concluding, thought about your paragraph.

CHAPTER 3 LESSON 5 CONTINUED

You might try a good compound sentence, such as, "I enjoy eating all kinds of foods, but my favorites will probably always be pizza, hamburgers, and ice cream." I will write this on the board under "Sentence #9: A concluding sentence." (*Demonstrate by writing the information below on the board. Read the sentence again to the students.*)

Sentence #9. A concluding sentence: I enjoy eating all kinds of foods, but my favorites will probably always be pizza, hamburgers, and ice cream.

370

TEACHING SCRIPT FOR CHECKING THE FINISHED PARAGRAPH

It is good to get in the habit of checking over your writing after you have finished. Just reading your finished paragraph several times slowly will help you see and hear things that you may want to correct. It also helps to have a checklist that tells specific areas to check to make sure you do not lose points for careless mistakes.

Look at your reference page as I read what it tells you to do as you write each sentence of your three-point paragraph. (*Read and discuss each section of the three-point paragraph example in Reference 14. Tell students to use this reference page if they need it when they write a three-point paragraph. It will help them organize their writing, and it will help them see the pattern of a three-point expository paragraph.*)

Teacher's Note: There was neither discussion nor guidelines provided for writing a title for the paragraph. Single paragraphs are often written without titles; the decision is left to the teacher or writer. Remind students that this is an expository paragraph, which means that its purpose is to inform or explain. The three-point format is a way of <u>organizing</u> an expository paragraph.

TEACHER INSTRUCTIONS FOR WRITING ASSIGNMENT #1

Give Writing Assignment #1 from the box below. Remind students to use the three-point paragraph example in Reference 14 on page 14 in the Reference Section if they need it. **If this is their first year in the program, tell students that this writing assignment will be done on a writing page in their books.** The writing page is already set up in a three-point format that will help them follow the form of the three-point paragraph. Direct students to page 55 in the Practice Section of their books. (*The practice page is reproduced for you at the end of this lesson on page 57.*)

Writing Assignment Box

Writing Assignment #1: Three-Point Expository Paragraph
Writing topic choices: My Favorite Foods   or My Favorite Sports/Hobbies   or My Favorite Sermons

---

After students have filled out the three-point practice page, have them transfer their sentences to a sheet of notebook paper or type them on a computer. Before students begin, go over the Writing Guidelines on the next page so they will know how to arrange their writing assignment on paper or on the computer.

CHAPTER 3 LESSON 5 CONTINUED

TEACHING SCRIPT FOR WRITING GUIDELINES

Today, we will go through some guidelines for your writing. Turn to page 13 in your book and look at Reference 13. You will use these guidelines every time you are given a writing assignment. (*Read and discuss the Writing Guidelines with your students.*)

Reference 13: Writing Guidelines
1. Label your writing assignment in the top right-hand corner of your page with the following information: A. Your Name   B. The Writing Assignment Number (*Example: WA#1, WA#2, etc.*)   C. Type of Writing (Examples: Expository Paragraph, Persuasive Essay, Descriptive Paragraph, etc.)   D. The title of the writing on the top of the first line   2. Think about the topic that you are assigned.   3. Think about the type of writing assigned, which is the purpose for the writing.   (*Is your writing intended to explain, persuade, describe, or narrate?*)   4. Think about the writing format, which is the organizational plan you are expected to use.   (*Is your assignment a paragraph, a 3-paragraph essay, a 5-paragraph essay, or a letter?*)   5. Use your writing time wisely.   (*Begin work quickly and concentrate on your assignment until it is finished.*)

TEACHING SCRIPT FOR USING THE WRITING PROCESS FOR WRITING ASSIGNMENT #1

As you begin this writing assignment, you will use the writing process discussed in Reference 13. I will give you a quick review of that writing process. First, you will think about your topic and gather any information you might need in order to do the writing. Second, you will write a rough draft. Remember that it is called a rough draft because it will be revised and edited. You do not have to worry about mistakes as you write your rough draft. After you write the first draft, you will make revisions, using the Revision Checklist in Reference 4. After you revise your writing, you will edit it, using the Beginning Editing Checklist in Reference 4. Finally, after you are satisfied with your revising and editing, you will write a final paper, using the Final Paper Checklist in Reference 4. You will then give the finished writing assignment to me.

TEACHER INSTRUCTIONS FOR CHECKING WRITING ASSIGNMENT #1

Read, check, and discuss Writing Assignment #1 after students have finished their final paper. Use the editing checklist (*Reference 4 on teacher's page 9*) as you check and discuss students' papers. Make sure students are using the editing checklist correctly. In the beginning, you must also check students' papers carefully for <u>form</u> mistakes. This will ensure that students are learning the three-point format correctly.

Teacher's Notes: It's okay for students to pattern their sentences after the examples. As they get stronger in this system and change topics, you will see more independent sentences. In fact, you will see a lot of variety in these paragraphs because students will probably choose at least two different foods and write different supporting sentences. Remind students that they now know how to add adjectives and adverbs to make their sentences more interesting and more expressive.

CHAPTER 3 LESSON 5 CONTINUED

Reference 14: Three-Point Paragraph Example

Topic: **My favorite foods**

Three main points: 1. **pizza**   2. **hamburgers**   3. **ice cream**

Sentence #1 – <u>Topic Sentence</u> (*Use words in the topic and tell how many points will be used.*)

I have three favorite foods.

Sentence #2 – <u>3-Point Sentence</u> (*List the 3 points in the order you will present them.*)

These foods are pizza, hamburgers, and ice cream.

Sentence #3 – <u>First Point</u>

My first favorite food is pizza.

Sentence #4 – <u>Supporting Sentence</u> for the first point.

I like pizza because of its great Italian taste.

Sentence #5 – <u>Second Point</u>

My second favorite food is hamburgers.

Sentence #6 – <u>Supporting Sentence</u> for the second point.

To me, the best kind is the hamburger that has all the trimmings, even onions.

Sentence #7 – <u>Third Point</u>

My third favorite food is ice cream.

Sentence #8 – <u>Supporting Sentence</u> for the third point.

I love ice cream because I love sweet, creamy things to eat.

Sentence #9 – <u>Concluding (final) Sentence</u>. (*Restate the topic sentence and add an extra thought.*)

I enjoy eating all kinds of foods, but my favorites will probably always be pizza, hamburgers, and ice cream.

SAMPLE PARAGRAPH　　　　　　　**My Favorite Foods**

    I have three favorite foods. These foods are pizza, hamburgers, and ice cream. My first favorite food is pizza. I like pizza because of its great Italian taste. My second favorite food is hamburgers. To me, the best kind is the hamburger that has all the trimmings, even onions. My third favorite food is ice cream. I love ice cream because I love sweet, creamy things to eat. I enjoy eating all kinds of foods, but my favorites will probably always be pizza, hamburgers, and ice cream.

CHAPTER 3 LESSON 5 CONTINUED

Chapter 3, Lesson 5, Practice Writing Page: Use the three-point outline form below to guide you as you write a three-point expository paragraph.

Write a topic: _____

Write 3 points to list about the topic.

1. _____ 2. _____ 3. _____

Sentence #1   Topic sentence (*Use words in the topic and tell how many points will be used.*)

_____

Sentence #2   3-point sentence (*List your 3 points in the order that you will present them.*)

_____

Sentence #3   State your first point in a complete sentence.

_____

Sentence #4   Write a supporting sentence for the first point.

_____

Sentence #5   State your second point in a complete sentence.

_____

Sentence #6   Write a supporting sentence for the second point.

_____

Sentence #7   State your third point in a complete sentence.

_____

Sentence #8   Write a supporting sentence for the third point.

_____

Sentence #9   Concluding sentence (*Restate the topic sentence and add an extra thought.*)

_____

Rewrite your nine-sentence paragraph on a sheet of notebook paper. Be sure to indent and use the checklists to help you edit your paragraph. Make sure you re-read your paragraph several times, slowly.

(End of lesson.)

CHAPTER 4 LESSON 1

New objectives: Grammar (Introductory Sentences, natural and inverted word order, Practice and Improved Sentences) and Vocabulary #1.

 JINGLE TIME

Have students turn to the Jingle Section of their books. The teacher will lead the students in reciting the previously-taught jingles.

 GRAMMAR TIME

Put the introductory sentences from the box below on the board. Use these sentences as you go through each new concept covered in your teaching script. For the greatest benefit, students must participate orally with the teacher. (*You might put the introductory sentences on notebook paper if you are doing one-on-one instruction with your students.*)

Chapter 4, Introductory Sentences for Lesson 1
1. _____ Yesterday, the huge snowflakes fell incredibly fast.
2. _____ The cranky little baby finally slept soundly.
3. _____ Surprisingly, the hungry seagulls swooped down very quickly.

TEACHING SCRIPT FOR NATURAL AND INVERTED WORD ORDER

In this lesson, we are going to add another part to the Question and Answer Flow. This new part will help us learn how to build variety into our sentences. Today, we will learn about **natural and inverted word order**. Turn to page 15 in the Reference Section of your book and look at Reference 15 as I explain natural and inverted word order.

Writers use inverted order to add variety to their sentences. Follow along as I read this important information to you. (*Read and discuss with your students all the information about natural and inverted word order in the reference box on the next page.*)

CHAPTER 4 LESSON 1 CONTINUED

Reference 15: Natural and Inverted Word Order

A **Natural Order** sentence has all subject parts first and all predicate parts after the verb. **Inverted Order** means that a sentence has predicate words in the complete subject. When a word is located in the complete subject but modifies the verb, it is a predicate word in the complete subject. A sentence with inverted order has one of these predicate words at the beginning of the complete subject: **an adverb, a helping verb, or a prepositional phrase**.

1. An adverb at the beginning of the sentence will modify the verb.

    (Example: <u>Tomorrow</u>, <u>we</u> / <u>will pick apples</u>.) (<u>We</u> / <u>will pick apples tomorrow</u>.)

2. A helping verb at the beginning of a sentence will always be part of the verb.

    (Example: <u>Have</u> <u>you</u> / <u>ordered a dessert</u>?) (<u>You</u> / <u>have ordered a dessert</u>.)

3. A prepositional phrase at the beginning of a sentence will often modify the verb.

    (Example: <u>During the night</u>, <u>we</u> / <u>heard sirens</u>.) (<u>We</u> / <u>heard sirens during the night</u>.)

To add inverted order to the Question and Answer Flow, say, *"Is this sentence in a natural or inverted order?"* If there are no predicate words in the complete subject, you say, *"Natural - No change."* If there are predicate words at the beginning of the complete subject, you say, *"Inverted - Underline the subject parts once and the predicate parts twice."* To identify the inverted order, draw one line under the subject parts and two lines under the predicate parts.

As we classify Sentences 1-3, we will add the **natural and inverted word order** to the Question and Answer Flows. Remember, the natural-and-inverted-word-order question will be added to the end of the Q & A Flow. We will identify only the adverb in this chapter. We will add the helping verb and the prepositional phrase after they have been taught. Begin.

Question and Answer Flow for Sentence 1: Yesterday, the huge snowflakes fell incredibly fast.

1. What fell incredibly fast? snowflakes - SN
2. What is being said about snowflakes?
    snowflakes fell - V
3. Fell how? fast - Adv
4. How fast? incredibly - Adv
5. What kind of snowflakes? huge - Adj
6. The - A
7. Fell when? yesterday - Adv

8. SN V P1 Check
9. Period, statement, declarative sentence
10. Go back to the verb - divide the complete subject from the complete predicate.
11. Is there an adverb exception? No.
12. Is this sentence in a natural or inverted order? Inverted - underline the subject parts once and the predicate parts twice.

Classified Sentence:

```
                       Adv      A  Adj     SN      V    Adv    Adv
            SN  V      Yesterday, the huge snowflakes / fell incredibly fast.  D
            P1
```

Question and Answer Flow for Sentence 2: The cranky little baby finally slept soundly.

1. Who finally slept soundly? baby - SN
2. What is being said about baby?
    baby slept - V
3. Slept how? soundly - Adv
4. Slept when? finally - Adv
5. What kind of baby? little - Adj
6. What kind of baby? cranky - Adj
7. The - A

8. SN V P1 Check
9. Period, statement, declarative sentence
10. Go back to the verb - divide the complete subject from the complete predicate.
11. Is there an adverb exception? Yes - change the line.
12. Is this sentence in a natural or inverted order? Natural - no change.

Classified Sentence:

```
                       A   Adj  Adj SN   Adv   V   Adv
            SN  V      The cranky little baby / finally slept soundly.  D
            P1
```

CHAPTER 4 LESSON 1 CONTINUED

Question and Answer Flow for Sentence 3: Surprisingly, the hungry seagulls swooped down very quickly.

1. What swooped down very quickly? seagulls - SN
2. What is being said about seagulls?
   seagulls swooped - V
3. Swooped where? down - Adv
4. Swooped how? quickly - Adv
5. How quickly? very - Adv
6. What kind of seagulls? hungry – Adj
7. The - A

8. Swooped how? surprisingly - Adv
9. SN V P1 Check
10. Period, statement, declarative sentence
11. Go back to the verb - divide the complete subject from the complete predicate.
12. Is there an adverb exception? No.
13. Is this sentence in a natural or inverted order? Inverted - underline the subject parts once and the predicate parts twice.

Classified Sentence:

```
                              Adv    A   Adj    SN        V      Adv  Adv  Adv
              SN V      Surprisingly, the hungry seagulls / swooped down very quickly.  D
              P1
```

TEACHER INSTRUCTIONS

Use Sentences 1-3 that you just classified with your students to do an Oral Skill Builder Check. Use the guidelines below.

Oral Skill Builder Check

1. **Noun check.**
   (Say the job and then say the noun. Circle each noun.)
2. **Identify the nouns as singular or plural.**
   (Write S or P above each noun.)
3. **Identify the nouns as common or proper.**
   (Follow established procedure for oral identification.)
4. **Do a vocabulary check.**
   (Follow established procedure for oral identification.)

5. **Identify the complete subject and the complete predicate.** (Underline the complete subject once and the complete predicate twice.)
6. **Identify the simple subject and simple predicate.**
   (Underline the simple subject once and the simple predicate twice. Bold, or highlight, the lines to distinguish them from the complete subject and complete predicate.)

TEACHING SCRIPT FOR THE PRACTICE SENTENCE

Sentences are the foundation of writing; so, you must first learn how sentences are put together. Next, you will learn how to improve and expand sentences, and then you will learn to combine sentences into paragraphs.

The first two areas we will address are how sentences are put together and how to improve them. In order to talk about sentences, we must know the vocabulary that is used to build sentences. If you are building a house, you need to know about hammers and nails. You need to know the names of the tools and materials that you will be using.

CHAPTER 4 LESSON 1 CONTINUED

In the same way, when you are building or writing sentences, you need to know the names of the parts you will be using and what to do with them. Your writing vocabulary will develop as you learn all the parts of a sentence. We will start by learning how to write a sentence from a given set of English labels. This is called a **Practice Sentence**.

A **Practice Sentence** is a sentence that is written following certain sentence labels (A, Adj, SN, V, Adv, etc.). The difficulty level of the sentence labels will increase as your ability increases. To write a Practice Sentence, you will follow the labels given to you in your assignment. You must think of words that fit the labels and that make sense.

Look at the Practice Sentence in Reference 16 on page 15 in your Reference Section. Since we have learned only four parts of a sentence so far, the Practice Sentence will demonstrate only these four parts. Notice that by using the four sentence parts - *subject noun, verb, adjective, article adjective,* and *adverb* - we can make a seven-word sentence: **The four busy workers talked very loudly**.

Reference 16: Practice Sentence						
Labels:	A	Adj	Adj	SN	V	Adv	Adv
Practice:	**The**	**four**	**busy**	**workers**	**talked**	**very**	**loudly.**

There are three adjectives used in this sentence: *the, four,* and *busy*. There are two adverbs: *very* and *loudly*. And, of course, there is the subject noun *workers,* and there is the verb *talked*. We could just as easily have written a sentence with the bare essentials: *the workers talked*. That is a correct sentence, but, by adding more parts, we are able to make the picture of the workers even clearer.

As you learn how to use more sentence parts to expand your sentences, you will use them automatically because they make your writing better.

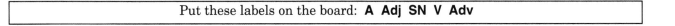

Put these labels on the board: **A Adj SN V Adv**

Look at the sentence labels on the board: **A Adj SN V Adv**. Now, I am going to guide you through the process of writing a sentence using all the parts that you have learned thus far. Most of these steps will become automatic in a very short time.

CHAPTER 4 LESSON 1 CONTINUED

Get out a sheet of notebook paper. On the top line of your notebook paper, write the title *Practice Sentence*. Copy the sentence labels from the board onto your notebook paper. Be sure to leave plenty of writing space between each label. Now, I will guide you through the process you will use whenever you write a Practice Sentence.

1. Go to the **SN** label for the subject noun. Think of a noun you want to use as your subject. Write the noun you have chosen on the line *under* the **SN** label.

2. Go to the **V** label for verb. Think of a verb that tells what your subject does. Make sure that your verb makes sense with the subject noun. Write the verb you have chosen on the line *under* the **V** label.

3. Go to the **Adv** label for the adverb. Go to the verb in your sentence and ask an adverb question. What are the adverb questions? (*how, when, where*) Choose one adverb question to ask and write your adverb answer *under* the **Adv** label.

4. Go to the **Adj** label for the adjective. Go to the subject noun of your sentence and ask an adjective question. What are the adjective questions? (*what kind, which one, how many*) Choose one adjective question to ask and write your adjective answer under the **Adj** label next to the subject noun. Always check to make sure your answers are making sense in the sentence.

5. Go to the **A** label for article adjective. What are the three article adjectives? (*a, an,* and *the*) You will choose the article adjective that makes the best sense in your sentence. Write the article adjective you have chosen *under* the **A** label.

6. Finally, check the Practice Sentence to make sure it has the necessary parts to be a complete sentence. What are the five parts of a complete sentence? (*subject, verb, complete sense, capital letter, and an end mark*) Does this Practice Sentence have all the parts necessary to make a complete sentence? (*Allow time for students' responses and for any corrections to be made on the board or on students' papers.*)

CHAPTER 4 LESSON 1 CONTINUED

TEACHING SCRIPT FOR AN IMPROVED SENTENCE

Now that we have written a correct sentence using all the parts that we have studied, we must now concentrate on improving what we have written. The result is called an **Improved Sentence**. An **Improved Sentence** is a sentence made from the Practice Sentence that is improved through the use of synonym changes, antonym changes, or complete-word changes. Writing Improved Sentences will help you make better word choices as you write because your writing vocabulary increases.

Look at the Improved Sentence in Reference 17 on page 15 in your Reference Section. The original English labels are on the first line. The sample Practice Sentence is on the second line. On the last line, you see an Improved Sentence made from synonyms, antonyms, and complete-word changes. Knowing how to make improvements in what you have written means that you are beginning to revise and edit. (*Read the Practice and Improved Sentences in the box as your students follow along. Make sure students see the difference that improving sentences can make.*)

Reference 17: Improved Sentence						
Labels:	A	Adj	Adj	SN	V	Adv	Adv
Practice:	The	four	busy	workers	talked	very	loudly.
Improved:	**A**	**few**	**industrious**	**employees**	**conversed**	**quite**	**softly.**
	(word change)	(word change)	(synonym)	(synonym)	(synonym)	(synonym)	(antonym)

Put these directions on the board or on paper:
Make at <u>least</u> one synonym change, one antonym change, and one complete-word change.

The directions on the board tell you to make these changes in your Practice Sentence: **Make at <u>least</u> one synonym change, one antonym change, and a complete-word change**. I am going to show you how to improve your Practice Sentence by making synonym, antonym, and complete-word changes in some of the words. The changed sentence will be called an **Improved Sentence** because you will make several improvements. Most of these steps will become automatic in a very short time. Now, on another line, under your Practice Sentence, write the title *Improved Sentence*.

1. Look at our Practice Sentence on the board. Let's find a word that can be improved with an antonym. (*Identify the word to be changed.*) Give me an antonym suggestion, and I will write your suggested antonym to improve, or change, the word.

Remember, antonyms are powerful because they completely change the direction or meaning of your sentence. (*Discuss several antonym suggestions from students.*) Let's write the antonym we have chosen *under* the word we want to change in the Practice Sentence. (*Write the antonym choice on the board and have students write it on their papers.*)

CHAPTER 4 LESSON 1 CONTINUED

2. Let's find a word in the Practice Sentence that can be improved with a synonym. *(Identify the word to be changed.)* Give me a synonym suggestion, and I will write your suggested synonym to improve the word. Remember, synonyms improve your writing vocabulary faster because they give you more word choices. *(Discuss several synonym suggestions from students.)* Let's write the synonym we have chosen *under* the word we want to improve in the Practice Sentence. *(Write the synonym choice on the board and have students write it on their papers.)*

3. Sometimes, you will think of a better word to use to improve your sentence that is not a synonym or antonym. We call this type of improvement a complete-word change. It will give you more flexibility as you work to improve your sentences. Look at the Practice Sentence again. Is there another word that we want to change by simply making a complete-word change? *(Discuss several complete-word change suggestions from students.)* Let's write the complete-word change we have chosen *under* the word we want to change in the Practice Sentence. *(Write the complete-word change on the board and have students write it on their papers.)* If you cannot think of a complete-word change, you can always use a synonym or antonym change.

4. Let's look at our Improved Sentence. Do you want to make any more improvements or changes? *(Discuss and then make extra improvements or changes as indicated by student participation.)*

5. Finally, let's check the Improved Sentence to make sure it has the necessary parts to be a complete sentence. Does our Improved Sentence have all the parts of a complete sentence? *(Allow time for students' responses and for corrections to be made on the board and on students' papers.)*

I want you to write your own Practice and Improved Sentences. Follow the same English labels given in Reference 17. Make sure you follow the procedures we have just gone through. Remember, any time you write an Improved Sentence, you are actually editing your writing, and that's why it is so important that you learn to write Improved Sentences. *(Check and discuss students' Practice and Improved Sentences after they have finished.)*

 VOCABULARY TIME

Assign Chapter 4, Vocabulary Words #1 on page 7 in the Reference Section for students to define in their Vocabulary notebooks. Tell students they are to use a dictionary or thesaurus to look up the meanings of the vocabulary words. After they write each word and its meaning, students are to write a sentence using the vocabulary word.

Chapter 4, Vocabulary Words #1
(coherent, ramble, deception, fraud)

(End of lesson.)

CHAPTER 4   LESSON 2

New objectives: Grammar (Practice Sentences) and Vocabulary #2.

JINGLE TIME

Have students turn to the Jingle Section of their books. The teacher will lead the students in reciting the previously-taught jingles.

GRAMMAR TIME

First-Year Option: Put the Practice Sentences from the box below on the board or notebook paper. Use these sentences as you practice the concepts that have been taught. For the greatest benefit, students must participate orally with the teacher. **Second-Year Option:** Have students classify the Practice Sentences independently on paper. Check students' sentences with the answers provided below. *(If you have the CDs for Practice Sentences, have students check their sentences with the CDs.)*

Chapter 4, Practice Sentences for Lesson 2
1. _____ The funny, furry caterpillar crawled very awkwardly away.
2. _____ Suddenly, a beautiful rainbow appeared brilliantly overhead.
3. _____ The huge spaceship swiftly traveled homeward today.

TEACHING SCRIPT FOR PRACTICING PATTERN 1 SENTENCES

We will classify three different sentences to practice the Question and Answer Flows. We will classify the sentences together. Begin. *(You might have your students write the labels above the sentences at this time.)*

Teacher's Notes: Make sure students say the **questions** and **answers** orally for each sentence. Be sure to lead them so they will say the Question and Answer Flows correctly.

Question and Answer Flow for Sentence 1: The funny, furry caterpillar crawled very awkwardly away.	
1. What crawled very awkwardly away? caterpillar - SN	8. The - A
2. What is being said about caterpillar? caterpillar crawled - V	9. SN V P1 Check
	10. Period, statement, declarative sentence
3. Crawled how? awkwardly - Adv	11. Go back to the verb - divide the complete subject
4. How awkwardly? very - Adv	from the complete predicate.
5. Crawled where? away - Adv	12. Is there an adverb exception? No.
6. What kind of caterpillar? furry - Adj	13. Is this sentence in a natural or inverted order?
7. What kind of caterpillar? funny - Adj	Natural - no change.

Classified Sentence:

```
                            A  Adj  Adj   SN       V    Adv   Adv   Adv
           SN  V            The funny, furry caterpillar / crawled very awkwardly away.  D
           P1
```

CHAPTER 4 LESSON 2 CONTINUED

Question and Answer Flow for Sentence 2: Suddenly, a beautiful rainbow appeared brilliantly overhead.

1. What appeared brilliantly overhead? rainbow - SN
2. What is being said about rainbow?
   rainbow appeared - V
3. Appeared how? brilliantly - Adv
4. Appeared where? overhead - Adv
5. What kind of rainbow? beautiful - Adj
6. A - A
7. Appeared when? suddenly - Adv

8. SN V P1 Check
9. Period, statement, declarative sentence
10. Go back to the verb - divide the complete subject from the complete predicate.
11. Is there an adverb exception? No.
12. Is this sentence in a natural or inverted order? Inverted - underline the subject parts once and the predicate parts twice.

Classified Sentence:

                                 Adv   A   Adj   SN   V   Adv   Adv

    __SN V__   Suddenly, a beautiful rainbow / appeared brilliantly overhead. D
     P1

Question and Answer Flow for Sentence 3: The huge spaceship swiftly traveled homeward today.

1. What traveled homeward today? spaceship - SN
2. What is being said about spaceship?
   spaceship traveled - V
3. Traveled where? homeward - Adv
4. Traveled when? today - Adv
5. Traveled how? swiftly - Adv
6. What kind of spaceship? huge - Adj
7. The - A

8. SN V P1 Check
9. Period, statement, declarative sentence
10. Go back to the verb - divide the complete subject from the complete predicate.
11. Is there an adverb exception? Yes - change the line.
12. Is this sentence in a natural or inverted order? Natural - no change.

Classified Sentence:

                                   A Adj   SN   Adv   V   Adv   Adv

    __SN V__   The huge spaceship / swiftly traveled homeward today. D
     P1

TEACHER INSTRUCTIONS

Use Sentences 1-3 that you just classified with your students to do an Oral Skill Builder Check. Use the guidelines below.

Oral Skill Builder Check

1. **Noun check.**
   (Say the job and then say the noun. Circle each noun.)
2. **Identify the nouns as singular or plural.**
   (Write S or P above each noun.)
3. **Identify the nouns as common or proper.**
   (Follow established procedure for oral identification.)
4. **Do a vocabulary check.**
   (Follow established procedure for oral identification.)

5. **Identify the complete subject and the complete predicate.** (Underline the complete subject once and the complete predicate twice.)
6. **Identify the simple subject and simple predicate.**
   (Underline the simple subject once and the simple predicate twice. Bold, or highlight, the lines to distinguish them from the complete subject and complete predicate.)

CHAPTER 4 LESSON 2 CONTINUED

TEACHING SCRIPT FOR AN EXPANDED PRACTICE SENTENCE

Put these labels on the board: **A Adj Adj SN V Adv Adv**

In the previous lesson, I guided you through the process of writing a Practice and Improved Sentence for practice. Today, I am going to step you through the same process again, but this time you will write an expanded sentence by adding a few more sentence labels. Look at the new sentence labels on the board: **A Adj Adj SN V Adv Adv**.

Get out a sheet of notebook paper and write the title *Practice Sentence* on the top line. Copy the labels on the board across the page: **A Adj Adj SN V Adv Adv**. Make sure you leave plenty of room for the words that you will write under the labels.

I will guide you through the process of writing a sentence using a given set of labels again. I will lead you each time we cover a new concept in Pattern 1. Writing a sentence using English labels is total sentence control. It is very easy if you know how, but it is also something very few people can do without training.

1. Go to the **SN** label for the subject noun. Think of a noun you want to use as your subject. Write the noun you have chosen on the line *under* the **SN** label.

2. Go to the **V** label for verb. Think of a verb that tells what your subject does. Make sure that your verb makes sense with the subject noun. Write the verb you have chosen on the line *under* the **V** label.

3. Go to the **Adv** label for the adverb. Go to the verb in your sentence and ask an adverb question. What are the adverb questions? (*how, when, where*) Choose one adverb question to ask and write your adverb answer *under* the first **Adv** label.

4. Go to the **Adv** label for another adverb. Go to the verb again and ask another adverb question. You can use the same adverb question, or you can use a different adverb question. Write another adverb *under* the second **Adv** label.

5. Go to the **Adj** label for the adjective. Go to the subject noun of your sentence and ask an adjective question. What are the adjective questions? (*what kind, which one, how many*) Choose one adjective question to ask and write your adjective answer under the **Adj** label next to the subject noun. Always check to make sure your answers are making sense in the sentence.

6. Go to the next **Adj** label for another adjective. Go to the subject noun again and ask another adjective question. You can use the same adjective question, or you can use a different adjective question. Write another adjective under the second **Adj** label.

7. Go to the **A** label for article adjective. What are the three article adjectives? (*a, an,* and *the*) Choose the article adjective that makes the best sense in your sentence. Write the article adjective you have chosen *under* the **A** label.

CHAPTER 4 LESSON 2 CONTINUED

8. Finally, check your Practice Sentence to make sure it has the necessary parts to be a complete sentence. What are the five parts of a complete sentence? (*subject, verb, complete sense, capital letter, and an end mark*) Does your Practice Sentence have the five parts of a complete sentence? (*Allow time for students to read over their sentences and to make any corrections they need to make.*)

9. Under your Practice Sentence, write the title *Improved Sentence* on another line. To improve your Practice Sentence, you will make two synonym changes, one antonym change, and your choice of a complete-word change or another synonym or antonym change.

   Since it is harder to find words that can be changed to an antonym, it is usually wise to go through your sentence to find an antonym change first. Then, look through your sentence again to find words that can be improved with synonyms. Finally, make a decision about whether your last change will be a complete-word change, a synonym change, or an antonym change.

I will give you time to write your Improved Sentence. (*Always encourage students to use a thesaurus, synonym-antonym book, or a dictionary to help them develop an interesting and improved writing vocabulary. After students have finished, check and discuss students' Practice and Improved Sentences.*)

 VOCABULARY TIME

Assign Chapter 4, Vocabulary Words #2 on page 7 in the Reference Section for students to define in their Vocabulary notebooks. Tell students they are to use a dictionary or thesaurus to look up the meanings of the vocabulary words. After they write each word and its meaning, students are to write a sentence using the vocabulary word.

Chapter 4, Vocabulary Words #2
(colleague, competitor, vacant, void)

(End of lesson.)

CHAPTER 4 LESSON 3

New objectives: Jingles (preposition, object of the prep, preposition flow), Grammar (adverb modifying an adjective, Practice Sentences), Skills (subject/verb agreement), and a Practice sheet.

 **JINGLE TIME**

Have students turn to the Jingle Section in their books and recite the previously-taught jingles. Then, lead students in reciting the new jingles (*Preposition, Object of the Preposition, and Preposition Flow*) below. Practice the new jingles several times until students can recite them smoothly. Emphasize reciting with rhythm. Students and teacher should be together! (*Do not try to explain the jingles at this time. Just have fun reciting them. Remember, add motions for more fun and laughter.*)

Teacher's Note: Again, do not spend a large amount of time practicing the new jingles. Students learn the jingles best by spending a small amount of time consistently, **every** day. The teacher should concentrate on the following areas while students are reciting the new jingles: togetherness, smoothness, volume, and enthusiasm.

Jingle 7: The Preposition Jingle

A PREP PREP PREPOSITION
Is a special group of words
That connects a
NOUN, NOUN, NOUN
Or a PRO, PRO, PRONOUN
To the rest of the sentence.

Jingle 8: Object of the Prep Jingle

Dum De Dum Dum!
An O-P is a N-O-U-N or a P-R-O
After the P-R-E-P
In a S-E-N-T-E-N-C-E.
Dum De Dum Dum - DONE!!

Jingle 9: Preposition Flow		
1. **Preposition, Preposition Starting with an A.** (Fast) aboard, about, above, across, after, against, (Slow) along, among, around, at.	2. **Preposition, Preposition Starting with a B.** (Fast) before, behind, below, beneath, beside, between, (Slow) beyond, but, by.	3. **Preposition, Preposition Starting with a D.** down (slow & long), during (snappy).
4. **Preposition, Preposition Don't go away. Go to the middle And see what we say. E-F-I and L-N-O** except, for, from, in, inside, into, like, near, of, off, on, out, outside, over.	5. **Preposition, Preposition Almost through. Start with P and end with W.** past, since, through, throughout, to, toward, under, underneath, until, up, upon, with, within, without.	6. **Preposition, Preposition Easy as can be. We're all finished, And aren't you pleased? We've just recited All 49 of these.**

CHAPTER 4 LESSON 3 CONTINUED

GRAMMAR TIME

First-Year Option: Put the Practice Sentences from the box below on the board or notebook paper. Use these sentences as you practice the concepts that have been taught. For the greatest benefit, students must participate orally with the teacher. **Second-Year Option:** Have students classify the Practice Sentences independently on paper. Check students' sentences with the answers provided below. (*If you have the CDs for Practice Sentences, have students check their sentences with the CDs.*)

Chapter 4, Practice Sentences for Lesson 3
1. _____ The extremely feeble old woman walked slowly away.
2. _____ A tardy student quietly sat down.
3. _____ Unintentionally, the young mother spoke quite harshly.

TEACHING SCRIPT FOR IDENTIFYING AN ADVERB THAT MODIFIES AN ADJECTIVE

Today, you will learn how to identify an adverb that modifies an adjective as we use the Question and Answer Flows to classify Practice Sentences for Pattern 1. We will classify the sentences together. Begin. (*You might have your students write the labels above the sentences at this time.*)

Teacher's Notes: Make sure students say the **questions** and **answers** orally for each sentence. Be sure to lead them so they will say the Question and Answer Flows correctly.

Question and Answer Flow for Sentence 1: The extremely feeble old woman walked slowly away.

1. Who walked slowly away? woman - SN
2. What is being said about woman? woman walked - V
3. Walked how? slowly - Adv
4. Walked where? away - Adv
5. What kind of woman? old - Adj
6. What kind of woman? feeble - Adj
7. How feeble? extremely - Adv
8. The - A

9. SN V P1 Check
10. Period, statement, declarative sentence
11. Go back to the verb - divide the complete subject from the complete predicate.
12. Is there an adverb exception? No.
13. Is this sentence in a natural or inverted order? Natural - no change.

Classified Sentence:

```
                        A    Adv    Adj  Adj  SN      V     Adv  Adv
        SN  V          The extremely feeble old woman / walked slowly away.  D
        P1
```

Question and Answer Flow for Sentence 2: A tardy student quietly sat down.

1. Who quietly sat down? student - SN
2. What is being said about student? student sat - V
3. Sat where? down - Adv
4. Sat how? quietly - Adv
5. What kind of student? tardy - Adj
6. A - A
7. SN V P1 Check

8. Period, statement, declarative sentence
9. Go back to the verb - divide the complete subject from the complete predicate.
10. Is there an adverb exception? Yes - change the line.
11. Is this sentence in a natural or inverted order? Natural - no change.

Classified Sentence:

```
                        A  Adj    SN     Adv  V  Adv
        SN  V          A tardy student / quietly sat down.  D
        P1
```

CHAPTER 4 LESSON 3 CONTINUED

Question and Answer Flow for Sentence 3: Unintentionally, the young mother spoke quite harshly.

1. Who spoke quite harshly? mother - SN
2. What is being said about mother? mother spoke - V
3. Spoke how? harshly - Adv
4. How harshly? quite - Adv
5. What kind of mother? young - Adj
6. The - A
7. Spoke how? unintentionally - Adv
8. SN V P1 Check

9. Period, statement, declarative sentence
10. Go back to the verb - divide the complete subject from the complete predicate.
11. Is there an adverb exception? No.
12. Is this sentence in a natural or inverted order? Inverted - underline the subject parts once and the predicate parts twice.

Classified Sentence:

```
                    Adv          A   Adj   SN        V    Adv   Adv
          SN V   Unintentionally, the young mother / spoke quite harshly.  D
          P1
```

SKILL TIME

TEACHING SCRIPT FOR SUBJECT / VERB AGREEMENT

A sentence must have correct subject-verb agreement. The word **agreement** means to work together; therefore, subject-verb agreement means the special way in which the subject and verb work together to make the sentence correct.

We will use this sentence to demonstrate the subject-verb agreement concept *(Put the following sentence on the board.)* **The young boy laughed at the clowns.** Whenever you work with subject-verb agreement, you must remember to work only with the subject and verb. Therefore, you must isolate the subject and verb before you begin. What are the subject and verb in the demonstration sentence? *(Boy laughed.)*

I will write only the subject and verb *Boy laughed* on a different section of the board so we can concentrate on what we need to do for subject-verb agreement. *(Write "Boy laughed" on a clean area of the board so you will have room to work without other sentences distracting students.)*

You only worry about subject-verb agreement with present tense verbs. To demonstrate this, look at the verb *laughed*. It ends in an "ed" or past tense form. It doesn't matter if the subject is singular or plural—the verb never changes its past tense or "ed" form.

Example: Boy laughed.   Boys laughed.

The example clearly demonstrates that we must change a past tense verb to present tense in order to work with singular and plural forms. How do we change *laughed* to present tense? *(Take off the -ed.)* Now that *laugh* is in present tense, we must check whether it agrees with its subject. If the subject is singular, we must use a singular verb form. If the subject is plural, we must use a plural verb form.

Is the subject *boy* singular or plural? *(Singular.)* Since the subject *boy* is singular, we must choose the singular form of the verb *laugh*. How do we make it singular? *(Add an **s** or **es** to the plain form to make the word **laughs**.)*

CHAPTER 4 LESSON 3 CONTINUED

Since we have checked to make sure the subject and verb are both singular, we know the subject agrees with the verb. Let's say both singular forms together so we can hear the singular combination as we say them. (*Have students say "boy laughs" several times to hear the subject-verb agreement forms.*)

We will work with the plural forms of the subject and verb. Since the subject *boy* is singular, how do we make it plural? (*Add an **s** to make the word **boys**.*) We must also change the verb to a plural form. The plural form of a present tense verb is called the <u>plain form</u> because it does not end in *s* or *es*.

How would we write the plural form of the verb *laughs*? (*l-a-u-g-h*) The verb *laugh* is plural because it does not end in *s* or *es*. Since we have changed both the subject and verb to plural forms, we know the subject agrees with the verb. Let's say both plural forms together so we can hear the plural combinations as we say them. (*Have students say "boys laugh" several times to hear the subject-verb agreement forms.*)

Sometimes, a word does not follow the regular rules because of spelling form. These are called exceptions. One such exception is the word *child*. In the sentence, *Child laughed*, what are the subject and verb? (*child laughed.*) What is the present tense of the verb *laughed*? (*laugh*) Is the subject *child* singular or plural? (singular) Since the subject is singular, we must use the singular verb form. How do we make the verb *laugh* singular? (*Add an **s** or **es** to the plain form to make the word **laughs**.*)

Since our subject and verb are both singular, we know the subject agrees with the verb. Let's say both singular forms together so we can hear the singular combination as we say them. (*Have students say "child laughs" several times to hear the subject-verb agreement forms.*)

We will work with the plural forms of the subject and verb. Since the subject *child* is singular, how do we make it plural? This is one of the exceptions. Some words are made plural by changing the spelling form, not by adding an "s" or "es". To make *child* plural, we must make a spelling change to make the plural word *children*. We must also change the verb to a plural form.

Remember, the plural form of a present tense verb is called the plain form because it does not end in *s* or *es*. What is the plural form of the verb *laughs*? (*laugh*) The verb *laugh* is plural because it does not end in *s* or *es*. Since we have changed both the subject and verb to plural forms, we know the subject agrees with the verb. Let's say both plural forms together so we can hear the plural combination as we say them. (*Have students say "children laugh" several times to hear the subject-verb agreement forms.*)

We will now discuss a set of rules that will also help you make the right subject-verb agreement choice with different kinds of verbs. Look at Reference 18 on page 15 in the Reference Section of your book. Rule 1 says that if you have a singular subject, you must use a singular verb form that ends in *s*: **is, was, has, does, or verbs ending with *s* or *es***. Notice that singular verb forms end in **s**. The "s" stands for singular verb forms. Remember, a singular subject agrees with a singular verb form that ends in **s**.

CHAPTER 4 LESSON 3 CONTINUED

Reference 18: Subject-Verb Agreement Rules
Rule 1: A singular subject must use a singular verb form that ends in **s**: *is, was, has, does, or verbs ending with **s** or **es**.*
Rule 2: A plural subject, a compound subject, or the subject **YOU** must use a plural verb form that has **no s** ending: *are, were, do, have, or verbs without **s** or **es** endings.* (A plural verb form is also called the *plain form*.)
Examples: For each sentence, do these four things: 1. Write the subject. 2. Write S if the subject is singular or P if the subject is plural. 3. Write the rule number. 4. Underline the correct verb in the sentence.

Subject	S or P	Rule		
dog	S	1	1.	The **dog** (chew, <u>**chews**</u>) on his bone.
pencil and paper	P	2	2.	The **pencil** and **paper** (is, <u>**are**</u>) in the drawer.
You	P	2	3.	**You** (<u>**make**</u>, makes) the bed.

Rule 2 says that if you have a plural subject, a compound subject, or the subject *YOU*, you must use these verbs: **are, were, have, do, or verbs without *s* or *es* endings** because these verbs are plural verb forms. Any time the pronoun YOU is the subject of a sentence, you do not have to decide whether it is singular or plural. The subject pronoun YOU always uses a plural verb, and you MUST choose a plural verb form. Remember, a plural subject agrees with a plural verb form that does not end in *s*.

Look at the examples under the rules. The directions say you must write the subject, then write S if the subject is singular or write P if the subject is plural. You must also write the rule number (Rule 1 or 2) from the rule box and then underline the correct verb in the sentence. What is the subject in Sentence 1? (*dog*) Is the subject *dog* singular or plural? (*singular*)

Since the subject is singular, you will go to the rule box and find the rule that tells you which verb to choose if you have a singular subject. Which rule do we put in the blank? (*Rule 1*) Notice that a number 1 has been written in the blank for Rule 1. Using the list of singular verbs in Rule 1, which verb would we choose to agree with the singular subject *dog*? (*Chews,* the verb with the *s* or *es ending*) The verb *chews* has been underlined as the correct verb choice.

What is the subject in Sentence 2? (*pencil and paper*) Is the subject *pencil* and *paper* singular or plural? (*Plural - because it is compound*) Since the subject is plural, you will go to the rule box and find the rule that tells you which verb to choose if you have a plural subject. Which rule do we put in the blank? (*Rule 2*) A number 2 has been written in the blank for Rule 2. Using the list of plural verbs in Rule 2, which verb would we choose to agree with the plural subject *pencil* and *paper*? (*are*) The verb *are* has been underlined as the correct verb choice.

What is the subject in Sentence 3? (*You*) Is the subject *you* singular or plural? (*plural*) Since the subject is plural, you will go to the rule box and find the rule that tells you which verb to choose if you have a plural subject. Which rule do we put in the blank? (*Rule 2*) A number 2 has been written in the blank for Rule 2. Using the list of plural verbs in Rule 2, which verb would we choose to agree with the plural subject *you*? (*make*) The verb *make* has been underlined as the correct verb choice.

Choosing verbs to agree with the subjects in the sentences on your test will be easy if you follow the rules you have just learned. Remember, first you must decide if the subject of the sentence is singular or plural. Next, you must look at the verb choices in parentheses in the sentence. Last, you must choose the verb that is listed under the singular or plural rule in the box. (*Discuss the subject **I** as an exception. The subject **I** takes a plural verb form. Examples: I have, I want, I walk, I talk, etc.*)

CHAPTER 4 LESSON 3 CONTINUED

Teacher's Note: The singular subject **I** and the verb **be** present a special case of subject-verb agreement. Use the following examples to demonstrate the verb forms used with the pronoun **I**.
Examples: I am. I was. I have. I walk. I talk.

 PRACTICE TIME

Have students turn to page 56 in the Practice Section of their book and find the skills under Chapter 4, Lesson 3, Practice (1-3). Go over the directions to make sure they understand what to do. Check and discuss the Practice after students have finished. (*Chapter 4, Lesson 3, Practice keys are given below.*)

Chapter 4, Lesson 3, Practice 1

Rule 1: A singular subject must use a singular verb form that ends in **s**: *is, was, has, does, or verbs ending with **s** or **es**.*
Rule 2: A plural subject, a compound subject, or the subject **YOU** must use a plural verb form that has **no s** ending: *are, were, do, have, or verbs without **s** or **es** endings.* (A plural verb form is also called the *plain form*.)

Examples: For each sentence, do these four things: 1. Write the subject. 2. Write S if the subject is singular or P if the subject is plural. 3. Write the rule number. 4. Underline the correct verb in the sentence.

Subject	S or P	Rule		
eagles	P	2	1.	The **eagles** (was, <u>**were**</u>) flying upside down.
Tom and sister	P	2	2.	**Tom** and his **sister** (is, <u>**are**</u>) good sports.
aunt	S	1	3.	My **aunt** (<u>**was**</u>, were) fearful of the plane ride.

Chapter 4, Lesson 3, Practice 2

On notebook paper, write a Practice and Improved Sentence, using these labels: **A Adj Adj SN V Adv Adv**

Chapter 4, Lesson 3, Practice 3

Put this 3-part assignment on notebook paper: (1) Write the four parts of speech that you have studied so far (in any order). (2) Write out the Question and Answer Flow in exact order for the sentence listed. (3) Classify the sentence.

1. noun	**2. verb**	**3. adjective**	**4. adverb**

Practice Sentence: Unintentionally, the young mother spoke quite harshly.

Question and Answer Flow Key for Practice Sentence: Unintentionally, the young mother spoke quite harshly.

1. Who spoke quite harshly? mother - SN
2. What is being said about mother? mother spoke - V
3. Spoke how? harshly - Adv
4. How harshly? quite - Adv
5. What kind of mother? young- Adj
6. The - A
7. Spoke how? unintentionally - Adv

8. SN V P1 Check
9. Period, statement, declarative sentence
10. Go back to the verb - divide the complete subject from the complete predicate.
11. Is there an adverb exception? No.
12. Is this sentence in a natural or inverted order? Inverted - underline the subject parts once and the predicate parts twice.

Classified Sentence:

Adv   A   Adj   SN   V   Adv   Adv
SN V   <u>Unintentionally, the young mother</u> / <u>spoke quite harshly.</u>   **D**
P1

(End of lesson.)

CHAPTER 4 LESSON 4

New objectives: Test and an Activity.

JINGLE TIME

Have students turn to the Jingle Section of their books. The teacher will lead the students in reciting the previously-taught jingles.

STUDY TIME

Have students study the vocabulary words in their vocabulary notebooks. Remind students that any vocabulary word in their notebooks could be on their test. Also, have students study any of the skills in the Practice Section they need to review.

TEST TIME

Have students turn to page 85 in the Test Section of their books and find the Chapter 4 Test. Remind them to pay attention and to think about what they are doing. Go over the directions to make sure they understand what to do. (*Chapter 4 Test key is on the next page.*)

CHECK TIME

After students have finished, check and discuss their test papers. Make sure they understand why their answers are right or wrong. (*For total points, count each required answer as a point.*)

ACTIVITY / ASSIGNMENT TIME

Make a list of five different animals. Write the name of each animal on an index card. On the back of each index card, write a descriptive sentence about the animal listed on the front. Be sure to include as many adjectives and adverbs as possible. Finally, play a guessing game with different members of your family. Read aloud or hold up the side of the card with the description and let family members guess which animal's name is written on the other side. Discuss which animals were the hardest and easiest to guess.

(End of lesson.)

Chapter 4 Test
(Student Page 85)

Exercise 1: Classify each sentence.

```
            Adv       A    Adj  Adj   SN        V    Adv    Adv
1. SN V ___ Yesterday, the sleek black corvette / stopped quite abruptly. D
   P1
```

```
            A   Adj   SN     V      Adv      Adv
2. SN V ___ The tired baby / wailed impatiently today. D
   P1
```

```
            A   Adj    SN       V      Adv    Adv
3. SN V ___ The weary hikers / trudged miserably home. D
   P1
```

Exercise 2: Use Sentence 2 to underline the complete subject once and the complete predicate twice and to complete the table below.

List the Noun Used	List the Noun Job	Singular or Plural	Common or Proper	Simple Subject	Simple Predicate
1. baby	2. SN	3. S	4. C	5. baby	6. wailed

Exercise 3: Name the four parts of speech that you have studied so far. *(Accept answers in any order.)*

1. **noun**	2. **verb**	3. **adjective**	4. **adverb**

Exercise 4: For each sentence, write the subject, then write S if the subject is singular or P if the subject is plural, write the rule number, and underline the correct verb in the sentence.

Rule 1: A singular subject must use a singular verb form that ends in **s**: *is, was, has, does, or verbs ending with **s** or **es**.*
Rule 2: A plural subject, a compound subject, or the subject **YOU** must use a plural verb form that has **no s** ending: *are, were, do, have, or verbs without **s** or **es** endings.* (A plural verb form is also called the *plain form*.)

Subject	S or P	Rule
snails	P	2
tablecloth	S	1
hikers	P	2
You	P	2
candle	S	1
shoes	P	2
mayor	S	1
Tiffany and Glen	P	2
computer	S	1
salamander	S	1
elephant	S	1
calendar	S	1

1. Some **snails** (has, <u>have</u>) long antenna.
2. This **tablecloth** (wrinkle, <u>wrinkles</u>) too easily.
3. (<u>Do</u>, Does) the **hikers** ever get lost?
4. **You** (has, <u>have</u>) a legitimate argument.
5. The **candle** (<u>is</u>, are) painfully dim.
6. My **shoes** (was, <u>were</u>) too tight.
7. The **mayor** (<u>has</u>, have) rescheduled the meeting.
8. **Tiffany** and **Glen** (was, <u>were</u>) twins.
9. (<u>Was</u>, Were) your **computer** new or used?
10. The **salamander** (do, <u>does</u>) not seem tired.
11. One **elephant** (<u>was</u>, were) terribly stubborn.
12. The **calendar** (<u>has</u>, have) a missing month.

Exercise 5: Identify each pair of words as synonyms or antonyms by putting parentheses ( ) around *syn* or *ant*.

1. void, vacant	**(syn)** ant	5. conceal, exhume	syn **(ant)**	9. debate, argue	**(syn)** ant
2. false, authentic	syn **(ant)**	6. deception, fraud	**(syn)** ant	10. acknowledge, admit	**(syn)** ant
3. fact, hypothesis	syn **(ant)**	7. coherent, ramble	syn **(ant)**	11. audacious, timid	syn **(ant)**
4. prodigy, genius	**(syn)** ant	8. abolish, destroy	**(syn)** ant	12. competitor, colleague	syn **(ant)**

Exercise 6: In your journal, write a paragraph summarizing what you have learned this week.

CHAPTER 4 LESSON 4 CONTINUED

TEACHER INSTRUCTIONS

Use the Question and Answer Flows below for the sentences on Chapter 4 Test.

Question and Answer Flow for Sentence 1: Yesterday, the sleek black corvette stopped quite abruptly.

1. What stopped quite abruptly? corvette - SN
2. What is being said about corvette? corvette stopped - V
3. Stopped how? abruptly - Adv
4. How abruptly? quite - Adv
5. What kind of corvette? black - Adj
6. What kind of corvette? sleek - Adj
7. The - A
8. Stopped when? yesterday - Adv

9. SN V P1 Check
10. Period, statement, declarative sentence
11. Go back to the verb - divide the complete subject from the complete predicate.
12. Is there an adverb exception? No.
13. Is this sentence in a natural or inverted order? Inverted - underline the subject parts once and the predicate parts twice.

Classified Sentence:

          Adv   A   Adj   Adj   SN   V   Adv   Adv

 <u>SN V</u>   <u>Yesterday, the sleek black corvette</u> / <u>stopped quite abruptly</u>. **D**
 P1

Question and Answer Flow for Sentence 2: The tired baby wailed impatiently today.

1. Who wailed impatiently today? baby - SN
2. What is being said about baby? baby wailed - V
3. Wailed how? impatiently - Adv
4. Wailed when? today - Adv
5. What kind of baby? tired - Adj
6. The - A

7. SN V P1 Check
8. Period, statement, declarative sentence
9. Go back to the verb - divide the complete subject from the complete predicate.
10. Is there an adverb exception? No.
11. Is this sentence in a natural or inverted order? Natural - no change.

Classified Sentence:

          A   Adj   SN   V   Adv   Adv

 <u>SN V</u>   The tired baby / wailed impatiently today.   **D**
 P1

Question and Answer Flow for Sentence 3: The weary hikers trudged miserably home.

1. Who trudged miserably home? hikers - SN
2. What is being said about hikers? hikers trudged - V
3. Trudged how? miserably - Adv
4. Trudged where? home - Adv
5. What kind of hikers? weary - Adj
6. The - A
7. SN V P1 Check

8. Period, statement, declarative sentence
9. Go back to the verb - divide the complete subject from the complete predicate.
10. Is there an adverb exception? No.
11. Is this sentence in a natural or inverted order? Natural - no change.

Classified Sentence:

          A   Adj   SN   V   Adv   Adv

 <u>SN V</u>   The weary hikers / trudged miserably home.   **D**
 P1

CHAPTER 4   LESSON 5

New objectives: Writing assignment #2.

 **WRITING TIME**

TEACHER INSTRUCTIONS FOR WRITING ASSIGNMENT

Give Writing Assignment #2 from the box below. Remind students to follow the Writing Guidelines as they prepare their writings.

> **Writing Assignment Box**
>
> **Writing Assignment #2: Three-Point Expository Paragraph**
> **Writing topic choices:**   **Qualities I Like in a Friend** or **My Favorite Places** or **My Favorite Bible Verses**

TEACHING SCRIPT FOR USING THE WRITING PROCESS FOR THIS WRITING ASSIGNMENT

As you begin this writing assignment, you will use the writing process again. First, you will think about your topic and gather any information you might need in order to do the writing. Second, you will write a rough draft. Remember, it is called a rough draft because it will be revised and edited. You do not have to worry about mistakes as you write your rough draft. After you write the first draft, you will make revisions, using the Revision Checklist in Reference 4. After you revise your writing, you will edit, using the Beginning Editing Checklist in Reference 4. Finally, after you are satisfied with your revising and editing, you will write a final paper, using the Final Paper Checklist in Reference 4. You will then give the finished writing assignment to me. (*Students should finish their writing during their free time if they do not finish during this lesson.*)

TEACHER INSTRUCTIONS FOR CHECKING WRITING ASSIGNMENT #2

Read, check, and discuss Writing Assignment #2 after students have finished their final papers. Use the editing checklist (*Reference 4 on teacher's page 9*) as you check and discuss students' papers. Make sure students are using the editing checklist correctly. In the beginning, you must also check students' papers carefully for <u>form</u> mistakes. This will ensure that students are learning the three-point format correctly.

CHAPTER 5   LESSON 1

New objectives: Grammar (Introductory Sentences, preposition, object of the preposition, prepositional phrase), Skills (Adding the object of the preposition to the Noun Check and Parts of Speech), and Vocabulary #1.

JINGLE TIME

Have students turn to the Jingle Section of their books. The teacher will lead the students in reciting the previously-taught jingles.

GRAMMAR TIME

Put the introductory sentences from the box below on the board. Use these sentences as you go through each new concept covered in your teaching script. For the greatest benefit, students must participate orally with the teacher. (*You might put the introductory sentences on notebook paper if you are doing one-on-one instruction with your students.*)

Chapter 5, Introductory Sentences for Lesson 1
1. _____ Nick sat silently in the seat by the aisle on the crowded plane.
2. _____ The members of the financial committee worked diligently on the new budget.
3. _____ The curious, fat raccoon sniffed along the outside of the fence.

TEACHING SCRIPT FOR PREPOSITION, OBJECT OF THE PREPOSITION, AND PREPOSITIONAL PHRASE

We will now begin the really "fun stuff" in English. We are going to start prepositions! The preposition jingles have already told you a lot about prepositions, but now we are going to learn even more. A **preposition** is a joining word. It joins a noun or a pronoun to the rest of the sentence. To know whether a word is a preposition, say the preposition word and ask *What* or *Whom*. If the answer is a noun or pronoun, then the word is a preposition. Prepositions are labeled with a *P*.

An **object of the preposition** is a noun or pronoun after the preposition in a sentence. An object of the preposition is labeled with an *OP*.

It is important for you to know the difference between prepositions and adverbs. Look at Reference 19 on page 15 as I explain how you can tell the difference between prepositions and adverbs.

A word can be a <u>preposition</u> or an <u>adverb</u>, depending on how it is used in a sentence. For example, the word *around* can be an adverb or a preposition. How do you decide if the word *around* is an adverb or a preposition? If *around* is used alone, with no noun after it, it is an adverb. If *around* has a noun after it that answers the question *what* or *whom*, then *around* is a preposition, and the noun after *around* is an object of the preposition. (*Have students follow along as you read and discuss the information in the reference box on the next page.*)

CHAPTER 5 LESSON 1 CONTINUED

Reference 19: Knowing the Difference Between Prepositions and Adverbs
Adv In the sample sentence, *Sam ran around*, the word *around* is an adverb because it does not have a noun after it.

In the sample sentence, *Sam ran around the track*, the word *around* is a preposition because it has the noun *track* (the object of the preposition) after it. To find the preposition and object of the preposition in the Question and Answer Flow, say: **around - P**   (Say: *around – preposition*)
around what? track - OP   (Say: *around what? track - object of the preposition*)

Today, we will learn about prepositional phrases. A **prepositional phrase** starts with the preposition and ends with the object of the preposition. It includes any modifiers between the preposition and the object of the preposition. A prepositional phrase adds meaning to a sentence and can be located anywhere in the sentence. Prepositional phrases can modify like adjectives or adverbs. For example, the prepositional phrase (*around the track*) tells where Sam ran. A single word that modifies a verb is called an adverb. A prepositional phrase that modifies a verb is called an adverb phrase or adverbial phrase. Prepositional phrases can also modify like adjectives. (*Students are not required to identify adjective and adverbial phrases in sentences until seventh grade. This is just extra information.*)

Prepositional phrases are identified in the Question and Answer Flow after you say the word *check*. Now, when you say *check*, you are also looking for prepositional phrases in the sentence. If you find a prepositional phrase, you will read the whole prepositional phrase and put parentheses around it. If there is more than one prepositional phrase in a sentence, read all prepositional phrases during this check time. For example, after you classify the sentence, ***Travis drove to town in a truck***, you say "Subject Noun Verb Pattern 1 - Check: (to town) - prepositional phrase; (in a truck) - prepositional phrase."

I will show you how to classify a preposition and an object of the preposition and how to identify a prepositional phrase by reciting the Question and Answer Flow for Sentence 1. (*Classify Sentence 1.*)

Question and Answer Flow for Sentence 1: Nick sat silently in the seat by the aisle on the crowded plane.

1. Who sat silently in the seat by the aisle on the crowded plane? Nick - SN
2. What is being said about Nick? Nick sat - V
3. Sat how? silently - Adv
4. In - P (Preposition)
5. In what? seat - OP (Object of the Preposition)

Note: To test whether a word is a preposition, say your preposition and ask "what" or "whom." If your answer is a noun or pronoun, you will have a preposition. All prepositions will have noun or pronoun objects. (*When the object of the preposition is a person ask "whom" instead of "what."*)

6. The - A
7. By - P (Preposition)
8. By what? aisle - OP (Object of the Preposition)
9. The - A
10. On - P (Preposition)
11. On what? plane - OP (Object of the Preposition)

12. What kind of plane? crowded - Adj
13. The - A
14. SN V P1 Check
15. (In the seat) - Prepositional phrase

Note: Say "in the seat – Prepositional phrase" as you put parentheses around the words. This also teaches your students how to read in phrases, so keep it smooth.

16. (By the aisle) - Prepositional phrase
17. (On the crowded plane) - Prepositional phrase
18. Period, statement, declarative sentence
19. Go back to the verb - divide the complete subject from the complete predicate.
20. Is there an adverb exception? No.
21. Is this sentence in a natural or inverted order? Natural - no change.

Classified Sentence:

		SN	V	Adv	P	A	OP	P	A	OP	P	A	Adj	OP
	SN V	Nick / sat silently (in the seat) (by the aisle) (on the crowded plane). D
	P1	

CHAPTER 5 LESSON 1 CONTINUED

I will now classify Sentence 1 again, but this time you classify it with me. I will lead you as we say the questions and answers together. Remember, it is very important that you say the questions with me as well as the answers. *(Classify Sentence 1 again with your students.)*

We will classify Sentences 2 and 3 together to practice the new parts of the Question and Answer Flow. You must say the **questions and answers** with me. By asking and answering the questions together, orally, you will learn everything faster because you see it, hear it, say it, and then do it. Begin.

Question and Answer Flow for Sentence 2: The members of the financial committee worked diligently on the new budget.

1. Who worked diligently on the new budget? members - SN
2. What is being said about members? members worked - V
3. Worked how? diligently - Adv
4. On - P (Preposition)
5. On what? budget - OP (Object of the preposition)
6. What kind of budget? new - Adj
7. The - A
8. Of - P
9. Of what? committee - OP
10. What kind of committee? financial - Adj
11. The - A
12. The - A
13. SN V P1 Check
14. (Of the financial committee) - Prepositional phrase
15. (On the new budget) - Prepositional phrase
16. Period, statement, declarative sentence
17. Go back to the verb - divide the complete subject from the complete predicate.
18. Is there an adverb exception? No.
19. Is this sentence in a natural or inverted order? Natural - no change.

Classified Sentence:

	A	SN	P	A	Adj	OP	V	Adv	P	A	Adj	OP

SN V
P1
    The members (of the financial committee) / worked diligently (on the new budget). **D**

Question and Answer Flow for Sentence 3: The curious, fat raccoon sniffed along the outside of the fence.

1. What sniffed along the outside of the fence? raccoon - SN
2. What is being said about raccoon? raccoon sniffed - V
3. Along - P
4. Along what? outside - OP
5. The - A
6. Of - P
7. Of what? fence - OP
8. The - A
9. What kind of raccoon? fat - Adj
10. What kind of raccoon? curious - Adj
11. The - A
12. SN V P1 Check
13. (Along the outside) - Prepositional phrase
14. (Of the fence) - Prepositional phrase
15. Period, statement, declarative sentence
16. Go back to the verb - divide the complete subject from the complete predicate.
17. Is there an adverb exception? No.
18. Is this sentence in a natural or inverted order? Natural - no change.

Classified Sentence:

	A	Adj	Adj	SN	V	P	A	OP	P	A	OP

SN V
P1
    The curious, fat raccoon / sniffed (along the outside) (of the fence). **D**

CHAPTER 5 LESSON 1 CONTINUED

TEACHING SCRIPT FOR ADDING THE OBJECT OF THE PREPOSITION TO THE NOUN CHECK

We are going to use the sentences we have just classified to do an Oral Skill Builder Check. You have already learned how to do a Noun Check with the subject of the sentence. Today, we are going to add another noun job to the Noun Check. Another job that nouns can do in a sentence is to act as the object of the preposition. Therefore, to find nouns, you will go to the words marked SN and OP in the classified sentences.

Look at Sentences 1-3 that we have just classified on the board. Remember, we will go to the subject nouns **and** the objects of the prepositions to find nouns. We will circle each noun as we find it.

Look at Sentence 1. You will say, "Number 1: subject noun *Nick, yes,* object of the preposition *seat, yes;* object of the preposition *aisle, yes;* object of the preposition *plane, yes;*" and I will circle each noun as you identify it. *(Have students repeat number 1 with you as you circle each noun identified.)* We will find and circle the nouns in Sentences 2 -3 the same way. *(Work through the rest of the sentences, identifying and circling the subject nouns and object-of-the-preposition nouns.)*

Use the same Skill Builder procedures that were taught in previous chapters to have students identify each noun as singular or plural. Ask students to tell which nouns are common and which are proper. Check the vocabulary words used for each sentence. Select the ones your students may not know and do a Vocabulary Check. For each word selected, make sure it is defined, used in a new sentence, and given a synonym and/or an antonym. You might also ask for synonyms and antonyms of several words just to check students' understanding of different words.

Now that you have finished the Noun Check, the Singular/Plural Check, the Common/Proper Check, and the Vocabulary Check, continue using Sentences 1-3 to do the rest of the Skill Builders from the checklist below. This checklist will always be given to you every time you do an Oral Skill Builder Check.

Teacher's Note: You will be given directions for a Skill Builder Check only with the first set of sentences in a chapter. You could do Skill Builder Checks with every set of sentences, but it is usually not necessary. Your time allotment and the needs of your students will influence your decision.

Oral Skill Builder Check	
1. Noun check. (Say the job and then say the noun. Circle each noun.) **2. Identify the nouns as singular or plural.** (Write S or P above each noun.) **3. Identify the nouns as common or proper.** (Follow established procedure for oral identification.) **4. Do a vocabulary check.** (Follow established procedure for oral identification.)	**5. Identify the complete subject and the complete predicate.** (Underline the complete subject once and the complete predicate twice.) **6. Identify the simple subject and simple predicate.** (Underline the simple subject once and the simple predicate twice. Bold, or highlight, the lines to distinguish them from the complete subject and complete predicate.)

CHAPTER 5 LESSON 1 CONTINUED

TEACHING SCRIPT FOR ADDING THE PREPOSITION TO THE PARTS OF SPEECH

Until now, we have had only four parts of speech. Do you remember the names of the four parts of speech we have already learned? _(noun, verb, adjective, and adverb)_ Today, we have learned about prepositions. A preposition is also a part of speech; so, we will add it to our list. We do not add the object of the preposition because it is a noun, and nouns are already on our list. Now, you know five of the eight parts of speech. What are the five parts of speech we have studied? _(noun, verb, adjective, adverb, and preposition)_

 VOCABULARY TIME

Assign Chapter 5, Vocabulary Words **#1** on page 7 in the Reference Section for students to define in their Vocabulary notebooks. Tell students they are to use a dictionary or thesaurus to look up the meanings of the vocabulary words. After they write each word and its meaning, students are to write a sentence using the vocabulary word.

Chapter 5, Vocabulary Words #1
(alliance, division, frugal, thrifty)

(End of lesson.)

CHAPTER 5 LESSON 2

New objectives: Grammar (Introductory Sentences, adding the prepositional phrase to inverted order and Practice and Improved sentence with a prepositional phrase) and Vocabulary #2.

JINGLE TIME

Have students turn to the Jingle Section of their books. The teacher will lead the students in reciting the previously-taught jingles.

GRAMMAR TIME

Put the introductory sentences from the box below on the board. Use these sentences as you go through each new concept covered in your teaching script. For the greatest benefit, students must participate orally with the teacher. (*You might put the introductory sentences on notebook paper if you are doing one-on-one instruction with your students.*)

Chapter 5, Introductory Sentences for Lesson 2
1. _____ During the debate, the second speaker spoke very audaciously.
2. _____ The star quarterback of the football team quit suddenly at the beginning of the season.
3. _____ The robbers in the stolen vehicle raced away from the police officer.

TEACHING SCRIPT FOR ADDING A PREPOSITIONAL PHRASE TO INVERTED ORDER

I want to do a quick review of the natural and inverted order of a sentence. Look at Reference 15 on page 15. A sentence with inverted order has one of these predicate words at the beginning of the complete subject: **an adverb, a helping verb, or a prepositional phrase**. (*See reference box in chapter 4 page 59.*) Today, we will identify an inverted-order sentence with a prepositional phrase at the beginning of the sentence. We will classify the sentences together. Begin. (*You might have your child write the labels above the sentences at this time.*)

Question and Answer Flow for Sentence 1: During the debate, the second speaker spoke very audaciously.	
1. Who spoke very audaciously? speaker - SN	10. SN V P1 Check
2. What is being said about speaker? speaker spoke - V	11. (During the debate) - Prepositional phrase
3. Spoke how? audaciously - Adv	12. Period, statement, declarative sentence
4. How audaciously? very - Adv	13. Go back to the verb - divide the complete subject from the complete predicate.
5. What kind of speaker? second - Adj	14. Is there an adverb exception? No.
6. The - A	15. Is this sentence in a natural or inverted order? Inverted - underline the subject parts once and the predicate parts twice.
7. During - P	
8. During what? debate - OP	
9. The - A	

Classified Sentence:

```
                          P    A   OP   A   Adj   SN      V    Adv   Adv
             SN  V      (During the debate), the second speaker / spoke very audaciously.  D
             P1
```

CHAPTER 5 LESSON 2 CONTINUED

Teacher's Notes: Make sure students say the **questions** and **answers** orally for each sentence. Be sure to lead them so they will say the Question and Answer Flows correctly.

Question and Answer Flow for Sentence 2: The star quarterback of the football team quit suddenly at the beginning of the season.

1. Who quit suddenly at the beginning of the season? quarterback - SN
2. What is being said about quarterback? quarterback quit - V
3. Quit how? suddenly - Adv
4. At - P
5. At what? beginning - OP
6. The - A
7. Of - P
8. Of what? season - OP
9. The - A
10. Of - P
11. Of what? team - OP
12. What kind of team? football - Adj
13. The - A

14. What kind of quarterback? star - Adj
15. The - A
16. SN V P1 Check
17. (Of the football team) - Prepositional phrase
18. (At the beginning) - Prepositional phrase
19. (Of the season) - Prepositional phrase
20. Period, statement, declarative sentence
21. Go back to the verb - divide the complete subject from the complete predicate.
22. Is there an adverb exception? No.
23. Is this sentence in a natural or inverted order? Natural - no change.

Classified Sentence:

	A	Adj	SN		P	A	Adj	OP	V	Adv	P	A	OP	P	A	OP

SN V
P1 The star quarterback (of the football team) / quit suddenly (at the beginning) (of the season). D

Question and Answer Flow for Sentence 3: The robbers in the stolen vehicle raced away from the police officer.

1. Who raced away from the police officer? robbers - SN
2. What is being said about robbers? robbers raced - V
3. Raced where? away - Adv
4. From - P
5. From whom? officer - OP

Note: When the object of the preposition is a person, use *whom* instead of *what*.

6. What kind of officer? police - Adj
7. The - A
8. In - P
9. In what? vehicle - OP

10. What kind of vehicle? stolen - Adj
11. The - A
12. The - A
13. SN V P1 Check
14. (In the stolen vehicle) - Prepositional phrase
15. (From the police officer) - Prepositional phrase
16. Period, statement, declarative sentence
17. Go back to the verb - divide the complete subject from the complete predicate.
18. Is there an adverb exception? No.
19. Is this sentence in a natural or inverted order? Natural - no change.

Classified Sentence:

	A	SN	P	A	Adj	OP	V	Adv	P	A	Adj	OP

SN V
P1 The robbers (in the stolen vehicle) / raced away (from the police officer). D

CHAPTER 5 LESSON 2 CONTINUED

TEACHING SCRIPT FOR A PRACTICE SENTENCE WITH A PREPOSITIONAL PHRASE

Put these labels on the board: **A Adj Adj SN V Adv P A Adj OP**

Look at the new sentence labels on the board: **A Adj Adj SN V Adv P A Adj OP**. I will guide you again through the process of writing a sentence to practice all the parts that you have learned.

Get out a sheet of notebook paper. On the top line of your notebook paper, write the title _Practice Sentence_. Copy the sentence labels from the board onto your notebook paper. Be sure to leave plenty of writing space between each label. Now, I will guide you through the process you will use whenever you write a Practice Sentence with a prepositional phrase.

1. Go to the **SN** label for the subject noun. Think of a noun you want to use as your subject. Write the noun you have chosen on the line _under_ the **SN** label.

2. Go to the **V** label for verb. Think of a verb that tells what your subject does. Make sure that your verb makes sense with the subject noun. Write the verb you have chosen on the line _under_ the **V** label.

3. Go to the **Adv** label for the adverb. Immediately go to the verb in your sentence and ask an adverb question. What are the adverb questions? (_how, when, where_) Choose one adverb question to ask and write your adverb answer _under_ the **Adv** label.

4. Go to the **P** label for the preposition. Think of a preposition word that tells something about your verb. You must be careful to choose a preposition word that makes sense with the noun you will choose for the object of the preposition in your next step. Write the word you have chosen for a preposition under the **P** label.

5. Go to the **OP** label for object of the preposition. If you like the noun you thought of while thinking of a preposition, write it down under the **OP** label. If you prefer, think of another noun by asking **what** or **whom** after your preposition. Check to make sure the preposition and object of the preposition make sense together and also make sense with the rest of the sentence. Remember, the object of the preposition will always answer the question **what** or **whom** after the preposition. Write the word you have chosen for the object of the preposition under the **OP** label.

6. Go to the **Adj** label for an adjective. Go to the object of the preposition that you just wrote and ask an adjective question to describe the object of the preposition noun. What are the adjective questions? (_what kind, which one, how many_) Choose one adjective question to ask and write your adjective answer under the **Adj** label next to the object of the preposition. Always check to make sure your answers are making sense in the sentence.

7. Go to the **A** label for the article adjective that is part of your prepositional phrase. What are the three article adjectives? (_a, an,_ and _the_) Choose the article adjective that makes the best sense in your sentence. Write the article adjective you have chosen _under_ the **A** label.

CHAPTER 5 LESSON 2 CONTINUED

8. Go to the **Adj** label for another adjective. Go to the subject noun of your sentence and ask an adjective question. What are the adjective questions again? (*what kind, which one, how many*) Choose one adjective question to ask and write your adjective answer under the **Adj** label next to the subject noun.

9. Go to the **Adj** label for a third adjective. Go to the subject noun again and ask another adjective question. You can use the same adjective question, or you can use a different adjective question. Write another adjective under the third **Adj** label.

10. Go to the **A** label for the article adjective in the subject area. What are the three article adjectives again? (*a, an,* and *the*) Choose the article adjective that makes the best sense in your sentence. Write the article adjective you have chosen *under* the **A** label.

11. Finally, check your Practice Sentence to make sure it has the necessary parts to be a complete sentence. What are the five parts of a complete sentence? (*subject, verb, complete sense, capital letter, and an end mark*) Does your Practice Sentence have the five parts of a complete sentence? (*Allow time for students to read over their sentences and to make any corrections they need to make.*)

TEACHING SCRIPT FOR THE IMPROVED SENTENCE

Under your Practice Sentence, write the title *Improved Sentence* on another line. To improve your Practice Sentence, you will make two synonym changes, one antonym change, and your choice of a complete word change or another synonym or antonym change.

Since it is harder to find words that can be changed to an antonym, it is usually wise to go through your sentence to find an antonym change first. Then, look through your sentence again to find words that can be improved with synonyms. Finally, make a decision about whether your last change will be a complete-word change, another synonym change, or another antonym change.

I will give you time to write your Improved Sentence. (*Always encourage students to use a thesaurus, synonym-antonym book, or a dictionary to help them develop an interesting and improved writing vocabulary. After students have finished, check and discuss students' Practice and Improved Sentences.*)

 VOCABULARY TIME

Assign Chapter 5, Vocabulary Words **#2** on page 7 in the Reference Section for students to define in their Vocabulary notebooks. Tell students they are to use a dictionary or thesaurus to look up the meanings of the vocabulary words. After they write each word and its meaning, students are to write a sentence using the vocabulary word.

Chapter 5, Vocabulary Words #2
(melodramatic, subdued, odious, hateful)

(End of lesson.)

CHAPTER 5   LESSON 3

New objectives: Jingles (pronoun, subject pronoun, possessive pronoun), Grammar (Practice Sentences), Practice sheet, and an Activity.

 **JINGLE TIME**

Have students turn to the Jingle Section in their books and recite the previously-taught jingles. Then, lead students in reciting the new jingles (*Pronoun, Subject Pronoun, Possessive Pronoun*) below. Practice the new jingles several times until students can recite them smoothly. Emphasize reciting with a rhythm. Students and teacher should be together! (*Do not try to explain the jingles at this time. Just have fun reciting them. Remember, add motions for more fun and laughter.*)

Teacher's Note: Again, do not spend a large amount of time practicing the new jingles. Students learn the jingles best by spending a small amount of time consistently, **every** day. The teacher should concentrate on the following areas while students are reciting the new jingles: togetherness, smoothness, volume, and enthusiasm.

Jingle 10: Pronoun Jingle	Jingle 11: Subject Pronoun Jingle	Jingle 12: Possessive Pronoun Jingle
These little pronouns, Hanging around, Take the place of all the nouns. With a smile and a nod And a twinkle of the eye, Give those pronouns a big high-five! Yea!	There are seven subject pronouns That are easy as can be: I and we, (clap twice) He and she, (clap twice) It and they and you. (clap three)	There are seven possessive pronouns That are easy as can be: My and our, (clap twice) His and her, (clap twice) Its and their and your. (clap three)

 GRAMMAR TIME

First-Year Option: Put the Practice Sentences from the box below on the board or notebook paper. Use these sentences as you practice the concepts that have been taught. For the greatest benefit, students must participate orally with the teacher. **Second-Year Option:** Have students classify the Practice Sentences independently on paper. Check students' sentences with the answers provided below. (*If you have the CDs for Practice Sentences, have students check their sentences with the CDs.*)

Chapter 5, Practice Sentences for Lesson 3
1. _____ Yesterday, the angry mob shouted furiously at the guards. 2. _____ During the tour, the young children in the group ran carelessly around the museum. 3. _____ A massive beast suddenly appeared on the screen!

CHAPTER 5 LESSON 3 CONTINUED

TEACHING SCRIPT FOR PRACTICING PATTERN 1 SENTENCES WITH PREPOSITIONAL PHRASES

We will classify three different sentences to practice using prepositional phrases in the Question and Answer Flows. We will classify the sentences together. Begin. (*You might have your students write the labels above the sentences at this time.*)

Question and Answer Flow for Sentence 1: Yesterday, the angry mob shouted furiously at the guards.

1. Who shouted furiously at the guards? mob - SN
2. What is being said about mob? mob shouted - V
3. Shouted how? furiously - Adv
4. At - P
5. At whom? guards - OP

Note: When the object of the preposition refers to people, use *whom* instead of *what*.

6. The - A
7. What kind of mob? angry - Adj
8. The - A
9. Shouted when? yesterday - Adv

10. SN V P1 Check
11. (At the guards) - Prepositional phrase
12. Period, statement, declarative sentence
13. Go back to the verb - divide the complete subject from the complete predicate.
14. Is there an adverb exception? No.
15. Is this sentence in a natural or inverted order? Inverted - underline the subject parts once and the predicate parts twice.

Classified Sentence:

		Adv	A	Adj	SN	V	Adv	P	A	OP
SN	V	Yesterday,	the	angry	mob /	shouted	furiously	(at	the	guards). D
P1										

Teacher's Notes: Make sure students say the **questions** and **answers** orally for each sentence. Be sure to lead them so they will say the Question and Answer Flows correctly.

Question and Answer Flow for Sentence 2: During the tour, the young children in the group ran carelessly around the museum.

1. Who ran carelessly around the museum? children - SN
2. What is being said about children? children ran - V
3. Ran how? carelessly - Adv
4. Around - P
5. Around what? museum - OP
6. The - A
7. In - P
8. In what? group - OP
9. The - A
10. What kind of children? young - Adj
11. The - A
12. During - P
13. During what? tour - OP

14. The - A
15. SN V P1 Check
16. (During the tour) - Prepositional phrase
17. (In the group) - Prepositional phrase
18. (Around the museum) - Prepositional phrase
19. Period, statement, declarative sentence
20. Go back to the verb - divide the complete subject from the complete predicate.
21. Is there an adverb exception? No.
22. Is this sentence in a natural or inverted order? Inverted - underline the subject parts once and the predicate parts twice.

Classified Sentence:

		P	A	OP	A	Adj	SN	P	A	OP	V	Adv	P	A	OP
SN	V	(During	the	tour),	the	young	children	(in	the	group) /	ran	carelessly	(around	the	museum). D
P1															

CHAPTER 5 LESSON 3 CONTINUED

Question and Answer Flow for Sentence 3: A massive beast suddenly appeared on the screen!

1. What appeared on the screen? beast - SN
2. What is being said about beast? beast appeared - V
3. On - P
4. On what? screen - OP
5. The - A
6. Appeared when? suddenly - Adv
7. What kind of beast? massive - Adj
8. A - A
9. SN V P1 Check

10. (On the screen) - Prepositional phrase
11. Exclamation point, strong feeling, exclamatory sentence
12. Go back to the verb - divide the complete subject from the complete predicate.
13. Is there an adverb exception? Yes - change the line.
14. Is this sentence in a natural or inverted order? Natural - no change.

Classified Sentence:

```
                          A   Adj   SN    Adv        V      P  A   OP
          SN  V      A massive beast / suddenly appeared (on the screen)!  E
          P1
```

PRACTICE TIME

Have students turn to page 56 in the Practice Section of their book and find the skills under Chapter 5, Lesson 3, Practice (1-2). Go over the directions to make sure they understand what to do. Check and discuss the Practice after students have finished. (*Chapter 5, Lesson 3, Practice keys are given below.*)

Chapter 5, Lesson 3, Practice 1: Write the five parts of speech that you have studied so far (in any order) on notebook paper.				
1. noun	2. verb	3. adjective	4. adverb	5. preposition

Chapter 5, Lesson 3, Practice 2
Choose one set of labels below and write a Practice and Improved Sentence on notebook paper.
A Adv Adj SN V Adv P A Adj OP or **A Adj Adj SN P A OP V Adv P A Adj OP**

ACTIVITY / ASSIGNMENT TIME

Have students clip prepositional phrases from articles and/or ads in newspapers and magazines and put them in a freezer bag for storage. Have students draw and color different shapes on a white poster board (*round shapes, square shapes, figure eight shapes, etc.*). Next, students are to glue their prepositional phrases in the different shapes. Have them explain and display their artistic creation. (*This project could take several days.*)

(End of lesson.)

CHAPTER 5   LESSON 4
New objectives: Test.

 **JINGLE TIME**

Have students turn to the Jingle Section of their books. The teacher will lead the students in reciting the previously-taught jingles.

 STUDY TIME

Have students study the vocabulary words in their vocabulary notebooks. Remind students that any vocabulary word in their notebooks could be on their test. Also, have students study any of the skills in the Practice Section that they need to review.

 TEST TIME

Have students turn to page 86 in the Test Section of their book and find the Chapter 5 Test section. Remind them to pay attention and think about what they are doing. Go over the directions to make sure they understand what to do. (*Chapter 5 Test key is on the next page.*)

 **CHECK TIME**

After students have finished, check and discuss their test papers. Make sure they understand why their answers are right or wrong. (*For total points, count each required answer as a point.*)

Chapter 5 Test
(Student Page 86)

Exercise 1: Classify each sentence.

```
            P    A      OP       A    SN        V     P    A   Adj      OP
1. SN V     (After the game), the spectators / moved (onto the basketball court). D
   P1

            A    Adj    SN    Adv    V    P   A    Adj    OP
2. SN V     The fascinated child / quickly rushed (for the drifting bubbles). D
   P1

            Adj   Adj     SN        V     Adv    P    A    Adj    OP
3. SN V     Eight mighty Olympians / dashed briskly (toward the finish line)! E
   P1
```

Exercise 2: Use Sentence 3 to underline the complete subject once and the complete predicate twice and to complete the table below.

List the Noun Used	List the Noun Job	Singular or Plural	Common or Proper	Simple Subject	Simple Predicate
1. Olympians	2. SN	3. P	4. P	5. Olympians	6. dashed
7. line	8. OP	9. S	10. C		

Exercise 3: Name the five parts of speech that you have studied so far. *(Accept answers in any order.)*

1. **Noun**   2. **Verb**   3. **Adjective**   4. **Adverb**   5. **Preposition**

Exercise 4: Identify each pair of words as synonyms or antonyms by putting parentheses ( ) around *syn* or *ant*.

1. authentic, false	syn	**(ant)**	5. ramble, coherent	syn	**(ant)**	9. alliance, division	syn	**(ant)**
2. frugal, thrifty	**(syn)**	ant	6. conceal, exhume	syn	**(ant)**	10. construction, dilapidation	syn	**(ant)**
3. fraud, deception	**(syn)**	ant	7. hateful, odious	**(syn)**	ant	11. mimic, imitate	**(syn)**	ant
4. destroy, abolish	**(syn)**	ant	8. pardon, amnesty	**(syn)**	ant	12. melodramatic, subdued	syn	**(ant)**

Exercise 5: For each sentence, write the subject, then write S if the subject is singular or P if the subject is plural, write the rule number, and underline the correct verb in the sentence.

> Rule 1: A singular subject must use a singular verb form that ends in **s**: *is, was, has, does,* or verbs ending with **s** or **es**.
> Rule 2: A plural subject, a compound subject, or the subject **YOU** must use a plural verb form that has **no s** ending: *are, were, do, have,* or verbs without **s** or **es** endings. (A plural verb form is also called the *plain form*.)

Subject	S or P	Rule
Jessica and Jason	P	2
keys	P	2
boys	P	2
parents	P	2
car	S	1
toothbrush and comb	P	2
kitten	S	1
Mom	S	1
Gloria and Wendi	P	2
company	S	1

1. **Jessica** and **Jason** (talk, talks) on the phone for hours.
2. The **keys** (was, were) locked in the car.
3. The **boys** (runs, run) to catch the frisbee.
4. Our **parents** (was, were) talking about the plans.
5. My **car** (look, looks) very dirty.
6. Your **toothbrush** and **comb** (is, are) in my drawer.
7. The **kitten** (was, were) licking its paws.
8. (Was, Were) **Mom** pleased with your grade?
9. **Gloria** and **Wendi** (is, are) going to the mall.
10. The **company** (has, have) many good employees.

Exercise 6: In your journal, write a paragraph summarizing what you have learned this week.

CHAPTER 5 LESSON 4 CONTINUED

TEACHER INSTRUCTIONS

Use the Question and Answer Flows below for the sentences on Chapter 5 Test.

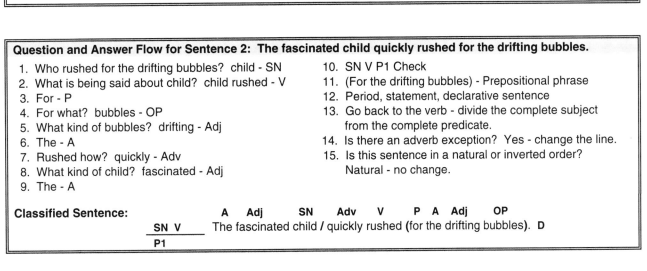

Question and Answer Flow for Sentence 1: After the game, the spectators moved onto the basketball court.

1. Who moved onto the basketball court? spectators - SN
2. What is being said about spectators? spectators moved - V
3. Onto - P
4. Onto what? court - OP
5. What kind of court? basketball - Adj
6. The - A
7. The - A
8. After - P
9. After what? game - OP
10. The - A
11. SN V P1 Check
12. (After the game) - Prepositional phrase
13. (Onto the basketball court) - Prepositional phrase
14. Period, statement, declarative sentence
15. Go back to the verb - divide the complete subject from the complete predicate.
16. Is there an adverb exception? No.
17. Is this sentence in a natural or inverted order? Inverted - underline the subject parts once and the predicate parts twice.

Classified Sentence:

```
                    P   A   OP    A    SN      V     P    A    Adj     OP
          SN V   (After the game), the spectators / moved (onto the basketball court).  D
          P1
```

Question and Answer Flow for Sentence 2: The fascinated child quickly rushed for the drifting bubbles.

1. Who rushed for the drifting bubbles? child - SN
2. What is being said about child? child rushed - V
3. For - P
4. For what? bubbles - OP
5. What kind of bubbles? drifting - Adj
6. The - A
7. Rushed how? quickly - Adv
8. What kind of child? fascinated - Adj
9. The - A
10. SN V P1 Check
11. (For the drifting bubbles) - Prepositional phrase
12. Period, statement, declarative sentence
13. Go back to the verb - divide the complete subject from the complete predicate.
14. Is there an adverb exception? Yes - change the line.
15. Is this sentence in a natural or inverted order? Natural - no change.

Classified Sentence:

```
                   A    Adj    SN     Adv    V    P   A   Adj     OP
          SN V   The fascinated child / quickly rushed (for the drifting bubbles).  D
          P1
```

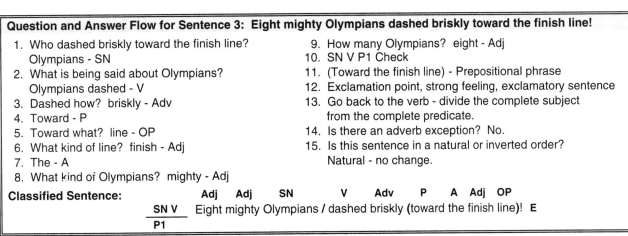

Question and Answer Flow for Sentence 3: Eight mighty Olympians dashed briskly toward the finish line!

1. Who dashed briskly toward the finish line? Olympians - SN
2. What is being said about Olympians? Olympians dashed - V
3. Dashed how? briskly - Adv
4. Toward - P
5. Toward what? line - OP
6. What kind of line? finish - Adj
7. The - A
8. What kind of Olympians? mighty - Adj
9. How many Olympians? eight - Adj
10. SN V P1 Check
11. (Toward the finish line) - Prepositional phrase
12. Exclamation point, strong feeling, exclamatory sentence
13. Go back to the verb - divide the complete subject from the complete predicate.
14. Is there an adverb exception? No.
15. Is this sentence in a natural or inverted order? Natural - no change.

Classified Sentence:

```
                  Adj   Adj    SN       V     Adv    P    A   Adj  OP
          SN V   Eight mighty Olympians / dashed briskly (toward the finish line)!  E
          P1
```

CHAPTER 5   LESSON 5
New objectives: Writing (point of view, writing in first and third person) and Writing Assignments #3 and #4, Bonus Option.

 **WRITING TIME**

TEACHING SCRIPT FOR INTRODUCING POINT OF VIEW AND WRITING IN FIRST AND THIRD PERSON

When you write, you usually write from a certain point of view. Point of view refers to the writer's use of personal pronouns to determine who is telling a story. There are commonly two points of view used in literature and writing: first person point of view and third person point of view.

Second person point of view is not used very often in writing except when you are telling someone how to do something. Second person point of view will use the second person pronouns *you, your, yours* to name the person or thing spoken to. Very few stories, paragraphs, or essays are written in second person. Mostly, second person point of view is used in giving directions, and it uses the pronoun **you** almost exclusively.

Since you will not be using second person point of view in your writing at this time, we will concentrate on learning how to write in first and third person. Look at Reference 20 on page 16 in the Reference Section of your book while I read the information.

Reference 20: Writing in First Person or Third Person
Events and stories can be told from different viewpoints. **First person Point of View** uses the first person pronouns *I, we, me, us, my, our, mine,* and *ours* to name the speaker. If any of the first person pronouns are used in a writing, the writing is usually considered a first person writing, even though second and third person pronouns may also be used. First person shows that you (*the writer*) are speaking, and that you (*the writer*) are personally involved in what is happening. (Examples: **I** am going fishing in **my** new boat. He likes **my** boat.) **Third person Point of View** uses the third person pronouns *he, his, him, she, her, hers, it, its, they, their, theirs,* and *them* to name the person or thing spoken about. You should <u>not</u> use the first person pronouns *I, we, us, me, my, mine,* and *ours* because using the first person pronouns usually puts a writing in a first person point of view. Third person means that you (*the writer*) must write as if you are watching the events take place. Third person shows that you are writing about another person, thing, or event. (Examples: **He** is going fishing in **his** new boat. **She** likes **his** boat.)

CHAPTER 5 LESSON 5 CONTINUED

It is simple to see the difference in first and third person by listening to the following paragraphs. Listen as I read a paragraph written in first person.

First person Point of View

Tomorrow, <u>my</u> brother and <u>I</u> will leave for New Orleans. <u>We</u> love the French Quarter, especially Jackson Square. In fact, <u>my</u> brother, who travels with guitar in hand, usually strums a tune or two as spectators watch the steamboats pass. Both of <u>us</u> are fascinated with the sounds and smells of the Quarter, and every meal <u>we</u> eat is either Cajun or Creole.

Listen as I read a second paragraph, this time in third person point of view. As I read, notice that the first person pronouns have been changed to third person or to a person's name. Remember that when you write in third person, you cannot use any of the first person pronouns (*I, we, us, me, my, mine,* and *ours*) because using any first person pronoun automatically puts a writing in a first person point of view. *(There are exceptions when you use quotations, but this is a good rule of thumb to follow.)*

Third person Point of View

Tomorrow, Sam and <u>his</u> brother will leave for New Orleans. <u>They</u> love the French Quarter, especially Jackson Square. In fact, <u>his</u> brother, who travels with guitar in hand, usually strums a tune or two as spectators watch the steamboats pass. Both of <u>them</u> are fascinated with the sounds and smells of the Quarter, and every meal <u>they</u> eat is either Cajun or Creole.

Remember, it is good to get in the habit of checking over your writing after you have finished. Just reading your finished paragraph several times slowly will help you see and hear things that you may want to correct.

TEACHER INSTRUCTIONS FOR WRITING ASSIGNMENTS

Give Writing Assignment #3 and Writing Assignment #4 from the box on the next page. Remind students to follow the Writing Guidelines as they prepare their writings. For Writing Assignment #3, have students underline all <u>first person pronouns</u> in their paragraph. For Writing Assignment #4, have students underline all <u>third person pronouns</u> in their paragraph.

CHAPTER 5 LESSON 5 CONTINUED

Writing Assignment Box

Writing Assignment #3: Three-Point Expository Paragraph (First Person)
(Remind students that first person pronouns are *I, we, me, us, my, our, mine,* and *ours.*)
Writing topic choices: Why Walking Is Good Exercise or **My Crazy Dream**

Writing Assignment #4: Three-Point Expository Paragraph (Third Person)
(Remind students that third person pronouns are *he, she, it, they, them, their, him,* and *her.*)
Writing topic choices: Why Walking Is Good Exercise or **His/Her Crazy Dream**

Bonus Option: Write the 12 disciples in your Journal from memory. Next, write a story, using only the names of eleven disciples. Be sure to edit your story using the editing checklist. Let a friend or family member read your story when you have finished. Can they name the disciple you left out of your story?

Simon(Peter), Andrew (Simon's brother), James (Son of Zebedee), John (James' brother), Phillip, Bartholomew, Thomas, Matthew (the tax collector), James (Son of Alphaeus), Thaddaeus, Simon of Zealot, and Judas Iscariot (who betrayed Jesus). Mathew 10:2

TEACHING SCRIPT FOR USING THE WRITING PROCESS FOR THIS WRITING ASSIGNMENT

As you begin this writing assignment, you will again go through the writing process. First, you will think about your topic and gather any information you might need in order to do the writing. Second, you will write a rough draft. Remember, it is called a rough draft because it will be revised and edited. You do not have to worry about mistakes as you write your rough draft. After you write the first draft, you will make revisions, using the Revision Checklist in Reference 4. After you revise your writing, you will edit, using the Beginning Editing Checklist in Reference 4. Finally, after you are satisfied with your revising and editing, you will write a final paper, using the Final Paper Checklist in Reference 4. You will then give the finished writing assignment to me. (*Students should finish their writing during their free time if they do not finish during this lesson.*)

TEACHER INSTRUCTIONS FOR CHECKING WRITING ASSIGNMENTS

Read, check, and discuss Writing Assignments #3 and #4 after students have finished their final papers. Use the editing checklist (*Reference 4 on teacher's page 9*) as you check and discuss students' papers. Make sure students are using the editing checklists correctly. In the beginning, you must also check students' papers carefully for <u>form</u> mistakes. This will ensure that students are learning the three-point format correctly.

(End of lesson.)

CHAPTER 6   LESSON 1

New objectives: Grammar (Practice Sentences), Practice sheet, and Vocabulary #1.

JINGLE TIME

Have students turn to the Jingle Section of their books. The teacher will lead the students in reciting the previously-taught jingles.

GRAMMAR TIME

First-Year Option: Put the Practice Sentences from the box below on the board or notebook paper. Use these sentences as you practice the concepts that have been taught. For the greatest benefit, students must participate orally with the teacher. **Second-Year Option:** Have students classify the Practice Sentences independently on paper. Check students' sentences with the answers provided below. (*If you have the CDs for Practice Sentences, have students check their sentences with the CDs.*)

Chapter 6, Practice Sentences for Lesson 1

1. _____ Today, the college students from three local universities protested at the political rally.
2. _____ A very large chemical truck turned over today in the highway median.
3. _____ The hungry fox cautiously crept toward the chicken coop during the night.

TEACHING SCRIPT FOR PRACTICING PATTERN 1 SENTENCES WITH PREPOSITIONAL PHRASES

We will practice classifying prepositional phrases in the Question and Answer Flows. We will classify the sentences together. Begin. (*You might have your students write the labels above the sentences at this time.*)

Question and Answer Flow for Sentence 1: Today, the college students from three local universities protested at the political rally.

1. Who protested at the political rally? students - SN
2. What is being said about students? students protested - V
3. At - P
4. At what? rally - OP
5. What kind of rally? political - Adj
6. The - A
7. From - P
8. From what? universities - OP
9. What kind of universities? local - Adj
10. How many universities? three - Adj
11. What kind of students? college - Adj
12. The - A
13. Protested when? today - Adv
14. SN V P1 Check
15. (From three local universities) - Prepositional phrase
16. (At the political rally) - Prepositional phrase
17. Period, statement, declarative sentence
18. Go back to the verb - divide the complete subject from the complete predicate.
19. Is there an adverb exception? No.
20. Is this sentence in a natural or inverted order? Inverted - underline the subject parts once and the predicate parts twice.

Classified Sentence:

            Adv   A   Adj   SN   P   Adj Adj   OP   V   P A   Adj   OP

SN V Today, the college students (from three local universities) / protested (at the political rally). D

P1

CHAPTER 6 LESSON 1 CONTINUED

Question and Answer Flow for Sentence 2: A very large chemical truck turned over today in the highway median.

1. What turned over today in the highway median? truck - SN
2. What is being said about truck? truck turned - V
3. Turned how? over - Adv
4. Turned when? today - Adv
5. In - P
6. In what? median - OP
7. What kind of median? highway - Adj
8. The - A
9. What kind of truck? chemical - Adj
10. What kind of truck? large - Adj

11. How large? very - Adv
12. A - A
13. SN V P1 Check
14. (In the highway median) - Prepositional phrase
15. Period, statement, declarative sentence
16. Go back to the verb - divide the complete subject from the complete predicate.
17. Is there an adverb exception? No.
18. Is this sentence in a natural or inverted order? Natural - no change.

Classified Sentence:

	A	Adv	Adj	Adj	SN	V	Adv	Adv	P	A	Adj	OP

SN V / P1   A very large chemical truck / turned over today (in the highway median). **D**

Question and Answer Flow for Sentence 3: The hungry fox cautiously crept toward the chicken coop during the night.

1. What crept toward the chicken coop during the night? fox - SN
2. What is being said about fox? fox crept - V
3. Toward - P
4. Toward what? coop - OP
5. What kind of coop? chicken - Adj
6. The - A
7. During - P
8. During what? night - OP
9. The - A
10. Crept how? cautiously - Adv

11. What kind of fox? hungry - Adj
12. The - A
13. SN V P1 Check
14. (Toward the chicken coop) - Prepositional phrase
15. (During the night) - Prepositional phrase
16. Period, statement, declarative sentence
17. Go back to the verb - divide the complete subject from the complete predicate.
18. Is there an adverb exception? Yes - change the line.
19. Is this sentence in a natural or inverted order? Natural - no change.

Classified Sentence:

	A	Adj	SN	Adv	V	P	A	Adj	OP	P	A	OP

SN V / P1   The hungry fox / cautiously crept (toward the chicken coop) (during the night). **D**

TEACHER INSTRUCTIONS

Use Sentences 1-3 that you just classified with your students to do an Oral Skill Builder Check. Use the guidelines on the next page.

CHAPTER 6 LESSON 1 CONTINUED

Oral Skill Builder Check

1. Noun check. (Say the job and then say the noun. Circle each noun.)	**5. Identify the complete subject and the complete predicate.** (Underline the complete subject once and the complete predicate twice.)
2. Identify the nouns as singular or plural. (Write S or P above each noun.)	**6. Identify the simple subject and simple predicate.** (Underline the simple subject once and the simple predicate twice. Bold, or highlight, the lines to distinguish them from the complete subject and complete predicate.)
3. Identify the nouns as common or proper. (Follow established procedure for oral identification.)	
4. Do a vocabulary check. (Follow established procedure for oral identification.)	

 PRACTICE TIME

Have students turn to page 56 in the Practice Section of their book and find the skills under Chapter 6, Lesson 1, Practice (*1-2*). Go over the directions to make sure they understand what to do. Check and discuss the Practice after students have finished. (*Chapter 6, Lesson 1, Practice keys are given below.*)

Chapter 6, Lesson 1, Practice 1				
Write the five parts of speech that you have studied so far (in any order) on notebook paper.				
1. noun	**2. verb**	**3. adjective**	**4. adverb**	**5. preposition**

Chapter 6, Lesson 1, Practice 2
Choose one set of labels below and write a Practice Sentence and Improved Sentence on notebook paper.   **A Adv Adj SN V Adv P A Adj OP P A OP** or **A Adj SN P A OP V P A Adj OP P A OP**

 VOCABULARY TIME

Assign Chapter 6, Vocabulary Words **#1** on page 7 in the Reference Section for students to define in their Vocabulary notebooks. Tell students they are to use a dictionary or thesaurus to look up the meanings of the vocabulary words. After they write each word and its meaning, students are to write a sentence using the vocabulary word.

Chapter 6, Vocabulary Words #1
(veritable, fictitious, perpetual, constant)

(End of lesson.)

CHAPTER 6   LESSON 2

New objectives: Grammar (Introductory Sentences, pronoun, subject pronoun, understood subject pronoun, Noun Checks with pronouns, adding the pronoun to the parts of speech), Activity, and Vocabulary #2.

 JINGLE TIME

Have students turn to the Jingle Section of their books. The teacher will lead the students in reciting the previously-taught jingles.

 GRAMMAR TIME

Put the introductory sentences from the box below on the board. Use these sentences as you go through each new concept covered in your teaching script. For the greatest benefit, students must participate orally with the teacher. (*You might put the introductory sentences on notebook paper if you are doing one-on-one instruction with your students.*)

Chapter 6, Introductory Sentences for Lesson 2
1. _____ He waved desperately at the passing motorist!
2. _____ Look very carefully for the keys in the desk.
3. _____ Today, they slowly jogged around the track for two hours.

TEACHING SCRIPT FOR THE PRONOUN AND THE SUBJECT PRONOUN

Today, we will learn about pronouns and the different kinds of pronouns. Let's look at the Pronoun Jingle again. It tells us that a **pronoun** takes the place of a noun. A pronoun may stand for a person, place, thing, or idea and can stand in place of any noun in a sentence. Without pronouns, everyone would be forced to repeat the same nouns again and again. Frequently-used pronouns are usually memorized.

The first kind of pronoun we will study is the subject pronoun. There are five things you should know about the subject pronoun.

1. A **subject pronoun** takes the place of a noun that is used as the subject of a sentence.
2. These are the most common subject pronouns: *I, we, he, she, it, they*, and *you*. Use the Subject Pronoun Jingle to remember the common subject pronouns.
3. To find a subject pronoun, ask the subject question *who* or *what*.
4. Label a subject pronoun with an *SP*.
5. Call the **SP** abbreviation a subject pronoun.

If you are ever in doubt about whether the subject is a noun or pronoun, just recite the subject pronoun jingle. The subject is a subject pronoun if it is one of the words in the subject pronoun jingle; otherwise, the subject is a subject noun. (*Have students recite the subject pronoun jingle.*)

CHAPTER 6 LESSON 2 CONTINUED

We will use that information as you classify Sentence 1 with me to find the subject pronoun. Remember, you use the same subject question, starting with *who* or *what*, to find the subject pronoun. Begin.

Question and Answer Flow for Sentence 1: He waved desperately at the passing motorist!

1. Who waved desperately at the passing motorist?
   He - SP (subject pronoun)
2. What is being said about he? he waved - V
3. Waved how? desperately - Adv
4. At - P
5. At whom? motorist - OP
6. What kind of motorist? passing - Adj
7. The - A

8. SN V P1 Check
9. (At the passing motorist) - Prepositional phrase
10. Exclamation point, strong feeling, exclamatory sentence
11. Go back to the verb - divide the complete subject from the complete predicate.
12. Is there an adverb exception? No.
13. Is this sentence in a natural or inverted order? Natural - no change.

Note: When writing the sentence pattern, write SN even though the subject may be a subject pronoun. See teacher's note below.

Classified Sentence:

	SP	V	Adv	P	A	Adj	OP
SN V	He / waved	desperately	(at	the	passing	motorist)!	E
P1							

Teacher's Note: Each sentence pattern is still identified with an *SN* even though the actual subject is identified and labeled as *SP* in the sentence. The *SN* is part of a consistent pattern of identification, not the actual identification of the subject in the sentence.

TEACHING SCRIPT FOR UNDERSTOOD SUBJECT PRONOUN

The second kind of pronoun we will study is the <u>understood subject pronoun</u>. There are four things you should know about the understood subject pronoun.

1. A sentence has an **understood subject** when someone gives a command or makes a request and leaves the subject unwritten or unspoken. It is understood that the unspoken subject will always be the pronoun *you.*
2. An imperative sentence gives a command or makes a request. It ends with a period or an exclamation point and always has the word *you* understood, but not expressed, as the subject.
3. The understood subject pronoun *you* is always written in parentheses at the beginning of the sentence with the label *SP* beside or above it: SP(You).
4. Call the abbreviation <u>SP(You)</u> an understood subject pronoun.

As you can see, an understood subject is not spoken or written down. Whenever a sentence gives a command or makes a request and leaves the subject unwritten and unspoken, the subject is always called an UNDERSTOOD SUBJECT. This understood subject will always be the pronoun YOU.

In this example, *Turn quickly,* who is being commanded to turn quickly? It is understood that someone is being commanded to turn quickly even though the name is not mentioned. The person receiving the command is always the understood subject pronoun YOU.

CHAPTER 6 LESSON 2 CONTINUED

Let's classify Sentence 2 for identification of the understood subject pronoun *you*.

Question and Answer Flow for Sentence 2: Look very carefully for the keys in the desk.

1. Who look very carefully for the keys in the desk?
   (You) - SP (Understood subject pronoun)

Note: Say, "you - understood subject pronoun." Demonstrate how to write (You) - SP above the pattern to the left of the sentence.

2. What is being said about you? you look - V
3. Look how? carefully - Adv
4. How carefully? very - Adv
5. For - P
6. For what? keys - OP
7. The - A
8. In - P
9. In what? desk - OP

10. The - A
11. SN V P1 Check
12. (For the keys) - Prepositional phrase
13. (In the desk) - Prepositional phrase
14. Period, command, imperative sentence

Note: Emphasize that when they have an understood subject pronoun, they will usually have an imperative sentence.

15. Go back to the verb - divide the complete subject from the complete predicate.
16. Is there an adverb exception? No.
17. Is this sentence in natural or inverted order?
    Natural - no change.

Classified Sentence:

(You) SP		V	Adv	Adv	P	A	OP	P	A	OP
SN V		/ Look very carefully (for the keys) (in the desk). **Imp**								
P1										

Teacher's Notes: Question and Answer Flow Disclaimer.

For consistency, the Question and Answer Flow will use the verb form that is written in each sentence to complete the subject question, regardless of whether the verb is singular or plural.

> Example: We <u>are</u> skating. Q & A: Who <u>are</u> skating?

If you prefer using the singular verb form, just make the necessary change whenever it occurs.

At this point, it is wise to note an exception because you will have to make decisions based on this knowledge. When a sentence has an understood subject pronoun, it will <u>usually</u> be an imperative sentence. The only time an imperative sentence is not classified as imperative is when it is a command that shows very strong feeling or excitement and has (or should have) an exclamation point. Then, it is classified as an exclamatory sentence. (*Example: Yell for help!*)

Question and Answer Flow for Sentence 3: Today, they slowly jogged around the track for two hours.

1. Who jogged around the track for two hours?
   they - SP (subject pronoun)
2. What is being said about they? they jogged - V
3. Around - P
4. Around what? track - OP
5. The - A
6. For - P
7. For what? hours - OP
8. How many hours? two - Adj
9. Jogged how? slowly - Adv
10. Jogged when? today - Adv

11. SN V P1 Check
12. (Around the track) - Prepositional phrase
13. (For two hours) - Prepositional phrase
14. Period, statement, declarative sentence
15. Go back to the verb - divide the complete subject from the complete predicate.
16. Is there an adverb exception? Yes - change the line.
17. Is this sentence in a natural or inverted order?
    Inverted - underline the subject parts once and the predicate parts twice.

Classified Sentence:

		Adv	SP	Adv	V	P	A	OP	P	Adj	OP
SN V		Today, they / slowly jogged (around the track) (for two hours). **D**									
P1											

Level 5 Homeschool Teacher's Manual

CHAPTER 6 LESSON 2 CONTINUED

TEACHING SCRIPT FOR A NOUN CHECK WHEN PRONOUNS ARE IN THE SENTENCES

A Noun Check is a check for nouns. Since nouns are located in noun jobs, it is essential to know the noun jobs so that you know where to go to find nouns. You have had two noun jobs so far: the subject-noun job and the object-of-the-preposition noun job.

Since we are looking for nouns, we will say the noun job, say the noun or pronoun, and then say *yes* if it is a noun or *no* if it is a pronoun. Let's start with number one and go through the Noun Check for Sentences 1-3, identifying nouns by using the procedure below.

Sentence 1: Subject pronoun *he*, no. Object of the preposition *motorist*, yes. *(Circle **motorist** because it is a noun.)*
Sentence 2: Understood subject pronoun *you*, no. Object of the preposition *keys*, yes. *(Circle **keys** because it is a noun.)* Object of the preposition *desk*, yes. *(Circle **desk** because it is a noun.)*
Sentence 3: Subject pronoun *they*, no. Object of the preposition *track*, yes. *(Circle **track** because it is a noun.)* Object of the preposition *hours, yes. (Circle **hours** because it is a noun.)*

Use Sentences 1-3 that you just classified with your students to do an Oral Skill Builder Check. Use the guidelines below.

Oral Skill Builder Check	
1. Noun check. (Say the job and then say the noun. Circle each noun.) **2. Identify the nouns as singular or plural.** (Write S or P above each noun.) **3. Identify the nouns as common or proper.** (Follow established procedure for oral identification.) **4. Do a vocabulary check.** (Follow established procedure for oral identification.)	**5. Identify the complete subject and the complete predicate.** (Underline the complete subject once and the complete predicate twice.) **6. Identify the simple subject and simple predicate.** (Underline the simple subject once and the simple predicate twice. Bold, or highlight, the lines to distinguish them from the complete subject and complete predicate.)

TEACHING SCRIPT FOR ADDING THE PRONOUN TO THE PARTS OF SPEECH

Do you remember that all words in the English language have been put into one of eight groups called the **Parts of Speech**? We learned that how a word is used in a sentence determines its part of speech. Do you remember the names of the five parts of speech we have already studied? *(noun, verb, adjective, adverb, and preposition)*

Today, we have learned about pronouns. A pronoun is also a part of speech; so, we will add it to our list. Now, you know six of the eight parts of speech. What are the six parts of speech? *(noun, verb, adjective, adverb, preposition, and pronoun) (Chant the six parts of speech that the students have learned several times for immediate reinforcement. Students will learn an Eight-Parts-of-Speech Jingle after the eight parts have been introduced.)*

CHAPTER 6 LESSON 2 CONTINUED

ACTIVITY / ASSIGNMENT TIME

Using the example activity below, show students how prepositional phrases are used to describe the activity. Tell students they are to pick two of the three activity assignments listed and write at least eight prepositional phrases describing each activity. Students may use the activities listed or select activities of your own. (*Put the activities and the example on the board.*)

Example Activity: **Practicing a play...**
in our costumes
from beginning to end
at the rehearsal
for a week
in the auditorium
on the stage
for a second time
by the script

Activity Assignments

Riding a four wheeler
Going to church
Playing basketball

VOCABULARY TIME

Assign Chapter 6, Vocabulary Words **#2** on page 7 in the Reference Section for students to define in their Vocabulary notebooks. Tell students they are to use a dictionary or thesaurus to look up the meanings of the vocabulary words. After they write each word and its meaning, students are to write a sentence using the vocabulary word.

Chapter 6, Vocabulary Words #2
(ethical, carnal, prodigal, wasteful)

(End of lesson.)

CHAPTER 6   LESSON 3

New objectives: Grammar (Introductory Sentences, possessive pronouns, Practice and Improved Sentences with pronouns) and an Activity.

 **JINGLE TIME**

Have students turn to the Jingle Section of their books. The teacher will lead the students in reciting the previously-taught jingles.

 GRAMMAR TIME

Put the introductory sentences from the box below on the board. Use these sentences as you go through each new concept covered in your teaching script. For the greatest benefit, students must participate orally with the teacher. (*You might put the introductory sentences on notebook paper if you are doing one-on-one instruction with your students.*)

Chapter 6, Introductory Sentences for Lesson 3

1. _____ He went eagerly to the soccer game with his friends.
2. _____ The thirsty dog anxiously rushed toward his water bowl.
3. _____ Yesterday, our celebration began with a big dance for our fifty-year anniversary.

TEACHING SCRIPT FOR POSSESSIVE PRONOUNS

The third kind of pronoun we will study is the possessive pronoun. There are six things you should know about the possessive pronoun. (*Read and discuss the information about possessive pronouns below.*)

1. A possessive pronoun takes the place of a possessive noun.

2. A possessive pronoun's spelling form makes it possessive. These are the most common possessive pronouns: *my, our, his, her, its, their,* and *your.* Use the possessive pronoun jingle to remember the most common possessive pronouns.

3. A possessive pronoun has two jobs: to show ownership or possession and to modify like an adjective.

4. When classifying a possessive pronoun, both jobs will be recognized by labeling it as a possessive pronoun adjective. Use the abbreviation **PPA** (possessive pronoun adjective).

5. Include possessive pronouns when you are asked to identify pronouns, possessives or adjectives.

6. To find a possessive pronoun, begin with the question *whose.* (*Whose book? His - PPA*)

You will use this information as you classify Sentence 1 with me to find the possessive pronoun. Remember, you use the question *whose* to find the possessive pronoun. Begin.

CHAPTER 6 LESSON 3 CONTINUED

Question and Answer Flow for Sentence 1: He went eagerly to the soccer game with his friends.

1. Who went eagerly to the soccer game with his friends? he - SP
2. What is being said about he? he went - V
3. Went how? eagerly - Adv
4. To - P
5. To what? game - OP
6. What kind of game? soccer - Adj
7. The - A
8. With - P
9. With whom? friends -OP
10. Whose friends? his - PPA (Possessive Pronoun Adjective)

11. SN V P1 Check
12. (To the soccer game) - Prepositional phrase
13. (With his friends) - Prepositional phrase
14. Period, statement, declarative sentence
15. Go back to the verb - divide the complete subject from the complete predicate.
16. Is there an adverb exception? No.
17. Is this sentence in natural or inverted order? Natural - no change.

Classified Sentence:

	SP	V	Adv	P	A	Adj	OP	P	PPA	OP

SN V / P1   He / went eagerly (to the soccer game) (with his friends). **D**

Question and Answer Flow for Sentence 2: The thirsty dog anxiously rushed toward his water bowl.

1. What rushed toward his water bowl? dog - SN
2. What is being said about dog? dog rushed - V
3. Toward - P
4. Toward what? bowl - OP
5. What kind of bowl? water - Adj
6. Whose bowl? his - PPA
7. Rushed how? anxiously - Adv
8. What kind of dog? thirsty - Adj
9. The - A

10. SN V P1 Check
11. (Toward his water bowl) - Prepositional phrase
12. Period, statement, declarative sentence
13. Go back to the verb - divide the complete subject from the complete predicate.
14. Is there an adverb exception? Yes - change the line.
15. Is this sentence in natural or inverted order? Natural - no change.

Classified Sentence:

	A	Adj	SN	Adv	V	P	PPA	Adj	OP

SN V / P1   The thirsty dog / anxiously rushed (toward his water bowl). **D**

Question and Answer Flow for Sentence 3: Yesterday, our celebration began with a big dance for our fifty-year anniversary.

1. What began with a big dance for our fifty-year anniversary? celebration - SN
2. What is being said about celebration? celebration began - V
3. With - P
4. With what? dance - OP
5. What kind of dance? big - Adj
6. A - A
7. For - P
8. For what? anniversary - OP
9. What kind of anniversary? fifty-year - Adj
10. Whose anniversary? our - PPA
11. Whose celebration? our - PPA

12. Began when? yesterday - Adv
13. SN V P1 Check
14. (With a big dance) - Prepositional phrase
15. (For our fifty-year anniversary) - Prepositional phrase
16. Period, statement, declarative sentence
17. Go back to the verb - divide the complete subject from the complete predicate.
18. Is there an adverb exception? No.
19. Is this sentence in a natural or inverted order? Inverted - underline the subject parts once and the predicate parts twice.

Classified Sentence:

	Adv	PPA	SN	V	P	A	Adj	OP	P	PPA	Adj	OP

SN V / P1   Yesterday, our celebration / began (with a big dance) (for our fifty-year anniversary). **D**

CHAPTER 6 LESSON 3 CONTINUED

TEACHING SCRIPT FOR A PRACTICE SENTENCE WITH PRONOUNS

Put these labels on the board: **SP V Adv P PPA Adj OP**

Look at the new sentence labels on the board: **SP V Adv P PPA Adj OP**. I will guide you through the process of writing a sentence to practice the new parts that you have learned.

Get out a sheet of notebook paper. On the top line of your notebook paper, write the title _Practice Sentence_. Copy the sentence labels from the board onto your notebook paper. Be sure to leave plenty of writing space between each label. I will guide you through the process you will use whenever you write a Practice Sentence with pronouns.

1. Go to the **SP** label for the subject pronoun. Repeat the Subject Pronoun Jingle to help you think of a pronoun you want to use as your subject. Write the pronoun you have chosen on the line _under_ the **SP** label.

2. Go to the **V** label for verb. Think of a verb that tells what your subject does. Make sure that your verb makes sense with the subject pronoun. Write the verb you have chosen on the line _under_ the **V** label.

3. Go to the **Adv** label for the adverb. Immediately go to the verb in your sentence and ask an adverb question. What are the adverb questions? (_how, when, where_) Choose one adverb question to ask and write your adverb answer _under_ the **Adv** label.

4. Go to the **P** label for the preposition. Think of a preposition word that tells something about your verb. You must be careful to choose a preposition word that makes sense with the noun you will choose for the object of the preposition in your next step. Write the word you have chosen for a preposition under the **P** label.

5. Go to the **OP** label for object of the preposition. If you like the noun you thought of while thinking of a preposition, write it down under the **OP** label. If you prefer, think of another noun by asking **what** or **whom** after your preposition. Check to make sure the preposition and object of the preposition make sense together and also make sense with the rest of the sentence. Remember, the object of the preposition will always answer the question **what** or **whom** after the preposition. Write the word you have chosen for the object of the preposition under the **OP** label.

6. Go to the **Adj** label for the adjective. Go to the object of the preposition that you just wrote and ask an adjective question to describe the object-of-the-preposition noun. What are the adjective questions? (_what kind, which one, how many_) Choose one adjective question to ask and write your adjective answer under the **Adj** label next to the object of the preposition. Always check to make sure your answers are making sense in the sentence.

7. Go to the **PPA** label for the possessive pronoun adjective that is part of your prepositional phrase. Repeat the possessive pronoun jingle to help you think of a pronoun you want to use as your possessive pronoun adjective. You will choose one of the possessive pronouns that makes the best sense in your sentence. Write the possessive pronoun you have chosen _under_ the **PPA** label.

CHAPTER 6 LESSON 3 CONTINUED

8. Finally, check your Practice Sentence to make sure it has the necessary parts to be a complete sentence. What are the five parts of a complete sentence? (*subject, verb, complete sense, capital letter, and an end mark*) Does your Practice Sentence have the five parts of a complete sentence? (*Allow time for students to read over their sentences and to make any corrections they need to make.*)

TEACHING SCRIPT FOR AN IMPROVED SENTENCE

Under your Practice Sentence, write the title *Improved Sentence* on another line. To improve your Practice Sentence, you will make two synonym changes, one antonym change, and your choice of a complete-word change or another synonym or antonym change.

Since it is harder to find words that can be changed to an antonym, it is usually wise to go through your sentence to find an antonym change first. Look through your sentence again to find words that can be improved with synonyms. Finally, make a decision about whether your last change will be a complete-word change, another synonym change, or another antonym change.

I will give you time to write your Improved Sentence. (*Always encourage students to use a thesaurus, synonym-antonym book, or a dictionary to help them develop an interesting and improved writing vocabulary. After students have finished, check and discuss students' Practice and Improved Sentences.*)

 ACTIVITY / ASSIGNMENT TIME

Down the left side of a sheet of paper, make a list of all the pronouns that are used in the pronoun jingles. Take your list with you when you sit down to watch your favorite television show.   Every time you hear a pronoun, place a tally mark beside that pronoun. At the end of the program, total up the number of times you heard pronouns used. Discuss the pronouns that you heard the most.

Try this experiment again with other television programs, radio talk shows, or various songs. Then, try to write the lyrics of your favorite song without using any pronouns. When you finish, sing your favorite song, without pronouns, to family members or friends. Give them a chance to try with a different song. Discuss the importance of pronouns in our communications.

Another way you can use this experiment in your home is to follow a family member around for an hour or two. Make a new list of all the pronouns that are used in the pronoun jingles. With this list in hand, record tally marks beside every pronoun that you hear the family member say. At the end of the designated time, total up the number of times each pronoun was used. Discuss the importance of pronouns in our communications.

(End of lesson.)

CHAPTER 6   LESSON 4

New objectives: Test.

 **JINGLE TIME**

Have students turn to the Jingle Section of their books. The teacher will lead the students in reciting the previously-taught jingles.

 STUDY TIME

Have students study the vocabulary words in their vocabulary notebooks. Remind students that any vocabulary word in their notebooks could be on their test. Also, have students study any of the skills in the Practice Section that they need to review.

 TEST TIME

Have students turn to page 87 in the Test Section of their book and find the Chapter 6 Test section. Remind them to pay attention and think about what they are doing. Go over the directions to make sure they understand what to do. (*Chapter 6 Test key is on the next page.*)

 **CHECK TIME**

After students have finished, check and discuss their test papers. Make sure they understand why their answers are right or wrong. (*For total points, count each required answer as a point.*)

Chapter 6 Test
(Student Page 87)

Exercise 1: Classify each sentence.

```
              SP    Adv    V      P   A  Adj    OP     P  A   OP
1.  SN V      She / quietly walked (through the dark hallway) (in the castle).  D
    P1

              SP    V     Adv   P  PPA  OP
2.  SN V      They / prayed daily (for our country).  D
    P1

    (You) SP     V   Adv   Adv   P  A    OP
3.  SN V       / Eat very slowly (in the cafeteria).  Imp
    P1
```

Exercise 2: Use Sentence 1 to underline the complete subject once and the complete predicate twice and to complete the table below.

List the Noun Used	List the Noun Job	Singular or Plural	Common or Proper	Simple Subject	Simple Predicate
1. **hallway**	2. **OP**	3. **S**	4. **C**	5. **She**	6. **walked**
7. **castle**	8. **OP**	9. **S**	10. **C**		

Exercise 3: Name the six parts of speech that you have studied so far. *(Accept answers in any order.)*

1. **noun**   2. **verb**   3. **adjective**   4. **adverb**   5. **preposition**   6. **pronoun**

Exercise 4: Identify each pair of words as synonyms or antonyms by putting parentheses ( ) around *syn* or *ant*.

1. frugal, thrifty	**(syn)** ant	5. hateful, odious	**(syn)** ant	9. vacant, void	**(syn)** ant
2. alliance, division	syn **(ant)**	6. perpetual, constant	**(syn)** ant	10. veritable, fictitious	syn **(ant)**
3. prodigy, genius	**(syn)** ant	7. pardon, amnesty	**(syn)** ant	11. prodigal, wasteful	**(syn)** ant
4. ethical, carnal	syn **(ant)**	8. withhold, bequeath	syn **(ant)**	12. fraud, deception	**(syn)** ant

Exercise 5: For each sentence, write the subject, then write S if the subject is singular or P if the subject is plural, write the rule number, and underline the correct verb in the sentence.

> Rule 1: A singular subject must use a singular verb form that ends in **s**: *is, was, has, does, or verbs ending with* **s** *or* **es**.
> Rule 2: A plural subject, a compound subject, or the subject **YOU** must use a plural verb form that has **no s** ending:
> *are, were, do, have, or verbs without* **s** *or* **es** *endings.* (A plural verb form is also called the *plain form*.)

Subject	S or P	Rule
tree	S	1
Chris and Shawna	P	2
stores	P	2
puppy	S	1
flowers	P	2
sister	S	1
food	S	1
students	P	2
painting	S	1
boys	P	2

1. The **tree** (<u>was</u>, were) a beautiful specimen.
2. **Chris** and **Shawna** (is, <u>are</u>) staying in Oxford.
3. The **stores** (has, <u>have</u>) great holiday sales.
4. That **puppy** (need, <u>needs</u>) some food.
5. The **flowers** (is, <u>are</u>) very beautifully arranged.
6. My **sister** (<u>was</u>, were) taken to the hospital.
7. The **food** (<u>is</u>, are) in the lower cabinet.
8. (<u>Do</u>, Does) those **students** have the homework?
9. The **painting** (seem, <u>seems</u>) to be missing.
10. The **boys** (was, <u>were</u>) enjoying their vacation.

Exercise 6: On a sheet of paper, write as many prepositions as you can.

Exercise 7: In your journal, write a paragraph summarizing what you have learned this week.

CHAPTER 6 LESSON 4 CONTINUED

TEACHER INSTRUCTIONS

Use the Question and Answer Flows below for the sentences on Chapter 6 Test.

Question and Answer Flow for Sentence 1: She quietly walked through the dark hallway in the castle.

1. Who walked through the dark hallway in the castle?
   she - SP
2. What is being said about she? she walked - V
3. Through - P
4. Through what? hallway - OP
5. What kind of hallway? dark - Adj
6. The - A
7. In - P
8. In what? castle - OP
9. The - A
10. Walked how? quietly - Adv

11. SN V P1 Check
12. (Through the dark hallway) - Prepositional phrase
13. (In the castle) - Prepositional phrase
14. Period, statement, declarative sentence
15. Go back to the verb - divide the complete subject from the complete predicate.
16. Is there an adverb exception? Yes - change the line.
17. Is this sentence in natural or inverted order?
    Natural - no change.

Classified Sentence:

```
                          SP    Adv    V        P    A  Adj   OP     P  A   OP
                  SN V    She / quietly walked (through the dark hallway) (in the castle).  D
                  P1
```

Question and Answer Flow for Sentence 2: They prayed daily for our country.

1. Who prayed daily for our country? they - SP
2. What is being said about they? they prayed - V
3. Prayed when? daily - Adv
4. For - P
5. For what? country - OP
6. Whose country? our - PPA
7. SN V P1 Check

8. (For our country) - Prepositional phrase
9. Period, statement, declarative sentence
10. Go back to the verb - divide the complete subject from the complete predicate.
11. Is there an adverb exception? No.
12. Is this sentence in natural or inverted order?
    Natural - no change.

Classified Sentence:

```
                         SP    V     Adv   P  PPA  OP
                 SN V    They / prayed daily (for our country).  D
                 P1
```

Question and Answer Flow for Sentence 3: Eat very slowly in the cafeteria.

1. Who eat very slowly in the cafeteria?
   (You) - SP (Understood subject pronoun)
2. What is being said about you? you eat - V
3. Eat how? slowly - Adv
4. How slowly? very - Adv
5. In - P
6. In what? cafeteria - OP
7. The - A
8. SN V P1 Check

9. (In the cafeteria) - Prepositional phrase
10. Period, command, imperative sentence
11. Go back to the verb - divide the complete subject from the complete predicate.
12. Is there an adverb exception? No.
13. Is this sentence in natural or inverted order?
    Natural - no change.

Classified Sentence:

```
                 (You) SP    V   Adv   Adv   P  A    OP
                 SN  V       / Eat very slowly (in the cafeteria).  Imp
                 P1
```

CHAPTER 6   LESSON 5

New objectives: Writing (changing plural categories to singular points) and Writing Assignments #5 and #6.

 WRITING TIME

TEACHING SCRIPT FOR CHANGING PLURAL CATEGORIES TO SINGULAR POINTS

When you have a topic such as *My favorite animals*, you will usually name your favorite animals by categories, or groups, like dolphins, giraffes, and penguins. When this happens, you need to change some plural points to singular points. I am going to use an example to show you some things you need to do. First, I will read the paragraph to you. Then, I will go through each of the three points in the paragraph and show you how to write it correctly. (*Put the following paragraph on the board to use as a visual aid while you discuss writing singular and plural points correctly. Read the paragraph to your students from beginning to end. Then, go through the teaching script given for each sentence in the paragraph.*)

Three-Point Expository Paragraph in First Person

Topic: My favorite animals
3-points: 1. dolphins   2. giraffes   3. penguins

    I have three favorite animals. These animals are dolphins, giraffes, and penguins. My first favorite animal is a dolphin. I love dolphins because they glide so smoothly through the ocean. My second favorite animal is a giraffe. I enjoy watching giraffes walk around gracefully on long legs. My third favorite animal is a penguin. I think penguins are fascinating because they can survive the frigid arctic weather. My three favorite animals are splendid creatures and I enjoy learning as much as I can about them.

Notice that I have written the topic first because it is the subject of the paragraph. Writing the topic first helps me to focus on what the paragraph is about. Next, I have listed the three points that I am going to discuss. Again, having the three points written down before I start helps me focus on what I will say in the paragraph.

I am now ready to begin my paragraph because I am clear about my topic and about the points I will cover as I write. I start with a topic sentence because it tells the reader what the paragraph is about: *I have three favorite animals.* Knowing what the paragraph is about helps the reader focus on the main points as the reader progresses through the paragraph.

My next sentence is the three-point sentence: *These animals are dolphins, giraffes, and penguins.* The three-point sentence lists the three main points that will be discussed in the paragraph, so in this paragraph we know the three main points are *dolphins, giraffes*, and *penguins*. Now, I want you to notice that each of the three points listed is plural (*dolphins, giraffes*, and *penguins*). These main points are actually categories, or groups, of animals, and that is why they are listed as plural words.

CHAPTER 6 LESSON 5 CONTINUED

Let's look at the sentence I have written for the first point. The sentence for the first point starts out like this: *My first favorite animal is.* Since this phrase is singular, I could change my plural listing to a singular listing to agree with the type of sentence I am writing. To do this, I will change *dolphins* from plural to singular: *My first favorite animal is a dolphin.* Usually, an article adjective is needed to make the sentence sound better.

Just remember: If your three points are plural, you usually make them singular as you name them for your first point, second point, and third point. Use an article adjective with your singular form to make it sound better. Notice that the second and third main points follow this same format. Look at the forms as I read them to you. (**2nd point:** *My second favorite animal is a giraffe.* **3rd point:** *My third favorite animal is a penguin.*)

After each main point, I have a supporting sentence. Supporting sentences make each point clearer by telling extra information about each main point. Remember, I have stated in my main points that dolphins, giraffes, and penguins are three of my favorite animals. Each supporting sentence should state some kind of information that proves each of the main points. (**1st Supporting sentence:** *I love dolphins because they glide so smoothly through the ocean.* **2nd Supporting sentence:** *I enjoy watching giraffes walk around gracefully on long legs.* **3rd Supporting sentence:** *I think penguins are fascinating because they can survive the frigid arctic weather.*) Notice that I also used the plural forms in the supporting sentences.

My last sentence is a concluding sentence. It summarizes my three points by restating some of the words in the topic sentence and by adding an extra thought that finalizes the paragraph. (**Concluding sentence:** *My three favorite animals are splendid creatures, and I enjoy learning as much as I can about them.*)

I will read you the same paragraph in third person. Notice the change in pronouns. Listen carefully. (*Put the paragraph below on the board to use as a visual aid while you discuss writing in third person. Read the paragraph to your class from beginning to end. Then, discuss the differences in the first person and third person paragraphs.*) (Remind students that third person is the point of view in writing that uses only the personal pronouns *he, she, it, they, them, their, him,* and *her.* Students <u>should not use any</u> of the first person pronouns: *I, me, my, mine,* or *we, us, our,* and *ours*).

Three-Point Expository Paragraph in Third Person

Topic: Shawna's favorite animals
3-points: 1. dolphins   2. giraffes   3. penguins

    Shawna has three favorite animals. These animals are dolphins, giraffes, and penguins. Shawna's first favorite animal is a dolphin. She loves dolphins because they glide so smoothly through the ocean. Shawana's second favorite animal is a giraffe. Shawana enjoys watching giraffes walk around gracefully on long legs. Shawna's third favorite animal is a penguin. She thinks penguins are fascinating because they can survive the frigid arctic weather. Shawna's three favorite animals are splendid creatures, and she enjoys learning as much as she can about them.

As we study the two paragraphs, make sure you know that *third person* pronouns may be used in first person writing without changing the first person point of view. (Example: <u>I</u> like <u>his</u> work.) Remember, if even **one first person pronoun** is used in a sentence or paragraph, it is identified as first person even though *third person* pronouns are also used. On the other hand, only *third person* pronouns should be used in third person writing. Not one **first person** pronoun (including **my**) should be used in most *third person* writing. First person pronouns are very powerful and will change any writing to a first person point of view.

CHAPTER 6 LESSON 5 CONTINUED

TEACHER INSTRUCTIONS FOR WRITING ASSIGNMENTS #5 AND #6

Give Writing Assignment #5 and Writing Assignment #6 from the box below. Remind students to follow the Writing Guidelines from Chapter 3 as they prepare their writings.

For Writing Assignment #5, students are to write a three-point paragraph in first person. Have students underline all first person pronouns in their paragraph. Remind students that they can use _third person_ pronouns in first person writing.

For Writing Assignment #6, students are to write a three-point paragraph in third person. Have students underline all third person pronouns in their second paragraph. Remind students that they normally would not use any first person pronouns (including _my_) in _third person_ writing.

Writing Assignment Box

Writing Assignment #5: Three-Point Expository Paragraph (First Person)
(Remind students that first person pronouns are _I, we, me, us, my, our, mine,_ and _ours_.)
Writing topic: My Favorite Animals

Writing Assignment #6: Three-Point Expository Paragraph (Third Person)
(Remind students that third person pronouns are _he, she, it, they, them, their, him,_ and _her_.)
Writing topic: (Person's Name) Favorite Animals

TEACHING SCRIPT FOR USING THE WRITING PROCESS FOR THIS WRITING ASSIGNMENT

As you begin this writing assignment, you will again go through the writing process. First, you will think about your topic and gather any information you might need in order to do the writing. Second, you will write a rough draft. Remember, it is called a rough draft because it will be revised and edited. You do not have to worry about mistakes as you write your rough draft. After you write the first draft, you will make revisions, using the Revision Checklist in Reference 4. After you revise your writing, you will edit, using the Beginning Editing Checklist in Reference 4. Finally, after you are satisfied with your revising and editing, you will write a final paper, using the Final Paper Checklist in Reference 4. You will then give the finished writing assignment to me.

TEACHER INSTRUCTIONS FOR CHECKING WRITING ASSIGNMENTS #5 AND #6

Read, check, and discuss Writing Assignments #5 and #6 after students have finished their final papers. Use the editing checklist (_Reference 4 on teacher's page 9_) as you check and discuss students' papers. Make sure students are using the editing checklist correctly. In the beginning, you must also check students' papers carefully for <u>form</u> mistakes. This will ensure that students are learning the three-point format correctly.

(End of lesson.)

CHAPTER 7 LESSON 1

New objectives: Grammar (Introductory Sentences, possessive noun, Noun Check with possessive nouns) and Vocabulary #1.

JINGLE TIME

Have students turn to the Jingle Section of their books. The teacher will lead the students in reciting the previously-taught jingles.

GRAMMAR TIME

Put the introductory sentences from the box below on the board. Use these sentences as you go through each new concept covered in your teaching script. For the greatest benefit, students must participate orally with the teacher. (*You might put the introductory sentences on notebook paper if you are doing one-on-one instruction with your students.*)

Chapter 7, Introductory Sentences for Lesson 1
1. _____ My friend's new puppy gleefully pranced across her mother's white carpet. 2. _____ Look through our catalog for the color of your choice. 3. _____ During the evening, the cattle in the pasture bellowed loudly for their grain.

TEACHING SCRIPT FOR POSSESSIVE NOUN

Today, we will learn about a very special noun: the possessive noun. Since there is not a jingle for a possessive noun, information about the possessive noun is listed in your Reference Section on page 16. Look at Reference 21. Follow along as I read the six things you should know about the possessive noun. (*Read and discuss the information about possessive nouns in the reference box below.*)

Reference 21: Possessive Nouns
1. A possessive noun is the name of a person, place, or thing that owns something. 2. A possessive noun will always have an apostrophe after it. It will have either an *apostrophe* before the <u>s</u> ('s) or an *apostrophe* after the <u>s</u> (s'). The apostrophe makes a noun show ownership. (*Tim's car*) 3. A possessive noun has two jobs: to show ownership or possession and to modify like an adjective. 4. When classifying a possessive noun, both jobs will be recognized by labeling it as a possessive noun adjective. Use the abbreviation **PNA** (possessive noun adjective). 5. Include possessive nouns when you are asked to identify possessive nouns or adjectives. Do not include possessive nouns when you are asked to identify regular nouns. 6. To find a possessive noun, begin with the question *whose*. (*Whose car? Tim's - PNA*)

Since you use the *whose* question to find a possessive noun and a possessive pronoun, you must remember one important fact about each one in order to tell them apart. Remember, all possessive nouns have an apostrophe, and the seven possessive pronouns are in the possessive pronoun jingle you have learned. (*You may want your students to recite the possessive pronoun jingle again to reinforce what you have just said.*) You will use this information as you classify Sentences 1-3 with me. Begin.

CHAPTER 7 LESSON 1 CONTINUED

Question and Answer Flow for Sentence 1: My friend's new puppy gleefully pranced across her mother's white carpet.

1. What pranced across her mother's white carpet?
   puppy - SN
2. What is being said about puppy? puppy pranced - V
3. Across - P
4. Across what? carpet - OP
5. What kind of carpet? white - Adj
6. Whose carpet? mother's - PNA (Possessive Noun Adjective)
7. Whose mother? her - PPA (Possessive Pronoun Adjective)
8. Pranced how? gleefully - Adv
9. What kind of puppy? new - Adj
10. Whose puppy? friend's - PNA

11. Whose friend? my - PPA
12. SN V P1 Check
13. (Across her mother's white carpet) -
    Prepositional phrase
14. Period, statement, declarative sentence
15. Go back to the verb - divide the complete subject
    from the complete predicate.
16. Is there an adverb exception? Yes - change the
    line.
17. Is this sentence in a natural or inverted order?
    Natural - no change.

Classified Sentence:

	PPA	PNA	Adj	SN	Adv	V	P	PPA	PNA	Adj	OP

SN V
P1   My friend's new puppy / gleefully pranced (across her mother's white carpet). **D**

Question and Answer Flow for Sentence 2: Look through our catalog for the color of your choice.

1. Who look through our catalog for the color of your
   choice? (You) - SP (Understood subject pronoun)
2. What is being said about you? you look - V
3. Through - P
4. Through what? catalog - OP
5. Whose catalog? our - PPA
6. For - P
7. For what? color - OP
8. The - A
9. Of - P
10. Of what? choice - OP

11. Whose choice? your - PPA
12. SN V P1 Check
13. (Through our catalog) - Prepositional phrase
14. (For the color) - Prepositional phrase
15. (Of your choice) - Prepositional phrase
16. Period, command, Imperative sentence
17. Go back to the verb - divide the complete subject
    from the complete predicate.
18. Is there an adverb exception? No.
19. Is this sentence in a natural or inverted order?
    Natural - no change.

Classified Sentence:

(You) SP	V	P	PPA	OP	P	A	OP	P	PPA	OP

SN V
P1   / Look (through our catalog) (for the color) (of your choice). **Imp**

Question and Answer Flow for Sentence 3: During the evening, the cattle in the pasture bellowed loudly for their grain.

1. What bellowed loudly for their grain? cattle - SN
2. What is being said about cattle? cattle bellowed - V
3. Bellowed how? loudly - Adv
4. For - P
5. For what? grain - OP
6. Whose grain? their - PPA
7. In - P
8. In what? pasture - OP
9. The - A
10. The - A
11. During - P
12. During what? evening - OP

13. The - A
14. SN V P1 Check
15. (During the evening) - Prepositional phrase
16. (In the pasture) - Prepositional phrase
17. (For their grain) - Prepositional phrase
18. Period, statement, declarative sentence
19. Go back to the verb - divide the complete subject
    from the complete predicate.
20. Is there an adverb exception? No.
21. Is this sentence in a natural or inverted order?
    Inverted - underline the subject parts once and
    the predicate parts twice.

Classified Sentence:

	P	A	OP	A	SN	P	A	OP	V	Adv	P	PPA	OP

SN V
P1   (During the evening), the cattle (in the pasture) / bellowed loudly (for their grain). **D**

CHAPTER 7 LESSON 1 CONTINUED

TEACHING SCRIPT FOR A NOUN CHECK WHEN POSSESSIVE NOUNS ARE IN THE SENTENCES

We will only do a Noun Check today to show you how to deal with possessive nouns when you are identifying nouns. A possessive noun's part of speech is an adjective. Remember, a Noun Check is a check for nouns. If there is a possessive noun, we will not identify it because we are looking only for noun jobs that give us regular nouns, not special nouns that function as possessives and adjectives. Let's start with number one and go through the noun check for Sentences 1-3, looking for nouns. *(Recite the information below with your students.)*

Sentence 1: Subject noun *puppy*, yes *(Circle **puppy** because it is a noun.)* Object of the preposition *carpet*, yes. *(Circle **carpet** because it is a noun.)*

Sentence 2: Understood subject pronoun *you*, no. Object of the preposition *catalog*, yes. *(Circle **catalog** because it is a noun.)* Object of the preposition *color*, yes. *(Circle **color** because it is a noun.)* Object of the preposition *choice*, yes. *(Circle **choice** because it is a noun.)*

Sentence 3: Object of the preposition *evening*, yes. *(Circle **evening** because it is a noun.)* Subject noun *cattle*, yes. *(Circle **cattle** because it is a noun.)* Object of the preposition *pasture*, yes. *(Circle **pasture** because it is a noun.)* Object of the preposition *grain*, yes. *(Circle **grain** because it is a noun.)*

Use Sentences 1-3 that you just classified with your students to do an Oral Skill Builder Check. Use the guidelines below.

Oral Skill Builder Check	
1. Noun check. (Say the job and then say the noun. Circle each noun.) **2. Identify the nouns as singular or plural.** (Write S or P above each noun.) **3. Identify the nouns as common or proper.** (Follow established procedure for oral identification.) **4. Do a vocabulary check.** (Follow established procedure for oral identification.)	**5. Identify the complete subject and the complete predicate.** (Underline the complete subject once and the complete predicate twice.) **6. Identify the simple subject and simple predicate.** (Underline the simple subject once and the simple predicate twice. Bold, or highlight, the lines to distinguish them from the complete subject and complete predicate.)

 VOCABULARY TIME

Assign Chapter 7, Vocabulary Words **#1** on page 7 in the Reference Section for students to define in their Vocabulary notebooks. Tell students they are to use a dictionary or thesaurus to look up the meanings of the vocabulary words. After they write each word and its meaning, students are to write a sentence using the vocabulary word.

Chapter 7, Vocabulary Words #1
(frivolous, grave, proverbial, notorious)

(End of lesson.)

CHAPTER 7   LESSON 2

New objectives: Grammar (Practice Sentences), Activity, and Vocabulary #2.

 JINGLE TIME

Have students turn to the Jingle Section of their books. The teacher will lead the students in reciting the previously-taught jingles.

 GRAMMAR TIME

First-Year Option: Put the Practice Sentences from the box below on the board or notebook paper. Use these sentences as you practice the concepts that have been taught. For the greatest benefit, students must participate orally with the teacher. **Second-Year Option:** Have students classify the Practice Sentences independently on paper. Check students' sentences with the answers provided below. (*If you have the CDs for Practice Sentences, have students check their sentences with the CDs.*)

Chapter 7, Practice Sentences for Lesson 2
1. _____ She paid for the shoes with her dad's hard-earned money.
2. _____ Study thoroughly for your test tomorrow.
3. _____ I prayed silently for my sister during her final operation.

TEACHING SCRIPT FOR PRACTICING PATTERN 1 SENTENCES WITH PRONOUNS AND POSSESSIVE NOUNS

We will classify three different sentences to practice the new skills in the Question and Answer Flows. We will classify the sentences together. Begin. (*You might have your students write the labels above the sentences at this time.*)

Question and Answer Flow for Sentence 1: She paid for the shoes with her dad's hard-earned money.

1. Who paid for the shoes with her dad's hard-earned money? she - SP
2. What is being said about she? she paid - V
3. For - P
4. For what? shoes - OP
5. The - A
6. With - P
7. With what? money - OP
8. What kind of money? hard-earned - Adj
9. Whose money? dad's - PNA
10. Whose dad? her - PPA
11. SN V P1 Check
12. (For the shoes) - Prepositional phrase
13. (With her dad's hard-earned money) - Prepositional phrase
14. Period, statement, declarative sentence
15. Go back to the verb - divide the complete subject from the complete predicate.
16. Is there an adverb exception? No.
17. Is this sentence in a natural or inverted order? Natural - no change.

Classified Sentence:

	SP	V	P	A	OP		P	PPA	PNA	Adj	OP
SN V	She /	paid	(for	the	shoes)		(with	her	dad's	hard-earned	money). **D**
P1											

CHAPTER 7 LESSON 2 CONTINUED

Question and Answer Flow for Sentence 2: Study thoroughly for your test tomorrow.

1. Who study thoroughly for your test tomorrow?
   (You) - SP (Understood subject pronoun)
2. What is being said about you? you study - V
3. Study how? thoroughly - Adv
4. For - P
5. For what? test - OP
6. Whose test? your - PPA

7. Study when? tomorrow - Adv
8. SN V P1 Check
9. (For your test) - Prepositional phrase
10. Period, command, imperative sentence
11. Is there an adverb exception? No.
12. Is this sentence in a natural or inverted order?
    Natural - no change.

Classified Sentence:

<pre>
              (You) SP   V   Adv   P PPA OP   Adv
              SN V   / Study thoroughly (for your test) tomorrow. Imp
              P1
</pre>

Question and Answer Flow for Sentence 3: I prayed silently for my sister during her final operation.

1. Who prayed silently for my sister during her final operation? I - SP
2. What is being said about I? I prayed - V
3. Prayed how? silently - Adv
4. For - P
5. For whom? sister - OP
6. Whose sister? my - PPA
7. During - P
8. During what? operation - OP
9. What kind of operation? final - Adj
10. Whose operation? her - PPA

11. SN V P1 Check
12. (For my sister) - Prepositional phrase
13. (During her final operation) - Prepositional phrase
14. Period, statement, declarative sentence
15. Go back to the verb - divide the complete subject from the complete predicate.
16. Is there an adverb exception? No.
17. Is this sentence in natural or inverted order?
    Natural - no change.

Classified Sentence:

<pre>
                        SP V   Adv   P PPA OP   P   PPA Adj   OP
              SN V   I / prayed silently (for my sister) (during her final operation). D
              P1
</pre>

TEACHING SCRIPT FOR THE PRACTICE SENTENCE

Put these labels on the board: **SP V Adv P PPA PNA Adj OP**

Look at the new sentence labels on the board: **SP V Adv P PPA PNA Adj OP**. I will guide you again through the process of writing a sentence to practice the different parts that you have learned.

Get out a sheet of notebook paper. On the top line of your notebook paper, write the title *Practice Sentence*. Copy the sentence labels from the board onto your notebook paper. Be sure to leave plenty of writing space between each label. I will guide you through the process you will use whenever you write a Practice Sentence with pronouns and possessive nouns.

CHAPTER 7 LESSON 2 CONTINUED

1. Go to the **SP** label for the subject pronoun. Repeat the Subject Pronoun Jingle to help you think of a pronoun you want to use as your subject. Write the pronoun you have chosen on the line *under* the **SP** label.

2. Go to the **V** label for verb. Think of a verb that tells what your subject does. Make sure that your verb makes sense with the subject pronoun. Write the verb you have chosen on the line *under* the **V** label.

3. Go to the **Adv** label for the adverb. Immediately go to the verb in your sentence and ask an adverb question. What are the adverb questions? (*how, when, where*) Choose one adverb question to ask and write your adverb answer *under* the **Adv** label.

4. Go to the **P** label for the preposition. Think of a preposition word that tells something about your verb. You must be careful to choose a preposition word that makes sense with the noun you will choose for the object of the preposition in your next step. Write the word you have chosen for a preposition under the **P** label.

5. Go to the **OP** label for object of the preposition. If you like the noun you thought of while thinking of a preposition, write it down under the **OP** label. If you prefer, think of another noun by asking **what** or **whom** after your preposition. Check to make sure the preposition and object of the preposition make sense together and also make sense with the rest of the sentence. Remember, the object of the preposition will always answer the question **what** or **whom** after the preposition. Write the word you have chosen for the object of the preposition under the **OP** label.

6. Go to the **Adj** label for the adjective. Go to the object of the preposition that you just wrote and ask an adjective question to describe the object of the preposition noun. What are the adjective questions? (*what kind, which one, how many*) Choose one adjective question to ask and write your adjective answer under the **Adj** label next to the object of the preposition. Always check to make sure your answers are making sense in the sentence.

7. Go to the **PNA** label for the possessive noun adjective that is part of your prepositional phrase. Think of a possessive noun that answers "whose" when you refer to the object of the preposition noun. Make sure the possessive noun makes sense in your sentence. Also, make sure you write the apostrophe correctly as you write the possessive noun you have chosen *under* the **PPA** label.

8. Go to the **PPA** label for the possessive pronoun adjective that is part of your prepositional phrase. Repeat the Possessive Pronoun Jingle to help you think of a pronoun you want to use as your possessive pronoun adjective. You will choose one of the possessive pronouns that makes the best sense in your sentence. Write the possessive pronoun you have chosen *under* the **PPA** label.

9. Finally, check your Practice Sentence to make sure it has the necessary parts to be a complete sentence. What are the five parts of a complete sentence? (*subject, verb, complete sense, capital letter, and an end mark*) Does your Practice Sentence have the five parts of a complete sentence? (*Allow time for students to read over their sentences and to make any corrections they need to make.*)

CHAPTER 7 LESSON 2 CONTINUED

TEACHING SCRIPT FOR THE IMPROVED SENTENCE

Under your Practice Sentence, write the title *Improved Sentence* on another line. To improve your Practice Sentence, you will make two synonym changes, one antonym change, and your choice of a complete-word change or another synonym or antonym change.

Since it is harder to find words that can be changed to an antonym, it is usually wise to go through your sentence to find an antonym change first. Then, look through your sentence again to find words that can be improved with synonyms. Finally, make a decision about whether your last change will be a complete-word change, another synonym change, or another antonym change.

I will give you time to write your Improved Sentence. *(Always encourage students to use a thesaurus, synonym-antonym book, or a dictionary to help them develop an interesting and improved writing vocabulary. After students have finished, check and discuss students' Practice and Improved Sentences.)*

 ACTIVITY / ASSIGNMENT TIME

Select a favorite storybook (*like a little Golden Book*). You will do two things. First, you will rewrite the story again and replace every noun with a pronoun. Do you know what the story is about? Why or why not? Second, you will rewrite the story and replace every pronoun with a noun. What happens when you try to read the story out loud? Compare the two stories. Discuss what you have discovered.

 VOCABULARY TIME

Assign Chapter 7, Vocabulary Words **#2** on page 7 in the Reference Section for students to define in their Vocabulary notebooks. Tell students they are to use a dictionary or thesaurus to look up the meanings of the vocabulary words. After they write each word and its meaning, students are to write a sentence using the vocabulary word.

Chapter 7, Vocabulary Words #2
(vague, specific, transparent, translucent)

(End of lesson.)

CHAPTER 7   LESSON 3
New objectives: Jingles (object pronoun), Grammar (Practice Sentences, object pronoun), and a Practice activity.

 JINGLE TIME

Have students turn to the Jingle Section in their books and recite the previously-taught jingles. Then, lead students in reciting the new jingle (*Object Pronoun*) below. Practice the new jingle several times until students can recite it smoothly. Emphasize reciting with a rhythm. Students and teacher should be together! (*Do not try to explain the jingles at this time. Just have fun reciting them. Remember, add motions for more fun and laughter.*)

Teacher's Note: Again, do not spend a large amount of time practicing the new jingles. Students learn the jingles best by spending a small amount of time consistently, **every** day. The teacher should concentrate on the following areas while students are reciting the new jingles: togetherness, smoothness, volume, and enthusiasm.

Jingle 13: Object Pronoun Jingle	
There are seven object pronouns	
That are easy as can be:	
Me and us,	(clap twice)
Him and her,	(clap twice)
It and them and you.	(clap three)

 GRAMMAR TIME

First-Year Option: Put the Practice Sentences from the box below on the board or notebook paper. Use these sentences as you practice the concepts that have been taught. For the greatest benefit, students must participate orally with the teacher. **Second-Year Option:** Have students classify the Practice Sentences independently on paper. Check students' sentences with the answers provided below. (*If you have the CDs for Practice Sentences, have students check their sentences with the CDs.*)

Chapter 7, Practice Sentences for Lesson 3
1. _____ The young man came to the United States from a small town in Honduras.
2. _____ The politicians at the convention talked politely to us.
3. _____ I glanced frantically at the unfamiliar surroundings!

CHAPTER 7 LESSON 3 CONTINUED

TEACHING SCRIPT FOR PRACTICING PATTERN 1 SENTENCES WITH PRONOUNS AND
POSSESSIVE NOUNS

We will classify three different sentences to practice using pronouns and possessive nouns in the Question and Answer Flows. We will classify the sentences together. Begin. (*You might have your students write the labels above the sentences at this time.*)

Question and Answer Flow for Sentence 1: The young man came to the United States from a small town in Honduras.

1. Who came to the United States from a small town in Honduras? man - SN
2. What is being said about man? man came - V
3. To - P
4. To what? United States - OP
5. The - A
6. From - P
7. From what? town - OP
8. What kind of town? small - Adj
9. A - A
10. In - P
11. In what? Honduras - OP
12. What kind of man? young - Adj
13. The - A
14. SN V P1 Check
15. (To the United States) - Prepositional phrase
16. (From a small town) - Prepositional phrase
17. (In Honduras) - Prepositional phrase
18. Period, statement, declarative sentence
19. Go back to the verb - divide the complete subject from the complete predicate.
20. Is there an adverb exception? No.
21. Is this sentence in a natural or inverted order? Natural - no change.

Classified Sentence:

	A	Adj	SN	V	P	A		OP		P	A	Adj	OP	P	OP
SN V	The	young	man	/ came	(to	the	United	States)		(from	a	small	town)	(in	Honduras).	D
P1															

Teacher's Notes: Make sure students say the **questions** and **answers** orally for each sentence. Be sure to lead them so they will say the Question and Answer Flows correctly.

Question and Answer Flow for Sentence 2: The politicians at the convention talked politely to us.

1. Who talked politely to us? politicians - SN
2. What is being said about politicians? politicians talked - V
3. Talked how? politely - Adv
4. To - P
5. To whom? us - OP
6. At - P
7. At what? convention - OP
8. The - A
9. The - A
10. SN V P1 Check
11. (At the convention) - Prepositional phrase
12. (To us) - Prepositional phrase
13. Period, statement, declarative sentence
14. Go back to the verb - divide the complete subject from the complete predicate.
15. Is there an adverb exception? No.
16. Is this sentence in a natural or inverted order? Natural - no change.

Classified Sentence:

	A	SN	P	A	OP	V	Adv	P	OP
SN V	The	politicians	(at	the	convention)	/ talked	politely	(to	us).	D
P1									

CHAPTER 7 LESSON 3 CONTINUED

Question and Answer Flow for Sentence 3: I glanced frantically at the unfamiliar surroundings!

1. Who glanced frantically at the unfamiliar surroundings? I - SP
2. What is being said about I? I glanced - V
3. Glanced how? frantically - Adv
4. At - P
5. At what? surroundings - OP
6. What kind of surroundings? unfamiliar - Adj
7. The - A
8. SN V P1 Check

9. (At the unfamiliar surroundings) - Prepositional phrase
10. Exclamation point, strong feeling, exclamatory sentence
11. Go back to the verb - divide the complete subject from the complete predicate.
12. Is there an adverb exception? No.
13. Is this sentence in a natural or inverted order? Natural - no change.

Classified Sentence:

<pre>
                        SP   V   Adv   P   A   Adj   OP
            SN V   I / glanced frantically (at the unfamiliar surroundings)! E
            P1
</pre>

TEACHING SCRIPT FOR OBJECT PRONOUN

We are now ready to learn another type of pronoun. But, first, let's review the two jingles that tell us about two other types of pronouns: the Subject Pronoun Jingle and the Possessive Pronoun Jingle. (*Recite the two jingles.*) Now, we are going to recite the Object Pronoun Jingle that you learned at the beginning of this lesson. (*Have students turn to the Jingle Section of their books and recite the object pronoun jingle with you.*)

There are three things you need to know about object pronouns.

1. If a pronoun does any job that has the word *object* in it, that pronoun is an object pronoun. Object pronouns can be used as objects of the prepositions, direct objects, or indirect objects. Did you notice that these jobs all have the word *object* in them? Listen to the list again. *Object* pronouns are used as *objects* of the prepositions, direct *objects*, and indirect *objects*.

2. The object pronouns are the ones listed in your Object Pronoun Jingle: *me, us, him, her, it, them*, and *you*.

3. An object pronoun does not have a special label. An object pronoun keeps the OP, DO, or IO label that tells its job. (*Review the object pronoun examples below.*)

Examples: Larry gave his lunch to *him*. The reporter interviewed *us*. Give *her* the directions. (*Write the examples above on the board as a visual aid for your students.*)

CHAPTER 7 LESSON 3 CONTINUED

As you can see, an object pronoun can perform many jobs. Remember, the object pronoun will not be labeled object pronoun. It will take the name of the pronoun job that you use when you classify the sentence. For example, the object pronoun is labeled *OP* for object of the preposition (*not object pronoun*). It may also be labeled *DO* for direct object or *IO* for indirect object. You will learn about the other object pronoun jobs in later sentence patterns. For now, we will concentrate on using the object pronoun as an object of the preposition.

Look at Sentence 1 that we have just classified. It has two prepositional phrases. In the first prepositional phrase, the object of the preposition is a noun. In the second prepositional phrase, the object of the preposition is a pronoun. Notice that we classify both objects of the prepositions as "OP."

(*Put this example sentence on the board: The trophy was presented **to me** during our banquet. Read and discuss the example sentence.*) Can we substitute other object pronouns for object pronoun that is used? (*Yes.*) What are some of the object pronouns that we could substitute? (***to her, to him, to them, to us***) How would you label the object pronouns that we could substitute? (*Keep the same OP label for the object of the preposition.*)

 PRACTICE TIME

Have students write the three sentences that they classified at the beginning of the lesson on a sheet of paper. (*See page 122.*) Have them tape-record the Question and Answer Flows for all three sentences. Students should write labels above the sentences as they classify them. They especially need the second practice if this is their first year in the program. (*After the students have finished, check the tape and sentence labels. Make sure students understand any mistakes they have made.*)

 WRITING TIME

Have students make an entry in their journals.

 STUDY TIME

Have students study the vocabulary words in their vocabulary notebooks. Tell students that any vocabulary word in their notebooks could be on their test. Also, have students study any of the skills in the Practice Section that they need to review.

(End of lesson.)

CHAPTER 7 LESSON 4

New objectives: Test.

 JINGLE TIME

Have students turn to the Jingle Section of their books. The teacher will lead the students in reciting the previously-taught jingles.

 STUDY TIME

Have students study the vocabulary words in their vocabulary notebooks. Remind students that any vocabulary word in their notebooks could be on their test. Also, have students study any of the skills in the Practice Section that they need to review.

 TEST TIME

To develop listening skills, give students a definition test orally. Have them get out one sheet of paper and number it 1-10. They should listen carefully to the questions and write the answers on their paper. Ask the questions listed below. After students have finished, check and discuss the answers together. Discuss strong areas as well as weak areas. (*You may or may not want to take a grade on this oral test. Bonus points usually work nicely in place of grades.*)

1. What are the three article adjectives? *an, an, the*
2. What are the five parts of a correct sentence? *subject, verb, complete sense, capital letter, and end mark*
3. What is an interrogative sentence? *a question*
4. What is the understood subject pronoun? *you*
5. What punctuation is used for possessive nouns? *an apostrophe or (')*
6. What are the three adverb questions? *how, when, where*
7. What are the three adjective questions? *what kind, which one, how many*
8. What is the definition of a pronoun? *A pronoun takes the place of a noun*.
9. What are the seven subject pronouns? *I, we, he, she, it, they, you*
10. What are the seven possessive pronouns? *my, our, his, her, its, their, your*

Have students turn to page 88 in the Test Section of their book and find the Chapter 7 Test section. Remind them to pay attention and think about what they are doing. Go over the directions to make sure they understand what to do. (*Chapter 7 Test key is on the next page.*)

 CHECK TIME

After students have finished, check and discuss their test papers. Make sure they understand why their answers are right or wrong. (*For total points, count each required answer as a point.*)

(End of lesson.)

Chapter 7 Test
(Student Page 88)

Exercise 1: Classify each sentence.

```
        Adv      A     PNA        SN       V      Adv        P    A     PNA        OP
1. SN V    Yesterday, the assassin's airplane / crashed directly (into the president's headquarters)!  E
   P1
```

```
            P      Adj    OP   SP    V       Adv      P  PPA     Adj    Adj  OP
2. SN V    (During biology class), we / reviewed endlessly (for our upcoming lab test).  D
   P1
```

```
   (You)SP      V    Adv    Adv       P    A    Adj    OP
3. SN V    / Drive very carefully (around the sharp curves).  Imp
   P1
```

Exercise 2: Use Sentence 1 to underline the complete subject once and the complete predicate twice and to complete the table below.

List the Noun Used	List the Noun Job	Singular or Plural	Common or Proper	Simple Subject	Simple Predicate
1. **airplane**	2. **SN**	3. **S**	4. **C**	5. **airplane**	6. **crashed**
7. **headquarters**	8. **OP**	9. **P**	10. **C**		

Exercise 3: Name the six parts of speech that you have studied so far. *(Accept answers in any order.)*

1. **noun**   2. **verb**   3. **adjective**   4. **adverb**   5. **preposition**   6. **pronoun**

Exercise 4: Identify each pair of words as synonyms or antonyms by putting parentheses ( ) around *syn* or *ant*.

1. carnal, ethical	syn	**(ant)**	4. fictitious, veritable	syn	**(ant)**	7. proverbial, notorious	**(syn)**	ant
2. vague, specific	syn	**(ant)**	5. prodigal, wasteful	**(syn)**	ant	8. colleague, competitor	syn	**(ant)**
3. frivolous, grave	syn	**(ant)**	6. perpetual, constant	**(syn)**	ant	9. transparent, translucent	**(syn)**	ant

Exercise 5: Finding One Part of Speech. For each sentence, write *SN* above the simple subject and *V* above the simple predicate. Underline the word(s) for the part of speech listed to the left of each sentence.

```
                                  SN          V
Adjective(s):    1. Several mallard ducks landed in my grandfather's reflection pond.
```
```
                     SP       V
Preposition(s):  2. I always jog in the park during the summer.
```
```
                    CSN        CSP  V
Pronoun(s):      3. My family and I cheered loudly for Steven from our seats in the stands.
```

Exercise 6: For each sentence, write the subject, then write S if the subject is singular or P if the subject is plural, write the rule number (Rule 1 for singular and Rule 2 for plural), and underline the correct verb in the sentence.

Subject	S or P	Rule		
stories	P	2	1.	Those **stories** (<u>sound</u>, sounds) quite interesting.
Dustin and girlfriend	P	2	2.	**Dustin** and his **girlfriend** (is, <u>are</u>) flying to Denver.
sun	S	1	3.	The **sun** (<u>was</u>, were) shining.
You	P	2	4.	**You** (was, <u>were</u>) great at playing the trombone.
dog	S	1	5.	(<u>Does</u>, Do) your **dog** bite?
parents	P	2	6.	(Doesn't, <u>Don't</u>) your **parents** wonder where you are?
friend	S	1	7.	My **friend** (live, <u>lives</u>) in another country.
clothes	P	2	8.	Those **clothes** in the basket (was, <u>were</u>) dirty.

Exercise 7: On a sheet of paper, write seven subject pronouns, seven possessive pronouns, and seven object pronouns.

Exercise 8: In your journal, write a paragraph summarizing what you have learned this week.

CHAPTER 7 LESSON 4 CONTINUED

TEACHER INSTRUCTIONS

Use the Question and Answer Flows below for the sentences on Chapter 7 Test.

Question and Answer Flow for Sentence 1: Yesterday, the assassin's airplane crashed directly into the president's headquarters!

1. What crashed directly into the president's headquarters? airplane - SN
2. What is being said about airplane? airplane crashed - V
3. Crashed where? directly - Adv
4. Into - P
5. Into what? headquarters - OP
6. Whose headquarters? president's - PNA
7. The - A
8. Whose airplane? assassin's - PNA
9. The - A
10. Crashed when? yesterday - Adv

11. SN V P1 Check
12. (Into the president's headquarters) - Prepositional phrase
13. Exclamation point, strong feeling, exclamatory sentence
14. Go back to the verb - divide the complete subject from the complete predicate.
15. Is there an adverb exception? No.
16. Is this sentence in natural or inverted order? Inverted - underline the subject parts once and the predicate parts twice.

		Adv	A	PNA	SN	V	Adv	P	A	PNA	OP
Classified Sentence:	SN V	Yesterday,	the	assassin's	airplane /	crashed	directly	(into	the	president's	headquarters)! **E**
	P1										

Question and Answer Flow for Sentence 2: During biology class, we reviewed endlessly for our upcoming lab test.

1. Who reviewed endlessly for our upcoming lab test? We - SP
2. What is being said about we? we reviewed - V
3. Reviewed how? endlessly - Adv
4. For - P
5. For what? test - OP
6. What kind of test? lab - Adj
7. What kind of test? upcoming - Adj
8. Whose test? our - PPA
9. During - P
10. During what? class - OP

11. What kind of class? biology - Adj
12. SN V P1 Check
13. (During biology class) - Prepositional phrase
14. (For our upcoming lab test) - Prepositional phrase
15. Period, statement, declarative sentence
16. Go back to the verb - divide the complete subject from the complete predicate.
17. Is there an adverb exception? No.
18. Is this sentence in natural or inverted order? Inverted - underline the subject parts once and the predicate parts twice.

		P	Adj	OP	SP	V	Adv	P	PPA	Adj	Adj	OP
Classified Sentence:	SN V	(During	biology	class),	we /	reviewed	endlessly	(for	our	upcoming	lab	test). **D**
	P1											

Question and Answer Flow for Sentence 3: Drive very carefully around the sharp curves.

1. Who drive very carefully around the sharp curves? (You) - SP (understood subject pronoun)
2. What is being said about you? you drive - V
3. Drive how? carefully - Adv
4. How carefully? very - Adv
5. Around - P
6. Around what? curves - OP
7. What kind of curves? sharp - Adj
8. The - A

9. SN V P1 Check
10. (Around the sharp curves) - Prepositional phrase
11. Period, command, Imperative sentence
12. Go back to the verb - divide the complete subject from the complete predicate.
13. Is there an adverb exception? No.
14. Is this sentence in a natural or inverted order? Natural - no change.

		(You) SP	V	Adv	Adv	P	A	Adj	OP
Classified Sentence:									
	SN V	/ Drive	very	carefully	(around	the	sharp	curves). **Imp**	
	P1								

CHAPTER 7   LESSON 5

New objectives: Writing (standard and time-order forms) and Writing Assignment #7, Bonus Option.

 WRITING TIME

TEACHING SCRIPT FOR STANDARD AND TIME-ORDER FORMS

When you learned to write a three-point paragraph, you learned to state your points by beginning each sentence that stated a point with an article adjective or a possessive pronoun. (**My** first favorite, **My** second favorite, **My** third favorite, or **The** first thing, **The** second thing, **The** third thing.) We will call what you have been doing the **standard form** because it is used often and is a good, reliable three-point form. But now you are ready to learn another way to state each point in a three-point paragraph. This will give you some versatility in your writing. We will call the new way to state each point the **time-order form**. You must remember this word of caution. Whichever form you choose, you must use that same form throughout your paragraph to introduce each of your points. You cannot mix forms in the same paragraph.

In the time-order form, you should begin each sentence that states a point with words that suggest a definite time or number order, such as *first, second, third*, etc. or *first, next, last,* or *finally,* etc. When you begin your sentence with time order words, you leave out the article adjectives and possessive pronouns. For example, instead of saying "**My first** favorite" you would say "**First**, I like."

I am going to use an example to show how to do this. First, I will read the paragraph to you. Next, I will go through each of the three points in the paragraph and show you how it was written in the non-standard form. Look at Reference 22 on pages 16 and 17 in the Reference Section of your book and follow along as I read the paragraph to you. (*After you read the paragraph, continue reading the teaching script.*)

Reference 22: Sample Paragraph in Time-Order Form
Topic: My favorite summer activities **3-points:** 1. camping   2. hiking   3. swimming
Example 1: Three-point paragraph using a standard topic sentence with non-standard points
I enjoy three different summer activities. These summer activities are camping, hiking, and swimming. <u>**First**</u>, I enjoy camping. I like the adventure of camping in remote areas. <u>**Second**</u>, I enjoy hiking. I love discovering the hidden beauty of nature when I hike. <u>**Third**</u>, I enjoy swimming. I especially like swimming after a long hike because it is very refreshing. My three favorite summer activities provide a lot of fun for me, and they help me enjoy the outdoors.

Notice that I have written the topic first because it helps me to focus on what the paragraph is about. Next, I have listed the three points that I am going to write about. Again, having the three points written down before I start helps me focus on what I will say in the paragraph.

I am now ready to begin my paragraph because I am clear about my topic and about the points I will cover as I write. I start with a topic sentence because it tells the reader what the paragraph is about. Knowing what the paragraph is about helps the reader focus on the main points as the reader progresses through the paragraph. My topic sentence is, "I enjoy three different summer activities."

My next sentence is the three-point sentence: *These summer activities are camping, hiking, and swimming.* The three-point sentence lists the three main points that will be discussed in the paragraph, so we know the three main points are *camping, hiking,* and *swimming.*

CHAPTER 7 LESSON 5 CONTINUED

Let's look at the sentence I have written for the first point. The sentence for the first point starts out like this: *First, I enjoy.* As you can see, I did not use the possessive pronoun *my* or the article *the* in front of the word *first*, and I put a comma after the order word because it is an introductory word.

Look at the second and third main points. Notice that each of the remaining points have been written in the same format selected for the first point. Look at their form as I read them to you. (**2nd point:** *Second, I enjoy hiking.* **3rd point:** *Third, I enjoy swimming.*) Another interesting detail is that you could use *finally* instead of *third* to introduce your last point.

After each main point, I have a supporting sentence. Each of my supporting sentences backs up the point that it follows. The supporting sentences make each point clearer by telling information that proves what I have stated in each point is true. Remember, I have stated in my main points that camping, hiking, and swimming are my three favorite summer activities. Each supporting sentence should state some kind of information that proves each of the main points. (**1st Supporting sentence:** *I like the adventure of **camping** in remote areas.* **2nd Supporting sentence:** *I love discovering the hidden beauty of nature when I **hike**.* **3rd Supporting sentence:** *I especially like **swimming** after a long hike because it is very refreshing.*)

My last sentence is a concluding sentence. It summarizes my three points by restating some of the words in the topic sentence and by adding an extra thought that finalizes the paragraph. (**Concluding sentence:** *My three favorite summer activities provide a lot of fun for me, and they help me enjoy the outdoors.*)

I will read the same paragraph to you again, but this time I will use different order words to introduce each point. In the first example, the order words are *first, second,* and *third*. In the second example, the order words will be *first, next,* and *last*. It is a minor change, but it definitely adds variety to the paragraph. (*Read the following paragraph from beginning to end. Emphasize the different words that introduce each point sentence.*)

Reference 22: Sample Paragraph in Time-Order Form, Continued

Example 2: Three-point paragraph using a standard topic sentence with time-order points

I enjoy three different summer activities. These summer activities are camping, hiking, and swimming. **First**, I enjoy camping. I like the adventure of camping in remote areas. **Next**, I enjoy hiking. I love discovering the hidden beauty of nature when I hike. **Last**, I enjoy swimming. I especially like swimming after a long hike because it is very refreshing. My three favorite summer activities provide a lot of fun for me, and they help me enjoy the outdoors.

Notice that this time I used the order words *first, next,* and *last* at the beginning of the point sentences. I also put a comma after the words, *first next,* and *last* as they are written in the paragraph. You could again use *finally* instead of *last* to introduce your last point.

As a review, I will go over the four things you need to know whenever you are using the time-order form to write a three-point paragraph. Listen carefully because I will ask you a few questions after I have finished the review. (*Go over the four items listed below.*)

Using the Time-Order Form

1. Use time-order words at the beginning of each of the main point sentences.
   (*first, second, third,* etc.) or (*first, next, last, finally,* etc.)
2. Do not use a possessive pronoun or article in front of the time-order word.
3. Put a comma after the introductory time-order word.
4. For consistency, use the same style to introduce each point in your paragraph.

Now, I will ask a few questions about what I have just discussed with you.

1. The words you use in the time-order form usually come in sets. We have discussed two sets. What are they? (*first, second, third,* etc.) or (*first, next, last, finally,* etc.)

CHAPTER 7 LESSON 5 CONTINUED

2. What two kinds of words are generally not used in the time-order form? (*possessive pronouns and articles*)

3. When you use time-order words to introduce the point sentences, they are introductory words. What punctuation is required after the time-order words when they are used as introductory words? (*comma*)

4. If I am writing a three-point paragraph using the standard form, what form do I use for each of the points I introduce? (*the standard form*) In the standard form, am I allowed to use possessive pronouns and articles to help introduce my points? (*yes*)

5. If I am writing a three-point paragraph using the time-order form, what form do I use for each of the points I introduce? (*the time-order form*) In the time-order form, am I allowed to use possessive pronouns and articles to help introduce my points? (*no*)

TEACHER INSTRUCTIONS FOR WRITING ASSIGNMENT

For Writing Assignment #7, students are to write a three-point paragraph in first person, using the time-order form. They are to <u>underline all time-order words</u> used at the beginning of each sentence that states a point. Remind students that they can use third person pronouns in first person writing. Have them follow the Writing Guidelines as they prepare their writing. Also, tell students to look up any words they cannot spell as they check over their writing. A spelling check is being added to the general editing list for the students. (*See "More Editing Skills" in Reference 4 on student page 11.*)

Writing Assignment Box

Writing Assignment #7: Three-Point Expository Paragraph (First Person, Time-Order Form)
(Remind students that first person pronouns are *I, we, me, us, my, our, mine, and ours.*)
Writing topic choices: Things That I Cherish the Most or **My Favorite Vacation Spots**

Bonus Option: Write this question in your Journal and today's date: What is the only book in the Bible that does not contain the word God? Leave space in your Journal to record this information: How long did it take you to find the answer? Where did you find the answer? Did you ask someone for the answer? How many people knew the answer? What did you learn in your search for the answer? (*Answer: Esther*)

TEACHING SCRIPT FOR USING THE WRITING PROCESS FOR THIS WRITING ASSIGNMENT

As you begin this writing assignment, you will start through the writing process. First, you will think about your topic and gather any information you might need in order to do the writing. Second, you will write a rough draft. Remember, it is called a rough draft because it will be revised and edited. You do not have to worry about mistakes as you write your rough draft. After you write the first draft, you will make revisions, using the Revision Checklist in Reference 4. After you revise your writing, you will edit, using the Beginning Editing Checklist in Reference 4. Finally, after you are satisfied with your revising and editing, you will write a final paper, using the Final Paper Checklist in Reference 4. You will then give the finished writing assignment to me.

TEACHER INSTRUCTIONS FOR CHECKING WRITING ASSIGNMENT

Read, check, and discuss Writing Assignment #7 after students have finished their final paper. Use the editing checklist (*Reference 4 on teacher's page 9*) as you check and discuss students' papers. Make sure students are using the editing checklist correctly. In the beginning, you must also check students' papers carefully for <u>form</u> mistakes. This will ensure that students are learning the three-point format correctly.

(End of lesson.)

CHAPTER 8 LESSON 1

New objectives: Jingles (the 23 helping verbs of the mean, lean verb machine), Grammar (Introductory Sentences, helping verb, **not** adverb, question verb), and Vocabulary #1.

 JINGLE TIME

Have students turn to the Jingle Section in their books and recite the previously-taught jingles. Then, lead students in reciting the new jingle (*The 23 Helping Verbs of the Mean, Lean Verb Machine*) below. Practice the new jingle several times until students can recite it smoothly. Emphasize reciting with a rhythm. Students and teacher should be together! (*Do not try to explain the jingle at this time. Just have fun reciting it. Remember, add motions for more fun and laughter.*)

Teacher's Note: Again, do not spend a large amount of time practicing the new jingles. Students learn the jingles best by spending a small amount of time consistently, **every** day. The teacher should concentrate on the following areas while students are reciting the new jingle: togetherness, smoothness, volume, and enthusiasm.

Jingle 14: The 23 Helping Verbs of the Mean, Lean Verb Machine Jingle

These 23 helping verbs will be on my test.
I gotta remember them so I can do my best.
I'll start out with 8 and finish with 15;
Just call me the mean, lean verb machine.

There are the 8 *be* verbs that are easy as can be:
  am, is, are --was and were,
  am, is, are --was and were,
  am, is, are --was and were,
  be, being, and been.
All together now, the 8 *be* verbs:
am, is, are -- was and were -- be, being, and been,
am, is, are -- was and were -- be, being, and been.

There're 23 helping verbs, and I've recited only 8.
That leaves fifteen more that I must relate:
  has, have, and had --do, does, and did,
  has, have, and had --do, does, and did,
  might, must, may --might, must, may.

Knowing these verbs will save my grade:
  can and could --would and should,
  can and could --would and should,
  shall and will,
  shall and will.
In record time, I did this drill.
I'm the mean, lean verb machine - STILL!

 GRAMMAR TIME

Put the introductory sentences from the box below on the board. Use these sentences as you go through each new concept covered in your teaching script. For the greatest benefit, students must participate orally with the teacher. (*You might put the introductory sentences on notebook paper if you are doing one-on-one instruction with your students.*)

Chapter 8, Introductory Sentences for Lesson 1

1. _____ The congregation in the huge cathedral has been listening attentively to the missionary for hours.
2. _____ They have not searched diligently for the sunken treasure off the coast of Florida.
3. _____ Has Elizabeth spoken to your committee about the advantages of computers in the classrooms?

CHAPTER 8 LESSON 1 CONTINUED

TEACHING SCRIPT FOR THE HELPING VERB

Today, we will learn about helping verbs. When there are two or more verbs, the verbs in front are known as the **helping verbs**, and the last verb is the main verb. Helping verbs are also called **auxiliary verbs**. The main verb and helping verbs together are called a **verb phrase**.

When directions are given to underline the verb, the helping verb and the main verb will be underlined because they are both part of the verb phrase. (For example: The fox **is running** for his life!) Helping verbs are labeled with *HV*. *Is running* is the verb phrase and both verbs would be underlined. If you are labeling *is running*, you would label the helping verb *is* with the letters *HV* and the main verb *running* with the letter *V*.

You will use this information as you classify Sentence 1 with me to find the helping verb. Remember, you use the same subject question, *who* or *what*, to start classifying all sentences. Begin.

Question and Answer Flow for Sentence 1: The congregation in the huge cathedral has been listening attentively to the missionary for hours.

1. Who has been listening attentively to the missionary for hours? congregation - SN
2. What is being said about congregation? congregation has been listening - V

Note: There are 3 verbs. *Listening* is the main verb and will be labeled with a <u>V</u>. *Has* and *been* are the helping verbs in front of *listening* and will be labeled with <u>HV</u>.

3. Has - HV (helping verb) (Write HV above *has*.)
4. Been - HV (helping verb) (Write HV above *been*.)
5. Listening how? attentively - Adv
6. To - P
7. To whom? missionary - OP
8. The - A
9. For - P
10. For what? hours - OP
11. In - P
12. In what? cathedral - OP
13. What kind of cathedral? huge - Adj
14. The - A
15. The - A
16. SN V P1 Check
17. (In the huge cathedral) - Prepositional phrase
18. (To the missionary) - Prepositional phrase
19. (For hours) - Prepositional phrase
20. Period, statement, declarative sentence
21. Go back to the verb - divide the complete subject from the complete predicate.
22. Is there an adverb exception? No.
23. Is this sentence in a natural or inverted order? Natural - no change.

Classified Sentence:

```
                                A      SN       P  A  Adj   OP      HV  HV   V      Adv     P  A
        SN  V      The congregation (in the huge cathedral) / has been listening attentively (to the
        P1                         OP       P  OP
                   missionary) (for hours).  D
```

---

*TEACHING SCRIPT FOR THE **NOT** ADVERB*

Even though the word *not* is not a verb, we will study it now because it is so often confused as part of a verb phrase. The helping verb can be split from the main verb by the adverb *NOT*. The word *NOT* is always an adverb telling *how*. Many negative words are adverbs telling *how* or *to what extent*. (For example: My friends **are** *not* **going** to the game tonight.) We will now classify Sentence 2 to find the "not" adverb. Begin.

CHAPTER 8 LESSON 1 CONTINUED

Question and Answer Flow for Sentence 2: They have not searched diligently for the sunken treasure off the coast of Florida.

1. Who have not searched diligently for the sunken treasure off the coast of Florida? they - SP
2. What is being said about they? they have searched - V
3. Have - HV
4. Have searched how? not - Adv
5. Have searched how? diligently - Adv
6. For - P
7. For what? treasure - OP
8. What kind of treasure? sunken - Adj
9. The - A
10. Off - P
11. Off what? coast - OP
12. The - A
13. Of - P
14. Of what? Florida - OP
15. SN V P1 Check
16. (For the sunken treasure) - Prepositional phrase
17. (Off the coast) - Prepositional phrase
18. (Of Florida) - Prepositional phrase
19. Period, statement, declarative sentence
20. Go back to the verb - divide the complete subject from the complete predicate.
21. Is there an adverb exception? No.
22. Is this sentence in a natural or inverted order? Natural - no change.

Classified Sentence:

```
                    SP  HV Adv  V      Adv    P A   Adj    OP     P A OP    P  OP
SN V    They / have not searched diligently (for the sunken treasure) (off the coast) (of Florida).  D
P1
```

TEACHING SCRIPT FOR THE QUESTION VERB

Earlier, we studied interrogative sentences. Now, we are going to review the interrogative sentence that starts with a helping verb. When the helping verb is placed before the subject, the sentence is usually a question. The subject will come between the helping verb and the main verb. You can check the parts of a question by making a statement: (For example: **Are** you **going** to the library? You **are going** to the library.)

Let's classify Sentence 3 for identification of the question verb. Begin.

Question and Answer Flow for Sentence 3: Has Elizabeth spoken to your committee about the advantages of computers in the classrooms?

1. Who has spoken to your committee about the advantages of computers in the classrooms? Elizabeth - SN
2. What is being said about Elizabeth? Elizabeth has spoken - V
3. Has - HV
4. To - P
5. To whom? committee - OP
6. Whose committee? your - PPA
7. About - P
8. About what? advantages - OP
9. The - A
10. Of - P
11. Of what? computers - OP
12. In - P
13. In what? classrooms - OP
14. The - A
15. SN V P1 Check
16. (To your committee) - Prepositional phrase
17. (About the advantages) - Prepositional phrase
18. (Of computers) - Prepositional phrase
19. (In the classrooms) - Prepositional phrase
20. Question mark, question, interrogative sentence
21. Go back to the verb - divide the complete subject from the complete predicate.
(With a question verb, divide in front of the main verb.)
22. Is there an adverb exception? No.
23. Is this sentence in a natural or inverted order? Inverted - underline the subject parts once and the predicate parts twice.
(The question verb is located in the subject of the sentence, but it is part of the predicate.)

Classified Sentence:

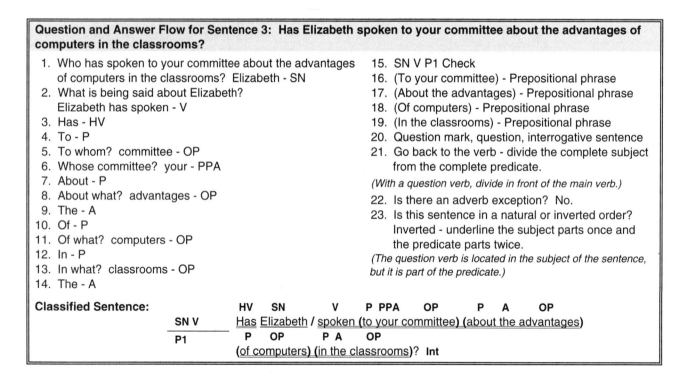

```
                    HV   SN       V    P PPA   OP      P   A    OP
SN V    Has Elizabeth / spoken (to your committee) (about the advantages)
P1                    P   OP    P A   OP
                    (of computers) (in the classrooms)?  Int
```

CHAPTER 8 LESSON 1 CONTINUED

TEACHER INSTRUCTIONS

Use Sentences 1-3 that you just classified with your students to do an Oral Skill Builder Check. Use the guidelines below.

Oral Skill Builder Check	
1. Noun check. (Say the job and then say the noun. Circle each noun.) **2. Identify the nouns as singular or plural.** (Write S or P above each noun.) **3. Identify the nouns as common or proper.** (Follow established procedure for oral identification.) **4. Do a vocabulary check.** (Follow established procedure for oral identification.)	**5. Identify the complete subject and the complete predicate.** (Underline the complete subject once and the complete predicate twice.) **6. Identify the simple subject and simple predicate.** (Underline the simple subject once and the simple predicate twice. Bold, or highlight, the lines to distinguish them from the complete subject and complete predicate.)

 VOCABULARY TIME

Assign Chapter 8, Vocabulary Words **#1** on page 7 in the Reference Section for students to define in their Vocabulary notebooks. Tell students they are to use a dictionary or thesaurus to look up the meanings of the vocabulary words. After they write each word and its meaning, students are to write a sentence using the vocabulary word.

Chapter 8, Vocabulary Words #1
(myth, fact, veracity, truth)

(End of lesson.)

CHAPTER 8   LESSON 2

New objectives: Grammar (Practice Sentences, Practice and Improved Sentence with helping verb), Practice activity, and Vocabulary #2.

 JINGLE TIME

Have students turn to the Jingle Section of their books. The teacher will lead the students in reciting the previously-taught jingles.

 GRAMMAR TIME

First-Year Option: Put the Practice Sentences from the box below on the board or notebook paper. Use these sentences as you practice the concepts that have been taught. For the greatest benefit, students must participate orally with the teacher. **Second-Year Option:** Have students classify the Practice Sentences independently on paper. Check students' sentences with the answers provided below. (*If you have the CDs for Practice Sentences, have students check their sentences with the CDs.*)

Chapter 8, Practice Sentences for Lesson 2
1. _____ Did the pink roses on your rosebush bloom early during the warm spring weather?
2. _____ The crowd in the large arena was yelling excitedly for the rodeo clown.
3. _____ The extremely shy professor has never spoken to a large group of people.

*TEACHING SCRIPT FOR PRACTICING HELPING VERBS AND THE **NOT** ADVERB*

We will classify three different sentences to practice our new skills in the Question and Answer Flows. We will classify the sentences together. Begin. (*You might have your child write the labels above the sentences at this time.*)

Question and Answer Flow for Sentence 1: Did the pink roses on your rosebush bloom early during the warm spring weather?	
1. What did bloom early during the warm spring weather? roses - SN	13. What kind of roses? pink - Adj
	14. The - A
2. What is being said about roses? roses did bloom - V	15. SN V P1 Check
3. Did – HV	16. (On your rosebush) - Prepositional phrase
4. Did bloom when? early - Adv	17. (During the warm spring weather) - Prepositional phrase
5. During - P	
6. During what? weather - OP	18. Question mark, question, interrogative sentence
7. What kind of weather? spring - Adj	19. Go back to the verb - divide the complete subject from the complete predicate.
8. What kind of weather? warm - Adj	
9. The - A	20. Is there an adverb exception? Yes – change the line.
10. On - P	
11. On what? rosebush - OP	21. Is this sentence in a natural or inverted order? Inverted - underline the subject parts once and the predicate parts twice.
12. Whose rosebush? your - PPA	

Classified Sentence:

```
                            HV  A  Adj  SN    P  PPA  OP        V   Adv   P   A  Adj   Adj
              SN V      Did the pink roses (on your rosebush) / bloom early (during the warm spring
              ‾‾‾‾         OP
               P1       weather)? Int
```

Level 5 Homeschool Teacher's Manual

CHAPTER 8 LESSON 2 CONTINUED

Question and Answer Flow for Sentence 2: The crowd in the large arena was yelling excitedly for the rodeo clown.

1. Who was yelling excitedly for the rodeo clown?
   crowd - SN
2. What is being said about crowd?
   crowd was yelling - V
3. Was - HV
4. Was yelling how? excitedly - Adv
5. For - P
6. For whom? clown - OP
7. What kind of clown? rodeo - Adj
8. The - A
9. In - P
10. In what? arena - OP
11. What kind of arena? large - Adj

12. The - A
13. The - A
14. SN V P1 Check
15. (In the large arena) - Prepositional phrase
16. (For the rodeo clown) - Prepositional phrase
17. Period, statement, declarative sentence
18. Go back to the verb - divide the complete subject from the complete predicate. (You will divide in front of the helping verb.)
19. Is there an adverb exception? No.
20. Is this sentence in a natural or inverted order? Natural - no change.

Classified Sentence:

```
                              A   SN      P A  Adj  OP   HV   V     Adv    P  A   Adj    OP
        SN   V        The crowd (in the large arena) / was yelling excitedly (for the rodeo clown).  D
        P1
```

Question and Answer Flow for Sentence 3: The extremely shy professor has never spoken to a large group of people.

1. Who has never spoken to a large group of people?
   professor - SN
2. What is being said about professor? professor has spoken - V
3. Has - HV
4. Has spoken when? never - Adv
5. To - P
6. To what? group - OP
7. What kind of group? large - Adj
8. A - A
9. Of - P
10. Of whom? people - OP
11. What kind of professor? shy - Adj

12. How shy? extremely - Adv
13. The - A
14. SN V P1 Check
15. (To a large group) - Prepositional phrase
16. (Of people) - Prepositional phrase
17. Period, statement, declarative sentence
18. Go back to the verb - divide the complete subject from the complete predicate.
19. Is there an adverb exception? No.
20. Is this sentence in a natural or inverted order? Natural - no change.

Classified Sentence:

```
                            A   Adv   Adj  SN       HV   Adv   V    P  A  Adj  OP    P   OP
        SN  V        The extremely shy professor / has never spoken (to a large group) (of people).  D
        P1
```

CHAPTER 8 LESSON 2 CONTINUED

TEACHING SCRIPT FOR A PRACTICE SENTENCE WITH HELPING VERB

Put these labels on the board: **HV A Adj SN V P PPA OP**

Look at the new sentence labels on the board: **HV A Adj SN V P PPA OP**. I will guide you through the process of writing a sentence to practice the new parts that you have learned.

Get out a sheet of notebook paper. On the top line of your notebook paper, write the title *Practice Sentence*. Copy the sentence labels from the board onto your notebook paper. Be sure to leave plenty of writing space between each label. I will guide you through the process you will use whenever you write a Practice Sentence with helping verbs.

1. Go to the **SN** label for the subject noun. Think of a noun you want to use as your subject. Write the noun you have chosen on the line *under* the **SN** label.

2. Go to the **V** label for verb. Think of a verb that tells what your subject does. Make sure that your verb makes sense with the subject noun. Write the verb you have chosen on the line *under* the **V** label.

3. Go to the **P** label for the preposition. Think of a preposition word that tells something about your verb. You must be careful to choose a preposition word that makes sense with the noun you will choose for the object of the preposition in your next step. Write the word you have chosen for a preposition under the **P** label.

4. Go to the **OP** label for object of the preposition. If you like the noun you thought of while thinking of a preposition, write it down under the **OP** label. If you prefer, think of another noun by asking **what** or **whom** after your preposition. Check to make sure the preposition and object of the preposition make sense together and also make sense with the rest of the sentence. Remember, the object of the preposition will always answer the question **what** or **whom** after the preposition. Write the word you have chosen for the object of the preposition under the **OP** label.

5. Go to the **PPA** label for the possessive pronoun adjective that is part of your prepositional phrase. Repeat the possessive pronoun jingle to help you think of a pronoun you want to use as your possessive pronoun adjective. Choose the possessive pronoun that makes the best sense in your sentence. Write the possessive pronoun you have chosen *under* the **PPA** label.

6. Go to the **Adj** label for the adjective. Go to the subject noun of your sentence and ask an adjective question. What are the adjective questions again? (*what kind, which one, how many*) Choose one adjective question to ask and write your adjective answer under the **Adj** label next to the subject noun.

7. Go to the **A** label for the article adjective in the subject area. What are the three article adjectives again? (*a, an, the*) Choose the adjective that makes the best sense in your sentence. Write the article adjective you have chosen *under* the **A** label.

CHAPTER 8 LESSON 2 CONTINUED

8. Go to the **HV** label for the helping verb. Choose a helping verb that asks a question and that makes sense in your sentence. Write the helping verb you have chosen *under* the **HV** label.

9. Finally, check your Practice Sentence to make sure it has the necessary parts to be a complete sentence. What are the five parts of a complete sentence? (*subject, verb, complete sense, capital letter, and an end mark*) Does your Practice Sentence have the five parts of a complete sentence? (*Allow time for students to read over their sentences and to make any corrections they need to make.*)

TEACHING SCRIPT FOR THE IMPROVED SENTENCE

Under your Practice Sentence, write the title *Improved Sentence* on another line. To improve your Practice Sentence, you will make two synonym changes, one antonym change, and your choice of a complete-word change or another synonym or antonym change.

Since it is harder to find words that can be changed to an antonym, it is usually wise to go through your sentence to find an antonym change first. Look through your sentence again to find words that can be improved with synonyms. Finally, make a decision about whether your last change will be a complete-word change, another synonym change, or another antonym change.

I will give you time to write your Improved Sentence. (*Always encourage students to use a thesaurus, synonym-antonym book, or a dictionary to help them develop an interesting and improved writing vocabulary. After students have finished, check and discuss students' Practice and Improved Sentences.*)

PRACTICE TIME

Have students write the three sentences that they classified at the beginning of the lesson on a sheet of paper. (*See page 136.*) Have them tape-record the Question and Answer Flows for all three sentences. Students should write labels above the sentences as they classify them. They especially need the second practice if this is their first year in the program. (*After students have finished, check the tape and sentence labels. Make sure students understand any mistakes they have made.*)

VOCABULARY TIME

Assign Chapter 8, Vocabulary Words **#2** on page 7 in the Reference Section for students to define in their Vocabulary notebooks. Tell students they are to use a dictionary or thesaurus to look up the meanings of the vocabulary words. After they write each word and its meaning, students are to write a sentence using the vocabulary word.

Chapter 8, Vocabulary Words #2
(spurious, accurate, condense, abbreviate)

(End of lesson.)

CHAPTER 8 LESSON 3

New objectives: Grammar (Practice Sentences, adding an irregular verb chart to the Skill Builder Check), Practice sheet, and an Activity.

 JINGLE TIME

Have students turn to the Jingle Section of their books. The teacher will lead the students in reciting the previously-taught jingles.

 GRAMMAR TIME

First-Year Option: Put the Practice Sentences from the box below on the board or notebook paper. Use these sentences as you practice the concepts that have been taught. For the greatest benefit, students must participate orally with the teacher. **Second-Year Option:** Have students classify the Practice Sentences independently on paper. Check students' sentences with the answers provided below. (*If you have the CDs for Practice Sentences, have students check their sentences with the CDs.*)

Chapter 8, Practice Sentences for Lesson 3
1. ____ She proudly cheered for her boyfriend during the hockey game.
2. ____ They did not stop by the church for choir practice tonight.
3. ____ After the long trip, the registered thoroughbred horses were delivered to their new owners.

---

*TEACHING SCRIPT FOR PRACTICING HELPING VERBS AND THE **NOT** ADVERB*

We will practice classifying the new concepts in the Question and Answer Flows. We will classify the sentences together. Begin. (*You might have your students write the labels above the sentences at this time.*)

Question and Answer Flow for Sentence 1: She proudly cheered for her boyfriend during the hockey game.

1. Who cheered for her boyfriend during the hockey game? she - SP
2. What is being said about she? she cheered - V
3. For - P
4. For whom? boyfriend - OP
5. Whose boyfriend? her - PPA
6. During - P
7. During what? game - OP
8. What kind of game? hockey - Adj
9. The - A
10. Cheered how? proudly - Adv
11. SN V P1 Check
12. (For her boyfriend) - Prepositional phrase
13. (During the hockey game) - Prepositional phrase
14. Period, statement, declarative sentence
15. Go back to the verb - divide the complete subject from the complete predicate.
16. Is there an adverb exception? Yes - change the line.
17. Is this sentence in a natural or inverted order? Natural - no change.

Classified		SP	Adv	V		P	PPA	P		P	A	Adj	OP	
Sentence:	SN V	She /	proudly	cheered	(for	her	boyfriend)	(during	the	hockey	game).	**D**
	P1											

CHAPTER 8 LESSON 3 CONTINUED

Question and Answer Flow for Sentence 2: They did not stop by the church for choir practice tonight.

1. Who did not stop by the church for choir practice tonight? they - SP
2. What is being said about they? they did stop - V
3. Did - HV
4. Did stop how? not - Adv
5. By - P
6. By what? church - OP
7. The - A
8. For - P
9. For what? practice - OP
10. What kind of practice? choir - Adj
11. Stop when? tonight - Adv
12. SN V P1 Check
13. (By the church) - Prepositional phrase
14. (For choir practice) - Prepositional phrase
15. Period, statement, declarative sentence
16. Go back to the verb - divide the complete subject from the complete predicate.
17. Is there an adverb exception? No.
18. Is this sentence in a natural or inverted order? Natural - no change.

Classified Sentence:

```
                    SP   HV  Adv  V    P   A    OP     P   Adj    OP     Adv
    SN   V          They / did not stop (by the church) (for choir practice) tonight. D
    P1
```

Question and Answer Flow for Sentence 3: After the long trip, the registered thoroughbred horses were delivered to their new owners.

1. What were delivered to their new owners? horses - SN
2. What is being said about horses? horses were delivered - V
3. Were - HV
4. To - P
5. To whom? owners - OP
6. What kind of owners? new - Adj
7. Whose owners? their - PPA
8. What kind of horses? thoroughbred - Adj
9. What kind of horses? registered - Adj
10. The - A
11. After - P
12. After what? trip - OP
13. What kind of trip? long - Adj
14. The - A
15. SN V P1 Check
16. (After the long trip) - Prepositional phrase
17. (To their new owners) - Prepositional phrase
18. Period, statement, declarative sentence
19. Go back to the verb - divide the complete subject from the complete predicate.
20. Is there an adverb exception? No.
21. Is this sentence in a natural or inverted order? Inverted - underline the subject parts once and the predicate parts twice.

Classified Sentence:

```
                    P    A   Adj OP  A    Adj      Adj         SN      HV       V
    SN   V          (After the long trip), the registered thoroughbred horses / were delivered
    P1              P   PPA  Adj   OP
                    (to their new owners). D
```

CHAPTER 8 LESSON 3 CONTINUED

TEACHER INSTRUCTIONS

Use Sentences 1-3 that you just classified with your students to do an Oral Skill Builder Check. Use the guidelines below.

Oral Skill Builder Check	
1. Noun check. (Say the job and then say the noun. Circle each noun.)	**5. Identify the complete subject and the complete predicate.** (Underline the complete subject once and the complete predicate twice.)
2. Identify the nouns as singular or plural. (Write S or P above each noun.)	**6. Identify the simple subject and simple predicate.** (Underline the simple subject once and the simple predicate twice. Bold, or highlight, the lines.)
3. Identify the nouns as common or proper. (Follow established procedure for oral identification.)	**7. Recite the irregular verb chart.** (This new skill is explained below.)
4. Do a vocabulary check. (Follow established procedure for oral identification.)	

TEACHING SCRIPT FOR ADDING AN IRREGULAR VERB CHART TO THE SKILL BUILDER CHECK

We will now add an Irregular Verb Chart to the Skill Builder Check. Look at the Irregular Verb Chart that is located in Reference 23 on page 17 in your book. (*The verb chart is reproduced for you on the next page.*) We will recite the irregular verb chart during Skill Builder Checks to help you learn the different principal parts of some irregular verbs.

Even though this is only a partial listing of irregular verbs, it will expose you to the correct forms on a consistent basis. We could add more irregular verbs as we think of them. (*You do not need to chant all of the verb chart for every Skill Builder Check. Pick only a few verbs to chant if your child does not have a problem with irregular verb usage.*)

If you use an irregular verb incorrectly, either spoken or written, I will say, "I need a correction for the verb ____," and you will be expected to recite the verb correctly two ways. You will recite the two corrections several times in short sentences. If you cannot remember how to use the two corrections in short sentences, you should use the chart to help you. (*Explain the example below.*)

Example: He **seen** the turkey.   Verb used incorrectly: **seen**

1. Correction with the past tense form: He **saw** it; He **saw** it; He **saw** it; He **saw** it.
2. Correction with a helping verb: He **has seen** it; He **has seen** it; He **has seen** it; He **has seen** it.

CHAPTER 8 LESSON 3 CONTINUED

Reference 23: Irregular Verb Chart						
PRESENT		PAST		PAST PARTICIPLE		PRESENT PARTICIPLE
become		became		(has)	become	(is)	becoming
blow		blew		(has)	blown	(is)	blowing
break		broke		(has)	broken	(is)	breaking
bring		brought		(has)	brought	(is)	bringing
burst		burst		(has)	burst	(is)	bursting
buy		bought		(has)	bought	(is)	buying
choose		chose		(has)	chosen	(is)	choosing
come		came		(has)	come	(is)	coming
drink		drank		(has)	drunk	(is)	drinking
drive		drove		(has)	driven	(is)	driving
eat		ate		(has)	eaten	(is)	eating
fall		fell		(has)	fallen	(is)	falling
fly		flew		(has)	flown	(is)	flying
freeze		froze		(has)	frozen	(is)	freezing
get		got		(has)	gotten	(is)	getting
give		gave		(has)	given	(is)	giving
grow		grew		(has)	grown	(is)	growing
know		knew		(has)	known	(is)	knowing
lie		lay		(has)	lain	(is)	lying
lay		laid		(has)	laid	(is)	laying
make		made		(has)	made	(is)	making
ride		rode		(has)	ridden	(is)	riding
ring		rang		(has)	rung	(is)	ringing
rise		rose		(has)	risen	(is)	rising
sell		sold		(has)	sold	(is)	selling
sing		sang		(has)	sung	(is)	singing
sink		sank		(has)	sunk	(is)	sinking
set		set		(has)	set	(is)	setting
sit		sat		(has)	sat	(is)	sitting
shoot		shot		(has)	shot	(is)	shooting
swim		swam		(has)	swum	(is)	swimming
take		took		(has)	taken	(is)	taking
tell		told		(has)	told	(is)	telling
throw		threw		(has)	thrown	(is)	throwing
wear		wore		(has)	worn	(is)	wearing
write		wrote		(has)	written	(is)	writing

CHAPTER 8 LESSON 3 CONTINUED

WRITING TIME

Have students make an entry in their journals.

PRACTICE TIME

To develop listening skills, give students a knowledge test orally. Have them get out one sheet of paper and number it 1-10. They should listen carefully to the questions and write the answers on their paper. Ask the questions listed below. After students have finished, check and discuss the answers together. Discuss strong areas as well as weak areas.

1. What part of speech is the word NOT? **adverb**
2. Name the understood subject pronoun. **you**
3. What is an imperative sentence? **a command**
4. What is a declarative sentence? **a statement**
5. What is an interrogative sentence? **a question**
6. What punctuation mark does a possessive noun always have? **an apostrophe**
7. What part of speech is a possessive noun classified as, and what is the abbreviation used? **adjective, PNA**

8. List the 8 *be* verbs.
   am, is, are, was, were, be, being, been
9. What are the parts of a verb phrase?
   helping verb and main verb
10. Name the seven subject pronouns.
    I, we, he, she, it, you, they
11. Name the seven possessive pronouns.
    my, our, his, her, its, their, your

ACTIVITY / ASSIGNMENT TIME

Write the letters of each of your family member's names vertically, including your own name. Beside each letter, write an adjective or short phrase that starts with that letter to describe each family member. Have students research the word **acrostic**. Discuss this type of poem. (*Write the example below on the board for your students.*)

Example:

C – caring
A – always polite
T – thinks of others
H – hardly ever late
Y – young at heart

STUDY TIME

Have students study the vocabulary words in their vocabulary notebooks. Tell students that any vocabulary word in their notebooks could be on their test. Also, have students study any of the skills in the Practice Section that they need to review.

(End of lesson.)

CHAPTER 8 LESSON 4

New objectives: Test.

JINGLE TIME

Have students turn to the Jingle Section of their books. The teacher will lead the students in reciting the previously-taught jingles.

STUDY TIME

Have students study the vocabulary words in their vocabulary notebooks. Remind students that any vocabulary word in their notebooks could be on their test. Also, have students study any of the skills in the Practice Section that they need to review.

TEST TIME

Have students turn to page 89 in the Test Section of their book and find the Chapter 8 Test. Remind them to pay attention and think about what they are doing. Go over the directions to make sure they understand what to do. (*Chapter 8 Test key is on the next page.*)

CHECK TIME

After students have finished, check and discuss their test papers. Make sure they understand why their answers are right or wrong. (*For total points, count each required answer as a point.*)

(End of lesson.)

Chapter 8 Test
(Student Page 89)

Exercise 1: Classify each sentence.

```
            HV   A   Adj   SN      V    P   A    OP        P     A    Adj     OP
1. SN V     Did the lead dancer / fall (across the stage) (during the spring musical)?  Int
   P1
```

```
             A  Adj  SN    P    OP      HV  HV  V     P    PPA   Adj     OP
2. SN V     The big flock (of turkeys) / could be seen (from our balcony window).  D
   P1
```

```
             A    Adj    SN     HV Adv  V    Adv       P   OP
3. SN V     The frightened rabbit / did not dash immediately (for cover).  D
   P1
```

Exercise 2: Use Sentence 2 to underline the complete subject once and the complete predicate twice and to complete the table below.

List the Noun Used	List the Noun Job	Singular or Plural	Common or Proper	Simple Subject	Simple Predicate
1. flock	2. SN	3. S	4. C	5. flock	6. could be seen
7. turkeys	8. OP	9. P	10. C		
11. window	12. OP	13. S	14. C		

Exercise 3: Name the six parts of speech that you have studied so far. *(Accept answers in any order.)*

1. noun	2. verb	3. adjective	4. adverb	5. preposition	6. pronoun

Exercise 4: For each sentence, write the subject, then write S if the subject is singular or P if the subject is plural, write the rule number (Rule 1 for singular and Rule 2 for plural), and underline the correct verb in the sentence.

Subject	S or P	Rule
sister	S	1
pictures	P	2
clothes	P	2
posters	P	2
team	S	1
you	P	2
Megan and Dylan	P	2

1. My **sister** (look, <u>looks</u>) beautiful today.
2. **Pictures** (was, <u>were</u>) taken of the crime scene.
3. (<u>Do</u>, Does) these **clothes** belong on the floor?
4. The **posters** (was, <u>were</u>) left in my car.
5. Our **team** (<u>is</u>, are) playing right now.
6. **You** (has, <u>have</u>) four dollars left.
7. **Megan** and **Dylan** (has, <u>have</u>) fed the dog.

Exercise 5: Finding One Part of Speech. For each sentence, write *SN* above the simple subject and *V* (or *HV* and V) above the simple predicate. Underline the word(s) for the part of speech listed to the left of each sentence.

```
                          SN                              V
Preposition(s):  1. The administrators of the school district gather for the first meeting of the year.
```

```
                            SP HV    V
Verb(s):         2. During the winter, we are driving to Lake Tahoe for our vacation.
```

```
                    SP HV    V
Pronoun(s):      3. He is not staying with our family this year.
```

Exercise 6: Identify each pair of words as synonyms or antonyms by putting parentheses ( ) around *syn* or *ant*.

1. void, vacant	**(syn)** ant	5. veracity, truth	**(syn)** ant	9. condense, abbreviate	**(syn)** ant
2. debate, argue	**(syn)** ant	6. frivolous, grave	syn **(ant)**	10. proverbial, notorious	**(syn)** ant
3. myth, fact	syn **(ant)**	7. mimic, imitate	**(syn)** ant	11. melodramatic, subdued	syn **(ant)**
4. vague, specific	syn **(ant)**	8. ethical, carnal	syn **(ant)**	12. spurious, accurate	syn **(ant)**

Exercise 7: In your journal, write a paragraph summarizing what you have learned this week.

CHAPTER 8 LESSON 4 CONTINUED

TEACHER INSTRUCTIONS

Use the Question and Answer Flows below for the sentences on Chapter 8 Test.

Question and Answer Flow for Sentence 1: Did the lead dancer fall across the stage during the spring musical?

1. Who did fall across the stage during the spring musical? dancer - SN
2. What is being said about dancer? dancer did fall - V
3. Did - HV
4. Across - P
5. Across what? stage - OP
6. The - A
7. During - P
8. During what? musical - OP
9. What kind of musical? spring - Adj
10. The - A
11. What kind of dancer? lead - Adj
12. The - A
13. SN V P1 Check
14. (Across the stage) - Prepositional phrase
15. (During the spring musical) - Prepositional phrase
16. Question mark, question, interrogative sentence
17. Go back to the verb - divide the complete subject from the complete predicate.
18. Is there an adverb exception? No.
19. Is this sentence in a natural or inverted order? Inverted - underline the subject parts once and the predicate parts twice.

Classified Sentence:

                                HV A Adj SN   V   P A OP   P A Adj   OP

       SN V   Did the lead dancer / fall (across the stage) (during the spring musical)? Int

       P1

Question and Answer Flow for Sentence 2: The big flock of turkeys could be seen from our balcony window.

1. What could be seen from our balcony window? flock - SN
2. What is being said about flock? flock could be seen - V
3. Could - HV
4. Be - HV
5. From - P
6. From what? window - OP
7. What kind of window? balcony - Adj
8. Whose window? our - PPA
9. Of - P
10. Of what? turkeys - OP
11. What kind of flock? big - Adj
12. The - A
13. SN V P1 Check
14. (Of turkeys) - Prepositional phrase
15. (From our balcony window) - Prepositional phrase
16. Period, statement, declarative sentence
17. Go back to the verb - divide the complete subject from the complete predicate.
18. Is there an adverb exception? No.
19. Is this sentence in a natural or inverted order? Natural - no change.

Classified Sentence:

                              A Adj SN P OP   HV HV V   P PPA Adj   OP

       SN V   The big flock (of turkeys) / could be seen (from our balcony window). D

       P1

Question and Answer Flow for Sentence 3: The frightened rabbit did not dash immediately for cover.

1. Who did dash immediately for cover? rabbit - SN
2. What is being said about rabbit? rabbit did dash - V
3. Did - HV
4. Did dash how? not - Adv
5. Did dash when? immediately - Adv
6. For - P
7. For what? cover - OP
8. What kind of rabbit? frightened - Adj
9. The - A
10. SN V P1 Check
11. (For cover) - Prepositional phrase
12. Period, statement, declarative sentence
13. Go back to the verb - divide the complete subject from the complete predicate.
14. Is there an adverb exception? No.
15. Is this sentence in a natural or inverted order? Natural - no change.

Classified Sentence:

                              A   Adj   SN HV Adv V   Adv   P OP

       SN V   The frightened rabbit / did not dash immediately (for cover). D

       P1

CHAPTER 8 LESSON 5

New objectives: Writing (topic sentences) and Writing Assignment #8.

 WRITING TIME

TEACHING SCRIPT FOR INTRODUCING ANOTHER WAY TO WRITE TOPIC SENTENCES WITHOUT STATING THE NUMBER OF POINTS

When we learned how to write a topic sentence, we listed three things we needed to know about a topic sentence in order to recognize it and to write one correctly. I will go over those three things again.

1. A topic sentence should tell the main idea of a paragraph. The topic sentence will give you a general overview of what the paragraph is going to be about. Notice that I said a **general** overview, not a detailed overview. A topic sentence does not give details because its job is to inform the reader very quickly what the reader can expect to find in the paragraph.

2. Most of the time, the topic sentence is the first sentence in the paragraph because most writers prefer to tell their readers at the very beginning what they can expect from the paragraph. Placing the topic sentence first also helps the writer stay focused on the topic of the paragraph. Occasionally, writers will place the topic sentence last or in the middle of a paragraph, but we will concentrate on what will happen the majority of the time.

3. A topic sentence usually tells the number of points that will be discussed in the paragraph. This helps narrow the topic and keeps the writer on target.

We are going to look more closely at the third thing a topic sentence usually does. It usually tells the number of points that will be discussed in the paragraph. Let's look at the topic sentence and the three-point sentence from our earlier paragraph about water sports. (*Write the following sentences on the board.* **Topic sentence**: *I am interested in three different water sports.* **Three-point**: *These water sports are water skiing, swimming, and canoeing.*)

Notice the topic sentence tells that there will be three points in the paragraph, and the points are then listed in the three-point sentence. Because this way of writing a topic sentence is used often and is a good reliable form in the three-point paragraph, it is called by the same name that we learned in the previous lesson: the **standard form**. But it is also important that you are aware that topic sentences do not always have to state the exact number of points, and that brings us to today's lesson on how to write a topic sentence using a **general form**.

CHAPTER 8 LESSON 5 CONTINUED

It is very simple to write a topic sentence in general form: You just don't state the exact number of points. I am going to show you how to rewrite this topic sentence without actually stating the total number of points. Instead, you will tell the number of points in the three-point sentence. An example of this change might be something like this:

Topic sentence: I enjoy participating in *several* summer activities.
Three-point sentence: Three of these activities are *camping, hiking, and swimming*.

Notice that words such as **several, many, some, numerous, etc.**, can be used in the topic sentence instead of the exact number of points you will discuss. When you choose to make the topic sentence more general by not stating the exact number of points, you force the three-point sentence to supply more information. The three-point sentence must now <u>state the number of points along with listing them</u>.

After you have written the general-topic sentence and the enumeration sentence, you may write the rest of your paragraph by using the original way of stating your point sentences (standard form) or by using the form you learned in the last lesson (time-order form).

I am going to read the third and fourth sample paragraphs to show you the different ways to combine the things you have learned about three-point paragraphs. (*Have students turn to Reference 22 on pages 16 and 17 and follow along as you read and discuss the paragraphs.*)

Reference 22: Sample Paragraph in Time-Order Form, Continued

Example 3: Three-point paragraph using a general topic sentence with standard points

    I enjoy participating in several summer activities. Three of these activities are camping, hiking, and swimming. <u>My first </u>favorite summer activity is camping. I like the adventure of camping in remote areas. <u>My second</u> favorite summer activity is hiking. I enjoy discovering the hidden beauty of nature when I hike. <u>My third </u>favorite summer activity is swimming. I especially like swimming after a long hike because it is very refreshing. My three favorite summer activities provide a lot of fun for me, and they help me enjoy the outdoors.

Example 4: Three-point paragraph using a general topic sentence with time-order points

    I enjoy participating in summer activities of all kinds. Three of these activities are camping, hiking, and swimming. <u>First</u>, I enjoy camping. I like the adventure of camping in remote areas. <u>Next</u>, I enjoy hiking. I enjoy discovering the hidden beauty of nature when I hike. <u>Last</u>, I enjoy swimming. (*or* **Finally**, *I enjoy swimming.*) I especially like swimming after a long hike because it is very refreshing. My three favorite summer activities provide a lot of fun for me, and they help me enjoy the outdoors.

TEACHER INSTRUCTIONS FOR WRITING ASSIGNMENT

Give Writing Assignment #8 from the box on the next page. For Writing Assignment #8, students are to write a three-point paragraph in first person, using the time-order form. They are to <u>underline all time-order words</u> used at the beginning of each sentence that states a point. Remind students that they can use third person pronouns in first person writing. Have them follow the Writing Guidelines as they prepare their writing.

CHAPTER 8 LESSON 5 CONTINUED

Writing Assignment Box

Writing Assignment #8: Three-Point Expository Paragraph (First Person, General and Time-Order Forms)
(Remind students that first person pronouns are *I, we, me, us, my, our, mine,* and *ours.*)

Writing topic choices: **Interesting Things I Have Learned** or **Strange Things That Have Happened to Me**

TEACHING SCRIPT FOR USING THE WRITING PROCESS FOR THIS WRITING ASSIGNMENT

As you begin this writing assignment, you will start through the writing process. First, you will think about your topic and gather any information you might need in order to do the writing. Second, you will write a rough draft. Remember, it is called a rough draft because it will be revised and edited. You do not have to worry about mistakes as you write your rough draft. After you write the first draft, you will make revisions, using the Revision Checklist in Reference 4. After you revise your writing, you will edit, using the Beginning Editing Checklist in Reference 4.

Finally, after you are satisfied with your revising and editing, you will write a final paper, using the Final Paper Checklist in Reference 4. You will then give the finished writing assignment to me.

TEACHER INSTRUCTIONS FOR CHECKING WRITING ASSIGNMENT

Read, check, and discuss Writing Assignment #8 after students have finished their final paper. Use the editing checklist (*Reference 4 on teacher's page 9*) as you check and discuss students' papers. Make sure students are using the editing checklist correctly. In the beginning, you must also check students' papers carefully for <u>form</u> mistakes. This will ensure that students are learning the three-point format correctly.

TEACHING SCRIPT FOR CHOOSING THE BEST WRITING FORM

The three forms for a three-point paragraph, the standard, time-order, and general forms, give you the ability to add variety to your paragraph writing. As you write three-point paragraphs, you may choose either the standard or the time-order form. Since both forms produce effective paragraphs, I will leave it up to you which form you choose each time. Some of you may enjoy the variety of choosing a different form each time you write a paragraph. Others may be more comfortable using only one paragraph form for your writing assignments.

Even though you are allowed to choose the form you use to write your paragraph, you must follow the directions given for writing in either first or third person. If a point of view is not assigned, you may choose to write in either first or third person. Be aware that the point of view you choose could make it necessary to change the wording of your title.

(End of lesson.)

CHAPTER 9 LESSON 1

New objectives: Jingles (the eight parts of speech), Grammar (Introductory Sentences, conjunctions, compound parts, interjection, eight parts of speech), Activity, and Vocabulary #1.

 JINGLE TIME

Have students turn to the Jingle Section in their books and recite the previously-taught jingles. Then, lead students in reciting the new jingle (*The Eight Parts of Speech*) below. Practice the new jingle several times until students can recite it smoothly. Emphasize reciting with a rhythm. Students and teacher should be together! (*Do not try to explain the jingle at this time. Just have fun reciting it. Remember, add motions for more fun and laughter.*)

Teacher's Note: Again, do not spend a large amount of time practicing the new jingles. Students learn the jingles best by spending a small amount of time consistently, **every** day. The teacher should concentrate on the following areas while students are reciting the new jingle: togetherness, smoothness, volume, and enthusiasm.

Jingle 15: The Eight Parts of Speech Jingle
Want to know how to write? Use the eight parts of speech - They're dynamite! **N**ouns, **V**erbs, and **P**ronouns - They rule! They're called the **NVP's**, and they're really cool! The **Double A's** are on the move; **A**djectives and **A**dverbs help you groove! Next come the **PIC's**, and then we're done! The **PIC's** are **P**reposition, **I**nterjection, and **C**onjunction! All together now, the eight parts of speech, abbreviations please: NVP, AA, PIC   NVP, AA, PIC!

 GRAMMAR TIME

Put the introductory sentences from the box below on the board. Use these sentences as you go through each new concept covered in your teaching script. For the greatest benefit, students must participate orally with the teacher. (*You might put the introductory sentences on notebook paper if you are doing one-on-one instruction with your students.*)

Chapter 9, Introductory Sentences for Lesson 1
1. _____ Rabbits and pheasants were pursued quickly by the hounds. 2. _____ The little dog barked and yelped at the mischievous squirrels. 3. _____ Wow! The clouds are churning and rumbling in the storm's wake!

CHAPTER 9 LESSON 1 CONTINUED

TEACHING SCRIPT FOR CONJUNCTIONS AND COMPOUND PARTS

Today, we will learn about conjunctions and compound parts. A **conjunction** is a word that joins words or groups of words together. The three most common conjunctions are *and, or,* and *but.* The conjunctions *and, or,* and *but* are used so often that they should be memorized. Since conjunctions are memorized, there are no questions to ask to find a conjunction. Conjunctions are labeled with a *C.* Let's chant the three most common conjunctions together several times. (*Have students chant the three most common conjunctions with you several times. Try "stand up, sit down, arms up in a V" as you recite them. Other motions will also work well.*)

When words or groups of words in a sentence are joined by a conjunction, the parts that are joined are called **compound parts.** The label *C* is written in front of the regular labels for the compound parts. Example: **CSN** for each compound subject noun or **CV** for each compound verb.

You will use what you have just learned as you classify Sentences 1-2 with me to find the conjunction and compound parts. We will classify the sentences together, and I will show you how to say the new part as we say the Question and Answer Flow. Begin.

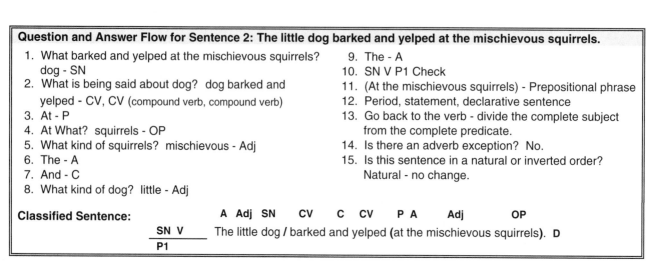

Question and Answer Flow for Sentence 1: Rabbits and pheasants were pursued quickly by the hounds.

1. What were pursued quickly by the hounds? rabbits and pheasants - CSN, CSN (compound subject noun, compound subject noun)
2. What is being said about rabbits and pheasants? rabbits and pheasants were pursued - V
3. Were - HV
4. Were pursued how? quickly - Adv
5. By - P
6. By what? hounds - OP
7. The - A

8. And - C
   Note: Say, "and - conjunction." Label "and" with a "C."
9. SN V P1 Check
10. (By the hounds) - Prepositional phrase
11. Period, statement, declarative sentence
12. Go back to the verb - divide the complete subject from the complete predicate.
13. Is there an adverb exception? No.
14. Is this sentence in a natural or inverted order? Natural - no change.

Classified Sentence:

```
                    CSN    C    CSN    HV    V    Adv   P  A    OP
         SN V    Rabbits and pheasants / were pursued quickly (by the hounds).  D
         P1
```

Question and Answer Flow for Sentence 2: The little dog barked and yelped at the mischievous squirrels.

1. What barked and yelped at the mischievous squirrels? dog - SN
2. What is being said about dog? dog barked and yelped - CV, CV (compound verb, compound verb)
3. At - P
4. At What? squirrels - OP
5. What kind of squirrels? mischievous - Adj
6. The - A
7. And - C
8. What kind of dog? little - Adj

9. The - A
10. SN V P1 Check
11. (At the mischievous squirrels) - Prepositional phrase
12. Period, statement, declarative sentence
13. Go back to the verb - divide the complete subject from the complete predicate.
14. Is there an adverb exception? No.
15. Is this sentence in a natural or inverted order? Natural - no change.

Classified Sentence:

```
                 A  Adj  SN    CV    C   CV    P  A    Adj         OP
         SN V    The little dog / barked and yelped (at the mischievous squirrels).  D
         P1
```

CHAPTER 9 LESSON 1 CONTINUED

TEACHING SCRIPT FOR INTERJECTION

We will now learn about interjections. An **interjection** is one or more words used to express mild or strong emotion. Interjections are usually located at the beginning of a sentence and are separated from the rest of the sentence with a punctuation mark. Mild interjections are followed by a comma or period; strong interjections are followed by an exclamation point. Example: **Oh! Well, Wow! Yes, Hey!**

Interjections are not to be considered when you are deciding whether a sentence is declarative, interrogative, exclamatory, or imperative. There are no questions to find interjections. Interjections are named and then labeled with the abbreviation *I* above them.

You will use what you have just learned about interjections as you classify Sentence 3 with me. We will classify the sentence together, and I will show you how to say the new part as we say the Question and Answer Flow. Begin.

Question and Answer Flow for Sentence 3: Wow! The clouds are churning and rumbling in the storm's wake!	
1. What are churning and rumbling in the storm's wake? clouds - SN	10. Wow - I
2. What is being said about clouds? clouds are churning and rumbling - CV, CV	**Note:** Say, "Wow - interjection." Label "Wow "with an 'I'.
3. Are - HV	11. SN V P1 Check
4. In - P	12. (In the storm's wake) - Prepositional phrase
5. In what? wake - OP	13. Exclamation point, strong feeling, exclamatory sentence
6. Whose wake? storm's - PNA	14. Go back to the verb - divide the complete subject from the complete predicate.
7. The - A	15. Is there an adverb exception? No.
8. And - C	16. Is this sentence in a natural or inverted order? Natural - no change.
9. The - A	

Classified Sentence:

<pre>
                        I   A   SN   HV   CV   C   CV   P   A   PNA   OP
        SN V   Wow! The clouds / are churning and rumbling (in the storm's wake)! E
        ─────
         P1
</pre>

TEACHER INSTRUCTIONS

Use Sentences 1-3 that you just classified with your students to do an Oral Skill Builder Check. Use the guidelines below.

Oral Skill Builder Check	
1. **Noun check.** (Say the job and then say the noun. Circle each noun.)	5. **Identify the complete subject and the complete predicate.** (Underline the complete subject once and the complete predicate twice.)
2. **Identify the nouns as singular or plural.** (Write S or P above each noun.)	6. **Identify the simple subject and simple predicate.** (Underline the simple subject once and the simple predicate twice. Bold, or highlight, the lines.)
3. **Identify the nouns as common or proper.** (Follow established procedure for oral identification.)	
4. **Do a vocabulary check.** (Follow established procedure for oral identification.)	7. **Recite the irregular verb chart.** (Located on student page 17 and teacher page 143.)

CHAPTER 9 LESSON 1 CONTINUED

TEACHING SCRIPT FOR ALL EIGHT PARTS OF SPEECH

We can add the final two parts of speech, conjunctions and interjections, to our eight parts of speech list. Remember, all words in the English language have been put into one of eight groups called the **Parts of Speech**. How a word is used in a sentence determines its part of speech.

It is very important to know the eight parts of speech because they are the vocabulary for writing. We will now celebrate learning the eight parts of speech by reciting the Eight Parts of Speech Jingle. This jingle will help you remember the eight parts of speech quickly and easily. Turn to page 4 in the Jingle Section of your books and recite Jingle 15, the Eight Parts of Speech Jingle.

 ACTIVITY / ASSIGNMENT TIME

Create a word search puzzle and a crossword puzzle, using all the English terms and English definitions that you have studied so far. Make a "key" for each puzzle. Continue to upgrade your puzzles as you have time. Your work on this project may take several days. If you use the computer for this project, generate several puzzles for friends and for other members of your family.

 VOCABULARY TIME

Assign Chapter 9, Vocabulary Words **#1** on page 7 in the Reference Section for students to define in their Vocabulary notebooks. Tell students they are to use a dictionary or thesaurus to look up the meanings of the vocabulary words. After they write each word and its meaning, students are to write a sentence using the vocabulary word.

Chapter 9, Vocabulary Words #1
(simultaneous, periodic, odd, quaint)

(End of lesson.)

CHAPTER 9 LESSON 2

New objectives: Grammar (Practice Sentences, Practice and Improved Sentence with conjunction and compound parts), Practice activity, and Vocabulary #2.

JINGLE TIME

Have students turn to the Jingle Section of their books. The teacher will lead the students in reciting the previously-taught jingles.

GRAMMAR TIME

First-Year Option: Put the Practice Sentences from the box below on the board or notebook paper. Use these sentences as you practice the concepts that have been taught. For the greatest benefit, students must participate orally with the teacher. **Second-Year Option:** Have students classify the Practice Sentences independently on paper. Check students' sentences with the answers provided below. (*If you have the CDs for Practice Sentences, have students check their sentences with the CDs.*)

Chapter 9, Practice Sentences for Lesson 2
1. _____ Do not drive in Boston during rush hours.
2. _____ My uncle's coat and scarf were stolen in a famous restaurant!
3. _____ The patience and kindness of my kindergarten teacher will never fade from my memory.

TEACHING SCRIPT FOR PRACTICING PATTERN 1 SENTENCES WITH THE 8 PARTS OF SPEECH

We will classify three different sentences to practice using the eight parts of speech in the Question and Answer Flows. We will classify the sentences together. Begin. (*You might have your students write the labels above the sentences at this time.*)

Question and Answer Flow for Sentence 1: Do not drive in Boston during rush hours.

1. Who do not drive in Boston during rush hours?
   (You) - SP (Understood subject pronoun)
2. What is being said about you? you do drive - V
3. Do - HV
4. Do drive how? not - Adv
5. In - P
6. In what? Boston - OP
7. During - P
8. During what? hours - OP
9. What kind of hours? rush - Adj
10. SN V P1 Check
11. (In Boston) - Prepositional phrase
12. (During rush hours) - Prepositional phrase
13. Period, command, imperative sentence
14. Go back to the verb - divide the complete subject from the complete predicate.
15. Is there an adverb exception? No.
16. Is this sentence in a natural or inverted order?
    Natural - no change.

Classified Sentence:

```
               (You) SP    HV  Adv  V    P    OP      P    Adj   OP
               SN  V     / Do  not drive (in Boston) (during rush hours). Imp
               P1
```

CHAPTER 9 LESSON 2 CONTINUED

Question and Answer Flow for Sentence 2: My uncle's coat and scarf were stolen in a famous restaurant!

1. What were stolen in a famous restaurant?
   coat and scarf - CSN, CSN
2. What is being said about coat and scarf?
   coat and scarf were stolen - V
3. Were - HV
4. In - P
5. In what? restaurant - OP
6. What kind of restaurant? famous - Adj
7. A - A
8. And - C

9. Whose coat and scarf? uncle's - PNA
10. Whose uncle? my - PPA
11. SN V P1 Check
12. (In a famous restaurant) - Prepositional phrase
13. Exclamation point, strong feeling, exclamatory sentence
14. Go back to the verb - divide the complete subject from the complete predicate.
15. Is there an adverb exception? No.
16. Is this sentence in a natural or inverted order? Natural - no change.

Classified Sentence:

		PPA	PNA	CSN	C	CSN	HV	V	OP	A	Adj	OP
SN V		My	uncle's	coat	and	scarf	/ were	stolen	(in a	famous		restaurant)! **E**
P1												

Question and Answer Flow for Sentence 3: The patience and kindness of my kindergarten teacher will never fade from my memory.

1. What will never fade from my memory?
   patience and kindness - CSN, CSN
2. What is being said about patience and kindness?
   patience and kindness will fade - V
3. Will - HV
4. Will fade when? never - Adv
5. From - P
6. From what? memory - OP
7. Whose memory? my - PPA
8. Of - P
9. Of whom? teacher - OP
10. What kind of teacher? kindergarten - Adj

11. Whose teacher? my - PPA
12. And - C
13. The - A
14. SN V P1 Check
15. (Of my kindergarten teacher) - Prepositional phrase
16. (From my memory) - Prepositional phrase
17. Period, statement, declarative sentence
18. Go back to the verb - divide the complete subject from the complete predicate.
19. Is there an adverb exception? No.
20. Is this sentence in a natural or inverted order? Natural - no change.

Classified Sentence:

		A	CSN	C	CSN	P	PPA	Adj	OP	HV	Adv	V	P	PPA	OP
SN V		The	patience	and	kindness	(of	my	kindergarten	teacher) /	will	never	fade	(from	my	memory). **D**
P1															

CHAPTER 9 LESSON 2 CONTINUED

TEACHING SCRIPT FOR THE PRACTICE SENTENCE WITH CONJUNCTION AND COMPOUND PARTS

Put these labels on the board: **I CSN C CSN HV V P PPA OP**

Look at the new sentence labels on the board: **I CSN C CSN HV V P PPA OP**. I will guide you again through the process of writing a sentence to practice the different parts that you have learned.

Get out a sheet of notebook paper. On the top line of your notebook paper, write the title _Practice Sentence_. Copy the sentence labels from the board onto your notebook paper. Be sure to leave plenty of writing space between each label. I will guide you through the process you will use whenever you write a Practice Sentence with pronouns and possessive nouns.

1. Go to the two **CSN** labels for compound subject nouns. Think of two nouns you want to use as your compound subject. Remember, these two nouns must make sense together and with the verb that you choose. Write the two nouns you have chosen on the line _under_ the two **CSN** labels.

2. Go to the **HV** and the **V** labels for the helping verb and the main verb. Think of a helping verb and a main verb that tell what your subjects do. Make sure that your verb makes sense with the two subject nouns. Also, check to make sure you have proper subject-verb agreement. Write the two verbs you have chosen on the line _under_ the **HV** and the **V** labels.

3. Go to the **P** label for the preposition. Think of a preposition word that tells something about your verb. You must be careful to choose a preposition word that makes sense with the noun you will choose for the object of the preposition in your next step. Write the word you have chosen for a preposition under the **P** label.

4. Go to the **OP** label for object of the preposition. If you like the noun you thought of while thinking of a preposition, write it down under the **OP** label. If you prefer, think of another noun by asking **what** or **whom** after your preposition. Check to make sure the preposition and object of the preposition make sense together and also make sense with the rest of the sentence. Remember, the object of the preposition will always answer the question **what** or **whom** after the preposition. Write the word you have chosen for the object of the preposition under the **OP** label.

5. Go to the **PPA** label for the possessive pronoun adjective that is part of your prepositional phrase. Repeat the possessive pronoun jingle to help you think of a pronoun you want to use as your possessive pronoun adjective. Choose the possessive pronoun that makes the best sense in your sentence. Write the possessive pronoun you have chosen _under_ the **PPA** label.

CHAPTER 9 LESSON 2 CONTINUED

6. Go to the **C** label for the conjunction in your sentence and choose a conjunction that makes sense. What are the three main conjunctions again? (*and, but, or*) Write the conjunction you have chosen under the **C** label.

7. Go to the **I** label for the interjection at the beginning of the sentence. Choose an interjection that makes the best sense in your sentence. Write the interjection you have chosen *under* the **I** label.

8. Finally, check your Practice Sentence to make sure it has the necessary parts to be a complete sentence. What are the five parts of a complete sentence? (*subject, verb, complete sense, capital letter, and an end mark*) Does your Practice Sentence have the five parts of a complete sentence? (*Allow time for students to read over their sentences and to make any corrections they need to make.*)

TEACHING SCRIPT FOR THE IMPROVED SENTENCE

Under your Practice Sentence, write the title *Improved Sentence* on another line. To improve your Practice Sentence, you will make two synonym changes, one antonym change, and your choice of a complete-word change or another synonym or antonym change.

Since it is harder to find words that can be changed to an antonym, it is usually wise to go through your sentence to find an antonym change first. Look through your sentence again to find words that can be improved with synonyms. Finally, make a decision about whether your last change will be a complete-word change, another synonym change, or another antonym change.

I will give you time to write your Improved Sentence. (*Always encourage students to use a thesaurus, synonym-antonym book, or a dictionary to help them develop an interesting and improved writing vocabulary.*) (*After students have finished, check and discuss students' Practice and Improved Sentences.*)

 PRACTICE TIME

Have students write the three sentences that they classified at the beginning of the lesson on a sheet of paper. (*See page 155.*) Have them tape-record the Question and Answer Flows for all three sentences. Students should write labels above the sentences as they classify them. They especially need the second practice if this is their first year in the program. (*After the students have finished, check the tape and sentence labels. Make sure students understand any mistakes they have made.*)

 VOCABULARY TIME

Assign Chapter 9, Vocabulary Words **#2** on page 7 in the Reference Section for students to define in their Vocabulary notebooks. Tell students they are to use a dictionary or thesaurus to look up the meanings of the vocabulary words. After they write each word and its meaning, students are to write a sentence using the vocabulary word.

Chapter 9, Vocabulary Words #2
(savory, bland, honesty, integrity)

(End of lesson.)

CHAPTER 9 LESSON 3

New objectives: Grammar (Practice Sentences), Skills (homonyms), and an Activity (continued).

 JINGLE TIME

Have students turn to the Jingle Section of their books. The teacher will lead the students in reciting the previously-taught jingles.

 GRAMMAR TIME

First-Year Option: Put the Practice Sentences from the box below on the board or notebook paper. Use these sentences as you practice the concepts that have been taught. For the greatest benefit, students must participate orally with the teacher. **Second-Year Option:** Have students classify the Practice Sentences independently on paper. Check students' sentences with the answers provided below. (*If you have the CDs for Practice Sentences, have students check their sentences with the CDs.*)

Chapter 9, Practice Sentences for Lesson 3
1. _____ The old cow and her calf had never ventured beyond their tiny barnyard.
2. _____ Yikes! A brawl erupted in the bleachers after the facemask penalty!
3. _____ Yesterday, we snickered and laughed aloud at the clown's antics.

TEACHING SCRIPT FOR PRACTICING PATTERN 1 SENTENCES WITH THE 8 PARTS OF SPEECH

We will classify three different sentences to practice using the eight parts of speech in the Question and Answer Flows. We will classify the sentences together. Begin. (*You might have your students write the labels above the sentences at this time.*)

Question and Answer Flow for Sentence 1: The old cow and her calf had never ventured beyond their tiny barnyard.

1. What had never ventured beyond their tiny barnyard?
   cow and calf - CSN, CSN
2. What is being said about cow and calf?
   cow and calf had ventured - V
3. Had - HV
4. Had ventured when? never - Adv
5. Beyond - P
6. Beyond what? barnyard - OP
7. What kind of barnyard? tiny - Adj
8. Whose barnyard? their - PPA
9. Whose calf? her - PPA

10. And - C
11. What kind of cow? old - Adj
12. The - A
13. SN V P1 Check
14. (Beyond their tiny barnyard) - Prepositional phrase
15. Period, statement, declarative sentence
16. Go back to the verb - divide the complete subject from the complete predicate.
17. Is there an adverb exception? No.
18. Is this sentence in a natural or inverted order?
   Natural - no change.

Classified Sentence:		A	Adj	CSN	C	PPA	CSN	HV	Adv	V	P	PPA	Adj	OP
SN V P1		The	old	cow	and	her	calf / had	never	ventured	(beyond	their	tiny	barnyard). **D**

CHAPTER 9 LESSON 3 CONTINUED

Question and Answer Flow for Sentence 2: Yikes! A brawl erupted in the bleachers after the facemask penalty!

1. What erupted in the bleachers after the facemask penalty? brawl - SN
2. What is being said about brawl? brawl erupted - V
3. In - P
4. In what? bleachers - OP
5. The - A
6. After - P
7. After what? penalty - OP
8. What kind of penalty? facemask - Adj
9. The - A
10. A - A

11. Yikes - I (Interjection)
12. SN V P1 Check
13. (In the bleachers) - Prepositional phrase
14. (After the facemask penalty) - Prepositional phrase
15. Exclamation point, strong feeling, exclamatory sentence
16. Go back to the verb - divide the complete subject from the complete predicate.
17. Is there an adverb exception? No.
18. Is this sentence in a natural or inverted order? Natural - no change.

Classified Sentence:

                                    I   A SN   V   P   A   OP   P   A   Adj   OP

            <u>SN V</u>   Yikes! A brawl / erupted (in the bleachers) (after the facemask penalty)! **E**
            P1

Question and Answer Flow for Sentence 3: Yesterday, we snickered and laughed aloud at the clown's antics.

1. Who snickered and laughed aloud at the clown's antics? we - SP
2. What is being said about we? we snickered and laughed - CV, CV
3. Snickered and laughed how? aloud - Adv
4. At - P
5. At what? antics - OP
6. Whose antics? clown's - PNA
7. The - A
8. And - C

9. Snickered and laughed when? yesterday - Adv
10. SN V P1 Check
11. (At the clown's antics) - Prepositional phrase
12. Period, statement, declarative sentence
13. Go back to the verb - divide the complete subject from the complete predicate.
14. Is there an adverb exception? No.
15. Is this sentence in a natural or inverted order? Inverted - underline the subject parts once and the predicate parts twice.

Classified Sentence:

                            Adv   SP   CV   C   CV   Adv P A PNA   OP

            <u>SN V</u>   <u>Yesterday, we</u> / <u>snickered and laughed aloud (at the clown's antics)</u>. **D**
            P1

SKILL TIME

TEACHING SCRIPT FOR HOMONYMS

Today, we will learn about homonyms. Look at Reference 24 on page 18 in the Reference section of your book. The definition says that homonyms are words that sound the same but have different meanings and different spellings. You should study the Homonym Chart until you are familiar enough with each homonym that you can choose the correct form easily. Since this is only a partial listing, you must look up homonyms that you do not know and that are not listed on the chart. (*The homonym chart is located on the next page.*)

Look at the examples for choosing the correct homonyms at the bottom of the reference box. The directions say to underline the correct homonym. Read number 1. Look at the homonym *council* and *counsel*. Go to the Homonym Chart and read the definition for each spelling. How do we spell the homonym that means *assembly*? (*c-o-u-n-c-i-l*) How do we spell the homonym that means *advice*? (*c-o-u-n-s-e-l*)

CHAPTER 9 LESSON 3 CONTINUED

Which homonym would you choose to complete the first sentence correctly? (*council*) How did you decide? It makes sense for Matthew to be a member of an assembly. The word *council* means the same thing as *assembly*.

Now, look at number 2. Which homonym would you choose to complete the second sentence correctly? (*counsel*) How did you decide? It makes sense for Mr. Jones to give advice about job opportunities. The word *counsel* means the same thing as *advice*. Always check the Homonym Chart or use a dictionary if you have a question about which homonym to use.

Reference 24: Homonym Chart		
Homonyms are words that sound the same but have different meanings and different spellings.		
1. **capital** - upper part, main	15. **lead** - metal	29. **their** - belonging to them
2. **capitol** - statehouse	16. **led** - guided	30. **there** - in that place
3. **coarse** - rough	17. **no -** not so	31. **they're** - they are
4. **course** - route	18. **know** - to understand	32. **threw** - did throw
5. **council** - assembly	19. **right** - correct	33. **through** -from end to end
6. **counsel** - advice	20. **write** - to form letters	34. **to** - toward, preposition
7. **forth** - forward	21. **principle** - a truth/rule/law	35. **too** - denoting excess
8. **fourth** - ordinal number	22. **principal** - chief/head person	36. **two** - a couple
9. **its** - possessive pronoun	23. **stationary** - motionless	37. **your** - belonging to you
10. **it's** - it is	24. **stationery** - paper	38. **you're** - you are
11. **hear** - to listen	25. **peace** - quiet	39. **weak** - not strong
12. **here** - in this place	26. **piece** - a part	40. **week** - seven days
13. **knew** - understood	27. **sent** - caused to go	41. **days** - more than one day
14. **new** - not old	28. **scent** - odor	42. **daze** - a confused state
Examples: Underline the correct homonym.		

1. Matthew is a member of the student (**council**, counsel) at school.
2. Mr. Jones (councils, **counsels**) the employees about their job opportunities.

WRITING TIME

Have students make an entry in their journals.

ACTIVITY / ASSIGNMENT TIME

Continue working on your word search puzzle and crossword puzzle. Make sure you are using all the English terms and English definitions that you have studied so far. Make a "key" for each puzzle. Give your finished project to family members and friends and have them complete your puzzles. Check the puzzles they work with your puzzle key. Keep notes in your Journal about your puzzles for future reference. Continue to upgrade your puzzles as you have time. Remember, if you use the computer for this project, generate several puzzles for friends and for other members of your family.

Also, you should study the skills in the Practice Section that you need to review. Study your homonym chart and your jingles. Chapter 9 Test will include homonyms and matching English definitions.

(End of lesson.)

CHAPTER 9   LESSON 4

New objectives: Test and an Activity (concluded).

JINGLE TIME

Have students turn to the Jingle Section of their books. The teacher will lead the students in reciting the previously-taught jingles.

STUDY TIME

Have students study the vocabulary words in their vocabulary notebooks. Remind students that any vocabulary word in their notebooks could be on their test. Also, have students study any of the skills in the Practice Section that they need to review.

TEST TIME

Have students turn to page 90 in the Test Section of their book and find Chapter 9 Test. Remind them to pay attention and think about what they are doing. Go over the directions to make sure they understand what to do. (*Chapter 9 Test key is on the next page.*)

CHECK TIME

After students have finished, check and discuss their test papers. Make sure they understand why their answers are right or wrong. (*For total points, count each required answer as a point.*)

ACTIVITY / ASSIGNMENT TIME

Today, you will evaluate your "puzzle" project. Write the evaluation of this project in your Journal. Tell what you enjoyed most about this project. Tell what you would do differently next time. Share the most interesting and inspiring part of the project. Share the most frustrating part of the project. Did you finish your project on time? Did you share your project and get feedback from friends and family members? Did you create more puzzles? Compare your creative efforts with other projects that you have done. Are you happy with the finished product? What grade would you give this project? Explain why.

(End of lesson.)

Chapter 9 Test
(Student Page 90)

Exercise 1: Classify each sentence.

```
                  A   Adj   CSN    C   PPA   CSN         V      P    Adj   Adj    OP
1. SN V     The city manager and his assistant / wrestled (with several fresh alternatives).  D
   P1
   (You) SP    HV  Adv   V     P    A     Adj      OP        P   A  Adj  OP    `P  A   OP
2. SN V     / Do not drive (across the flooded highway) (after a big rain) (in the spring).  Imp
   P1
               HV   A   Adj      Adj      SN      V        Adv        P    A    Adj    Adj    OP
3. SN V     Did the old swaybacked mare / collapse unexpectedly (during the charity horse race)?  Int
   P1
```

Exercise 2: Use Sentence 2 to underline the complete subject once and the complete predicate twice and to complete the table below.

List the Noun Used	List the Noun Job	Singular or Plural	Common or Proper	Simple Subject	Simple Predicate
1. highway	2. OP	3. S	4. C	5. You	6. do drive
7. rain	8. OP	9. S	10. C		
11. spring	12. OP	13. S	14. C		

Exercise 3: Name the eight parts of speech that you have studied. *(Accept answers in any order.)*

| 1. **noun** | 2. **verb** | 3. **adjective** | 4. **adverb** | 5. **preposition** | 6. **pronoun** | 7. **conjunction** | 8. **interjection** |

Exercise 4: Answer each question below on a sheet of notebook paper.

1. List the 8 *be* verbs. **am, is, are, was, were, be, being, been**

2. What are the parts of a verb phrase? **helping verb and main verb**

3. Name the seven subject pronouns. **I, we, he, she, it, you, they**

4. Name the seven possessive pronouns. **my, our, his, her, its, their, your**

5. Name the seven object pronouns. **me, us, him, her, it, them, you**

6. What part of speech is the word NOT? **adverb**

Exercise 5: Identify each pair of words as synonyms or antonyms by putting parentheses ( ) around *syn* or *ant*.

1. odd, quaint	**(syn)** ant	5. veracity, truth	**(syn)** ant	9. honesty, integrity	**(syn)** ant
2. vague, specific	syn **(ant)**	6. spurious, accurate	syn **(ant)**	10. simultaneous, periodic	syn **(ant)**
3. fact, myth	syn **(ant)**	7. savory, bland	syn **(ant)**	11. condense, abbreviate	**(syn)** ant
4. odious, hateful	**(syn)** ant	8. fraud, deception	**(syn)** ant	12. transparent, translucent	**(syn)** ant

Exercise 6: Underline the correct homonym in each sentence.

1. When I finished the race, I was pathetically (<u>weak</u>, week).

2. There are no (<u>capital</u>, capitol) letters in common nouns.

3. The priest (lead, <u>led</u>) his parishioners on a religious pilgrimage.

4. Janet said (their, <u>they're</u>) still planning to go.

5. Be sure to type your reply on letterhead (stationary, <u>stationery</u>).

6. He (<u>knew</u>, new) better than to ask me that question.

7. Together, they set (<u>forth</u>, fourth) on a new crusade.

8. Ethiopia has not seen (piece, <u>peace</u>) in years.

Exercise 7: In your journal, write a paragraph summarizing what you have learned this week.

CHAPTER 9 LESSON 4 CONTINUED

TEACHER INSTRUCTIONS

Use the Question and Answer Flows below for the sentences on Chapter 9 Test.

Question and Answer Flow for Sentence 1: The city manager and his assistant wrestled with several fresh alternatives.

1. Who wrestled with several fresh alternatives? manager and assistant - CSN, CSN
2. What is being said about manager and assistant? manager and assistant wrestled - V
3. With - P
4. With what? alternatives - OP
5. What kind of alternatives? fresh - Adj
6. How many alternatives? several - Adj
7. Whose assistant? his - PPA
8. And - C

9. What kind of manager? city - Adj
10. The - A
11. SN V P1 Check
12. (With several fresh alternatives) - Prepositional phrase
13. Period, statement, declarative sentence
14. Go back to the verb - divide the complete subject from the complete predicate.
15. Is there an adverb exception? No.
16. Is this sentence in a natural or inverted order? Natural - no change.

Classified Sentence:

	A	Adj	CSN	C	PPA	CSN	V	P	Adj	Adj	OP
SN V	The	city	manager	and	his	assistant	/ wrestled	(with	several	fresh	alternatives). D
P1

Question and Answer Flow for Sentence 2: Do not drive across a flooded highway after a big rain in the spring.

1. Who do not drive across a flooded highway after a big rain in the spring? (You) - SP (Understood subject pronoun)
2. What is being said about you? you do drive - V
3. Do - HV
4. Do drive how? not - Adv
5. Across - P
6. Across what? highway - OP
7. What kind of highway? flooded - Adj
8. A - A
9. After - P
10. After what? rain - OP
11. What kind of rain? big - Adj
12. A - A
13. In - P

14. In what? spring - OP
15. The - A
16. SN V P1 Check
17. (Across a flooded highway) - Prepositional phrase
18. (After a big rain) - Prepositional phrase
19. (In the spring) - Prepositional phrase
20. Period, command, imperative sentence
21. Go back to the verb - divide the complete subject from the complete predicate.
22. Is there an adverb exception? No.
23. Is this sentence in a natural or inverted order? Natural - no change.

Classified Sentence:

	(You) SP	HV	Adv	V	P	A	Adj	OP	P	A	Adj	OP	P	A	OP
SN V	/ Do	not	drive	(across	a	flooded	highway)	(after	a	big	rain)	(in	the	spring). Imp
P1

Question and Answer Flow for Sentence 3: Did the old swaybacked mare collapse unexpectedly during the charity horse race?

1. What did collapse unexpectedly during the charity horse race? mare - SN
2. What is being said about mare? mare did collapse - V
3. Did - HV
4. Did collapse how? unexpectedly - Adv
5. During - P
6. During what? race - OP
7. What kind of race? horse - Adj
8. What kind of race? charity - Adj
9. The - A
10. What kind of mare? swaybacked - Adj

11. What kind of mare? old - Adj
12. The - A
13. SN V P1 Check
14. (During the charity horse race) - Prepositional phrase
15. Question mark, question, interrogative sentence
16. Go back to the verb - divide the complete subject from the complete predicate.
17. Is there an adverb exception? No.
18. Is this sentence in a natural or inverted order? Inverted - underline the subject parts once and the predicate parts twice.

Classified Sentence:

	HV	A	Adj	Adj	SN	V	Adv	P	A	Adj	Adj	OP
SN V	Did	the	old	swaybacked	mare	/ collapse	unexpectedly	(during	the	charity	horse	race)? Int
P1

Level 5 Homeschool Teacher's Manual

CHAPTER 9   LESSON 5
New objectives: Writing (essay) and Writing Assignments #9 and #10.

 **WRITING TIME**

TEACHING SCRIPT FOR INTRODUCING AN ESSAY

You have been writing expository paragraphs in a three-point paragraph format. Remember, writing in a three-point paragraph format is a way to organize your paragraph by defining your topic, listing each of your points, supporting each of your points, and ending with a conclusion. Now, in this writing section, you will learn to expand your basic three-point format into several paragraphs. When you write several paragraphs about a certain topic, it is called an essay.

The essay is an easy and fun form of writing. The **essay** is a written discussion of one idea and is made up of several paragraphs. It might be interesting to know that the word *essay* comes from the French word *essai*, meaning "a trial" or "a try." Many students consider essay writing a real "trial." However, with the Shurley Method, you will find essay writing quite easy and even pleasant. In fact, anyone who reads your essays will be very impressed with your ability to organize and discuss any writing topic.

In this writing section, you will write expository essays. **Expository essays** give facts or directions, explain ideas, or define words, just like the expository paragraphs. Expository writing is often used for writing assignments in different subject areas. Any time you do an expository writing, whether it is an essay or a paragraph, you should focus on making your meaning clear and understandable. The three-point format you use will help your reader understand exactly what you mean. You will now learn to expand a three-point paragraph into an expository essay.

TEACHING SCRIPT FOR INTRODUCING HOW TO WRITE A 3-PARAGRAPH ESSAY

To make essay writing easier, you will first learn how to develop a three-paragraph essay using the three-point format. Remember, the three-point format is a way of organizing your essay that will help make your meaning clear and understandable.

A three-paragraph essay has three parts: **1. Introduction 2. Body 3. Conclusion**. All these parts will always be written in that order. Although a title will be the first item appearing at the top of your essay, you will not write the title until you have finished the essay. In a three-paragraph essay, there will be three paragraphs, no more and no fewer. The introduction forms the first paragraph, the body forms the second paragraph, and the conclusion forms the third paragraph of the essay.

As you are learning to write a three-paragraph essay, it will help to remember the outline for the three-point paragraph that you have already learned. Look at the two outlines in Reference 25 on page 18 in your book. Let's compare and discuss the differences in the paragraph and essay. Notice that there are more sentences in the introduction and conclusion for the essay. Of course, the second paragraph contains all the points and their supporting sentences. (*Reference 25 is on the next page.*)

CHAPTER 9 LESSON 5 CONTINUED

Reference 25: Three-Point Paragraph and Essay

Outline of a Three-Point Paragraph	Outline of a Three-Paragraph Essay
I. Title	I. Title
II. Paragraph (9 sentences)	II. Paragraph 1 - Introduction (3 sentences)
A. Topic sentence	A. Topic and general number sentence
B. A three-point sentence	B. Extra information about the topic sentence
C. A **first-point** sentence	C. Three-point sentence
D. A **supporting** sentence for the first point	III. Paragraph 2 - Body (6-9 sentences)
E. A **second-point** sentence	A. **First-point** sentence
F. A **supporting** sentence for the second point	B. One or two **supporting** sentences for the first point
G. A **third-point** sentence	C. **Second-point** sentence
H. A **supporting** sentence for the third point	D. One or two **supporting** sentences for the second point
I. A concluding sentence	E. **Third-point** sentence
	F. One or two **supporting** sentences for the third point
	IV. Paragraph 3 - Conclusion (2 sentences)
	A. Concluding general statement
	B. Concluding summary sentence

You will learn how to write each sentence and paragraph in the three-paragraph expository essay by following the steps in Reference 26 on pages 19 and 20 in your book. (*Read and discuss Reference 26 with your students.*)

Reference 26: Steps in Writing a Three-Paragraph Expository Essay

WRITING TOPIC: Stamp-Collecting

LIST THE POINTS FOR THE TOPIC

♦ Select three points to list about the topic.
  1. **Is inexpensive**
  2. **Gives sense of history**
  3. **Teaches one to observe**

WRITING THE INTRODUCTION AND TITLE

1. Sentence #1 – Topic Sentence
   Write the topic sentence by using the words in your topic and adding a general number word, such as *several, many, some,* or *numerous,* instead of the exact number of points you will discuss. **(Quite by accident, I discovered that, as a hobby, stamp-collecting offers many rewards.)**

2. Sentence #2 – Extra Information about the topic sentence
   This sentence can clarify, explain, define, or just be an extra interesting comment about the topic sentence. If you need another sentence to complete your information, write the extra sentence here. If you write an extra sentence, your introductory paragraph will have four sentences in it instead of three sentences. **(Although some of my friends collect other things, like coins and rocks, I think I like my hobby best.)**

3. Sentence #3 – Three-point sentence
   This sentence will list the three points to be discussed in the order that you will present them in the Body of your paper. You can list the points with or without the specific number in front. **(As hobbies go, it is inexpensive, it gives one a sense of history, and it teaches one to be a careful observer.) or (My three favorite things about stamp-collecting are these: it's an inexpensive hobby, it gives one a sense of history, and it teaches one to be a careful observer.)**

CHAPTER 9 LESSON 5 CONTINUED

Reference 26: Steps in Writing a Three-Paragraph Expository Essay, Continued

♦ <u>The Title</u> - Since there are many possibilities for titles, look at the topic and the three points listed about the topic. Use some of the words in the topic and write a phrase to tell what your paragraph is about. Your title can be short or long. Capitalize the first, last, and important words in your title. **(Why Stamp Collecting Is a Worthwhile Hobby)**

WRITING THE BODY

4. <u>Sentence #4 - First Point</u> –Write a sentence stating your first point.
   (One of the reasons I enjoy stamp collecting is that it is inexpensive.)

5. <u>Sentence #5 – Supporting Sentence(s)</u> – Write one or two sentences that give more information about your first point. **(One simply has to remove the postage stamps from each day's mail.)**

6. <u>Sentence #6 - Second Point</u> - Write a sentence stating your second point.
   (Another reason I enjoy stamp collecting is that it gives one a sense of history.)

7. <u>Sentence #7 – Supporting Sentence(s)</u> – Write one or two sentences that give more information about your second point. **(Stamps feature historical figures and major events in our country's history.)**

8. <u>Sentence #8 - Third Point</u> - Write a sentence stating your third point.
   (I also enjoy stamp collecting because it teaches one to be a careful observer.)

9. <u>Sentence #9 – Supporting Sentence(s)</u> – Write one or two sentences that give more information about your third point. **(Especially with many of the older stamps, one has to look carefully at the lettering and whether the words "U.S. Postage" are located at the top or bottom of each one.)**

WRITING THE CONCLUSION

10. <u>Sentence #10 – Concluding General Statement</u> - Read the topic sentence again and then rewrite it, using some of the same words to say the same thing in a different way.
    (To be sure, there are many advantages to stamp collecting.)

11. <u>Sentence #11 – Concluding Summary (Final) Sentence</u> - Read the three-point sentence again and then rewrite it using some of the same words to say the same thing in a different way.
    (For those who collect stamps, the hobby can be extremely rewarding in more ways than one.)

SAMPLE THREE-PARAGRAPH ESSAY
Why Stamp Collecting Is a Worthwhile Hobby

Quite by accident, I discovered that, as a hobby, stamp collecting offers many rewards. Although some of my friends collect other things, like coins and rocks, I think I like my hobby best. As hobbies go, it is inexpensive, it gives one a sense of history, and it teaches one to be a careful observer.

One of the reasons I enjoy stamp-collecting is that it is inexpensive. One simply has to remove the postage stamps from each day's mail. Another reason I enjoy stamp collecting is that it gives one a sense of history. Stamps feature historical figures and major events in our country's history. I also enjoy stamp collecting because it teaches one to be a careful observer. Especially with many of the older stamps, one has to look carefully at the lettering and whether the words "U.S. Postage" are located at the top or bottom of each one.

To be sure, there are many advantages to stamp collecting. For those who collect stamps, the hobby can be extremely rewarding in more ways than one.

CHAPTER 9 LESSON 5 CONTINUED

TEACHER INSTRUCTIONS FOR WRITING ASSIGNMENTS

Give Writing Assignment #9 and Writing Assignment #10 from the box below. Remind students to follow the Writing Guidelines as they prepare their writings. For Writing Assignment #9, students are to write a three-point **paragraph** in first person. Have students underline all first person pronouns in their paragraph. Remind students that they can use third person pronouns in first person writing.

For Writing Assignment #10, students are to write a **three-paragraph essay** in first person. Use the three-paragraph essay steps and the essay outline to do the writing assignment below. After students have finished writing their essay, have them circle the capital letter and end mark at the beginning and end of each sentence.

Writing Assignment Box

Writing Assignment #9: Three-Point Expository Paragraph (First Person)
(Remind students that first person pronouns are *I, we, me, us, my, our, mine, and ours.*)

Writing topic: A Special Weekend Breakfast or **What Happens When You Lose Your Homework**

Writing Assignment #10: Three-Paragraph Expository Essay (First Person)
Remind students that the 3-paragraph essay has four parts: 1. Title 2. Introduction 3. Body 4. Conclusion

Writing topic: Why I Would/Would Not Like to Be a Circus Clown or **Why Everyone Should Learn to Swim**

TEACHING SCRIPT FOR USING THE WRITING PROCESS FOR THIS WRITING ASSIGNMENT

As you begin this writing assignment, you will start through the writing process. First, you will think about your topic and gather any information you might need in order to do the writing. Second, you will write a rough draft. Remember, it is called a rough draft because it will be revised and edited. You do not have to worry about mistakes as you write your rough draft. After you write the first draft, you will make revisions, using the Revision Checklist in Reference 4. After you revise your writing, you will edit, using the Beginning Editing Checklist in Reference 4. Finally, after you are satisfied with your revising and editing, you will write a final paper, using the Final Paper Checklist in Reference 4. You will then give the finished writing assignment to me.

TEACHER INSTRUCTIONS FOR CHECKING WRITING ASSIGNMENTS

Read, check, and discuss Writing Assignments #9 and #10 after students have finished their final papers. Use the editing checklist (*Reference 4 on teacher's page 9*) as you check and discuss students' papers. Make sure students are using the editing checklist correctly. In the beginning, you must also check students' papers carefully for <u>form</u> mistakes. This will ensure that students are learning the three-point essay format correctly.

(End of lesson.)

Level 5 Homeschool Teacher's Manual

CHAPTER 10   LESSON 1

New objectives: Grammar (Practice Sentences), Skills (capitalization), Activity, and Vocabulary #1.

JINGLE TIME

Have students turn to the Jingle Section of their books. The teacher will lead the students in reciting the previously-taught jingles.

GRAMMAR TIME

First-Year Option: Put the Practice Sentences from the box below on the board or notebook paper. Use these sentences as you practice the concepts that have been taught. For the greatest benefit, students must participate orally with the teacher. **Second-Year Option:** Have students classify the Practice Sentences independently on paper. Check students' sentences with the answers provided below. (*If you have the CDs for Practice Sentences, have students check their sentences with the CDs.*)

Chapter 10, Practice Sentences for Lesson 1

1. _____ Was the returned manila envelope received today?
2. _____ Beware of that narrow bridge across the gorge!

TEACHING SCRIPT FOR PRACTICING PATTERN 1 SENTENCES

We will practice classifying Pattern 1 Sentences. We will classify the sentences together. Begin. (*You might have your students write the labels above the sentences at this time.*)

Question and Answer Flow for Sentence 1: Was the returned manila envelope received today?

1. What was received today? envelope - SN
2. What is being said about envelope? envelope was received - V
3. Was - HV
4. Was received when? today - Adv
5. What kind of envelope? manila - Adj
6. What kind of envelope? returned - Adj
7. The - A

8. SN V P1 Check
9. No prepositional phrases.
10. Question mark, question, interrogative sentence
11. Go back to the verb - divide the complete subject from the complete predicate.
12. Is there an adverb exception? No.
13. Is this sentence in a natural or inverted order? Inverted - underline the subject parts once and the predicate parts twice.

Classified Sentence:

		HV	A	Adj	Adj	SN	V	Adv
SN	V	Was	the	returned	manila	envelope /	received	today? **Int**
P1								

CHAPTER 10 LESSON 1 CONTINUED

Question and Answer Flow for Sentence 2: Beware of that narrow bridge across the gorge!

1. Who beware of that narrow bridge across the gorge?
   (You) - SP (Understood subject pronoun)
2. What is being said about you? you beware - V
3. Of - P
4. Of what? bridge - OP
5. What kind of bridge? narrow - Adj
6. Which bridge? that - Adj
7. Across - P
8. Across what? gorge - OP
9. The - A

10. SN V P1 Check
11. (Of that narrow bridge) - Prepositional phrase
12. (Across the gorge) - Prepositional phrase
13. Exclamation point, strong feeling, exclamatory sentence
14. Go back to the verb - divide the complete subject from the complete predicate.
15. Is there an adverb exception? No.
16. Is this sentence in a natural or inverted order? Natural - no change.

Classified Sentence:

```
              (You) SP      V      P Adj Adj  OP      P  A  OP
              _____   / Beware (of that narrow bridge) (across the gorge)!  E
              SN  V
              _____
              P1
```

Use Sentences 1-2 that you just classified with your students to do an Oral Skill Builder Check. Use the guidelines below.

Oral Skill Builder Check

1. **Noun check.**
   (Say the job and then say the noun. Circle each noun.)
2. **Identify the nouns as singular or plural.**
   (Write S or P above each noun.)
3. **Identify the nouns as common or proper.**
   (Follow established procedure for oral identification.)
4. **Do a vocabulary check.**
   (Follow established procedure for oral identification.)

5. **Identify the complete subject and the complete predicate.** (Underline the complete subject once and the complete predicate twice.)
6. **Identify the simple subject and simple predicate.** (Underline the simple subject once and the simple predicate twice. Bold, or highlight, the lines.)
7. **Recite the irregular verb chart.** (Located on student page 17 and teacher page 143.)

SKILL TIME

TEACHING SCRIPT FOR INTRODUCING THE CAPITALIZATION RULES

Turn to pages 20 and 21 in the Reference Section and look at Reference 27 in your student book. These are the rules for capitalization. The capitalization rules are organized into sections of similar rules. (*Read and discuss each section and the rules contained in each section.*) Your knowledge of capitalization rules will help you as you write and edit your writing. You will find that readers appreciate writers who use capitalization rules well. (*The capitalization rules are reproduced for you on page 172.*)

CHAPTER 10 LESSON 1 CONTINUED

ACTIVITY / ASSIGNMENT TIME

Today, you will begin preparations to make a Capitalization Collage. Look up the word **collage**. Know the definition and ways to make different collages. (*Students could look on the internet or in art books for more information and examples of collages.*) Your assignment is to <u>make a collage of things that are capitalized.</u>

Write the key word **Capitalization** with a black magic marker in the middle of a posterboard. (*You could also use other creative ways to spell out Capitalization. For instance, you could cut black paper into little pieces and glue the pieces on the poster board to form the word Capitalization. You might also use different-colored paper scraps for a different look.*)

Using the capitalization rule page as a guide, try to find as many examples of each rule as possible. Look through magazines, newspapers, and the internet to find **words, phrases, sentences,** and **paragraphs** that show how the different capitalization rules are used. Put them in a freezer bag to use later. Be sure to add pictures of people, places, or things that would also be capitalized. Keep collecting words and pictures for your Capitalization Collage throughout the week. You will put it together in another lesson.

VOCABULARY TIME

Assign Chapter 10, Vocabulary Words **#1** on page 7 in the Reference Section for students to define in their Vocabulary notebooks. Tell students they are to use a dictionary or thesaurus to look up the meanings of the vocabulary words. After they write each word and its meaning, students are to write a sentence using the vocabulary word.

Chapter 10, Vocabulary Words #1
(spontaneous, forced, burn, smolder)

(End of lesson.)

CHAPTER 10 LESSON 1 CONTINUED

Reference 27: Capitalization Rules

SECTION 1: CAPITALIZE THE FIRST WORD

1. The first word of a sentence. (*He likes to take a nap.*)

2. The first word in the greeting and closing of letters. (*Dear, Yours truly*)

3. The first and last word and important words in titles of literary works.
   (*books, songs, short stories, poems, articles, movie titles, magazines*)
   (*Note: Conjunctions, articles, and prepositions with fewer than five letters are not capitalized unless they are the first or last word.*)

4. The first word of a direct quotation. (*Dad said, "We are going home."*)

5. The first word in each line of a topic outline.

SECTION 2: CAPITALIZE NAMES, INITIALS, AND TITLES OF PEOPLE

6. The pronoun I. (*May I go with you?*)

7. The names and nicknames of people. (*Sam, Joe, Jones, Slim, Shorty*)

8. Family names when used in place of or with the person's name.
   (*Grandmother, Auntie, Uncle Joe, Mother – Do NOT capitalize <u>my mother</u>.*)

9. Titles used with, or in place of, people's names.
   (*Mr., Ms., Miss, Dr. Smith, Doctor, Captain, President, Sir*)

10. People's initials. (*J.D., C. Smith*)

SECTION 3: CAPITALIZE WORDS OF TIME

11. The days of the week and months of the year. (*Monday, July*)

12. The names of holidays. (*Christmas, Thanksgiving, Easter*)

13. The names of historical events, periods, laws, documents, conflicts, and distinguished awards.
    (*Civil War, Middle Ages, Medal of Honor*)

SECTION 4: CAPITALIZE NAMES OF PLACES

14. The names and abbreviations of cities, towns, counties, states, countries, and nations.
    (*Dallas, Texas, Fulton County, Africa, America, USA, AR, TX*)

15. The names of avenues, streets, roads, highways, routes, and post office boxes.
    (*Main Street, Jones Road, Highway 89, Rt. 1, Box 2, P.O. Box 45*)

16. The names of lakes, rivers, oceans, mountain ranges, deserts, parks, stars, planets, and
    constellations. (*Beaver Lake, Rocky Mountains, Venus*)

17. The names of schools and specific school courses.
    (*Walker Elementary School, Mathematics II*)

18. North, south, east, and west when they refer to sections of the country.
    (*up North, live in the East, out West*)

SECTION 5: CAPITALIZE NAMES OF OTHER NOUNS AND PROPER ADJECTIVES

19. The names of pets. (*Spot, Tweety Bird, etc.*)

20. The names of products. (*Campbell's soup, Kelly's chili, Ford cars, etc.*)

21. The names of companies, buildings, stores, ships, planes, space ships.
    (*Empire State Building, Titanic, IBM, The Big Tire Co.*)

22. Proper adjectives. (*the English language, Italian restaurant, French test*)

23. The names of clubs, organizations, or groups. (*Lion's Club, Jaycees, Beatles*)

24. The names of political parties, religious preferences, nationalities, and races.
    (*Democratic party, Republican, Jewish synagogue, American*)

CHAPTER 10   LESSON 2
New objectives: Grammar (Practice Sentences), Skills (punctuation), Activity, and Vocabulary #2.

JINGLE TIME

Have students turn to the Jingle Section of their books. The teacher will lead the students in reciting the previously-taught jingles.

GRAMMAR TIME

First-Year Option: Put the Practice Sentences from the box below on the board or notebook paper. Use these sentences as you practice the concepts that have been taught. For the greatest benefit, students must participate orally with the teacher. **Second-Year Option:** Have students classify the Practice Sentences independently on paper. Check students' sentences with the answers provided below. (*If you have the CDs for Practice Sentences, have students check their sentences with the CDs.*)

Chapter 10, Practice Sentences for Lesson 2
1. _____ The parents, teachers, and students were clapping loudly after the final performance of the operetta.
2. _____ Were Clyde's corn and beans completely destroyed from recent rainfall?

TEACHING SCRIPT FOR PRACTICING PATTERN 1 SENTENCES

Today, we will practice classifying Pattern 1 Sentences. We will classify the sentences together. Begin.
(*You might have your students write the labels above the sentences at this time.*)

Question and Answer Flow for Sentence 1: The parents, teachers, and students were clapping loudly after the final performance of the operetta.	
1. Who were clapping loudly after the final performance of the operetta? parents, teachers, and students - CSN, CSN, CSN	11. The - A
	12. And - C
	13. The - A
2. What is being said about parents, teachers, and students? parents, teachers, and students were clapping - V	14. SN V P1 Check
	15. (After the final performance) - Prepositional phrase
3. Were - HV	16. (Of the operetta) - Prepositional phrase
4. Clapping how? loudly - Adv	17. Period, statement, declarative sentence
5. After - P	18. Go back to the verb - divide the complete subject
6. After what? performance - OP	from the complete predicate.
7. What kind of performance? final - Adj	19. Is there an adverb exception? No.
8. The - A	20. Is this sentence in a natural or inverted order?
9. Of - P	Natural - no change.
10. Of what? operetta - OP	

Classified
Sentence:

		A	CSN	CSN	C	CSN	HV	V	Adv	P	A	Adj	OP
SN	V	The parents, teachers, and students **/** were clapping loudly **(**after the final performance**)**											

P A OP
(of the operetta). **D**

P1

CHAPTER 10 LESSON 2 CONTINUED

Question and Answer Flow for Sentence 2: Were Clyde's corn and beans completely destroyed from recent rainfall?

1. What were destroyed from recent rainfall? corn and beans - CSN, CSN
2. What is being said about corn and beans? corn and beans were destroyed - V
3. Were - HV
4. From - P
5. From what? rainfall - OP
6. Which rainfall? recent - Adj
7. Were destroyed how? completely - Adv
8. And - C
9. Whose corn and beans? Clyde's - PNA

10. SN V P1 Check
11. (From recent rainfall) - Prepositional phrase
12. Question mark, question, interrogative sentence
13. Go back to the verb - divide the complete subject from the complete predicate.
14. Is there an adverb exception? Yes - change the line.
15. Is this sentence in a natural or inverted order? Inverted - underline the subject parts once and the predicate parts twice.

Classified Sentence:

	HV	PNA	CSN	C	CSN	Adv	V	P	Adj	OP
SN V	Were	Clyde's	corn	and	beans /	completely	destroyed	(from	recent	rainfall)? **Int**
P1										

TEACHING SCRIPT FOR INTRODUCING A PATTERN 1 PRACTICE SENTENCE

Put these words on the board: **Pattern 1 Sentence**

Get out a sheet of notebook paper. On the top line of your notebook paper, write the title *Pattern 1 Practice Sentence*. Look at the new words on the board: **Pattern 1 Sentence**. I will guide you again through the process as we learn to write a Pattern 1 sentence.

You have already learned how to write a Practice Sentence according to labels that have been provided for you. Today, you will learn how to write a Practice Sentence in which you select the parts of the sentence and the order they appear in your sentence. You will use only sentence parts of a Pattern 1 sentence.

Name the parts of a Pattern 1 sentence that YOU MUST USE. (*All Pattern 1 sentences must have a subject and a verb.*) Now, name the parts of a sentence that YOU CAN CHOOSE to add to your sentence. (*adjectives, adverbs, article adjectives, prepositional phrases, subject pronouns, possessive nouns, possessive pronouns, helping verbs, conjunctions, and interjections.*)

Let's write the labels for a Pattern 1 sentence on a sheet of notebook paper. First, write the *SN* and *V* labels that a Pattern 1 sentence must have, on your paper. Be sure to place them in the middle of your paper. (*Demonstrate by writing the SN and V labels on the board.*) Now, using what you know about writing Practice Sentences, we will decide what other parts we want to add to our Pattern 1 sentence. But first, we will look at a Reference box that will list all the parts that we can use. Turn to page 21 and look at Reference 28. (*Read and discuss the information in Reference 28 with your students. Reference 28 is reproduced for you on the next page.*)

CHAPTER 10 LESSON 2 CONTINUED

Reference 28: Sentence Parts That Can Be Used for a Pattern 1 Sentence

1. Nouns
Use only subject nouns or object of the preposition nouns.

2. Adverbs
Tell how, when, or where.
Can be placed before or after verbs, at the beginning or end of a sentence, and in front of adjectives or other adverbs.

3. Adjectives
Tell what kind, which one, or how many.
Can be placed in front of nouns. Sometimes two or three adjectives can modify the same noun.
Articles
Adjectives that are used in front of nouns (a, an, the).

4. Verbs *(Can include helping verbs.)*

5. Prepositional Phrases
Can be placed before or after nouns, after verbs, adverbs, or other prepositional phrases, and at the beginning or end of a sentence.

6. Pronouns
(subjective, possessive, or objective)

7. Conjunctions
Connecting words for compound parts: and, or, but.

8. Interjections
Usually found at the beginning of a sentence. Can show strong or mild emotion.

Teacher's Note: You may want to make a poster of the information in the box above to show students that they are actually using the eight parts of speech from which to choose the different sentence parts that can be used for a Pattern 1 Sentence.

TEACHER INSTRUCTIONS

Use the information in the box above to help your students choose other parts to add to a Pattern 1 sentence. Help students select sentence labels and place them in the order in which they have decided. As students choose the sentence parts they want in their sentence, you should write the labels in the designated order on the board. Students should write the labels on their papers when they are ready to write a Pattern 1 Sentence. (*Students will have the same sentence labels in the same order this first time.*)

After your students have finished writing the teacher-guided Pattern 1 Practice Sentences on their papers, each student should then write his or her own Pattern 1 sentence, choosing their own labels. Tell students they can use any sentence part listed in Reference 28 every time they write an independent Pattern 1 Sentence. Some students may add only adjectives, adverbs, and one or two prepositional phrases the first time. Other students may have the confidence to use a variety of sentence parts: pronouns, possessives, inverted order, adverb exceptions, etc.

TEACHING SCRIPT FOR THE IMPROVED SENTENCE

Under your Practice Sentence, write the title *Improved Sentence* on another line. To improve your Practice Sentence, you will make two synonym changes, one antonym change, and your choice of a complete-word change or another synonym or antonym change. I will give you time to write your Improved Sentence. (*Always encourage students to use a thesaurus, synonym-antonym book, or a dictionary to help them develop an interesting and improved writing vocabulary.*) (*After students have finished, check and discuss students' Practice and Improved Sentences.*)

CHAPTER 10 LESSON 2 CONTINUED

SKILL TIME

TEACHING SCRIPT FOR INTRODUCING THE PUNCTUATION RULES

Turn to pages 22 and 23 in the Reference Section and look at Reference 29A and 29B in your student book. These are the rules for punctuation. The punctuation rules are organized into sections of similar rules. (_Read and discuss each section and the rules under each section._) Your knowledge of punctuation rules will help you as you write and as you edit your writing. You will find that readers also appreciate writers who use punctuation rules well. Correct use of punctuation keeps writing clear and easy to understand. (_The punctuation rules are reproduced for you on the next two pages._)

ACTIVITY / ASSIGNMENT TIME

Today, you will begin preparations to make a Punctuation Collage. First, write the key word **Punctuation** with a black magic marker in the middle of a posterboard. (_You could also use other ways to spell out Punctuation. You could use the same method that you used for your Capitalization Collage, or you could think of another artistic way to put "Punctuation" on your posterboard_).

Using the punctuation-rules pages as a guide, try to find as many examples of each rule as possible. Look through magazines, newspapers, and the internet to find **words, phrases, sentences** and **paragraphs** that show how the different punctuation rules are used. Put them in a freezer bag to use later. Be sure to add pictures to illustrate or emphasize different types of punctuation. Keep collecting material for your Punctuation collage throughout the week. You will put it together in another lesson.

VOCABULARY TIME

Assign Chapter 10, Vocabulary Words **#2** on page 7 in the Reference Section for students to define in their Vocabulary notebooks. Tell students they are to use a dictionary or thesaurus to look up the meanings of the vocabulary words. After they write each word and its meaning, students are to write a sentence using the vocabulary word.

Chapter 10, Vocabulary Words #2
(repulsive, amiable, escalate, expand)

(End of lesson.)

CHAPTER 10 LESSON 2 CONTINUED

Reference 29A: Punctuation Rules

SECTION 6: END MARK PUNCTUATION

1. Use a (.) for the end punctuation of a sentence that makes a statement.
   (*Mom baked us a cake.*)
2. Use a (?) for the end punctuation of a sentence that asks a question.
   (*Are you going to town?*)
3. Use an (!) for the end punctuation of a sentence that expresses strong feeling.
   (*That bee stung me!*)
4. Use a (.) for the end punctuation of a sentence that gives a command or makes a request.
   (*Close the door.*)

SECTION 7: COMMAS TO SEPARATE TIME WORDS

5. Use a comma between the day of the week and the month. (*Friday, July 23*)
   Use a comma between the day and year. (*July 23, 2009*)
6. Use a comma to separate the year from the rest of the sentence when the year follows the month or the month and the day.
   (*We spent May, 2001, with Mom. We spent July 23, 2001, with Dad.*)

SECTION 8: COMMAS TO SEPARATE PLACE WORDS

7. Use a comma to separate the city from the state or country.
   (*I will go to Dallas, Texas. He is from Paris, France.*)
8. Use a comma to separate the state or country from the rest of the sentence when the name of the state or country follows the name of a city.
   (*We flew to Dallas, Texas, in June. We flew to Paris, France, in July.*)

SECTION 9: COMMAS TO MAKE MEANINGS CLEAR

9. Use a comma to separate words or phrases in a series.
   (*We had soup, crackers, and milk.*)
10. Use commas to separate introductory words such as *Yes, Well, Oh,* and *No* from the rest of a sentence.
    (*Oh, I didn't know that.*)
11. Use commas to set off most appositives. An appositive is a word, phrase, title, or degree used directly after another word or name to explain it or to rename it.
    (*Sue, the girl next door, likes to draw.*)
    One-word appositives can be written two different ways: *(1) My brother, Tim, is riding in the horse show. (2) My brother Tim is riding in the horse show.* Your assignments will require one-word appositives to be set off with commas.
12. Use commas to separate a noun of direct address (the name of a person directly spoken to) from the rest of the sentence.
    (*Mom, do I really have to go?*)

SECTION 10: PUNCTUATION IN GREETINGS AND CLOSINGS OF LETTERS

13. Use a comma (,) after the salutation (greeting) of a friendly letter. (*Dear Sam,*)
14. Use a comma (,) after the closing of any letter. (*Yours truly,*)
15. Use a colon (:) after the salutation (greeting) of a business letter. (*Dear Sir:*)

CHAPTER 10 LESSON 2 CONTINUED

Reference 29B: Punctuation Rules

SECTION 11: PERIODS

16. Use a period after most abbreviations or titles that are accepted in formal writing. (*Mr., Ms., Dr., Capt., St., Ave., St. Louis*) (*Note: These abbreviations cannot be used by themselves. They must always be used with a proper noun.*)

    In the abbreviations of many well-known organizations or words, periods are not required. (*USA, GM, TWA, GTE, AT&T, TV, AM, FM, GI, etc.*) Use only one period after an abbreviation at the end of a statement. Do not put an extra period for the end mark punctuation.

17. Use a period after initials. (*C. Smith, D.J. Brewton, Thomas A. Jones*)

18. Place a period after Roman numerals, Arabic numbers, and letters of the alphabet in an outline. (*II., IV., 5., 25., A., B.*)

SECTION 12: APOSTROPHES

19. Form a contraction by using an apostrophe in place of a letter or letters that have been left out. (*I'll, he's, isn't, wasn't, can't*)

20. Form the possessive of singular and plural nouns by using an apostrophe. (*boy's ball, boys' ball, children's ball*)

21. Form the plurals of letters, symbols, numbers, and signs with the apostrophe plus *s* (*'s*). (*9's, B's, b's*)

SECTION 13: UNDERLINING

22. Use underlining or italics for titles of books, magazines, works of art, ships, newspapers, motion pictures, etc. (*A famous movie is <u>Gone With the Wind</u>. Our newspaper is the <u>Cabot Star Herald</u>.*) (*<u>Titanic, Charlotte's Web</u>, etc.*)

SECTION 14: QUOTATION MARKS

23. Use quotation marks to set off the titles of songs, short stories, short poems, articles, essays, short plays, and book chapters. (*Do you like to sing the song "America" in music class?*)

24. Quotation marks are used at the beginning and end of the person's words to separate what the person actually said from the rest of the sentence. Since the quotation tells what is being said, it will always have quotation marks around it.

25. The words that tell who is speaking are the explanatory words. Do not set explanatory words off with quotation marks. (*Fred said, "I'm here."*) (***Fred said** is explanatory and should not be set off with quotations.*)

26. A new paragraph is used to indicate a change of speaker.

27. When a speaker's speech is longer than one paragraph, quotation marks are used at the beginning of each paragraph and at the end of the last paragraph of that speaker's speech.

28. Use single quotation marks to enclose a quotation within a quotation. (*"My teddy bear says 'I love you' four different ways," said little Amy.*)

29. Use a period at the end of explanatory words that come at the end of a sentence.

30. Use a comma to separate a direct quotation from the explanatory words.

CHAPTER 10   LESSON 3

New objectives: Grammar (Practice Sentences), Skills (capitalization and punctuation), and a Practice sheet.

 JINGLE TIME

Have students turn to the Jingle Section of their books. The teacher will lead the students in reciting the previously-taught jingles.

 GRAMMAR TIME

First-Year Option: Put the Practice Sentences from the box below on the board or notebook paper. Use these sentences as you practice the concepts that have been taught. For the greatest benefit, students must participate orally with the teacher. **Second-Year Option:** Have students classify the Practice Sentences independently on paper. Check students' sentences with the answers provided below. (*If you have the CDs for Practice Sentences, have students check their sentences with the CDs.*)

Chapter 10, Practice Sentences for Lesson 3
1. _____ Her chauffeur suddenly turned into my sister's driveway.
2. _____ Were you and your husband surprised by January's festive parades?

TEACHING SCRIPT FOR PRACTICING PATTERN 1 SENTENCES

Today, we will practice classifying Pattern 1 Sentences. We will classify the sentences together. Begin.
(*You might have your students write the labels above the sentences at this time.*)

Question and Answer Flow for Sentence 1: Her chauffeur suddenly turned into my sister's driveway.	
1. Who turned into my sister's driveway? chauffeur - SN	9. SN V P1 Check
2. What is being said about chauffeur? chauffeur turned - V	10. (Into my sister's driveway) - Prepositional phrase
3. Into - P	11. Period, statement, declarative sentence
4. Into what? driveway - OP	12. Go back to the verb - divide the complete subject from the complete predicate.
5. Whose driveway? sister's - PNA	13. Is there an adverb exception? Yes - change the line.
6. Whose sister? my - PPA	
7. Turned how? suddenly - Adv	14. Is this sentence in a natural or inverted order? Natural - no change.
8. Whose chauffeur? her - PPA	

Classified Sentence:

```
              PPA   SN       Adv     V     P  PPA PNA     OP
   SN  V      Her chauffeur / suddenly turned (into my sister's driveway).  D
   P1
```

CHAPTER 10 LESSON 3 CONTINUED

Question and Answer Flow for Sentence 2: Were you and your husband surprised by January's festive parades?

1. Who were surprised by January's festive parades?
   you and husband - CSP, CSN
2. What is being said about you and husband?
   you and husband were surprised - V
3. Were - HV
4. By - P
5. By what? parades - OP
6. What kind of parades? festive - Adj
7. Whose parades? January's - PNA
8. Whose husband? your - PPA

9. And - C
10. SN V P1 Check
11. (By January's festive parades) - Prepositional phrase
12. Question mark, question, interrogative sentence
13. Go back to the verb - divide the complete subject from the complete predicate.
14. Is there an adverb exception? No.
15. Is this sentence in a natural or inverted order?
    Inverted - underline the subject parts once and the predicate parts twice.

Classified Sentence:

```
                        HV  CSP  C  PPA  CSN      V        P   PNA     Adj     OP
         SN  V          Were you and your husband / surprised (by January's festive parades)?  Int
         P1
```

SKILL TIME

TEACHING SCRIPT FOR CAPITALIZATION AND PUNCTUATION

You are ready to learn how to use the rules for capitalization and punctuation to edit sentences, paragraphs, and letters. It is important for you to know how to capitalize and punctuate any type of writing correctly. Expertise comes with years of practice and being able to apply all capitalization and punctuation rules automatically to edit your writing.

Teacher's Note: You will find a copy of the capitalization rules at the end of Lesson 1 and the punctuation rules at the end of Lesson 2 in this chapter. Refer to them as needed.

Look at References 27, 29A, and 29B for the capitalization and punctuation rules on pages 20, 21, 22, and 23 in the Reference Section of your book. You should know most of these rules by now, but I want you to know how the rules pages are set up with similar rules grouped in a given section. Let's read over the titles of all the sections on the rules pages. If you can find the right section, you'll be able to find the specific rule number.

TEACHER INSTRUCTIONS

Go over the different sections and one or two specific rules in each section of all three rules pages at this time. Reading over every capitalization and punctuation rule is not necessary. Students will get plenty of practice finding and applying these rules as they correct errors in the different exercises. They will learn the rules by using them over and over again while they are correcting the errors. You may have your students color-code the different sections. To make sure the color of their marker does not cover the rules or rule numbers, have students draw a box around each section instead of coloring each section.

Teacher's Note: Make sure students understand the concept of proper adjectives during the discussion of the capitalization rules. Ask for examples of proper adjectives.

CHAPTER 10 LESSON 3 CONTINUED

I'm going to show you how to use capitalization and punctuation rules to correct capitalization and punctuation errors. You will correct all capitalization errors first so you don't have to work with more than one page of rules at a time. For capitalization corrections, you will use only Reference 27, the capitalization rules page. You will correct all punctuation errors, using only the punctuation rules pages in Reference 29A and 29B. Using this method will prevent you from flipping back and forth from page to page for every correction.

Look at the *Capitalization and Punctuation Examples* on Reference 30 on page 23 in the Reference Section. Look at number 1. All capitalization errors have been corrected and bolded so we can clearly see them. Our job in this format is to supply only the correct rule numbers above the corrections that were made.

Look at the editing guide that is located under Sentence 1. The number beside CAPITALS in the editing guide tells how many total capitalization errors are in that sentence. There is a number 5 after the word CAPITALS. This means that there are 5 capitalization errors to correct. You are to write the rule number above each of the five corrections. Let's look at one bolded correction at a time and find the rule number listed on the rules page that matches the correction. (*Have students look up each capitalization rule number to see how it relates to each bolded correction.*)

Reference 30: Capitalization and Punctuation Examples

   1   6   14   14   11

1. **Yes, I'll** go to **Lincoln, Nebraska,** in **J**uly for our family reunion.

     10 19   7   8   1

Editing Guide for Sample 1 Sentence: Capitals: 5   Commas: 3   Apostrophes: 1   End Marks: 1

   N   P

2. **no, peaches,** our **neighbor's** new golden **retriever,** is not a house **dog.**

Editing Guide for Sample 2 Sentence: Capitals: 2   Commas: 3   Apostrophes: 1   End marks: 1

We will check the editing guide for the specific punctuation errors. If you see a number beside the word PERIODS, it is for the periods used after abbreviations and initials within the sentence. A period at the end of a sentence is listed beside the words END MARKS in the editing guide. (*Have students look up each punctuation rule number to see how it relates to each bolded correction.*)

Look at Sentence 2. For this sentence, we will make corrections only. We do not have to put the rule numbers. Look at how you are to correct capitalization mistakes. Do you see how a capital letter is put above each small letter that needs to be capitalized?

Now, look at the punctuation examples. Do you see how you are to write each punctuation correction? Since punctuation is sometimes hard to see, you are to bold your punctuation answers by making them a little bigger and darker than normal. (*Lead students in a discussion of the corrections and why they were made.*)

CHAPTER 10 LESSON 3 CONTINUED

 PRACTICE TIME

Have students turn to page 57 in the Practice Section of their book and find Chapter 10, Lesson 3, Practice. Go over the directions to make sure they understand what to do. Check and discuss the Practice after students have finished. (*Chapter 10, Lesson 3, Practice key is given below.*)

Chapter 10, Lesson 3, Practice
Use the Editing Guide below each sentence to know how many capitalization and punctuation errors to correct. For Sentence 1, write the capitalization and punctuation rule numbers for each correction in bold. For Sentence 2, write the capitalization and punctuation corrections. Use the capitalization and punctuation rule pages to help you.

    1 6   14   14   11

1. **No, I**'ve not been to **Bangor, Maine,** in **April** for their white birch events.
  10 19   7   8   1

Editing Guide for Example 1 Sentence: Capitals: 5   Commas: 3   Apostrophes: 1   End Marks: 1

  W   L

2. well, lester, my mother**'**s oldest brother, is a hermit.

Editing Guide for Example 2 Sentence: Capitals: 2   Commas: 3   Apostrophes: 1   End marks: 1

Teacher's Note: Remind students to look at the Editing Guide several times for the total number of capitalization and punctuation mistakes.

 WRITING TIME

Have students make an entry in their journals.

 STUDY TIME

Have students study the vocabulary words in their vocabulary notebooks. Tell students that any vocabulary word in their notebooks could be on their test. Have students study any of the skills in the Practice Section that they need to review.   Students should also study their homonym chart.

(End of lesson.)

                                    Level 5 Homeschool Teacher's Manual

CHAPTER 10   LESSON 4

New objectives: Test and an Activity (concluded).

JINGLE TIME

Have students turn to the Jingle Section of their books. The teacher will lead the students in reciting the previously-taught jingles.

STUDY TIME

Have students study the vocabulary words in their vocabulary notebooks. Remind students that any vocabulary word in their notebooks could be on their test. Also, have students study any of the skills in the Practice Section that they need to review.

TEST TIME

Have students turn to page 91 in the Test Section of their book and find the Chapter 10 Test. Students must use the Reference Section in their books to find the capitalization and punctuation rule numbers to edit the friendly letter (*References 27, 29A, or 29B*). Remind them to pay attention and think about what they are doing. Go over the directions to make sure they understand what to do. (*Chapter 10 Test key is on the next page.*)

CHECK TIME

After students have finished, check and discuss their test papers. Make sure they understand why their answers are right or wrong. (*For total points, count each required answer as a point.*)

ACTIVITY / ASSIGNMENT TIME

You have collected words and pictures for your Capitalization and Punctuation collages throughout the week. Now, you will finish the two collages. Make sure you have the key words "**Capitalization**" and "**Punctuation**" in the middle of each piece of poster board. Paste the words and pictures that you collected earlier on the poster boards around the key words. Arrange them in a pattern that is pleasing and colorful. Put your name on the collages and share them with family members and friends.

(End of lesson.)

Chapter 10 Test
(Student Page 91)

Exercise 1: Classify each sentence.

```
              A      SN        P   A   Adj   OP     V     P   PNA      OP       P    PPA    OP
1.  SN  V     The teakettle (on the wood stove) / grated (on Mom's nerves) (during her naptime).  D
    P1

                    I    PPA   SN       V    P   A    Adj    OP
2.  SN  V     Whew!  My goldfish / landed (in the kitchen sink)!  E
    P1

              A    Adj    SN    HV   Adv   CV      P    A     OP    C    HV     CV
3.  SN  V     The excited toddler / was eagerly running (after the balloon) and was squealing
    P1              Adv        P    A    OP
              delightedly (during the chase).  D
```

Exercise 2: Use Sentence 3 to underline the complete subject once and the complete predicate twice and to complete the table below.

List the Noun Used	List the Noun Job	Singular or Plural	Common or Proper	Simple Subject	Simple Predicate
1. toddler	2. SN	3. S	4. C	5. toddler	6.was running/ was squealing
7. balloon	8. OP	9. S	10. C		
11. chase	12. OP	13. S	14. C		

Exercise 3: Name the eight parts of speech that you have studied. *(Accept answers in any order.)*

1. **noun**   2. **verb**   3. **adjective**   4. **adverb**   5. **preposition**   6. **pronoun**   7. **conjunction**   8. **interjection**

Exercise 4: Identify each pair of words as synonyms or antonyms by putting parentheses ( ) around *syn* or *ant*.

1. burn, smolder	**(syn)** ant	5. frugal, thrifty	**(syn)** ant	9. acknowledge, admit	**(syn)** ant
2. bland, savory	syn **(ant)**	6. conceal, exhume	syn **(ant)**	10. honesty, integrity	**(syn)** ant
3. timid, audacious	syn **(ant)**	7. amiable, repulsive	syn **(ant)**	11. spontaneous, forced	syn **(ant)**
4. odd, quaint	**(syn)** ant	8. escalate, expand	**(syn)** ant	12. periodic, simultaneous	syn **(ant)**

Exercise 5: Underline the correct homonym in each sentence.

1. Melissa looked at Chris and shook her head (<u>no</u>, know).
2. I bought a (knew, <u>new</u>) pair of shoes yesterday.
3. Steven already (<u>knew</u>, new) the answer to the question.
4. You will make a (write, <u>right</u>) turn after you pass the blue house.
5. The flower's fresh (cent, <u>scent</u>) filled the room.
6. Mom (<u>sent</u>, cent) Kyle to his room.
7. I (<u>know</u>, no) that tomorrow is your birthday.
8. Don't forget to (right, <u>write</u>) your grandmother a thank-you note.

Exercise 6: Use the Editing Guide below each sentence to know how many capitalization and punctuation errors to correct. For Sentence 1, write the capitalization and punctuation rule numbers for each correction in bold. For Sentence 2, write the capitalization and punctuation corrections. Use the capitalization and punctuation rule pages to help you.

```
     1              9   7                        17     17     17        11
1.  Did you know that Dr. Speer has been teaching at Eastern Technical College since August 12, 1972?
                    16                                                               5    2
```

Editing Guide: Capitals: 7   Commas: 1   Periods: 1   Apostrophes: 0   End Marks: 1

```
     O        H                            D   B                                        J
2.  our trip to honduras was so successful that dr. baker said he would take another group this july.
```

Editing Guide: Capitals: 5   Commas: 0   Periods: 1   Apostrophes: 0   End Marks: 1

Exercise 7: In your journal, write a paragraph summarizing what you have learned this week.

CHAPTER 10 LESSON 4 CONTINUED

TEACHER INSTRUCTIONS

Use the Question and Answer Flows below for the sentences on Chapter 10 Test.

Question and Answer Flow for Sentence 1: The teakettle on the wood stove grated on Mom's nerves during her naptime.

1. What grated on Mom's nerves during her naptime?
   teakettle - SN
2. What is being said about teakettle?
   teakettle grated - V
3. On - P
4. On what? nerves - OP
5. Whose nerves? Mom's - PNA
6. During - P
7. During what? naptime - OP
8. Whose naptime? her - PPA
9. On - P
10. On what? stove - OP
11. What kind of stove? wood - Adj

12. The - A
13. The - A
14. SN V P1 Check
15. (On the wood stove) - Prepositional phrase
16. (On Mom's nerves) - Prepositional phrase
17. (During her naptime) - Prepositional phrase
18. Period, statement, declarative sentence
19. Go back to the verb - divide the complete subject from the complete predicate.
20. Is there an adverb exception? No.
21. Is this sentence in a natural or inverted order? Natural - no change.

Classified Sentence:

         A   SN   P A Adj OP   V   P PNA   OP   P   PPA   OP

SN V   The teakettle (on the wood stove) / grated (on Mom's nerves) (during her naptime). **D**
P1

Question and Answer Flow for Sentence 2: Whew! My goldfish landed in the kitchen sink!

1. What landed in the kitchen sink? goldfish - SN
2. What is being said about goldfish?
   goldfish landed - V
3. In - P
4. In what? sink - OP
5. What kind of sink? kitchen - Adj
6. The - A
7. Whose goldfish? my - PPA
8. Whew - I

9. SN V P1 Check
10. (In the kitchen sink) - Prepositional phrase
11. Exclamation point, strong feeling, exclamatory sentence
12. Go back to the verb - divide the complete subject from the complete predicate.
13. Is there an adverb exception? No.
14. Is this sentence in a natural or inverted order? Natural - no change.

Classified Sentence:

                   I   PPA SN   V   P A Adj   OP

SN V   Whew! My goldfish / landed (in the kitchen sink)! **E**
P1

Question and Answer Flow for Sentence 3: The excited toddler was eagerly running after the balloon and was squealing delightedly during the chase.

1. Who was eagerly running after the balloon and was squealing delightedly during the chase? toddler - SN
2. What is being said about toddler?
   toddler was running and was squealing - CV, CV
3. Was - HV
4. Was - HV
5. Was squealing how? delightedly - Adv
6. During - P
7. During what? chase - OP
8. The - A
9. And - C
10. After - P
11. After what? balloon - OP

12. The - A
13. Was running how? eagerly - Adv
14. What kind of toddler? excited - Adj
15. The - A
16. SN V P1 Check
17. (After the balloon) - Prepositional phrase
18. (During the chase) - Prepositional phrase
19. Period, statement, declarative sentence
20. Go back to the verb - divide the complete subject from the complete predicate.
21. Is there an adverb exception? No.
22. Is this sentence in a natural or inverted order? Natural - no change.

Classified Sentence:

         A   Adj   SN   HV   Adv   CV   P A OP   C HV   CV

SN V   The excited toddler / was eagerly running (after the balloon) and was squealing
P1   Adv   P A   OP

    delightedly (during the chase). **D**

CHAPTER 10   LESSON 5
New objectives: Writing (5-paragraph essay) and Writing Assignment #11, Bonus Option.

 WRITING TIME

Teacher's Note:

1. Students will name or list three points they want to discuss about their topic.

2. As you work through the steps below, be sure to show students how an essay is divided into 5 paragraphs: the introduction, the first-point paragraph, the second-point paragraph, the third-point paragraph, and the conclusion.

3. Remind students that this is an expository essay, which means that its purpose is to inform or explain. The five-point format is another way of organizing an expository essay.

TEACHING SCRIPT FOR INTRODUCING HOW TO WRITE A 5-PARAGRAPH ESSAY

You have already learned how to write a three-paragraph essay. You also learned that an essay has three main parts: 1. Introduction 2. Body 3. Conclusion.

Today, you will learn how to write a five-paragraph essay. In a five-paragraph expository essay, there will be five paragraphs, no more and no fewer. The five-paragraph essay will also have the same three main parts: the introduction, body, and conclusion. The introduction forms the first paragraph, the body forms the second, third, and fourth paragraphs, and the conclusion forms the fifth paragraph of the essay.

As you are learning to write a five-paragraph essay, it will help you to remember the outline for the three-paragraph essay that you have already learned. Look at the two outlines in Reference 31 on page 24 in your book.

Let's compare and discuss the differences between the three-paragraph essay and the five-paragraph essay. Notice that the introduction and conclusion are the same for both essays. Also, notice that the body of the five-paragraph essay has three paragraphs. Each point and its supporting sentences are a separate paragraph in the body of the five-paragraph essay.

CHAPTER 10 LESSON 5 CONTINUED

Reference 31: Three- Paragraph Essay and Five-Paragraph Essay	
Outline of a 3-Paragraph Essay	**Outline of a 5-Paragraph Essay**
I. Title	I. Title

II. Paragraph 1 – Introduction (3 sentences)
  A. Topic and general number sentence
  B. Extra information about the topic sentence
  C. Three-point sentence
	II. Paragraph 1 - Introduction (3 sentences)
	  A. Topic and general number sentence
	  B. Extra information about the topic sentence
	  C. Three-point sentence

III. Paragraph 2 – Body   (6-9 sentences)
  A. **First-point** sentence
  B. One or two **supporting** sentences
     for the first point
  C. **Second-point** sentence
  D. One or two **supporting** sentence
     for the second point
  E. **Third-point** sentence
  F. One or two **supporting** sentences
     for the third point
	III. Paragraph 2 - First Point Body (3-4 sentences)
	  A. **First-point** sentence
	  B. Two or three **supporting** sentences for the first point
	
	IV. Paragraph 3 – Second Point Body (3-4 sentences)
	  A. **Second-point** sentence
	  B. Two or three **supporting** sentences for the second
	     point
	
	V. Paragraph 4 – Third Point Body (3-4 sentences)
	  A. **Third-point** sentence
	  B. Two or three **supporting** sentences for the third point

IV. Paragraph 3 – Conclusion (2 sentences)
  A. Concluding general statement
  B. Concluding summary sentence
	VI. Paragraph 5 – Conclusion (2 sentences)
	  A. Concluding general statement
	     (Restatement of the topic sentence)
	  B. Concluding summary sentence
	     (Restatement of the enumeration sentence)

You will learn how to write each sentence and paragraph in the five-paragraph expository essay by following the steps in Reference 32 on pages 25 and 26 in your book. (*Read and discuss Reference 30 with your students. The reference box is located on the next page.*)

CHAPTER 10 LESSON 5 CONTINUED

Reference 32: Steps in Writing a Five-Paragraph Expository Essay

WRITING TOPIC: Stamp-Collecting

THREE MAIN POINTS

♦ Select the points to list about the topic.
    1. Is inexpensive
    2. Gives sense of history
    3. Teaches one to observe

WRITING THE INTRODUCTION AND TITLE

1. <u>Sentence #1 - Topic Sentence</u>
Write the topic sentence by using the words in your topic and adding a general number word, such as *several, many, some*, or *numerous*, instead of the exact number of points you will discuss.
(Quite by accident, I discovered that, as a hobby, stamp collecting offers many rewards.)

2. <u>Sentence #2 - Extra Information about the topic sentence</u>
This sentence can clarify, explain, define, or just be an extra interesting comment about the topic sentence. If you need another sentence to complete your information, write an extra sentence here. If you write an extra sentence, your introductory paragraph will have four sentences in it instead of three and that is okay.
(Although some of my friends collect other things, like coins and rocks, I think I like my hobby best.)

3. <u>Sentence #3 – Three-point sentence</u>
This sentence will list the three points to be discussed in the order that you will present them in the body of your paper. You can list the points with or without the specific number in front.
(As hobbies go, it is inexpensive, it gives one a sense of history, and it teaches one to be a careful observer.) or **(My three favorite things about stamp collecting are these: it's an inexpensive hobby, it gives one a sense of history, and it teaches one to observe.)**

♦ <u>The Title</u> - Since there are many possibilities for titles, look at the topic and the three points listed about the topic. Use some of the words in the topic and write a phrase to tell what your paragraph is about. Your title can be short or long. Capitalize the first, last, and important words in your title.
(Why Stamp Collecting Is a Worthwhile Hobby)

WRITING THE BODY

4. <u>Sentence #4 - First Point</u> –Write a sentence stating your first point.
(One of the reasons I enjoy stamp collecting is that it is inexpensive.)

5. <u>Sentences #5 - #7 – Supporting Sentences</u> - Write two or three sentences that give more information about your first point.
(For one thing, rather than having to buy new stamps, one simply has to remove the postage stamps from each day's mail.) (Other than the cost of an album, which is nominal, and a package of gummed hinges for mounting, there are no other expenses.) (To be sure, one can collect stamps and not go broke.)

6. <u>Sentence #8 - Second Point</u> - Write a sentence stating your second point.
(Another reason I enjoy stamp collecting is that it gives one a sense of history.)

7. <u>Sentences #9 -#11 – Supporting Sentences</u> - Write two or three sentences that give more information about your second point.
(For example, stamps feature historical figures in our country's history – people like presidents, inventors, scientists, and authors of all types.) (They also feature major events in our nation's past – events such as natural disasters, wars, treaties, and various "firsts" in the fields of transportation and communication.) (Stamp collecting, as one can see, is a means of gaining perspective on what brought us as a nation to where we are today.)

                Level 5 Homeschool Teacher's Manual

CHAPTER 10 LESSON 5 CONTINUED

Reference 32: Steps in Writing a Five-Paragraph Expository Essay, Continued

8. <u>Sentence #12 - Third Point</u> – Write a sentence stating your third point.
   (I also enjoy stamp collecting because it teaches one to be a careful observer.)

9. <u>Sentences #13 - #15 – Supporting Sentences</u> - Write two or three sentences that give more information about your third point.
   (In order to place stamps properly on the pages of an album, one has to be sure the lettering corresponds – same style, same size, and same location.) (Besides that, one has to note whether the words "U. S. Postage" are located at the top or bottom of each stamp.) (Particularly with the early stamps, whose coloring in the various series remained the same, one has to observe the wording and its placement very carefully in order to place the stamps properly in the album.)

WRITING THE CONCLUSION

10. <u>Sentence #16 – Concluding General Statement</u> – Read the topic sentence again and then rewrite it using some of the same words to say the same thing in a different way.
    (To be sure, there are many advantages to stamp collecting.)

11. <u>Sentence #17 – Concluding Summary Sentence</u> - Read the three-point sentence again and then rewrite it, using some of the same words to say the same thing in a different way.
    (For those who collect stamps, the hobby can be extremely rewarding in more ways than one.)

SAMPLE FIVE-PARAGRAPH ESSAY

Why Stamp Collecting Is a Worthwhile Hobby

Quite by accident, I discovered that, as a hobby, stamp collecting offers many rewards. Although some of my friends collect other things, like coins and rocks, I think I like my Bobby best. As hobbies go, it is inexpensive, it gives one a sense of history, and it teaches one to be a careful observer.

One of the reasons that I enjoy stamp collecting is that it is inexpensive. For one thing, rather than having to buy new stamps, one simply has to remove the postage stamps from each day's mail. Other than the cost of an album, which is nominal, and a package of gummed hinges for mounting, there are no other expenses. To be sure, one can collect stamps and not go broke.

Another reason I enjoy stamp collecting is that it gives one a sense of history. For example, stamps feature historical figures in our country's history – people like presidents, inventors, scientists, and authors of all types. They also feature major events in our nation's past – events such as natural disasters, wars, treaties, and various "firsts" in the fields of transportation and communication. Stamp collecting, as one can see, is a means of gaining perspective on what brought us as a nation to where we are today.

I also enjoy stamp collecting because it teaches one to be a careful observer. In order to place stamps properly on the pages of an album, one has to be sure the lettering corresponds – same style, same size, and same location. Besides that, one has to note whether the words "U.S. Postage" are located at the top or bottom of each stamp. Particularly with the early stamps, whose coloring in the various series remained the same, one has to observe the wording and its placement very carefully in order to place the stamps properly in the album.

To be sure, there are many advantages to stamp collecting. For those who collect stamps, the hobby can be extremely rewarding in more ways than one.

CHAPTER 10 LESSON 5 CONTINUED

TEACHER INSTRUCTIONS FOR WRITING ASSIGNMENT

Give Writing Assignment #11 from the box below. For this writing assignment, students are to write a five-paragraph essay in first person. Remind students to follow the Writing Guidelines from Chapter 3 as they prepare their writings. Students are also encouraged to use the five-paragraph essay example and the essay outline in their Reference Section to do the writing assignment below.

Writing Assignment Box

Writing Assignment #11: Five-Paragraph Expository Essay (First Person)
Remind students that the 5-paragraph essay still has three parts: 1. Introduction 2. Body 3. Conclusion. The body now has three paragraphs instead of one.

Writing topic: Presidents/People I Admire or **My Favorite Movies**

Bonus Option: Write Psalms 23 in your Journal from memory. Then, write an essay that explains what this chapter in the Bible means to you.

TEACHING SCRIPT FOR USING THE WRITING PROCESS FOR THIS WRITING ASSIGNMENT

As you begin this writing assignment, you will start through the writing process. First, you will think about your topic and gather any information you might need in order to do the writing. Second, you will write a rough draft. Remember, it is called a rough draft because it will be revised and edited. You do not have to worry about mistakes as you write your rough draft. After you write the first draft, you will make revisions, using the Revision Checklist in Reference 4. After you revise your writing, you will edit, using the Beginning Editing Checklist in Reference 4. Finally, after you are satisfied with your revising and editing, you will write a final paper, using the Final Paper Checklist in Reference 4. You will then give the finished writing assignment to me.

TEACHER INSTRUCTIONS FOR CHECKING WRITING ASSIGNMENT

Read, check, and discuss Writing Assignment #11 after students have finished their final paper. Use the editing checklist (*Reference 4 on teacher's page 9*) as you check and discuss students' papers. Make sure students are using the editing checklist correctly. In the beginning, you must also check students' papers carefully for <u>form</u> mistakes. This will ensure that students are learning the three-point format correctly.

(End of lesson.)

Level 5 Homeschool Teacher's Manual

CHAPTER 11   LESSON 1

New objectives: Grammar (Practice Sentences), Skills (capitalization and punctuation of a friendly letter using rule numbers), Practice sheet, and Vocabulary #1.

 JINGLE TIME

Have students turn to the Jingle Section of their books. The teacher will lead the students in reciting the previously-taught jingles.

 GRAMMAR TIME

First-Year Option: Put the Practice Sentences from the box below on the board or notebook paper. Use these sentences as you practice the concepts that have been taught. For the greatest benefit, students must participate orally with the teacher. **Second-Year Option:** Have students classify the Practice Sentences independently on paper. Check students' sentences with the answers provided below. (*If you have the CDs for Practice Sentences, have students check their sentences with the CDs.*)

Chapter 11, Practice Sentences for Lesson 1
1. _____ Before the game, the coaches and players stood at the flagpole for devotions and introductions.
2. _____ Goodness! That deer almost ran into us on the dark highway near Traci's house!

TEACHING SCRIPT FOR PRACTICING PATTERN 1 SENTENCES

We will practice classifying Pattern 1 Sentences. We will classify the sentences together. Begin. (*You might have your students write the labels above the sentences at this time.*)

Question and Answer Flow for Sentence 1: Before the game, the coaches and players stood at the flagpole for devotions and introductions.	
1. Who stood at the flagpole for devotions and introductions? coaches and players - CSN, CSN	13. The - A
2. What is being said about coaches and players? coaches and players stood - V	14. SN V P1 Check
3. At - P	15. (Before the game) - Prepositional phrase
4. At what? flagpole - OP	16. (At the flagpole) - Prepositional phrase
5. The - A	17. (For devotions and introductions) - Prepositional phrase
6. For - P	18. Period, statement, declarative sentence
7. For what? devotions and introductions - COP, COP (compound object of the preposition, compound object of the preposition)	19. Go back to the verb - divide the complete subject from the complete predicate.
8. And - C	20. Is there an adverb exception? No.
9. And - C	21. Is this sentence in a natural or inverted order? Inverted - underline the subject parts once and the predicate parts twice.
10. The - A	
11. Before - P	
12. Before what? game - OP	

Classified Sentence:

```
                      P    A   OP   A  CSN   C  CSN    V    P   A   OP
          SN  V    (Before the game), the coaches and players / stood (at the flagpole)
          P1         P   COP    C    COP
                   (for devotions and introductions). D
```

CHAPTER 11 LESSON 1 CONTINUED

Question and Answer Flow for Sentence 2: Goodness! That deer almost ran into us on the dark highway near Traci's house!

1. What ran into us on the dark highway near Traci's house? deer - SN
2. What is being said about deer? deer ran - V
3. Into - P
4. Into whom? us - OP
5. On - P
6. On what? highway - OP
7. What kind of highway? dark - Adj
8. The - A
9. Near - P
10. Near what? house - OP
11. Whose house? Traci's - PNA
12. Ran how? almost - Adv
13. Which deer? that - Adj
14. Goodness - I
15. SN V P1 Check
16. (Into us) - Prepositional phrase
17. (On the dark highway) - Prepositional phrase
18. (Near Traci's house) - Prepositional phrase
19. Exclamation point, strong feeling, exclamatory sentence
20. Go back to the verb - divide the complete subject from the complete predicate.
21. Is there an adverb exception? Yes - change the line.
22. Is this sentence in a natural or inverted order? Natural - no change.

Classified		I		Adj	SN	Adv	V	P	OP	P	A	Adj	OP		P	PNA	OP	
Sentence:	SN V	Goodness! That deer / almost ran (into us) (on the dark highway) (near Traci's house)!																E
	P1																	

Use Sentences 1-2 that you just classified with your students to do an Oral Skill Builder Check. Use the guidelines below.

Oral Skill Builder Check

1. **Noun check.**
   (Say the job and then say the noun. Circle each noun.)

2. **Identify the nouns as singular or plural.**
   (Write S or P above each noun.)

3. **Identify the nouns as common or proper.**
   (Follow established procedure for oral identification.)

4. **Do a vocabulary check.**
   (Follow established procedure for oral identification.)

5. **Identify the complete subject and the complete predicate.** (Underline the complete subject once and the complete predicate twice.)

6. **Identify the simple subject and simple predicate.**
   (Underline the simple subject once and the simple predicate twice. Bold, or highlight, the lines.)

7. **Recite the irregular verb chart.**
   (Located on student page 17 and teacher page 143.)

CHAPTER 11 LESSON 1 CONTINUED

SKILL TIME

TEACHING SCRIPT FOR CAPITALIZATION AND PUNCTUATION OF A FRIENDLY LETTER, USING RULE NUMBERS ONLY

Today, you will learn how to apply the capitalization and punctuation rules to a friendly letter. A friendly letter is a letter written to talk to a friend or relative. The capitalization and punctuation rules apply to friendly letters in the same way they apply to any other type of writing. The only difference is that there are more address-related punctuation rules and a few new terms that you will learn as you punctuate letters. You do not have to learn the friendly letter form at this time because it has already been set up for you.

The first friendly letter you will use in Practice Time has already been corrected. The corrections are identified in bold type. You need only to put the rule number that justifies each capitalization or mark of punctuation in the bold type. I must also remind you to look at the editing guide to find the total number of errors you need to correct in each section. Remember that the end-mark total tells you how many sentences need end mark punctuation. For instance, if you have the number *five* beside the words END MARKS in your editing guide, it means there are five sentences in your letter. Also, make sure you pay attention to the greeting and closing of a friendly letter.

PRACTICE TIME

Have students turn to page 57 in the Practice Section of their books and find the skill under Chapter 11, Lesson 1, Practice. Go over the directions to make sure they understand what to do. Students must use the Reference Section in their books to find the capitalization and punctuation rule numbers to edit the friendly letter. They will write a rule number for each correction in bold type. Check and discuss the Practice after students have finished. (*Chapter 11, Lesson 1 Practice key is given on the next page.*)

VOCABULARY TIME

Assign Chapter 11, Vocabulary Words **#1** on page 7 in the Reference section for students to define in their Vocabulary notebooks. Tell students they are to use a dictionary or thesaurus to look up the meanings of the vocabulary words. After they write each word and its meaning, students are to write a sentence using the vocabulary word.

Chapter 11, Vocabulary Words #1
(solicitude, indifference, mandatory, required)

(End of lesson.)

CHAPTER 11 LESSON 1 CONTINUED

Chapter 11, Lesson 1, Practice 1

Write the capitalization and punctuation rule numbers for each correction in bold.

15   **15**
700 College Ave.
       16
14   **14**   **14**
Bigelow, South Carolina 73086
      7
11
May 4, 20—
     5

2   **7**
Dear Alicia,
     13

(1 or 8) **7**   **21**   **21**
Aunt Linda surprised me with two front row tickets to the concert at Wallace Arena

        11   **(1 or 7)** **7**   **23**   **1**
on the first day of June. Cindy Martin and the Marletts will be performing. Yes, I know
         1   **1** **10**

         1   **6**   **(1 or 6)**
you love their music. That is why I want you to take my other ticket.   I hope you can make
        1   **1**

       11   **1**
the concert in June. Write back soon.
       1   **1**

2
Your cousin,
      14
7
Ashley

Editing Guide: Capitals: 24   Commas: 5   Periods: 1   End marks: 6

CHAPTER 11   LESSON 2

New objectives: Grammar (Practice Sentences), Skills (capitalization and punctuation of a friendly letter using corrections), Practice sheet, and Vocabulary #2.

 JINGLE TIME

Have students turn to the Jingle Section of their books. The teacher will lead the students in reciting the previously-taught jingles.

 GRAMMAR TIME

First-Year Option: Put the Practice Sentences from the box below on the board or notebook paper. Use these sentences as you practice the concepts that have been taught. For the greatest benefit, students must participate orally with the teacher. **Second-Year Option:** Have students classify the Practice Sentences independently on paper. Check students' sentences with the answers provided below. (*If you have the CDs for Practice Sentences, have students check their sentences with the CDs.*)

Chapter 11, Practice Sentences for Lesson 2
1. _____ My dad's boss did not go on the company cruise.
2. _____ My dentist and his assistant are driving to Wisconsin in August for a dental seminar.

TEACHING SCRIPT FOR PRACTICING PATTERN 1 SENTENCES

We will practice classifying Pattern 1 Sentences. We will classify the sentences together. Begin. (*You might have your students write the labels above the sentences at this time.*)

Question and Answer Flow for Sentence 1: My dad's boss did not go on the company cruise.

1. Who did not go on the company cruise? boss - SN
2. What is being said about boss? boss did go - V
3. Did - HV
4. Did go how? not - Adv
5. On - P
6. On what? cruise - OP
7. What kind of cruise? company - Adj
8. The - A
9. Whose boss? dad's - PNA
10. Whose dad? my - PPA
11. SN V P1 Check
12. (On the company cruise) - Prepositional phrase
13. Period, statement, declarative sentence
14. Go back to the verb - divide the complete subject from the complete predicate.
15. Is there an adverb exception? No.
16. Is this sentence in a natural or inverted order? Natural - no change.

Classified Sentence:

```
                  PPA PNA   SN   HV Adv V   P  A   Adj    OP
          SN V    My  dad's boss / did not go (on the company cruise). D
          ——————
          P1
```

CHAPTER 11 LESSON 2 CONTINUED

Question and Answer Flow for Sentence 2: My dentist and his assistant are driving to Wisconsin in August for a dental seminar.

1. Who are driving to Wisconsin in August for a dental seminar? dentist and assistant - CSN, CSN
2. What is being said about dentist and assistant? dentist and assistant are driving - V
3. Are - HV
4. To - P
5. To what? Wisconsin - OP
6. In - P
7. In what? August - OP
8. For - P
9. For what? seminar - OP
10. What kind of seminar? dental - Adj
11. A - A

12. Whose assistant? his - PPA
13. And - C
14. Whose dentist? my - PPA
15. SN V P1 Check
16. (To Wisconsin) - Prepositional phrase
17. (In August) - Prepositional phrase
18. (For a dental seminar) - Prepositional phrase
19. Period, statement, declarative sentence
20. Go back to the verb - divide the complete subject from the complete predicate.
21. Is there an adverb exception? No.
22. Is this sentence in a natural or inverted order? Natural - no change.

Classified Sentence:

```
                    PPA CSN  C PPA CSN    HV  V    P   OP    P  OP    P  A  Adj
           SN  V    My dentist and his assistant / are driving (to Wisconsin) (in August) (for a dental
           P1                 OP
                    seminar).  D
```

TEACHER INSTRUCTIONS FOR A PATTERN 1 SENTENCE

Tell students that their sentence writing assignment today is to write a Pattern 1 sentence. They are to follow the same procedure used in the previous lessons. They should decide on their labels, arrange them in a selected order, write their sentences, and edit their sentences for improved word choices. (*Students do not have to write an Improved Sentence at this point unless you feel they need more one-on-one word choice writing practice.*) Make sure students check Reference 28 in Chapter 10 (*Student page 21*) for the sentence parts that can be used in a Pattern 1 sentence. Check and discuss the Pattern 1 sentence after students have finished. (*Independent sentence assignments will be given in an assignment box like the one below.*)

Sentence Writing Assignment Box

Independent Pattern 1 Sentence

(In order to write a Pattern 1 sentence, students should decide on their labels, arrange them in a selected order, write their sentences, and edit their sentences for improved word choices.)

SKILL TIME

TEACHING SCRIPT FOR CAPITALIZATION AND PUNCTUATION OF A FRIENDLY LETTER, USING CORRECTIONS ONLY

Your second friendly letter has not been punctuated. You are to write capitalization corrections above the capitalization mistakes and write the punctuation corrections where they belong in the letter. I must again remind you to look at the editing guide to find the total number of errors you need to correct in each section. Remember that the end mark total tells you how many sentences need end mark punctuation. You may also use your capitalization and punctuation rules as a reference if you need them.

CHAPTER 11 LESSON 2 CONTINUED

 PRACTICE TIME

Have students turn to page 58 in the Practice Section of their book and find the skill under Chapter 11, Lesson 2, Practice. Go over the directions to make sure they understand what to do. Remind students to look at the editing guide to find the total number of errors they need to correct in each section. Students may also use their capitalization and punctuation rules as a reference if they need them. Check and discuss the Practice after students have finished. (*Chapter 11, Lesson 2, Practice key is given below.*)

Chapter 11, Lesson 2, Practice 1

Write the capitalization and punctuation corrections only.

W   E   B
504 west egg blvd.
M   L   M
meadow lake, montana
S
september 16, 20—

D   U   C
dear uncle charles,

   I   I   S   H   P   A   B
    i heard about the honor you received at the indiana state highway police awards banquet.
W   C
we are very proud of your achievement. congratulations on such a high honor!

Y
your only nephew,
C
collin

Editing Guide:	Capitals: 21	Commas: 4	Periods: 1	End marks: 3

 VOCABULARY TIME

Assign Chapter 11, Vocabulary Words **#2** on page 7 in the Reference Section for students to define in their Vocabulary notebooks. Tell students they are to use a dictionary or thesaurus to look up the meanings of the vocabulary words. After they write each word and its meaning, students are to write a sentence using the vocabulary word.

Chapter 11, Vocabulary Words #2
(reprehensible, admirable, knoll, mound)

(End of lesson.)

CHAPTER 11 LESSON 3
New objectives: Grammar (Practice Sentences) and Test.

 JINGLE TIME

Have students turn to the Jingle Section of their books. The teacher will lead the students in reciting the previously-taught jingles.

 GRAMMAR TIME

First-Year Option: Put the Practice Sentences from the box below on the board or notebook paper. Use these sentences as you practice the concepts that have been taught. For the greatest benefit, students must participate orally with the teacher. **Second-Year Option:** Have students classify the Practice Sentences independently on paper. Check students' sentences with the answers provided below. (*If you have the CDs for Practice Sentences, have students check their sentences with the CDs.*)

Chapter 11, Practice Sentences for Lesson 3
____1. My niece and nephew finally camped near a small stream for the night.
____2. Did the guilty party confess to the theft of the highly-treasured seashell?

TEACHING SCRIPT FOR PRACTICING PATTERN 1 SENTENCES

We will practice classifying Pattern 1 Sentences. We will classify the sentences together. Begin.

Question and Answer Flow for Sentence 1: **My niece and nephew finally camped near a small stream for the night.**	
1. Who camped near a small stream for the night? niece and nephew - CSN, CSN	10. Camped when? finally - Adv
	11. And - C
2. What is being said about niece and nephew? niece and nephew camped - V	12. Whose niece and nephew? my - PPA
	13. SN V P1 Check
3. Near - P	14. (Near a small stream) - Prepositional phrase
4. Near what? stream - OP	15. (For the night) - Prepositional phrase
5. What kind of stream? small - Adj	16. Period, statement, declarative sentence
6. A -A	17. Go back to the verb - divide the complete subject from the complete predicate.
7. For - P	
8. For what? night - OP	18. Is there an adverb exception? Yes - change the line.
9. The - A	19. Is this sentence in a natural or inverted order? Natural - no change.

Classified Sentence:		PPA	CSN	C	CSN	Adv	V	P	A	Adj	OP	P	A	OP	
	SN V **P1**	My	niece	and	nephew /	finally	camped	(near	a	small	stream)	(for	the	night).	**D**

CHAPTER 11 LESSON 3 CONTINUED

Question and Answer Flow for Sentence 2: Did the guilty party confess to the theft of the highly-treasured seashell?

1. Who did confess to the theft of the highly-treasured seashell? party - SN
2. What is being said about party? party did confess - V
3. Did - HV
4. To - P
5. To what? theft - OP
6. The - A
7. Of - P
8. Of what? seashell - OP
9. What kind of seashell? highly-treasured - Adj
10. The - A
11. What kind of party? guilty - Adj

12. The - A
13. SN V P1 Check
14. (To the theft) - Prepositional phrase
15. (Of the highly-treasured seashell) - Prepositional phrase
16. Question mark, question, interrogative sentence
17. Go back to the verb - divide the complete subject from the complete predicate.
18. Is there an adverb exception? No.
19. Is this sentence in a natural or inverted order? Inverted - underline the subject parts once and the predicate parts twice.

Classified
Sentence:

		HV	A	Adj	SN		V		P	A	OP	P	A	Adj		OP	

SN V P1 Did the guilty party / confess (to the theft) (of the highly-treasured seashell)? Int

---

 STUDY TIME

Have students study the vocabulary words in their vocabulary notebooks. Tell students that any vocabulary word in their notebooks could be on their test. Also, have students study any of the skills in the Practice Section that they need to review. Students should also study their homonym chart.

 TEST TIME

Have students turn to page 92 in the Test Section of their book and find Chapter 11 Test A. Students should use the Reference Section in their books to find the capitalization and punctuation rule numbers to edit the sentence and friendly letter. Remind them to pay attention and think about what they are doing. Go over the directions to make sure they understand what to do. (*Chapter 11A Test key is on the next page.*)

 CHECK TIME

After students have finished, check and discuss their test papers. Make sure they understand why their answers are right or wrong. (*For total points, count each required answer as a point.*)

 WRITING TIME

Have students make an entry in their journals.

(End of lesson.)

Chapter 11 Test A
(Student Page 92)

Exercise 1: <u>Sentence</u>: Write the capitalization and punctuation rule numbers for each correction in bold.

```
     1            9  10 10 7                  13           13                    3              3
1. My teacher, Ms. E.L. Summers, won the Caldecott Award for her story Thanksgiving Blessings.
            11   16  17 17          11                                              22              22
```

Editing Guide:	Capitals: 9	Commas: 2	Periods: 3	End marks: 1	Underlining: 1

Exercise 2: <u>Friendly Letter</u>: Write the capitalization and punctuation corrections only.

```
                                                                P        D
                                                                927 pickwick drive
                                                                A    K
                                                                alex, kentucky
                                                                A
                                                                aug. 21, 20—
   D     A   C
   dear aunt carol,
        T                                               C            I
      thank you for the digital camera you gave us for christmas.  it's so much fun to take snapshots
                    M        I                                                    I
   of the new baby.  mom and i have been putting all the pictures into a scrapbook.  i can't wait

   for you to see it.

                                                                Y
                                                                your grateful niece,
                                                                P        P
                                                                photo phyllis
```

Editing Guide:	Capitals: 17	Commas: 4	Periods: 1	Apostrophes: 2	End marks: 4

Exercise 3: Name the eight parts of speech that you have studied. *(Accept answers in any order.)*

1. **noun**   2. **verb**   3. **adjective**   4. **adverb**   5. **preposition**   6. **pronoun**   7. **conjunction**   8. **interjection**

Exercise 4: Identify each pair of words as synonyms or antonyms by putting parentheses ( ) around *syn* or *ant*.

1. knoll, mound	**(syn)** ant	5. void, vacant	**(syn)** ant	9. mandatory, required	**(syn)** ant
2. myth, fact	syn **(ant)**	6. perpetual, constant	**(syn)** ant	10. spontaneous, forced	syn **(ant)**
3. ethical, carnal	syn **(ant)**	7. solicitude, indifference	syn **(ant)**	11. repulsive, amiable	syn **(ant)**
4. truth, veracity	**(syn)** ant	8. escalate, expand	**(syn)** ant	12. reprehensible, admirable	syn **(ant)**

Exercise 5: Underline the correct homonym in each sentence.

1. The pastor knelt at the (<u>altar</u>, alter).
2. We have a beautiful (<u>calendar</u>, calender) in our office.
3. The teacher (cent, <u>sent</u>, scent) her to the office.
4. Mary was (<u>confident</u>, confidant) that she would win the award.
5. Sam loves chocolate (desert, <u>dessert</u>).
6. The books were a (fare, <u>fair</u>) price.
7. The pipes were full of (<u>leaks</u>, leeks).
8. My mother had a (<u>tear</u>, tier) in her eye.

Exercise 6: In your journal, write a paragraph summarizing what you have learned this week.

Level 5 Homeschool Teacher's Manual

CHAPTER 11   LESSON 4

New objectives: Test and an Activity.

TEST TIME

Have students turn to page 93 in the Test Section of their book and find Chapter 11 Test B. Students should use the Reference Section in their books to find the capitalization and punctuation rule numbers to edit the sentence and friendly letter. Remind them to pay attention and think about what they are doing. Go over the directions to make sure they understand what to do. (*Chapter 11B Test key is on the next page.*)

CHECK TIME

After students have finished, check and discuss their test papers. Make sure they understand why their answers are right or wrong. (*For total points, count each required answer as a point.*)

ACTIVITY / ASSIGNMENT TIME

Using Reference 30 on page 23 as an example, create a test for capitalization and punctuation. Compose a letter and a sentence that must be corrected. Make an editing guide that tells how many mistakes are in each one. Write directions to tell what should be done. Make a key that shows the correct answers. Give your capitalization and punctuation test to a family member or friend. Check the test after it has been completed. (*Discuss what students learned as they completed this project.*)

(End of lesson.)

Chapter 11 Test B
(Student Page 93)

Exercise 1: Classify each sentence.

```
              P  A     Adj       OP   SP   V        Adv            P   PPA   Adj    OP
1. SN  V     (In an argumentative tone), they / debated mercilessly (about their senior trip).  D
   P1
              (You) SP    V   P   A    OP      P   A    Adj   OP     P    A     OP
2. SN  V     / Wait (at the crosswalk) (for the traffic light) (during the procession).  D
   P1
                 A    Adj     SN    P   OP     Adv     V    P   A    Adj    OP
3. SN  V     An unbelievable number (of inmates) / recently escaped (from the prison farm).  D
   P1
```

Exercise 2: <u>Sentence</u>: Write the capitalization and punctuation corrections only.

```
   I              T          L    R    I              R
```
1. i thought of the <u>titanic</u> when larry, ricky, and i boarded our ship for russia.

Editing Guide: Capitals: 6   Commas: 2   Underline: 1   End marks: 1

Exercise 3: <u>Friendly Letter</u>: Write the capitalization and punctuation rule numbers for each correction in bold.

15   15   15
20178 North Birch Street

14   14   14
Russell Falls, Oregon 91218
                    7
11
May 23, 20—
                5

2   7
Dear Martin,
   13

    (1 or 6)   (1 or 6) 9 7 (1 or 6)

I just graduated from college with my degree in medicine. I am now Dr. Lee. I can hardly
                                                                   1   16   1

        1   21   21

believe it! It seems like just yesterday that we walked across the platform at Westville Stadium.
      3   1

(1)   9 7   1

Do you remember when Mr. Harding handed us our high school diploma? Those were the days!
                        16   2   3

(1 or 6)   1   9 7

I am looking forward to coming to your graduation soon. Best wishes, Dr. Adams!
                                                    1   12 16   3
                                                                          2

Your best bud,
            14
7   7
Allen Lee

Editing Guide: Capitals: 28   Commas: 5   Periods: 3   Apostrophes: 0   End marks: 8

CHAPTER 11 LESSON 4 CONTINUED

TEACHER INSTRUCTIONS

Use the Question and Answer Flows below for the sentences on Chapter 11B Test.

Question and Answer Flow for Sentence 1: In an argumentative tone, they debated mercilessly about their senior trip.

1. Who debated mercilessly about their senior trip? they - SP
2. What is being said about they? they debated - V
3. Debated how? mercilessly - Adv
4. About - P
5. About what? trip - OP
6. What kind of trip? senior - Adj
7. Whose trip? their - PPA
8. In - P
9. In what? tone - OP
10. What kind of tone? argumentative - Adj
11. An - A

12. SN V P1 Check
13. (In an argumentative tone) - Prepositional phrase
14. (About their senior trip) - Prepositional phrase
15. Period, statement, declarative sentence
16. Go back to the verb - divide the complete subject from the complete predicate.
17. Is there an adverb exception? No.
18. Is this sentence in natural or inverted order? Inverted - underline the subject parts once and the predicate parts twice.

Classified Sentence:

<pre>
                          P A   Adj   OP   SP   V   Adv   P PPA Adj OP
        SN V   (In an argumentative tone), they / debated mercilessly (about their senior trip). D
        P1
</pre>

Question and Answer Flow for Sentence 2: Wait at the crosswalk for the traffic light during the procession.

1. Who wait at the crosswalk for the traffic light during the procession? (You) - SP (understood subject pronoun)
2. What is being said about you? you wait - V
3. At - P
4. At what? crosswalk - OP
5. The - A
6. For - P
7. For what? light - OP
8. What kind of light? traffic - Adj
9. The - A
10. During - P
11. During what? procession - OP

12. The - A
13. SN V P1 Check
14. (At the crosswalk) - Prepositional phrase
15. (For the traffic light) - Prepositional phrase
16. (During the procession) - Prepositional phrase
17. Period, command, imperative sentence
18. Go back to the verb - divide the complete subject from the complete predicate.
19. Is there an adverb exception? No.
20. Is this sentence in a natural or inverted order? Natural - no change.

Classified Sentence:

<pre>
               (You) SP   V   P A   OP   P A   Adj OP   P   A   OP
        SN V   / Wait (at the crosswalk) (for the traffic light) (during the procession). Imp
        P1
</pre>

Question and Answer Flow for Sentence 3: An unbelievable number of inmates recently escaped from the prison farm.

1. Who escaped from the prison farm? number - SN
2. What is being said about number? number escaped - V
3. From - P
4. From what? farm - OP
5. What kind of farm? prison - Adj
6. The - A
7. Escaped when? recently - Adv
8. Of - P
9. Of whom? inmates - OP
10. Which number? unbelievable - Adj

11. An - A
12. SN V P1 Check
13. (Of inmates) - Prepositional phrase
14. (From the prison farm) - Prepositional phrase
15. Period, statement, declarative sentence
16. Go back to the verb - divide the complete subject from the complete predicate.
17. Is there an adverb exception? Yes - change the line.
18. Is this sentence in a natural or inverted order? Natural - no change.

Classified Sentence:

<pre>
               A   Adj   SN   P   OP   Adv   V   P   A   Adj   OP
        SN V   An unbelievable number (of inmates) / recently escaped (from the prison farm). D
        P1
</pre>

CHAPTER 11   LESSON 5

New objectives: Writing (persuasive essay) and Writing Assignment #12.

 WRITING TIME

TEACHING SCRIPT FOR A PERSUASIVE ESSAY

Persuasion means getting other people to see things your way. When you write a persuasive essay, you choose for your topic something you want to "persuade" people to do or believe. A persuasive essay expresses an opinion and tries to convince the reader that this opinion is correct. Persuading someone to agree with you requires careful thinking and planning. As the writer, you must make the issue clear and present facts and reasons that give strong support to your opinion. You are encouraging your audience to take a certain action or to feel the same way you do.

In attempting to persuade anyone to your way of thinking, it is VERY important to consider just who the reader is that you are trying to persuade. Your reader is your audience. When you know who your reader is, you must use persuasive reasoning that will appeal to that reader. Know your reader well enough to use arguments that will appeal to him/her. You would not use the same kind of argument to persuade your five-year-old sister to tell you where she hid your skates that you would use to persuade your parents to allow you to have friends over for the night.

The three-point writing format is one of the best ways to present your persuasive argument because it gives you an organized way of stating your opinion and supporting it. The persuasive writing format is the same as your earlier expository writing format. They both use the three-point organization. The differences between persuasive and expository writings are your purpose for writing, the content of your paper, and the wording of your sentences.

You will find that the main difference is that the topic sentence is an opinion statement. In addition, all the points and supporting sentences are persuasive in nature and are intended to back up the opinion statement. Remember, persuasive writing states your opinion with supporting facts that try to convince your reader to think or act in a certain way, and expository writing attempts to give an explanation or information to your reader.

We will go through the steps for writing a persuasive essay by reading and discussing the guidelines for a three-paragraph persuasive essay in Reference 33 on page 27 in your book. You actually have two guidelines in your reference box. Let's go through the persuasive essay first so you will know all the parts.

Your first paragraph is an introductory paragraph and will have three sentences. Sentence #1 is the <u>Topic Sentence.</u> You will state your opinion in the topic sentence:
Every town needs biking trails.

Sentence #2 is the <u>Reason Sentence.</u> You will give a general reason why you think the topic sentence is true:
They would provide safety for children who especially enjoy riding bikes, either alone or with their friends.

Sentence #3 is the <u>General Number Sentence.</u> You will use a general number word and restate the main idea in the topic sentence:
There are some obvious safety benefits for bikers and non-bikers that would come from biking trails.

CHAPTER 11 LESSON 5 CONTINUED

The second paragraph is the body of the essay and will have 6 sentences. Sentence #4 is the <u>First-Point Persuasive Sentence.</u> You will give your first reason to support your opinion:
One of the obvious benefits of a biking trail is that it would keep children off the streets.
Sentence #5 is the <u>First-Point Supporting Sentence.</u> You will give an example that supports and explains your first point:
Since streets are heavily traveled, biking trails would lessen the risk of bicycle accidents.

Sentence #6 is the <u>Second-Point Persuasive Sentence.</u> You will give your second reason to support your opinion:
Another benefit of a biking trail is that it would free the sidewalks for pedestrian traffic.
Sentence #7 is the <u>Second-Point Supporting Sentence.</u> You will give an example that supports and explains your second point:
In most instances, sidewalks will not accommodate both bikers and walkers without someone being hurt or inconvenienced.

Sentence #8 is the <u>Third-Point Persuasive Sentence.</u> You will give your third reason to support your opinion:
A third reason for a biking trail is that it would give bikers better exposure to the outdoors.
Sentence #9 is the <u>Third-Point Supporting Sentence.</u> You will give an example that supports and explains your third point:
Bikers could enjoy the luxuries of wildflowers and wildlife of various types on a biking trail and without the impediments of intersections and stop signs.

The third paragraph is the conclusion of the essay and will have two concluding sentences. The first concluding sentence is simply a restatement sentence that forcefully restates your original opinion in the topic sentence and usually starts with IN CONCLUSION. Sentence #10 is the <u>In Conclusion Sentence:</u>
In conclusion, in every community, the young and old alike would benefit from a biking trail.

The second concluding sentence is a summary sentence. This sentence summarizes one or more of the reasons stated. Sentence #11 is the <u>Final Summary Sentence:</u>
A biking trail would increase the security and pleasure of bikers, walkers, and drivers alike.

You have just learned how to write a three-paragraph persuasive essay. With that knowledge, I will now show you how to expand a three-paragraph persuasive essay into a five-paragraph persuasive essay. It will be just like the five-paragraph expository essay. Let's go over the steps.

1. The first paragraph has three sentences: the <u>Topic</u> sentence, the <u>Reason</u> sentence, and the <u>General</u> number sentence.
2. The second paragraph has the <u>First</u> point and two or three <u>Supporting</u> sentences for the first point.
3. The third paragraph has the <u>Second</u> point and two or three <u>Supporting</u> sentences for the second point.
4. The fourth paragraph has the <u>Third</u> point and two or three <u>Supporting</u> sentences for the third point.
5. The fifth paragraph has two sentences: the <u>In-conclusion</u> sentence and the <u>Final Summary</u> sentence.

Sometimes, you will only want to write a persuasive paragraph, not an essay. We will now go through the persuasive paragraph so you will know all the parts and will be familiar with the patterns for persuasive paragraphs and essays. Look at the persuasive paragraph guidelines in Reference 33. (*Read and discuss the guidelines for a persuasive paragraph and a persuasive essay in the reference box on the next page with your students. Make sure you use the sample essay to point out how each sentence is made.*)

CHAPTER 11 LESSON 5 CONTINUED

Reference 33: Persuasive Paragraph and Essay Guidelines	
Guidelines for a Persuasive Paragraph	Guidelines for a 3-Paragraph Persuasive Essay

Paragraph   (10-13 sentences)
A. **Topic** sentence (opinion statement)
B. **General number** sentence
C. **First-point** persuasive sentence
D. 1 or 2 **supporting** sentences for the first point
E. **Second-point** persuasive sentence
F. 1 or 2 **supporting** sentences for the second point
G. **Third-point** persuasive sentence
H. 1 or 2 **supporting** sentences for the third point
I. **In conclusion** sentence (Repeat topic idea)
J. **Final summary** sentence (Summarize reasons)
	1. Paragraph 1 – Introduction (3 sentences)
	  A. **Topic** sentence (opinion statement)
	  B. **Reason** sentence
	  C. **General number** sentence
	2. Paragraph 2 – Body (6-9 sentences)
	  A. **First-point** persuasive sentence
	  B. 1 or 2 **supporting** sentences for the first point
	  C. **Second-point** persuasive sentence
	  D. 1 or 2 **supporting** sentences for the second point
	  E. **Third-point** persuasive sentence
	  F. 1 or 2 **supporting** sentences for the third point
	3. Paragraph 3 - Conclusion (2 sentences)
	  A. **In conclusion** sentence (Repeat topic idea)
	  B. **Final summary** sentence (Summarize reasons)

Need for Biking Trails

Every town needs biking trails. They would provide safety for children who especially enjoy riding bikes, either alone or with their friends. There are some obvious safety benefits for bikers and non-bikers that would come from biking trails.

One of the obvious benefits of a biking trail is that it would keep children off the streets. Since streets are heavily traveled, biking trails would lessen the risk of bicycle accidents. Another benefit of a biking trail is that it would free the sidewalks for pedestrian traffic. In most instances, sidewalks will not accommodate both bikers and walkers without someone being hurt or inconvenienced. A third reason for a biking trail is that it would give bikers better exposure to the outdoors. Bikers could enjoy the luxuries of wildflowers and wildlife of various types on a biking trail and without the impediments of intersections and stop signs.

In conclusion, in every community, the young and old alike would benefit from a biking trail. A biking trail would increase the security and pleasure of bikers, walkers, and drivers alike.

Now, you will write, revise, and edit a persuasive essay. As you edit, make sure you use all the checklists in Reference 4. Remember to read through the whole essay, starting with the title. After you are satisfied with your revising and editing, you will write a final paper, using the Final Paper Checklist in Reference 4. You will then give the finished writing assignment to me.

Writing Assignment Box

Writing Assignment #12: Three-Paragraph Persuasive Essay (First Person)
(Remind students that first-person pronouns are *I, we, me, us, my, our, mine,* and *ours.*)
Writing topic choices: Why an Education Is Important   or   Why Praying Is Important

---

Read, check, and discuss the final paper for Writing Assignment #12 after students have finished writing, revising, and editing their writing assignment. Use the checklists in Reference 4 as you check and discuss students' papers.

(End of lesson.)

CHAPTER 12   LESSON 1

New objectives: Jingles (the direct object), Grammar (Introductory Sentences, direct objects, transitive verbs, adding direct objects to the Noun Check), Vocabulary #1, and an Activity.

 **JINGLE TIME**

Have students turn to the Jingle Section in their books and recite the previously-taught jingles. Then, lead students in reciting the new jingle (*The Direct Object*) below. Practice the new jingle several times until students can recite it smoothly. Emphasize reciting with a rhythm. Students and teacher should be together! (*Do not try to explain the jingle at this time. Just have fun reciting it.*)

Teacher's Note: Do not spend a large amount of time practicing the new jingles. Students learn the jingles best by spending a small amount of time consistently, **every** day.

Jingle 16:   The Direct Object Jingle
1. A direct object is a noun or pronoun.
2. A direct object completes the meaning of the sentence.
3. A direct object is located after the verb-transitive.
4. To find the direct object, ask WHAT or WHOM after your verb.

 GRAMMAR TIME

Put the introductory sentences from the box below on the board. Use these sentences as you go through each new concept covered in your teaching script. For the greatest benefit, students must participate orally with the teacher. (*You might put the introductory sentences on notebook paper if you are doing one-on-one instruction with your students.*)

Chapter 12, Introductory Sentences for Lesson 1
1. _____ The custodians waxed the floors.
2. _____ For a week, the conscientious custodians earnestly waxed the floors.
3. _____ Could the elderly folks on your street hear the sirens?

TEACHING SCRIPT FOR DIRECT OBJECTS AND TRANSITIVE VERBS

We have been studying Pattern 1, which has only the subject noun and verb as its main parts (N V). Now, we will learn a new sentence pattern. This new sentence pattern is called Pattern 2, and it will have some new parts that you will learn today. Pattern 2 is different from Pattern 1 because its main parts are noun, verb, noun (N V N). The second noun is called a direct object. There are five things you need to know about a direct object. For this information, look at Reference 34 on page 24 in the Reference Section of your book and follow along as I read this information to you.

CHAPTER 12 LESSON 1 CONTINUED

I want you to notice that these five things are very similar to the direct object jingle. You will read the example with me so you will know what to say when you classify Pattern 2 sentences. (*Read the information about direct objects to your students. Then, have students read and classify the sample sentence orally, with you.*)

Reference 34: Direct Object, Verb-transitive, and Pattern 2

1. A **direct object** is a noun or pronoun after the verb that completes the meaning of the sentence.

2. A **direct object** is labeled as DO.

3. To find the **direct object**, ask WHAT or WHOM after the verb.

4. A **direct object** must be verified to mean someone or something different from the subject noun.

5. A **verb-transitive** is an action verb with a direct object after it and is labeled V-t. (Whatever receives the action of a transitive verb is the direct object.)

Sample Sentence for the exact words to say to find the direct object and transitive verb.

1. Larry rides a mule.
2. Who rides a mule? Larry - SN
3. What is being said about Larry? Larry rides - V
4. Larry rides what? mule - verify the noun
5. Does mule mean the same thing as Larry? No.
6. Mule - DO (*Say: mule - direct object.*)
7. Rides - V-t (*Say: rides - verb-transitive.*)
8. A - A

9. SN V-t DO P2 Check (*Say: Subject Noun, Verb-transitive, Direct Object, Pattern 2, Check.*) (*This first check is to make sure the "t" is added to the verb.*)
10. Verb-transitive - check again. (*"Check again" means to check for prepositional phrases and then go through the rest of the question and answer flow.*)
11. No prepositional phrases.
12. Period, statement, declarative sentence.
13. Go back to the verb - divide the complete subject from the complete predicate.
14. Is there an adverb exception? No.
15. Is this sentence in a natural or inverted order? Natural - no change.

Earlier you learned that nouns can have different jobs, or functions, in a sentence. You have studied two of these jobs already: A noun can be a subject, or a noun can be an object of a preposition. You must remember, however, that a noun used as a subject is a <u>core part of a sentence pattern</u> (like **SN V**). But a noun that is used as an object of a preposition is not a core part of a sentence pattern. Nouns used as objects of prepositions can be used with every sentence pattern since they are not part of the core in the pattern.

You will now study how nouns function in different sentence patterns. The first pattern, **Pattern 1**, has a *Noun Verb* for the core sentence pattern and is written **N V**. However, notice that when you write Pattern 1 in Shurley English, you write **SN V** because you name the job of each core part as well, which is *Subject Noun / Verb.* You will also add the pattern number to each pattern to make it easier to identify. Therefore, the **first pattern** in Shurley English is *subject noun / verb / Pattern 1,* and it is written as **SN V P1**.

In the new sentence pattern, **Pattern 2**, there are two nouns in the core sentence pattern: **N V N.** The first noun is a subject noun and is still written as **SN**. The second noun will always come after the verb (*as its position in the pattern indicates*) and is required to complete the meaning of the sentence. This second noun is called a direct object and is written with the abbreviation **DO**. Any time there is a direct object in a sentence pattern, the verb is transitive and is written as **V-t** to indicate that it is an action verb used with a direct object noun. The **second pattern** in Shurley English is *subject noun / verb-transitive / direct object / Pattern 2,* and it is written as **SN V-t DO P2**.

CHAPTER 12 LESSON 1 CONTINUED

What is Pattern 2? (*SN V-t DO*) What are the core parts of a Pattern 2 sentence? (*SN V-t DO*) What parts of speech are used in a Pattern 2 sentence? (*N V N*) You will use what you have just learned as you classify Sentences 1-3 with me to find the direct object and verb-transitive. As we classify the sentences together, I will show you how to say the new part as we say the Question and Answer Flow. Begin.

Question and Answer Flow for Sentence 1: The custodians waxed the floors.

1. Who waxed the floors? custodians - SN
2. What is being said about custodians? custodians waxed - V
3. Custodians waxed what? floors - verify the noun

Note: "Verify the noun" is a check to make sure the second noun does not mean the same thing as the subject noun. If it does not, then the second noun is a direct object.

4. Do floors mean the same thing as custodians? No.
5. Floors – DO (Direct object)
6. Waxed - V-t (Verb-transitive)

Note: Always ask the WHAT question immediately after finding the SN and V to get the DO. Mark the verb with a V until the DO has been identified. After you verify that the noun is a direct object, mark your verb as transitive by adding the "t" to the main verb.

The verb is changed to a V-t when a direct object has been identified. Always get the core, SN V-t DO, before you classify the rest of the sentence.

7. The - A
8. The - A
9. SN V-t DO P2 Check
(Subject noun, Verb-transitive, Direct object, Pattern 2 Check)
(Write *SN V-t DO P2* in the blank beside the sentence.)

Note: Check for the "t" on the verb by saying, verb transitive. Check for prepositional phrases by saying, "check again".

10. Verb-transitive - Check again.
11. No prepositional phrases.
12. Period, statement, declarative sentence
13. Go back to the verb - divide the complete subject from the complete predicate.
14. Is there an adverb exception? No.
15. Is this sentence in a natural or inverted order? Natural - no change.

Classified Sentence:

```
                        A    SN      V-t   A    DO
        SN  V-t      The custodians / waxed the floors.  D
        DO  P2
```

Teacher's Notes: A verb-transitive check has been added for Pattern 2 sentences because students tend to forget to add the "t" to the verb, even after they say verb-transitive while classifying the direct object. If they leave the "t" off, it is wrong. This is the reason the verb-transitive check is so important for them to remember.

Question and Answer Flow for Sentence 2: For a week, the conscientious custodians earnestly waxed the floors.

1. Who waxed the floors? custodians - SN
2. What is being said about custodians? custodians waxed - V
3. Custodians waxed what? floors - verify the noun
4. Do floors mean the same thing as custodians? No.
5. Floors - DO
6. Waxed - V-t
7. The - A
8. Waxed how? earnestly - Adv
9. What kind of custodians? conscientious - Adj
10. The - A
11. For - P
12. For what? week - OP

13. A - A
14. SN V-t DO P2 Check
15. Verb-transitive - Check again.
16. (For a week) - Prepositional phrase
17. Period, statement, declarative sentence
18. Go back to the verb - divide the complete subject from the complete predicate.
19. Is there an adverb exception? Yes - change the line.
20. Is this sentence in a natural or inverted order? Inverted - underline the subject parts once and the predicate parts twice.

Classified Sentence:

```
                     P   A  OP   A     Adj        SN       Adv    V-t   A   DO
        SN  V-t   (For a week), the conscientious custodians / earnestly waxed the floors.  D
        DO  P2
```

CHAPTER 12 LESSON 1 CONTINUED

Question and Answer Flow for Sentence 3: Could the elderly folks on your street hear the sirens?

1. Who could hear the sirens? folks - SN
2. What is being said about folks? folks could hear - V
3. Could - HV
4. Folks could hear what? sirens - verify the noun
5. Do sirens mean the same thing as folks? No.
6. Sirens - DO
7. Hear - V-t
8. The - A
9. On - P
10. On what? street - OP
11. Whose street? your - PPA
12. What kind of folks? elderly - Adj
13. The - A
14. SN V-t DO P2 Check
15. Verb-transitive - Check again.
16. (On your street) - Prepositional phrase
17. Question mark, question, interrogative sentence
18. Go back to the verb - divide the complete subject from the complete predicate.
19. Is there an adverb exception? No.
20. Is this sentence in a natural or inverted order? Inverted - underline the subject parts once and the predicate parts twice.

Classified Sentence:

          HV   A   Adj   SN   P   PPA   OP   V-t   A   DO
SN V-t   Could the elderly folks (on your street) / hear the sirens? Int
DO P2

Teacher's Notes: Question and Answer Flow Notice.

For consistency, the Question and Answer Flow will verify the direct object by using the verb **Do** if the direct object is plural and **Does** if the direct object is singular.

Example: He bought two trucks. Q & A: <u>Do trucks</u> mean the same thing as he?

On the other hand, you may prefer to use the singular form because you are actually saying, "Does the **word** *trucks* mean the same thing as he?" Therefore, if you choose to use the singular verb form, just make the necessary change whenever it occurs.

Example: He bought two trucks. Q & A: <u>Does trucks</u> mean the same thing as he?

TEACHING SCRIPT FOR ADDING THE DIRECT OBJECTS TO THE NOUN CHECK

Name the noun jobs we have had before today. (*SN and OP*) Today, we have added another noun job. What is the new noun job that we have just added? (*direct object—DO*) So, if I want to find nouns in a sentence, where would I go? (*To the SN, OP, and DO jobs*) After I go to the subject noun, object of the preposition, and direct object jobs, what do I do next? (*Check each job to see if the word is a noun or a pronoun. If it is a pronoun, move to the next job. If it is a noun, circle it to indicate that it is a noun.*)

Oral Skill Builder Check

1. **Noun check.**
   (Say the job and then say the noun. Circle each noun.)

2. **Identify the nouns as singular or plural.**
   (Write S or P above each noun.)

3. **Identify the nouns as common or proper.**
   (Follow established procedure for oral identification.)

4. **Do a vocabulary check.**
   (Follow established procedure for oral identification.)

5. **Identify the complete subject and the complete predicate.** (Underline the complete subject once and the complete predicate twice.)

6. **Identify the simple subject and simple predicate.**
   (Underline the simple subject once and the simple predicate twice. Bold, or highlight, the lines.)

7. **Recite the irregular verb chart.**
   (Located on student page 17 and teacher page 143.)

CHAPTER 12 LESSON 1 CONTINUED

WRITING TIME

Have students make an entry in their journals.

VOCABULARY TIME

Assign Chapter 12, Vocabulary Words **#1** on page 7 in the Reference Section for students to define in their Vocabulary notebooks. Tell students they are to use a dictionary or thesaurus to look up the meanings of the vocabulary words. After they write each word and its meaning, students are to write a sentence using the vocabulary word.

Chapter 12, Vocabulary Words #1
(marginal, significant, ecstatic, blissful)

ACTIVITY / ASSIGNMENT TIME

Have students use the directions below to create a **personality poem** that uses parts of speech. Have students create a **personality poem** for themselves and one for each of their family members and for a friend. (*Write the directions and the example below on the board for your students.*)

Directions for each line of a personality poem:

1. Write your first name.
2. Write two adjectives that describe your personality.
3. Write four words that describe your appearance.
   (*adjective, noun, adjective, noun*).
4. Write five nouns naming things you enjoy.
5. Write any descriptive word you choose about yourself.

Example:

Dustin
Friendly, cheerful
Brown eyes, big smile
Friends, church, science, debates, music
Generous

(End of lesson.)

CHAPTER 12 LESSON 2

New objectives: Grammar (Practice Pattern 2 Sentences,), Vocabulary #2, and an Activity.

 JINGLE TIME

Have students turn to the Jingle Section of their books. The teacher will lead the students in reciting the previously-taught jingles.

 GRAMMAR TIME

First-Year Option: Put the Practice Sentences from the box below on the board or notebook paper. Use these sentences as you practice the concepts that have been taught. For the greatest benefit, students must participate orally with the teacher. **Second-Year Option:** Have students classify the Practice Sentences independently on paper. Check students' sentences with the answers provided below. (*If you have the CDs for Practice Sentences, have students check their sentences with the CDs.*)

Chapter 12, Practice Sentences for Lesson 2

1. _____ The professional photographers took pictures of the models on stage.
2. _____ For a year, the eager musicians slowly and thoroughly memorized the tunes.
3. _____ The wily magician cheerfully accepted the applause of the captive audience.

TEACHING SCRIPT FOR PRACTICING PATTERN 2 SENTENCES

We will classify three different sentences to practice Pattern 2 sentences. We will classify the sentences together. Begin. (*You might have your students write the labels above the sentences at this time.*)

Question and Answer Flow for Sentence 1: The professional photographers took pictures of the models on stage.

1. Who took pictures of the models on stage? photographers - SN
2. What is being said about photographers? photographers took - V
3. Photographers took what? pictures - verify the noun
4. Do pictures mean the same thing as photographers? No.
5. Pictures - DO
6. Took - V-t
7. Of - P
8. Of whom? models - OP
9. The - A
10. On - P
11. On what? stage - OP
12. What kind of photographers? professional - Adj
13. The - A
14. SN V-t DO P2 Check
15. Verb-transitive - Check again.
16. (Of the models) - Prepositional phrase
17. (On stage) - Prepositional phrase
18. Period, statement, declarative sentence
19. Go back to the verb - divide the complete subject from the complete predicate.
20. Is there an adverb exception? No.
21. Is this sentence in a natural or inverted order? Natural - no change.

Classified Sentence:

		A	Adj	SN	V-t	DO	P	A	OP	P	OP
SN V-t		The professional photographers / took pictures (of the models) (on stage). **D**									
DO P2											

CHAPTER 12 LESSON 2 CONTINUED

Question and Answer Flow for Sentence 2: For a year, the eager musicians slowly and thoroughly memorized the tunes.

1. Who memorized the tunes? musicians - SN
2. What is being said about musicians? musicians memorized - V
3. Musicians memorized what? tunes - verify the noun
4. Do tunes mean the same thing as musicians? No.
5. Tunes - DO
6. Memorized - V-t
7. The - A
8. Memorized how? slowly and thoroughly - CAdv, Cadv (Compound Adverb, compound adverb)
9. And - C
10. What kind of musicians? eager - Adj
11. The - A
12. For - P
13. For what? year - OP
14. A - A
15. SN V-t DO P2 Check
16. Verb-transitive - Check again.
17. (For a year) - Prepositional phrase
18. Period, statement, declarative sentence
19. Go back to the verb - divide the complete subject from the complete predicate.
20. Is there an adverb exception? Yes - change the line.
21. Is this sentence in a natural or inverted order? Inverted - underline the subject parts once and the predicate parts twice.

Classified Sentence:

```
              P   A  OP    A   Adj    SN     CAdv  C  CAdv     V-t      A   DO
 SN  V-t    (For a year), the eager musicians / slowly and thoroughly memorized the tunes.  D
 DO  P2
```

Question and Answer Flow for Sentence 3: The wily magician cheerfully accepted the applause of the captive audience.

1. Who accepted the applause of the captive audience? magician - SN
2. What is being said about magician? magician accepted - V
3. Magician accepted what? applause - verify the noun
4. Does applause mean the same thing as magician? No.
5. Applause - DO
6. Accepted - V-t
7. The - A
8. Of - P
9. Of whom? audience - OP
10. What kind of audience? captive - Adj
11. The - A
12. Accepted how? cheerfully - Adv
13. What kind of magician? wily - Adj
14. The - A
15. SN V-t DO P2 Check
16. Verb-transitive - Check again.
17. (Of the captive audience) - Prepositional phrase
18. Period, statement, declarative sentence
19. Go back to the verb - divide the complete subject from the complete predicate.
20. Is there an adverb exception? Yes - change the line.
21. Is this sentence in a natural or inverted order? Natural - no change.

Classified Sentence:

```
              A  Adj   SN      Adv      V-t    A   DO   P  A  Adj    OP
 SN  V-t    The wily magician / cheerfully accepted the applause (of the captive audience).  D
 DO  P2
```

TEACHER INSTRUCTIONS

Use Sentences 1-3 that you just classified with your students to do an Oral Skill Builder Check. Use the guidelines on the next page.

CHAPTER 12 LESSON 2 CONTINUED

Oral Skill Builder Check	
1. Noun check. (Say the job and then say the noun. Circle each noun.) **2. Identify the nouns as singular or plural.** (Write S or P above each noun.) **3. Identify the nouns as common or proper.** (Follow established procedure for oral identification.) **4. Do a vocabulary check.** (Follow established procedure for oral identification.)	**5. Identify the complete subject and the complete predicate.** (Underline the complete subject once and the complete predicate twice.) **6. Identify the simple subject and simple predicate.** (Underline the simple subject once and the simple predicate twice. Bold, or highlight, the lines.) **7. Recite the irregular verb chart.** (Located on student page 17 and teacher page 143.)

TEACHING SCRIPT FOR INTRODUCING A PATTERN 2 PRACTICE SENTENCE

Put these words on the board: **Pattern 2 Practice Sentence**

Get out a sheet of notebook paper. On the top line of your notebook paper, write the title *Pattern 2 Practice Sentence*. Look at the new words on the board: **Pattern 2 Practice Sentence**. I will guide you again through the process as we learn to write a Pattern 2 sentence.

You have already learned how to write an independent Pattern 1 sentence according to labels you select. You will now learn how to write an independent Pattern 2 sentence the same way. First, you start out with the core labels for a Pattern 2 sentence. This means that you <u>must always have a subject, a verb-transitive, and a direct object before you add any extra parts.</u> (*SN V-t DO*)

Next, you build the rest of your Pattern 2 sentence from the regular sentence parts learned in Pattern 1. I will ask you a few questions to make sure you understand. What are the parts of a Pattern 2 sentence that YOU MUST USE? (*All Pattern 2 sentences must have a subject, a verb-transitive, and a direct object.*) I want you to name the extra sentence parts that you can use with your sentence. There are ten parts. (*adjectives, adverbs, articles, prepositional phrases, subject pronouns, possessive nouns, possessive pronouns, helping verbs, conjunctions, and interjections*) Remember, you will use the core parts of a Pattern 2 sentence and then add the extra parts that you want your sentence to have.

Let's write the labels for a Pattern 2 sentence on a sheet of notebook paper. First, on your paper, write the *SN V-t* and *DO* labels that a Pattern 2 sentence must have. Be sure to place them in the middle of your paper. (*Demonstrate by writing the SN V-t DO labels on the board.*) Using what you know about writing Practice Sentences, you decide the other parts you want to add to your Pattern 2 Practice Sentence. (*Have students finish writing a Pattern 2 sentence and turn it in to you. Students do not have to write an Improved Sentence at this point unless you feel they need the practice. If your students cannot handle this much independence so soon, give them the labels you want them to follow for a Pattern 2 sentence. (Example: A Adj SN V-t DO P A OP P OP) Check and discuss students' sentences after they have finished.*)

CHAPTER 12 LESSON 2 CONTINUED

 VOCABULARY TIME

Assign Chapter 12, Vocabulary Words **#2** on page 7 in the Reference Section for students to define in their Vocabulary notebooks. Tell students they are to use a dictionary or thesaurus to look up the meanings of the vocabulary words. After they write each word and its meaning, students are to write a sentence using the vocabulary word.

Chapter 12, Vocabulary Words #2
(precarious, stable, zeppelin, balloon)

 ACTIVITY / ASSIGNMENT TIME

Have students write the three sentences that they classified at the beginning of the lesson on a sheet of paper. (*See page 212.*) Have them tape-record the Question and Answer Flows for all three sentences. Students should write labels above the sentences as they classify them. They especially need the second practice if this is their first year in the program. (*After the students have finished, check the tape and sentence labels. Make sure students understand any mistakes they have made.*)

(End of lesson.)

CHAPTER 12   LESSON 3

New objectives: Grammar (Practice Sentence), Skills (Editing Checklist), and a Practice sheet.

 JINGLE TIME

Have students turn to the Jingle Section of their books. The teacher will lead the students in reciting the previously-taught jingles.

 GRAMMAR TIME

First-Year Option: Put the Practice Sentences from the box below on the board or notebook paper. Use these sentences as you practice the concepts that have been taught. For the greatest benefit, students must participate orally with the teacher. **Second-Year Option:** Have students classify the Practice Sentences independently on paper. Check students' sentences with the answers provided below. (*If you have the CDs for Practice Sentences, have students check their sentences with the CDs.*)

Chapter 12, Practice Sentences for Lesson 3
1. _____ Will they require a resume before my interview?
2. _____ Print Linda's name inside her collar in bold letters.
3. _____ A missionary from our church gave the sermon.

TEACHING SCRIPT FOR PRACTICING PATTERN 2 SENTENCES

We will classify three different sentences to practice Pattern 2 sentences. We will classify the sentences together. Begin. (*You might have your students write the labels above the sentences at this time.*)

Question and Answer Flow for Sentence 1: Will they require a resume before my interview?
1. Who will require a resume before my interview? they - SP
2. What is being said about they? they will require - V
3. Will - HV
4. They will require what? resume - verify the noun
5. Does resume mean the same thing as they? No.
6. Resume - DO
7. Require - V-t
8. A - A
9. Before - P
10. Before what? interview - OP
11. Whose interview? my - PPA
12. SN V-t DO P2 Check
13. Verb-transitive - Check again.
14. (Before my interview) - Prepositional phrase
15. Question mark, question, interrogative sentence
16. Go back to the verb - divide the complete subject from the complete predicate.
17. Is there an adverb exception? No.
18. Is this sentence in a natural or inverted order? Inverted - underline the subject parts once and the predicate parts twice.

Classified Sentence:

```
                        HV  SP    V-t  A  DO     P   PPA   OP
         SN  V-t     Will they / require a resume (before my interview)? Int
         DO  P2
```

CHAPTER 12 LESSON 3 CONTINUED

Question and Answer Flow for Sentence 2: Print Linda's name inside her collar in bold letters.

1. Who print Linda's name inside her collar in bold letters? (You) - SP (Understood subject pronoun)
2. What is being said about you? you print - V
3. You print what? name - verify the noun
4. Does name mean the same thing as you? No.
5. Name - DO
6. Print - V-t
7. Whose name? Linda's - PNA
8. Inside - P
9. Inside what? collar - OP
10. Whose collar? her - PPA
11. In - P

12. In what? letters - OP
13. What kind of letters? bold - Adj
14. SN V-t DO P2 Check
15. Verb-transitive - Check again.
16. (Inside her collar) - Prepositional phrase
17. (In bold letters) - Prepositional phrase
18. Period, command, imperative sentence
19. Go back to the verb - divide the complete subject from the complete predicate.
20. Is there an adverb exception? No.
21. Is this sentence in a natural or inverted order? Natural - no change.

Classified Sentence:

```
                  (You) SP    V-t  PNA    DO   P   PPA  OP   P  Adj  OP
                  SN  V-t   / Print Linda's name (inside her collar) (in bold letters).  Imp
                  DO  P2
```

Question and Answer Flow for Sentence 3: A missionary from our church gave the sermon.

1. Who gave the sermon? missionary - SN
2. What is being said about missionary? missionary gave - V
3. Missionary gave what? sermon - verify the noun
4. Does sermon mean the same thing as missionary? No.
5. Sermon - DO
6. Gave - V-t
7. The - A
8. From - P
9. From what? church - OP

10. Whose church? our - PPA
11. A - A
12. SN V-t DO P2 Check
13. Verb-transitive - Check again.
14. (From our church) - Prepositional phrase
15. Period, statement, declarative sentence
16. Go back to the verb - divide the complete subject from the complete predicate.
17. Is there an adverb exception? No.
18. Is this sentence in a natural or inverted order? Natural - no change.

Classified Sentence:

```
                     A    SN       P  PPA  OP    V-t  A   DO
            SN  V-t   A missionary (from our church) / gave the sermon.  D
            DO  P2
```

SKILL TIME

TEACHING SCRIPT FOR INTRODUCING A REGULAR EDITING CHECKLIST

The process of finding and correcting errors in writing is called editing. Remember, the writing that you edit is called a rough draft. Before we begin detailed editing, I want you to know that total editing is a slow, meticulous (careful) process. You do not get in a hurry when you edit. It is like being a detective. You have all the clues, but you must study the clues carefully in order to solve the editing mystery. After a while, the editing process will become automatic, but you must remember that editing is never a fast process. As you mature in your writing ability, editing will become more and more important because without it, you just cannot have a top-quality piece of writing. Editing is like icing on a cake: It puts the finishing touches on a product.

CHAPTER 12 LESSON 3 CONTINUED

To make regular editing easier, you must have a system. If you have a system when you edit, you will get the maximum benefit of editing. The Shurley English editing system is simple: Use a checklist. All high-tech businesses use checklists to keep track of everything that's important and productive. They are simple but very effective when used correctly. Editing should become an automatic process that enables you to produce a top-quality writing product every time you write.

You have been using the Beginning Editing Checklist. That is a good checklist, but now you are ready to use the regular editing checklist. It is more detailed and establishes an editing routine that will be easy for you to follow. We will now go over the regular editing checklist, and then I will show you how to use it to edit a rough draft. Look at Reference 35 on page 28 in your Reference section. *(The Editing Checklist below includes a few skills that students have not had. Add these skills as they are introduced during Skill Time.)*

Reference 35: Regular Editing Checklist

Read each sentence and go through the Sentence Checkpoints below.

_____ E1. Sentence sense check. (Check for words left out or words repeated.)

_____ E2. First word, capital letter check. End mark check. Any other capitalization check. Any other punctuation check.

_____ E3. Sentence structure and punctuation check. (Check for correct construction and correct punctuation of a simple sentence, a simple sentence with compound parts, a compound sentence, or a complex sentence.)

_____ E4. Spelling and homonym check. (Check for misspelled words and incorrect homonym choices.)

_____ E5. Usage check. (Check subject-verb agreement, a/an choice, pronoun/antecedent agreement, pronoun cases, degrees of adjectives, double negatives, verb tenses, and contractions.)

Read each paragraph and go through the Paragraph Checkpoints below.

_____ E6. Check to see that each paragraph is indented.

_____ E7. Check each paragraph for a topic sentence.

_____ E8. Check each sentence to make sure it supports the topic of the paragraph.

_____ E9. Check the content for interest and creativity. Do not begin all sentences with the same word, and use a variety of simple, compound, and complex sentences.

_____ E10. Check the type and format of the writing assigned.

Notice that each checkpoint on the editing guide has a capital *E* and a number beside it. The capital *E* refers to the editing checklist (*E* for editing). The number indicates which skill area is listed beside each checkpoint. So, *E1* means you are editing the first skill area. We will call *E1* checkpoint 1. What is being checked in checkpoint 1? (**E1:** *Sentence sense check. Check for words left out or words repeated.*) What is being checked in checkpoint 2? (**E2:** *First word, capital letter check. End mark check. Any other capitalization check. Any other punctuation check.*) What is being checked in checkpoint 3? (**E3:** *Sentence structure and sentence structure punctuation check. Check for correct construction and correct punctuation of a simple sentence, a simple sentence with compound parts, a compound sentence, or a complex sentence.*)

CHAPTER 12 LESSON 3 CONTINUED

What is being checked in checkpoint 4? (**E4:** *Spelling and homonym check. Check for misspelled words and incorrect homonym choices.*) What is being checked in checkpoint 5? (**E5:** *Usage check. Check subject-verb agreement, a/an choice, pronoun/antecedent agreement, pronoun cases, degrees of adjectives, double negatives, verb tenses, and contractions.*)

These first five checkpoints will be used for each sentence as you do a sentence-by-sentence edit. The second five checkpoints are done as you check each paragraph. What are the five paragraph checkpoints? (**E6:** *Check to see that each paragraph is indented.* **E7:** *Check each paragraph for a topic sentence.* **E8:** *Check each sentence to make sure it supports the topic of the paragraph.* **E9:** *Check the content for interest and creativity. Do not begin all sentences with the same word, and use a variety of simple, compound, and complex sentences.* **E10:** *Check the type and format of the writing assigned.*)

Remember, editing is a slow, careful process that works best when you use your system. Your papers are not very long at this point, and it is crucial that you get in the habit of going through each sentence five times, one time for each sentence checkpoint. You'll know your paper pretty well by the time you finish, but that's the whole idea of editing. You should know your paper well enough to have corrected every mistake in it. The Shurley system may take you a little longer at the beginning, but it will save you from having to redo a poor editing job due to improper editing techniques.

I will guide you through an expository essay that has been edited so you can see the editing process. Look at the bottom of Reference 36 on page 29 in your book. *(Use the reference box below as you go through the teaching script that follows. Make sure you point out that all corrections are written on the line above each mistake.)* *(Do not go over the rough draft and final paper sections at this time. They will be discussed in later lessons.)*

Reference 36: Editing Example
Topic: **Application of theater skills**   Three main points: (**1. Speak clearly   2. Speak extemporaneously   3. Exhibit poise**)

Major
Reasons to major in Theater

→   a   there
Being a theater major can teach an person a number of invaluable lessons. Although their may
                              (,)
be few opportunities to act professionally one can take the performing skills and apply them in other
    (.)T   (,)
professions three important lessons one can apply in a host of professions are speaking clearly
                          (,)
speaking extemporaneously and exhibiting poise.
One→
one of the important application skills of a theater major is the art of speaking clearly. Proper
                not   a
enunciation of words knot only makes for effective communication, but it also creates an positive
        A   who
impression on others. another of the application skills is that of impromptu speaking. People whom
                    clearly   always
an
are able to think quickly and clear can almost alway convince others to their way of thinking; they exude a
                                                                            is
unmistakable confidence in their use of language. Another application of theater skills are exhibiting poise
                        Their
in front of a group of people. There "stage presence" enables them to carry on.
        conclusion   to
    In Conclusion, a host of theater skills can be applied too many different professions. To
                                                            to
be able to speak clearly and without preparation and with poise are keys too success in any walk of life.

Total Mistakes: 23
Editing Guide: Sentence checkpoints: **E1, E2, E3, E4, E5**   Paragraph checkpoints: **E6, E7, E8, E9, E10**

CHAPTER 12 LESSON 3 CONTINUED

1. Check the title for capitalization and spelling mistakes. (***Capitalization check****-correct* <u>major</u> *with a capital M.*

2. **Read the first sentence.** (Being a theater major can teach an person a number of invaluable lessons.)

3. Are there any mistakes for checkpoint 1? *(Read checkpoint 1 and check the sentence.)* (***Sentence sense check****-no mistakes.)*

4. Are there any mistakes for checkpoint 2? *(Read checkpoint 2 and check the sentence.)* (***First word, capital letter check****--no mistakes.* ***End mark check****—no mistakes.* ***Any other capitalization check****—no mistakes.* ***Any other punctuation check****--no mistakes.)*

5. Are there any mistakes for checkpoint 3? *(Read checkpoint 3 and check the sentence.)* (***Sentence structure and sentence structure punctuation check****--no mistakes.)*

6. Are there any mistakes for checkpoint 4? *(Read checkpoint 4 and check the sentence.)* (***Spelling and homonym check****--no mistakes.)*

7. Are there any mistakes for checkpoint 5? You have to do a usage by-usage-check in checkpoint 5 because there are too many different skills to check as a group. *(Read checkpoint 5 and check the sentence.)* *(Subject-verb agreement check--no mistakes.* ***A-An check****—Article an should be changed to article a..* *Pronoun/antecedent agreement check--no mistakes. Pronoun case check--no mistakes. Double negative check--no mistakes. Verb tense check--no mistakes. Contraction check--no mistakes.)*

Now we start the checkpoints over again on the next sentence. You will make very few editing mistakes if you stick with this system until it becomes automatic. As soon as editing becomes automatic, you will go through the editing process with ease, so trust me on this. Begin.

1. **Read the second sentence.** (Although their may be few opportunities to act professionally one can take the performing skills and apply them in other professions)

2. Are there any mistakes for checkpoint 1? *(Checkpoint 1:* ***Sentence sense check****-no mistakes.)*

3. Are there any mistakes for checkpoint 2? *(Checkpoint 2:* (***First word, capital letter check****—no mistakes* **A.** ***End mark check****—correct with a period.* ***Any other capitalization check****--no mistakes.* ***Any other punctuation check****--no mistakes.)*

4. Are there any mistakes for checkpoint 3? *(Checkpoint 3:* ***Sentence structure and sentence structure punctuation check****--no mistakes.)* *(They have not had a complex sentence yet, so just tell them the sentence is correct.)*

5. Are there any mistakes for checkpoint 4? *(Checkpoint 4:* ***Spelling and homonym check****—no mistakes*

6. Are there any mistakes for checkpoint 5? *(Checkpoint 5:* ***Subject-verb agreement check****--no mistakes.* ***A-An check****--no mistakes.* ***Pronoun/antecedent agreement check****--no mistakes.* ***Pronoun case check****--no mistakes.* ***Double negative check****--no mistakes.* ***Verb tense check****--no mistakes.* ***Contraction check****--no mistakes.)*

1. **Read the third sentence.** (Three important lessons one can apply in a host of professions are speaking clearly speaking extemporaneously and exhibiting poise.)

2. Are there any mistakes for checkpoint 1? *(Checkpoint 1:* ***Sentence sense check****-no mistakes.)*

3. Are there any mistakes for checkpoint 2? *(Checkpoint 2:* ***First word, capital letter check****—correct first word with a capital T.* ***End mark check****—no mistakes.* ***Any other capitalization check****--no mistakes.* ***Any other punctuation check****—put a comma after* <u>clearly</u> *and after* <u>extemporaneously</u> *to separate items in a series.)*

4. Are there any mistakes for checkpoint 3? *(Checkpoint 3:* ***Sentence structure and sentence structure punctuation check****--no mistakes.)*

CHAPTER 12 LESSON 3 CONTINUED

5. Are there any mistakes for checkpoint 4? *(Checkpoint 4: **Spelling and homonym check**--no mistakes.)*

6. Are there any mistakes for checkpoint 5? *(Checkpoint 5: **Subject-verb agreement check**--no mistakes. **A-An check**--no mistakes. **Pronoun/antecedent agreement check**—no mistakes.. **Pronoun case check**--no mistakes. **Double negative check**--no mistakes. **Verb tense check**--no mistakes. **Contraction check**--no mistakes.)*

Look at the first paragraph. Now we will do a paragraph check for the last five checkpoints.

1. Are there any mistakes for checkpoint 6? *(Read checkpoint 6 and check the first paragraph.) (No corrections.)*
2. Are there any mistakes for checkpoint 7? *(Read checkpoint 7 and check the first paragraph.) (No corrections.)*
3. Are there any mistakes for checkpoint 8? *(Read checkpoint 8 and check the first paragraph.) (No corrections.)*
4. Are there any mistakes for checkpoint 9? *(Read checkpoint 9 and check the first paragraph.) (No corrections.)*
5. Are there any mistakes for checkpoint 10? *(Read checkpoint 10 and check the first paragraph.) (No corrections.)*

*(Work through the remaining sentences in the last two paragraphs. **Make sure you take the time now to establish the editing routine that you want your students to follow.**)*

 PRACTICE TIME

Have students turn to page 58 in the Practice Section of their book and find the skill under Chapter 12, Lesson 3, Practice. Go over the directions to make sure they understand what to do. Check and discuss the Practice after students have finished. *(Chapter 12, Lesson 3, Practice key is given below.)*

Chapter 12, Lesson 3, Practice
Make corrections to the following paragraph.

(indent)   **surprises**   **are**   **roam**
Hiking in the woods can be full of suprises. There is all kinds of critters that rome the woods,
                    turtles   **(.) One**   **a**
everything from squirrels and snakes to turtels of various kinds one needs to be prepared for an host of
           grow   **(,)**
eventualities. Also, many wildflowers grows in the shade of full-grown trees flowers such as bluets,
                                        new
jack-in-the-pulpit, and coral bells. Anyone looking for adventure can discover something knew
              (.)
each time he "hits the trail"   **Total Mistakes: 12**

 WRITING TIME

Have students make an entry in their journals. After they have finished, have students study the vocabulary words in their vocabulary notebooks and any of the skills in the Practice Section that they need to review.

(End of lesson.)

CHAPTER 12   LESSON 4

New objectives: Test.

JINGLE TIME

Have students turn to the Jingle Section of their books. The teacher will lead the students in reciting the previously-taught jingles.

STUDY TIME

Have students study the vocabulary words in their vocabulary notebooks. Remind students that any vocabulary word in their notebooks could be on their test. Also, have students study any of the skills in the Practice Section that they need to review.

TEST TIME

Have students turn to page 94 in the Test Section of their book and find the Chapter 12 Test. Students are allowed to use the Reference Section to help them remember the new information and to check the capitalization and punctuation rules while they correct capitalization and punctuation errors in the sentences. Remind them to pay attention and think about what they are doing. Go over the directions to make sure they understand what to do. (*Chapter 12 Test key is on the next page.*)

CHECK TIME

After students have finished, check and discuss their test papers. Make sure they understand why their answers are right or wrong. (*For total points, count each required answer as a point.*)

(End of lesson.)

Chapter 12 Test
(Student Page 94)

Exercise 1: Classify each sentence.

```
            SN      V-t    Adj Adj   DO      Adv      Adv
1.  SN V-t   Steve / challenges all new opponents quite convincingly.  D
    DO P2
                 Adv   A    SN    P   A   Adj    OP      CV-t  C  CV-t      PNA     DO
2.  SN V-t   Today, the driver (of the blue convertible) / passed and sideswiped Eleanor's van.  D
    DO P2
                 I       A    SN       V     Adj    CDO  C  Adj  CDO   P   PPA
3.  SN V-t   Horrors!  The hurricane / uprooted towering palms and ancient oaks (during its
    DO P2    Adj    OP     P  A   OP
             savage attack) (on the coastline)!  E
```

Exercise 2: Use Sentence 3 to underline the complete subject once and the complete predicate twice and to complete the table below.

List the Noun Used	List the Noun Job	Singular or Plural	Common or Proper	Simple Subject	Simple Predicate
1. hurricane	2. SN	3. S	4. C	5. hurricane	6. uprooted
7. palms	8. DO	9. P	10. C		
11. oaks	12. DO	13. P	14. C		
15. attack	16. OP	17. S	18. C		
19. coastline	20. OP	21. S	22. C		

Exercise 3: Identify each pair of words as synonyms or antonyms by putting parentheses ( ) around *syn* or *ant*.

1. mimic, imitate	**(syn)** ant	5. wasteful, prodigal	**(syn)** ant	9. ecstatic, blissful	**(syn)** ant
2. stable, precarious	syn **(ant)**	6. savory, bland	syn **(ant)**	10. mandatory, required	**(syn)** ant
3. abolish, destroy	**(syn)** ant	7. odd, quaint	**(syn)** ant	11. marginal, significant	syn **(ant)**
4. alliance, division	syn **(ant)**	8. balloon, zeppelin	**(syn)** ant	12. repulsive, amiable	syn **(ant)**

Exercise 4: Underline the correct homonym in each sentence.

1. Give dad a (<u>piece</u>, peace) of pie.
2. My knee is very (<u>weak</u>, week) after surgery.
3. We parked (<u>by</u>, buy) a black truck.
4. Are we meeting (<u>here</u>, hear) today?
5. Our house has (<u>lead</u>, led) pipes.
6. My sister (<u>blew</u>, blue) her nose loudly.
7. Juneau is the (<u>capital</u>, capitol) of Alaska.
8. Days of the week start with a (<u>capital</u>, capitol) letter.

Exercise 5: <u>For Sentences 1 and 2</u>: Write the capitalization and punctuation corrections only.
<u>For Sentence 3</u>: Write the capitalization and punctuation rule numbers for each correction in bold.

```
    L        R                    S     F    S    D                         G     C
1.  lucy, did the russian immigrants see sioux falls, south dakota, on their way to the grand canyon?
```

Editing Guide: Capitals: 8	Commas: 3	End marks: 1

```
    N    M   D      I         M      R         S     F    N    M         J
2.  no, mr. davis and i did not go to a mexican restaurant in santa fe, new mexico, in june.
```

Editing Guide: Capitals: 10	Commas: 3	Periods: 1	End marks: 1

```
    1        9  10 10 7                         16      16           14      14
3.  Our guide, Mr. J. C. Notingham, took us hiking around Lake Conway near Denver, Colorado.
       11  16 17 17            11                                           7         1
```

Editing Guide: Capitals: 9	Commas: 3	Periods: 3	End marks: 1

Exercise 6: In your journal, write a paragraph summarizing what you have learned this week.

CHAPTER 12 LESSON 4 CONTINUED

TEACHER INSTRUCTIONS

Use the Question and Answer Flows below for the sentences on Chapter 12 Test.

Question and Answer Flow for Sentence 1: Steve challenges all new opponents quite convincingly.

1. Who challenges all new opponents quite convincingly? Steve - SN
2. What is being said about Steve? Steve challenges - V
3. Steve challenges whom? opponents - verify the noun
4. Do opponents mean the same thing as Steve? No.
5. Opponents - DO
6. Challenges - V-t
7. What kind of opponents? new - Adj
8. How many opponents? all - Adj
9. Challenges how? convincingly - Adv
10. How convincingly? quite - Adv
11. SN V-t DO P2 Check
12. Verb-transitive - Check again.
13. No prepositional phrases.
14. Period, statement, declarative sentence
15. Go back to the verb - divide the complete subject from the complete predicate.
16. Is there an adverb exception? No.
17. Is this sentence in a natural or inverted order? Natural - no change.

Classified Sentence:

	SN	V-t	Adj	Adj	DO	Adv	Adv
SN V-t DO P2	Steve /	challenges	all	new	opponents	quite	convincingly. **D**

Question and Answer Flow for Sentence 2: Today, the driver of the blue convertible passed and sideswiped Eleanor's van.

1. Who passed and sideswiped Eleanor's van? driver - SN
2. What is being said about driver? driver passed and sideswiped - CV, CV
3. Driver passed and sideswiped what? van - verify the noun
4. Does van mean the same thing as driver? No.
5. Van - DO
6. Passed and sideswiped - CV-t, CV-t
7. Whose van? Eleanor's - PNA
8. And - C
9. Of - P
10. Of what? convertible - OP
11. What kind of convertible? blue - Adj
12. The - A
13. The - A
14. Passed and sideswiped when? today - Adv
15. SN V-t DO P2 Check
16. Verb-transitive Check again.
17. (Of the blue convertible) - Prepositional phrase
18. Period, statement, declarative sentence
19. Go back to the verb - divide the complete subject from the complete predicate.
20. Is there an adverb exception? No.
21. Is this sentence in a natural or inverted order? Inverted - underline the subject parts once and the predicate parts twice.

Classified Sentence:

	Adv	A	SN	P	A	Adj	OP	CV-t	C	CV-t	PNA	DO
SN V-t DO P2	Today,	the	driver	(of	the	blue	convertible) /	passed	and	sideswiped	Eleanor's	van. **D**

Level 5—Shurley English—Homeschool Edition

CHAPTER 12 LESSON 4 CONTINUED

Question and Answer Flow for Sentence 3: Horrors! The hurricane uprooted towering palms and ancient oaks during its savage attack on the coastline!

1. What uprooted towering palms and ancient oaks during its savage attack on the coastline? hurricane - SN
2. What is being said about hurricane? hurricane uprooted - V
3. Hurricane uprooted what? palms and oaks - verify the nouns
4. Do palms and oaks mean the same thing as hurricane? No.
5. Palms and oaks - CDO, CDO
6. Uprooted - V-t
7. What kind of palms? towering - Adj
8. And - C
9. What kind of oaks? ancient - Adj
10. During - P
11. During what? attack - OP
12. What kind of attack? savage - Adj
13. Whose attack? its - PPA
14. On - P
15. On what? coastline - OP
16. The - A
17. The - A
18. Horrors - I
19. SN V-t DO P2 Check
20. Verb-transitive - Check again.
21. (During its savage attack) - Prepositional phrase
22. (On the coastline) - Prepositional phrase
23. Exclamation point, strong feeling, exclamatory sentence
24. Go back to the verb - divide the complete subject from the complete predicate.
25. Is there an adverb exception? No.
26. Is this sentence in natural or inverted order? Natural - no change.

Classified Sentence:

```
                    I    A    SN      V-t     Adj   CDO   C   Adj   CDO   P   PPA
   SN  V-t    Horrors!  The hurricane / uprooted towering palms and ancient oaks (during its
   DO  P2    Adj    OP      P   A    OP
             savage attack) (on the coastline)!  E
```

(End of lesson.)

Level 5 Homeschool Teacher's Manual

© SHURLEY INSTRUCTIONAL MATERIALS, INC.

CHAPTER 12   LESSON 5

Introduce these objectives: Writing Assignment #13 and #14, Bonus Option.

 WRITING TIME

TEACHING SCRIPT FOR PRACTICING DIFFERENT KINDS OF WRITING

Today, you are assigned two different kinds of writing. You will write a five-paragraph persuasive essay and a three-paragraph expository essay. <u>You will revise and edit the five-paragraph persuasive essay.</u> (*Read the box below for more information about students' writing assignment.*) As you edit, make sure you use the checkpoints in the editing checklist provided in Reference 35. Remember to read through the whole essay, starting with the title, and then edit, sentence-by-sentence, using the five-sentence checkpoints for each sentence. Use the paragraph checkpoints to check each paragraph. You should use the Beginning Checklists for all other instructions. Remember, your editing is now more detailed and more comprehensive, so take your time.

Writing Assignment Box #1

Writing Assignment #13: Five-Paragraph Persuasive Essay (First Person)
(Remember, first person pronouns are *I, we, me, us, my, our, mine, and ours.*)
Remind students that the 5-paragraph essay has three parts: 1. Introduction 2. Body 3. Conclusion. The body has three paragraphs instead of one. Have students use their regular editing checklist to edit this assignment.

Writing topic: Why Computers Are Necessary or **Why Grandparents are Important**

Your second writing assignment is to write a three-paragraph expository essay. (*Read the box below for more information about students' writing assignment.*) You do not have to edit this assignment with the editing checklist.

Writing Assignment Box #2

Writing Assignment #14: Three-Paragraph Expository Essay (First Person)
(Remember, first person pronouns are *I, we, me, us, my, our, mine, and ours.*)
Remind students that the 3-paragraph essay has three parts: 1. Introduction 2. Body 3. Conclusion. The body has one paragraph instead of three. Have students use their regular editing checklist to edit this assignment.

Writing topic: Family Vacation Places or **Things You Need for Inventing Something New**

Bonus Option: Do you have a Biblical name? Do you know someone who does? Research in books and on the Internet to find out the origin of your name and other family members' names.

Read, check, and discuss Writing Assignment #13 after students have finished their final papers. Use the checklists as you check and discuss students' papers. Make sure students are using the regular editing checklist correctly. Read and discuss Writing Assignment #14 for fun and enrichment.

(End of lesson.)

CHAPTER 13 LESSON 1

New objectives: Grammar (Practice Sentences), Skills (identify complete sentences and sentence fragments, correcting sentence fragments), Practice sheet, and Vocabulary #1.

 JINGLE TIME

Have students turn to the Jingle Section of their books. The teacher will lead the students in reciting the previously-taught jingles.

 GRAMMAR TIME

First-Year Option: Put the Practice Sentences from the box below on the board or notebook paper. Use these sentences as you practice the concepts that have been taught. For the greatest benefit, students must participate orally with the teacher. **Second-Year Option:** Have students classify the Practice Sentences independently on paper. Check students' sentences with the answers provided below. (*If you have the CDs for Practice Sentences, have students check their sentences with the CDs.*)

Chapter 13, Practice Sentences for Lesson 1
1. _____ He suddenly recognized the weird symbol on the door.
2. _____ Did your sister eat the raisins in her cereal today?

TEACHING SCRIPT FOR PRACTICING PATTERN 2 SENTENCES

We will practice classifying Pattern 2 sentences. We will classify the sentences together. Begin. (*You might have your students write the labels above the sentences at this time.*)

Question and Answer Flow for Sentence 1: He suddenly recognized the weird symbol on the door.	
1. Who recognized the weird symbol on the door? he - SP	12. Recognized when? suddenly - Adv
2. What is being said about he? he recognized - V	13. SN V-t DO P2 Check
3. He recognized what? symbol - verify the noun	14. Verb-transitive - Check again.
4. Does symbol mean the same thing as he? No.	15. (On the door) - Prepositional phrase
5. Symbol - DO	16. Period, statement, declarative sentence
6. Recognized - V-t	17. Go back to the verb - divide the complete subject from the complete predicate.
7. What kind of symbol? weird – Adj	18. Is there an adverb exception? Yes - change the line.
8. The – A	
9. On – P	19. Is this sentence in a natural or inverted order? Natural - no change.
10. On what? door – OP	
11. The - A	

Classified Sentence:
```
                      SP    Adv      V-t     A    Adj   DO    P   A   OP
       SN  V-t        He / suddenly recognized the weird symbol (on the door).  D
       DO  P2
```

CHAPTER 13 LESSON 1 CONTINUED

Question and Answer Flow for Sentence 2: Did your sister eat the raisins in her cereal today?

1. Who did eat the raisins in her cereal today? sister - SN
2. What is being said about sister? sister did eat - V
3. Did - HV
4. Sister did eat what? raisins - verify the noun
5. Do raisins mean the same thing as sister? No.
6. Raisins - DO
7. Eat - V-t
8. The - A
9. In - P
10. In what? cereal - OP
11. Whose cereal? her - PPA
12. Did eat when? today - Adv

13. Whose sister? your - PPA
14. SN V-t DO P2 Check
15. Verb-transitive - Check again.
16. (In her cereal) - Prepositional phrase
17. Question mark, question, interrogative sentence
18. Go back to the verb - divide the complete subject from the complete predicate.
19. Is there an adverb exception? No.
20. Is this sentence in a natural or inverted order? Inverted - underline the subject parts once and the predicate parts twice.

Classified Sentence:

	HV	PPA	SN		V-t	A		DO	P	PPA	OP	Adv

SN V-t / DO P2

Did your sister / eat the raisins (in her cereal) today? Int

Use Sentences 1-2 that you just classified with your students to do an Oral Skill Builder Check. Use the guidelines below.

Oral Skill Builder Check

1. **Noun check.**
(Say the job and then say the noun. Circle each noun.)
2. **Identify the nouns as singular or plural.**
(Write S or P above each noun.)
3. **Identify the nouns as common or proper.**
(Follow established procedure for oral identification.)
4. **Do a vocabulary check.**
(Follow established procedure for oral identification.)

5. **Identify the complete subject and the complete predicate.** (Underline the complete subject once and the complete predicate twice.)
6. **Identify the simple subject and simple predicate.** (Underline the simple subject once and the simple predicate twice. Bold, or highlight, the lines.)
7. **Recite the irregular verb chart.** (Located on student page 17 and teacher page 143.)

SKILL TIME

TEACHING SCRIPT FOR IDENTIFYING COMPLETE SENTENCES AND SENTENCE FRAGMENTS

You should feel comfortable using a variety of sentences in your writing. You should also be skilled in constructing long or short sentences that are simple, compound, or complex. A basic knowledge of different kinds of sentence structure is necessary for you to become a writer who is confident and effective. Today, we will learn to recognize and work with simple sentences and sentence fragments.

First, we are going to learn the difference between a complete sentence and a fragment. Most of the time you will have no trouble writing a complete sentence because you know the five rules to make a correct sentence. Let's repeat the Sentence jingle again to make sure we are all focused on the same thing. (*Repeat the Sentence jingle.*) When you are writing, sometimes you will put a thought down without checking the five parts. If your sentence **does not have a subject, a verb, and a complete thought**, you could have a sentence fragment. This lesson will teach you how to recognize and prevent sentence fragments so all your sentences can be written correctly.

CHAPTER 13 LESSON 1 CONTINUED

Next, we will learn more about the simple sentence. A **simple sentence is one complete sentence**. It is also known as **one complete thought**. Adjectives, adverbs, and prepositional phrases add greater meaning, more life, and more color to simple sentences, but they are not necessary for a sentence to be a complete thought. A simple or complete sentence must have **a subject, a verb, and be a complete thought**. The abbreviation for a simple sentence is the letter **S**. A sentence fragment does not express a complete thought because it always has one or more of the core parts missing. The abbreviation for a fragment is the letter **F**.

Find Reference 37 on page 29 in your book. Let's read the directions together. (*Read and discuss the directions.*) We will identify whether each sentence is a fragment or a simple sentence. After we decide what type of sentence it is, we will put the correct abbreviation in the blank at the left of each group of words. The abbreviations that you use are found in the directions. Remember, check each group of words for the main parts that make it a sentence: a subject, a verb, and a complete thought. (*Work through sentences 1–5, showing students how to identify each type of sentence and write the abbreviation in the blank.*)

Reference 37: Complete Sentences and Sentence Fragments		
Identifying simple sentences and fragments: Write S for a complete sentence and F for a sentence fragment on the line beside each group of words below.		
F	1.	The huge mountains in the distance.
S	2.	Babies squealed.
F	3.	For the biggest prize.
F	4.	Scaling the steepest cliffs.
S	5.	Life preservers are essential.
Reference 37: Part 2: Sentence Fragments		
Fragment Examples: (1) falling down the steps (2) the funny monkeys at the zoo (3) as I talked to my mom (4) for a bottle of milk.		

Look at the title "Fragment Examples" under Part 2 in the reference box. I am going to read several things about a fragment. As I read each one, you will read the fragment example that illustrates that point. I'll tell you when to read by saying "read." (*Teacher reads sentences 1-4 below. After each one, teacher says, "Read." Students will read the fragment in parentheses that illustrates the point just read by the teacher. You may want to do this part of the exercise again after your students realize what you are doing.*)

1. A fragment is a group of words that does not have a subject. Read: (falling down the steps)
2. A fragment is a group of words that does not have a verb. Read: (the funny monkeys at the zoo)
3. A fragment is a group of words that does not complete a thought. Read: (as I talked to my mom)
4. Sentence fragments should not be punctuated as complete sentences. Read: (for a bottle of milk.)

Remember, if a sentence is missing one of these three parts, a <u>subject</u>, a <u>verb</u>, or a <u>complete thought,</u> you probably have a sentence fragment.

TEACHING SCRIPT FOR CORRECTING SENTENCE FRAGMENTS

I want you to know how to add missing subject parts or missing predicate parts to make sentences complete. The third part of Reference 37 will help you learn how to correct fragments. Look at the third part of Reference 37 as I go over it with you. These are all sentence fragments. We will make them complete sentences by adding the underlined part. (*Read the directions and work through the third part with your students. Part 3 is located on the next page.*)

CHAPTER 13 LESSON 1 CONTINUED

Reference 37: Part 3: Correcting Sentence Fragments

Directions: Add the part that is underlined in parentheses to make each fragment into a complete sentence.

1. On the edge of the diving board for a brief moment. (subject part, predicate part, <u>both the subject and predicate</u>)
   (**The first diver poised** on the edge of the diving board for a brief moment.)

2. The excited fans. (subject part, <u>predicate part</u>, both the subject and predicate)
   (The excited fans **clapped and yelled loudly for the players**.)

3. Was rolling down the hill. (<u>subject part</u>, predicate part, both the subject and predicate)
   (**My expensive camera** was rolling down the hill.)

 PRACTICE TIME

Have students turn to pages 58 and 59 in the Practice Section of their book and find Chapter 13, Lesson 1, Practice (*1-2*). Go over the directions to make sure they understand what to do. Check and discuss the Practices after students have finished. (*Chapter 13, Lesson 1 Practice keys are given below.*)

Chapter 13, Lesson 1, Practice 1: On notebook paper, add the part that is underlined in the parentheses to make each fragment into a complete sentence. *(Sentences will vary.)*

1. Inside the shed behind the house   (subject part, predicate part, <u>both the subject and predicate</u>)
2. Slipped and slid on the snowy hillside   (<u>subject part</u>, predicate part, both the subject and predicate)
3. The unusually large painting in the foyer   (subject part, <u>predicate part</u>, both the subject and predicate)

Chapter 13, Lesson 1, Practice 2: Identify each kind of sentence by writing the abbreviation in the blank. (S, F).

S	1.	The big hawk swooped toward the frightened mouse.
S	2.	Summer squash ripened early.
F	3.	Lying abandoned near the shore.
S	4.	Interest skyrockets.
F	5.	Weird noises.

 WRITING TIME

Have students make an entry in their journals.

 VOCABULARY TIME

Assign Chapter 13, Vocabulary Words **#1** on page 7 in the Reference Section for students to define in their Vocabulary notebooks. Tell students they may use a dictionary or thesaurus. After they write each word and its meaning, students are to write a sentence using the vocabulary word.

Chapter 13, Vocabulary Words #1
(luminous, obscure, bangle, bracelet)

(End of lesson.)

CHAPTER 13   LESSON 2
New objectives: Grammar (Practice Sentences), Skills (simple sentence with compound parts, run-on sentence), Practice sheet, and Vocabulary #2.

 JINGLE TIME

Have students turn to the Jingle Section of their books. The teacher will lead the students in reciting the previously-taught jingles.

 GRAMMAR TIME

First-Year Option: Put the Practice Sentences from the box below on the board or notebook paper. Use these sentences as you practice the concepts that have been taught. For the greatest benefit, students must participate orally with the teacher. **Second-Year Option:** Have students classify the Practice Sentences independently on paper. Check students' sentences with the answers provided below. (*If you have the CDs for Practice Sentences, have students check their sentences with the CDs.*)

Chapter 13, Practice Sentences for Lesson 2
1. _____ Mercy! Their car lost a front tire on the freeway!
2. _____ Kenny's more experienced players very quickly won the game during the tournament.

TEACHING SCRIPT FOR PRACTICING PATTERN 2 SENTENCES

We will practice classifying Pattern 2 sentences. We will classify the sentences together. Begin. (*You might have your students write the labels above the sentences at this time.*)

Question and Answer Flow for Sentence 1: Mercy! Their car lost a front tire on the freeway!

1. What lost a front tire on the freeway? car - SN
2. What is being said about car? car lost - V
3. Car lost what? tire - verify the noun
4. Does tire mean the same thing as car? No.
5. Tire - DO
6. Lost - V-t
7. What kind of tire? front - Adj
8. A - A
9. On - P
10. On what? freeway - OP
11. The - A
12. Whose car? their - PPA
13. Mercy - I
14. SN V-t DO P2 Check
15. Verb-transitive - Check again.
16. (On the freeway) - Prepositional phrase
17. Exclamation point, strong feeling, exclamatory sentence.
18. Go back to the verb - divide the complete subject from the complete predicate.
19. Is there an adverb exception? No.
20. Is this sentence in a natural or inverted order? Natural - no change.

Classified Sentence:

```
            I   PPA SN  V-t A Adj  DO  P  A    OP
SN V-t    Mercy! Their car / lost a front tire (on the freeway)! E
DO P2
```

Question and Answer Flow for Sentence 2: Kenney's more experienced players very quickly won the game during the tournament.

1. Who won the game during the tournament? players -SN
2. What is being said about players? players won - V
3. Players won what? game - verify the noun
4. Does game mean the same thing as players? No.
5. Game - DO
6. Won - V-t
7. The - A
8. During - P
9. During what? tournament - OP
10. The - A
11. Won how? quickly - Adv
12. How quickly? very - Adv

13. What kind of players? experienced - Adj
14. How experienced? more - Adv
15. Whose players? Kenney's - PNA
16. SN V-t DO P2 Check
17. Verb-transitive - Check again.
18. (During the tournament) - Prepositional phrase
19. Period, statement, declarative sentence
20. Go back to the verb - divide the complete subject from the complete predicate.
21. Is there an adverb exception? Yes - change the line.
22. Is this sentence in a natural or inverted order? Natural - no change.

Classified Sentence:		PNA	Adv	Adj	SN	Adv	Adv	V-t	A	DO	P	A	OP
SN V-t DO P2		Kenney's	more	experienced	players **/**	very	quickly	won	the	game	(during	the	tournament). **D**

TEACHER INSTRUCTIONS FOR A PATTERN 2 SENTENCE

Tell students that their sentence writing assignment today is to write a Pattern 2 sentence. They are to follow the same procedure used in the previous lessons. They should decide on their labels, arrange them in a selected order, write their sentences, and edit their sentences for improved word choices. (*Students do not have to write an Improved Sentence at this point unless you feel they need more one-on-one word choice writing practice.*) Check and discuss the Pattern 2 sentence after students have finished.

 SKILL TIME

TEACHING SCRIPT FOR A SIMPLE SENTENCE WITH COMPOUND PARTS

In the previous lesson, we learned about the three core parts that make a complete sentence. What are the three main parts? (*subject, verb, complete sense.*) We also learned that the abbreviation for a simple sentence is the letter **S** and the abbreviation for a fragment is the letter **F**.

Turn to Reference 38 on page 30 in your Reference Section. (*Reference 38 is located on the next page.*) Look at Example 1. This is an example of a simple sentence. Let's read the simple sentence together: **The little girl looked shyly at her teacher. (S)** (*Do not read the (S) on the end.*) The (*S*) abbreviation in parentheses at the end is an identification symbol that indicates it is a simple sentence.

CHAPTER 13 LESSON 2 CONTINUED

Reference 38: Simple Sentences, Compound Parts, and Fragments

Example 1: The little girl looked shyly at her teacher. (S)
Example 2: Carla's <u>mom and dad</u> attended her graduation. (SCS)
Example 3: Jennifer <u>jumped and twirled</u> during the dance rehearsal. (SCV)

Part 2: Identify each kind of sentence by writing the abbreviation in the blank. (S, SS, F, SCS, SCV)

<u>SCV</u> 1. The children ran and shouted during recess.
<u>SCS</u> 2. The rain and sleet fell steadily.
<u>F</u> 3. During the picnic at noon in the park.
<u>S</u> 4. Our electricity went off during the ice storm.
<u>SS</u> 5. I watched a movie. It was good.

Part 3: Put a slash to separate each run-on sentence below. Then, correct the run-on sentences by rewriting them as indicated by the labels in parentheses at the end of each sentence.

1. The wasps were swarming **/** they were upset. (SS)
   The wasps were swarming. They were upset.
2. The horse is in the barn **/** the cow is in the barn. (SCS)
   The horse and cow are in the barn.
3. The ambulance parked **/** it waited for a call. (SCV)
   The ambulance parked and waited for a call.

A simple sentence may have **compound parts, such as a compound subject or a compound verb,** even though it expresses only one complete thought. The abbreviation for a simple sentence with a compound subject is **SCS** (*simple sentence, compound subject*). The abbreviation for a simple sentence with a compound verb is **SCV** (*simple sentence, compound verb*).

Let's read the Example 2 and Example 3 sentences in your box together. Notice that the abbreviation at the end tells us what kind of sentence it is. (*Read the two sentences with your students.*) Example 2: **Carla's mom and dad attended her graduation.** (SCS)   Example 3: **Jennifer jumped and twirled during the dance rehearsal.** (SCV)

Look at Part 2. We will identify whether each sentence is a fragment, a simple sentence, two simple sentences, a simple sentence with a compound subject, or a simple sentence with a compound verb. After we decide what type of sentence it is, we will put the correct abbreviation in the blank at the left of each sentence. The abbreviations that you use are found at the end of the directions. (*Read the directions and work through sentences 1–5, showing students how to identify each type of sentence and then write the abbreviation in the blank.*)

TEACHING SCRIPT FOR A RUN-ON SENTENCE

If two sentences are written together as one sentence without being punctuated correctly, it is called a run-on sentence. Go to Part 3 in your reference box and look at number 1: **The wasps were swarming they were upset (SS)**. Is the first sentence "The wasps were swarming" a complete thought? (*yes*) Is the second sentence "they were upset" a complete thought? (*yes*) There are two complete thoughts expressed in number 1. The two thoughts are run together because they are written as one sentence.

CHAPTER 13 LESSON 2 CONTINUED

There are several ways to correct a run-on sentence, but today we will concentrate on three ways to use the simple sentence to correct a run-on sentence. First, we will put a slash between the two thoughts that are run together so we can see each sentence clearly. (*The wasps were swarming / they were upset.*) Then, we will look at the abbreviation in parentheses at the end of number 1 to see how we are to correct this run-on sentence. Look at the end of number 1. The **(SS)** in parentheses tells us to correct the run-on sentence by making it into two simple sentences.

Let's step back and observe the facts. We have a run-on sentence that needs to be corrected. We know that we are to correct it by making it into two simple sentences. So, how do we punctuate this run-on sentence to show that it is now two separate sentences? (*The first word of each sentence must be capitalized, and each sentence must have end mark punctuation.*)

Notice that I have corrected the run-on sentence by writing it as two simple sentences. Writing it as two simple sentences now matches the instructions in parentheses on how to correct it. The **(SS)** in parentheses tells me to make simple sentences. (*Read the two simple sentences:* **The wasps were swarming. They were upset.**)

We will now look at a second way to use the simple sentence to correct a run-on sentence. Look at number 2: **The horse is in the barn the cow is in the barn. (SCS)** This is a run-on sentence that needs to be corrected. First, we will put a slash between the two thoughts that are run together so we can see each sentence clearly. (*The horse is in the barn / the cow is in the barn.*)

Then, we will look at the abbreviation in parentheses at the end of number 2 to see how we are to correct the run-on sentence. Look at the end of number 2. The **(SCS)** in parentheses tells us to correct the run-on sentence by writing a simple sentence with a compound subject. When each sentence has a different subject, join the two subjects together with the conjunction *AND*. That will make a compound subject. If the subjects have additional subject words, include them as you write the compound subjects. (**The horse and cow.**)

Since both sentences have the same verb and complete predicate, the verb and complete predicate will stay the same except for one change. This change is a subject-verb agreement change. When *horse* and *cow* were used as singular subjects, they each used the singular verb *is*. Now that *horse* and *cow* have become a compound subject, the singular verb *is* MUST be changed to the plural verb *are* because a compound subject uses a plural verb. This new sentence is called a simple sentence with a compound subject. (**The horse and cow are in the barn.**)

We will look at a third way to use the simple sentence to correct a run-on sentence. Look at number 3: **The ambulance parked it waited for a call. (SCV)** This is a run-on sentence that needs to be corrected. First, we will put a slash between the two thoughts that are run together so we can see each sentence clearly. (*The ambulance parked / it waited for a call.*)

We will look at the abbreviation in parentheses at the end of number 3 to see how we are to correct the run-on sentence. Look at the end of number 3. The **(SCV)** in parentheses tells us to correct the run-on sentence by writing a simple sentence with a compound verb. Since both sentences have the same subject (***ambulance*** and ***it*** *are the same thing*), the subject noun *ambulance* is used.

CHAPTER 13 LESSON 2 CONTINUED

Next, we look at the verbs. Since each sentence has a different verb, the two verbs are joined together with the conjunction *AND*. Joining the verbs together with a conjunction makes a compound verb. If the verbs have additional predicate words, the predicate words are always included as the compound verbs are written. (**parked and waited**). This new sentence is called a simple sentence with a compound verb: **The ambulance parked and waited for a call.**

 PRACTICE TIME

Have students turn to page 59 in the Practice Section of their book and find Chapter 13, Lesson 2, Practice (1 and 2). Go over the directions to make sure they understand what to do. Check and discuss the Practices after students have finished. (*Chapter 31, Lesson 2 Practice keys are given below.*)

Chapter 13, Lesson 2, Practice 1: Put a slash to separate each run-on sentence below. Then, correct the run-on sentences by rewriting them as indicated by the labels in parentheses at the end of each sentence.

1. The children were playing **/** they were happy. (SS)
   The children were playing. They were happy.
2. The car is in the garage **/** the bicycle is in the garage. (SCS)
   The car and bicycle are in the garage.
3. The boys washed the car **/** they waxed the car. (SCV)
   The boys washed and waxed the car.

Chapter 13, Lesson 2, Practice 2: Identify each kind of sentence by writing the abbreviation in the blank. (S, SS, F, SCS, SCV)

F	1.	Alongside the narrow road.
SS	2.	The faucet sprung a leak. Dad fixed it.
SCV	3.	The astronauts put on their helmets and walked in space.
S	4.	Mom lit all of the candles on the cake.
SCS	5.	Parsley and marjoram are her favorite spices.

 VOCABULARY TIME

Assign Chapter 13, Vocabulary Words **#2** on page 7 in the Reference Section for students to define in their Vocabulary notebooks. Tell students they are to use a dictionary or thesaurus to look up the meanings of the vocabulary words. After they write each word and its meaning, students are to write a sentence using the vocabulary word.

Chapter 13, Vocabulary Words #2
(innate, acquired, entourage, followers)

(End of lesson.)

CHAPTER 13   LESSON 3

New objectives: Grammar (Practice Sentences), Skills (compound sentence, comma splice), and a Practice sheet.

 JINGLE TIME

Have students turn to the Jingle Section of their books. The teacher will lead the students in reciting the previously-taught jingles.

 GRAMMAR TIME

First-Year Option: Put the Practice Sentences from the box below on the board or notebook paper. Use these sentences as you practice the concepts that have been taught. For the greatest benefit, students must participate orally with the teacher. **Second-Year Option:** Have students classify the Practice Sentences independently on paper. Check students' sentences with the answers provided below. (*If you have the CDs for Practice Sentences, have students check their sentences with the CDs.*)

Chapter 13, Practice Sentences for Lesson 3

1. _____ In two days, the accountant notified him about the refund.
2. _____ The counselor's kind words lessened Amy's apprehension.

TEACHING SCRIPT FOR PRACTICING PATTERN 2 SENTENCES

We will practice classifying Pattern 2 sentences. We will classify the sentences together. Begin. (*You might have your students write the labels above the sentences at this time.*)

Question and Answer Flow for Sentence 1: In two days, the accountant notified him about the refund.

1. Who notified him about the refund? accountant - SN
2. What is being said about accountant? accountant notified - V
3. Accountant notified whom? him - verify the pronoun
4. Does him mean the same thing as accountant? No.
5. Him - DO
6. Notified - V-t
7. About - P
8. About what? refund - OP
9. The - A
10. The - A
11. In - P
12. In what? days - OP
13. How many days? two - Adj
14. SN V-t DO P2 Check
15. Verb-transitive - Check again.
16. (In two days) - Prepositional phrase
17. (About the refund) - Prepositional phrase
18. Period, statement, declarative sentence
19. Go back to the verb - divide the complete subject from the complete predicate.
20. Is there an adverb exception? No.
21. Is this sentence in a natural or inverted order? Inverted - underline the subject parts once and the predicate parts twice.

Classified Sentence:

```
                          P  Adj  OP   A    SN       V-t  DO   P    A   OP
        SN V-t      (In two days), the accountant / notified him (about the refund).  D
        DO P2
```

CHAPTER 13 LESSON 3 CONTINUED

Question and Answer Flow for Sentence 2: The counselor's kind words lessened Amy's apprehension.

1. What lessened Amy's apprehension? words - SN
2. What is being said about words? words lessened - V
3. Words lessened what? apprehension - verify the noun
4. Does apprehension mean the same thing as words? No.
5. Apprehension - DO
6. Lessened - V-t
7. Whose apprehension? Amy's - PNA
8. What kind of words? kind - Adj
9. Whose words? counselor's - PNA
10. The - A

11. SN V-t DO P2 Check
12. Verb-transitive - Check again.
13. No prepositional phrases.
14. Period, statement, declarative sentence
15. Go back to the verb - divide the complete subject from the complete predicate.
16. Is there an adverb exception? No.
17. Is this sentence in a natural or inverted order? Natural - no change.

Classified Sentence:

                     A   PNA   Adj SN   V-t   PNA   DO

  SN V-t   The counselor's kind words **/** lessened Amy's apprehension. **D**
  DO P2

SKILL TIME

TEACHING SCRIPT FOR THE COMPOUND SENTENCE, A COMMA SPLICE, AND A REVIEW OF THE RUN-ON SENTENCE

Another kind of sentence you need to be able to recognize and write is the compound sentence. Look at the information about the compound sentence in Reference 39 on page 30 in your book. Pay special attention to the ways you can correctly join the parts of a compound sentence. (*Read the information about a compound sentence, comma splice, and run-on sentence with the class. This information is reproduced below.*)

Reference 39: The Compound Sentence

1. Compound means two. A compound sentence is two complete sentences joined together correctly.

2. <u>The first way to join two sentences</u> to make a compound sentence is to <u>use a comma and a conjunction</u>. The formula for you to follow will always be given at the end of the sentence. The formula gives the abbreviation for "compound sentence" and lists the conjunction to use (**CD, but**). Remember to place the comma BEFORE the conjunction.
      Example: She studied for her driver's **test, but** she did not pass it. (CD, but)

3. <u>The second way to join two sentences</u> and make a compound sentence is to <u>use a semicolon and a connective (conjunctive) adverb</u>. The formula to follow is given at the end of the sentence. The formula gives the abbreviation for "compound sentence" and lists the connective adverb to use (**CD; however,**). Remember to place a semicolon BEFORE the connective adverb and a comma AFTER the connective adverb. (This method is particularly useful when you are working with longer sentences.)   **Example:** She studied for her driver's test; **however,** she did not pass it. (CD; however,)

4. <u>The third way to join two sentences</u> and make a compound sentence is to <u>use a semicolon only</u>. The formula to follow is given at the end of the sentence and lists the semicolon after the abbreviation for "compound sentence" (**CD;**). Remember, there is no conjunction or connective adverb when the semicolon is used alone. (This method is usually used with short sentences that are closely related in thought.)   **Example:** She studied for her driver's **test; she** did not pass it. (CD;)

5. Compound sentences should be closely related in thought and importance.
   <u>Correct</u>:   She studied for her driver's **test, but** she did not pass it.
   <u>Incorrect</u>: She studied for her driver's test, but she preferred toast.

CHAPTER 13 LESSON 3 CONTINUED

When the parts of a compound sentence are not joined together correctly, you have a **comma splice or a run-on sentence.** (*Put the sample sentences below on the board.*)

1. **A comma splice** is two or more sentences incorrectly connected with a comma and no conjunction. To correct a comma splice: Put a conjunction (*and, or, but*) after the comma.

   Incorrect: She studied for her driver's **test, she** did not pass it.
   Correct: She studied for her driver's **test, but she** did not pass it.

2. **A run-on sentence** is two or more sentences written together as one sentence, or two or more sentences written with a conjunction and no comma.

   Incorrect: She studied for her driver's **test she** did not pass it.
   Incorrect: She studied for her driver's **test but she** did not pass it.

3. There are three ways to correct a run-on sentence:

   1. Put a comma and a conjunction between the two complete thoughts.
   2. Put a semicolon and a connective adverb between the two complete thoughts.
   3. Put a semicolon between the two complete thoughts.

      Correct: She studied for her driver's **test, but she** did not pass it.
      Correct: She studied for her driver's **test; however, she** did not pass it.
      Correct: She studied for her driver's **test; she** did not pass it.

As you have just learned, compound sentences are correctly joined with conjunctions, semicolons, and connective adverbs. Now, we are going to learn more about the joining words that connect two sentences to form a compound sentence. We are going to learn more about conjunctions.

You have already learned that conjunctions join words or groups of words together, and the three most common conjunctions are *and, or*, and *but*. Since there are different kinds of conjunctions, you will now learn the names of conjunctions that join, or connect. Conjunctions that join are called **coordinate conjunctions, or coordinating conjunctions**. Coordinate conjunctions join things of equal importance, like compound subjects, compound verbs, or compound sentences.

The conjunctions *and, but, or, nor,* and *yet* are coordinate conjunctions. They join together words, phrases, or sentences that have equal importance. Sometimes, the word *so* is used as a coordinate conjunction. You will know to use *so* as a coordinate conjunction if it means *as a result*. Put a comma before *so* if it is used as a coordinate conjunction. Do not put a comma before *so* if you can substitute the words "so that" as you read the sentence.

Examples: We caught our **flight, so** we will arrive on time. We left early **so (that)** we wouldn't miss our plane.

The connective (or conjunctive) adverb acts as an adverb and conjunction. It modifies the sentence that it introduces, and it works with the semicolon to connect two simple sentences into a compound sentence. It must be used with a semicolon and is usually followed by a comma. (**Example:** I came early**; therefore,** I left early.)

The coordinate conjunctions and some of the connective adverbs are listed in a chart in Reference 40 on page 30 to help make it easy for you to use them. (*Read and discuss the chart on the next page with your students.*)

CHAPTER 13 LESSON 3 CONTINUED

Reference 40: Coordinate Conjunction and Connective Adverb Chart				
Type of Conj / Adv	More Information	Contrast/Choice	Alternative	As a result
Coordinate Conjunction	,and ,nor	,but ,yet	,or	,so (as a result) so (that) - no comma
Connective Adverbs	;moreover, ;furthermore, ;besides, ;also, ;likewise,	;however, ;nevertheless,	;otherwise,	;therefore, ;hence, ;thus, ;consequently, ;accordingly,

Look at the practice examples in Reference 41. We will work through the examples together. We will read the directions first to be sure we know what to do. (*Read the directions for Reference 41.*)

Reference 41: Examples Using S, SCS, SCV, and CD to Correct Run-On Sentences
Put a slash to separate the two complete thoughts in each run-on sentence. Correct the run-on sentences or fragments as indicated by the labels in parentheses at the end of each sentence.

1. Dave plans to move **/** he doesn't like packing. (CD, but)
   Dave plans to move, but he doesn't like packing.

2. George will drive to Denver **/** there is a snow advisory posted. (CD; however,)
   George will drive to Denver; however, there is a snow advisory posted.

3. I always climb the flights of stairs **/** the exercise is healthy. (CD;)
   I always climb the flights of stairs; the exercise is healthy.

4. Kimberly gathered daisies along the roadside **/** Kimberly gathered rocks along the roadside. (S)
   Kimberly gathered daisies and rocks along the roadside. (*Simple sentences can have other compound parts.*)

5. Larry woke at 6:00 **/** Sue woke at 6:00. (SCS)
   Larry and Sue woke at 6:00.

6. For recreation, Judy plays the piano **/** she writes songs. (SCV)
   For recreation, Judy plays the piano and writes songs.

Look at number 1. Is "Dave plans to move" a complete sentence? (*Yes, except for an end mark.*) Is "he doesn't like packing" a complete sentence? (*Yes - except for a capital letter and end mark.*) The directions tell us to put a slash between these two complete thoughts. (*Show students how the run-on sentence is divided with a slash.*)

Next, look at the end of number 1. The (**CD, but**) in parentheses tells us how to make these two sentences into a compound sentence. The (**CD**) stands for compound sentence, and the (**but**) tells which coordinate conjunction to use. Remember, we must also use a comma in front of the conjunction in order to punctuate the compound sentence correctly.

As you can see, the compound sentence has been written by using the information in parentheses (**CD, but**). (*Read the compound sentence: **Dave plans to move, but he doesn't like packing**.*) These two sentences are made into a compound sentence by using a comma and the coordinate conjunction *but* to join them.

CHAPTER 13 LESSON 3 CONTINUED

TEACHER INSTRUCTIONS

Work through the rest of the Practice Sentences 2-6 in the same way. Make sure your students understand that the abbreviations in parentheses at the end of the sentences give directions on how to correct the run-on sentences and fragments.

Have students look at Reference 42. Read the directions and work through Parts 1 and 2. Make sure students understand how each example was done because they will be tested in each format. (*In Part 2, point out that number 13 is a compound sentence because it has two sentences joined by a comma and conjunction. Number 14 is a simple sentence with a compound verb because it is only one sentence with a conjunction connecting two verbs. It does not have a second sentence and requires no commas.*)

Reference 42: Identifying S, F, SCS, SCV, and CD
Part 1: Identify each kind of sentence by writing the abbreviation in the blank (S, F, SCS, SCV, CD).
_CD_ 1. Jeff did not study last night; therefore, he is in a panic now.
_F_ 2. Beside a creek where a grove of trees stood.
SCV 3. We flew into Chicago and took a taxi to the stadium.
_S_ 4. After school, Josh mows yards three nights a week.
SCS 5. The superintendent and principal met behind closed doors.
_CD_ 6. Rhonda wrapped the presents, and she took them to her mother's.
Part 2: On your paper, use the ways listed below to correct this run-on sentence: **The vase cracked it did not break.**
7. CD, but **The vase cracked, but it did not break.** 8. SCV **The vase cracked but did not break.**

 PRACTICE TIME

Have students turn to page 60 in the Practice Section of their book and find Chapter 13, Lesson 3, Practice (*1-3*). Go over the directions to make sure they understand what to do. Check and discuss the Practices after students have finished. (*Chapter 13, Lesson 3 Practice keys are reproduced below.*)

Chapter 13, Lesson 3, Practice 1: Put a slash to separate each run-on sentence below. Then, correct the run-on sentences by rewriting them as indicated by the labels in parentheses at the end of each sentence.

1. The disgruntled wrestler argued with the referee / the referee would not change his mind. (CD, but)
   The disgruntled wrestler argued with the referee, but the referee would not change his mind.
2. The disgruntled wrestler argued with the referee / the referee would not change his mind. (CD; however,)
   The disgruntled wrestler argued with the referee; however, the referee would not change his mind.
3. The disgruntled wrestler argued with the referee / he fought with the referee. (SCV)
   The disgruntled wrestler argued and fought with the referee.
4. The disgruntled wrestler argued with the referee / the referee would not change his mind. (CD;)
   The disgruntled wrestler argued with the referee; the referee would not change his mind.

Chapter 13, Lesson 3, Practice 2:	**Chapter 13, Lesson 3, Practice 3:**
Identify each kind of sentence by writing the abbreviation in the blank. (S, F, SCS, SCV, CD)	Write three compound sentences using these labels to guide you:
	① (CD, but) ② (CD; therefore,) ③(CD;)
SCV 1. The buzzard swooped and grabbed the kitten.	
_F_ 2. Put into a defenseless position.	
_CD_ 3. Mom fixed the soup; Lori baked a pie.	(End of lesson.)
SCS 4. His warmth and kindness were appreciated.	

CHAPTER 13   LESSON 4

New objectives: Test and an Activity.

 JINGLE TIME

Have students turn to the Jingle Section of their books. The teacher will lead the students in reciting the previously-taught jingles.

 STUDY TIME

Have students study the vocabulary words in their vocabulary notebooks. Remind students that any vocabulary word in their notebooks could be on their test. Also, have students study any of the skills in the Practice Section that they need to review.

 TEST TIME

Have students turn to page 95 in the Test Section of their book and find Chapter 13 Test. Go over the directions to make sure they understand what to do. (*Chapter 13 Test key is on the next page.*)

 CHECK TIME

After students have finished, check and discuss their test papers. Make sure they understand why their answers are right or wrong. (*For total points, count each required answer as a point.*)

 ACTIVITY / ASSIGNMENT TIME

The **limerick** is a popular type of rhymed poem consisting of five lines. The poet Ogden Nash popularized it in the United States. The intent of the **limerick** is to evoke a smile or chuckle in the reader. Almost all **limericks** are humorous and are fun to write. The rules are simple. The first, second, and fifth lines contain three accents and rhyme with each other. The third and fourth lines contain two accents and rhyme with each other. Read and discuss the example below. Have students write their own limerick and then share it with others.

> An old miser by the name of Fred
> Is lucky he isn't dead.
> He was hateful and cruel
> To others, as a rule,
> And thought with a hollow head.

(End of lesson.)

Chapter 13 Test
(Student Page 95)

Exercise 1: Classify each sentence.

```
           P    A    OP    A    SN      Adv    V-t A  Adj    DO
1. SN  V-t  (Across the street), the builders / quickly erected a retaining wall.  D
   DO P2
```

```
           CSN  C    CSN      V-t A Adj DO  P A    OP      P A   OP
2. SN  V-t  Bill and Rhonda / rode a city bus (to the concert) (in the park).  D
   DO P2
```

Exercise 2: Use Sentence 2 to underline the complete subject once and the complete predicate twice and to complete the table below.

List the Noun Used	List the Noun Job	Singular or Plural	Common or Proper	Simple Subject	Simple Predicate
1. **Bill**	2. **CSN**	3. **S**	4. **P**	5. **Bill and Rhonda**	6. **rode**
7. **Rhonda**	8. **CSN**	9. **S**	10. **P**		
11. **bus**	12. **DO**	13. **S**	14. **C**		
15. **concert**	16. **OP**	17. **S**	18. **C**		
19. **park**	20. **OP**	21. **S**	22. **C**		

Exercise 3: Identify each pair of words as synonyms or antonyms by putting parentheses ( ) around *syn* or *ant*.

1. ecstatic, blissful	**(syn)** ant	5. bracelet, bangle	**(syn)** ant	9. proverbial, notorious	**(syn)** ant
2. innate, acquired	syn **(ant)**	6. knoll, mound	**(syn)** ant	10. entourage, followers	**(syn)** ant
3. audacious, timid	syn **(ant)**	7. precarious, stable	syn **(ant)**	11. luminous, obscure	syn **(ant)**
4. burn, smolder	**(syn)** ant	8. zeppelin, balloon	**(syn)** ant	12. marginal, significant	syn **(ant)**

Exercise 4: Put a slash to separate each run-on sentence below. Then, correct the run-on sentences by rewriting them as indicated by the labels in parentheses at the end of each sentence.

1. Horns were honking / sirens were blaring. (CD;)
   Horns were honking; sirens were blaring.
2. The girls washed the windows / the boys washed the windows. (SCS)
   The girls and boys washed the windows.
3. The secretary signed the letters / she stuffed them in envelopes. (SCV)
   The secretary signed the letters and stuffed them in envelopes.
4. The secretary signed the letters / she stuffed them in envelopes. (CD, and)
   The secretary signed the letters, and she stuffed them in envelopes.
5. Ray rebuilt the fence / Warren helped him. (SCS)
   Ray and Warren rebuilt the fence.
6. The girls boiled a dozen eggs / they colored them for Easter. (SCV)
   The girls boiled a dozen eggs and colored them for Easter.

Exercise 5: Identify each kind of sentence by writing the abbreviation in the blank. (S, F, SCS, SCV, CD)

S	1.	The August drought left the lake nearly dry.
CD	2.	She tried to volunteer, yet no one would give her a chance.
SCS	3.	The hoe and shovel will go with me to the garden.
F	4.	Wrapped around the electric pole at the end of our street.
CD	5.	My aunt died; consequently, I have a trip to make.
SCV	6.	The usher held her hand and led her to her seat.
F	7.	Only because we had no other choice.

Exercise 6: Write four sentences using these labels to guide you: (S), (SCS), (SCV), (CD). **Answers will vary.**

Exercise 7: In your journal, write a paragraph summarizing what you have learned this week.

CHAPTER 13 LESSON 4 CONTINUED

TEACHER INSTRUCTIONS

Use the Question and Answer Flows below for the sentences on Chapter 13 Test.

Question and Answer Flow for Sentence 1: Across the street, the builders quickly erected a retaining wall.

1. Who erected a retaining wall? builders - SN
2. What is being said about builders? builders erected - V
3. Builders erected what? wall - verify the noun
4. Does wall mean the same thing as builders? No.
5. Wall - DO
6. Erected - V-t
7. What kind of wall? retaining - Adj
8. A - A
9. Erected how? quickly - Adv
10. The - A
11. Across - P
12. Across what? street - OP
13. The - A
14. SN V-t DO P2 Check
15. Verb-transitive - Check again.
16. (Across the street) - Prepositional phrase
17. Period, statement, declarative sentence
18. Go back to the verb - divide the complete subject from the complete predicate.
19. Is there an adverb exception? Yes - change the line.
20. Is this sentence in a natural or inverted order? Inverted - underline the subject parts once and the predicate parts twice.

Classified Sentence:

```
                          P    A   OP   A   SN     Adv    V-t   A   Adj    DO
        SN  V-t    (Across the street), the builders / quickly erected a retaining wall.  D
        DO  P2
```

Question and Answer Flow for Sentence 2: Bill and Rhonda rode a city bus to the concert in the park.

1. Who rode a city bus to the concert in the park? Bill and Rhonda - CSN, CSN
2. What is being said about Bill and Rhonda? Bill and Rhonda rode - V
3. Bill and Rhonda rode what? bus - verify the noun
4. Does bus mean the same thing as Bill and Rhonda? No.
5. Bus - DO
6. Rode - V-t
7. What kind of bus? city - Adj
8. A - A
9. To - P
10. To what? concert - OP
11. The - A
12. In - P
13. In what? park - OP
14. The - A
15. And - C
16. SN V-t DO P2 Check
17. Verb-transitive - Check again.
18. (To the concert) - Prepositional phrase
19. (In the park) - Prepositional phrase
20. Period, statement, declarative sentence
21. Go back to the verb - divide the complete subject from the complete predicate.
22. Is there an adverb exception? No.
23. Is this sentence in a natural or inverted order? Natural - no change.

Classified Sentence:

```
                     CSN  C   CSN     V-t  A Adj DO    P  A   OP      P  A   OP
        SN  V-t    Bill and Rhonda / rode a city bus (to the concert) (in the park).  D
        DO  P2
```

CHAPTER 13   LESSON 5

Introduce these objectives: Writing Assignments #15 and #16.

 WRITING TIME

TEACHING SCRIPT FOR PRACTICING DIFFERENT KINDS OF WRITING

Today, you are assigned two different kinds of writing. You will write a five-paragraph expository essay and a three-paragraph persuasive essay. <u>You will revise and edit the five-paragraph expository essay</u>. (*Read the box below for more information about students' writing assignment.*) As you edit, make sure you use the checkpoints in the editing checklist provided in Reference 35. Remember to read through the whole essay, starting with the title, and then edit, sentence-by-sentence, using the five sentence checkpoints for each sentence. Use the paragraph checkpoints to check each paragraph. Remember, your editing is now more detailed and more comprehensive, so take your time.

Writing Assignment Box #1

Writing Assignment #15: Five-Paragraph Expository Essay (First Person)
(Remember, first person pronouns are *I, we, me, us, my, our, mine, and ours.*)
Remind students that the 5-paragraph essay has three parts: 1. Introduction 2. Body 3. Conclusion. The body has three paragraphs instead of one. Have students use their regular editing checklist to edit this assignment.

Writing topic: Why Staying in a Motel is Fun or **Why Some Kids Keep Messy/Neat Rooms** or **Why I Dream**

Your second writing assignment is to write a three-paragraph persuasive essay. (*Read the box below for more information about the students' writing assignment.*) You do not have to edit this assignment with the editing checklist.

Writing Assignment Box #2

Writing Assignment #16: Three-Paragraph Persuasive Essay (First Person)
(Remember, first person pronouns are *I, we, me, us, my, our, mine, and ours.*)
Remind students that the 3-paragraph essay has three parts: 1. Introduction 2. Body 3. Conclusion. The body has one paragraph instead of three. Have students use their regular editing checklist to edit this assignment.

Writing topic: Why Too Much TV is Unhealthy or **Why My Friends Should Not Smoke**
            or **Why a Hobby/Laughter is Important**

Read, check, and discuss Writing Assignment #15 after students have finished their final papers. Use the checklists as you check and discuss students' papers. Make sure students are using the regular editing checklist correctly. Read and discuss Writing Assignment #16 for fun and enrichment.

(End of lesson.)

CHAPTER 14 LESSON 1

New objectives: Grammar (Practice Sentences), Skills (complex sentences, subordinate conjunctions), Practice sheet, and Vocabulary #1.

JINGLE TIME

Have students turn to the Jingle Section of their books. The teacher will lead the students in reciting the previously-taught jingles.

GRAMMAR TIME

First-Year Option: Put the Practice Sentences from the box below on the board or notebook paper. Use these sentences as you practice the concepts that have been taught. For the greatest benefit, students must participate orally with the teacher. **Second-Year Option:** Have students classify the Practice Sentences independently on paper. Check students' sentences with the answers provided below. (*If you have the CDs for Practice Sentences, have students check their sentences with the CDs.*)

Chapter 14, Practice Sentences for Lesson 1
1. _____ Citizens need a clear set of choices at election time.
2. _____ The huge flashing sign alerted the passing motorists to the hazardous travel conditions.

TEACHING SCRIPT FOR PRACTICING PATTERN 2 SENTENCES

We will practice classifying Pattern 2 sentences. We will classify the sentences together. Begin. (*You might have your students write the labels above the sentences at this time.*)

Question and Answer Flow for Sentence 1: Citizens need a clear set of choices at election time.	
1. Who need a clear set of choices at election time? citizens - SN	12. At what? time - OP
2. What is being said about citizens? citizens need - V	13. What kind of time? election - Adj
3. Citizens need what? set - verify the noun	14. SN V-t DO P2 Check
4. Does set mean the same thing as citizens? No.	15. Verb-transitive - Check again.
5. Set - DO	16. (Of choices) - Prepositional phrase
6. Need - V-t	17. (At election time) - Prepositional phrase
7. What kind of set? clear - Adj	18. Period, statement, declarative sentence
8. A - A	19. Go back to the verb - divide the complete subject from the complete predicate.
9. Of - P	20. Is there an adverb exception? No.
10. Of what? choices - OP	21. Is this sentence in a natural or inverted order? Natural - no change.
11. At - P	

Classified Sentence:

```
                              SN        V-t  A  Adj  DO  P   OP      P   Adj  OP
               SN V-t     Citizens / need a clear set (of choices) (at election time). D
               DO P2
```

CHAPTER 14 LESSON 1 CONTINUED

Question and Answer Flow for Sentence 2: The huge flashing sign alerted the passing motorists to the hazardous travel conditions.

1. What alerted the passing motorists to the hazardous travel conditions? sign - SN
2. What is being said about sign? sign alerted - V
3. Sign alerted whom? motorists - verify the noun
4. Do motorists mean the same thing as sign? No.
5. Motorists - DO
6. Alerted - V-t
7. What kind of motorists? passing - Adj
8. The - A
9. To - P
10. To what? conditions - OP
11. What kind of conditions? travel - Adj
12. What kind of conditions? hazardous - Adj

13. The - A
14. What kind of sign? flashing - Adj
15. What kind of sign? huge - Adj
16. The - A
17. SN V-t DO P2 Check
18. Verb-transitive - Check again.
19. (To the hazardous travel conditions) - Prepositional phrase
20. Period, statement, declarative sentence
21. Go back to the verb - divide the complete subject from the complete predicate.
22. Is there an adverb exception? No.
23. Is this sentence in a natural or inverted order? Natural - no change.

Classified Sentence:

<u>SN V-t</u>
DO P2

A   Adj   Adj   SN   V-t   A   Adj   DO   P   A   Adj   Adj   OP
The huge flashing sign / alerted the passing motorists (to the hazardous travel conditions). **D**

Use Sentences 1-2 that you just classified with your students to do an Oral Skill Builder Check. Use the guidelines below.

Oral Skill Builder Check

1. **Noun check.**
   (Say the job and then say the noun. Circle each noun.)
2. **Identify the nouns as singular or plural.**
   (Write S or P above each noun.)
3. **Identify the nouns as common or proper.**
   (Follow established procedure for oral identification.)
4. **Do a vocabulary check.**
   (Follow established procedure for oral identification.)

5. **Identify the complete subject and the complete predicate.** (Underline the complete subject once and the complete predicate twice.)
6. **Identify the simple subject and simple predicate.**
   (Underline the simple subject once and the simple predicate twice. Bold, or highlight, the lines.)
7. **Recite the irregular verb chart.**
   (Located on student page 17 and teacher page 143.)

SKILL TIME

TEACHING SCRIPT FOR COMPLEX SENTENCES AND SUBORDINATE CONJUNCTIONS

Today, you will study one of the most powerful kinds of sentences used in writing. It is called the complex sentence. The complex sentence is a great writing tool because it is very easy to use and because it gives your writing more versatility and more power than any other kind of sentence.

(Have students open their books to Reference 43 on page 32 so they can follow the examples as you teach complex sentences. Read the definition of the complex sentence in the reference box, then continue with the teaching script. This information is located on the next page.)

CHAPTER 14 LESSON 1 CONTINUED

Reference 43: The Complex Sentence and Subordinate Conjunctions

Definition: A complex sentence is made by correctly joining two sentences: an independent sentence and a subordinate sentence.

1. **Independent sentence:** He won the spelling bee.
2. **Subordinate sentence:** <u>After</u> he won the spelling bee.
3. **Complex sentence:**   <u>After</u> he won the spelling bee, <u>he earned the respect of his classmates.</u>

Example 1: he won the spelling bee he earned the respect of his classmates. (CX, after 1)
   After he won the spelling bee, he earned the respect of his classmates.
Example 2: he earned the respect of his classmates he won the spelling bee. (CX, after 2)
   He earned the respect of his classmates after he won the spelling bee.
Example 3: After he won the spelling bee, he earned the respect of his classmates.
Example 4: He earned the respect of his classmates **after he won the spelling bee**.

Review

A. A sentence becomes a complex sentence when you add a subordinate conjunction to one of the two sentences that make up a complex sentence.
B. Any independent sentence can be made subordinate (dependent) by simply adding a subordinate conjunction to the beginning of that sentence.
   Subordinate sentences: (After he won) **(When** he won) **(Because** he won) **(Until** he won)

A LIST OF THE MOST COMMON SUBORDINATE CONJUNCTIONS

A subordinate conjunction is a conjunction that always introduces a subordinate sentence. Since there are many subordinate conjunctions, only a few of the most common subordinate conjunctions are provided in the list below.

after	because	except	so that	though	when
although	before	if	than	unless	where
as, or as soon as	even though	since	that	until	while

A complex sentence is made by correctly joining two sentences: an independent sentence and a subordinate sentence. An **independent sentence** is a regular sentence. It has a subject and a verb and expresses a complete thought. It can stand alone as a simple sentence because it is independent. (*Have students look at number 1 while you read the independent sentence to the class.*)

   1. **Independent sentence:** He won the spelling bee.

A **subordinate sentence** is a dependent sentence. It cannot stand alone. It is made by adding one powerful sentence-changing word (*called a subordinate conj*unction) to the beginning of a regular, independent sentence. A subordinate sentence has a subject, a verb, and a subordinate conjunction, but it does not express a complete thought by itself. It must be joined to an independent sentence in order to complete its meaning. (*Have students look at number 2 while you read the subordinate sentence to the class.*)

   2. **Subordinate sentence:** <u>After</u> he won the spelling bee.

CHAPTER 14 LESSON 1 CONTINUED

To help you write complex sentences, you will be given a run-on sentence and a formula to follow at the end of the run-on sentence. The formula gives the abbreviation of the complex sentence (*CX*), lists the subordinate conjunction to use (*when*), and indicates whether to put the subordinate conjunction on the first sentence or second sentence by a number one (*1*) or a number two (*2*). (*Have students look at Examples 1 and 2 while you read them to the class.*)

Example 1: he won the spelling bee he earned the respect of his classmates. (CX, after 1)
After he won the spelling bee, he earned the respect of his classmates.
Example 2: he earned the respect of his classmates he won the spelling bee. (CX, after 2)
He earned the respect of his classmates after he won the spelling bee.

If the subordinate sentence comes before the independent sentence, a comma is usually required at the end of the subordinate sentence. (*Have students look at Example 3 while you read it to the class.*)

Example 3: After he won the spelling bee, he earned the respect of his classmates.

If the subordinate sentence comes after the independent sentence, a comma is normally not required at the end of the independent sentence. (*Have students look at Example 4 while you read it to the class.*)

Example 4: He earned the respect of his classmates **after he won the spelling bee**.

I want you to look at the review in your reference box. Follow along as I go over it with you. (*Read and discuss the review reproduced below with your students.*)

Review

A. A sentence becomes a complex sentence when you add a subordinate conjunction to one of the two sentences that make up a complex sentence.
B. Any independent sentence can be made subordinate (dependent) by simply adding a subordinate conjunction to the beginning of that sentence.

Subordinate sentences: (After he won) **(When** he won) **(Because** he won) **(Until** he won)

As you can see, a sentence becomes a complex sentence when you add a subordinate conjunction to one of the two sentences that make up a complex sentence.

Look at the bottom of your reference box at the subordinate conjunctions. A subordinate conjunction is a conjunction that introduces a subordinate sentence. Since there are many subordinate conjunctions, only a few of the most common subordinate conjunctions are provided for you in the reference box. Let's recite the list together. (*Recite the list below.*)

A LIST OF THE MOST COMMON SUBORDINATE CONJUNCTIONS					
after	because	except	so that	though	when
although	before	if	than	unless	where
as, or as soon as	even though	since	that	until	while

CHAPTER 14 LESSON 1 CONTINUED

TEACHING SCRIPT FOR WRITING COMPLEX SENTENCES

We will practice the two ways to write a complex sentence by going through the examples in Reference 44. The examples in this reference box will give you an easy step-by- step method to identify and write complex sentences. Remember, we always read the directions first. Look at Part 1 as I read the directions. (*Read the directions for Part 1.*)

Reference 44: Examples of Complex Sentences	
Part 1: Put a slash to separate each sentence. Rewrite and correct the run-on sentences as indicated by the labels in parentheses.	**Part 2:** Identify each kind of sentence by writing the abbreviation in the blank (S, F, SCS, SCV, CD, CX).
1. Larry fell down **/** he broke his arm. **(CX, when 1)** 2. He overslept **/** he was late for work. **(CX, because 1)** 3. You will not graduate **/** you do not study. **(CX, if 2)** 4. The phone rang **/** I burned my finger. **(CX, before 1)**	5. __S__ After midnight, the tornado warning sirens blared. 6. __CX__ As he left, he threw us a kiss. 7. __SCV__ My tutor broke her arm and quit. 8. __SCS__ Tomorrow, you and the other team captain will lead the parade.
Key for 1-4: 1. When Larry fell down, he broke his arm. 3. You will not graduate if you do not study.	2. Because he overslept, he was late for work. 4. Before the phone rang, I burned my finger.

Look at number 1. Is **Larry fell down** a complete sentence? (*Yes, except for an end mark.*) Is **he broke his arm** a complete sentence? (*Yes - except for a capital letter and an end mark.*) The directions tell us to put a slash between these two complete thoughts. (*The run-on sentence is divided with a slash.*) We have now identified the two simple sentences that will be made into a complex sentence.

Now, look at the end of number 1. The (**CX, when, 1**) in parentheses tells us **how** to make these two sentences into a complex sentence. The (**CX**) stands for complex sentence; the (**when**) tells which subordinate conjunction to use; and the (**1**) tells which sentence will begin with the subordinate conjunction.

Notice that the complex sentence was written by using the information given to us in parentheses. (*The first complex sentence looks like this:* **When Larry fell down, he broke his arm.**)

These two sentences are made into a complex sentence by using the subordinate conjunction **when** at the beginning of the first sentence. When the first sentence is the subordinate sentence, it will usually have a comma after it. (*Work through the rest of the Part 1 sample sentences in the same way.*)

Make sure your students understand that a complex sentence will always have one sentence with a subordinate conjunction at the beginning and one sentence that is an independent sentence. Then, read the directions and work through the guided examples for Part 2.

CHAPTER 14 LESSON 1 CONTINUED

 PRACTICE TIME

Have students turn to page 61 in the Practice Section of their book and find Chapter 14, Lesson 1, Practice (*1-2*). Go over the directions to make sure they understand what to do. Guide students closely as they write complex sentences for the first time. Make sure they know to underline the <u>subordinate</u> sentence in each of the complex sentences they write. (*Students may use the Reference section in their books to help them remember the new information.* Check and discuss the Practice after students have finished. (*Chapter 14, Lesson 1, Practice keys are given below.*)

Chapter 14, Lesson 1, Practice 1: Put a slash to separate each run-on sentence below. Then, correct the run-on sentences by rewriting them as indicated by the labels in parentheses ( ) at the end of each sentence.

1. Dad unleashed the dog **/** the cat took cover. (CX, when) (1)
   When Dad unleashed the dog, the cat took cover.

2. Dad unleashed the dog **/** the cat took cover. (CX, when) (2)
   Dad unleashed the dog when the cat took cover.

Chapter 14, Lesson 1, Practice 2: Identify each kind of sentence by writing the abbreviation in the blank. (S, F, SCS, SCV, CD, CX)

F	1. Because her cupboard was bare.
CD	2. The traffic light did not work; however, there was a stop sign.
SCS	3. After the storm subsided, Joe and his wife returned home.
CX	4. The phone quit ringing before I got to it.
SCV	5. The nearly voiceless cheerleaders jumped and shouted with joy.
CD	6. We gave them warning, but they totally ignored us.

 WRITING TIME

Have students make an entry in their journals.

 VOCABULARY TIME

Assign Chapter 14, Vocabulary Words **#1** on page 7 in the Reference Section for students to define in their Vocabulary notebooks. Tell students they are to use a dictionary or thesaurus to look up the meanings of the vocabulary words. After they write each word and its meaning, students are to write a sentence using the vocabulary word.

Chapter 14, Vocabulary Words #1
(impenetrable, vulnerable, equestrian, rider)

(End of lesson.)

CHAPTER 14   LESSON 2

New objectives: Grammar(Practice Sentences), Practice sheet, and Vocabulary #2.

 JINGLE TIME

Have students turn to the Jingle Section of their books. The teacher will lead the students in reciting the previously-taught jingles.

 GRAMMAR TIME

First-Year Option: Put the Practice Sentences from the box below on the board or notebook paper. Use these sentences as you practice the concepts that have been taught. For the greatest benefit, students must participate orally with the teacher. **Second-Year Option:** Have students classify the Practice Sentences independently on paper. Check students' sentences with the answers provided below. (*If you have the CDs for Practice Sentences, have students check their sentences with the CDs.*)

Chapter 14, Practice Sentences for Lesson 2

1. _____ Do full-grown crocodiles warn their prey adequately before an attack?
2. _____ Heavy tropical rains darkened the heavens for days at a time.

TEACHING SCRIPT FOR PRACTICING PATTERN 2 SENTENCES

We will practice classifying Pattern 2 sentences. We will classify the sentences together. Begin. (*You might have your students write the labels above the sentences at this time.*)

Question and Answer Flow for Sentence 1: Do full-grown crocodiles warn their prey adequately before an attack?

1. What warn their prey adequately before an attack? crocodiles - SN
2. What is being said about crocodiles? crocodiles do warn - V
3. Do - HV
4. Crocodiles do warn what? prey - verify the noun
5. Does prey mean the same thing as crocodiles? No.
6. Prey - DO
7. Warn - V-t
8. Whose prey? their - PPA
9. Do warn how? adequately - Adv
10. Before - P
11. Before what? attack - OP
12. An - A
13. What kind of crocodiles? full-grown - Adj
14. SN V-t DO P2 Check
15. Verb-transitive - Check again.
16. (Before an attack) - Prepositional phrase
17. Question mark, question, interrogative sentence
18. Go back to the verb - divide the complete subject from the complete predicate.
19. Is there an adverb exception? No.
20. Is this sentence in a natural or inverted order? Inverted - underline the subject parts once and the predicate parts twice.

Classified Sentence:

```
                          HV    Adj      SN      V-t  PPA  DO     Adv      P    A    OP
              SN V-t      Do full-grown crocodiles / warn their prey adequately (before an attack)? Int
              DO P2
```

CHAPTER 14 LESSON 2 CONTINUED

Question and Answer Flow for Sentence 2: Heavy tropical rains darkened the heavens for days at a time.

1. What darkened the heavens for days at a time? rains - SN
2. What is being said about rains? rains darkened - V
3. Rains darkened what? heavens - verify the noun
4. Do heavens mean the same thing as rains? No.
5. Heavens - DO
6. Darkened - V-t
7. The - A
8. For - P
9. For what? days - OP
10. At - P
11. At what? time - OP
12. A - A

13. What kind of rains? tropical - Adj
14. What kind of rains? heavy - Adj
15. SN V-t DO P2 Check
16. Verb-transitive - Check again.
17. (For days) - Prepositional phrase
18. (At a time) - Prepositional phrase
19. Period, statement, declarative sentence
20. Go back to the verb - divide the complete subject from the complete predicate.
21. Is there an adverb exception? No.
22. Is this sentence in a natural or inverted order? Natural - no change.

Classified Sentence:

```
                          Adj   Adj   SN      V-t    A    DO    P   OP    P  A  OP
        SN  V-t   Heavy tropical rains / darkened the heavens (for days) (at a time).  D
        DO  P2
```

TEACHER INSTRUCTIONS FOR A PATTERN 2 SENTENCE

Tell students that their sentence writing assignment today is to write a Pattern 2 sentence. They are to follow the same procedure used in the previous lessons. They should decide on their labels, arrange them in a selected order, write their sentence, and edit the sentence for improved word choices. (*Students do not have to write an Improved Sentence at this point unless you feel they need more one-on-one word choice writing practice.*) Check and discuss the Pattern 2 sentence after students have finished.

CHAPTER 14 LESSON 2 CONTINUED

 PRACTICE TIME

Students will continue identifying and writing complex sentences during Practice Time. Have students turn to page 62 in the Practice Section of their book and find Chapter 14, Lesson 2, Practice (*1-3*). Go over the directions to make sure they understand what to do. If students need a review, have them study the information and examples of complex sentences in the Reference Section of their book. Check and discuss the Practices after students have finished. (*Chapter 14, Lesson 2, Practice keys are given below.*)

Chapter 14, Lesson 2, Practice 1: Put a slash to separate each run-on sentence below. Then, correct the run-on sentences by rewriting them as indicated by the labels in parentheses ( ) at the end of each sentence.

1. Dad unleashed the dog **/** the cat took cover. (CX, after)(1)
   After Dad unleashed the dog, the cat took cover.

2. Sue gathered the eggs **/** she put on her sunbonnet. (CX, before)(1)
   Before Sue gathered the eggs, she put on her sunbonnet.

3. The little boy fell **/** his shoelaces came untied. (CX, when)(2)
   The little boy fell when his shoelaces came untied.

Chapter 14, Lesson 2, Practice 2: Identify each kind of sentence by writing the abbreviation in the blank. (S, F, SCS, SCV, CD, CX)

CD	1.	There was constant turmoil; consequently, we left.
CX	2.	Since the road was closed, we had to detour.
SCS	3.	The boys and girls watched football yesterday.
F	4.	Only because no one else had asked.
S	5.	The water was nearly as high as the bridge.
CX	6.	We ran to the window before the rainbow disappeared.
SCV	7.	Jeremy sat and twiddled his thumbs after dinner.

Chapter 14, Lesson 2, Practice 3: On a sheet of paper, write three complex sentences. Underline each <u>subordinate</u> sentence. (*Answers will vary.*)

 VOCABULARY TIME

Assign Chapter 14, Vocabulary Words **#2** on page 7 in the Reference Section for students to define in their Vocabulary notebooks. Tell students they are to use a dictionary or thesaurus to look up the meanings of the vocabulary words. After they write each word and its meaning, students are to write a sentence using the vocabulary word.

Chapter 14, Vocabulary Words #2
(cordial, hostile, equilibrium, balance)

(End of lesson.)

CHAPTER 14   LESSON 3

New objectives: Grammar (Practice Sentences) and a Practice sheet.

 **JINGLE TIME**

Have students turn to the Jingle Section of their books. The teacher will lead the students in reciting the previously-taught jingles.

 GRAMMAR TIME

First-Year Option: Put the Practice Sentences from the box below on the board or notebook paper. Use these sentences as you practice the concepts that have been taught. For the greatest benefit, students must participate orally with the teacher. **Second-Year Option:** Have students classify the Practice Sentences independently on paper. Check students' sentences with the answers provided below. (*If you have the CDs for Practice Sentences, have students check their sentences with the CDs.*)

Chapter 14, Practice Sentences for Lesson 3
1. _____ After his stroke, Marie's dad could not give specific instructions to his family.
2. _____ Yesterday, she purchased a new skirt and blouse at the shopping mall downtown.

TEACHING SCRIPT FOR PRACTICING PATTERN 2 SENTENCES

We will practice classifying Pattern 2 sentences. We will classify the sentences together. Begin. (*You might have your students write the labels above the sentences at this time.*)

Question and Answer Flow for Sentence 1: After his stroke, Marie's dad could not give specific instructions to his family.

1. Who could not give specific instructions to his family? dad – SN
2. What is being said about dad? dad could give - V
3. Could – HV
4. Could give how? not - Adv
5. Dad could give what? instructions - verify the noun
6. Do instructions mean the same thing as dad? No.
7. Instructions - DO
8. Give - V-t
9. What kind of instructions? specific - Adj
10. To – P
11. To whom? family - OP
12. Whose family? his - PPA
13. Whose dad? Marie's - PNA

14. After - P
15. After what? stroke - OP
16. Whose stroke? his - PPA
17. SN V-t DO P2 Check
18. Verb-transitive - Check again.
19. (After his stroke) - Prepositional phrase
20. (To his family) - Prepositional phrase
21. Period, statement, declarative sentence
22. Go back to the verb - divide the complete subject from the complete predicate.
23. Is there an adverb exception? No.
24. Is this sentence in a natural or inverted order? Inverted - underline the subject parts once and the predicate parts twice.

Classified   P   PPA   OP   PNA   SN   HV Adv V-t   Adj   DO   P PPA OP
Sentence: SN V-t   (After his stroke), Marie's dad / could not give specific instructions (to his family). **D**
                 DO P2

CHAPTER 14 LESSON 3 CONTINUED

Question and Answer Flow for Sentence 2: Yesterday, she purchased a new skirt and blouse at the shopping mall downtown.

1. Who purchased a new skirt and blouse at the shopping mall downtown? she - SP
2. What is being said about she? she purchased - V
3. She purchased what? skirt and blouse - verify the nouns
4. Do skirt and blouse mean the same thing as she? No.
5. Skirt and blouse - CDO, CDO
6. Purchased - V-t
7. What kind of skirt? new - Adj
8. A – A
9. And – C
10. At – P
11. At what? mall - OP
12. What kind of mall? shopping - Adj
13. The - A
14. Purchased where? downtown - Adv
15. Purchased when? yesterday - Adv
16. SN V-t DO P2 Check
17. Verb-transitive - Check again.
18. (At the shopping mall) - Prepositional phrase
19. Period, statement, declarative sentence
20. Go back to the verb - divide the complete subject from the complete predicate.
21. Is there an adverb exception? No.
22. Is this sentence in a natural or inverted order? Inverted - underline the subject parts once and the predicate parts twice.

Classified Sentence:		Adv	SP	V-t	A Adj CDO	C CDO	P A	Adj	OP	Adv
	SN V-t	Yesterday, she / purchased a new skirt and blouse (at the shopping mall) downtown. D
	DO P2	

PRACTICE TIME

Students will continue identifying and writing complex sentences during Practice Time. Have students turn to page 63 in the Practice Section of their book and find Chapter 14, Lesson 3, Practice (1-4). Go over the directions to make sure they understand what to do. If students need a review, have them study the information and examples of complex sentences in the Reference Section of their book. Check and discuss the Practices after students have finished. (*Chapter 14, Lesson 3, Practice keys are given below.*)

Chapter 14, Lesson 3, Practice 1: Put a slash to separate each run-on sentence below. Then, correct the run-on sentences by rewriting them as indicated by the labels in parentheses ( ) at the end of each sentence.

1. Mom opened the door **/** the puppies ran outside. (CX, after) (1)
   After Mom opened the door, the puppies ran outside.

2. The tiny baby cried **/** her bottle was empty. (CX, when) (2)
   The tiny baby cried when her bottle was empty.

Chapter 14, Lesson 3, Practice 2: Identify each kind of sentence by writing the abbreviation in the blank. (S, F, SCS, SCV, CD, CX)

CD	1.	The storm passed through; however, we escaped injury.
CX	2.	When I balanced my checkbook, I heaved a sigh of relief.
S	3.	He sometimes drove in the middle of the road to avoid the potholes.
SCS	4.	The robins and mockingbirds declared war on each other.
F	5.	Just as he crested the hill.

Chapter 14, Lesson 3, Practice 3: On a sheet of paper, write three complex sentences. Underline each <u>subordinate</u> sentence.

Chapter 14, Lesson 3, Practice 4: On a sheet of paper, write three compound sentences, using these labels to guide you: ① (CD, but) ② (CD; therefore,) ③ (CD;)

(End of lesson.)

CHAPTER 14   LESSON 4

New objectives: Test and an Activity.

 JINGLE TIME

Have students turn to the Jingle Section of their books. The teacher will lead the students in reciting the previously-taught jingles.

 STUDY TIME

Have students study the vocabulary words in their vocabulary notebooks. Remind students that any vocabulary word in their notebooks could be on their test. Also, have students study any of the skills in the Practice Section that they need to review.

 TEST TIME

Have students turn to page 96 in the Test Section of their book and find Chapter 14 Test. Go over the directions to make sure they understand what to do. (*Chapter 14 Test key is on the next page.*)

 CHECK TIME

After students have finished, check and discuss their test papers. Make sure they understand why their answers are right or wrong. (*For total points, count each required answer as a point.*)

 ACTIVITY / ASSIGNMENT TIME

The **Parts-of-Speech Poem** is a directional poem in which one employs various parts of speech that follow a prescribed formula. Teachers or students can design their own formulas to create different effects. Read and discuss the example below. Have students write their own **Parts-of-Speech Poem** using the directions below. Have them share their poems with others.

Line 1—One interjection	Good grief!
Line 2—Two subject nouns	Julie and Jill
Line 3—One verb and one direct object	misplaced their car
Line 4—One prepositional phrase	At the shopping mall
Line 5—Two prepositional phrase	On the far side of town
Line 6—One adverb	Yesterday.

(End of lesson.)

Chapter 14 Test
(Student Page 96)

Exercise 1: Classify each sentence.

          SN   V-t A   DO   P PPA   OP   P COP   C   COP

1. <u>SN V-t</u>   Henry / rode a motorcycle (to his interviews) (in Kansas and Nebraska). **D**
   DO P2

                   P   Adj   OP   A   SN   V-t   DO   P A   Adj

2. <u>SN V-t</u>   (<u>After twenty years</u>), <u>the congregation / surprised him (with an appreciation</u>
   DO P2
           OP
   <u>banquet</u>). **D**

Exercise 2: Use Sentence 2 to underline the complete subject once and the complete predicate twice and to complete the table below.

List the Noun Used	List the Noun Job	Singular or Plural	Common or Proper	Simple Subject	Simple Predicate
1. **years**	2. **OP**	3. **P**	4. **C**	5. **congregation**	6. **surprised**
7. **congregation**	8. **SN**	9. **S**	10. **C**		
11. **banquet**	12. **OP**	13. **S**	14. **C**		

Exercise 3: Identify each pair of words as synonyms or antonyms by putting parentheses ( ) around *syn* or *ant*.

1. rider, equestrian	**(syn)** ant	5. honesty, integrity	**(syn)** ant	9. equilibrium, balance	**(syn)** ant
2. timid, audacious	syn **(ant)**	6. zeppelin, balloon	**(syn)** ant	10. construction, dilapidation	syn **(ant)**
3. cordial, hostile	syn **(ant)**	7. frivolous, grave	syn **(ant)**	11. solicitude, indifference	syn **(ant)**
4. odious, hateful	**(syn)** ant	8. escalate, expand	**(syn)** ant	12. impenetrable, vulnerable	syn **(ant)**

Exercise 4: Put a slash to separate each run-on sentence below. Then, correct the run-on sentences by rewriting them as indicated by the labels in parentheses at the end of each sentence.

1. The pigs ate all the corn / they seemed contented. (CX, after 1)
   After the pigs ate all the corn, they seemed contented.
2. The pigs ate all the corn / they seemed contented. (CD, and)
   The pigs ate all the corn, and they seemed contented.
3. The pigs ate all the corn / they seemed contented. (SCV)
   The pigs ate all the corn and seemed contented.
4. The pigs ate all the corn / they seemed contented. (CD;)
   The pigs ate all the corn; they seemed contented.
5. The pigs ate all the corn / the chickens ate all the corn. (SCS)
   The pigs and chickens ate all the corn.

Exercise 5: Identify each kind of sentence by writing the abbreviation in the blank (S, F, SCS, SCV, CD, CX).

  CD   1. She lost her billfold; moreover, she lost her keys.
  CX   2. When the doorbell rang, she nearly jumped out of her shoes.
  SCS 3. Students and teachers alike were ready for vacation.
  F   4. Whenever I get the oil changed.
  CD   5. My pen is out of ink, and I have no stamps.
  F   6. Besides being home for Christmas.
  SCV 7. Jared drove his truck into the creek and got stuck.

Exercise 6: On a sheet of paper, write three complex sentences. Underline each <u>subordinate</u> sentence.

Exercise 7: On a sheet of paper, write five sentences, using these labels to guide you: (S), (SCS), (SCV), (CD), (CX). (Answers will vary.)

Exercise 8: In your journal, write a paragraph summarizing what you have learned this week.

CHAPTER 14 LESSON 4 CONTINUED

TEACHER INSTRUCTIONS

Use the Question and Answer Flows below for the sentences on Chapter 14 Test.

Question and Answer Flow for Sentence 1: Henry rode a motorcycle to his interviews in Kansas and Nebraska.

1. Who rode a motorcycle to his interviews in Kansas and Nebraska? Henry - SN
2. What is being said about Henry? Henry rode - V
3. Henry rode what? motorcycle - verify the noun
4. Does motorcycle mean the same thing as Henry? No.
5. Motorcycle - DO
6. Rode - V-t
7. A - A
8. To - P
9. To what? interviews - OP
10. Whose interviews? his - PPA
11. In - P

12. In what? Kansas and Nebraska - COP, COP
13. And - C
14. SN V-t DO P2 Check
15. Verb-transitive - Check again.
16. (To his interviews) - Prepositional phrase
17. (In Kansas and Nebraska) - Prepositional phrase
18. Period, statement, declarative sentence
19. Go back to the verb - divide the complete subject from the complete predicate.
20. Is there an adverb exception? No.
21. Is this sentence in a natural or inverted order? Natural - no change.

Classified Sentence:

		SN	V-t	A	DO	P PPA	OP	P	COP	C	COP

SN V-t Henry / rode a motorcycle (to his interviews) (in Kansas and Nebraska). **D**
DO P2

Question and Answer Flow for Sentence 2: After twenty years, the congregation surprised him with an appreciation banquet.

1. Who surprised him with an appreciation banquet? congregation - SN
2. What is being said about congregation? congregation surprised - V
3. Congregation surprised whom? him - verify the pronoun
4. Does him mean the same thing as congregation? No.
5. Him - DO
6. Surprised - V-t
7. With - P
8. With what? banquet - OP
9. What kind of banquet? appreciation - Adj
10. An - A
11. The - A
12. After - P

13. After what? years - OP
14. How many years? twenty - Adj
15. SN V-t DO P2 Check
16. Verb-transitive - Check again.
17. (After twenty years) - Prepositional phrase
18. (With an appreciation banquet) - Prepositional phrase
19. Period, statement, declarative sentence
20. Go back to the verb - divide the complete subject from the complete predicate.
21. Is there an adverb exception? No.
22. Is this sentence in a natural or inverted order? Inverted - Underline the subject parts once and the predicate parts twice.

Classified Sentence:

	P	Adj	OP	A	SN	V-t	DO	P	A	Adj	OP

SN V-t (After twenty years), the congregation / surprised him (with an appreciation banquet). **D**
DO P2

CHAPTER 14   LESSON 5

New objectives: Writing Assignments #17 and #18.

 **WRITING TIME**

TEACHING SCRIPT FOR PRACTICING DIFFERENT KINDS OF WRITING

Today, you are assigned two different kinds of writing. You will write a five-paragraph persuasive essay and a three-paragraph expository essay. <u>You will revise and edit the five-paragraph persuasive essay.</u> (*Read the box below for more information about students' writing assignment.*) As you edit, make sure you use the checkpoints in the editing checklist provided in Reference 35. Remember to read through the whole essay, starting with the title, and then edit, sentence-by-sentence, using the five-sentence checkpoints for each sentence. Use the paragraph checkpoints to check each paragraph. Remember, your editing is now more detailed and more comprehensive, so take your time.

Writing Assignment Box #1

Writing Assignment #17: Five-Paragraph Persuasive Essay (First Person)
(Remember, first person pronouns are *I, we, me, us, my, our, mine, and ours.*)
Remind students that the 5-paragraph essay has three parts: 1. Introduction 2. Body 3. Conclusion. The body has three paragraphs instead of one. Have students use their regular editing checklist to edit this assignment.

Writing topic: Why Good Friends Are Important or **Why We Need Fingernails** or **Why We Need Traffic Lights**

Your second writing assignment is to write a three-paragraph expository essay. (*Read the box below for more information about students' writing assignment.*) You do not have to edit this assignment with the editing checklist.

Writing Assignment Box #2

Writing Assignment #18: Three-Paragraph Expository Essay (First Person)
(Remember, first person pronouns are *I, we, me, us, my, our, mine, and ours.*)
Remind students that the 3-paragraph essay has three parts: 1. Introduction 2. Body 3. Conclusion. The body has one paragraph instead of three. Have students use their regular editing checklist to edit this assignment.

Writing topic: Ways to Be Courteous or **Things I Enjoy Doing** or **Why I Appreciate My Parents**

Read, check, and discuss Writing Assignment #17 after students have finished their final papers. Use the checklists as you check and discuss students' papers. Make sure students are using the regular editing checklist correctly. Read and discuss Writing Assignment #18 for fun and enrichment.

(End of lesson.)

CHAPTER 15   LESSON 1

New objectives: Grammar (Practice Sentences), Skills (possessive nouns), Practice sheet, and Vocabulary #1.

JINGLE TIME

Have students turn to the Jingle Section of their books. The teacher will lead the students in reciting the previously-taught jingles.

GRAMMAR TIME

First-Year Option: Put the Practice Sentences from the box below on the board or notebook paper. Use these sentences as you practice the concepts that have been taught. For the greatest benefit, students must participate orally with the teacher. **Second-Year Option:** Have students classify the Practice Sentences independently on paper. Check students' sentences with the answers provided below. (*If you have the CDs for Practice Sentences, have students check their sentences with the CDs.*)

Chapter 15, Practice Sentences for Lesson 1

1. _____ That menacing look in his eye actually aroused fear inside me!
2. _____ Those towering oaks provide shade for the house and the yard.

TEACHING SCRIPT FOR PRACTICING PATTERN 2 SENTENCES

We will practice classifying Pattern 2 sentences. We will classify the sentences together. Begin. (*You might have your child write the labels above the sentences at this time.*)

Question and Answer Flow for Sentence 1: That menacing look in his eye actually aroused fear inside me!

1. What aroused fear inside me? look - SN
2. What is being said about look? look aroused - V
3. Look aroused what? fear - verify the noun
4. Does fear mean the same thing as look? No.
5. Fear - DO
6. Aroused - V-t
7. Inside - P
8. Inside whom? me - OP
9. Aroused how? actually - Adv
10. In - P
11. In what? eye - OP
12. Whose eye? his – PPA
13. What kind of look? menacing - Adj

14. Which look? that - Adj
15. SN V-t DO P2 Check
16. Verb-transitive - Check again.
17. (In his eye) - Prepositional phrase
18. (Inside me) - Prepositional phrase
19. Exclamation point, strong feeling, exclamatory sentence
20. Go back to the verb - divide the complete subject from the complete predicate.
21. Is there an adverb exception? Yes - change the line.
22. Is this sentence in a natural or inverted order? Natural - no change.

Classified Sentence:

		Adj	Adj	SN	P PPA OP	Adv	V-t	DO	P	OP
SN V-t		That	menacing	look	(in his eye) **/**	actually	aroused	fear	(inside	me)! **E**
DO P2										

Level 5 Homeschool Teacher's Manual

CHAPTER 15 LESSON 1 CONTINUED

Question and Answer Flow for Sentence 2: Those towering oaks provide shade for the house and the yard.	
1. What provide shade for the house and the yard? oaks - SN	12. What kind of oaks? towering - Adj
2. What is being said about oaks? oaks provide - V	13. Which oaks? those - Adj
3. Oaks provide what? shade - verify the noun	14. SN V-t DO P2 Check
4. Does shade mean the same thing as oaks? No.	15. Verb-transitive - Check again.
5. Shade - DO	16. (For the house and the yard) - Prepositional phrase
6. Provide - V-t	17. Period, statement, declarative sentence
7. For - P	18. Go back to the verb - divide the complete subject from the complete predicate.
8. For what? house and yard - COP, COP	19. Is there an adverb exception? No.
9. The - A	20. Is this sentence in a natural or inverted order? Natural - no change.
10. And - C	
11. The - A	

Classified Sentence:

```
            Adj     Adj     SN      V-t     DO      P   A   COP  C  A  COP
   SN V-t   Those towering oaks / provide shade (for the house and the yard).  D
   DO P2
```

Use Sentences 1-2 that you just classified with your students to do an Oral Skill Builder Check. Use the guidelines below.

Oral Skill Builder Check	
1. **Noun check.** (Say the job and then say the noun. Circle each noun.)	5. **Identify the complete subject and the complete predicate.** (Underline the complete subject once and the complete predicate twice.)
2. **Identify the nouns as singular or plural.** (Write S or P above each noun.)	6. **Identify the simple subject and simple predicate.** (Underline the simple subject once and the simple predicate twice. Bold, or highlight, the lines.)
3. **Identify the nouns as common or proper.** (Follow established procedure for oral identification.)	7. **Recite the irregular verb chart.** (Located on student page 17 and teacher page 143.)
4. **Do a vocabulary check.** (Follow established procedure for oral identification.)	

SKILL TIME

TEACHING SCRIPT FOR MAKING NOUNS POSSESSIVE

Learning how to make nouns possessive is the next skill you will learn. This skill is really simple, but, again, students and adults alike have a lot of trouble with it when they write. The more practice you have in making nouns possessive, the more likely you will use possessive nouns correctly in your writing.

In order to form possessive nouns that show ownership, you must first decide if the noun is singular or plural before you add the apostrophe. After you know whether a noun is singular or plural, you can then use three rules to tell you how to make the noun possessive.

CHAPTER 15 LESSON 1 CONTINUED

Look at Reference 45 on page 32 in the Reference Section of your book and follow along as we go through the three rules and practice examples. (*The information and practice examples are reproduced for you below.*) Remember, we always read the directions first. Listen carefully because you have several things to do. (*Read the directions for Part A and Part B below.*)

Reference 45: Making Nouns Possessive						
1. For a singular noun - add (**'s**) **Rule 1: boy's**		2. For a plural noun that ends in **s** - add (**'**) **Rule 2: boys'**		3. For a plural noun that does not end in **s** – add (**'s**) **Rule 3: men's**		
Part A: Underline each noun to be made possessive and write singular or plural (S-P), the rule number, and the possessive form. Part B: Write each noun as singular possessive and then as plural possessive.						
Part A	**S-P**	**Rule**	**Possessive Form**	**Part B**	**Singular Poss**	**Plural Poss**
1. <u>oyster</u> pearl	S	1	**oyster's pearl**	5. class	**class's**	**classes'**
2. <u>ducks</u> feathers	P	2	**ducks' feathers**	6. child	**child's**	**children's**
3. <u>baboon</u> grin	S	1	**baboon's grin**	7. roof	**roof's**	**roofs'**
4. <u>kittens</u> cries	P	2	**kittens' cries**	8. Jones	**Jones's**	**Jones'**

For Part A, let's review the four things that the directions tell us to do. First, we decide which noun is to be made possessive and underline it. Second, we are going to identify the noun as singular or plural. Third, we are going to write the number of the rule to be followed from the rule box. Last, we are going to write the correct possessive form in the blank.

Look at number 1. The first thing we must do is underline the noun to be made possessive. An easy way to test for the correct noun to be made possessive is to do the "of" test. We would say "the pearl **of** the oyster, not the oyster **of** the pearl!" Now, we know the noun to make possessive. The word *oyster* is underlined, as shown in the example.

Next, we must decide whether our underlined noun is singular or plural before we can make it possessive. Is *oyster* singular or plural? (*singular*) The letter *S* is written in the blank under the column marked *S-P*.

Now, we will look at the rule box for making nouns possessive. Which rule do we use since *oyster* is singular? (*Rule 1*) A number 1 is written in the blank under the column marked *Rule*. What does Rule 1 tell us to do? (*For a singular noun, add an apostrophe and **s**.*) The singular possessive noun *oyster's* is written under the column marked *Possessive Form*. (*Work through the rest of Part A in the same way to make sure your students understand how to use the rule box for making nouns possessive.*)

TEACHING SCRIPT FOR MAKING NOUNS POSSESSIVE, PART B

Look at Part B. Every noun listed is singular. The directions tell us to do two things. First, we are going to write the singular possessive form of the noun. Second, we are going to change the singular noun to plural and then write the plural possessive form of the noun. That means you may need to check a dictionary for the correct plural spelling of the noun. Dictionaries should always be available for looking up words.

Look at number 5 under Part B. It says *class*. Since we know that *class* is singular, we go to Rule 1 so it will tell us how to make the word *class* possessive. What does Rule 1 tell us to do? (*For a singular noun, add an apostrophe and **s**.*) The word *class's* is written under the column marked *Singular Possessive*.

CHAPTER 15 LESSON 1 CONTINUED

We must change *class* to its plural form before we can make it plural possessive. How do we make *class* plural? (By adding an es: *classes*.) We still need to make the plural word *classes* possessive. Since the plural form of *classes* ends in an s, which rule do we need to follow? *(Rule 2)* What does Rule 2 say to add to *classes* to make it possessive? *(An apostrophe.)* The word *classes'* is written with an apostrophe in the *Plural Possessive* column. *(Work through the rest of Part B in the same way. After the singular possessive form has been demonstrated and discussed, make sure your students understand how the plural form of the noun is written before making it possessive with the apostrophe by following Rule 2 or Rule 3. Always encourage your students to use the dictionary to check plural spellings.)*

 PRACTICE TIME

Have students turn to page 64 in the Practice Section of their book and find Chapter 15, Lesson 1, Practice. Go over the directions to make sure they understand what to do. Guide students closely as they do the practice exercises for the first time. *(Students may use the Reference section in their books to help them remember the new information.)* Check and discuss the Practice after students have finished. *(Chapter 15, Lesson 1, Practice key is given below.)*

Chapter 15, Lesson 1, Practice: Part A: Underline each noun to be made possessive and write singular or plural (S-P), the rule number, and the possessive form. Part B: Write each noun as singular possessive and then as plural possessive.

1. For a singular noun - add ('s)				2. For a plural noun that ends in *s* - add (')		3. For a plural noun that does not end in *s* - add ('s)		
Rule 1: boy's				**Rule 2: boys'**		**Rule 3: men's**		
Part A	**S-P**	**Rule**	**Possessive Form**	**Part B**		**Singular Poss**	**Plural Poss**	
1. <u>wind</u> velocity	S	1	**wind's velocity**	5. egret		**egret's**	**egrets'**	
2. <u>donkeys</u> tails	P	2	**donkeys' tails**	6. woman		**woman's**	**women's**	
3. <u>patients</u> rights	P	2	**patients' rights**	7. pansy		**pansy's**	**pansies'**	
4. <u>children</u> pleas	P	3	**children's pleas**	8. wife		**wife's**	**wives'**	

 WRITING TIME

Have students make an entry in their journals.

 VOCABULARY TIME

Assign Chapter 15, Vocabulary Words **#1** on page 7 in the Reference Section for students to define in their Vocabulary notebooks. Tell students they are to use a dictionary or thesaurus to look up the meanings of the vocabulary words. After they write each word and its meaning, students are to write a sentence using the vocabulary word.

Chapter 15, Vocabulary Words #1
(gullible, dubious, fatigue, exhaustion)

(End of lesson.)

CHAPTER 15   LESSON 2

New objectives: Grammar (Practice Sentences) and a Practice sheet.

JINGLE TIME

Have students turn to the Jingle Section of their books. The teacher will lead the students in reciting the previously-taught jingles.

GRAMMAR TIME

Put the Practice Sentences from the box below on the board. Use these sentences as you practice the concepts that have been taught. For the greatest benefit, students must participate orally with the teacher. (*You might put the Practice Sentences on notebook paper if you are doing one-on-one instruction with your child.*)

Chapter 15, Practice Sentences for Lesson 2
1. _____ With an encouraging smile and firm handshake, he introduced the new manager to his first assignment.
2. _____ Manley Hopkins investigates with genuine curiosity the intricacies of the larger universe.

TEACHING SCRIPT FOR PRACTICING PATTERN 2 SENTENCES

We will practice classifying Pattern 2 sentences. We will classify the sentences together. Begin. (*You might have your child write the labels above the sentences at this time.*)

Question and Answer Flow for Sentence 1: With an encouraging smile and firm handshake, he introduced the new manager to his first assignment.

1. Who introduced the new manager to his first assignment? he - SP
2. What is being said about he? he introduced - V
3. He introduced whom? manager - verify the noun
4. Does manager mean the same thing as he? No.
5. Manager - DO
6. Introduced - V-t
7. What kind of manager? new - Adj
8. The - A
9. To - P
10. To what? assignment - OP
11. What kind of assignment? first - Adj
12. Whose assignment? his - PPA
13. With - P
14. With what? smile and handshake - COP, COP

15. What kind of handshake? firm - Adj
16. And - C
17. What kind of smile? encouraging - Adj
18. An - A
19. SN V-t DO P2 Check
20. Verb-transitive - Check again.
21. (With an encouraging smile and firm handshake) - Prepositional phrase
22. (To his first assignment) - Prepositional phrase
23. Period, statement, declarative sentence
24. Go back to the verb - divide the complete subject from the complete predicate.
25. Is there an adverb exception? No.
26. Is this sentence in a natural or inverted order? Inverted - underline the subject parts once and the predicate parts twice.

Classified
Sentence:
                    P   A   Adj   COP   C   Adj   COP   SP   V-t   A   Adj   DO
          SN V-t   (With an encouraging smile and firm handshake), he / introduced the new manager
          DO P2   P PPA Adj   OP
          (to his first assignment). D

CHAPTER 15 LESSON 2 CONTINUED

Question and Answer Flow for Sentence 2: Manley Hopkins investigates with genuine curiosity the intricacies of the larger universe.

1. Who investigates with genuine curiosity the intricacies of the larger universe? Manley Hopkins - SN
2. What is being said about Manley Hopkins? Manley Hopkins investigates - V
3. Manley Hopkins investigates what? intricacies - verify the noun
4. Do intricacies mean the same thing as Manley Hopkins? No.
5. Intricacies - DO
6. Investigates - V-t
7. With - P
8. With what? curiosity - OP
9. What kind of curiosity? genuine - Adj
10. The - A
11. Of - P
12. Of what? universe - OP
13. What kind of universe? larger - Adj
14. The - A
15. SN V-t DO P2 Check
16. Verb-transitive - Check again.
17. (With genuine curiosity) - Prepositional phrase
18. (Of the larger universe) - Prepositional phrase
19. Period, statement, declarative sentence
20. Go back to the verb - divide the complete subject from the complete predicate.
21. Is there an adverb exception? No.
22. Is this sentence in a natural or inverted order? Natural - no change.

Classified Sentence:	SN	V-t		P	Adj	OP	A	DO	P	A	Adj	OP

<u>SN V-t
DO P2</u> Manley Hopkins / investigates (with genuine curiosity) the intricacies (of the larger universe). **D**

TEACHER INSTRUCTIONS FOR A PATTERN 2 PRACTICE SENTENCE

Tell students that their sentence writing assignment today is to write a Pattern 2 sentence. They are to follow the same procedure used in the previous lessons. They should decide on their labels, arrange them in a selected order, write their sentence, and edit the sentence for improved word choices. (*Students do not have to write an Improved Sentence at this point unless you feel they need more one-on-one word choice writing practice.*) Check and discuss the Pattern 2 sentence after students have finished.

 PRACTICE TIME

Students will continue their practice of making nouns possessive. Have students turn to page 64 in the Practice Section of their book and find Chapter 15, Lesson 2, Practice. Go over the directions to make sure they understand what to do. Check and discuss the Practice after students have finished. (*Chapter 15, Lesson 2, Practice key is given below.*)

Chapter 15, Lesson 2, Practice: Part A: Underline each noun to be made possessive and write singular or plural (S-P), the rule number, and the possessive form. Part B: Write each noun as singular possessive and then as plural possessive.

1. For a singular noun - add (**'s**)			2. For a plural noun that ends in *s* - add (**'**)		3. For a plural noun that does not end in *s* - add (**'s**)	
Rule 1: boy's			Rule 2: boys'		Rule 3: men's	
Part A	**S-P**	**Rule**	**Possessive Form**	**Part B**	**Singular Poss**	**Plural Poss**
1. <u>hens</u> eggs	P	2	hens' eggs	5. deer	**deer's**	**deer's**
2. <u>officer</u> badge	S	1	officer's badge	6. angel	**angel's**	**angels'**
3. <u>tractor</u> muffler	S	1	tractor's muffler	7. eel	**eel's**	**eels'**
4. <u>Arnold</u> mother	S	1	Arnold's mother	8. child	**child's**	**children's**

(End of lesson.)

CHAPTER 15   LESSON 3

New objectives: Grammar (Practice Sentences), Practice sheet, and Vocabulary #2.

 **JINGLE TIME**

Have students turn to the Jingle Section of their books. The teacher will lead the students in reciting the previously-taught jingles.

 GRAMMAR TIME

First-Year Option: Put the Practice Sentences from the box below on the board or notebook paper. Use these sentences as you practice the concepts that have been taught. For the greatest benefit, students must participate orally with the teacher. **Second-Year Option:** Have students classify the Practice Sentences independently on paper. Check students' sentences with the answers provided below. (*If you have the CDs for Practice Sentences, have students check their sentences with the CDs.*)

Chapter 15, Practice Sentences for Lesson 3

1. _____ During lunch, the over-worked waitresses toiled their way between the tables.
2. _____ The elderly spinster clearly needed the attention of the nursing staff.

TEACHING SCRIPT FOR PRACTICING PATTERN 2 SENTENCES

We will practice classifying Pattern 2 sentences. We will classify the sentences together. Begin. (*You might have your students write the labels above the sentences at this time.*)

Question and Answer Flow for Sentence 1: During lunch, the over-worked waitresses toiled their way between the tables.

1. Who toiled their way between the tables? waitresses - SN
2. What is being said about waitresses? waitresses toiled - V
3. Waitresses toiled what? way - verify the noun
4. Does way mean the same thing as waitresses? No.
5. Way - DO
6. Toiled - V-t
7. Whose way? their - PPA
8. Between - P
9. Between what? tables - OP
10. The - A
11. What kind of waitresses? over-worked - Adj
12. The - A
13. During - P
14. During what? lunch - OP
15. SN V-t DO P2 Check
16. Verb-transitive - Check again.
17. (During lunch) - Prepositional phrase
18. (Between the tables) - Prepositional phrase
19. Period, statement, declarative sentence
20. Go back to the verb - divide the complete subject from the complete predicate.
21. Is there an adverb exception? No.
22. Is this sentence in a natural or inverted order? Inverted - underline the subject parts once and the predicate parts twice.

Classified		P	OP	A	Adj	SN	V-t PPA DO	P	A	OP
Sentence:	SN V-t	(During lunch),	the over-worked waitresses /	toiled their way (between the tables). D						
	DO P2									

CHAPTER 15 LESSON 3 CONTINUED

Question and Answer Flow for Sentence 2: The elderly spinster clearly needed the attention of the nursing staff.

1. Who needed the attention of the nursing staff? spinster - SN
2. What is being said about spinster? spinster needed - V
3. Spinster needed what? attention - verify the noun
4. Does attention mean the same thing as spinster? No.
5. Attention - DO
6. Needed - V-t
7. The - A
8. Of - P
9. Of what? staff - OP
10. What kind of staff? nursing - Adj
11. The - A
12. Needed how? clearly - Adv

13. What kind of spinster? elderly - Adj
14. The - A
15. SN V-t DO P2 Check
16. Verb-transitive - Check again.
17. (Of the nursing staff) - Prepositional phrase
18. Period, statement, declarative sentence
19. Go back to the verb - divide the complete subject from the complete predicate.
20. Is there an adverb exception? Yes - change the line.
21. Is this sentence in a natural or inverted order? Natural - no change.

Classified Sentence:

SN V-t / DO P2

    A   Adj   SN   Adv   V-t   A   DO   P A   Adj   OP
The elderly spinster / clearly needed the attention (of the nursing staff). D

PRACTICE TIME

Students will continue their practice of making nouns possessive. Have students turn to page 64 in the Practice Section of their book and find Chapter 15, Lesson 3, Practice. Go over the directions to make sure they understand what to do. Check and discuss the Practice after students have finished. (*Chapter 15, Lesson 3, Practice key is given below.*)

Chapter 15, Lesson 3, Practice: Part A: Underline each noun to be made possessive and write singular or plural (S-P), the rule number, and the possessive form. Part B: Write each noun as singular possessive and then as plural possessive.

| 1. For a singular noun - add ('s) | | 2. For a plural noun that ends in **s** - add (') | | 3. For a plural noun that does not end in **s** - add ('s) | |
| Rule 1: boy's | | Rule 2: boys' | | Rule 3: men's | |

Part A	S-P	Rule	Possessive Form	Part B	Singular Poss	Plural Poss
1. jewelers rings	P	2	jewelers' rings	5. monkey	monkey's	monkeys'
2. pilot itinerary	S	1	pilot's itinerary	6. wolf	wolf's	wolves'
3. dogs fleas	P	2	dogs' fleas	7. ox	ox's	oxen's
4. Leo suitcase	S	1	Leo's suitcase	8. blizzard	blizzard's	blizzards'

VOCABULARY TIME

Assign Chapter 15, Vocabulary Words **#2** on page 7 in the Reference Section for students to define in their Vocabulary notebooks. After they write each word and its meaning, students are to write a sentence using the vocabulary word. Have students study the vocabulary words when they have finished.

Chapter 15, Vocabulary Words #2
(gaudy, tasteful, grandiose, impressive)

(End of lesson.)

CHAPTER 15   LESSON 4

New objectives: Test and an Activity.

 JINGLE TIME

Have students turn to the Jingle Section of their books. The teacher will lead the students in reciting the previously-taught jingles.

 STUDY TIME

Have students study the vocabulary words in their vocabulary notebooks. Remind students that any vocabulary word in their notebooks could be on their test. Also, have students study any of the skills in the Practice Section that they need to review.

 TEST TIME

Have students turn to page 97 in the Test Section of their book and find Chapter 15 Test. Go over the directions to make sure they understand what to do. (*Chapter 15 Test key is on the next page.*)

 CHECK TIME

After students have finished, check and discuss their test papers. Make sure they understand why their answers are right or wrong. (*For total points, count each required answer as a point.*)

 ACTIVITY / ASSIGNMENT TIME

Read and discuss the new **Parts-of-Speech** formula and the example below. Have students write another **Parts-of-Speech Poem**, using the new formula below. Have them share their poems with others.

Line 1 - Write one noun (*the topic of your poem*).
Line 2 - Write two adjectives to describe the noun.
Line 3 - Write one verb with a direct object.
Line 4 - Write one adverb describing the verb.
Line 5 - Write one prepositional phrase.
Line 6 - Write a sentence about the noun.

Thunder
Loud and rumbling
Makes its way
Effortlessly
Across the sky.
Thunder rules the night.

(End of lesson.)

Level 5 Homeschool Teacher's Manual

Chapter 15 Test
(Student Page 97)

Exercise 1: Classify each sentence.

```
           Adj    Adj       Adj       SN      V-t  A  Adj  DO    P  A   OP     P    PPA   OP
1. SN V-t  Two skillful, dedicated pastors / built a small church (on the land) (behind our farm).  D
   DO P2
              A    Adj      SN     HV      V-t     CDO   C   CDO      P   OP
2. SN V-t  The energetic children / have collected papers and magazines (at church).  D
   DO P2
```

Exercise 2: Use Sentence 1 to underline the complete subject once and the complete predicate twice and to complete the table below.

List the Noun Used	List the Noun Job	Singular or Plural	Common or Proper	Simple Subject	Simple Predicate
1. **pastors**	2. **SN**	3. **P**	4. **C**	5. **pastors**	6. **built**
7. **church**	8. **DO**	9. **S**	10. **C**		
11. **land**	12. **OP**	13. **S**	14. **C**		
15. **farm**	16. **OP**	17. **S**	18. **C**		

Exercise 3: Identify each pair of words as synonyms or antonyms by putting parentheses ( ) around *syn* or *ant*.

1. thrifty, frugal	**(syn)** ant	5. rider, equestrian	**(syn)** ant	9. fatigue, exhaustion	**(syn)** ant
2. argue, debate	**(syn)** ant	6. gullible, dubious	syn **(ant)**	10. cordial, hostile	syn **(ant)**
3. gaudy, tasteful	syn **(ant)**	7. fact, hypothesis	syn **(ant)**	11. grandiose, impressive	**(syn)** ant
4. prodigy, genius	**(syn)** ant	8. bracelet, bangle	**(syn)** ant	12. innate, acquired	syn **(ant)**

Exercise 4: Part A: Underline each noun to be made possessive and write singular or plural (S-P), the rule number, and the possessive form. Part B: Write each noun as singular possessive and then as plural possessive.

. For a singular noun - add (**'s**) Rule 1: **boy's**		2. For a plural noun that ends in **s** - add (**'**) Rule 2: **boys'**		3. For a plural noun that does not end in **s** - add (**'s**) Rule 3: **men's**		
Part A	**S-P**	**Rule**	**Possessive Form**	**Part B**	**Singular Poss**	**Plural Poss**
1. <u>flags</u> waving	P	2	**flags' waving**	12. ax	**ax's**	**axe's**
2. <u>Dennis</u> courtesy	S	1	**Dennis's courtesy**	13. roof	**roof's**	**roofs'**
3. <u>fence</u> height	S	1	**fence's height**	14. wolf	**wolf's**	**wolves'**
4. <u>diner</u> menu	S	1	**diner's menu**	15. cousin	**cousin's**	**cousins'**
5. <u>letter</u> intent	S	1	**letter's intent**	16. turkey	**turkey's**	**turkeys'**
6. <u>fielders</u> errors	P	2	**fielders' errors**	17. child	**child's**	**children's**
7. <u>judge</u> verdict	S	1	**judge's verdict**	18. mirror	**mirror's**	**mirrors'**
8. <u>parents</u> worries	P	2	**parents' worries**	19. gentleman	**gentleman's**	**gentlemen's**
9. <u>flight</u> delay	S	1	**flight's delay**	20. pirate	**pirate's**	**pirates'**
10. <u>crows</u> footprints	P	2	**crows' footprints**	21. igloo	**igloo's**	**igloos'**
11. <u>barbers</u> prices	P	2	**barbers' prices**	22. woman	**woman's**	**women's**

Exercise 5: On a sheet of paper, write one sentence for each of these labels: ① (S) ② (SCS) ③ (SCV) ④ (CD) ⑤ (CX). (Answers will vary.)

Exercise 6: In your journal, write a paragraph summarizing what you have learned this week.

CHAPTER 15 LESSON 4 CONTINUED

TEACHER INSTRUCTIONS

Use the Question and Answer Flows below for the sentences on Chapter 15 Tests.

Question and Answer Flow for Sentence 1: Two skillful, dedicated pastors built a small church on the land behind our farm.

1. Who built a small church on the land behind our farm? pastors - SN
2. What is being said about pastors? pastors built - V
3. Pastors built what? church - verify the noun
4. Does church mean the same thing as pastors? No.
5. Church - DO
6. Built - V-t
7. What kind of church? small - Adj
8. A - A
9. On - P
10. On what? land - OP
11. The - A
12. Behind - P
13. Behind what? farm - OP
14. Whose farm? our - PPA
15. What kind of pastors? dedicated - Adj
16. What kind of pastors? skillful - Adj
17. How many pastors? two - Adj
18. SN V-t DO P2 Check
19. Verb-transitive - Check again.
20. (On the land) - Prepositional phrase
21. (Behind our farm) - Prepositional phrase
22. Period, statement, declarative sentence
23. Go back to the verb - divide the complete subject from the complete predicate.
24. Is there an adverb exception? No.
25. Is this sentence in a natural or inverted order? Natural - no change.

Classified Sentence:

		Adj	Adj	Adj	SN	V-t	A	Adj	DO	P	A	OP	P	PPA	OP
SN V-t	Two skillful, dedicated pastors / built a small church (on the land) (behind our farm). D

DO P2

Question and Answer Flow for Sentence 2: The energetic children have collected papers and magazines at church.

1. Who have collected papers and magazines at church? children - SN
2. What is being said about children? children have collected - V
3. Have - HV
4. Children have collected what? papers and magazines - verify the nouns
5. Do papers and magazines mean the same thing as children? No.
6. Papers, magazines - CDO, CDO
7. Collected - V-t
8. And - C
9. At - P
10. At what? church - OP
11. What kind of children? energetic - Adj
12. The - A
13. SN V-t DO P2 Check
14. Verb-transitive - Check again.
15. (At church) - Prepositional phrase
16. Period, statement, declarative sentence
17. Go back to the verb - divide the complete subject from the complete predicate.
18. Is there an adverb exception? No.
19. Is this sentence in a natural or inverted order? Natural - no change.

Classified Sentence:

		A	Adj	SN	HV	V-t	CDO	C	CDO	P	OP
SN V-t	The energetic children / have collected papers and magazines (at church). D

DO P2

CHAPTER 15   LESSON 5

New objectives: Writing Assignments #19 and #20, Bonus Option.

 **WRITING TIME**

TEACHING SCRIPT FOR PRACTICING DIFFERENT KINDS OF WRITING

Today, you are assigned two different kinds of writing. You will write a five-paragraph expository essay and a three-paragraph persuasive essay. <u>You will revise and edit the five-paragraph expository essay.</u> (_Read the box below for more information about students' writing assignment._) As you edit, make sure you use the checkpoints in the editing checklist provided in Reference 35. Remember to read through the whole essay, starting with the title, and then edit, sentence-by-sentence, using the five-sentence checkpoints for each sentence. Use the paragraph checkpoints to check each paragraph. Remember, your editing is now more detailed and more comprehensive, so take your time.

Writing Assignment Box #1

Writing Assignment #19: Five-Paragraph Expository Essay (First Person)
(Remember, first person pronouns are _I, we, me, us, my, our, mine, and ours._)
Remind students that the 5-paragraph essay has three parts: 1. Introduction 2. Body 3. Conclusion. The body has three paragraphs instead of one. Have students use their regular editing checklist to edit this assignment.

Writing topic: The Kind of Parent I Want To Be or **Things Money Can't Buy**
               or **Why I Am Glad I Have a Brother(s) and/or Sister(s)**

Your second writing assignment is to write a three-paragraph persuasive essay. (_Read the box below for more information about students' writing assignment._) You do not have to edit this assignment with the editing checklist.

Writing Assignment Box #2

Writing Assignment #20: Three-Paragraph Persuasive Essay (First Person)
(Remember, first person pronouns are _I, we, me, us, my, our, mine, and ours._)
Remind students that the 3-paragraph essay has three parts: 1. Introduction 2. Body 3. Conclusion. The body has one paragraph instead of three. Have students use their regular editing checklist to edit this assignment.

Writing topic: Telephone Courtesy Is Important or **Why I Need An Allowance**
               or **Why I Need a Raise in My Allowance**

Bonus Option: How many books are in the Old Testament? (_39_) **Look up all the books of the Old Testament and list them in your Journal. Next, create a word search that contains all the books of the Old Testament. Be careful to spell all the names correctly. Give the word search to a family member to complete. Make a key so you can check the finished word search.**

Read, check, and discuss Writing Assignment #19 after students have finished their final papers. Use the checklists as you check and discuss students' papers. Make sure students are using the regular editing checklist correctly. Read and discuss Writing Assignment #20 for fun and enrichment.

(End of lesson.)

CHAPTER 16   LESSON 1
New objectives: Jingle (the indirect object), Grammar (Introductory Sentences, indirect objects, adding the indirect object to the Noun Check), Vocabulary #1, and an Activity.

 **JINGLE TIME**

Have students turn to the Jingle Section in their books and recite the previously-taught jingles. Then, lead students in reciting the new jingle (*The Indirect Object*) below. Practice the new jingle several times until students can recite it smoothly. Emphasize reciting with a rhythm. Students and teacher should be together! (*Do not try to explain the jingle at this time. Just have fun reciting it.*)

Teacher's Note: Again, do not spend a large amount of time practicing the new jingles. Students learn the jingles best by spending a small amount of time consistently, **every** day. The teacher should concentrate on the following areas while students are reciting the new jingle: togetherness, smoothness, volume, and enthusiasm.

Jingle 17:   The Indirect Object Jingle
1. An indirect object is a noun or pronoun.
2. An indirect object receives what the direct object names.
3. An indirect object is located between the verb-transitive and the direct object.
4. To find the indirect object, ask TO WHOM or FOR WHOM after the direct object.

 GRAMMAR TIME

Put the introductory sentences from the box below on the board. Use these sentences as you go through each new concept covered in your teaching script. For the greatest benefit, students must participate orally with the teacher. (*You might put the introductory sentences on notebook paper if you are doing one-on-one instruction with your students.*)

Chapter 16, Introductory Sentences for Lesson 1
1. _____ Janice's sister handed Josh a funny birthday card.
2. _____ Yesterday, Laura's husband drew Alex and Walter a cartoon character.
3. _____ Would you buy him hiking boots?

TEACHING SCRIPT FOR INDIRECT OBJECTS

Earlier, you learned that nouns can have different jobs, or functions, in a sentence. You have studied three of these jobs already: A noun can be a subject, an object of a preposition, or a direct object. You must remember, however, that a noun used as a subject or direct object is a core part of a sentence pattern (like SN V or SN V-t DO). But a noun that is used as an object of a preposition is not part of a core sentence pattern.

CHAPTER 16 LESSON 1 CONTINUED

In the new sentence pattern, **Pattern 3**, there are three nouns in the core sentence pattern: **N V N N**. The <u>first</u> noun is a subject noun and is still written as **SN**. The <u>third</u> noun is a direct object and is still written as **DO**. The verb is labeled **V-t** after identifying the direct object. The <u>second</u> noun is called an indirect object and is written with the abbreviation **IO**. The indirect object will *always* come between the verb and direct object. This third pattern in Shurley English is *subject noun / verb-transitive / indirect object / direct object / Pattern 3*, and it is written as **SN V-t IO DO P3**.

There are five basic things you need to know about an indirect object. For this information, look at Reference 46 on page 33 in the Reference Section of your book and follow along as I read this information to you. I want you to notice that these five things are very similar to the indirect object jingle. You will read the Question and Answer Flow for the Sample Sentence with me so you will know what to say when you classify Pattern 3 sentences. (*Read the information about indirect objects to your students. Then, have students read and classify the Sample Sentence orally with you.*)

Reference 46: Indirect Object and Pattern 3

1. An **indirect object** is a noun or pronoun.

2. An **indirect object** receives what the direct object names.

3. An **indirect object** is located between the verb-transitive and the direct object.

4. An **indirect object** is labeled as IO.

5. To find the **indirect object**, ask TO WHOM or FOR WHOM after the direct object.

Sample Sentence for the exact words to say to find the indirect object.

1. Chris sang her a lullaby.
2. Who sang her a lullaby? Chris - SN
3. What is being said about Chris? Chris sang - V
4. Chris sang what? lullaby - verify the noun
5. Does lullaby mean the same thing as Chris? No.
6. Lullaby - DO
7. Sang - V-t
8. Chris sang lullaby for whom? her - IO (*Say: her - indirect object.*)
9. A - A

10. SN V-t IO DO P3 Check (*Say: Subject Noun, Verb-transitive, Indirect Object, Direct Object, Pattern 3, Check.*) (*This first check is to make sure the "t" is added to the verb.*)

11. Verb-transitive - check again. (*"Check again" means to check for prepositional phrases and then go through the rest of the question and answer flow.*)

12. No prepositional phrases.

13. Period, statement, declarative sentence.

14. Go back to the verb - divide the complete subject from the complete predicate.

15. Is there an adverb exception? No.

16. Is this sentence in a natural or inverted order? Natural - no change.

What is Pattern 3? (*SN V-t IO DO*) What is the sentence core of a Pattern 3 sentence? (*SN V-t IO DO*) What parts of speech does a Pattern 3 sentence use? (*N V N N*) You will use the information you have just learned as you classify this first set of sentences with me to find the indirect object. Begin.

CHAPTER 16 LESSON 1 CONTINUED

Question and Answer Flow for Sentence 1: Janice's sister handed Josh a funny birthday card.

1. Who handed Josh a funny birthday card? sister - SN
2. What is being said about sister? sister handed - V
3. Sister handed what? card - verify the noun
4. Does card mean the same thing as sister? No.
5. Card - DO
6. Handed - V-t

Note: Ask the indirect object question after the direct object has been identified.

7. Sister handed card to whom? Josh - IO (Indirect object)

Note: Always get the core, SN V-t IO DO, before you classify the rest of the sentence.

8. What kind of card? birthday - Adj

9. What kind of card? funny - Adj
10. A - A
11. Whose sister? Janice's - PNA
12. SN V-t IO DO P3 Check
    (Subject noun, verb transitive, indirect object, direct object Pattern 3 Check)
13. Verb-transitive - Check again.
14. No prepositional phrases.
15. Period, statement, declarative sentence
16. Go back to the verb - divide the complete subject from the complete predicate.
17. Is there an adverb exception? No.
18. Is this sentence in a natural or inverted order? Natural - no change.

Classified Sentence:

		PNA	SN		V-t	IO	A	Adj	Adj	DO

<u>SN V-t</u> Janice's sister / handed Josh a funny birthday card. **D**
<u>IO DO P3</u>

Teacher's Notes: The verb-transitive check is continued for Pattern 3 because students might forget to add the "t" to the verb. If they leave the "t" off, it is wrong. This is the reason the verb-transitive check is so important for them to remember.

Question and Answer Flow for Sentence 2: Yesterday, Laura's husband drew Alex and Walter a cartoon character.

1. Who drew Alex and Walter a cartoon character? husband - SN
2. What is being said about husband? husband drew - V
3. Husband drew what? character - verify the noun
4. Does character mean the same thing as husband? No.
5. Character - DO
6. Drew - V-t
7. Husband drew character for whom? Alex and Walter - CIO, CIO (compound indirect object, compound indirect object)
8. What kind of character? cartoon - Adj
9. A - A
10. And - C

11. Whose husband? Laura's - PNA
12. Drew when? yesterday - Adv
13. SN V-t IO DO P3 Check
14. Verb-transitive - Check again.
15. No prepositional phrases.
16. Period, statement, declarative sentence
17. Go back to the verb - divide the complete subject from the complete predicate.
18. Is there an adverb exception? No.
19. Is this sentence in a natural or inverted order? Inverted - underline the subject parts once and the predicate parts twice.

Classified Sentence:

		Adv	PNA	SN		V-t	CIO	C	CIO	A	Adj	DO

<u>SN V-t</u> <u>Yesterday, Laura's husband</u> / <u>drew Alex and Walter a cartoon character</u>. **D**
<u>IO DO P3</u>

CHAPTER 16 LESSON 1 CONTINUED

Question and Answer Flow for Sentence 3: Would you buy him hiking boots?

1. Who would buy him hiking boots? you - SP
2. What is being said about you? you would buy - V
3. Would - HV
4. You would buy what? boots - verify the noun
5. Do boots mean the same thing as you? No.
6. Boots - DO
7. Buy - V-t
8. You would buy boots for whom? him - IO
9. What kind of boots? hiking - Adj
10. SN V-t IO DO P3 Check

11. Verb-transitive - Check again.
12. No prepositional phrases.
13. Question mark, question, interrogative sentence
14. Go back to the verb - divide the complete subject from the complete predicate.
15. Is there an adverb exception? No.
16. Is this sentence in a natural or inverted order? Inverted - underline the subject parts once and the predicate parts twice.

Classified Sentence:

```
                         HV   SP   V-t  IO  Adj   DO
          SN  V-t      Would you / buy him hiking boots? Int
          IO DO  P3
```

Teacher's Notes: If your students need a smoother recitation of the Question and Answer Flows, you have the option of classifying the sentences a second time to reinforce the new concepts. (*Suggestion: You can erase the labels and have students re-label or have students trace over the teacher's labels. Check for any problems during this second classifying.*)

TEACHING SCRIPT FOR ADDING THE INDIRECT OBJECTS TO THE NOUN CHECK

Name the noun jobs we have had before today. (*SN, OP, and DO*) Today, we have added another noun job. What is the new noun job that we have just added? (*indirect object—IO*) So, if I want to find nouns in a sentence, where would I go? (*To the SN, OP, DO, or IO jobs*) After I go to the subject noun, object of the preposition, direct object, and indirect object jobs, what do I do next? (*Check each job to see if the word is a noun or a pronoun. If it is a pronoun, move to the next job. If it is a noun, circle it to indicate that it is a noun.*)

Oral Skill Builder Check	
1. **Noun check.** (Say the job and then say the noun. Circle each noun.)	5. **Identify the complete subject and the complete predicate.** (Underline the complete subject once and the complete predicate twice.)
2. **Identify the nouns as singular or plural.** (Write S or P above each noun.)	6. **Identify the simple subject and simple predicate.** (Underline the simple subject once and the simple predicate twice. Bold, or highlight, the lines.)
3. **Identify the nouns as common or proper.** (Follow established procedure for oral identification.)	7. **Recite the irregular verb chart.** (Located on student page 17 and teacher page 143.)
4. **Do a vocabulary check.** (Follow established procedure for oral identification.)	

 WRITING TIME

Have students make an entry in their journals.

CHAPTER 16 LESSON 1 CONTINUED

VOCABULARY TIME

Assign Chapter 16, Vocabulary Words **#1** on page 8 in the Reference Section for students to define in their Vocabulary notebooks. Tell students they are to use a dictionary or thesaurus to look up the meanings of the vocabulary words. After they write each word and its meaning, students are to write a sentence using the vocabulary word.

Chapter 16, Vocabulary Words #1
(flippant, polite, camouflage, conceal)

ACTIVITY / ASSIGNMENT TIME

Put the two examples of Definition Poems below on the board for your students. Read and discuss the following information about Definition Poems and the two examples. Have students write one or two definition poems. Have them share the definition poems they create.

Definition Poems. Almost always, a **Definition Poem** is written about an abstraction. Abstractions are intangible things that one cannot see, hear, smell, taste, or touch. Think of the many words in our language that are mental concepts only—*love, courage, patience, cruelty*, and hundreds of others. No one can see a *love* or a courage; no one can see a *patience* or a *cruelty*. **Definition Poems,** through the use of concrete examples, attempt to define the abstraction the poem is written about. *(Write the examples below on the board and discuss them with your students.)*

EXAMPLES:

Trust is...
> taking directions from a stranger,
> loaning money to a neighbor,
> agreeing to an anesthetic,
> ordering merchandise over the computer,
> and sharing a secret with a friend.

Courage is...
> taking a stand against the majority,
> not yielding to peer pressure,
> proclaiming your beliefs at the risk of ridicule,
> drafting a living will,
> and helping to break up a fight.

(End of lesson.)

CHAPTER 16 LESSON 2

New objectives: Grammar (Practice Pattern 3 Sentences), Vocabulary #2, and a Practice activity.

 JINGLE TIME

Have students turn to the Jingle Section of their books. The teacher will lead the students in reciting the previously-taught jingles.

 GRAMMAR TIME

First-Year Option: Put the Practice Sentences from the box below on the board or notebook paper. Use these sentences as you practice the concepts that have been taught. For the greatest benefit, students must participate orally with the teacher. **Second-Year Option:** Have students classify the Practice Sentences independently on paper. Check students' sentences with the answers provided below. (*If you have the CDs for Practice Sentences, have students check their sentences with the CDs.*)

Chapter 16, Practice Sentences for Lesson 2

1. _____ Would you pass me some strawberry jam for my toast?
2. _____ Gary gave me two explanations for the skid marks in front of the elementary school.
3. _____ My teacher gave me a different assignment for my homework.

TEACHING SCRIPT FOR PRACTICING PATTERN 3 SENTENCES

We will classify three different sentences to practice Pattern 3 sentences. We will classify the sentences together. Begin. (*You might have your students write the labels above the sentences at this time.*)

Question and Answer Flow for Sentence 1: Would you pass me some strawberry jam for my toast?

1. Who would pass me some strawberry jam for my toast? you - SP
2. What is being said about you? you would pass - V
3. Would - HV
4. You would pass what? jam - verify the noun
5. Does jam mean the same thing as you? No.
6. Jam - DO
7. Pass - V-t
8. You would pass jam to whom? me - IO
9. What kind of jam? strawberry - Adj
10. How much jam? some - Adj
11. For - P

12. For what? toast - OP
13. Whose toast? my - PPA
14. SN V-t IO DO P3 Check
15. Verb-transitive - Check again.
16. (For my toast) - Prepositional phrase
17. Question mark, question, interrogative sentence
18. Go back to the verb - divide the complete subject from the complete predicate.
19. Is there an adverb exception? No.
20. Is this sentence in a natural or inverted order? Inverted - underline the subject parts once and the predicate parts twice.

Classified Sentence:

		HV	SP	V-t	IO	Adj	Adj	DO	P PPA OP	
SN V-t		Would	you	/ pass	me	some	strawberry	jam	(for my toast)	? Int
IO DO P3										

CHAPTER 16 LESSON 2 CONTINUED

Question and Answer Flow for Sentence 2: Gary gave me two explanations for the skid marks in front of the elementary school.

1. Who gave me two explanations for the skid marks in front of the elementary school? Gary - SN
2. What is being said about Gary? Gary gave - V
3. Gary gave what? explanations - verify the noun
4. Do explanations mean the same thing as Gary? No.
5. Explanations - DO
6. Gave - V-t
7. Gary gave explanations to whom? me - IO
8. How many explanations? two - Adj
9. For - P
10. For what? marks - OP
11. What kind of marks? skid - Adj
12. The - A
13. In - P
14. In what? front - OP
15. Of - P
16. Of what? school - OP
17. What kind of school? elementary - Adj
18. The - A
19. SN V-t IO DO P3 Check
20. Verb-transitive - Check again.
21. (For the skid marks) - Prepositional phrase
22. (In front) - Prepositional phrase
23. (Of the elementary school) - Prepositional phrase
24. Period, statement, declarative sentence
25. Go back to the verb - divide the complete subject from the complete predicate.
26. Is there an adverb exception? No.
27. Is this sentence in a natural or inverted order? Natural - no change.

Classified	SN	V-t	IO Adj	DO	P A Adj OP	P OP	P A Adj	OP

Classified Sentence: SN V-t / IO DO P3 — Gary / gave me two explanations (for the skid marks) (in front) (of the elementary school). **D**

Question and Answer Flow for Sentence 3: My teacher gave me a different assignment for my homework.

1. Who gave me a different assignment for my homework? teacher - SN
2. What is being said about teacher? teacher gave - V
3. Teacher gave what? assignment - verify the noun
4. Does assignment mean the same thing as teacher? No.
5. Assignment - DO
6. Gave - V-t
7. Teacher gave assignment to whom? me - IO
8. What kind of assignment? different - Adj
9. A - A
10. For - P
11. For what? homework - OP
12. Whose homework? my - PPA
13. Whose teacher? my - PPA
14. SN V-t IO DO P3 Check
15. Verb-transitive - Check again.
16. (For my homework) - Prepositional phrase
17. Period, statement, declarative sentence
18. Go back to the verb - divide the complete subject from the complete predicate.
19. Is there an adverb exception? No.
20. Is this sentence in a natural or inverted order? Natural - no change.

Classified Sentence: PPA SN V-t IO A Adj DO P PPA OP

SN V-t / IO DO P3 — My teacher / gave me a different assignment (for my homework). **D**

TEACHER INSTRUCTIONS

Use Sentences 1-3 that you just classified with your students to do an Oral Skill Builder Check.

Oral Skill Builder Check

1. **Noun check.**
   (Say the job and then say the noun. Circle each noun.)
2. **Identify the nouns as singular or plural.**
   (Write S or P above each noun.)
3. **Identify the nouns as common or proper.**
   (Follow established procedure for oral identification.)
4. **Do a vocabulary check.**
   (Follow established procedure for oral identification.)
5. **Identify the complete subject and the complete predicate.** (Underline the complete subject once and the complete predicate twice.)
6. **Identify the simple subject and simple predicate.**
   (Underline the simple subject once and the simple predicate twice. Bold, or highlight, the lines.)
7. **Recite the irregular verb chart.**
   (Located on student page 17 and teacher page 143.)

CHAPTER 16 LESSON 2 CONTINUED

TEACHING SCRIPT FOR INTRODUCING A PATTERN 3 PRACTICE SENTENCE

Get out a sheet of notebook paper. On the top line of your notebook paper, write the title *Pattern 3 Practice Sentence*. Put this title on the board: **Pattern 3 Sentence**. I will guide you through the process as we learn to write a Pattern 3 sentence.

You have already learned how to write independent Pattern 1 and Pattern 2 sentences according to labels you select. You will now learn how to write an independent Pattern 3 sentence the same way. First, you start out with the core labels for a Pattern 3 sentence. This means that you <u>must always have a subject, a</u> <u>verb-transitive, an indirect object, and a direct object before you add any extra parts.</u>

You build the rest of your Pattern 3 sentence from the regular sentence parts learned in Pattern 1. I will ask you a few questions to make sure you understand. What are the parts of a Pattern 3 sentence that YOU MUST USE. (*All Pattern 3 sentences must have a subject, a verb-transitive, an indirect object, and a direct object.*) I want you to name the extra sentence parts that you can use with your sentence. There are ten parts. (*adjectives, adverbs, articles, prepositional phrases, subject pronouns, possessive nouns, possessive pronouns, helping verbs, conjunctions, and interjections*) Remember, you will use the core parts of a Pattern 3 sentence and then add the extra parts that you want to use in your sentence.

Let's write the labels for a Pattern 3 sentence on a sheet of notebook paper. First, write the *SN V-t DO* and *IO* labels that a Pattern 3 sentence must have on your paper. Be sure to place them in the middle of your paper. (*Demonstrate by writing the SN V-t IO DO labels on the board.*) Using what you know about writing Practice Sentences, you must decide what other parts you want to add to your Pattern 3 sentence. (*Have students finish writing a Pattern 3 sentence and turn it in to you. Students do not have to write an Improved Sentence at this point unless you feel they need the practice. If your students cannot handle this much independence so soon, give them the labels you want them to follow for a Pattern 3 sentence. Sample:* (*A Adj Adj SN V-t PPA IO A Adj Adj DO P PPA OP) Check and discuss students' sentences after they have finished.*)

 VOCABULARY TIME

Assign Chapter 16, Vocabulary Words **#2** on page 8 in the Reference Section for students to define in their Vocabulary notebooks. Tell students they are to use a dictionary or thesaurus to look up the meanings of the vocabulary words. After they write each word and its meaning, students are to write a sentence using the vocabulary word.

Chapter 16, Vocabulary Words #2
(exquisite, gauche, scrutinize, examine)

 PRACTICE TIME

Have students write the three sentences that they classify at the beginning of the lesson on a sheet of paper. (*See page 277.*) Have them tape-record the Question and Answer Flows for all three sentences. Students should write labels above the sentences as they classify them. They especially need the second practice if this is their first year in the program. (*After the students have finished, check the tape and sentence labels. Make sure students understand any mistakes they have made.*)

(End of lesson.)

CHAPTER 16   LESSON 3

New objectives: Grammar (Practice Sentences), Skills (pronoun cases), and a Practice sheet.

JINGLE TIME

Have students turn to the Jingle Section of their books. The teacher will lead the students in reciting the previously-taught jingles.

GRAMMAR TIME

First-Year Option: Put the Practice Sentences from the box below on the board or notebook paper. Use these sentences as you practice the concepts that have been taught. For the greatest benefit, students must participate orally with the teacher. **Second-Year Option:** Have students classify the Practice Sentences independently on paper. Check students' sentences with the answers provided below. (*If you have the CDs for Practice Sentences, have students check their sentences with the CDs.*)

Chapter 16, Practice Sentences for Lesson 3
1. _____ The publisher sent me a tempting contract for my manuscript.
2. _____ Yeah! The curator gladly gave us an extremely generous contribution for our arrowhead collection!
3. _____ The frail little girl gave my sister and me some tender smiles.

TEACHING SCRIPT FOR PRACTICING PATTERN 3 SENTENCES

We will classify three different sentences to practice Pattern 3 sentences. We will classify the sentences together. Begin. (*You might have your students write the labels above the sentences at this time.*)

Question and Answer Flow for Sentence 1: The publisher sent me a tempting contract for my manuscript.

1. Who sent me a tempting contract for my manuscript? publisher - SN
2. What is being said about publisher? publisher sent - V
3. Publisher sent what? contract - verify the noun
4. Does contract mean the same thing as publisher? No.
5. Contract - DO
6. Sent - V-t
7. Publisher sent contract to whom? me - IO
8. What kind of contract? tempting - Adj
9. A - A
10. For - P
11. For what? manuscript - OP

12. Whose manuscript? my - PPA
13. The - A
14. SN V-t IO DO P3 Check
15. Verb-transitive - Check again.
16. (For my manuscript) - Prepositional phrase
17. Period, statement, declarative sentence
18. Go back to the verb - divide the complete subject from the complete predicate.
19. Is there an adverb exception? No.
20. Is this sentence in a natural or inverted order? Natural - no change.

Classified Sentence:

```
                        A   SN        V-t IO A  Adj     DO    P PPA     OP
         SN V-t    The publisher / sent me a tempting contract (for my manuscript).  D
         IO DO P3
```

CHAPTER 16 LESSON 3 CONTINUED

Question and Answer Flow for Sentence 2: Yeah! The curator gladly gave us an extremely generous contribution for our arrowhead collection!

1. Who gave us an extremely generous contribution for our arrowhead collection? curator - SN
2. What is being said about curator? curator gave - V
3. Curator gave what? contribution - verify the noun
4. Does contribution mean the same thing as curator? No.
5. Contribution - DO
6. Gave - V-t
7. Curator gave contribution to whom? us - IO
8. What kind of contribution? generous - Adj
9. How generous? extremely - Adv
10. An - A
11. For - P
12. For what? collection - OP
13. What kind of collection? arrowhead - Adj
14. Whose collection? our - PPA
15. Gave how? gladly - Adv
16. The - A
17. Yeah - I
18. SN V-t IO DO P3 Check
19. Verb-transitive - Check again.
20. (For our arrowhead collection) - Prepositional phrase
21. Exclamation point, strong feeling, exclamatory sentence
22. Go back to the verb - divide the complete subject from the complete predicate.
23. Is there an adverb exception? Yes - change the line.
24. Is this sentence in a natural or inverted order? Natural - no change.

Classified Sentence:

```
                    I   A   SN    Adv  V-t  IO  A    Adv     Adj      DO
 SN  V-t     Yeah! The curator / gladly gave us an extremely generous contribution
 IO DO P3    P  PPA     Adj      OP
             (for our arrowhead collection)!  E
```

Question and Answer Flow for Sentence 3: The frail little girl gave my sister and me some tender smiles.

1. Who gave my sister and me some tender smiles? girl - SN
2. What is being said about girl? girl gave - V
3. Girl gave what? smiles - verify the noun
4. Do smiles mean the same thing as girl? No.
5. Smiles - DO
6. Gave - V-t
7. Girl gave smiles to whom? sister and me - CIO, CIO
8. What kind of smiles? tender - Adj
9. How many smiles? some - Adj
10. And - C
11. Whose sister? my - PPA
12. What kind of girl? little - Adj
13. What kind of girl? frail - Adj
14. The - A
15. SN V-t IO DO P3 Check
16. Verb-transitive - Check again.
17. No prepositional phrases.
18. Period, statement, declarative sentence
19. Go back to the verb - divide the complete subject from the complete predicate.
20. Is there an adverb exception? No.
21. Is this sentence in a natural or inverted order? Natural - no change.

Classified Sentence:

```
                    A  Adj  Adj  SN   V-t  PPA  CIO  C  CIO  Adj    Adj    DO
 SN  V-t     The frail little girl / gave my sister and me some tender smiles.  D
 IO DO P3
```

CHAPTER 16 LESSON 3 CONTINUED

SKILL TIME

TEACHING SCRIPT FOR INTRODUCING PRONOUN CASES

You have already learned about subject pronouns, possessive pronouns, object pronouns and the jingles that list them. Let's recite these pronoun jingles right now. (*Lead your students in the pronoun jingles as a review.*) You are going to learn how to use these pronouns correctly. Look at Reference 47 on page 33 for information about pronoun cases. (*Read and discuss the information about the pronoun cases, numbers 1-3, in the reference box below.*)

Reference 47: Subjective, Objective, and Possessive Pronoun Cases

1. The **subject** pronouns are in the **subjective case:** *I, we, he, she, it, they,* and *you.*
   Use subjective case pronouns for subjects or predicate pronouns.
2. The **object** pronouns are in the **objective case:** *me, us, him, her, it, them,* and *you.*
   Use objective case pronouns for objects: object of a preposition, direct object, or indirect object.
3. The **possessive** pronouns are in the **possessive case:** *my, our, his, her, its, their, your,* and *mine.*
   Use possessive case pronouns to show ownership.

Practice Section: For Sentences 1-4, replace each underlined pronoun by writing the correct form in the first blank and **S** or **O** for **S**ubjective or **O**bjective case in the second blank.

1. Molly and <u>me</u> are waiting on Tim.   <u> I </u> <u> S </u>   3. Do you want <u>she</u> and <u>I</u> to choose? <u>her and me</u> <u> O </u>
2. Dad wants to invite Howard and <u>they</u>. <u> them </u> <u> O </u>   4. Did you speak to <u>he</u> or <u>I</u>? <u>him or me</u> <u> O </u>

Until it becomes automatic, you must make a determined effort to choose the correct pronoun when you write or speak. Since the subjective and objective cases give us the most trouble, we will concentrate on them as we practice correct pronoun usage. You must know how and when to use the subjective and objective pronouns. To give you practice in choosing pronouns according to their case, look at the practice section provided at the bottom of Reference 47.

Look at sentences 1-4. The underlined pronouns in these sentences are used incorrectly because they are in the wrong case. In this practice, you will learn how to choose the correct pronouns to use in each sentence. Let's look at Sentence 1. Why is the pronoun *me* incorrect? (*The job of the underlined pronoun should be a subject pronoun. The pronoun **me** is an object pronoun and cannot be used as the subject.*)

Since we need a subject pronoun, which subject pronoun would replace the pronoun *me* in this sentence? (*I*) The directions say to write the correct pronoun in the first blank. What is written in the first blank? (*The pronoun I.*) The directions also say to write *S* or *O* in the second blank to show whether the pronoun is subjective or objective. Is the pronoun *I* subjective or objective? (*subjective*) What is written in the second blank? (*The letter S.*) (*Work through sentences 2-4 in the same way.*)

CHAPTER 16 LESSON 3 CONTINUED

 PRACTICE TIME

Do an oral review of pronoun cases by identifying pronouns as subjective, objective, or possessive. As you say the pronoun, have students tell you the pronoun case. Make this a fun review. (*This chant will sound like a cheer. Students do not have a copy of this chant, so they will follow your lead.*)

I say **they**; you say (*subjective*): **they**: *subjective*   I say **me**; you say (*objective*): **me**: *objective*
I say **your**; you say (*possessive*): **your**: *possessive*   I say **my**; you say (*possessive*): **my**: *possessive*
I say **him**; you say (*objective*): **him**: *objective*   I say **I**; you say (*subjective*): **I**: *subjective*
I say **he**; you say (*subjective*): **he**: *subjective*   I say **its**; you say (*possessive*): **its**: *possessive*
I say **our**; you say (*possessive*): **our**: *possessive*   I say **his**; you say (*possessive*): **his**: *possessive*
I say **us**; you say (*objective*): **us**: *objective*   I say **we**; you say (*subjective*): **we**: *subjective*
I say **mine**; you say (*possessive*): **mine**: *possessive*   I say **them**; you say (*objective*): **them**: *objective*
I say **their**; you say (*possessive*): **their**: *possessive*   I say **she**; you say (*subjective*): **she**: *subjective*

In the next chant, the pronouns will have two possible cases, depending on how they are used in a sentence. Your response will include the two possible cases.

I say **it**; you say (*subjective or objective*): **it**: *subjective* or *objective*
I say **you**; you say (*subjective or objective*): **you**: *subjective* or *objective*
I say **her**; you say (*objective or possessive*): **her**: *objective* or *possessive*

Have students turn to page 65 in the Practice Section of their book and find Chapter 16, Lesson 3, Practice. Go over the directions to make sure they understand what to do. Check and discuss the Practice after students have finished. (*Chapter 16, Lesson 3, Practice key is given below.*)

Chapter 16, Lesson 3, Practice: For sentences 1-4, replace each underlined pronoun by writing the correct form in the first blank and **S** or **O** for subjective or objective case in the second blank.

1. <u>Us</u> volunteers were eager to help. <u>We</u>   <u>S</u>   3. Make a reservation for Mom and <u>they</u>. <u>them</u>   <u>O</u>
2. Win a vacation from <u>we</u> ladies. <u>us</u>   <u>O</u>   4. Mark and <u>us</u> will probably drive. <u>we</u>   <u>S</u>

 WRITING TIME

Have students make an entry in their journals.

 STUDY TIME

Have students study the vocabulary words in their vocabulary notebooks. Tell students that any vocabulary word in their notebooks could be on their test. Also, have students study any of the skills in the Practice Section that they need to review.

(End of lesson.)

CHAPTER 16   LESSON 4

New objectives: Test.

JINGLE TIME

Have students turn to the Jingle Section of their books. The teacher will lead the students in reciting the previously-taught jingles.

STUDY TIME

Have students study the vocabulary words in their vocabulary notebooks. Remind students that any vocabulary word in their notebooks could be on their test. Also, have students study any of the skills in the Practice Section that they need to review.

TEST TIME

Have students turn to page 98 in the Test Section of their book and find Chapter 16 Test. Go over the directions to make sure they understand what to do. (*Chapter 16 Test key is on the next page.*)

CHECK TIME

After students have finished, check and discuss their test papers. Make sure they understand why their answers are right or wrong. (*For total points, count each required answer as a point.*)

(End of lesson.)

Chapter 16 Test
(Student Page 98)

Exercise 1: Classify each sentence.

```
       (You) SP    V-t  PPA  IO   Adj   Adj      DO     P  PPA   OP
1.  SN V-t      / Give your cousin those sparkly earrings (for her birthday).  Imp
    IO DO P3
                 A   SN    P    A   Adj     OP      V-t  IO  A   Adj     DO
2.  SN V-t      The waiter (at the new restaurant) / served us an excellent dessert.  D
    IO DO P3
                 HV  SP   V-t   CIO  C   CIO   A   DO    P  PPA    OP
3.  SN V-t      Have you / given Gene and Laura the note (from your mom)?  Int
    IO DO P3
```

Exercise 2: Use Sentence 3 to underline the complete subject once and the complete predicate twice and to complete the table below.

List the Noun Used	List the Noun Job	Singular or Plural	Common or Proper	Simple Subject	Simple Predicate
1. Gene	2. CIO	3. S	4. P	5. you	6. have given
7. Laura	8. CIO	9. S	10. P		
11. note	12. DO	13. S	14. C		
15. mom	16. OP	17. S	18. C		

Exercise 3: Identify each pair of words as synonyms or antonyms by putting parentheses ( ) around *syn* or *ant*.

1. odd, quaint	(syn) ant	5. flippant, polite	syn (ant)	9. scrutinize, examine	(syn) ant
2. ethical, carnal	syn (ant)	6. exquisite, gauche	syn (ant)	10. impenetrable, vulnerable	syn (ant)
3. mimic, imitate	(syn) ant	7. gullible, dubious	syn (ant)	11. conceal, camouflage	(syn) ant
4. gaudy, tasteful	syn (ant)	8. prodigal, wasteful	(syn) ant	12. luminous, obscure	syn (ant)

Exercise 4: Underline the correct homonym in each sentence.

1. We drove (threw, <u>through</u>) the tunnel at night.
2. The kitten cut (<u>its</u>, it's) paw on the barbed wire.
3. Put (<u>your</u>, you're) pajamas in my suitcase.
4. He has been our (<u>principal</u>, principle) for ten years now.
5. It is so easy (<u>to</u>, too, two) throw caution to the wind.
6. He seemed to be on the right (coarse, <u>course</u>) for success.

Exercise 5: Identify these pronouns by writing **S** (subjective), **O** (objective), or **P** (possessive) in each blank.

P 1. their   **P** 2. our   **S** 3. we   **O** 4. them   **S/O** 5. it   **O** 6. us   **P** 7. your   **S** 8. she

Exercise 6: For Sentences 1-4, replace each underlined pronoun by writing the correct form in the first blank and **S** or **O** for subjective or objective case in the second blank.

1. No one asked Jim or <u>I</u>. me   O
2. It is too cold for <u>we</u>. us   O
3. The principal summoned <u>they</u> to the office. them   O
4. Mark and <u>her</u> are dating now. she   S

Exercise 7: Identify each kind of sentence by writing the abbreviation in the blank. (S, F, SCS, SCV, CD, CX)

F 1. As long as there are no detours.
SCV 2. The jalopy coughed and sputtered to a stop.
CD 3. I forgot her number; moreover, I don't have time to call.
CX 4. Because the ice storm came, travel was imperiled.
SCS 5. The post office and jail were destroyed in the fire.

Exercise 8: There are three ways to connect compound sentences. Write a sentence demonstrating each one.

Exercise 9: In your journal, write a paragraph summarizing what you have learned this week.

Level 5 Homeschool Teacher's Manual   Page 285
© SHURLEY INSTRUCTIONAL MATERIALS, INC.

CHAPTER 16 LESSON 4 CONTINUED

TEACHER INSTRUCTIONS

Use the Question and Answer Flows below for the sentences on Chapter 16 Test.

Question and Answer Flow for Sentence 1: Give your cousin those sparkly earrings for her birthday.

1. Who give your cousin those sparkly earrings for her birthday? (You) - SP (Understood subject pronoun)
2. What is being said about you? you give - V
3. You give what? earrings - verify the noun
4. Do earrings mean the same thing as you? No.
5. Earrings - DO
6. Give - V-t
7. You give earrings to whom? cousin - IO
8. What kind of earrings? sparkly - Adj
9. Which earrings? those - Adj
10. For - P
11. For what? birthday - OP
12. Whose birthday? her - PPA
13. Whose cousin? your - PPA
14. SN V-t IO DO P3 Check
15. Verb-transitive - Check again.
16. (For her birthday) - Prepositional phrase
17. Period, command, imperative sentence
18. Go back to the verb - divide the complete subject from the complete predicate.
19. Is there an adverb exception? No.
20. Is this sentence in a natural or inverted order? Natural - no change.

Classified Sentence:

```
             (You) SP    V-t  PPA   IO   Adj   Adj    DO     P  PPA  OP
             SN V-t    / Give your cousin those sparkly earrings (for her birthday). Imp
             IO DO  P3
```

Question and Answer Flow for Sentence 2: The waiter at the new restaurant served us an excellent dessert.

1. Who served us an excellent dessert? waiter - SN
2. What is being said about waiter? waiter served - V
3. Waiter served what? dessert - verify the noun
4. Does dessert mean the same thing as waiter? No.
5. Dessert - DO
6. Served - V-t
7. Waiter served dessert to whom? us - IO
8. What kind of dessert? excellent - Adj
9. An - A
10. At - P
11. At what? restaurant - OP
12. What kind of restaurant? new - Adj
13. The - A
14. The - A
15. SN V-t IO DO P3 Check
16. Verb-transitive - Check again.
17. (At the new restaurant) - Prepositional phrase
18. Period, statement, declarative sentence
19. Go back to the verb - divide the complete subject from the complete predicate.
20. Is there an adverb exception? No.
21. Is this sentence in a natural or inverted order? Natural - no change.

Classified Sentence:

```
                 A   SN    P   A   Adj    OP      V-t   IO  A   Adj     DO
      SN V-t    The waiter (at the new restaurant) / served us an excellent dessert. D
      IO DO  P3
```

Question and Answer Flow for Sentence 3: Have you given Gene and Laura the note from your mom?

1. Who have given Gene and Laura the note from your mom? you - SP
2. What is being said about you? you have given - V
3. Have - HV
4. You have given what? note - verify the noun
5. Does note mean the same thing as you? No.
6. Note - DO
7. Given - V-t
8. You have given note to whom? Gene and Laura - CIO, CIO
9. The - A
10. From - P
11. From whom? mom - OP
12. Whose mom? your - PPA
13. And - C
14. SN V-t IO DO P3 Check
15. Verb-transitive - Check again.
16. (From your mom) - Prepositional phrase
17. Question mark, question, interrogative sentence
18. Go back to the verb - divide the complete subject from the complete predicate.
19. Is there an adverb exception? No.
20. Is this sentence in a natural or inverted order? Inverted - underline the subject parts once and the predicate parts twice.

Classified Sentence:

```
                  HV   SP   V-t   CIO   C   CIO   A   DO    P  PPA   OP
      SN V-t     Have you / given Gene and Laura the note (from your mom)? Int
      IO DO  P3
```

CHAPTER 16   LESSON 5

New objectives: Writing Assignments #21 and #22.

 **WRITING TIME**

TEACHING SCRIPT FOR PRACTICING DIFFERENT KINDS OF WRITING

Today, you are assigned two different kinds of writing. You will write a five-paragraph persuasive essay and a three-paragraph expository essay. <u>You will revise and edit the five-paragraph persuasive essay.</u> (*Read the box below for more information about students' writing assignment.*) As you edit, make sure you use the checkpoints in the editing checklist provided in Reference 35. Remember to read through the whole essay, starting with the title, and then edit, sentence-by-sentence, using the five-sentence checkpoints for each sentence. Use the paragraph checkpoints to check each paragraph. Remember, your editing is now more detailed and more comprehensive, so take your time.

Writing Assignment Box #1

Writing Assignment #21: Five-Paragraph Persuasive Essay (First or Third Person)
(Remember, first person pronouns are *I, we, me, us, my, our, mine, and ours.*)
Remind students that the 5-paragraph essay has three parts: 1. Introduction 2. Body 3. Conclusion. The body has three paragraphs instead of one. Have students use their regular editing checklist to edit this assignment.

Writing topic: Why I Should Vote or **Why Everyone Needs to See a Dentist Once a Year** or **Why I Need a Pet**

Your second writing assignment is to write a three-paragraph expository essay. (*Read the box below for more information about students' writing assignment.*) You do not have to edit this assignment with the editing checklist.

Writing Assignment Box #2

Writing Assignment #22: Three-Paragraph Expository Essay (First Third Person)
(Remember, first person pronouns are *I, we, me, us, my, our, mine, and ours.*)
Remind students that the 3-paragraph essay has three parts: 1. Introduction 2. Body 3. Conclusion. The body has one paragraph instead of three. Have students use their regular editing checklist to edit this assignment.

Writing topic: Things I Want To Do After I Graduate or **Why I Like Birthdays** or **My Favorite Songs**

Read, check, and discuss Writing Assignment #21 after students have finished their final papers. Use the checklists as you check and discuss students' papers. Make sure students are using the regular editing checklist correctly. Read and discuss Writing Assignment #22 for fun and enrichment.

(End of lesson.)

CHAPTER 17   LESSON 1

New objectives: Grammar (Practice Sentences), Skills (beginning quotes, ending quotes), Practice sheet, and Vocabulary #1.

JINGLE TIME

Have students turn to the Jingle Section of their books. The teacher will lead the students in reciting the previously-taught jingles.

GRAMMAR TIME

First-Year Option: Put the Practice Sentences from the box below on the board or notebook paper. Use these sentences as you practice the concepts that have been taught. For the greatest benefit, students must participate orally with the teacher. **Second-Year Option:** Have students classify the Practice Sentences independently on paper. Check students' sentences with the answers provided below. (*If you have the CDs for Practice Sentences, have students check their sentences with the CDs.*)

Chapter 17, Practice Sentences for Lesson 1

1. _____ Edna told us a story about her school days in Kentucky.
2. _____ Send Mom the biscuit recipe promptly and accurately.

TEACHING SCRIPT FOR PRACTICING PATTERN 3 SENTENCES

We will practice Classifying Pattern 3 sentences. We will classify the sentences together. Begin. (*You might have your students write the labels above the sentences at this time.*)

Question and Answer Flow for Sentence 1: Edna told us a story about her school days in Kentucky.

1. Who told us a story about her school days in Kentucky?
   Edna - SN
2. What is being said about Edna? Edna told - V
3. Edna told what? story - verify the noun
4. Does story mean the same thing as Edna? No.
5. Story - DO
6. Told - V-t
7. Edna told a story to whom? us - IO
8. A - A
9. About - P
10. About what? days - OP
11. Which days? school - Adj
12. Whose days? her - PPA

13. In - P
14. In what? Kentucky - OP
15. SN V-t IO DO P3 Check
16. Verb-transitive - Check again.
17. (About her school days) - Prepositional phrase
18. (In Kentucky) - Prepositional phrase
19. Period, statement, declarative sentence
20. Go back to the verb - divide the complete subject from the complete predicate.
21. Is there an adverb exception? No.
22. Is this sentence in a natural or inverted order?
   Natural - no change.

Classified Sentence:

<pre>
                          SN   V-t IO A DO   P PPA Adj OP   P OP
          SN V-t   Edna / told us a story (about her school days) (in Kentucky). D
          IO DO P3
</pre>

CHAPTER 17 LESSON 1 CONTINUED

Question and Answer Flow for Sentence 2: Send Mom the biscuit recipe promptly and accurately.

1. Who send Mom the biscuit recipe promptly and accurately?
   (You) - SP (Understood subject pronoun)
2. What is being said about you? you send - V
3. You send what? recipe - verify the noun
4. Does recipe mean the same thing as you? No.
5. Recipe - DO
6. Send - V-t
7. You send the recipe to whom? Mom - IO
8. What kind of recipe? biscuit - Adj
9. The - A
10. Send how? promptly and accurately - CAdv, CAdv

11. And - C
12. SN V-t IO DO P3 Check
13. Verb-transitive - Check again.
14. No prepositional phrases.
15. Period, command, imperative sentence
16. Go back to the verb - divide the complete subject from the complete predicate.
17. Is there an adverb exception? No.
18. Is this sentence in a natural or inverted order? Natural - no change.

Classified Sentence: (You) SP   V-t   IO   A   Adj   DO   CAdv   C   CAdv
                          SN V-t   / Send Mom the biscuit recipe promptly and accurately. **Imp**
                          IO DO P3

Use Sentences 1-2 that you just classified with your students to do an Oral Skill Builder Check. Use the guidelines below.

Oral Skill Builder Check

1. **Noun check.**
   (Say the job and then say the noun. Circle each noun.)
2. **Identify the nouns as singular or plural.**
   (Write S or P above each noun.)
3. **Identify the nouns as common or proper.**
   (Follow established procedure for oral identification.)
4. **Do a vocabulary check.**
   (Follow established procedure for oral identification.)

5. **Identify the complete subject and the complete predicate.** (Underline the complete subject once and the complete predicate twice.)
6. **Identify the simple subject and simple predicate.**
   (Underline the simple subject once and the simple predicate twice. Bold, or highlight. the lines.)
7. **Recite the irregular verb chart.**
   (Located on student page 17 and teacher page 143.)

SKILL TIME

TEACHING SCRIPT FOR BEGINNING QUOTES

I am going to read you two short stories. It is the same story, but it is written two different ways. When I am finished, I want you to tell me if you enjoyed Story 1 or Story 2 the best.

Story 1

This was Tammy's first babysitting job, and she showed all the patience in the world. Her little nephew was only two months old, and she felt very responsible for his well-being. She promised her Aunt Lydia that little Tyler would have excellent care.

Although Tammy was looking forward to her first earnings, she was more concerned about making a good impression on her aunt. She knew that if she did a good job, her aunt would give her a good recommendation when she applied for other jobs during the summer.

CHAPTER 17 LESSON 1 CONTINUED

Story 2

> "I'm so thrilled to have this job, Aunt Lydia, and you know I will take good care of Tyler." Tammy was quick to assure her aunt that Tyler was in good hands.
>
> "Tammy, I know that. This little guy is so lucky to have someone as responsible as you to take care of him." Aunt Lydia replied gratefully.
>
> As she anticipated earning her first paycheck, Tammy asked her aunt a question. "Aunt Lydia, if I prove myself in this job, would you give me a good recommendation for other jobs during the summer?" Tammy waited anxiously for her aunt's reply.
>
> "Why, certainly," Aunt Lydia replied. "You know I would".

Did you enjoy Story 1 or Story 2 the best? (*Discuss reasons your students give for their preferences.*) Quotations are used to make your writing come alive and to make your readers believe that they are right in the middle of the action. Quotations help build pictures for your readers as the story unfolds. In Story 2, the action was direct, vigorous, and strong. In Story 1, the action was indirect, limp, and a little weak, even though the meanings of the two stories were almost identical. You will use quotations more if you understand how to write them correctly. Quotations are fun to use, but as all good writers know, it requires a little effort to learn the basic rules.

Quotations are words spoken by someone, and quotation marks are used to set off the exact words that are spoken. The words set off by quotation marks are usually called a direct quotation. In your writing, you will often find it necessary to tell what someone has said, and you will need to know several rules of punctuation in order to write quotations.

We will start with how to punctuate beginning quotes. Look at Reference 48 on page 34 in the Reference Section of your book. We will go through each rule as we punctuate the guided sample sentence in the rule box for beginning quotes. (*It would be best to put the guided sentence on the board so students can follow each step as you write it. Follow the teaching script below the rule box on the next page.*)

Reference 48: Quotation Rules for Beginning Quotes

1. **Pattern: "C** -quote- **(,!?) "** <u>explanatory words (.)</u>
   (Quotation marks, capital letter, quote, end punctuation choice, quotation marks closed, explanatory words, period)
2. Underline **end explanatory words** and use a period at the end.
3. You should see the **beginning quote** – Use quotation marks at the beginning and end of what is said. Then, put a comma, question mark, or exclamation point (no period) after the quote but in front of the quotation mark.
4. **Capitalize** the beginning of a quote and any proper nouns or the pronoun *I*.
5. **Punctuate** the rest of the sentence by checking for any apostrophes, periods, or commas that may be needed within the sentence.

Guided Practice

Sentence: the poets and i are reading poetry on tuesday with m k miller the director said

1. Pattern: **"C** -quote- **(,!?) "** <u>explanatory words (.)</u>
2. the poets and i are reading poetry on tuesday with m k miller **the director said**(.)
3. "the poets and i are reading poetry on tuesday with m k miller**,"** <u>the director said</u>.
4. "**T**he poets and **I** are reading poetry on **T**uesday with **M K M**iller," <u>the director said</u>.
5. "The poets and I are reading poetry on Tuesday with M. K. Miller," <u>the director said</u>.
6. **Corrected Sentence:** "The poets and I are reading poetry on Tuesday with M. K. Miller," the director said.

You will never have trouble punctuating beginning quotations if you follow these simple quotation rules because they tell you exactly what to do to the whole sentence. Look at the sentence under the Guided Practice and read the sentence with me: (*the poets and i are reading poetry on tuesday with m k miller the director said*). We will break it up into sections, and then we will punctuate each section. First, you always write a pattern to follow, so we will write the pattern for a beginning quote. That's number one under your rules. Let's read what the pattern says: **"C** *-quote-* **(,!?) "** *explanatory words* **(.)**. I will translate the pattern for you: quotation marks, capital letter to begin a quote, the quote itself, a choice of end mark (,!?), quotation marks, explanatory words, and a period. You will understand it better as I explain each part to you.

Look at Rule 2. Rule 2 says to underline *end explanatory words* and use a period at the end. Explanatory words are the words that explain who is talking but are not part of the actual quote. Any time you have a beginning quote, your explanatory words will be at the end. What are the explanatory words at the end of this sentence? (*the director said*) (*Underline these explanatory words and put a period at the end.*)

Look at Rule 3. Rule 3 says, for beginning quotes, to use quotation marks at the beginning and end of what is said. Which words need quotation marks at the beginning and end? (*"the poets and i are reading poetry on tuesday with m k miller "*) (*Put quotation marks around these words.*) Rule 3 also says to put a comma, question mark, or exclamation point (but no period) after the quote but in front of the quotation mark. Which punctuation mark would you use and why? (*Use a comma because the sentence is a statement, not a question or an exclamation.*) (*Put a comma after* **miller** *but in front of the quotation marks.*)

Look at Rule 4. Rule 4 says to capitalize the beginning of the quote, any proper nouns, or the pronoun *I*. Which words would be capitalized in this sentence? (*The, I, Tuesday, M K Miller*) (*Capitalize these words.*)

Look at Rule 5. Rule 5 says to punctuate the rest of the sentence by checking for any apostrophes, periods, or commas that may be needed within the sentence. What punctuation is needed in this sentence? (*A period is needed after M. and after K. because they are a person's initials.*) (*Punctuate these initials.*)

Now, we have a corrected sentence. Wasn't that easy? For a final check, I will go through the corrected sentence using the quotation pattern only. You will still have to remember to capitalize and punctuate the rest of the sentence, but this pattern will help you remember how to punctuate a beginning quote correctly. (*As you read each part of the quotation pattern, point out that part in the corrected sentence.*) **"C** *-quote-* **(,!?) "** *explanatory words* **(.)**

TEACHING SCRIPT FOR ENDING QUOTES

Look at Reference 49 for end quotes on page 34. We will go through each rule as we punctuate the guided sample sentence in the rule box for end quotes. (*It would be best to put the guided sentence on the board so students can follow each step as you write it. Read the step-by-step teaching script for end quotes on the next page.*)

CHAPTER 17 LESSON 1 CONTINUED

Reference 49: Quotation Rules for End Quotes

1. **Pattern: C –explanatory words(,) "C -quote- (.!?) "**
   (Capital letter, explanatory words, comma, quotation marks, capital letter, quote, end punctuation choice, quotation marks closed)
2. Underline **beginning explanatory words** and use a comma after them.
3. You should see the **end quote** – Use quotation marks at the beginning and end of what is said. Then, put a period, question mark, or exclamation point (no comma) after the quote, usually in front of the quotation mark.
4. **Capitalize** the first of the explanatory words at the beginning of a sentence, the beginning of the quote, and any proper nouns or the pronoun *I*.
5. **Punctuate** the rest of the sentence by checking for any apostrophes, periods, or commas that may be needed within the sentence.

Guided Practice

Sentence: the director said the poets and i are reading poetry on tuesday with m k miller

1. Pattern: **C -explanatory words(,) "C –quote- (.!?) "**

2. **<u>the director said</u>(,)** the poets and i are reading poetry on tuesday with m k miller

3. <u>the director said</u>, "the poets and i are reading poetry on tuesday with m k miller**. "**

4. <u>The director said</u>, "**T**he poets and **I** are reading poetry on **T**uesday with **M K M**iller."

5. <u>The director said,</u> "The poets and I are reading poetry on Tuesday with M**.** K**.** Miller."

6. **Corrected Sentence:** The director said, "The poets and I are reading poetry on Tuesday with M. K. Miller."

You will never have trouble punctuating end quotations if you follow these simple rules because they tell you exactly what to do to the whole sentence. Look at the sentence under the Guided Practice and read the sentence with me: (*the director said the poets and i are reading poetry on tuesday with m k miller*). We will break it up into sections, and then we will punctuate each section. First, you always write a pattern to follow, so we will write the pattern for an end quote. That's number one under your rules. Let's read what the pattern says: *C -explanatory words(,) "C -quote- (.!?) "*. I will translate the pattern for you: capital letter to begin the explanatory words, the explanatory words, comma, quotation marks, capital letter to begin the quotation, a choice of end marks (.!?), and quotation marks.

Look at Rule 2. Rule 2 says to underline *beginning explanatory words* and use a comma after them. Remember, explanatory words are the words that explain who is talking but are not part of the actual quote. What are the explanatory words at the beginning of this sentence? (*the director said*) (*Underline these explanatory words and put a comma after **said**.*)

Look at Rule 3. Rule 3 says, for end quotes, to use quotation marks at the beginning and end of what is said. What words need quotation marks around them? (*"the poets and i are reading poetry on tuesday with m k miller "*) (*Put quotation marks around these words.*) Rule 3 also says to put a period, question mark, or exclamation point (but no comma) after the quote but in front of the quotation mark. Which punctuation mark would you use and why? (*Use a period because the sentence is a statement, not a question or an exclamation.*) (*Put a period after **miller** but in front of the quotation marks.*)

Look at Rule 4. Rule 4 says to capitalize the first of the explanatory words at the beginning of a sentence, the beginning of the quote, any proper nouns, or the pronoun *I*. Which words would be capitalized in this sentence? (*The, I, Tuesday, M K Miller*) (*Capitalize these words.*)

CHAPTER 17 LESSON 1 CONTINUED

Look at Rule 5. Rule 5 says to punctuate the rest of the sentence by checking for any apostrophes, periods, or commas that may be needed within the sentence. What punctuation is needed in this sentence? (*A period is needed after M. and after K. because they are a person's initials.*) (*Punctuate these initials.*)

Now, we have a corrected sentence. For a final check, I will go through the corrected sentence using the quotation pattern only. You will still have to remember to capitalize and punctuate the rest of the sentence, but this pattern will help you remember how to punctuate end quotes correctly. (*As you read each part of the quotation pattern, point out that part in the corrected sentence.*)
<u>C -explanatory words</u>(,) "C -quote- (.!?) "

PRACTICE TIME

Have students turn to page 65 in the Practice Section of their book and find Chapter 17, Lesson 1, Practice. Go over the directions to make sure they understand what to do. Guide students closely as they do the practice exercises for the first time. (*Students may use the Reference section in their books to help them remember the new information.*) Check and discuss the Practice after students have finished. (*Chapter 17, Lesson 1, Practice key is given below.*)

Chapter 17, Lesson 1, Practice: Use the Quotation Rules to help punctuate the quotations below. Underline the explanatory words.

    R   S   T
1. <u>reverend simms remarked</u>, "the time for forgiveness has come**.**"

    T   R   S
2. "the time for forgiveness has come," <u>reverend simms remarked</u>**.**

    I   P   C   M
3. <u>i whispered to patty before the christmas dance</u>, "mind your manners."

    M   I   P   C
4. "mind your manners," i whispered to patty before the christmas dance**.**

WRITING TIME

Have students make an entry in their journals.

VOCABULARY TIME

Assign Chapter 17, Vocabulary Words **#1** on page 8 in the Reference Section for students to define in their Vocabulary notebooks. After they write each word and its meaning, students are to write a sentence using the vocabulary word.

Chapter 17, Vocabulary Words #1
(diligent, negligent, contemplate, ponder)

(End of lesson.)

CHAPTER 17 LESSON 2

New objectives: Grammar (Practice Sentences), Skills (split quotes, other quotation rules), Practice sheet, and Vocabulary #2.

JINGLE TIME

Have students turn to the Jingle Section of their books. The teacher will lead the students in reciting the previously-taught jingles.

GRAMMAR TIME

First-Year Option: Put the Practice Sentences from the box below on the board or notebook paper. Use these sentences as you practice the concepts that have been taught. For the greatest benefit, students must participate orally with the teacher. **Second-Year Option:** Have students classify the Practice Sentences independently on paper. Check students' sentences with the answers provided below. (*If you have the CDs for Practice Sentences, have students check their sentences with the CDs.*)

Chapter 17, Practice Sentences for Lesson 2

1. _____ Pastor Johnson sent Pat and Muriel applications for the job.
2. _____ Ted and Larry promptly mailed me instructions for their essay contest.

TEACHING SCRIPT FOR PRACTICING PATTERN 3 SENTENCES

We will practice classifying Pattern 3 sentences. We will classify the sentences together. Begin. (*You might have your students write the labels above the sentences at this time.*)

Question and Answer Flow for Sentence 1: Pastor Johnson sent Pat and Muriel applications for the job.

1. Who sent Pat and Muriel applications for the job?
   Pastor Johnson - SN
2. What is being said about Pastor Johnson?
   Pastor Johnson sent - V
3. Pastor Johnson sent what? applications - verify the noun
4. Do applications mean the same thing as Pastor Johnson?
   No.
5. Applications - DO
6. Sent - V-t
7. Pastor Johnson sent applications to whom?
   Pat and Muriel - CIO, CIO
8. For - P

9. For what? job - OP
10. The - A
11. And - C
12. SN V-t IO DO P3 Check
13. Verb-transitive - Check again.
14. (For the job) - Prepositional phrase
15. Period, statement, declarative sentence
16. Go back to the verb - divide the complete subject from the complete predicate.
17. Is there an adverb exception? No.
18. Is this sentence in a natural or inverted order?
    Natural - no change.

Classified Sentence:

```
                              SN        V-t  CIO  C   CIO      DO        P  A  OP
        SN V-t      Pastor Johnson / sent Pat and Muriel applications (for the job).  D
        IO DO  P3
```

CHAPTER 17 LESSON 2 CONTINUED

Question and Answer Flow for Sentence 2: Ted and Larry promptly mailed me instructions for their essay contest.

1. Who mailed me instructions for their essay contest?
   Ted and Larry - CSN, CSN
2. What is being said about Ted and Larry?
   Ted and Larry mailed - V
3. Ted and Larry mailed what? instructions - verify the noun
4. Do instructions mean the same thing as Ted and Larry?
   No.
5. Instructions - DO
6. Mailed - V-t
7. Ted and Larry mailed instructions to whom? me - IO
8. For - P
9. For what? contest - OP
10. What kind of contest? essay - Adj

11. Whose contest? their - PPA
12. Mailed how? promptly - Adv
13. And - C
14. SN V-t IO DO P3 Check
15. Verb-transitive - Check again.
16. (For their essay contest) - Prepositional phrase
17. Period, statement, declarative sentence
18. Go back to the verb - divide the complete subject from the complete predicate.
19. Is there an adverb exception? Yes - change the line.
20. Is this sentence in a natural or inverted order? Natural - no change.

Classified Sentence:

		CSN	C	CSN	Adv	V-t	IO	DO	P	PPA	Adj	OP
SN	V-t	Ted and Larry / promptly mailed me instructions (for their essay contest).										D
	IO DO P3											

TEACHER INSTRUCTIONS FOR A PATTERN 3 PRACTICE SENTENCE

Tell students that their sentence writing assignment today is to write a Pattern 3 Practice Sentence. They are to follow the same procedure used in the previous lessons. They should decide on their labels, arrange them in a selected order, write their sentence, and edit the sentence for improved word choices. (*Students do not have to write an Improved Sentence at this point unless you feel they need more one-on-one word choice writing practice.*) Check and discuss the Pattern 3 Practice Sentence after students have finished.

 SKILL TIME

TEACHING SCRIPT FOR SPLIT QUOTES

Look at Reference 50 for split quotes on page 35. We will go through each rule as we punctuate the guided sample sentence in the rule box for split quotes. (*It would be best to put the guided sentence on the board so students can follow each step as you write it. Read the step-by-step teaching script for split quotes on the next page.*)

CHAPTER 17 LESSON 2 CONTINUED

Reference 50: Quotation Rules for Split Quotes

1. **Pattern:** "**C** -quote- **(,)** "**c** –explanatory words**(,**) "**c** –quote- **(.!?)** "
   (Quotation marks, capital letter, first part of quote, comma, quotation marks, explanatory words, comma, quotation marks again, second part of quote, end punctuation choice, quotation marks.)
2. Underline **middle explanatory words** and use a comma after them.
3. You should see the **first part of a split quote** - Use quotation marks at the beginning and end of the first part of what is said. Then, put a comma after the first part of the quote but in front of the quotation mark.
4. You should see the **second part of a split quote** – Use quotation marks at the beginning and end of the second part of what is said. Then, put end mark punctuation (no comma) after the quote but usually in front of the quotation mark.
5. **Capitalize** the beginning of a quote and any proper nouns or the pronoun *I*. (Do not capitalize the first word of the second part unless it is a proper noun or the pronoun *I*.)
6. **Punctuate** the rest of the sentence by checking for any apostrophes, periods, or commas that may be needed within the sentence.

Guided Practice

Sentence: the poets and i the director said are reading poetry on tuesday with m k miller

1. Pattern: "**C** -quote- **(,)** "**c** –explanatory words**(,**) "**c** -quote- **(.!?)** "
2. the poets and i **the director said(,)** are reading poetry on tuesday with m k miller
3. "the poets and i**,**" the director said, are reading poetry on tuesday with m k miller
4. "the poets and i," the director said, "are reading poetry on tuesday with m k miller**(.)**"
5. "**The** poets and **I**," the director said, "are reading poetry on **T**uesday with **M K M**iller."
6. "The poets and I," the director said, "are reading poetry on Tuesday with M. K. Miller."
7. **Corrected Sentence:** "The poets and I," the director said, "are reading poetry on Tuesday with M. K. Miller."

Note: When you enclose two sentences in quotation marks, you still have two sentences, not a split quote. "The poets and I are reading poetry on Tuesday," the director said. "I think they need the experience."

You will never have trouble punctuating split quotations if you follow these simple rules because they tell you exactly what to do to the whole sentence. Look at the sentence under the Guided Practice and read the sentence with me: (*the poets and i the director said are reading poetry on tuesday with m k miller*) We will break it up into sections, and then we will punctuate each section.

First, you always write a pattern to follow, so we will write the pattern for a split quote. That's number one under your rules. Let's read what the pattern says: "**C** *-quote-* **(,)** "**c** *-explanatory words***(,**) "**c** *-quote-* **(.!?)** ". I will translate the pattern for you: quotation marks, capital letter to begin the quote, the quotation, comma, quotation marks, the explanatory words, comma, quotation marks, small letter to begin the quotation, the quotation, a choice of end marks (.!?), and quotation marks.

CHAPTER 17 LESSON 2 CONTINUED

Look at Rule 2. Rule 2 says to underline *middle explanatory words* and use a comma at the end of them. Middle explanatory words are the words in the middle of the sentence that explain who is talking but are not part of the actual quote. What are the explanatory words in the middle of this sentence? (*the director said*) (*Underline these explanatory words and put a comma after* **said**.)

Since the explanatory words are in the middle of the sentence, the words at the beginning and at the end of the sentence are the split quote. Look at Rule 3. Rule 3 says, for the first part of split quotes, to use quotation marks at the beginning and end of the first part of what is said. What words need quotation marks at the beginning and end? (*"the poets and i"*) (*Put quotation marks around these words.*) Rule 3 also says to put a comma after the first part of the quote but in front of the quotation mark. (*Put a comma after* **i**.)

Rule 4 says for the second part of the split quote to use quotation marks at the beginning and end of the second part of what is said. What words need quotation marks at the beginning and end? (*"are reading poetry on tuesday with m k miller"*) (*Put quotation marks around these words.*) Now, Rule 4 says to put end mark punctuation, but no comma, after the second part of the quote but in front of the quotation mark. Which punctuation mark would you use and why? (*Use a period because the sentence is a statement, not a question or an exclamation.*) (*Put a period after* **miller** *but in front of the quotation mark.*)

Look at Rule 5. Rule 5 says to capitalize the beginning of the quote, any proper nouns, or the pronoun *I*. Which words would be capitalized in this sentence? (*The, I, Tuesday, M K Miller*) (*Capitalize these words.*)

Look at Rule 6. Rule 6 says to punctuate the rest of the sentence by checking for any apostrophes, periods, or commas that may be needed within the sentence. What punctuation is needed in this sentence? (*A period is needed after M. and after K. because they are a person's initials.*) (*Punctuate these initials.*)

Now, we have a corrected sentence. For a final check, I will go through the corrected sentence using the quotation pattern only. You will still have to remember to capitalize and punctuate the rest of the sentence, but this pattern will help you remember how to punctuate split quotes correctly. (*As you read each part of the quotation pattern, point out that part in the corrected sentence.*)
"**C** -quote- (**,**) "**c** -explanatory words(**,) **"c** -quote- (**.!?**) "

TEACHING SCRIPT FOR OTHER QUOTATION RULES

There are a few more rules that apply to different kinds of quotations. For a list of these rules, look at Reference 51 on page 36 in your Reference Section. (*Read and discuss this information and the examples with your class. Pay particular attention to the examples as you go over each one to explain a concept. This reference page is reproduced for you on the next page.*)

CHAPTER 17 LESSON 2 CONTINUED

Reference 51: Other Quotation Rules

1. Longer Quotes

A. When a quotation consists of several sentences, put quotation marks only at the beginning and at the end of the whole quotation, not around each sentence in the quotation.

Cathy repeated, "I do not work on Fridays. If you want to go shopping then, I'll be available."

B. When one person has a lengthy quote which is longer than one paragraph, quotation marks are used at the beginning of each paragraph and at the end of the last paragraph of that speaker's quote. Then, when the speaker changes, a new paragraph is started.

"_____

_____ (same speaker continues)

"_____

_____" (same speaker ends)

"_____" (new speaker begins and ends)

2. A Quote Within a Quote

Single quotation marks are used to punctuate a quotation within a quotation.

"Did she say, 'Scotland is my homeland'?" Charlie asked.

3. Quotation Marks to Punctuate Titles

Quotation marks are used to punctuate titles of songs, poems, short stories, chapters of books, articles, TV programs, and short plays. (*Capitalize the first word, last word, and every word except for articles, short prepositions, and short conjunctions.*)

Her favorite poem is "Two Tramps in Mud Time."

4. Direct Quotations, Indirect Quotations, and Statements

A. A direct quotation occurs when you show exactly what someone says by using quotation marks.

Direct quotation: Al said yesterday, "I'd like to buy a ranch."

B. An indirect quotation occurs when you simply describe what someone says without using his exact words.

Indirect quotation: Al said he would like to buy a ranch.

C. A statement occurs when no speaker is mentioned and no quotation is used.

Statement: Al would like to buy a ranch.

CHAPTER 17 LESSON 2 CONTINUED

 PRACTICE TIME

Students will continue punctuating direct quotations. Have students turn to pages 65 and 66 in the Practice Section of their book and find Chapter 17, Lesson 2, Practice (*1-2*). Go over the directions to make sure they understand what to do. Check and discuss the Practice after students have finished. (*Chapter 17, Lesson 2, Practice keys are given below*.)

Chapter 17, Lesson 2, Practice 1: Use the Quotation Rules to help punctuate the quotations below. Underline the explanatory words.

    L   L
1. "look out the window!" <u>lucy shouted</u>.

    W   I   M   T
2. "where can i reach you in memphis?" <u>todd asked</u>.

    H   M   C
3. "head south, " <u>she said</u>, "into montgomery county. "

    W   I   P   M   I
4. "when i climbed pinnacle mountain," <u>she gasped</u>, "i nearly fainted. "

    A   H   A
5. <u>albert inquired</u>, "how far is albuquerque from here? "

    S   Y
6. <u>sheila insisted</u>, "your taxes are due tomorrow. "

Chapter 17, Lesson 2, Practice 2: On a sheet of paper, write three sentences demonstrating each of the three quotations: Beginning quote, end quote, and split quote. (Answers will vary.)

 VOCABULARY TIME

Assign Chapter 17, Vocabulary Words **#2** on page 8 in the Reference Section for students to define in their Vocabulary notebooks. Tell students they are to use a dictionary or thesaurus to look up the meanings of the vocabulary words. After they write each word and its meaning, students are to write a sentence using the vocabulary word.

Chapter 17, Vocabulary Words #2
(delusion, reality, enunciation, pronounce)

(End of lesson.)

CHAPTER 17   LESSON 3
New objectives: Grammar (Practice Sentences) and a Practice sheet.

JINGLE TIME

Have students turn to the Jingle Section of their books. The teacher will lead the students in reciting the previously-taught jingles.

GRAMMAR TIME

First-Year Option: Put the Practice Sentences from the box below on the board or notebook paper. Use these sentences as you practice the concepts that have been taught. For the greatest benefit, students must participate orally with the teacher. **Second-Year Option:** Have students classify the Practice Sentences independently on paper. Check students' sentences with the answers provided below. (*If you have the CDs for Practice Sentences, have students check their sentences with the CDs.*)

Chapter 17, Practice Sentences for Lesson 3
1. _____ The antique dealer gave my mother and me a guided tour.
2. _____ She frequently fixed him a bowl of cereal for his breakfast.

TEACHING SCRIPT FOR PRACTICING PATTERN 3 SENTENCES

We will practice classifying Pattern 3 sentences. We will classify the sentences together. Begin. (*You might have your students write the labels above the sentences at this time.*)

Question and Answer Flow for Sentence 1: The antique dealer gave my mother and me a guided tour.
1. Who gave my mother and me a guided tour? dealer - SN
2. What is being said about dealer? dealer gave - V
3. Dealer gave what? tour - verify the noun
4. Does tour mean the same thing as dealer? No.
5. Tour - DO
6. Gave - V-t
7. Dealer gave tour to whom? mother and me - CIO, CIO
8. What kind of tour? guided - Adj
9. A - A
10. And - C
11. Whose mother? my - PPA

| 12. What kind of dealer? antique - Adj |
| 13. The - A |
| 14. SN V-t IO DO P3 Check |
| 15. Verb-transitive - Check again. |
| 16. No prepositional phrases. |
| 17. Period, statement, declarative sentence |
| 18. Go back to the verb - divide the complete subject from the complete predicate. |
| 19. Is there an adverb exception? No. |
| 20. Is this sentence in a natural or inverted order? Natural - no change. |

Classified Sentence:

                     A   Adj   SN   V-t PPA CIO   C CIO A Adj   DO

<u>SN V-t</u>   The antique dealer **/** gave my mother and me a guided tour. **D**

IO DO P3

CHAPTER 17 LESSON 3 CONTINUED

Question and Answer Flow for Sentence 2: She frequently fixed him a bowl of cereal for his breakfast.

1. Who fixed him a bowl of cereal for his breakfast? she - SP
2. What is being said about she? she fixed - V
3. She fixed what? bowl - verify the noun
4. Does bowl mean the same thing as she? No.
5. Bowl - DO
6. Fixed - V-t
7. She fixed bowl for whom? him - IO
8. A - A
9. Of - P
10. Of what? cereal - OP
11. For - P
12. For what? breakfast - OP
13. Whose breakfast? his - PPA

14. Fixed how? frequently - Adv
15. SN V-t IO DO P3 Check
16. Verb-transitive - Check again.
17. (Of cereal) - Prepositional phrase
18. (For his breakfast) - Prepositional phrase
19. Period, statement, declarative sentence
20. Go back to the verb - divide the complete subject from the complete predicate.
21. Is there an adverb exception? Yes - change the line.
22. Is this sentence in a natural or inverted order? Natural - no change.

Classified Sentence:

	SP	Adv	V-t	IO	A	DO	P	OP	P	PPA	OP
SN V-t	She / frequently fixed him a bowl (of cereal) (for his breakfast). **D**										
IO DO P3											

 **PRACTICE TIME**

Students will continue punctuating direct quotations. Have students turn to page 66 in the Practice Section of their book and find Chapter 17, Lesson 3, Practice (*1-2*). Go over the directions to make sure they understand what to do. Check and discuss the Practice after students have finished. (*Chapter 17, Lesson 3, Practice keys are given below.*)

Chapter 17, Lesson 3, Practice 1: Use the Quotation Rules to help punctuate the quotations below. Underline the explanatory words.

     M   B
1. "marsha, did you see the aardvark at the zoo? " <u>inquired bert</u>.

     B   M
2. <u>Bert inquired</u>, "marsha, did you see the aardvark at the zoo?"

     M   B
3. "marsha," <u>bert inquired</u>, "did you see the aardvark at the zoo?"

     M   B   I
4. "marsha, did you see the aardvark at the zoo?" <u>inquired bert</u>. "i was hoping you got to pet it. "

Chapter 17, Lesson 3, Practice 2: On a sheet of paper, write three sentences demonstrating each of the three quotations: Beginning quote, end quote, and split quote. (Answers will vary.)

 STUDY TIME

Have students study the vocabulary words in their vocabulary notebooks.   Also, have students study any of the skills in the Practice Section that they need to review.

(End of lesson.)

CHAPTER 17   LESSON 4

New objectives: Test and an Activity.

 JINGLE TIME

Have students turn to the Jingle Section of their books. The teacher will lead the students in reciting the previously-taught jingles.

 STUDY TIME

Have students study the vocabulary words in their vocabulary notebooks. Remind students that any vocabulary word in their notebooks could be on their test. Also, have students study any of the skills in the Practice Section that they need to review.

 TEST TIME

Have students turn to page 99 in the Test Section of their books and find Chapter 17 Test. Go over the directions to make sure they understand what to do. (*Chapter 17 Test key is on the next page.*)

 CHECK TIME

After students have finished, check and discuss their test papers. Make sure they understand why their answers are right or wrong. (*For total points, count each required answer as a point.*)

 ACTIVITY / ASSIGNMENT TIME

Have students create their own **Parts-of-Speech Poem** formula. Then, have students design their own Parts-of-Speech poem, following the directions of their formula. Read and discuss their poems; then, have them share their poems with others.

(End of lesson.)

Chapter 17 Test
(Student Page 99)

Exercise 1: Classify each sentence.

   (You) SP   V-t CIO C CIO A   DO   P PPA Adj   OP

1. **SN V-t**   / Give Jim and Ed the directions (to your summer camp). **Imp**
   IO DO P3

                 A SN   Adv V-t A IO   Adj   DO   P   PPA   OP

2. **SN V-t**   The guard / calmly gave the inmates detailed instructions (about their release). **D**
   IO DO P3

Exercise 2: Use Sentence 1 to underline the complete subject once and the complete predicate twice and to complete the table below.

List the Noun Used	List the Noun Job	Singular or Plural	Common or Proper	Simple Subject	Simple Predicate
1. **Jim**	2. **CIO**	3. **S**	4. **P**	5. **you**	6. **give**
7. **Ed**	8. **CIO**	9. **S**	10. **P**		
11. **directions**	12. **DO**	13. **P**	14. **C**		
15. **camp**	16. **OP**	17. **S**	18. **C**		

Exercise 3: Identify each pair of words as synonyms or antonyms by putting parentheses ( ) around *syn* or *ant*.

1. ecstatic, blissful	**(syn)** ant	5. precarious, stable	syn **(ant)**	9. contemplate, ponder	**(syn)** ant
2. cordial, hostile	syn **(ant)**	6. withhold, bequeath	syn **(ant)**	10. entourage, followers	**(syn)** ant
3. delusion, reality	syn **(ant)**	7. diligent, negligent	syn **(ant)**	11. enunciate, pronounce	**(syn)** ant
4. bangle, bracelet	**(syn)** ant	8. mandatory, required	**(syn)** ant	12. veritable, fictitious	syn **(ant)**

Exercise 4: For Sentences 1-4, replace each underlined pronoun by writing the correct form in the first blank and **S** or **O** for subjective or objective case in the second blank.

1. Invite Velma and I sometime.   **me**   **O**   3. Winter gave my sister and I colds.   **me** **O**
2. Mike and me ate pizza last night.   **I**   **S**   4. The finalists were Boyd and me.   **I**   **S**

Exercise 5: Use the Quotation Rules to help punctuate the quotations below. Underline the explanatory words.

      W   I   T

1. "why did i think you were a cowboy**?**,**"** <u>inquired tom with a smile</u>**.**

      W   I   I   R

2. "when i was younger, i was," <u>ronnie replied</u>.

     S   T   I

3. "so," <u>tom said,</u> "what do you do now, if i might ask**?** ".

     L   T   R   I   K   M

4. <u>looking tom straight in the eye, ronnie retorted,</u> "i haul cotton in kennett, missouri**!** "

Exercise 6: On a sheet of paper, write one sentence for each of these labels: ① (S) ② (SCS) ③ (SCV) ④ (CD) ⑤(CX).

Exercise 7: On a sheet of paper, write three sentences, demonstrating each of the three quotations: Beginning quote, end quote, and split quote. (Answers will vary.)

Exercise 8: In your journal, write a paragraph summarizing what you have learned this week.

CHAPTER 17 LESSON 4 CONTINUED

TEACHER INSTRUCTIONS

Use the Question and Answer Flows below for the sentences on Chapter 17 Tests.

Question and Answer Flow for Sentence 1: Give Jim and Ed the directions to your summer camp.

1. Who give Jim and Ed the directions to your summer camp? (You) - SP (understood subject pronoun)
2. What is being said about you? you give - V
3. You give what? directions - verify the noun
4. Do directions mean the same thing as you? No.
5. Directions - DO
6. Give - V-t
7. You give directions to whom? Jim and Ed - CIO, CIO
8. The - A
9. To - P
10. To what? camp - OP
11. What kind of camp? summer - Adj
12. Whose camp? your - PPA
13. And - C
14. SN V-t IO DO P3 Check
15. Verb-transitive - Check again.
16. (To your summer camp) - Prepositional phrase
17. Period, command, imperative sentence
18. Go back to the verb - divide the complete subject from the complete predicate.
19. Is there an adverb exception? No.
20. Is this sentence in a natural or inverted order? Natural - no change.

Classified Sentence:

	(You) SP	V-t	CIO C CIO	A	DO	P PPA Adj	OP

SN V-t / Give Jim and Ed the directions (to your summer camp). **Imp**
IO DO P3

Question and Answer Flow for Sentence 2: The guard calmly gave the inmates detailed instructions about their release.

1. Who gave the inmates detailed instructions about their release? guard - SN
2. What is being said about guard? guard gave - V
3. Guard gave what? instructions - verify the noun
4. Do instructions mean the same thing as guard? No.
5. Instructions - DO
6. Gave - V-t
7. Guard gave instructions to whom? inmates - IO
8. What kind of instructions? detailed - Adj
9. About - P
10. About what? release - OP
11. Whose release? their - PPA
12. The - A
13. Gave how? calmly - Adv
14. The - A
15. SN V-t IO DO P3 Check
16. Verb-transitive - Check again.
17. (About their release) - Prepositional phrase
18. Period, statement, declarative sentence
19. Go back to the verb - divide the complete subject from the complete predicate.
20. Is there an adverb exception? Yes - change the line.
21. Is this sentence in a natural or inverted order? Natural - no change.

Classified Sentence:

	A SN	Adv V-t	A	IO	Adj	DO	P PPA	OP

SN V-t The guard / calmly gave the inmates detailed instructions (about their release). **D**
IO DO P3

CHAPTER 17   LESSON 5

New objectives: Writing (narrative, writing with dialogue and without dialogue) and Writing Assignments #23 and #24.

 WRITING TIME

TEACHING SCRIPT FOR INTRODUCING NARRATIVE WRITING

Narrative writing is simply the telling of a story. When you compose stories, you are actually writing what professional writers call narratives, or short stories. Short stories have certain characteristics that make them different from other types of writing. You will study five characteristics known as Story Elements. These Story Elements are main idea, setting, characters, plot, and ending. Your narrative writing skills will be developed through the use of Story Elements. Narrative writing will have a beginning, a middle, and an end.

You will learn how to use the five Story Elements—main idea, setting, characters, plot, and ending—to make a Story Elements outline. This outline will help keep your writing focused and help you choose details and events that support the main idea of your story. Before you begin every story writing assignment, you will complete a Story Elements outline like the one in Reference 52 on page 37. (*Have students go to Reference 52 on student page 37. Read and discuss the Story Elements and sample story with them.*)

Reference 52: Story Elements Outline

1. **Main Idea (Tell the problem or situation that needs a solution.)**
   Jared knew his mom was not feeling well and wanted to do something nice for her.
2. **Setting (Tell when and where the story takes place, either clearly stated or implied.)**
   When - The story takes place when Jared's mother could use some help. Where – The story takes place at Jared's home.
3. **Character (Tell whom or what the story is about.)**
   The two characters are Jared and his mother.
4. **Plot (Tell what the characters in the story do and what happens to them.)**
   The story is about a young man who sets out to surprise his mother and whose thoughtfulness overwhelms her.
5. **Ending (Use a strong ending that will bring the story to a close.)**
   The story ends with the mother's being overcome with emotion.

Jared's Surprise

   Jared didn't very often get the urge to do household chores. But, yesterday, he thought he'd do something nice for his mom because she hadn't been feeling well lately.

   "Mom, you just rest," he said. "I'm going to surprise you." With that, he turned and walked down the long hall toward the laundry room. "Whites," he said to himself thoughtfully. "Whites only in this load!" He had to keep reminding himself of the things he had heard his mother say as she did the laundry.

   When his mom heard the washer running, she got up from her bed to see what was happening. As she turned the corner into the laundry room, she stopped dead in her tracks. "Jared, what are you doing?"

   "Surprise!" he replied happily, grinning from ear to ear. "Just one thing less you'll need to worry about when you start feeling better. I did all our laundry!" Jared beamed as he gave his mother a hug.

   "Jared, I can't tell you how much I appreciate your thoughtfulness," said Jared's mom as she looked at the piles of clothes scattered all over the laundry room. With one last look at the pink sheets, Jared's mom gave her son another hug as she made her way back to bed.

CHAPTER 17 LESSON 5 CONTINUED

You will make a Story Elements outline when you get ready to write. I want to tell you about another special element that makes narrative writing especially interesting, and that is conversation. Remember, another word for conversation is **dialogue**. Writers use dialogue, or conversation, in their short stories because it helps move the plot along, and it helps the reader understand the characters better.

Dialogue often "shows" instead of "tells" in narratives. Dialogue also "shows" what a character is like. It is much better than the writer's "telling" what a character is like. A character's personal quotations show the readers a great deal about the character.

Listen as I review the main punctuation rules to observe when working with dialogue.

1. Dialogue is always placed in quotation marks. This placement will separate dialogue from any explanatory words or other words that develop the plot of the story.
2. Periods, commas, question marks, and exclamation marks that punctuate dialogue always go INSIDE the quotation marks. You follow the rules for punctuating quotations that you have already learned.
3. If more than one character is speaking, you must indent and create a new paragraph each time a different character speaks.

TEACHING SCRIPT FOR WRITING WITH DIALOGUE AND WITHOUT DIALOGUE

You will do two narrative writing assignments. The first narrative writing assignment will be a story without dialogue. The second narrative writing assignment will be the <u>same story</u> with dialogue. Both rough drafts will go through the revision and editing stages. (*Read the boxes below for more information about students' writing assignment.*) You will choose the point of view for each assignment.

Writing Assignment Box #1

Writing Assignment #23: A Narrative without dialogue (First or Third Person)
(Remember, first person pronouns are *I, we, me, us, my, our, mine,* and *ours.*)
Remind students to make a Story Elements outline.

Writing topic: The Lost Puppy or **My First Attempt at Cooking/Driving** or **The Mystery Gift** or **The Prayer List**

Writing Assignment Box #2

Writing Assignment #24: A Narrative with dialogue (First or Third Person)
(Remember, first person pronouns are *I, we, me, us, my, our, mine,* and *ours.*)
Students will use the same Story Elements outline from Writing Assignment #23.

Writing topic: The Lost Puppy or **My First Attempt at Cooking/Driving** or **The Mystery Gift** or **The Prayer List**

Read, check, and discuss Writing Assignment #23 and #24 after students have finished their final papers. Use the checklists as you check and discuss students' papers. Make sure students are using the regular editing checklist and quotations rules correctly.

(End of lesson.)

CHAPTER 18   LESSON 1

New objectives: Grammar (Practice Sentences), Skills (regular and irregular verbs, simple verb tenses, tenses of helping verbs), and a Practice sheet.

JINGLE TIME

Have students turn to the Jingle Section of their books. The teacher will lead the students in reciting the previously-taught jingles.

GRAMMAR TIME

First-Year Option: Put the Practice Sentences from the box below on the board or notebook paper. Use these sentences as you practice the concepts that have been taught. For the greatest benefit, students must participate orally with the teacher. **Second-Year Option:** Have students classify the Practice Sentences independently on paper. Check students' sentences with the answers provided below. (*If you have the CDs for Practice Sentences, have students check their sentences with the CDs.*)

Chapter 18, Practice Sentences for Lesson 1

1. _____ The lapidary showed me the first design for his turquoise ring.
2. _____ My aunt sent me a sprig of wild lilac.

Question and Answer Flow for Sentence 1: The lapidary showed me the first design for his turquoise ring.

1. Who showed me the first design for his turquoise ring? lapidary - SN
2. What is being said about lapidary? lapidary showed - V
3. Lapidary showed what? design - verify the noun
4. Does design mean the same thing as lapidary? No.
5. Design - DO
6. Showed - V-t
7. Lapidary showed design to whom? me - IO
8. Which design? first - Adj
9. The - A
10. For - P
11. For what? ring - OP

12. What kind of ring? turquoise - Adj
13. Whose ring? his - PPA
14. The - A
15. SN V-t IO DO P3 Check
16. Verb-transitive - Check again.
17. (For his turquoise ring) - Prepositional phrase
18. Period, statement, declarative sentence
19. Go back to the verb - divide the complete subject from the complete predicate.
20. Is there an adverb exception? No.
21. Is this sentence in a natural or inverted order? Natural - no change.

Classified Sentence:

```
                      A   SN        V-t  IO  A  Adj  DO    P PPA  Adj   OP
            SN V-t    The lapidary / showed me the first design (for his turquoise ring).  D
            IO DO P3
```

CHAPTER 18 LESSON 1 CONTINUED

Question and Answer Flow for Sentence 2: My aunt sent me a sprig of wild lilac.

1. Who sent me a sprig of wild lilac? aunt - SN
2. What is being said about aunt? aunt sent - V
3. Aunt sent what? sprig - verify the noun
4. Does sprig mean the same thing as aunt? No.
5. Sprig - DO
6. Sent - V-t
7. Aunt sent sprig to whom? me - IO
8. A - A
9. Of - P
10. Of what? lilac - OP
11. What kind of lilac? wild - Adj

12. Whose aunt? my - PPA
13. SN V-t IO DO P3 Check
14. Verb-transitive - Check again.
15. (Of wild lilac) - Prepositional phrase
16. Period, statement, declarative sentence
17. Go back to the verb - divide the complete subject from the complete predicate.
18. Is there an adverb exception? No.
19. Is this sentence in a natural or inverted order? Natural - no change.

Classified Sentence:

<pre>
                        PPA SN   V-t IO A DO   P Adj OP
        SN V-t   My aunt / sent me a sprig (of wild lilac). D
        IO DO P3
</pre>

Use Sentences 1-2 that your students classified to do an Oral Skill Builder Check.

Oral Skill Builder Check

1. **Noun check.**
   (Say the job and then say the noun. Circle each noun.)

2. **Identify the nouns as singular or plural.**
   (Write S or P above each noun.)

3. **Identify the nouns as common or proper.**
   (Follow established procedure for oral identification.)

4. **Do a vocabulary check.**
   (Follow established procedure for oral identification.)

5. **Identify the complete subject and the complete predicate.** (Underline the complete subject once and the complete predicate twice.)

6. **Identify the simple subject and simple predicate.**
   (Underline the simple subject once and the simple predicate twice. Bold, or highlight, the lines.)

7. **Recite the irregular verb chart.**
   (Located on student page 17 and teacher page 143.)

SKILL TIME

TEACHING SCRIPT FOR IDENTIFYING REGULAR AND IRREGULAR VERBS, SIMPLE VERB TENSES, AND THE TENSES OF HELPING VERBS

You are going to learn three interesting things about verbs that will help you make correct verb choices when you speak and write. You will learn how to identify regular and irregular verbs, how to identify the simple verb tenses, and how to identify the tenses of helping verbs. You will use References 53- 55 on pages 36- 38. We will start with Reference 53 on page 36. Follow along as I go over this important information with you.

CHAPTER 18 LESSON 1 CONTINUED

(Read the information to your students and work through the guided examples provided for each concept. This information and the guided examples are reproduced for you below and on the next page.)

Reference 53: Regular and Irregular Verbs

Most verbs are **regular verbs**. This means that they form the past tense merely by adding **-ed**, **-d**, or **-t** to the main verb: *race, raced*. This simple procedure makes regular verbs easy to identify. Some verbs, however, do not form their past tense in this regular way. For this reason, they are called **irregular verbs**. Most irregular verbs form the past tense by having a **vowel spelling change** in the word. For example: *sing, sang, sung* or *eat, ate, eaten*.

To decide if a verb is regular or irregular, remember these two things:

1. Look only at the main verb. If the main verb is made past tense with an *-ed, -d, or -t* ending, it is a regular verb. (race, raced, raced)
2. Look only at the main verb. If the main verb is made past tense with a vowel spelling change, it is an irregular verb. (sing, sang, sung)

A partial listing of the most common irregular verbs is on the irregular verb chart located in Reference 23 on page 17 in the student book. *(Page 143 in the Teacher's Manual.)* Refer to this chart whenever necessary.

Example: Identify each verb as regular or irregular and put R or I in the blank. Then, write the past tense form.

eat __I__ ___ate___   pay __R__ ___paid___   tempt __R__ ___tempted___

jump __R__ ___jumped___   forget __I__ ___forgot___   swim __I__ ___swam___

Reference 54: Simple Verb Tenses

When you are writing paragraphs, you must use verbs that are in the same tense. Tense means time. The tense of a verb shows the time of the action. There are three basic tenses that show when an action takes place. They are **present tense, past tense,** and **future tense**. These tenses are known as the simple tenses.

1. The **simple present tense** shows that something is happening now, in the present. The present tense form usually has *s, es or plain endings*.
(Regular present tense form: cheer, cheers) (Irregular present tense form: fall, falls)
(**Examples:** The fans <u>cheer</u> for their team. The rain <u>falls</u> slowly.)

2. The **simple past tense** shows that something has happened sometime in the past. The regular past tense form ends in *-ed, -d, -t*. Most irregular past tense forms should be memorized.
(Regular past tense form: cheered) (Irregular past tense form: fell)
(**Examples:** The fans <u>cheered</u> for their team. The rain <u>fell</u> slowly.)

3. The **future tense** shows that something will happen sometime in the future. The future tense form always has the helping verb *will* or *shall* before the main verb.
(Regular future tense form: will cheer) (Irregular future tense form: will fall)
(**Examples:** The fans <u>will cheer</u> for their team. The rain <u>will fall</u> slowly.)

Simple Present Tense	Simple Past Tense	Simple Future Tense
What to look for: **one verb** with s, es, or plain ending.	What to look for: **one verb** with -ed, -d, -t or irr spelling change.	What to look for: **will** or **shall** with a main verb.
1. He <u>stands</u> on his head. 2. She <u>plays</u> the harmonica.	3. He <u>stood</u> on his head. 4. She <u>played</u> the harmonica.	5. He <u>will stand</u> on his head. 6. She <u>will play</u> the harmonica.

CHAPTER 18 LESSON 1 CONTINUED

Reference 55: Tenses of Helping Verbs

1. If there is only a main verb in a sentence, the tense is determined by the main verb and will be either present tense or past tense.
2. If there is a helping verb with a main verb, the tense of both verbs will be determined by the helping verb, not the main verb.

Since the helping verb determines the tense, it is important to learn the tenses of the 14 helping verbs you will be using. You should memorize the list below so you will never have trouble with tenses.

> **Present tense helping verbs: am, is, are, has, have, do, does**
> **Past tense helping verbs: was, were, had, did, been**
> **Future tense helping verbs: will, shall**

If you use one of the present tense helping verbs, you are considered in present tense even though the main verb has an -ed ending and even though it doesn't sound like present tense. (*I have walked - present tense.*) In later grades, you will learn that certain helping verbs help form other tenses called the perfect tenses.

Example 1: Underline each verb or verb phrase. Identify the verb tense by writing a number 1 for present tense, a number 2 for past tense, and a number 3 for future tense. Write the past tense form and R or I for Regular or Irregular.

Verb Tense		Main Verb Past Tense Form	R or I
1	1. The boy <u>rides</u> his bicycle.	rode	I
2	2. The engineer <u>had</u> <u>consulted</u> the mayor.	consulted	R
3	3. Tomorrow, I <u>will</u> <u>stain</u> the deck.	stained	R

Example 2: List the present tense and past tense helping verbs below.

Present tense:	1. **am**	2. **is**	3. **are**	4. **has**	5. **have**	6. **do**	7. **does**
Past tense:	8. **was**	9. **were**	10. **had**	11. **did**	12. **been**		

 PRACTICE TIME

Have students turn to page 66 in the Practice Section of their book and find Chapter 18, Lesson 1, Practice. Go over the directions to make sure they understand what to do. Check and discuss the Practice after students have finished. (*Chapter 18, Lesson 1, Practice key is given below.*)

Chapter 18 Lesson 1, Practice: Underline each verb or verb phrase. Identify the verb tense by writing a number **1** for present tense, a number **2** for past tense, and a number **3** for future tense. Write the past tense form and **R** or **I** for Regular or Irregular.

Verb Tense		Main Verb Past Tense Form	R or I
2	1. Dad <u>coughed</u> all night long.	coughed	R
1	2. They <u>are</u> <u>sitting</u> in the parlor.	sat	I
1	3. The boys <u>have</u> <u>lost</u> their tournament.	lost	I
3	4. Dana <u>will</u> <u>pretend</u> she is ill.	pretended	R
2	5. They <u>had</u> <u>jumped</u> in icy water.	jumped	R
2	6. The birds <u>were</u> <u>flying</u> south?	flew	I
1	7. Richard <u>sleeps</u> in his tent.	slept	I

CHAPTER 18   LESSON 2

New objectives: Grammar (Practice Sentences), Skills (principal parts of verbs), Practice sheet, and Vocabulary #1 and #2.

JINGLE TIME

Have students turn to the Jingle Section of their books. The teacher will lead the students in reciting the previously-taught jingles.

GRAMMAR TIME

First-Year Option: Put the Practice Sentences from the box below on the board or notebook paper. Use these sentences as you practice the concepts that have been taught. For the greatest benefit, students must participate orally with the teacher. **Second-Year Option:** Have students classify the Practice Sentences independently on paper. Check students' sentences with the answers provided below. (*If you have the CDs for Practice Sentences, have students check their sentences with the CDs.*)

Chapter 18, Practice Sentences for Lesson 2

1. _____ Alas! The scientist unwittingly gave the spy his secret password!
2. _____ Did your Spanish interpreter teach you the correct pronunciation of proper nouns?

Question and Answer Flow for Sentence 1: Alas! The scientist unwittingly gave the spy his secret password!

1. Who gave the spy his secret password? scientist - SN
2. What is being said about scientist? scientist gave - V
3. Scientist gave what? password - verify the noun
4. Does password mean the same thing as scientist? No.
5. Password - DO
6. Gave - V-t
7. Scientist gave password to whom? spy - IO
8. What kind of password? secret - Adj
9. Whose password? his - PPA
10. The - A
11. Gave how? unwittingly - Adv
12. The - A
13. Alas - I

14. SN V-t IO DO P3 Check
15. Verb-transitive - Check again.
16. No prepositional phrases.
17. Exclamation point, strong feeling, exclamatory sentence
18. Go back to the verb - divide the complete subject from the complete predicate.
19. Is there an adverb exception? Yes - change the line.
20. Is this sentence in a natural or inverted order? Natural - no change.

Classified Sentence:

```
                              I    A    SN      Adv      V-t   A   IO  PPA  Adj      DO
             SN V-t        Alas!  The  scientist / unwittingly gave the spy his secret password! E
             IO DO P3
```

CHAPTER 18 LESSON 2 CONTINUED

Question and Answer Flow for Sentence 2: Did your Spanish interpreter teach you the correct pronunciation of proper nouns?

1. Who did teach you the correct pronunciation of proper nouns? interpreter - SN
2. What is being said about interpreter? Interpreter did teach - V
3. Did - HV
4. Interpreter did teach what? pronunciation - verify the noun
5. Does pronunciation mean the same thing as interpreter? No.
6. Pronunciation - DO
7. Teach - V-t
8. Interpreter did teach pronunciation to whom? you - IO
9. What kind of pronunciation? correct - Adj
10. The - A
11. Of - P
12. Of what? nouns - OP
13. What kind of nouns? proper - Adj
14. What kind of interpreter? Spanish - Adj
15. Whose interpreter? your - PPA
16. SN V-t IO DO P3 Check
17. Verb-transitive Check again.
18. (Of proper nouns) - Prepositional phrase
19. Question mark, question, interrogative sentence
20. Go back to the verb - divide the complete subject from the complete predicate.
21. Is there an adverb exception? No.
22. Is this sentence in a natural or inverted order? Inverted - underline the subject parts once and the predicate parts twice.

	HV PPA Adj SN	V-t IO A Adj DO P Adj OP
Classified Sentence: SN V-t IO DO P3	Did your Spanish interpreter /	teach you the correct pronunciation (of proper nouns)? Int

TEACHER INSTRUCTIONS FOR A PATTERN 3 PRACTICE SENTENCE

Tell students that their sentence writing assignment today is to write a Pattern 3 Practice Sentence. They are to follow the same procedure used in the previous lessons. They should decide on their labels, arrange them in a selected order, write their sentence, and edit the sentence for improved word choices. (*Students do not have to write an Improved Sentence at this point unless you feel they need more one-on-one word choice writing practice.*) Check and discuss the Pattern 3 Practice Sentence after students have finished.

SKILL TIME

TEACHING SCRIPT FOR PRINCIPAL PARTS OF VERBS

You are going to learn the four principal parts of verbs to help you better understand how verbs function. Look at Reference 56 on page 38 while I go over this important information with you. (*Read the information to your students and work through the guided examples provided. This information is reproduced for you on the next page.*)

CHAPTER 18 LESSON 2 CONTINUED

Reference 56: Principal Parts of Verbs

Every main verb has four principal forms, or parts. All the forms of a main verb are made by using one of the four principal parts. The four principal parts of main verbs are called **present, present participle, past,** and **past participle**. The principal parts are the same for regular and irregular verbs.

1. **Present principal part** - has a present tense main verb and no helping verb.
   (He <u>walks</u> home. They <u>walk</u> home.) (He <u>grows</u> fast. They <u>grow</u> fast.)
2. **Past principal part** - has a past tense main verb and no helping verb.
   (He <u>walked</u> home.) (He <u>grew</u> fast.)
3. **Past participle principal part** - has past tense main verb and present or past tense helping verb.
   (He <u>has walked</u> home.) (He <u>has grown</u> fast.)
4. **Present participle principal part** - has a main verb ending in *-ing* and a present or past tense helping verb.
   (He <u>is walking</u> home.) (He <u>is growing</u> fast.)

Examples: Principal parts of the regular verb *walk*: walk(s), walked, has walked, is walking
Examples: Principal parts of the irregular verb *grow*: grow(s), grew, has grown, is growing

Remember, you must not confuse the past principal part of the verb with the past participle principal part. The past principal part never has a helping verb. The past participle principal part always has a helping verb.

 PRACTICE TIME

Students will continue identifying verb tenses and regular/irregular verbs. Have students turn to page 67 in the Practice Section of their book and find Chapter 18, Lesson 2, Practice. Go over the directions to make sure they understand what to do. Check and discuss the Practice after students have finished. (*Chapter 18, Lesson 2, Practice key is given below.*)

Chapter 18, Lesson 2, Practice: Underline each verb or verb phrase. Identify the verb tense by writing a number **1** for present tense, a number **2** for past tense, and a number **3** for future tense. Write the past tense form and **R** or **I** for Regular or Irregular.

Verb Tense			Main Verb Past Tense Form	R or I
1	1.	She <u>is</u> <u>driving</u> to Kansas City.	drove	I
2	2.	Jack <u>called</u> from Alaska last night.	called	R
1	3.	Barry <u>has</u> <u>entered</u> the seminary.	entered	R
3	4.	I <u>will</u> <u>buy</u> a new truck this summer.	bought	I
1	5.	We <u>have</u> <u>eaten</u> the whole watermelon.	ate	I
1	6.	She <u>sings</u> in the local choir.	sang	I
2	7.	He <u>had</u> twice <u>interrupted</u> the parade.	interrupted	R
1	8.	The fire <u>is</u> <u>burning</u> out of control.	burned	R
3	9.	The show <u>will</u> <u>begin</u> at 8:00.	began	I

CHAPTER 18 LESSON 2 CONTINUED

 **WRITING TIME**

Have students make an entry in their journals.

 VOCABULARY TIME

Assign Chapter 18, Vocabulary Words **#1** and **#2** on page 8 in the Reference Section for students to define in their Vocabulary notebooks. Tell students they are to use a dictionary or thesaurus to look up the meanings of the vocabulary words. After they write each word and its meaning, students are to write a sentence using the vocabulary word. (*Students are assigned both sets of vocabulary words in this lesson.*)

Chapter 18, Vocabulary Words #1
(deception, candor, forfeit, relinquish)

Chapter 18, Vocabulary Words #2
(vanquish, escape, solitary, alone)

(End of lesson.)

CHAPTER 18   LESSON 3

New objectives: Grammar (Practice Sentences), Skills (changing verbs to different tenses in a paragraph), and a Practice sheet.

 JINGLE TIME

Have students turn to the Jingle Section of their books. The teacher will lead the students in reciting the previously-taught jingles.

 GRAMMAR TIME

First-Year Option: Put the Practice Sentences from the box below on the board or notebook paper. Use these sentences as you practice the concepts that have been taught. For the greatest benefit, students must participate orally with the teacher. **Second-Year Option:** Have students classify the Practice Sentences independently on paper. Check students' sentences with the answers provided below. (*If you have the CDs for Practice Sentences, have students check their sentences with the CDs.*)

Chapter 18, Practice Sentences for Lesson 3

1. _____ Show me the winner's trophy in the museum.
2. _____ Yesterday, Natalie's beau sent her a bouquet for her birthday.

Question and Answer Flow for Sentence 1: Show me the winner's trophy in the museum.

1. Who show me the winner's trophy in the museum?
   You - SP (Understood subject pronoun)
2. What is being said about you? you show - V
3. You show what? trophy - verify the noun
4. Does trophy mean the same thing as you? No.
5. Trophy - DO
6. Show - V-t
7. You show trophy to whom? me - IO
8. Whose trophy? winner's - PNA
9. The - A
10. In - P
11. In what? museum - OP
12. The - A
13. SN V-t IO DO P3 Check
14. Verb-transitive - Check again.
15. (In the museum) - Prepositional phrase
16. Period, command, imperative sentence
17. Go back to the verb - divide the complete subject from the complete predicate.
18. Is there an adverb exception? No.
19. Is this sentence in a natural or inverted order? Natural - no change.

Classified Sentence:

```
                    (You) SP      V-t IO  A  PNA      DO    P  A   OP
                    SN  V-t      / Show me the winner's trophy (in the museum).  Imp
                    IO DO  P3
```

CHAPTER 18 LESSON 3 CONTINUED

Question and Answer Flow for Sentence 2: Yesterday, Natalie's beau sent her a bouquet for her birthday.

1. Who sent her a bouquet for her birthday? beau - SN
2. What is being said about beau? beau sent - V
3. Beau sent what? bouquet - verify the noun
4. Does bouquet mean the same thing as beau? No.
5. Bouquet - DO
6. Sent - V-t
7. Beau sent bouquet to whom? her - IO
8. A - A
9. For - P
10. For what? birthday - OP
11. Whose birthday? her - PPA
12. Whose beau? Natalie's - PNA
13. Sent when? yesterday - Adv
14. SN V-t IO DO P3 Check
15. Verb-transitive - Check again.
16. (For her birthday) - Prepositional phrase
17. Period, statement, declarative sentence
18. Go back to the verb - divide the complete subject from the complete predicate.
19. Is there an adverb exception? No.
20. Is this sentence in a natural or inverted order? Inverted - underline the subject parts once and the predicate parts twice.

Classified Sentence:

| | Adv | PNA | SN | V-t | IO | A | DO | P | PPA | OP |
| SN V-t | Yesterday, | Natalie's | beau / | sent | her | a | bouquet | (for | her | birthday). D |
| IO DO P3 |

SKILL TIME

TEACHING SCRIPT FOR CHANGING VERBS TO DIFFERENT TENSES IN A PARAGRAPH

It is very important to study verb tenses because you will use what you learn in your writing. Remember, verb tenses in sentences are used to tell the reader the time period that an event takes place. In writing, one of the most common mistakes students make is mixing present tense and past tense verbs. Mixing verb tenses can make your writing awkward and confusing to your reader. Look at this example. (_Put the example on the board_.) Example: **My sister talked and grins as she hugs her new puppy.**

In this sentence, _talked_ is past tense, and _grins_ and _hugs_ are present tense. The shift from past to present leaves your reader wondering about the time these actions take place. To make your writing clear and effective, choose a verb tense, or time, for your writing and stick to it.

We will now work with verb tenses in a paragraph format. We will do several things to help you understand how the different tenses are used. First, we will identify the tense used in a sample paragraph as either present tense or past tense. Next, we will change from one tense to another tense in a paragraph. Then, we will work with mixed tenses. This means that a paragraph has a mixture of present and past tense verbs. Since past tense and present tense are usually not used together in the same paragraph, we will change all the mixed verbs to the tense indicated.

As I read the sample paragraph to you orally, listen very carefully to the verbs. After I have finished, I will ask you the tense of the paragraph. (_Read the sample paragraph in Reference 57 on the next page to your students. Do not have them look at the paragraph in their books, yet._) What is the tense of the paragraph? (_present tense_) We will now change the paragraph to past tense. To do this, we must change each verb to past tense, one at a time. After we have finished, I will read both paragraphs again so you can train your ear to hear the difference between present tense and past tense. (_Have students go to the first guided example in Reference 57 on page 39 and follow along as you show them how to change each present tense verb to a past tense verb._)

CHAPTER 18 LESSON 3 CONTINUED

The young couple is so excited. They are going on their first vacation. Their two children are also excited.

Reference 57: Changing Tenses in Paragraphs

Guided Example 1 : Change the underlined present tense verbs in Paragraph 1 to past tense verbs in Paragraph 2.

Paragraph 1: Present Tense

On weekends, Sarah **makes** pancakes for her family's breakfast. As soon as she **hears** footsteps in the distance, she **starts** mixing the batter and **begins** heating the griddle. Once the procession of husband and daughters **arrives** at the kitchen door, she **pours** batter the size of quarters on the hot griddle. As the flapjacks **sizzle** in hot oil, Sarah **urges** everyone to take a seat. The feast **is** about to begin.

Paragraph 2: Past Tense

On weekends, Sarah **made** pancakes for her family's breakfast. As soon as she **heard** footsteps in the distance, she **started** mixing the batter and **began** heating the griddle. Once the procession of husband and daughters **arrived** at the kitchen door, she **poured** batter the size of quarters on the hot griddle. As the flapjacks **sizzled** in hot oil, Sarah **urged** everyone to take a seat. The feast **was** about to begin.

Guided Example 2: Change the underlined mixed tense verbs in Paragraph 1 to past tense verbs in Paragraph 2.

Paragraph 3: Mixed Tenses

The excited couple **is planning** a trip to the beach for their anniversary. They eagerly **contacted** a local travel agent. The agent **suggests** renting a condo for a week on the Mississippi shoreline. Their two children **look** at pictures of beaches in travel magazines. The family carefully **saves** every extra penny for their vacation. Finally, the big day **arrives**, but no one **was going**. They all **have** chicken pox!

Paragraph 4: Past Tense

The excited couple **was planning** a trip to the beach for their anniversary. They eagerly **contacted** a local travel agent. The agent **suggested** renting a condo for a week on the Mississippi shoreline. Their two children **looked** at pictures of beaches in travel magazines. The family carefully **saved** every extra penny for their vacation. Finally, the big day **arrived**, but no one **was going**. They all **had** chicken pox!

 PRACTICE TIME

Students will continue their practice of verb tenses. Have students turn to pages 67-69 in the Practice Section of their books and find Chapter 18, Lesson 3, Practice (*1-3*). Go over the directions to make sure they understand what to do. Check and discuss the Practices after students have finished. (*Chapter 18, Lesson 3, Practice keys are given below and on the next page.*)

Chapter 18, Lesson 3, Practice 1: Underline each verb or verb phrase. Identify the verb tense by writing a number **1** for present tense, a number **2** for past tense, and a number **3** for future tense. Write the past tense form and **R** or **I** for Regular or Irregular.

Verb Tense		Main Verb Past Tense Form	R or I
3	1. The clouds <u>will</u> <u>be</u> <u>invading</u> soon.	invaded	R
1	2. He <u>is</u> <u>writing</u> a novel.	wrote	I
2	3. <u>Did</u> you <u>empty</u> the trash?	emptied	R
1	4. Today, they <u>are</u> <u>climbing</u> the mountain.	climbed	R

CHAPTER 18 LESSON 3 CONTINUED

Chapter 18, Lesson 3, Practice 2 Change the underlined present tense verbs in Paragraph 1 to past tense verbs in Paragraph 2.

Paragraph 1: Present Tense

When somebody new **moves** into the neighborhood, my mom **greets** them with open arms. She **makes** them feel welcome with little effort. Her homemade coffee cake **is** always a big hit, of course, but her inviting smile **speaks** more than a thousand words. She **believes** in making newcomers feel welcome and **treats** them like family.

Paragraph 2: Past Tense

When somebody new **moved** into the neighborhood, my mom **greeted** them with open arms. She **made** them feel welcome with little effort. Her homemade coffee cake **was** always a big hit, of course, but her inviting smile **spoke** more than a thousand words. She **believed** in making newcomers feel welcome and **treated** them like family.

Chapter 18, Lesson 3, Practice 3: Write the seven present tense helping verbs, the five past tense helping verbs, and the two future tense helping verbs. **The order of the answers may vary.** (Present: am, is, are, has, have, do, does; Past: was, were, had, did, been; Future: will, shall)

Chapter 18, Lesson 3, Practice 4: Change the underlined mixed tense verbs in Paragraph 1 to present tense verbs in Paragraph 2.

Paragraph 1: Mixed Tenses

Sometimes, I **took** my shoes off when I **waded** in the creek. The water **is** so invigorating! I **loved** to feel the ripples **pass** through my toes. On warm days, I **sit** on a rock in the middle of the creek and **felt** like I **was** in heaven.

Paragraph 2: Present Tense

Sometimes, I **take** my shoes off when I **wade** in the creek. The water **is** so invigorating! I **love** to feel the ripples **pass** through my toes. On warm days, I **sit** on a rock in the middle of the creek and **feel** like I **am** in heaven.

 STUDY TIME

Have students study the vocabulary words in their vocabulary notebooks. Tell students that any vocabulary word in their notebooks could be on their test. Also, have students study any of the skills in the Practice Section that they need to review.

(End of lesson.)

CHAPTER 18   LESSON 4

New objectives: Test.

JINGLE TIME

Have students turn to the Jingle Section of their books. The teacher will lead the students in reciting the previously-taught jingles.

STUDY TIME

Have students study the vocabulary words in their vocabulary notebooks. Remind students that any vocabulary word in their notebooks could be on their test. Also, have students study any of the skills in the Practice Section that they need to review.

TEST TIME

Have students turn to pages 100 and 101 in the Test Section of their books and find Chapter 18A and 18B Tests. Go over the directions to make sure they understand what to do. (*Chapter 18A and 18B Test keys are on the next two pages.*)

CHECK TIME

After students have finished, check and discuss their test papers. Make sure they understand why their answers are right or wrong. (*For total points, count each required answer as a point.*)

(End of lesson.)

Chapter 18A Test
(Student Page 100)

Exercise 1: Classify each sentence.

```
              SN   V-t     CIO    C   CIO    CDO     C    CDO      P  PPA  OP      P    OP
1.  SN  V-t      Kim / packed Gary and me broccoli and cauliflower (for our snack) (at work).  D
    IO DO P3

                 HV   SP   V-t  IO   PPA    Adj     DO    P    OP
2.  SN  V-t      Would you / fax me your purchase order (on Monday)?  Int
    IO DO P3
```

Exercise 2: Use Sentence 2 to underline the complete subject once and the complete predicate twice and to complete the table below.

List the Noun Used	List the Noun Job	Singular or Plural	Common or Proper	Simple Subject	Simple Predicate
1. order	2. **DO**	3. **S**	4. **C**	5. **you**	6. **would fax**
7. **Monday**	8. **OP**	9. **S**	10. **P**		

Exercise 3: Identify each pair of words as synonyms or antonyms by putting parentheses ( ) around *syn* or *ant*.

1. veracity, truth	**(syn)** ant	5. forfeit, relinquish	**(syn)** ant	9. grandiose, impressive	**(syn)** ant
2. vanquish, escape	syn **(ant)**	6. deception, candor	syn **(ant)**	10. solicitude, indifference	syn **(ant)**
3. coherent, ramble	syn **(ant)**	7. repulsive, amiable	syn **(ant)**	11. transparent, translucent	**(syn)** ant
4. solitary, alone	**(syn)** ant	8. fatigue, exhaustion	**(syn)** ant	12. marginal, significant	syn **(ant)**

Exercise 4: Underline each verb or verb phrase. Identify the verb tense by writing a number **1** for present tense, a number **2** for past tense, and a number **3** for future tense. Write the past tense form and **R** or **I** for Regular or Irregular.

Verb Tense		Main Verb Past Tense Form	R or I
2	1. He <u>purchased</u> the house at auction.	purchased	R
3	2. <u>Will</u> you <u>walk</u> home?	walked	R
1	3. I <u>have eaten</u> already.	ate	I
1	4. He <u>stands</u> alone on the issue.	stood	I
3	5. You <u>will be receiving</u> a subpoena.	received	R
1	6. She <u>is painting</u> her toenails.	painted	R
2	7. My sister <u>swallowed</u> the gum.	swallowed	R
2	8. We <u>had driven</u> all night.	drove	I
3	9. He <u>will fly</u> to the islands.	flew	I
2	10. He <u>had combined</u> wheat before.	combined	R
1	11. Roy <u>has left</u> the team again.	left	I
1	12. She <u>has written</u> me before.	wrote	I

Exercise 5: Identify each kind of sentence by writing the abbreviation in the blank. (S, F, SCS, SCV, CD, CX)

SCS	1.	The boys and girls stood in line almost an hour.
CX	2.	We can't get out when the road is flooded.
SCV	3.	The wasp attacked and stung me on the arm.
F	4.	The canoe in the middle of the river.
CD	5.	The tickets are too expensive; besides, I have another commitment.

Exercise 6: Change the underlined present tense verbs in Paragraph 1 to past tense verbs in Paragraph 2.

Paragraph 1: Present Tense

Grandma **makes** applesauce every October. She **gathers** apples from the trees in her orchard. She **places** them in her summer kitchen to ripen. Once they **are** ripe, she **removes** the cores and **quarters** them. She barely **covers** the fruit with water and **cooks** it on low heat until it **is** mushy. Then, she **strains** it through a colander and **adds** the necessary spices to give it a tangy flavor.

Paragraph 2: Past Tense

Grandma **made** applesauce every October. She **gathered** apples from the trees in her orchard. She **placed** them in her summer kitchen to ripen. Once they **were** ripe, she **removed** the cores and **quartered** them. She barely **covered** the fruit with water and **cooked** it on low heat until it **was** mushy. Then, she **strained** it through a colander and **added** the necessary spices to give it a tangy flavor.

Exercise 7: Change the underlined mixed tense verbs in Paragraph 1 to present tense verbs in Paragraph 2.

Paragraph 1: Mixed Tenses

Our mother **played** with dolls. She **designs** their clothes, houses, and cars. She **laughed** at night as she **tells** us about their adventures. She **brought** home examples of new products. We **gather** excitedly around the table as she **demonstrated** the newest fashions and trends. Our mother **hugged** us to her and **tells** us the same thing every night. We **were** her most precious dolls.

Paragraph 2: Present Tense

Our mother **plays** with dolls. She **designs** their clothes, houses, and cars. She **laughs** at night as she **tells** us about their adventures. She **brings** home examples of new products. We **gather** excitedly around the table as she **demonstrates** the newest fashions and trends. Our mother **hugs** us to her and **tells** us the same thing every night. We **are** her most precious dolls!

Exercise 8: On a sheet of paper, write one sentence for each of these labels: ① (S) ② (SCS) ③ (SCV) ④ (CD) ⑤ (CX). (Answers will vary.)

Exercise 9: On a sheet of paper, write three sentences, demonstrating each of the three quotations: Beginning quote, end quote, and split quote. (Answers will vary.)

Exercise 10: On a sheet of paper, write the seven present tense helping verbs, the five past tense helping verbs, and the two future tense helping verbs. **The order of the answers may vary.** (Present: am, is, are, has, have, do, does; Past: was, were, had, did, been; Future: will, shall)

Exercise 11: In your journal, write a paragraph summarizing what you have learned this week.

CHAPTER 18 LESSON 4 CONTINUED

TEACHER INSTRUCTIONS

Use the Question and Answer Flows below for the sentences on Chapter 18 Tests.

Question and Answer Flow for Sentence 1: Kim packed Gary and me broccoli and cauliflower for our snack at work.

1. Who packed Gary and me broccoli and cauliflower for our snack at work? Kim - SN
2. What is being said about Kim? Kim packed - V
3. Kim packed what? broccoli and cauliflower - verify the nouns
4. Do broccoli and cauliflower mean the same thing as Kim? No.
5. Broccoli and cauliflower - CDO, CDO
6. Packed - V-t
7. Kim packed broccoli and cauliflower for whom? Gary and me - CIO, CIO
8. And - C
9. For - P
10. For what? snack - OP
11. Whose snack? our - PPA
12. At - P
13. At what? work - OP
14. And - C
15. SN V-t IO DO P3 Check
16. Verb-transitive - Check again.
17. (For our snack) - Prepositional phrase
18. (At work) - Prepositional phrase
19. Period, statement, declarative sentence
20. Go back to the verb - divide the complete subject from the complete predicate.
21. Is there an adverb exception? No.
22. Is this sentence in a natural or inverted order? Natural - no change.

Classified Sentence:

SN   V-t   CIO C CIO CDO   C   CDO   P PPA OP   P OP

SN V-t / IO DO P3   Kim **/** packed Gary and me broccoli and cauliflower **(for our snack) (at work). D**

Question and Answer Flow for Sentence 2: Would you fax me your purchase order on Monday?

1. Who would fax me your purchase order on Monday? you - SP
2. What is being said about you? you would fax - V
3. Would - HV
4. You would fax what? order - verify the noun
5. Does order mean the same thing as you? No.
6. Order - DO
7. Fax - V-t
8. You would fax order to whom? me - IO
9. What kind of order? purchase - Adj
10. Whose order? your - PPA
11. On - P
12. On what? Monday - OP
13. SN V-t IO DO P3 Check
14. Verb-transitive - Check again.
15. (On Monday) - Prepositional phrase
16. Question mark, question, interrogative sentence
17. Go back to the verb - divide the complete subject from the complete predicate.
18. Is there an adverb exception? No.
19. Is this sentence in a natural or inverted order? Inverted - underline the subject parts once and the predicate parts twice.

Classified Sentence:

HV   SP   V-t IO PPA   Adj   DO   P OP

SN V-t / IO DO P3   Would you **/** fax me your purchase order **(on Monday)? Int**

CHAPTER 18   LESSON 5

New objectives: Writing Assignments #25 and #26, Bonus Option.

 **WRITING TIME**

TEACHING SCRIPT FOR NARRATIVE WRITING ASSIGNMENTS

You will do two narrative writing assignments. The first narrative writing assignment will be a story without dialogue. The second narrative writing assignment will be a <u>different story</u> with dialogue. You will make a Story Elements outline for both stories. Both rough drafts will go through the revision and editing stages. (*Read the boxes below for more information about the students' writing assignment.*) You will choose the point of view for each assignment.

Writing Assignment Box #1

Writing Assignment #25: Narrative Essay Without Dialogue (First or Third Person)

Remind students to make a Story Elements Outline.

Writing topic: The Morning I Overslept or **History Repeats Itself**

Writing Assignment Box #2

Writing Assignment #26: Narrative Essay With Dialogue (First or Third Person)

Remind students to make a Story Elements Outline.

Writing topic: Grandpa And The Computer or **A Wedding/Day/Person I Will Never Forget**

Bonus Option: How many books are in the New Testament? (*27*) **Look up all the books of the New Testament and list them in your Journal. Next, create a word search that contains all the books of the New Testament. Be careful to spell all the names correctly. Give the word search to a family member to complete. Make a key so you can check the finished word search.**

TEACHER INSTRUCTIONS FOR CHECKING WRITING ASSIGNMENT #25 AND #26

Read, check, and discuss Writing Assignments #25 and #26 after students have finished their final papers. Use the editing checklist as you check and discuss students' papers. Make sure students are using the editing checklist correctly.

(End of lesson.)

CHAPTER 19   LESSON 1

New objectives: Jingles (predicate noun), Grammar (Introductory Sentences, predicate nouns, linking verbs, adding the predicate noun to the Noun Check), Vocabulary #1, and an Activity.

 **JINGLE TIME**

Have students turn to the Jingle Section in their books and recite the previously-taught jingles. Then, lead students in reciting the new jingles (*The Predicate Noun Jingles*) below. Practice the new jingles several times until students can recite them smoothly. Emphasize reciting with a rhythm. Students and teacher should be together! (*Do not try to explain the jingles at this time. Just have fun reciting them.*)

Jingle 18:   The Predicate Noun Jingle

1. A predicate noun is a noun or a pronoun.
2. A predicate noun means the same thing as the subject word.
3. A predicate noun is located after a linking verb.
4. To find the predicate noun, ask WHAT or WHO after the verb.

Jingle 19:   Another Predicate Noun Jingle

Listen, my comrades, and you shall hear About predicate nouns from far and near. No one knows the time or year When the predicate nouns will appear. Listen now to all the facts, So you will know when the **Pred's** are back!	Dum De Dum Dum! **A pred**icate noun is a special noun in the predicate That means the same thing as the subject word. **To find a pred**icate noun, ask *what* or *who* After a linking verb.

 GRAMMAR TIME

Put the introductory sentences from the box below on the board. Use these sentences as you go through each new concept covered in your teaching script. For the greatest benefit, students must participate orally with the teacher. (*You might put the introductory sentences on notebook paper if you are doing one-on-one instruction with your students.*)

Chapter 19, Introductory Sentences for Lesson 1

1. _____ The waitress in the café was a very nice lady.
2. _____ The road is a narrow, dirt-covered trail between Idaho and Montana.
3. _____ Our pastor is an unusually dedicated person.

CHAPTER 19 LESSON 1 CONTINUED

TEACHING SCRIPT FOR PREDICATE NOUNS AND LINKING VERBS

Earlier, you learned that nouns have different jobs, or functions, in a sentence. You have studied four of these jobs already: A noun can be a subject, an object of a preposition, an indirect object, or a direct object. Again, you must remember that a noun used as an object of a preposition is not a core part of a sentence pattern.

In the new sentence pattern, **Pattern 4**, there are only two nouns in the basic sentence pattern: **N LV N.** The first noun is a subject noun and is still written as **SN.** The second noun is called a predicate noun and is written with the abbreviation **PrN.** Notice that in this new pattern, there is a different kind of verb in the core sentence pattern. This verb is a linking verb, and it will always be written with the abbreviation **LV.** A predicate noun will always come after a linking verb. This fourth pattern in Shurley English is *subject noun / linking verb / predicate noun / Pattern 4*, and it is written as **SN LV PrN P4.**

There are six basic things you need to know about a predicate noun. For this information, look at Reference 58 on page 43 in the Reference Section of your book and follow along as I read this information to you. I want you to notice that these six things are very similar to the predicate noun jingle. You will read the sample sentence with me so you will know what to say when you classify Pattern 4 sentences. (*Read the information about predicate nouns to your students. Then, have students read and classify the sample sentence orally with you.*)

Reference 58: Predicate Noun and Linking Verb

1. A **predicate noun** is a noun or pronoun after the verb that means the same thing as the subject.

2. A **predicate noun** is labeled as *PrN*.

3. To find the **predicate noun**, ask WHAT? or WHOM? after the verb.

4. A **predicate noun** is often called a predicate nominative.

5. A **predicate noun** always comes after a linking verb.

6. A **linking verb** links, or connects, the subject to a predicate noun or a predicate pronoun.

Example Sentence for the exact words to say to find the linking verb and predicate noun.

1. Sue is an excellent swimmer.	10. SN LV PrN P4 Check *(Say: Subject Noun, Linking Verb, Predicate Noun, Pattern 4, Check.) (This first check is to make sure the "L" is added to the verb.)*
2. Who is an excellent swimmer? Sue - SN	
3. What is being said about Sue? Sue is - V	11. Linking verb - check again. *("Check again" means to check for prepositional phrases and then go through the rest of the Question and Answer Flow.)*
4. Sue is what? swimmer - verify the noun	
5. Does swimmer mean the same thing as Sue? Yes.	12. No prepositional phrases.
6. Swimmer - PrN *(Say: swimmer - predicate noun.)*	13. Period, statement, declarative sentence.
7. Is - LV *(Say: Is - linking verb.)*	14. Go back to the verb - divide the complete subject from the complete predicate.
8. What kind of swimmer? excellent - Adj	15. Is there an adverb exception? No.
9. An - A	16. Is this sentence in a natural or inverted order? Natural - no change.

I will ask a few questions about what you have just learned. What is the design of a Pattern 4 sentence? (*SN LV PrN*) What is the sentence core of a Pattern 4 sentence? (*SN LV PrN*) What parts of speech does a Pattern 4 sentence use? (*N LV N*) You will use the information you have just learned as you classify this first set of sentences with me to find the predicate noun and linking verb. Begin.

CHAPTER 19 LESSON 1 CONTINUED

Teacher's Notes:
The verb check is now changed to a linking verb check because students tend to forget to add the "L" to the verb. If they leave the "L" off, it is wrong. This is the reason the linking verb check is so important for them to remember.

Question and Answer Flow for Sentence 1: The waitress in the café was a very nice lady.

1. Who was a very nice lady? waitress - SN
2. What is being said about waitress? waitress was - V
3. Waitress was what? lady - verify the noun
4. Does lady mean the same thing as waitress? Yes.
5. Lady - PrN (Predicate noun)
6. Was - LV
7. What kind of lady? nice - Adj
8. How nice? very - Adv
9. A - A
10. In - P
11. In what? café - OP
12. The - A
13. The - A
14. SN LV PrN P4 Check
15. Linking verb - Check again.
16. (In the café) - Prepositional phrase
17. Period, statement, declarative sentence
18. Go back to the verb - divide the complete subject from the complete predicate.
19. Is there an adverb exception? No.
20. Is this sentence in a natural or inverted order? Natural - no change.

Classified Sentence:

	A	SN		P	A	OP	LV	A	Adv	Adj	PrN

SN LV / PrN P4

The waitress (in the café) / was a very nice lady. **D**

Question and Answer Flow for Sentence 2: The road is a narrow, dirt-covered trail between Idaho and Montana.

1. What is a narrow, dirt-covered trail between Idaho and Montana? road - SN
2. What is being said about road? road is - V
3. Road is what? trail - verify the noun
4. Does trail mean the same thing as road? Yes.
5. Trail - PrN
6. Is - LV
7. What kind of trail? dirt-covered - Adj
8. What kind of trail? narrow - Adj
9. A - A
10. Between - P
11. Between what? Idaho and Montana - COP, COP (compound object of the preposition, compound object of the preposition)
12. And - C
13. The - A
14. SN LV PrN P4 Check
15. Linking verb - Check again.
16. (Between Idaho and Montana) - Prepositional phrase
17. Period, statement, declarative sentence
18. Go back to the verb - divide the complete subject from the complete predicate.
19. Is there an adverb exception? No.
20. Is this sentence in a natural or inverted order? Natural - no change.

Classified Sentence:

A SN LV A Adj Adj PrN P COP C COP

SN LV / PrN P4

The road / is a narrow, dirt-covered trail (between Idaho and Montana). **D**

Question and Answer Flow for Sentence 3: Our pastor is an unusually dedicated person.

1. Who is an unusually dedicated person? pastor - SN
2. What is being said about pastor? pastor is - V
3. Pastor is who? person - verify the noun
4. Does person mean the same thing as pastor? Yes.
5. Person - PrN
6. Is - LV
7. What kind of person? dedicated - Adj
8. How dedicated? unusually - Adv
9. An - A
10. Whose pastor? our - PPA
11. SN LV PrN P4 Check
12. Linking verb - Check again.
13. No prepositional phrases.
14. Period, statement, declarative sentence
15. Go back to the verb - divide the complete subject from the complete predicate.
16. Is there an adverb exception? No.
17. Is this sentence in a natural or inverted order? Natural - no change.

Classified Sentence:

PPA SN LV A Adv Adj PrN

SN LV / PrN P4

Our pastor / is an unusually dedicated person. **D**

CHAPTER 19 LESSON 1 CONTINUED

TEACHING SCRIPT FOR ADDING THE PREDICATE NOUNS TO THE NOUN CHECK

Name the noun jobs we have had previously. (*SN, OP, DO, and IO*) Today, we have added another noun job. What is the new noun job that we have just added? (*predicate noun—PrN*) So, if I want to find nouns in a sentence, where would I go? (*To the SN, OP, DO, IO, and PrN jobs*) After I go to the **subject noun, object of the preposition, direct object, indirect object, and predicate noun** jobs, what do I do next? (*Check each job to see if the word is a noun or a pronoun. If it is a pronoun, move to the next job. If it is a noun, circle it to indicate that it is a noun.*)

Oral Skill Builder Check	
1. Noun check. (Say the job and then say the noun. Circle each noun.) **2. Identify the nouns as singular or plural.** (Write S or P above each noun.) **3. Identify the nouns as common or proper.** (Follow established procedure for oral identification.) **4. Do a vocabulary check.** (Follow established procedure for oral identification.)	**5. Identify the complete subject and the complete predicate.** (Underline the complete subject once and the complete predicate twice.) **6. Identify the simple subject and simple predicate.** (Underline the simple subject once and the simple predicate twice. Bold, or highlight, the lines.) **7. Recite the irregular verb chart.** (Located on student page 17 and teacher page 143.)

WRITING TIME

Have students make an entry in their journals.

VOCABULARY TIME

Assign Chapter 19, Vocabulary Words #1 on page 8 in the Reference Section for students to define in their Vocabulary notebooks. Tell students they are to use a dictionary or thesaurus to look up the meanings of the vocabulary words. After they write each word and its meaning, students are to write a sentence using the vocabulary word.

Chapter 19, Vocabulary Words #1
(contemptible, admirable, adversity, misfortune)

ACTIVITY / ASSIGNMENT TIME

Put the directions and example of the color poem below on the board. After discussing the example with your students, have them follow the directions and write their own color poem.

Directions:

1. Pick a color as your title
2. Think of all the things that make you think of that color.
3. Tell about your color in complete sentences.
4. Your sentences do not have to rhyme.

Example:

Purple is...
Purple is a cluster of grapes.
Purple is a royal kingly robe.
It's plums and popsicles and pretty paint.
Purple is an angry face.
Purple is a hard word to describe.

(End of lesson.)

CHAPTER 19   LESSON 2

New objectives: Grammar (Practice Pattern 4 Sentences,), Vocabulary #2, and a Practice activity.

 JINGLE TIME

Have students turn to the Jingle Section of their books. The teacher will lead the students in reciting the previously-taught jingles.

 GRAMMAR TIME

First-Year Option: Put the Practice Sentences from the box below on the board or notebook paper. Use these sentences as you practice the concepts that have been taught. For the greatest benefit, students must participate orally with the teacher. **Second-Year Option:** Have students classify the Practice Sentences independently on paper. Check students' sentences with the answers provided below. (*If you have the CDs for Practice Sentences, have students check their sentences with the CDs.*)

Chapter 19, Practice Sentences for Lesson 2
1. _____ Fishing, sunning, and surfing are pastimes in the Florida Keys.
2. _____ The borders around the new pavilion are warm and restful colors.
3. _____ A pediatrician is an asset to the medical staff in a hospital.

TEACHING SCRIPT FOR PRACTICING PATTERN 4 SENTENCES

We will practice classifying Pattern 4 sentences. We will classify the sentences together. Begin. (*You might have your students write the labels above the sentences at this time.*)

Question and Answer Flow for Sentence 1: Fishing, sunning, and surfing are pastimes in the Florida Keys.

1. What are pastimes in the Florida Keys?
   fishing, sunning, and surfing - CSN, CSN, CSN
2. What is being said about fishing, sunning, and surfing?
   fishing, sunning, and surfing are - V
3. Fishing, sunning, and surfing are what?
   pastimes - verify the noun
4. Do pastimes mean the same thing as fishing, sunning, and surfing? Yes.
5. Pastimes - PrN
6. Are - LV
7. In - P
8. In what? Florida Keys - OP
9. The - A
10. And - C
11. SN LV PrN P4 Check
12. Linking verb - Check again.
13. (In the Florida Keys) - Prepositional phrase
14. Period, statement, declarative sentence
15. Go back to the verb - divide the complete subject from the complete predicate.
16. Is there an adverb exception? No.
17. Is this sentence in a natural or inverted order?
   Natural - no change.

Classified Sentence:

                      CSN   CSN   C   CSN   LV   PrN   P A   OP

        <u>SN LV</u>   Fishing, sunning, and surfing **/** are pastimes (in the Florida Keys). **D**

        PrN P4

CHAPTER 19 LESSON 2 CONTINUED

Question and Answer Flow for Sentence 2: The borders around the new pavilion are warm and restful colors.

1. What are warm and restful colors? borders - SN
2. What is being said about borders? borders are - V
3. Borders are what? colors - verify the noun
4. Do colors mean the same thing as borders? Yes.
5. Colors - PrN
6. Are - LV
7. What kind of colors? warm and restful - CAdj, CAdj
8. And - C
9. Around - P
10. Around what? pavilion - OP
11. What kind of pavilion? new - Adj

12. The - A
13. The - A
14. SN LV PrN P4 Check
15. Linking verb - Check again.
16. (Around the new pavilion) - Prepositional phrase
17. Period, statement, declarative sentence
18. Go back to the verb - divide the complete subject from the complete predicate.
19. Is there an adverb exception? No.
20. Is this sentence in a natural or inverted order? Natural - no change.

Classified Sentence:

<pre>
                     A   SN   P   A   Adj OP   LV CAdj C CAdj PrN
        SN LV   The borders (around the new pavilion) / are warm and restful colors. D
        ‾‾‾‾‾
        PrN P4
</pre>

Question and Answer Flow for Sentence 3: A pediatrician is an asset to the medical staff in a hospital.

1. Who is an asset to the medical staff in a hospital? pediatrician - SN
2. What is being said about pediatrician? pediatrician is - V
3. Pediatrician is what? asset - verify the noun
4. Does asset mean the same thing as pediatrician? Yes.
5. Asset - PrN
6. Is - LV
7. An - A
8. To - P
9. To what? staff - OP
10. What kind of staff? medical - Adj
11. The - A
12. In - P

13. In what? hospital - OP
14. A - A
15. A - A
16. SN LV PrN P4 Check
17. Linking verb - Check again.
18. (To the medical staff) - Prepositional phrase
19. (In a hospital) - Prepositional phrase
20. Period, statement, declarative sentence
21. Go back to the verb - divide the complete subject from the complete predicate.
22. Is there an adverb exception? No.
23. Is this sentence in a natural or inverted order? Natural - no change.

Classified Sentence:

<pre>
                     A   SN   LV A PrN P A   Adj   OP   P A OP
        SN LV   A pediatrician / is an asset (to the medical staff) (in a hospital). D
        ‾‾‾‾‾
        PrN P4
</pre>

TEACHER INSTRUCTIONS

Use Sentences 1-3 that you just classified with your students to do an Oral Skill Builder Check. Use the guidelines on the next page.

CHAPTER 19 LESSON 2 CONTINUED

Oral Skill Builder Check	
1. Noun check. (Say the job and then say the noun. Circle each noun.) **2. Identify the nouns as singular or plural.** (Write S or P above each noun.) **3. Identify the nouns as common or proper.** (Follow established procedure for oral identification.) **4. Do a vocabulary check.** (Follow established procedure for oral identification.)	**5. Identify the complete subject and the complete predicate.** (Underline the complete subject once and the complete predicate twice.) **6. Identify the simple subject and simple predicate.** (Underline the simple subject once and the simple predicate twice. Bold, or highlight, the lines.) **7. Recite the irregular verb chart.** (Located on student page 17 and teacher page 143.)

TEACHING SCRIPT FOR INTRODUCING A PATTERN 4 PRACTICE SENTENCE

Put these words on the board: **Pattern 4 Sentence**

Get out a sheet of notebook paper. On the top line of your notebook paper, write the title *Pattern 4 Practice Sentence*. Look at the new words on the board: **Pattern 4 Sentence**. I will guide you again through the process as we learn to write a Pattern 4 sentence.

You have already learned how to write independent Pattern 1, Pattern 2, and Pattern 3 sentences according to labels you select. You will now learn how to write an independent Pattern 4 sentence the same way. First, you start out with the core labels for a Pattern 4 sentence. This means that you <u>must always have a subject, a linking verb, and a predicate noun before you add any extra parts.</u>

You build the rest of your Pattern 4 sentence from the regular sentence parts learned in Pattern 1. I will ask you a few questions to make sure you understand. What are the parts of a Pattern 4 sentence that YOU MUST USE? (*All Pattern 4 sentences must have a subject, a linking verb, and a predicate noun.*) I want you to name the extra sentence parts that that you can use with your sentence. There are ten parts. (*adjectives, adverbs, articles, prepositional phrases, subject pronouns, possessive nouns, possessive pronouns, helping verbs, conjunctions, and interjections*) Remember, you will use the core parts of a Pattern 4 sentence and then add the extra parts that you want your sentence to have.

Let's write the labels for a Pattern 4 sentence on a sheet of notebook paper. First, write the *SN LV PrN* labels that a Pattern 4 sentence must have on your paper. Be sure to place them in the middle of your paper. (*Demonstrate by writing the SN LV PrN labels on the board.*) Using what you know about writing practice sentences, you must decide what other parts you want to add to your Pattern 4 sentence. (*Have students finish writing a Pattern 4 sentence and turn it in to you. Students do not have to write an Improved Sentence at this point unless you feel they need the practice. If your students cannot handle this much independence so soon, give them the labels you want them to follow for a Pattern 4 sentence. Check and discuss students' sentences after they have finished.*)

CHAPTER 19 LESSON 2 CONTINUED

 VOCABULARY TIME

Assign Chapter 19, Vocabulary Words **#2** on page 8 in the Reference Section for students to define in their Vocabulary notebooks. Tell students they are to use a dictionary or thesaurus to look up the meanings of the vocabulary words. After they write each word and its meaning, students are to write a sentence using the vocabulary word.

Chapter 19, Vocabulary Words #2
(conceited, humble, creditor, lender)

 PRACTICE TIME

Have students write the three sentences that they classified at the beginning of the lesson on a sheet of paper. (*See page 328.*) Have them tape-record the Question and Answer Flows for all three sentences. Students should write labels above the sentences as they classify them. They especially need the second practice if this is their first year in the program. (*After the students have finished, check the tape and sentence labels. Make sure students understand any mistakes they have made.*)

(End of lesson.)

CHAPTER 19   LESSON 3
New objectives: Grammar (Practice Sentences), Skills (contractions), Practice sheet, and an Activity.

 **JINGLE TIME**

Have students turn to the Jingle Section of their books. The teacher will lead the students in reciting the previously-taught jingles.

 GRAMMAR TIME

First-Year Option: Put the Practice Sentences from the box below on the board or notebook paper. Use these sentences as you practice the concepts that have been taught. For the greatest benefit, students must participate orally with the teacher. **Second-Year Option:** Have students classify the Practice Sentences independently on paper. Check students' sentences with the answers provided below. (*If you have the CDs for Practice Sentences, have students check their sentences with the CDs.*)

Chapter 19, Practice Sentences for Lesson 3
1. _____ The handsome man in the dark suit is my father.
2. _____ The small stray dog became my grandmother's devoted companion.
3. _____ The swing on the deck is a gift from my uncle's cousin.

TEACHING SCRIPT FOR PRACTICING PATTERN 4 SENTENCES

We will practice classifying Pattern 4 sentences. We will classify the sentences together. Begin. (*You might have your students write the labels above the sentences at this time.*)

Question and Answer Flow for Sentence 1: The handsome man in the dark suit is my father.	
1. Who is my father? man - SN	12. What kind of man? handsome - Adj
2. What is being said about man? man is - V	13. The - A
3. Man is what? father - verify the noun	14. SN LV PrN P4 Check
4. Does father mean the same thing as man? Yes.	15. Linking verb - Check again.
5. Father - PrN	16. (In the dark suit) - Prepositional phrase
6. Is - LV	17. Period, statement, declarative sentence
7. Whose father? my - PPA	18. Go back to the verb - divide the complete subject from the complete predicate.
8. In - P	
9. In what? suit - OP	19. Is there an adverb exception? No.
10. What kind of suit? dark - Adj	20. Is this sentence in a natural or inverted order? Natural - no change.
11. The - A	

Classified Sentence:

A   Adj   SN   P   A   Adj   OP   LV   PPA   PrN
SN LV   The handsome man (in the dark suit) / is my father. **D**
PrN P4

CHAPTER 19 LESSON 3 CONTINUED

Question and Answer Flow for Sentence 2: The small stray dog became my grandmother's devoted companion.

1. What became my grandmother's devoted companion? dog - SN
2. What is being said about dog? dog became - V
3. Dog became what? companion - verify the noun
4. Does companion mean the same thing as dog? Yes.
5. Companion - PrN
6. Became - LV
7. What kind of companion? devoted - Adj
8. Whose companion? grandmother's - PNA
9. Whose grandmother my - PPA
10. What kind of dog? stray - Adj
11. What kind of dog? small - Adj
12. The - A
13. SN LV PrN P4 Check
14. Linking verb - Check again.
15. No prepositional phrases.
16. Period, statement, declarative sentence
17. Go back to the verb - divide the complete subject from the complete predicate.
18. Is there an adverb exception? No.
19. Is this sentence in a natural or inverted order? Natural - no change.

Classified Sentence:

	A	Adj	Adj	SN	LV	PPA	PNA	Adj	PrN
SN LV	The	small	stray	dog /	became	my	grandmother's	devoted	companion. **D**
PrN P4

Question and Answer Flow for Sentence 3: The swing on the deck is a gift from my uncle's cousin.

1. What is a gift from my uncle's cousin? swing - SN
2. What is being said about swing? swing is - V
3. Swing is what? gift - verify the noun
4. Does gift mean the same thing as swing? Yes.
5. Gift - PrN
6. Is - LV
7. A - A
8. From - P
9. From whom? cousin - OP
10. Whose cousin? uncle's - PNA
11. Whose uncle? my - PPA
12. On - P
13. On what? deck - OP
14. The - A
15. The - A
16. SN LV PrN P4 Check
17. Linking verb - Check again.
18. (On the deck) - Prepositional phrase
19. (From my uncle's cousin) - Prepositional phrase
20. Period, statement, declarative sentence
21. Go back to the verb - divide the complete subject from the complete predicate.
22. Is there an adverb exception? No.
23. Is this sentence in a natural or inverted order? Natural - no change.

Classified Sentence:

	A	SN	P	A	OP	LV	A	PrN	P	PPA	PNA	OP
SN LV	The	swing	(on	the	deck) /	is	a	gift	(from	my	uncle's	cousin). **D**
PrN P4

SKILL TIME

TEACHING SCRIPT FOR INTRODUCING CONTRACTIONS

A contraction is two words shortened into one word, and the new word always has an apostrophe. The apostrophe takes the place of the letters that have been left out. When we worked with homonyms, you learned how important it was to choose the correct word. You had to constantly be aware of the spelling of certain words and their meanings. This will still be important as you work with contractions. You must know how to spell contractions correctly and which contraction is correct. And, of course, some contractions can be confused with possessive pronouns, so you must always be aware of the right choices.

CHAPTER 19 LESSON 3 CONTINUED

Look at Reference 59 on page 40. I want you to repeat with me the words from which the contraction is made and then repeat the contraction. (*Go over all the contractions in this manner. This will help your students see them, say them, and hear them correctly. Develop a sing-song chant that has enough rhythm to sound good and to be fun at the same time. The contraction chart is reproduced for you on the next page.*)

 PRACTICE TIME

Have students turn to page 69 in the Practice Section of their book and find the skill under Chapter 19, Lesson 3, Practice. Go over the directions to make sure they understand what to do. Check and discuss the Practice after students have finished. (*Use the contraction chart on the next page to help students check the Lesson 3, Practice below.*)

Chapter 19, Lesson 3, Practice: Copy the following words on another sheet of paper. Write the correct contraction beside each word. **Key: can't, let's, don't, wasn't, they're, aren't, hadn't, isn't, she's, who's, you're, didn't, it's, we're, weren't, doesn't, hasn't, I'm, I've, I'd, won't, I'll, wouldn't, I'd, shouldn't, couldn't, they'd**
Words: cannot, let us, do not, was not, they are, are not, had not, is not, she is, who is, you are, did not, it is, we are, were not, does not, has not, I am, I have, I had, will not, I will, would not, I would, should not, could not, they would

 WRITING TIME

Have students make an entry in their journals.

 ACTIVITY / ASSIGNMENT TIME

Discuss the following information about similes and metaphors. When a writer uses words to draw a picture of two things that he is comparing, it is called a figure of speech. Two figures of speech that writers use most often are **simile** and **metaphor**.

A simile: draws a picture by comparing one noun to another noun in the sentence using "like" or "as."

           Examples: The road was as winding as unraveled thread. The diagnosis was as threatening as a
                  guerilla attack. The little boy walks like a tarantula. My toothache hurt like a bad sunburn.

A metaphor: draws a picture by showing how two very different things can be alike. It will use linking verbs (*am, is, are, was, were*) to connect the noun in the predicate to the subject.

           Examples: His prolonged absence was a mirror of an Alaskan winter night. The stars are angels'
                  flashlights shining in distant darkness.

Assignment: Have students write ten sentences using similes (*like* or *as*) and five sentences using metaphors (*linking verb and predicate noun*). Discuss the similes and metaphors in students' sentences. Act out some of the sentences if possible. Option: Write and share a short story using similes and metaphors.

(End of lesson.)

CHAPTER 19 LESSON 3 CONTINUED

Reference 59: Contraction Chart			Pronoun	Contraction
AM				
I am	–	I'm		
IS				**its**	**it's**
is not	–	isn't		
he is	–	he's		
she is	–	she's		
it is	–	it's		
who is	–	who's		
that is	–	that's		
what is	–	what's		
there is	–	there's		

AM
I am — I'm

IS
is not — isn't
he is — he's
she is — she's
it is — it's
who is — who's
that is — that's
what is — what's
there is — there's

ARE
are not — aren't
you are — you're
we are — we're
they are — they're

WAS, WERE
was not — wasn't
were not — weren't

DO, DOES, DID
do not — don't
does not — doesn't
did not — didn't

CAN
cannot — can't

LET
let us — let's

HAS
has not — hasn't
he has — he's
she has — she's

HAVE
have not — haven't
I have — I've
you have — you've
we have — we've
they have — they've

HAD
had not — hadn't
I had — I'd
he had — he'd
she had — she'd
you had — you'd
we had — we'd
they had — they'd

WILL /SHALL
will not — won't
I will — I'll
he will — he'll
she will — she'll
you will — you'll
we will — we'll
they will — they'll

WOULD
would not — wouldn't
I would — I'd
he would — he'd
she would — she'd
you would — you'd
we would — we'd
they would — they'd

SHOULD, COULD
should not — shouldn't
could not — couldn't

Pronoun / Contraction

its (owns) *its coat* — **it's** (it is) *it's cute*

your (owns) *your car* — **you're** (you are) *you're right*

their (owns) *their house* — **they're** (they are) *they're gone*

whose (owns) *whose cat* — **who's** (who is) *who's going*

CHAPTER 19   LESSON 4

New objectives: Test.

 JINGLE TIME

Have students turn to the Jingle Section of their books. The teacher will lead the students in reciting the previously-taught jingles.

 STUDY TIME

Have students study the vocabulary words in their vocabulary notebooks. Remind students that any vocabulary word in their notebooks could be on their test. Also, have students study any of the skills in the Practice Section that they need to review.

 TEST TIME

Have students turn to page 102 in the Test Section of their book and find Chapter 19 Test. Go over the directions to make sure they understand what to do. (*Chapter 19 Test key is on the next page.*)

 CHECK TIME

After students have finished, check and discuss their test papers. Make sure they understand why their answers are right or wrong. (*For total points, count each required answer as a point.*)

(End of lesson.)

Chapter 19 Test
(Student Page 102)

Exercise 1: Classify each sentence.

```
          A    SN    LV A  Adj   Adj    PrN   P A    Adj      OP
1. SN LV  The iguana / is a large tropical lizard (of the Iguanidae family). D
   PrN P4

          SN  LV  A   PrN      P    OP
2. SN LV  Sue / was a missionary (in Africa). D
   PrN P4

          A    SN    LV A  Adv   Adj   PrN
3. SN LV  The sunset / is a very lovely sight. D
   PrN P4
```

Exercise 2: Identify each pair of words as synonyms or antonyms by putting parentheses ( ) around *syn* or *ant*.

1. burn, smolder	**(syn)** ant	5. adversity, misfortune	**(syn)** ant	9. contemplate, ponder	**(syn)** ant
2. flippant, polite	syn **(ant)**	6. delusion, reality	syn **(ant)**	10. colleague, competitor	syn **(ant)**
3. exquisite, gauche	syn **(ant)**	7. conceited, humble	syn **(ant)**	11. equilibrium, balance	**(syn)** ant
4. creditor, lender	**(syn)** ant	8. scrutinize, examine	**(syn)** ant	12. contemptible, admirable	syn **(ant)**

Exercise 3: Change the underlined mixed tense verbs in Paragraph 1 to past tense verbs in Paragraph 2.

Paragraph 1: Mixed Tenses

Bolivar **is** my constant companion. He **followed** me everywhere I **go** and **protects** me from potential harm. He **loved** the attention I **give** him and **likes** to be petted. We **take** long walks in the woods on warm days and often **sat** on the bank of the pond where we **listen** to a chorus of frogs.

Paragraph 2: Past Tense

Bolivar **was** my constant companion. He **followed** me everywhere I **went** and **protected** me from potential harm. He **loved** the attention I **gave** him and **liked** to be petted. We **took** long walks in the woods on warm days and often **sat** on the bank of the pond where we **listened** to a chorus of frogs.

Exercise 4: Copy the following words on another sheet of paper. Write the correct contraction beside each word. **(Key: you've, there's, isn't, they'll, won't, it's, he'll, let's, we'd, I'll, you'll, wasn't, don't, they've, I'm, doesn't, haven't.)** Words: you have, there is, is not, they will, will not, it is, he will, let us, we would, I will, you will, was not, do not, they have, I am, does not, have not.

Exercise 5: Copy the following contractions on another sheet of paper. Write the correct word beside each contraction. **(Key: they are, he is or he has, you are, has not, you had or you would, we have, does not, had not, cannot, I had, do not.)** Contractions: they're, he's, you're, hasn't, you'd, we've, doesn't, hadn't, can't, I'd, don't.

Exercise 6: Write the seven present tense helping verbs, the five past tense helping verbs, and the two future tense helping verbs. **The order of the answers may vary.** (Present: am, is, are, has, have, do, does; Past: was, were, had, did, been; Future: will, shall)

Exercise 7: In your journal, write a paragraph summarizing what you have learned this week.

CHAPTER 19 LESSON 4 CONTINUED

TEACHER INSTRUCTIONS

Use the Question and Answer Flows below for the sentences on Chapter 19 Tests.

Question and Answer Flow for Sentence 1: The iguana is a large tropical lizard of the Iguanidae family.

1. What is a large tropical lizard of the Iguanidae family? iguana - SN
2. What is being said about iguana? iguana is - V
3. Iguana is what? lizard - verify the noun
4. Does lizard mean the same thing as iguana? Yes.
5. Lizard - PrN
6. Is - LV
7. What kind of lizard? tropical - Adj
8. What kind of lizard? large - Adj
9. A - A
10. Of - P
11. Of what? family - OP
12. What kind of family? Iguanidae - Adj
13. The - A
14. The - A
15. SN LV PrN P4 Check
16. Linking verb - Check again.
17. (Of the Iguanidae family) - Prepositional phrase
18. Period, statement, declarative sentence
19. Go back to the verb - divide the complete subject from the complete predicate.
20. Is there an adverb exception? No.
21. Is this sentence in a natural or inverted order? Natural - no change.

Classified Sentence:

<u>SN LV</u>
PrN P4

A   SN   LV A Adj   Adj   PrN   P A   Adj   OP
The iguana / is a large tropical lizard (of the Iguanidae family). **D**

Question and Answer Flow for Sentence 2: Sue was a missionary in Africa.

1. Who was a missionary in Africa? Sue - SN
2. What is being said about Sue? Sue was - V
3. Sue was what? missionary - verify the noun
4. Does missionary mean the same thing as Sue? Yes.
5. Missionary - PrN
6. Was - LV
7. A - A
8. In - P
9. In what? Africa - OP
10. SN LV PrN P4 Check
11. Linking verb - Check again.
12. (In Africa) - Prepositional phrase
13. Period, statement, declarative sentence
14. Go back to the verb - divide the complete subject from the complete predicate.
15. Is there an adverb exception? No.
16. Is this sentence in a natural or inverted order? Natural - no change.

Classified Sentence:

<u>SN LV</u>
PrN P4

SN   LV A   PrN   P   OP
Sue / was a missionary (in Africa). **D**

Question and Answer Flow for Sentence 3: The sunset is a very lovely sight.

1. What is a very lovely sight? sunset - SN
2. What is being said about sunset? sunset is - V
3. Sunset is what? sight - verify the noun
4. Does sight mean the same thing as sunset? Yes.
5. Sight - PrN
6. Is - LV
7. What kind of sight? lovely - Adj
8. How lovely? very - Adv
9. A - A
10. The - A
11. SN LV PrN P4 Check
12. Linking verb - Check again.
13. No prepositional phrases.
14. Period, statement, declarative sentence
15. Go back to the verb - divide the complete subject from the complete predicate.
16. Is there an adverb exception? No.
17. Is this sentence in a natural or inverted order? Natural - no change.

Classified Sentence:

<u>SN LV</u>
PrN P4

A   SN   LV A Adv   Adj   PrN
The sunset / is a very lovely sight. **D**

CHAPTER 19 LESSON 5

New objectives: Writing Assignments #27 and #28.

 WRITING TIME

TEACHING SCRIPT FOR WRITING ASSIGNMENTS

You will do two writing assignments. The first writing assignment will be a narrative essay with dialogue. The second writing assignment will be a five-paragraph expository essay. You should make a Story Elements outline for the narrative writing. Both rough drafts will go through the revision and editing stages. As you revise and edit, make sure you use the checkpoints in the Regular Editing Checklist provided in Reference 35. (*Read the boxes below for more information about students' writing assignment.*)

Writing Assignment Box

Writing Assignment #27: Three-Paragraph Narrative Essay With Dialogue (First or Third Person)

Remind students to make a Story Elements outline for their story.

Writing topic choices: Flat Tire or The Best Day That I Almost Didn't Have
or Funny Things That Happen At Church

Writing Assignment Box

Writing Assignment #28: Five-Point Expository Paragraph (First Person)

Writing topic choices: Good Manners or Cell Phones or Bible Truths

---

Read, check, and discuss Writing Assignments #27 and #28 after students have finished their final papers. Use the editing checklist as you check and discuss students' papers.

(End of lesson.)

CHAPTER 20   LESSON 1

New objectives: Grammar (Practice Sentences), Skills (degrees of adjectives), Practice sheet, and Vocabulary #1.

 **JINGLE TIME**

Have students turn to the Jingle Section of their books. The teacher will lead the students in reciting the previously-taught jingles.

 GRAMMAR TIME

First-Year Option: Put the Practice Sentences from the box below on the board or notebook paper. Use these sentences as you practice the concepts that have been taught. For the greatest benefit, students must participate orally with the teacher. **Second-Year Option:** Have students classify the Practice Sentences independently on paper. Check students' sentences with the answers provided below. (*If you have the CDs for Practice Sentences, have students check their sentences with the CDs.*)

Chapter 20, Practice Sentences for Lesson 1

1. _____ Mexico is a country along the border of the United States.
2. _____ The patient salesman with a considerate manner and attitude is he.

Question and Answer Flow for Sentence 1: Mexico is a country along the border of the United States.

1. What is a country along the border of the United States? Mexico - SN
2. What is being said about Mexico? Mexico is - V
3. Mexico is what? country - verify the noun
4. Does country mean the same thing as Mexico? Yes.
5. Country - PrN
6. Is - LV
7. A - A
8. Along - P
9. Along what? border - OP
10. The - A
11. Of - P
12. Of what? United States - OP
13. The - A
14. SN LV PrN P4 Check
15. Linking verb - Check again.
16. (Along the border) - Prepositional phrase
17. (Of the United States) - Prepositional phrase
18. Period, statement, declarative sentence
19. Go back to the verb - divide the complete subject from the complete predicate.
20. Is there an adverb exception? No.
21. Is this sentence in a natural or inverted order? Natural - no change.

Classified Sentence:

```
                        SN   LV  A  PrN      P   A   OP    P   A    OP
             SN  LV   Mexico / is  a country (along  the  border) (of  the  United States).  D
             PrN P4
```

CHAPTER 20 LESSON 1 CONTINUED

Question and Answer Flow for Sentence 2: The patient salesman with a considerate manner and attitude is he.

1. Who is he? salesman - SN
2. What is being said about salesman? salesman is - V
3. Salesman is who? he - verify the pronoun
4. Does *he* mean the same thing as salesman? Yes.
5. He - PrP *(Say, "He - Predicate Pronoun")*
6. Is - LV
7. With - P
8. With what? manner and attitude - COP, COP
9. And - C
10. What kind of manner and attitude? considerate - Adj
11. A - A

12. What kind of salesman? patient - Adj
13. The - A
14. SN LV PrN P4 Check
15. Linking verb - Check again.
16. (With a considerate manner and attitude) - Prepositional phrase
17. Period, statement, declarative sentence
18. Go back to the verb - divide the complete subject from the complete predicate.
19. Is there an adverb exception? No.
20. Is this sentence in a natural or inverted order? Natural - no change.

Classified Sentence:

<u>SN LV</u>
PrN P4

A Adj SN P A Adj COP C COP LV PrP
The patient salesman (with a considerate manner and attitude) / is he. **D**

Use Sentences 1-2 that you just classified with your students to do an Oral Skill Builder Check. Use the guidelines below.

Oral Skill Builder Check

1. **Noun check.**
   (Say the job and then say the noun. Circle each noun.)
2. **Identify the nouns as singular or plural.**
   (Write S or P above each noun.)
3. **Identify the nouns as common or proper.**
   (Follow established procedure for oral identification.)
4. **Do a vocabulary check.**
   (Follow established procedure for oral identification.)

5. **Identify the complete subject and the complete predicate.** (Underline the complete subject once and the complete predicate twice.)
6. **Identify the simple subject and simple predicate.**
   (Underline the simple subject once and the simple predicate twice. Bold, or highlight, the lines.)
7. **Recite the irregular verb chart.**
   (Located on student page 17 and teacher page 143.)

SKILL TIME

TEACHING SCRIPT FOR DEGREES OF ADJECTIVES

We have learned a lot about how adjectives and adverbs make a major contribution to writing sentences. Now, you are going to learn three more things about adjectives. (*You may also apply this information to adverbs, but degrees of adverbs are not presented in Shurley English until Level 7.*) I am going to write three terms on the board. (*Write "Simple Form," "Comparative Form," and "Superlative Form" on the board. Leave plenty of space between each one.*)

CHAPTER 20 LESSON 1 CONTINUED

Listen carefully. Adjectives have three forms, or degrees, which we use in making comparisons. These forms, called degrees of comparison, are the simple form (*sometimes called positive form*), the comparative form, and the superlative form. The comparative and superlative forms of adjectives not only describe individual items, but they also give you the ability to compare one item with another.

Before we get into a deeper discussion of the three degrees of adjectives, I want to demonstrate what I have just told you. We will use strips of paper to demonstrate the three degrees of adjectives. (*Cut six strips of paper. They will represent different lengths. Tape the shortest strip of paper under the "Simple Form" title on the board.*) **This strip of paper is long**. We only have one strip of paper, so it cannot be compared to another strip of paper. When nothing is compared, it is the simple form.

Next, I will use two strips of paper to demonstrate the comparative form. (*Put a number 1 on the longest strip and a number two on the shorter strip. Tape the two strips of paper under the "Comparative Form" title on the board.*) Now, we have two strips of paper, so we can do a comparison. Any time you have two people, places, or things, you can compare one to the other. **Strip 1 is longer than Strip 2.** (*Student's name*) is more nervous than (*friend's name*). When two people, places, or things are compared, it is called the comparative form.

Last, I will use three strips of paper to demonstrate the superlative form. (*Put a number 3 on the longest strip and numbers one and two on the shorter strips. Tape the three strips of paper under the "Superlative Form" title on the board.*) **Strip 3 is the longest of all three strips**. Now, we have three strips of paper, so we can do another kind of comparison for three or more people, places, or things. (*Student's name*) runs the fastest of all three friends. (*Student's name*) is the most nervous of the three friends. When three or more are compared, it is called the superlative form.

Look on the board at the examples. If you have only one, it is the simple form, with nothing to compare. If you have two, it is the comparative form, with only two things to compare. If you have three or more, it is the superlative form, with three or more things to compare. Remember, one, two, three: simple, comparative, superlative. Let's say it several times so we will remember it: **one, two, three: simple, comparative, superlative**. (*Repeat the basic information in bold several times.*)

Now, we will read and discuss the rule box for making comparative and superlative comparisons. (*Direct your students to Reference 60 on student page 41. The reference box is reproduced for you on the next page.*)

Teacher's Note: As you read over these rules, write *-er* and *more* above the Comparative Form on the board and write *-est* and *most* above the Superlative Form on the board. As you go over the examples at the bottom of the chart, write the words under the correct forms on the board.

CHAPTER 20 LESSON 1 CONTINUED

Reference 60: Degrees of Adjectives

The **Simple Form** is used when no comparison is made. There are no rules for the simple form. (**fast, nervous**)

The **Comparative Form** is used to compare **TWO** people, places, or things.	The **Superlative Form** is used to compare **THREE** or more people, places, or things.
Rule 1. Use *-er* with most 1 or 2 syllable words. (**faster**) Use *more* with *-ful* words or whenever the *–er* sounds awkward. (**more nervous**) Use *more* for all 3-or-more syllable words.	**Rule 2.** Use *-est* with most 1 or 2 syllable words. (**fastest**) Use *most* with *-ful* words or whenever the *-est* sounds awkward. (**most nervous**) Use *most* for all 3-or-more syllable words.

Irregular Adjectives Have No Rule Numbers and Have to be Memorized

Simple Adjective		Comparative		Superlative	
1. good	3. little (amount)	5. better	7. less or lesser	9. best	11. least
2. bad, ill	4. much, many	6. worse	8. more	10. worst	12. most

Sentence Examples

1. Daniel bought a good hat.   2. Daniel bought a better hat than Scott.   3. Daniel bought the best hat of all the other students.

Practice: Write the rule numbers and the different forms for the adjectives below. For irregular forms, write **Irr** in the box.

Simple Adjective Form	Rule Box	Comparative Adjective Form	Rule Box	Superlative Adjective Form
1. agreeable	1	more agreeable	2	most agreeable
2. lucky	1	luckier	2	luckiest
3. ill	Irr	worse	Irr	worst

4. I am **taller** than Sam. (tall)   5. Of all the girls, she was the **most eager** to go. (eager)   6. She reads **better** than Sue. (good)

Some adjectives do not use the basic rules and have to be memorized. Those are irregular forms. (*Read and discuss these irregular forms from the reference chart with your students.*)

We will put what we have learned into practice as we work through the practice examples. Look at the first example. I will read the directions, and then I will guide you through each part.

Look at number 1. Find the word *agreeable*. Is the word *agreeable* in the simple, comparative, or superlative form? (*Simple form.*) How many syllables does the word *agreeable* have? (*Four.*) The comparative form compares how many people or things? (*Two.*) Go to the rule box and find the rule number that tells us how to write a comparative form for *agreeable*. (*Rule 1.*) How does it say to write *agreeable* in the comparative form? (*more agreeable.*) (*Write Rule 1 and more agreeable on the board.*)

Now, we will look at the superlative form. The superlative form compares how many people or things? (*Three or more.*) Go to the rule box and find the rule number that tells us how to write a superlative form for the word *agreeable*. (*Rule 2, most agreeable.*)

Now for a quick review of the three degrees or forms of the word *agreeable*. What is the simple form? (*agreeable*) What is the comparative form? (*more agreeable*) What is the superlative form? (*most agreeable*) What is another word sometimes used for simple form? (*positive form*)

(*Work through examples 2-3 in the same way. Make sure students understand how the rule box will help them decide how to write the different forms.*)

CHAPTER 20 LESSON 1 CONTINUED

 PRACTICE TIME

Have students turn to pages 69 and 70 in the Practice Section of their book and find Chapter 20, Lesson 1, Practice *(1-2)*. Go over the directions to make sure they understand what to do. Guide students closely as they do the practice exercises for the first time. *(Students may use the Reference section in their books to help them remember the new information.)* Check and discuss the Practice after students have finished. *(Chapter 20, Lesson 1, Practice keys are given below.)*

Chapter 20, Lesson 1, Practice 1: Write the rule numbers and the different forms for the adjectives below. For irregular forms write **Irr.**
Comparative: Rule 1: Use **-er** with 1 or 2 syllable words and **more** with -ful words, awkward words, or words with 3 or more syllables.
Superlative: Rule 2: Use **-est** with 1 or 2 syllable words and **most** with -ful words, awkward words, or words with 3 or more syllables.

Simple Adjective Form	Rule Box	Comparative Adjective Form	Rule Box	Superlative Adjective Form
1. easy	1	easier	2	easiest
2. turbulent	1	more turbulent	2	most turbulent
3. little	Irr	less	Irr	least
4. fair	1	fairer	2	fairest
5. gracious	1	more gracious	2	most gracious
6. much	Irr	more	Irr	most
7. eager	1	more eager	2	most eager

Chapter 20, Lesson 1, Practice 2: In each blank, write the correct form of the adjective in parentheses to complete the sentences.

1. Eric's training was **more extensive** than Brian's. (extensive)

2. Your answer is **better** than the one in the book. (good)

3. He is a **worthier** candidate than his brother. (worthy)

4. John is never anything but **kind**. (kind)

5. Lance bought the **most expensive** diamond in the store. (expensive)

 WRITING TIME

Have students make an entry in their journals.

 VOCABULARY TIME

Assign Chapter 20, Vocabulary Words **#1** on page 8 in the Reference Section for students to define in their Vocabulary notebooks. Tell students they are to use a dictionary or thesaurus to look up the meanings of the vocabulary words. After they write each word and its meaning, students are to write a sentence using the vocabulary word.

Chapter 20, Vocabulary Words #1
(component, humble, expense, disbursement)

(End of lesson.)

Level 5 Homeschool Teacher's Manual

CHAPTER 20   LESSON 2

New objectives: Grammar (Practice Sentences), Skills (double negatives), Practice sheet, Vocabulary #2, and an Activity.

JINGLE TIME

Have students turn to the Jingle Section of their books. The teacher will lead the students in reciting the previously-taught jingles.

GRAMMAR TIME

First-Year Option: Put the Practice Sentences from the box below on the board or notebook paper. Use these sentences as you practice the concepts that have been taught. For the greatest benefit, students must participate orally with the teacher. **Second-Year Option:** Have students classify the Practice Sentences independently on paper. Check students' sentences with the answers provided below. (*If you have the CDs for Practice Sentences, have students check their sentences with the CDs.*)

Chapter 20, Practice Sentences for Lesson 2
1. _____ My favorite comedian became a frequent guest on a weekly talk show.   2. _____ The cartwheel and backhand spring are difficult gymnastic movements for many beginners.

Question and Answer Flow for Sentence 1: My favorite comedian became a frequent guest on a weekly talk show.

1. Who became a frequent guest on a weekly talk show? comedian - SN
2. What is being said about comedian? comedian became - V
3. Comedian became what? guest - verify the noun
4. Does guest mean the same thing as comedian? Yes.
5. Guest - PrN
6. Became - LV
7. What kind of guest? frequent - Adj
8. A - A
9. On - P
10. On what? show - OP
11. What kind of show? talk - Adj
12. What kind of show? weekly - Adj
13. A - A
14. What kind of comedian? favorite - Adj
15. Whose comedian? my - PPA
16. SN LV PrN P4 Check
17. Linking verb - Check again.
18. (On a weekly talk show) - Prepositional phrase
19. Period, statement, declarative sentence
20. Go back to the verb - divide the complete subject from the complete predicate.
21. Is there an adverb exception? No.
22. Is this sentence in a natural or inverted order? Natural - no change.

Classified Sentence:		PPA Adj	SN	LV	A Adj	PrN	P A Adj Adj OP
	SN LV PrN P4	My favorite comedian **/** became a frequent guest (on a weekly talk show). **D**					

CHAPTER 20 LESSON 2 CONTINUED

Question and Answer Flow for Sentence 2: The cartwheel and back handspring are difficult gymnastic movements for many beginners.

1. What are difficult gymnastic movements for many beginners? cartwheel and handspring - CSN, CSN
2. What is being said about cartwheel and handspring? cartwheel and handspring are - V
3. Cartwheel and handspring are what? movements - verify the noun
4. Do movements mean the same thing as cartwheel and handspring? Yes.
5. Movements - PrN
6. Are - LV
7. What kind of movements? gymnastic - Adj
8. What kind of movements? difficult - Adj
9. For - P
10. For whom? beginners - OP
11. How many beginners? many - Adj
12. What kind of handspring? back - Adj
13. And - C
14. The - A
15. SN LV PrN P4 Check
16. Linking verb - Check again.
17. (For many beginners) - Prepositional phrase
18. Period, statement, declarative sentence
19. Go back to the verb - divide the complete subject from the complete predicate.
20. Is there an adverb exception? No.
21. Is this sentence in a natural or inverted order? Natural - no change.

Classified
Sentence:

| | A | CSN | C Adj | CSN | LV | Adj | Adj | PrN | P | Adj | OP |

SN LV The cartwheel and back handspring / are difficult gymnastic movements (for many beginners). D
PrN P4

TEACHER INSTRUCTIONS FOR A PATTERN 4 PRACTICE SENTENCE

Tell students that their sentence writing assignment today is to write a Pattern 4 Practice Sentence. They are to follow the same procedure used in the previous lessons. They should decide on their labels, arrange them in a selected order, write their sentence, and edit the sentence for improved word choices. *(Students do not have to write an Improved Sentence at this point unless you feel they need more one-on-one word choice writing practice.)* Check and discuss the Pattern 4 Practice Sentence after students have finished.

SKILL TIME

TEACHING SCRIPT FOR DOUBLE NEGATIVES

Today, we are going to learn how to correct double negative mistakes in writing. The first thing we need to know is what it means to have a double negative mistake. Double means TWO, and negative means NOT. We have a **double negative** mistake when we use two negative words that both mean NOT in the same sentence. Most negative words begin with the letter *n*. Other negative words do not begin with the letter *n* but are negative in meaning. There are also some prefixes that give words a negative meaning.

Look at Reference 61 on page 41 in your book. First, we will go over the most commonly used negative words and prefixes. Then, we'll learn three ways to correct double negatives, and finally, we'll see different ways to change negative words to positive words. *(Read and discuss the information in Reference 61 on the next page with your students.)*

CHAPTER 20 LESSON 2 CONTINUED

Reference 61: Double Negatives			
Negative Words That Begin With *N*		**Other Negative Words**	**Negative Prefixes**
neither no no one not (n't) nowhere never nobody none nothing		barely, hardly, scarcely	dis, non, un

Three Ways to Correct a Double Negative
Rule 1: **Change** the second negative to a positive: Wrong: Walter **couldn't** eat **nothing**.　　Right: Walter **couldn't** eat **anything**. Rule 2: **Take out** the negative part of a contraction: Wrong: Samantha **shouldn't** ask **nothing**.　　Right: Samantha **should** ask **nothing**. Rule 3: **Remove** the first negative word (possibility of a verb change): Wrong: Warren **didn't** want **nothing**.　　Right: Warren **wanted nothing**.

Changing Negative Words to Positive Words
1. Change *no* or *none* to *any*.　　4. Change *nothing* to *anything*.　　7. Change *neither* to *either*. 2. Change *nobody* to *anybody*.　　5. Change *nowhere* to *anywhere*.　　8. Remove the *n't* from a 3. Change *no one* to *anyone*.　　6. Change *never* to *ever*.　　　　　contraction.

Examples: Underline the negative words in each sentence. Rewrite each sentence and correct the double negative mistake as indicated by the rule number in parentheses at the end of the sentence.

1. Sarah <u>doesn't</u> have <u>no</u> money for the fair. (Rule 3) **Sarah has no money for the fair.**
2. He <u>can't</u> <u>hardly</u> wait for our science contest. (Rule 2) **He can hardly wait for our science contest.**
3. She <u>hasn't</u> done <u>nothing</u> for the fundraiser. (Rule 1) **She hasn't done anything for the fundraiser.**

Go through the guided examples with your class. Make sure students know how to make the double negative correction according to the rule provided at the end of each sentence. (*Remember, the reference answers are keyed to give students guided examples.*)

 PRACTICE TIME

Students will continue identifying verb tenses and regular/irregular verbs. Have students turn to page 70 in the Practice Section of their book and find Chapter 20, Lesson 2, Practice (*1-2*). Go over the directions to make sure they understand what to do. Check and discuss the Practice after students have finished. (*Chapter 20, Lesson 2, Practice key is given below.*)

Chapter 20, Lesson 2, Practice 1: Underline the negative words in each sentence. Rewrite each sentence and correct the double negative mistake as indicated by the rule number in parentheses at the end of the sentence.

Rule 1	Rule 2	Rule 3
Change the second negative to a positive.	Take out the negative part of a contraction.	Remove the first negative word (verb change).

1. She <u>couldn't</u> see <u>nothing</u> in the distance. (Rule 1)
   She couldn't see anything in the distance.
2. He <u>doesn't</u> have <u>no</u> common sense. (Rule 3)
   He has no common sense.
3. She <u>hasn't</u> <u>never</u> stayed home alone. (Rule 2)
   She has never stayed home alone.
4. Sue <u>doesn't</u> <u>never</u> come home for Christmas. (Rule 1)
   Sue doesn't ever come home for Christmas.
5. There <u>isn't</u> <u>no</u> right answer. (Rule 2)
   There is no right answer.
6. I <u>didn't</u> find <u>nothing</u> in that desk. (Rule 3)
   I found nothing in that desk.
7. Joe <u>hadn't</u> <u>never</u> fried eggs before. (Rule 2)
   Joe had never fried eggs before.
8. She <u>hasn't</u> eaten <u>no</u> lunch today. (Rule 1)
   She hasn't eaten any lunch today.

CHAPTER 20 LESSON 2 CONTINUED

Chapter 20, Lesson 2, Practice 2: On a sheet of paper, make a list of fifteen contractions, then write the words from which the contractions come. (*Answers will vary.*) (*Use the contraction chart to check students' work.*)

 WRITING TIME

Have students make an entry in their journals.

 VOCABULARY TIME

Assign Chapter 20, Vocabulary Words **#2** on page 8 in the Reference Section for students to define in their Vocabulary notebooks. Tell students they are to use a dictionary or thesaurus to look up the meanings of the vocabulary words. After they write each word and its meaning, students are to write a sentence using the vocabulary word.

Chapter 20, Vocabulary Words #2
(candid, sly, mandatory, required)

 ACTIVITY / ASSIGNMENT TIME

Have students make a booklet and title it, "Little Known Facts About Interesting People." They should interview one or two people a week for several weeks and organize their facts into a pleasing format. They may want to add photographs, artwork, etc. (*This can also be done on the computer.*) Students may use the suggestions below as they compile information for their folders. Suggested people to interview: grandparents, parents, relatives, mayor, police chief, nurse, doctor, preacher, etc.

City of residence, Birth date and place, Date of marriage, How I met my spouse, Details about my family, Occupation, Community activities, I drive a ..., My favorite room in the house is..., My favorite month is..., My Favorite author is, The last book I read was..., My favorite kind of music is..., My two favorite movies are..., My favorite TV show is..., My favorite restaurant is..., My favorite food is..., My favorite junk food is..., My teenage idol was..., My favorite childhood memory is..., When I was a kid, I wanted to be..., The greatest invention during my lifetime is..., My favorite school subject was..., My best vacation was..., If I could live in another time period, I'd choose..., If I could go anywhere in the world, I'd go to..., If I won a million dollars, I'd..., My proudest accomplishment is..., I wish I was better at..., If I've learned one thing in life, it's..., My pet peeve is..., When I'm nervous I..., My hobbies are..., The person who influenced me the most was..., I like people who..., My proudest accomplishments are..., My words of wisdom for others are...

(End of lesson.)

CHAPTER 20   LESSON 3

New objectives: Grammar (Practice Sentences) and a Practice sheet.

JINGLE TIME

Have students turn to the Jingle Section of their books. The teacher will lead the students in reciting the previously-taught jingles.

GRAMMAR TIME

First-Year Option: Put the Practice Sentences from the box below on the board or notebook paper. Use these sentences as you practice the concepts that have been taught. For the greatest benefit, students must participate orally with the teacher. **Second-Year Option:** Have students classify the Practice Sentences independently on paper. Check students' sentences with the answers provided below. (*If you have the CDs for Practice Sentences, have students check their sentences with the CDs.*)

Chapter 20, Practice Sentences for Lesson 3
1. _____ Attitude and personality are the outstanding qualities of this successful contestant. .
2. _____ The captain was an accomplished pilot of the sternwheeler and pontoon.

Question and Answer Flow for Sentence 1: Attitude and personality are the outstanding qualities of this successful contestant.

1. What are the outstanding qualities of this successful contestant? attitude and personality - CSN, CSN
2. What is being said about attitude and personality? attitude and personality are - V
3. Attitude and personality are what? qualities - verify the noun
4. Do qualities mean the same thing as attitude and personality? Yes.
5. Qualities - PrN
6. Are - LV
7. Which qualities? outstanding - Adj
8. The - A
9. Of - P
10. Of whom? contestant - OP
11. What kind of contestant? successful - Adj
12. Which contestant? this - Adj
13. And - C
14. SN LV PrN P4 Check
15. Linking verb - Check again.
16. (Of this successful contestant) - Prepositional phrase
17. Period, statement, declarative sentence
18. Go back to the verb - divide the complete subject from the complete predicate.
19. Is there an adverb exception? No.
20. Is this sentence in a natural or inverted order? Natural - no change.

Classified		**CSN**	**C**	**CSN**	**LV**	**A**	**Adj**	**PrN**	**P Adj**	**Adj**	**OP**
Sentence:	SN LV	Attitude and personality / are the outstanding qualities (of this successful contestant). D									
	PrN P4										

CHAPTER 20 LESSON 3 CONTINUED

Question and Answer Flow for Sentence 2: The captain was an accomplished pilot of the sternwheeler and pontoon.

1. Who was an accomplished pilot of the sternwheeler and pontoon? captain - SN
2. What is being said about captain? captain was - V
3. Captain was who? pilot - verify the noun
4. Does pilot mean the same thing as captain? Yes.
5. Pilot - PrN
6. Was - LV
7. What kind of pilot? accomplished - Adj
8. An - A
9. Of - P
10. Of what? sternwheeler and pontoon - COP, COP
11. And - C

12. The - A
13. The - A
14. SN LV PrN P4 Check
15. Linking verb - Check again.
16. (Of the sternwheeler and pontoon) - Prepositional phrase
17. Period, statement, declarative sentence
18. Go back to the verb - divide the complete subject from the complete predicate.
19. Is there an adverb exception? No.
20. Is this sentence in a natural or inverted order? Natural - no change.

Classified Sentence:

	A	SN	LV	A	Adj	PrN	P	A	COP	C	COP

SN LV
_____ The captain / was an accomplished pilot (of the sternwheeler and pontoon). **D**
PrN P4

PRACTICE TIME

Students will continue their practice of skills. Have students turn to pages 71 and 72 in the Practice Section of their books and find Chapter 20, Lesson 3, Practice (*1-6*). Go over the directions to make sure they understand what to do. If students need a review, have them study the information and examples in the Reference Section of their books. Check and discuss the Practices after students have finished. (*Chapter 20, Lesson 3, Practice keys are given below and on the next page.*)

Chapter 20, Lesson 3, Practice 1: Underline the negative words in each sentence. Rewrite each sentence and correct the double negative mistake as indicated by the rule number in parentheses at the end of the sentence.

Rule 1	Rule 2	Rule 3
Change the second negative to a positive.	Take out the negative part of a contraction.	Remove the first negative word (verb change).

1. Kay <u>didn't</u> insist on <u>nothing</u> today. (Rule 1)
   Kay didn't insist on anything today.
2. She <u>wasn't</u> <u>never</u> inconsiderate. (Rule 2)
   She was never inconsiderate.
3. He <u>wouldn't</u> ask <u>no one</u> for a pen. (Rule 1)
   He wouldn't ask anyone for a pen.
4. Kevin <u>hadn't</u> <u>never</u> milked a cow. (Rule 3)
   Kevin never milked a cow.

5. Nancy <u>hadn't</u> <u>never</u> traveled overseas. (Rule 2)
   Nancy had never traveled overseas.
6. He d<u>oesn't</u> <u>never</u> wear shoes in the summer. (Rule 3)
   He never wears shoes in the summer.
7. The judge <u>didn't</u> want <u>no</u> flimsy excuses. (Rule 1)
   The judge didn't want any flimsy excuses.
8. The applicant <u>didn't</u> want <u>no</u> special privileges. (Rule 3)
   The applicant wanted no special privileges.

Chapter 20, Lesson 3, Practice 2: On a sheet of paper, write three sentences in which you demonstrate each of the double negative rules above. Underline the negative word in each sentence.

CHAPTER 20 LESSON 3 CONTINUED

Chapter 20, Lesson 3, Practice 3: Write the rule numbers and the different forms for the adjectives below. For irregular forms, write **Irr**.

Comparative: Rule 1: Use **-er** with 1 or 2 syllable words and **more** with -ful words, awkward words, or words with 3 or more syllables.
Superlative: Rule 2: Use **-est** with 1 or 2 syllable words and **most** with -ful words, awkward words, or words with 3 or more syllables.

Simple Adjective Form	Rule Box	Comparative Adjective Form	Rule Box	Superlative Adjective Form
1. vocal	1	more vocal	2	most vocal
2. well	Irr	better	Irr	best
3. painful	1	more painful	2	most painful
4. vicious	1	more vicious	2	most vicious
5. smart	1	smarter	2	smartest
6. ill	Irr	worse	Irr	worst
7. wise	1	wiser	2	wisest

Chapter 20, Lesson 3, Practice 4: On a sheet of paper, write three sentences, demonstrating each of the three degrees of adjectives. Identify the form you used by writing **simple, comparative,** or **superlative** at the end of each sentence.

Chapter 20, Lesson 3, Practice 5: In each blank, write the correct form of the adjective in parentheses to complete the sentences.

1. Troy is the <u>most impatient</u> player on the team. (impatient)

2. Roy has a very <u>outgoing</u> personality. (outgoing)

3. Those were the <u>best</u> pancakes I'd ever tasted. (good)

4. These pretzels are <u>saltier</u> than those chips. (salty)

5. She is the <u>most vigilant</u> resident on the street. (vigilant)

Chapter 20, Lesson 3, Practice 6: On a sheet of paper, make a list of ten contractions, then write the words from which the contractions come. (*Answers will vary.*) (*Use the contraction chart to check students' work.*)

 STUDY TIME

Have students study the vocabulary words in their vocabulary notebooks. Tell students that any vocabulary word in their notebooks could be on their test. Also, have students study any of the skills in the Practice Section that they need to review.

(End of lesson.)

CHAPTER 20   LESSON 4

New objectives: Test and an Activity.

 JINGLE TIME

Have students turn to the Jingle Section of their books. The teacher will lead the students in reciting the previously-taught jingles.

 STUDY TIME

Have students study the vocabulary words in their vocabulary notebooks. Remind students that any vocabulary word in their notebooks could be on their test. Also, have students study any of the skills in the Practice Section that they need to review.

 TEST TIME

Have students turn to page 103 in the Test Section of their books and find Chapter 20 Test. Go over the directions to make sure they understand what to do. (*Chapter 20 Test key is on the next page.*)

 CHECK TIME

After students have finished, check and discuss their test papers. Make sure they understand why their answers are right or wrong. (*For total points, count each required answer as a point.*)

 ACTIVITY / ASSIGNMENT TIME

Read and discuss the example below of a color poem containing similes with your students. Have them follow the directions given to write their own color poem. (*Write the poem and directions on the board.*)

1. Choose a color for a title.
2. Write similes using *like* or *as*. Write one line for each of the five senses below:
    sight
    smell
    taste
    hearing
    touch

Brown

Looks like rusted metal
Smells like cured hay
Tastes as bland as rice cakes
Sounds as crisp as starched collars
And feels as dry as sunburnt skin

(End of lesson.)

Chapter 20 Test
(Student Page 103)

Exercise 1: Classify each sentence.

             PPA PNA   Adj Adj SN   LV   PrN

1. **SN LV**   My cousin's last two dogs **/** were Dalmatians. **D**
   PrN P4

                P   A OP   A   SN   LV   PrN   P A OP   P Adj   OP

2. **SN LV**   (During the storm), the tourists **/** became guests (of the hotel) (for three days). **D**
   PrN P4

Exercise 2: Identify each pair of words as synonyms or antonyms by putting parentheses ( ) around *syn* or *ant*.

1. delusion, reality	syn **(ant)**	4. vanquish, escape	syn **(ant)**	7. expense, disbursement	**(syn)** ant
2. solitary, alone	**(syn)** ant	5. component, whole	syn **(ant)**	8. mandatory, required	**(syn)** ant
3. candid, sly	syn **(ant)**	6. creditor, lender	**(syn)** ant	9. contemptible, admirable	syn **(ant)**

Exercise 3: Underline the negative words in each sentence. Rewrite each sentence and correct the double negative mistake as indicated by the rule number in parentheses at the end of the sentence.

Rule 1	Rule 2	Rule 3
Change the second negative to a positive.	Take out the negative part of a contraction.	Remove the first negative word (verb change).

1. Amy <u>doesn't</u> <u>never</u> stay home. (Rule 3)
   Amy never stays home.

2. Matt <u>doesn't</u> have <u>no</u> excuse. (Rule 1)
   Matt doesn't have any excuse.

3. I <u>won't</u> say <u>nothing</u> to her. (Rule 1)
   I won't say anything to her.

4. We <u>didn't</u> do <u>nothing</u> wrong. (Rule 3)
   We did nothing wrong.

5. He <u>couldn't</u> see <u>nothing</u> in the dark. (Rule 1)
   He couldn't see anything in the dark.

6. My dad <u>wouldn't</u> <u>never</u> dispute my mom's word. (Rule 2)
   My dad would never dispute my mom's word.

7. Tommy <u>can't</u> find <u>no</u> scissors. (Rule 2)
   Tommy can find no scissors.

8. Earl <u>doesn't</u> <u>never</u> answer the phone. (Rule 3)
   Earl never answers the phone.

Exercise 4: Write the rule numbers and the different forms for the adjectives below. For irregular forms, write **Irr**.

Comparative: Rule 1: Use **-er** with 1 or 2 syllable words and **more** with -ful words, awkward words, or words with 3 or more syllables.
Superlative: Rule 2: Use **-est** with 1 or 2 syllable words and **most** with -ful words, awkward words, or words with 3 or more syllables.

Simple Adjective Form	Rule Box	Comparative Adjective Form	Rule Box	Superlative Adjective Form
1. cold	1	colder	2	coldest
2. bad	Irr	worse	Irr	worst
3. brave	1	braver	2	bravest
4. inventive	1	more inventive	2	most inventive
5. many	Irr	more	Irr	most
6. warm	1	warmer	2	warmest
7. apparent	1	more apparent	2	most apparent

Exercise 5: In each blank, write the correct form of the adjective in parentheses to complete the sentences.

1. Annette was the <u>most attentive</u> student in the class. (attentive)

2. Mrs. Montgomery was a <u>wonderful</u> substitute. (wonderful)

3. Lisa is <u>younger</u> than her sister. (young)

4. Metal parts are <u>more durable</u> than plastic. (durable)

Exercise 6: In your journal, write a paragraph summarizing what you have learned this week.

CHAPTER 20 LESSON 4 CONTINUED

TEACHER INSTRUCTIONS

Use the Question and Answer Flows below for the sentences on Chapter 20 Tests.

Question and Answer Flow for Sentence 1: My cousin's last two dogs were Dalmatians.

1. What were Dalmatians? dogs - SN
2. What is being said about dogs? dogs were - V
3. Dogs were what? Dalmatians - verify the noun
4. Does Dalmatians mean the same thing as dogs? Yes.
5. Dalmatians - PrN
6. Were - LV
7. How many dogs? two - Adj
8. Which dogs? last - Adj
9. Whose dogs? cousin's - PNA
10. Whose cousin? my - PPA
11. SN LV PrN P4 Check
12. Linking verb - Check again.
13. No prepositional phrases.
14. Period, statement, declarative sentence
15. Go back to the verb - divide the complete subject from the complete predicate.
16. Is there an adverb exception? No.
17. Is this sentence in a natural or inverted order? Natural - no change.

Classified Sentence:

```
                    PPA  PNA   Adj Adj SN      LV      PrN
         SN LV     My cousin's last two dogs / were Dalmatians.  D
         PrN P4
```

Question and Answer Flow for Sentence 2: During the storm, the tourists became guests of the hotel for three days.

1. Who became guests of the hotel for three days? tourists - SN
2. What is being said about tourists? tourists became - V
3. Tourists became what? guests - verify the noun
4. Do guests mean the same thing as tourists? Yes.
5. Guests - PrN
6. Became - LV
7. Of - P
8. Of what? hotel - OP
9. The - A
10. For - P
11. For what? days - OP
12. How many days? three - Adj
13. The - A
14. During - P
15. During what? storm - OP
16. The - A
17. SN LV PrN P4 Check
18. Linking verb - Check again.
19. (During the storm) - Prepositional phrase
20. (Of the hotel) - Prepositional phrase
21. (For three days) - Prepositional phrase
22. Period, statement, declarative sentence
23. Go back to the verb - divide the complete subject from the complete predicate.
24. Is there an adverb exception? No.
25. Is this sentence in a natural or inverted order? Inverted - Underline the subject parts once and the predicate parts twice.

Classified Sentence:

```
                 P      A  OP    A  SN      LV    PrN    P  A  OP    P Adj  OP
      SN LV     (During the storm), the tourists / became guests (of the hotel) (for three days).  D
      PrN P4
```

CHAPTER 20   LESSON 5

New objectives: Writing (descriptive) and Writing Assignments #29 and #30, Bonus Option.

 **WRITING TIME**

TEACHING SCRIPT FOR INTRODUCING DESCRIPTIVE WRITING

An artist paints a picture on canvas with paint. A descriptive writer paints a picture on paper with words. Both the artist and writer must select what they will include in their picture. Descriptive writing **shows** the reader what is being described. It does not just **tell** him about it.

Even though you can use description in expository, narrative, and persuasive writing, sometimes you are asked to write only a descriptive piece of writing. Then, you must know that a **descriptive paragraph** gives a detailed picture of a person, place, thing, or idea.

A descriptive paragraph will usually start with an overall impression of what you are describing. That will be your topic sentence. Then, you will add supporting sentences that give details about the topic. To make a description clear and vivid, these detail sentences should include as much information as possible about how the topic looks, sounds, feels, or tastes. The sensory details that you include will depend on what you are describing. Since all the senses are not significant in all situations, the following guidelines about descriptive writing will give you the types of details that you should consider when you are describing certain topics.

Look at Reference 62 on page 42 in your Reference Section. Follow along as I read the guidelines for descriptive writing. This reference will give you ideas and help guide you as you write descriptive paragraphs. (*Read and discuss Reference 62 below with your students. You might even want to make a descriptive-guidelines poster for the wall so students can have a visual guide as they write descriptive paragraphs.*)

Reference 62: Guidelines for Descriptive Writing
1. **When describing people,** it is helpful to notice these types of details: appearance, walk, voice, manner, gestures, personality traits, any special incident related to the person being described, and any striking details that will help make that person stand out in your mind.
2. **When describing places or things,** it is helpful to notice these types of details: the physical features of a place or thing (color, texture, smell, shape, size, age), any unusual features, any special incident related to the place or thing being described, and whether or not the place or thing is special to you.
3. **When describing nature,** it is helpful to notice these types of details: the special features of the season, the sights, smells, sounds, colors, animals, insects, birds, and any special incident related to the scene being described.
4. **When describing an incident or an event,** it is helpful to notice these types of details: the order in which the event takes place, any specific facts that will keep the story moving from a beginning to an ending, the answers to any of the *who, what, when, where, why,* and *how* questions that the reader needs to know, and especially the details that will create a clear picture, such as how things look, sound, smell, feel, etc.

CHAPTER 20 LESSON 5 CONTINUED

Look at Reference 63 on page 42. Follow along as I go over the steps in writing a descriptive paragraph. (*Read the steps and samples below as students follow the guidelines in the reference box.*)

♦ Writing Topic: **A Picnic at the Park**
♦ <u>The Title</u> - Since there are many possibilities for titles, decide if you want to leave the topic as your title or if you want to write a different phrase to tell what your paragraph is about.
   (A Picnic at the Park)

1. Sentence #1 - Write a topic sentence that introduces what is being described.
   (Every Fourth of July, my aunt and uncle pack a picnic basket and have lunch at one of the wildlife parks.)

2. Sentences #2 - #8 -Write sentences that give a description of your topic. (*Use the descriptive writing guidelines in Reference 62 to help you.*)

   (Despite the pesky ants, they enjoy grilling hamburgers and hot dogs over an open fire. And while they are enjoying their sandwiches, they can watch and listen to a variety of birds in flight. Occasionally, an almost-tame deer wanders out of nearby woods and adds magic to their outing. They find that eating out in the open and breathing in the fresh air is invigorating.)

3. Sentence #9 -Write a concluding (final) sentence that summarizes your paragraph or relates it back to the topic sentence. Read the topic sentence again and then restate it by using some of the same words to say the same thing in a different way.
   (It is hard to imagine that my aunt and uncle would ever surrender this ritual.)

Reference 63: Descriptive Paragraph Guidelines

A. Sentence 1 is the topic sentence that introduces **what is being described**.
B. For sentences 2-8, use **the descriptive details** in Reference 62.
C. Sentence 6 is a concluding sentence that **restates or relates back to the topic sentence**.

A Picnic at the Park

   Every Fourth of July, my aunt and uncle pack a picnic basket and have lunch at one of the wildlife parks. Despite the pesky ants, they enjoy roasting hamburgers and hot dogs over an open fire. And while they are enjoying their sandwiches, they can watch and listen to a variety of birds in flight. Occasionally, an almost-tame deer wanders out of nearby woods and adds magic to their outing. They find that eating out in the open and breathing in the fresh air is invigorating. It is hard to imagine that my aunt and uncle would ever surrender this ritual.

CHAPTER 20 LESSON 5 CONTINUED

Teacher's Notes: The descriptive writing guideline is a suggested guide to help students as they learn to write descriptive paragraphs. However, some students will be able to organize their ideas and stick to the topic without following the guideline exactly. The number of sentences may also vary.

You will write two descriptive paragraphs. You should use the descriptive guidelines to help you notice and describe different types of details. Your rough drafts will go through the revision and editing stages. (*Read the boxes below for more information about students' writing assignment.*)

Writing Assignment Box 1

Writing Assignment #29: Descriptive paragraph (First Person)

Writing topic choices: The Cow That Wanted to Be a Horse or **My Best Friend** or **Your choice of topics**

Writing Assignment Box 2

Writing Assignment #30: Descriptive paragraph (First or Third Person)

Writing topic choices: (1) **Field Trips**　　(2) **Church Camp**　　(3) **My Pastor**　　(4) **Your choice of topics**

Bonus Option: Sometimes, stories can have a hidden theme. Write a story that contains at least 15 different names of books of the Bible. Weave the names into the story so that they seem very normal. Apostrophes and other slight changes can be made when necessary.

Example: <u>John</u> *called from the* <u>King's</u> *Cafe and wanted to speak first to* <u>Timothy</u> *and then to* <u>Ruth</u> *about his job.*

Create your story and edit it carefully for mistakes. Be sure to edit the story for meaning. Do all the sentences flow together and make sense? Then, give your story to several family members to see if they can find all the books of the Bible that you incorporated in your story. (Don't forget to make a key that shows the books you used in your story so you can check it quickly.)

Read, check, and discuss Writing Assignments #29 and #30 after students have finished their final papers. Use the editing checklist as you check and discuss students' papers. Make sure students are using the editing checklist correctly.

(End of lesson.)

CHAPTER 21   LESSON 1

New objectives: Grammar (Practice Sentences), Skills (personal pronouns and their antecedents), Practice sheet, and Vocabulary #1.

JINGLE TIME

Have students turn to the Jingle Section of their books. The teacher will lead the students in reciting the previously-taught jingles.

GRAMMAR TIME

First-Year Option: Put the Practice Sentences from the box below on the board or notebook paper. Use these sentences as you practice the concepts that have been taught. For the greatest benefit, students must participate orally with the teacher. **Second-Year Option:** Have students classify the Practice Sentences independently on paper. Check students' sentences with the answers provided below. (*If you have the CDs for Practice Sentences, have students check their sentences with the CDs.*)

Chapter 21, Practice Sentences for Lesson 1

1. _____ The best spellers in our school are Bridgett and David.
2. _____ Dr. Lamb is a very important man in our community.

Question and Answer Flow for Sentence 1: The best spellers in our school are Bridgett and David.

1. Who are Bridgett and David? spellers - SN
2. What is being said about spellers? spellers are - V
3. Spellers are who? Bridgett and David - verify the nouns
4. Do Bridgett and David mean the same thing as spellers? Yes.
5. Bridgett and David - CPrN, CPrN
6. Are - LV
7. And - C
8. In - P
9. In what? school - OP
10. Whose school? our - PPA
11. What kind of spellers? best - Adj
12. The - A
13. SN LV PrN P4 Check
14. Linking verb - Check again.
15. (In our school) - Prepositional phrase
16. Period, statement, declarative sentence
17. Go back to the verb - divide the complete subject from the complete predicate.
18. Is there an adverb exception? No.
19. Is this sentence in a natural or inverted order? Natural - no change.

Classified Sentence:

$$\underset{\text{PrN P4}}{\underset{\text{SN LV}}{}}\quad \overset{\text{A Adj SN}}{\text{The best spellers}}\ \overset{\text{P PPA OP}}{\text{(in our school)}}\ /\ \overset{\text{LV CPrN C CPrN}}{\text{are Bridgett and David.}}\ \textbf{D}$$

CHAPTER 21 LESSON 1 CONTINUED

Question and Answer Flow for Sentence 2: Dr. Lamb is a very important man in our community.

1. Who is a very important man in our community?
   Dr. Lamb - SN
2. What is being said about Dr. Lamb? Dr. Lamb is - V
3. Dr. Lamb is who? man - verify the noun
4. Does man mean the same thing as Dr. Lamb? Yes.
5. Man - PrN
6. Is - LV
7. What kind of man? important - Adj
8. How important? very - Adv
9. A - A
10. In - P
11. In what? community - OP
12. Whose community? our - PPA
13. SN LV PrN P4 Check
14. Linking verb - Check again.
15. (In our community) - Prepositional phrase
16. Period, statement, declarative sentence
17. Go back to the verb - divide the complete subject from the complete predicate.
18. Is there an adverb exception? No.
19. Is this sentence in a natural or inverted order? Natural - no change.

Classified Sentence:

```
                          SN      LV A Adv    Adj     PrN P PPA   OP
           SN LV    Dr. Lamb / is a very important man (in our community). D
           PrN P4
```

Use Sentences 1 and 2 that you just classified with your students to do an Oral Skill Builder Check. Use the guidelines below.

Oral Skill Builder Check

1. **Noun check.**
   (Say the job and then say the noun. Circle each noun.)
2. **Identify the nouns as singular or plural.**
   (Write S or P above each noun.)
3. **Identify the nouns as common or proper.**
   (Follow established procedure for oral identification.)
4. **Do a vocabulary check.**
   (Follow established procedure for oral identification.)
5. **Identify the complete subject and the complete predicate.** (Underline the complete subject once and the complete predicate twice.)
6. **Identify the simple subject and simple predicate.** (Underline the simple subject once and the simple predicate twice. Bold, or highlight, the lines.)
7. **Recite the irregular verb chart.** (Located on student page 17 and teacher page 143.)

SKILL TIME

TEACHING SCRIPT FOR PERSONAL PRONOUNS AND THEIR ANTECEDENTS

You will now learn about personal pronouns and their antecedents. The more practice you have in working with pronouns and antecedents, the more likely you will be to use them correctly in your writing. The most common pronouns are known as personal pronouns. These are used to refer to yourself and to other people. You have learned most of the personal pronouns already through the subject pronoun jingle, possessive pronoun jingle, and object pronoun jingle. (*I, she, his, him, them, themselves, etc.*)

Any time a personal pronoun is used in a sentence, it usually refers to a noun or another pronoun. The noun or pronoun to which a pronoun refers is called the **antecedent** of that pronoun. The antecedent can be in the same sentence as the pronoun is, or it can be in a different sentence.

CHAPTER 21 LESSON 1 CONTINUED

Turn to page 43 and look at the two sample sentences in Reference 64. (*Read the two examples to your students: 1. The nanny fell and broke her foot. 2. The nanny fell. She somehow broke her foot.*) In the first example, the noun **nanny** is the antecedent of the pronoun **her** because the pronoun **her** refers to the noun **nanny**. In the second example, the noun **nanny** is the antecedent of the pronouns **she** and **her** because the pronouns **she** and **her** refer to the noun **nanny** in the first sentence. The second noun *foot* is not an antecedent because there is not a pronoun that refers to the noun *foot*.

Since antecedents determine the pronouns used, it is important for the pronoun to be as similar to the antecedent as possible in number and gender. The two guidelines for number and gender in Reference 64 will help you. (*Read and explain the rest of the information in Reference 64 with your students. Then, read and discuss the guided practice for antecedent agreement.*)

Reference 64: Personal Pronoun-Antecedent Agreement

      antecedent   pronoun   antecedent pronoun   pronoun
1. The *nanny* fell and broke *her* foot. 2. The *nanny* fell. *She* somehow broke *her* foot.

1. Decide if the antecedent is singular or plural, and then choose the pronoun that agrees in number.

   If the antecedent is singular, the pronoun must be singular. (man - he, him, his, etc.)
   If the antecedent is plural, the pronoun must be plural. (men - they, them, their, etc.)

2. Decide if the antecedent is male or female, and then choose the pronoun that agrees in gender.

   If the antecedent is masculine, the pronoun must be masculine gender. (boy-he)
   If the antecedent is feminine, the pronoun must be feminine gender. (girl-she)
   If the antecedent is neither masculine nor feminine, the pronoun must be neuter gender. (book-it)
   (The plural pronouns *they* and *them* also show neuter gender. The **trees** are dead. **They** burned in the fire.)

Guided Practice for Pronoun-Antecedent Agreement

Choose an answer from the pronoun choices in parentheses. Then, fill in the rest of the columns according to the titles. (S or P stands for singular or plural.)

Pronoun-Antecedent Agreement	Pronoun choice	S or P	Antecedent	S or P
1. The snake arched (<u>its</u>, their) back in self-defense.	its	S	snake	S
2. The actress stared at (<u>her</u>, their) audience lovingly.	her	S	actress	S
3. Her uncles need (his, <u>their</u>) black shoes.	their	P	uncles	P

Oral Review

To develop listening skills, give students a review of antecedent agreement orally. Repeat the nouns in bold and have students respond with the correct pronoun that would refer to the noun.

Glove—its	**Doctors**—their	**Kangaroo**—its	**Cabbage**—its
Patients—their	**Senator**—his/her	**Goalie**—his/her	**Aunt**—her
Uncle—his	**Stewardess**—her	**Groom**—his	**Patrons**—their
Packages—their	**Computer**—its	**Rivers**—their	**Manager**—his/her
Parakeet—its	**Cereal**—its	**Artist**—his/her	**Diamonds**—their
Mother—her	**Vitamins**—their	**Sister**—her	**Newspaper**—its

CHAPTER 21 LESSON 1 CONTINUED

 PRACTICE TIME

Have students turn to page 72 in the Practice Section of their book and find Chapter 21, Lesson 1, Practice. Go over the directions to make sure they understand what to do. Guide students closely as they do the practice exercises for the first time. Check and discuss the Practice after students have finished. (*Chapter 21, Lesson 1, Practice key is given below.*)

Chapter 21, Lesson 1, Practice: Choose an answer from the pronoun choices in parentheses. Fill in the other columns according to the titles. (S or P stands for singular or plural.)

Pronoun-antecedent agreement

1. The bride looked at (<u>her</u>, their) mother.
2. Dad will call at (<u>his</u>, their) convenience.
3. Margie tripped on (<u>her</u>, their) shoelaces.
4. The raccoons crowded back into (its, <u>their</u>) den.
5. My aunts got lost on (her, <u>their</u>) trip.

Pronoun Choice	S or P	Antecedent	S or P
her	S	bride	S
his	S	Dad	S
her	S	Margie	S
their	P	raccoons	P
their	P	aunts	P

 WRITING TIME

Have students make an entry in their journals.

 VOCABULARY TIME

Assign Chapter 21, Vocabulary Words **#1** on page 8 in the Reference Section for students to define in their Vocabulary notebooks. Tell students they are to use a dictionary or thesaurus to look up the meanings of the vocabulary words. After they write each word and its meaning, students are to write a sentence using the vocabulary word.

Chapter 21, Vocabulary Words #1
(brusque, diplomatic, amateur, beginner)

(End of lesson.)

CHAPTER 21   LESSON 2

New objectives: Grammar (Practice Sentences), Practice sheet, and Vocabulary #2.

JINGLE TIME

Have students turn to the Jingle Section of their books. The teacher will lead the students in reciting the previously-taught jingles.

GRAMMAR TIME

First-Year Option: Put the Practice Sentences from the box below on the board or notebook paper. Use these sentences as you practice the concepts that have been taught. For the greatest benefit, students must participate orally with the teacher. **Second-Year Option:** Have students classify the Practice Sentences independently on paper. Check students' sentences with the answers provided below. (*If you have the CDs for Practice Sentences, have students check their sentences with the CDs.*)

Chapter 21, Practice Sentences for Lesson 2
1. _____ The turbulent weather was the source of many sleepless nights for the weather forecaster. 2. _____ New England is the former residence and burial place of Robert Frost.

Question and Answer Flow for Sentence 1: The turbulent weather was the source of many sleepless nights for the weather forecaster.

1. What was the source of many sleepless nights for the weather forecaster? weather - SN
2. What is being said about weather? weather was - V
3. Weather was what? source - verify the noun
4. Does source mean the same thing as weather? Yes.
5. Source - PrN
6. Was - LV
7. The - A
8. Of - P
9. Of what? nights - OP
10. What kind of nights? sleepless - Adj
11. How many nights? many - Adj
12. For - P
13. For whom? forecaster - OP
14. What kind of forecaster? weather - Adj
15. The - A
16. What kind of weather? turbulent - Adj
17. The - A
18. SN LV PrN P4 Check
19. Linking verb - Check again.
20. (Of many sleepless nights) - Prepositional phrase
21. (For the weather forecaster) - Prepositional phrase
22. Period, statement, declarative sentence
23. Go back to the verb - divide the complete subject from the complete predicate.
24. Is there an adverb exception? No.
25. Is this sentence in a natural or inverted order? Natural - no change.

Classified
Sentence:

	A	Adj	SN		LV	A	PrN	P	Adj	Adj	OP	P	A	Adj
<u>SN LV</u>	The	turbulent	weather	/	was	the	source	(of	many	sleepless	nights)	(for	the	weather

PrN P4   OP

forecaster). **D**

CHAPTER 21 LESSON 2 CONTINUED

Question and Answer Flow for Sentence 2: New England is the former residence and burial place of Robert Frost.

1. What is the former residence and burial place of Robert Frost? New England - SN
2. What is being said about New England? New England is - V
3. New England is what? residence and place - verify the nouns
4. Do residence and place mean the same thing as New England? Yes.
5. Residence and place - CPrN, CPrN
6. Is - LV
7. What kind of residence? former - Adj
8. The - A
9. And - C
10. What kind of place? burial - Adj
11. Of - P
12. Of whom? Robert Frost - OP
13. SN LV PrN P4 Check
14. Linking verb - Check again.
15. (Of Robert Frost) - Prepositional phrase
16. Period, statement, declarative sentence
17. Go back to the verb - divide the complete subject from the complete predicate.
18. Is there an adverb exception? No.
19. Is this sentence in a natural or inverted order? Natural - no change.

Classified Sentence:

```
                          SN        LV  A   Adj    CPrN    C  Adj CPrN  P    OP
           SN  LV    New England / is the former residence and burial place (of Robert Frost).  D
           PrN P4
```

TEACHER INSTRUCTIONS FOR A PATTERN 4 PRACTICE SENTENCE

Tell students that their sentence writing assignment today is to write a Pattern 4 Practice Sentence. They are to follow the same procedure used in the previous lessons. They should decide on their labels, arrange them in a selected order, write their sentence, and edit the sentence for improved word choices. (*Students do not have to write an Improved Sentence at this point unless you feel they need more one-on-one word choice writing practice.*) Check and discuss the Pattern 4 Practice Sentence after students have finished.

 PRACTICE TIME

Students will continue identifying verb tenses and regular/irregular verbs. Have students turn to page 73 in the Practice Section of their book and find Chapter 21, Lesson 2, Practice. Go over the directions to make sure they understand what to do. If students need a review, have them study the information and examples of quotations in the Reference Section of their book. Check and discuss the Practice after students have finished. (*Chapter 21, Lesson 2, Practice key is given below.*)

Chapter 21, Lesson 2, Practice: Choose an answer from the choices in parentheses. Fill in the other columns according to the titles. (S or P stands for singular or plural.)

Pronoun-antecedent agreement

1. One member of the band dropped (<u>his</u>, their) oboe.
2. The antiques had no prices on (it, <u>them</u>).
3. The senator offered (<u>his</u>, their) resignation.
4. The trainees raised (his/her, <u>their</u>) hands.
5. The farmer wrapped (<u>his</u>, their) bales of hay.
6. The postman made (<u>his</u>, their) rounds early.

Pronoun Choice	S or P	Antecedent	S or P
his	S	member	S
them	P	antiques	P
his	S	senator	S
their	P	trainees	P
his	S	farmer	S
his	S	postman	S

CHAPTER 21 LESSON 2 CONTINUED

 WRITING TIME

Have students make an entry in their journals.

 VOCABULARY TIME

Assign Chapter 21, Vocabulary Words **#2** on page 8 in the Reference Section for students to define in their Vocabulary notebooks. Tell students they are to use a dictionary or thesaurus to look up the meanings of the vocabulary words. After they write each word and its meaning, students are to write a sentence using the vocabulary word.

Chapter 21, Vocabulary Words #2
(superficial, genuine, aggressive, hostile)

(End of lesson.)

CHAPTER 21   LESSON 3

New objectives: Grammar (Practice Sentences) and a Practice sheet.

JINGLE TIME

Have students turn to the Jingle Section of their books. The teacher will lead the students in reciting the previously-taught jingles.

GRAMMAR TIME

First-Year Option: Put the Practice Sentences from the box below on the board or notebook paper. Use these sentences as you practice the concepts that have been taught. For the greatest benefit, students must participate orally with the teacher. **Second-Year Option:** Have students classify the Practice Sentences independently on paper. Check students' sentences with the answers provided below. (*If you have the CDs for Practice Sentences, have students check their sentences with the CDs.*)

Chapter 21, Practice Sentences for Lesson 3
1. _____ The crunchy stuff in the salad is sunflower seeds from the salad bar.
2. _____ The best chemistry students in the class are Tami and Matt.

Question and Answer Flow for Sentence 1: The crunchy stuff in the salad is sunflower seeds from the salad bar.

1. What is sunflower seeds from the salad bar? stuff - SN
2. What is being said about stuff? stuff is - V
3. Stuff is what? seeds - verify the noun
4. Do seeds mean the same thing as stuff? Yes.
5. Seeds - PrN
6. Is - LV
7. What kind of seeds? sunflower - Adj
8. From - P
9. From what? bar - OP
10. What kind of bar? salad - Adj
11. The - A
12. In - P
13. In what? salad - OP
14. The - A
15. What kind of stuff? crunchy - Adj
16. The - A
17. SN LV PrN P4 Check
18. Linking verb - Check again.
19. (In the salad) - Prepositional phrase
20. (From the salad bar) - Prepositional phrase
21. Period, statement, declarative sentence
22. Go back to the verb - divide the complete subject from the complete predicate.
23. Is there an adverb exception? No.
24. Is this sentence in a natural or inverted order? Natural - no change.

Classified Sentence:

		A	Adj	SN	P	A	OP	LV	Adj	PrN	P	A	Adj	OP
SN	LV	The	crunchy	stuff	(in	the	salad)	/ is	sunflower	seeds	(from	the	salad	bar). D
PrN	P4													

CHAPTER 21 LESSON 3 CONTINUED

Question and Answer Flow for Sentence 2: The best chemistry students in the class are Tami and Matt.

1. Who are Tami and Matt? students - SN
2. What is being said about students? students are - V
3. Students are who? Tami and Matt - verify the nouns
4. Do Tami and Matt mean the same thing as students? Yes.
5. Tami and Matt - CPrN, CPrN
6. Are - LV
7. And - C
8. In - P
9. In what? class - OP
10. The - A
11. What kind of students? chemistry - Adj

12. What kind of students? best - Adj
13. The - A
14. SN LV PrN P4 Check
15. Linking verb - Check again.
16. (In the class) - Prepositional phrase
17. Period, statement, declarative sentence
18. Go back to the verb - divide the complete subject from the complete predicate.
19. Is there an adverb exception? No.
20. Is this sentence in a natural or inverted order? Natural - no change.

Classified Sentence:

           A   Adj   Adj   SN   P A   OP   LV CPrN C CPrN
 SN LV   The best chemistry students (in the class) / are Tami and Matt. **D**
 PrN P4

 PRACTICE TIME

Students will continue their practice of skills. Have students turn to page 73 in the Practice Section of their books and find Chapter 21, Lesson 3, Practice. Go over the directions to make sure they understand what to do. If students need a review, have them study the information and examples in the Reference Section of their books. Check and discuss the Practice after students have finished. (*Chapter 21,Lesson 3, Practice key is given below.*)

Chapter 21, Lesson 3, Practice: Choose an answer from the choices in parentheses. Fill in the other columns according to the titles. (S or P stands for singular or plural.)

Pronoun-antecedent agreement	Pronoun Choice	S or P	Antecedent	S or P
1. The players misplaced (his, <u>their</u>) helmets.	their	P	players	P
2. Something in the hole stuck (<u>its</u>, their) tongue out.	its	S	something	S
3. The pilots got (its, <u>their</u>) way at contract time.	their	P	pilots	P
4. The comedian displayed (<u>his</u>, their) natural wit.	his	S	comedian	S
5. My sister lost (<u>her</u>, their) bracelet at the zoo.	her	S	sister	S
6. The lobster attacked with (<u>its</u>, their) claws.	its	S	lobster	S
7. The soldiers lost (his/her, <u>their</u>) way.	their	P	soldiers	P
8. My mattress has lost (<u>its</u>, their) firmness.	its	S	mattress	S
9. The deacon gave (<u>his</u>, their) testimony.	his	S	deacon	S
10. Azaleas in the front yard lost (its, <u>their</u>) luster.	their	P	Azaleas	P

(End of lesson.)

CHAPTER 21   LESSON 4

New objectives: Test and an Activity.

JINGLE TIME

Have students turn to the Jingle Section of their books. The teacher will lead the students in reciting the previously-taught jingles.

STUDY TIME

Have students study the vocabulary words in their vocabulary notebooks. Remind students that any vocabulary word in their notebooks could be on their test. Also, have students study any of the skills in the Practice Section that they need to review.

TEST TIME

Have students turn to page 104 in the Test Section of their books and find Chapter 21 Test. Remind them to pay attention and think about what they are doing. Go over the directions to make sure they understand what to do. (*Chapter 21 Test key is on the next page.*)

CHECK TIME

After students have finished, check and discuss their test papers. Make sure they understand why their answers are right or wrong. (*For total points, count each required answer as a point.*)

ACTIVITY / ASSIGNMENT TIME

Have students write a song from memory that they like. Have them sing the song or make up a new song that is funny or describes how they feel about something.

(End of lesson.)

Chapter 21 Test
(Student Page 104)

Exercise 1: Classify each sentence.

	PPA	PNA	Adj	Adj	SN	LV A	Adj	PrN	

1. **SN LV** My uncle's impressive stamp collection / is a noteworthy item. **D**
   PrN P4

        CSN   C   CSN   LV Adj   PrN   P Adj PPA OP

2. **SN LV** Meat and vegetables / are essential ingredients (of all our meals). **D**
   PrN P4

Exercise 2: Identify each pair of words as synonyms or antonyms by putting parentheses ( ) around *syn* or *ant*.

1. diligent, negligent	syn **(ant)**	4. brusque, diplomatic	syn **(ant)**	7. enunciation, pronounce	**(syn)** ant
2. deception, candor	syn **(ant)**	5. superficial, genuine	syn **(ant)**	8. camouflage, conceal	**(syn)** ant
3. aggressive, hostile	**(syn)** ant	6. amateur, beginner	**(syn)** ant	9. melodramatic, subdued	syn **(ant)**

Exercise 3: Choose an answer from the choices in parentheses. Fill in the other columns according to the titles. (S or P stands for singular or plural.)

Pronoun-antecedent agreement

	Pronoun Choice	S or P	Antecedent	S or P
1. The books on the shelves are missing (its, <u>their</u>) dust jackets.	their	P	books	P
2. His petition for a repeal lost (<u>its</u>, their) appeal.	its	S	petition	S
3. The foreign missionaries lost (his, <u>their</u>) plane tickets.	their	P	missionaries	P
4. Ultimately, the fever ran (<u>its</u>, their) course.	its	S	fever	S

Exercise 4: Underline the negative words in each sentence. Rewrite each sentence and correct the double negative mistake as indicated by the rule number in parentheses at the end of the sentence.

Rule 1	**Rule 2**	**Rule 3**
Change the second negative to a positive.	Take out the negative part of a contraction.	Remove the first negative word (verb change).

1. She <u>didn't</u> want <u>no</u> sympathy. (Rule 3)
   She wanted no sympathy.

2. They <u>don't</u> <u>never</u> take a lunch break. (Rule 3)
   They never take a lunch break.

3. He <u>wasn't</u> <u>never</u> unruly. (Rule 2)
   He was never unruly.

4. Mom <u>didn't</u> get <u>no</u> bread at the store. (Rule 1)
   Mom didn't get any bread at the store.

Exercise 5: On a sheet of paper, write three sentences, demonstrating each of the three degrees of adjectives. Identify the form you used by writing **simple, comparative,** or **superlative** at the end of each sentence.

Exercise 6: On a sheet of paper, write three sentences in which you demonstrate each of the double negative rules. Underline the negative word in each sentence.

Exercise 7: Write the seven present tense helping verbs, the five past tense helping verbs, and the two future tense helping verbs. **The order of the answers may vary.** (Present: am, is, are, has, have, do, does; Past: was, were, had, did, been; Future: will, shall)

Exercise 8: On a sheet of paper, write one sentence for each of these labels: ① (S) ② (SCS) ③ (SCV) ④(CD) ⑤(CX). (Answers will vary.)

Exercise 9: In your journal, write a paragraph summarizing what you have learned this week.

CHAPTER 21 LESSON 4 CONTINUED

TEACHER INSTRUCTIONS

Use the Question and Answer Flows below for the sentences on Chapter 21 Tests.

Question and Answer Flow for Sentence 1: My uncle's impressive stamp collection is a noteworthy item.

1. What is a noteworthy item? collection - SN
2. What is being said about collection? collection is - V
3. Collection is what? item - verify the noun
4. Does item mean the same thing as collection? Yes.
5. Item - PrN
6. Is - LV
7. What kind of item? noteworthy - Adj
8. A - A
9. What kind of collection? stamp - Adj
10. What kind of collection? impressive - Adj
11. Whose collection? Uncle's - PNA
12. Whose uncle? my - PPA
13. SN LV PrN P4 Check
14. Linking verb - Check again.
15. No prepositional phrases.
16. Period, statement, declarative sentence
17. Go back to the verb - divide the complete subject from the complete predicate.
18. Is there an adverb exception? No.
19. Is this sentence in a natural or inverted order? Natural - no change.

Classified Sentence:

	PPA	PNA	Adj	Adj	SN	LV	A	Adj	PrN
SN LV	My	uncle's	impressive	stamp	collection /	is	a	noteworthy	item. **D**
PrN P4									

Question and Answer Flow for Sentence 2: Meat and vegetables are essential ingredients of all our meals.

1. What are essential ingredients of all our meals? meat and vegetables - CSN, CSN
2. What is being said about meat and vegetables? meat and vegetables are - V
3. Meat and vegetables are what? Ingredients - verify the noun
4. Do ingredients mean the same thing as meat and vegetables? Yes.
5. Ingredients - PrN
6. Are - LV
7. Which ingredients? essential - Adj
8. Of - P
9. Of what? meals - OP
10. Whose meals? our - PPA
11. How many meals? all - Adj
12. And - C
13. SN LV PrN P4 Check
14. Linking verb - Check again.
15. (Of all our meals) - Prepositional phrase
16. Period, statement, declarative sentence
17. Go back to the verb - divide the complete subject from the complete predicate.
18. Is there an adverb exception? No.
19. Is this sentence in a natural or inverted order? Natural - no change.

Classified Sentence:

	CSN	C	CSN	LV	Adj	PrN	P	Adj	PPA	OP
SN LV	Meat	and	vegetables /	are	essential	ingredients	(of	all	our	meals). **D**
PrN P4										

CHAPTER 21   LESSON 5

New objectives: Writing Assignments #31 and #32, Bonus Option.

 WRITING TIME

TEACHING SCRIPT FOR WRITING ASSIGNMENTS

Today, you are assigned two different kinds of writing. You will write a five-paragraph persuasive essay and a descriptive paragraph. <u>You will revise and edit the five-paragraph persuasive essay.</u> (*Read the box below for more information about students' writing assignment.*) As you edit, make sure you use the checkpoints in the editing checklist. Remember to read through the whole essay, starting with the title, and then edit, sentence-by-sentence, using the five-sentence checkpoints for each sentence. Use the paragraph checkpoints to check each paragraph. Remember, your editing is now more detailed and more comprehensive, so take your time.

Writing Assignment Box #1

Writing Assignment #31: Five-Paragraph Persuasive Essay (First or Third Person)
(Remember, first person pronouns are *I, we, me, us, my, our, mine,* and *ours.*)
Remind students that the 5-paragraph essay has three parts: 1. Introduction 2. Body 3. Conclusion. The body has three paragraphs instead of one. Have students use their regular editing checklist to edit this assignment.

Writing topic: Why a Firm Handshake Is Important or **Why I Think _____ Is an Admirable Person**

Your second writing assignment is to write a descriptive paragraph. (*Read the box below for more information about students' writing assignment.*) You do not have to edit this assignment with the editing checklist.

Writing Assignment Box #2

Writing Assignment #32: Descriptive paragraph (First or Third Person)

Writing topic choices: My Dad Asleep in His Chair or **My Best Friend's Personality** or **Your choice of topics**

Bonus Option: Write all the scriptures you have memorized in your Journal. Have family members give you hints to help you remember as many as possible. From which book of the Bible have you memorized the most verses? Compare your memorized list with lists from other family members or friends. Make a list of scripture you want to memorize in the future. Memorize at least two of these verses to recite next week. Record the date in your Journal to see how long it takes you.

Read, check, and discuss Writing Assignment #31 after students have finished their final papers. Use the checklists as you check and discuss students' papers. Make sure students are using the regular editing checklist correctly. Read and discuss Writing Assignment #32 for fun and enrichment.

(End of lesson.)

CHAPTER 22   LESSON 1

New objectives: Grammar (Introductory Sentences, Mixed Patterns), Vocabulary #1, and an Activity.

 JINGLE TIME

Have students turn to the Jingle Section of their books. The teacher will lead the students in reciting the previously-taught jingles.

 GRAMMAR TIME

Put the introductory sentences from the box below on the board. Use these sentences as you go through each new concept covered in your teaching script. (*You might put the introductory sentences on notebook paper if you are doing one-on-one instruction with your students.*)

Chapter 22, Introductory Sentences for Lesson 1
1. _____ The huge freight train traveled swiftly along the tracks through our town.   2. _____ Teresa provided comfort to the soldiers and bandaged the wounds of the injured.   3. _____ The types of meats in the freezer are beef, chicken, pork, and venison.

TEACHING SCRIPT FOR INTRODUCING MIXED PATTERNS

You have studied each sentence pattern separately. Today, we will mix up the patterns in a set of sentences. You must decide if a sentence is a Pattern 1, Pattern 2, Pattern 3, or Pattern 4. Then, you should write the correct pattern in the blank after you classify the sentence. Remember, the three sentences can be any pattern, 1-4.

We will classify the three sentences to practice identifying the different sentence patterns. Begin. (*Students could write the labels above the sentences at this time.*)

Question and Answer Flow for Sentence 1: The huge freight train traveled swiftly along the tracks through our town.

1. What traveled swiftly along the tracks through our town? train - SN
2. What is being said about train? train traveled - V
3. Traveled how? swiftly - Adv
4. Along - P
5. Along what? tracks - OP
6. The - A
7. Through - P
8. Through what? town - OP
9. Whose town? our - PPA
10. What kind of train? freight - Adj
11. What kind of train? huge - Adj
12. The - A
13. SN V P1 Check
14. (Along the tracks) - Prepositional phrase
15. (Through our town) - Prepositional phrase
16. Period, statement, declarative sentence
17. Go back to the verb - divide the complete subject from the complete predicate.
18. Is there an adverb exception? No.
19. Is this sentence in a natural or inverted order? Natural - no change.

Classified Sentence:

	A	Adj	Adj	SN	V	Adv	P	A	OP	P	PPA	OP
SN V P1	The	huge	freight	train /	traveled	swiftly	(along	the	tracks)	(through	our	town). D

CHAPTER 22 LESSON 1 CONTINUED

Question and Answer Flow for Sentence 2: Teresa provided comfort to the soldiers and bandaged the wounds of the injured.

1. Who provided comfort to the soldiers and bandaged the wounds of the injured? Teresa - SN
2. What is being said about Teresa? Teresa provided and bandaged - CV, CV
3. Teresa provided what? comfort - verify the noun
4. Does comfort mean the same thing as Teresa? No.
5. Comfort - DO
6. Provided - CV-t
7. Teresa bandaged what? wounds - verify the noun
8. Do wounds mean the same thing as Teresa? No.
9. Wounds - DO
10. Bandaged - CV-t
11. The - A
12. Of - P
13. Of whom? injured - OP
14. The - A

15. And - C
16. To - P
17. To whom? soldiers - OP
18. The - A
19. SN V-t DO P2 Check
20. Verb-transitive - Check again.
21. (To the soldiers) - Prepositional phrase
22. (Of the injured) - Prepositional phrase
23. Period, statement, declarative sentence
24. Go back to the verb - divide the complete subject from the complete predicate.
25. Is there an adverb exception? No.
26. Is this sentence in a natural or inverted order? Natural - no change.

Classified	SN	CV-t	DO	P	A	OP	C	CV-t	A	DO	P	A	OP
Sentence:													

SN V-t DO P2   Teresa / provided comfort (to the soldiers) and bandaged the wounds (of the injured). **D**

Question and Answer Flow for Sentence 3: The types of meats in the freezer are beef, poultry, pork, and venison.

1. What are beef, poultry, pork, and venison? types - SN
2. What is being said about types? types are - V
3. Types are what? beef, poultry, pork, and venison - verify the nouns
4. Do beef, poultry, pork, and venison mean the same thing as types? Yes.
5. Beef, poultry, pork, and venison - CPrN, CPrN, CPrN, CPrN
6. Are - LV
7. And - C
8. In - P
9. In what? freezer - OP
10. The - A

11. Of - P
12. Of what? meats - OP
13. The - A
14. SN LV PrN P4 Check
15. Linking verb - Check again.
16. (Of meats) - Prepositional phrase
17. (In the freezer) - Prepositional phrase
18. Period, statement, declarative sentence
19. Go back to the verb - divide the complete subject from the complete predicate.
20. Is there an adverb exception? No.
21. Is this sentence in a natural or inverted order? Natural - no change.

Classified Sentence:	A	SN	P	OP	P	A	OP	LV	CPrN	CPrN	CPrN	C	CPrN

SN LV PrN P4   The types (of meats) (in the freezer) / are beef, poultry, pork, and venison. **D**

Use Sentences 1-3 that you just classified with your students to do an Oral Skill Builder Check.

Oral Skill Builder Check

1. **Noun check.**
   (Say the job and then say the noun. Circle each noun.)
2. **Identify the nouns as singular or plural.**
   (Write S or P above each noun.)
3. **Identify the nouns as common or proper.**
   (Follow established procedure for oral identification.)
4. **Do a vocabulary check.**
   (Follow established procedure for oral identification.)

5. **Identify the complete subject and the complete predicate.** (Underline the complete subject once and the complete predicate twice.)
6. **Identify the simple subject and simple predicate.** (Underline the simple subject once and the simple predicate twice. Bold, or highlight, the lines.)
7. **Recite the irregular verb chart.** (Located on student page 17 and teacher page 143.)

CHAPTER 22 LESSON 1 CONTINUED

WRITING TIME

Have students make an entry in their journals.

VOCABULARY TIME

Assign Chapter 22, Vocabulary Words **#1** on page 8 in the Reference Section for students to define in their Vocabulary notebooks. Tell students they are to use a dictionary or thesaurus to look up the meanings of the vocabulary words. After they write each word and its meaning, students are to write a sentence using the vocabulary word.

Chapter 22, Vocabulary Words #1
(summit, base, attire, apparel)

ACTIVITY / ASSIGNMENT TIME

You are a well-known developer. You must decide what million-dollar project you will develop for your state. You will be presenting your project to the state planning committee (your family and/or friends.) You must include a written description of the project, an illustration of the project, and a cost estimate of the project. (*Check with family members for estimated cost or look it up on the Internet.*)

Draw pictures to illustrate your project. These pictures will be used during your presentation. Good luck at the presentation! (*Students will share their projects in Chapter 23 during Lesson 4.*)

(End of lesson.)

CHAPTER 22   LESSON 2

New objectives: Grammar (Practice Sentences, the difference between action verbs and linking verbs), Practice sheet, and Vocabulary #2.

 JINGLE TIME

Have students turn to the Jingle Section of their books. The teacher will lead the students in reciting the previously-taught jingles.

 GRAMMAR TIME

First-Year Option: Put the Practice Sentences from the box below on the board or notebook paper. Use these sentences as you practice the concepts that have been taught. For the greatest benefit, students must participate orally with the teacher. **Second-Year Option:** Have students classify the Practice Sentences independently on paper. Check students' sentences with the answers provided below. (*If you have the CDs for Practice Sentences, have students check their sentences with the CDs.*)

Chapter 22, Practice Sentences for Lesson 2

1. _____ The proud coach showed them the trophy case during their tour.
2. _____ My friend's sister scheduled a long vacation in the Bahamas.
3. _____ The famous author rose from her chair and bowed to the audience.

TEACHING SCRIPT FOR PRACTICING MIXED PATTERNS

We will practice classifying Mixed Patterns. We will classify the sentences together. Begin. (*You might have your students write the labels above the sentences at this time.*)

Question and Answer Flow for Sentence 1: The proud coach showed them the trophy case during their tour.

1. Who showed them the trophy case during their tour? coach - SN
2. What is being said about coach? coach showed - V
3. Coach showed what? case - verify the noun
4. Does case mean the same thing as coach? No.
5. Case - DO
6. Showed - V-t
7. Coach showed case to whom? them - IO
8. What kind of case? trophy - Adj
9. The - A
10. During - P
11. During what? tour - OP

12. Whose tour? their - PPA
13. What kind of coach? proud - Adj
14. The - A
15. SN V-t IO DO P3 Check
16. Verb-transitive - Check again.
17. (During their tour) - Prepositional phrase
18. Period, statement, declarative sentence
19. Go back to the verb - divide the complete subject from the complete predicate.
20. Is there an adverb exception? No.
21. Is this sentence in a natural or inverted order? Natural - no change.

Classified Sentence:

          A Adj   SN   V-t   IO   A Adj   DO   P   PPA OP
SN V-t   The proud coach / showed them the trophy case (during their tour). **D**
IO DO P3

Question and Answer Flow for Sentence 2: My friend's sister scheduled a long vacation in the Bahamas.

1. Who scheduled a long vacation in the Bahamas?
   sister - SN
2. What is being said about sister? sister scheduled - V
3. Sister scheduled what? vacation - verify the noun
4. Does vacation mean the same thing as sister? No.
5. Vacation - DO
6. Scheduled - V-t
7. What kind of vacation? long - Adj
8. A - A
9. In - P
10. In what? Bahamas - OP
11. The - A

12. Whose sister? friend's - PNA
13. Whose friend? my - PPA
14. SN V-t DO P2 Check
15. Verb-transitive - Check again.
16. (In the Bahamas) - Prepositional phrase
17. Period, statement, declarative sentence
18. Go back to the verb - divide the complete subject from the complete predicate.
19. Is there an adverb exception? No.
20. Is this sentence in a natural or inverted order? Natural - no change.

Classified Sentence:

		PPA	PNA	SN	V-t	A	Adj	DO	P	A	OP

SN V-t / DO P2

My friend's sister /scheduled a long vacation (in the Bahamas). **D**

Question and Answer Flow for Sentence 3: The famous author rose from her chair and bowed to the audience.

1. Who rose from her chair and bowed to the audience?
   author - SN
2. What is being said about author? author rose and bowed - CV, CV
3. To - P
4. To whom? audience - OP
5. The - A
6. And - C
7. From - P
8. From what? chair - OP
9. Whose chair? her - PPA

10. What kind of author? famous - Adj
11. The - A
12. SN V P1 Check
13. (From her chair) - Prepositional phrase
14. (To the audience) - Prepositional phrase
15. Period, statement, declarative sentence
16. Go back to the verb - divide the complete subject from the complete predicate.
17. Is there an adverb exception? No.
18. Is this sentence in a natural or inverted order? Natural - no change.

Classified Sentence:

A Adj SN CV P PPA OP C CV P A OP

SN V / P1

The famous author / rose (from her chair) and bowed (to the audience). **D**

TEACHER INSTRUCTIONS FOR A PRACTICE SENTENCE

Tell students that their sentence writing assignment today is to write a sentence pattern of their choice. They may choose any Pattern, 1-5, for a Practice Sentence. They are to follow the same procedure used in the previous lessons. They should decide on their labels, arrange them in a selected order, write their sentence, and edit the sentence for improved word choices. (*Students do not have to write an Improved Sentence at this point unless you feel they need more one-on-one word choice writing practice.*) Check and discuss the sentence pattern chosen after students have finished.

TEACHING SCRIPT FOR THE DIFFERENCE BETWEEN ACTION VERBS AND LINKING VERBS

The verbs that you have studied in Patterns 1-3 are action verbs because they show what the subjects do. Today, you will continue your study of the linking verb. Remember, the linking verb does not show action. The linking verb does exactly what its name says it does: it links or connects the subject to a word in the predicate.

CHAPTER 22 LESSON 2 CONTINUED

You have already studied predicate nouns and linking verbs. It is time to learn more information about linking verbs. Turn to Reference 65 on page 44 in the Reference Section of your book. Follow along as I read additional information about the two kinds of verbs.

Reference 65: The Difference Between Action Verbs and Linking Verbs

An action verb shows action. It tells what the subject does. A linking verb does not show action. It does not tell what the subject does. A linking verb is called a state of being verb because it tells **what the subject is or is like**. To decide if a verb is linking or action, remember these two things:

1. A linking verb may have a noun in the predicate that means the same thing as the subject:

To show what the subject **is** means the linking verb connects the subject to a noun in the predicate that means the same thing as the subject. This noun is called a predicate noun and is identified with the abbreviation **PrN**.

SN LV PrN	SP LV PrN	SN LV PrN	SN LV PrN
Arnold **was** a (gymnast).	She **is** a (teacher).	The tour **is** an (education).	His car **was** a (jalopy).

2. A linking verb may also have an adjective in the predicate that tells what kind of subject it is:

To show what the subject **is like** means the linking verb connects the subject to an adjective in the predicate that tells what kind of subject it is. This adjective is called a predicate adjective and is identified with the abbreviation **PA**. *(What kind of dog? hungry – PA) (What kind of boat? expensive – PA) (What kind of cheese? moldy – PA)*

SN LV PA	SN LV PA	SN LV PA	SN LV PA
That dog **is** (hungry).	The boat **was** (expensive).	The cheese **is** (moldy).	The roads **are** (crooked).

These are the most common linking verbs: *am, is, are, was, were, be, been, seem, become.*

These sensory verbs can be linking or action: *taste, sound, smell, feel, look.*

Good rule to follow: If a sentence has a predicate noun (PrN) or a predicate adjective (PA), it has a linking verb. If a sentence does not have a predicate noun (PrN) or a predicate adjective (PA), it has an action verb.

Example: Underline each subject and fill in each column according to the title.

	List each Verb	Write PrN, PA, or None	Write L or A
1. The groceries are heavy.	are	PA	L
2. An apricot is a fruit.	is	PrN	L
3. The gnat buzzed in my ear.	buzzed	None	A

 PRACTICE TIME

Have students turn to page 74 in the Practice Section of their book and find the instructions under Chapter 22, Lesson 2, Practice. Go over the directions to make sure they understand what to do. If students need a review, have them study the information and examples in the Reference Section of their books. Check and discuss the Practice after students have finished. *(Chapter 22, Lesson 2, Practice key is on the next page.)*

CHAPTER 22 LESSON 2 CONTINUED

Chapter 22, Lesson 2, Practice: Underline each subject and fill in each column according to the title.

	List each Verb	Write PrN, PA, or None	Write L or A
1. <u>Grapes</u> are expensive.	are	PA	L
2. Those <u>details</u> are important.	are	PA	L
3. His <u>passport</u> is lost.	is	PA	L
4. <u>We</u> ate at the diner today.	ate	None	A
5. <u>Hawaii</u> is our fiftieth state.	is	PrN	L
6. <u>Patience</u> is a virtue.	is	PrN	L
7. The <u>answer</u> is too vague.	is	PA	L
8. <u>I</u> called him late last night.	called	None	A
9. <u>We</u> left the car at the airport.	left	None	A
10. <u>Toby</u> was totally surprised.	was	PA	L
11. <u>Aspirin</u> relieved his headache.	relieved	None	A
12. The <u>judges</u> were clearly impartial.	were	PA	L
13. <u>She</u> painted the foyer gold.	painted	None	A
14. <u>He</u> believes in ghosts.	believes	None	A
15. <u>Charlie</u> is my hero.	is	PrN	L

VOCABULARY TIME

Assign Chapter 22, Vocabulary Words **#2** on page 8 in the Reference Section for students to define in their Vocabulary notebooks. After they write each word and its meaning, students are to write a sentence using the vocabulary word.

Chapter 22, Vocabulary Words #2
(repeal, pass, chaperon, escort)

(End of lesson.)

CHAPTER 22 LESSON 3

New objectives: Grammar (Practice Sentences), Skills (forming plurals of nouns with different endings), and a Practice sheet.

 JINGLE TIME

Have students turn to the Jingle Section of their books. The teacher will lead the students in reciting the previously-taught jingles.

 GRAMMAR TIME

First-Year Option: Put the Practice Sentences from the box below on the board or notebook paper. Use these sentences as you practice the concepts that have been taught. For the greatest benefit, students must participate orally with the teacher. **Second-Year Option:** Have students classify the Practice Sentences independently on paper. Check students' sentences with the answers provided below. (*If you have the CDs for Practice Sentences, have students check their sentences with the CDs.*)

Chapter 22, Practice Sentences for Lesson 3
1. _____ Draw me two birds with feathers.
2. _____ The microwave is a valuable invention for the fast-food industry.
3. _____ The impaired soldier gingerly climbed the hill to the nearest highway.

TEACHING SCRIPT FOR PRACTICING MIXED PATTERNS

We will practice classifying Mixed Patterns. We will classify the sentences together. Begin. (*You might have your students write the labels above the sentences at this time.*)

Question and Answer Flow for Sentence 1: Draw me two birds with feathers.

1. Who draw me two birds with feathers?
   (You) - SP (Understood subject pronoun)
2. What is being said about you? you draw - V
3. You draw what? birds - verify the noun
4. Do birds mean the same thing as you? No.
5. Birds - DO
6. Draw - V-t
7. You draw birds for whom? me - IO
8. How many birds? two - Adj
9. With - P
10. With what? feathers - OP

11. SN V-t IO DO P3 Check
12. Verb-transitive Check again.
13. (With feathers) - Prepositional phrase
14. Period, command, imperative sentence
15. Go back to the verb - divide the complete subject from the complete predicate.
16. Is there an adverb exception? No.
17. Is this sentence in a natural or inverted order? Natural - no change.

Classified Sentence:

    (You) SP   V-t IO Adj DO   P   OP
    SN V-t   / Draw me two birds (with feathers). Imp
    IO DO P3

CHAPTER 22 LESSON 3 CONTINUED

Question and Answer Flow for Sentence 2: The microwave is a valuable invention for the fast-food industry.

1. What is a valuable invention for the fast-food industry? microwave - SN
2. What is being said about microwave? microwave is - V
3. Microwave is what? invention - verify the noun
4. Does invention mean the same thing as microwave? Yes.
5. Invention - PrN
6. Is - LV
7. What kind of invention? valuable - Adj
8. A - A
9. For - P
10. For what? industry - OP
11. What kind of industry? fast-food - Adj
12. The – A
13. The –A
14. SN LV PrN P4 Check
15. Linking verb - Check again.
16. (For the fast-food industry) - Prepositional phrase
17. Period, statement, declarative sentence
18. Go back to the verb - divide the complete subject from the complete predicate.
19. Is there an adverb exception? No.
20. Is this sentence in a natural or inverted order? Natural - no change.

Classified Sentence:

```
                      A     SN    LV A  Adj     PrN      P A    Adj      OP
        SN LV         The microwave / is a valuable invention (for the fast-food industry).  D
        PrN P4
```

Question and Answer Flow for Sentence 3: The impaired soldier gingerly climbed the hill to the nearest highway.

1. Who climbed the hill to the nearest highway? soldier - SN
2. What is being said about soldier? soldier climbed - V
3. Soldier climbed what? hill - verify the noun
4. Does hill mean the same thing as soldier? No.
5. Hill - DO
6. Climbed - V-t
7. The - A
8. To - P
9. To what? highway - OP
10. Which highway? nearest - Adj
11. The - A
12. Climbed how? gingerly - Adv
13. What kind of soldier? impaired - Adj
14. The - A
15. SN V-t DO P2 Check
16. Verb-transitive - Check again.
17. (To the nearest highway) - Prepositional phrase
18. Period, statement, declarative sentence
19. Go back to the verb - divide the complete subject from the complete predicate.
20. Is there an adverb exception? Yes - change the line.
21. Is this sentence in a natural or inverted order? Natural - no change.

Classified Sentence:

```
                      A   Adj    SN    Adv     V-t   A  DO  P A  Adj     OP
        SN V-t        The impaired soldier / gingerly climbed the hill (to the nearest highway).  D
        DO P2
```

SKILL TIME

TEACHING SCRIPT FOR HOW TO FORM THE PLURALS OF NOUNS WITH DIFFERENT ENDINGS

Today, we will learn how to form the plurals of nouns with different endings. Look at Reference 66 on page 44. This is a box of rules that will make it a little easier to form the plurals of nouns with different endings. Let's read the rules and discuss how each one is used. (_Read and discuss the rules in the reference box on the next page._)

CHAPTER 22 LESSON 3 CONTINUED

Reference 66: Rules for the Plurals of Nouns with Different Endings	
1. "ch, sh, z, s, ss, x," add "es."	6. "f" or "ff," add "s."
2. a vowel plus "y," add an "s."	7. a vowel plus "o," add "s."
3. a consonant plus "y," change "y" to "i" and add "es."	8. a consonant plus "o," add "es."
4. "f" or "fe," change the "f" or "fe" to "v" and add "es."	9. stays the same for S and P.
5. irregular nouns-change spellings completely.	10. regular nouns, add "s."

Use the rules above to write the correct plural form of these nouns:

1. obey	2	obeys	2. half	4	halves
3. hoof	6 or 4	hoofs or hooves	4. fish	9 or 1	fish or fishes

After reading the rules, we know 3 things:

1. Which rule you choose will usually depend on the last two letters of a word.

2. You will have to decide whether some letters are vowels or consonants before you can choose a rule.

3. There are some plurals that you will just have to memorize if you don't want to look them up in a dictionary.

I am going to help you form the plurals of a few words so you will see how the rules work. Look at the word OBEY on your sheet. What are the two letters at the end of obey? *(ey)* Is the 'e' a consonant or vowel? *(vowel)* What is the number of the rule that tells you what to do when you have a vowel plus 'y'? *(Rule 2)*

We will put the number 2 in the small blank beside OBEY. Now, we will read Rule 2 to find out how to make OBEY plural. What does Rule 2 tell you to do to make OBEY plural? *(add an s)* How do you spell the plural of obey? *(o-b-e-y-s)* Write the correct plural spelling in the blank beside OBEY.

Look at the next two words on your sheet. They are HALF and HOOF. What is the letter at the end of each of these words? *(f)* What two rules deal with the letter 'f'? *(Rules 4 and 6)* By just reading these two rules, can you tell how to make HALF and HOOF plural? *(no)*

The only time you know for sure you can use Rule 4 is when you have a word that ends in "fe" *(like knife – knives)*. The only time you know for sure you can use Rule 6 is when you have a word that ends in "ff." Words that end only in "f" *(like half and hoof)* must be looked up in the dictionary if you do not already know how to form their plurals. The correct spelling for words like HALF and HOOF that do not follow a definite rule will have to be memorized.

At this point, either look up HALF and HOOF in the dictionary or ask your students to spell these plurals correctly. Write the words on the board for the students to see. Encourage students to use the dictionary when they are not sure of the spellings. This is a valuable skill that will carry into adult life. *(You could even allow them to use a dictionary on their test; it will help them remember the words they do not know.)*

Have your students write the rule numbers and correct plural spellings for HALF and HOOF on their papers. Work through a few more words on their sheets. If your class needs you to work through all the words, please do so. Show them how to find the rules that will help them spell the plural words correctly.

CHAPTER 22 LESSON 3 CONTINUED

PRACTICE TIME

Have students turn to pages 74 and 75 in the Practice Section of their book and find Chapter 22, Lesson 3, Practice (1-3). Go over the directions to make sure they understand what to do. Check and discuss the Practice after students have finished.

Chapter 22, Lesson 3, Practice 1: Write the rule numbers from Reference 66 and the correct plural form of the nouns below.

		Rule	Plural Form				Rule	Plural Form
1.	donkey	2	donkeys		6.	monopoly	3	monopolies
2.	wolf	4	wolves		7.	fish	9 or 1	fish or fishes
3.	tax	1	taxes		8.	barnacle	10	barnacles
4.	ox	5	oxen		9.	reef	6	reefs
5.	tornado	8	tornadoes		10.	monkey	2	monkeys

Chapter 22, Lesson 3, Practice 2: On another sheet of paper, make a list of ten contractions, then write the words from which the contractions come. *(Answers will vary.) (Use the contraction chart to check students' work.)*

Chapter 22, Lesson 3, Practice 3: Underline each subject and fill in each column according to the title.

List each Verb	Write PrN, PA, or None	Write L or A
are	PA	L
drove	None	A
is	PrN	L
ravaged	None	A
is	PA	L
are	PrN	L

1. <u>Kiwis</u> are delicious.
2. <u>Kent</u> drove to the lake.
3. <u>Warren</u> is president this year.
4. Menacing <u>crows</u> ravaged the corn crop.
5. Her <u>address</u> is incorrect.
6. His <u>parents</u> are reporters.

WRITING TIME

Have students make an entry in their journals.

STUDY TIME

Have students study the vocabulary words in their vocabulary notebooks. Tell students that any vocabulary word in their notebooks could be on their test. Also, have students study any of the skills in the Practice Section that they need to review.

(End of lesson.)

CHAPTER 22   LESSON 4

New objectives: Test.

JINGLE TIME

Have students turn to the Jingle Section of their books. The teacher will lead the students in reciting the previously-taught jingles.

STUDY TIME

Have students study the vocabulary words in their vocabulary notebooks. Remind students that any vocabulary word in their notebooks could be on their test. Also, have students study any of the skills in the Practice Section that they need to review.

TEST TIME

Have students turn to page 105 in the Test Section of their book and find Chapter 22 Test. Remind them to pay attention and think about what they are doing. Go over the directions to make sure they understand what to do. (*Chapter 22 Test key is on the next page.*)

CHECK TIME

After students have finished, check and discuss their test papers. Make sure they understand why their answers are right or wrong. (*For total points, count each required answer as a point.*)

(End of lesson.)

Chapter 22 Test
(Student Page 105)

Exercise 1: Classify each sentence.

          CSN C   CSN   LV A   Adj   PrN   P OP

1. **SN LV**   Diet and exercise **/** are the central focus (of wellness). **D**
  PrN P4

             A   SN   P PPA   OP   CV   P   OP   C   CV   P   OP

2. **SN V**   The president (of our organization) **/** went (to South America) and talked (about peace). **D**
  P1

           A   SN   V-t IO A DO   P   A   Adj   OP

3. **SN V-t**   The sirens **/** gave us a warning (about the approaching tornado)! **E**
  IO DO P3

Exercise 2: Use Sentence 3 to underline the complete subject once and the complete predicate twice and complete the table below.

List the Noun Used	List the Noun Job	Singular or Plural	Common or Proper	Simple Subject	Simple Predicate
1. **sirens**	2. **SN**	3. **P**	4. **C**	5. **sirens**	6. **gave**
7. **warning**	8. **DO**	9. **S**	10. **C**		
11. **tornado**	12. **OP**	13. **S**	14. **C**		

Exercise 3: Identify each pair of words as synonyms or antonyms by putting parentheses ( ) around *syn* or *ant*.

1. summit, base	syn **(ant)**	4. component, whole	syn **(ant)**	7. forfeit, relinquish	**(syn)** ant
2. repeal, pass	syn **(ant)**	5. chaperon, escort	**(syn)** ant	8. brusque, diplomatic	syn **(ant)**
3. attire, apparel	**(syn)** ant	6. adversity, misfortune	**(syn)** ant	9. expense, disbursement	**(syn)** ant

Exercise 4: Write the rule numbers from Reference 66 and the correct plural forms of the nouns below.

		Rule	Plural Form			Rule	Plural Form
1.	witch	1	**witches**	10.	donkey	2	**donkeys**
2.	rodeo	7	**rodeos**	11.	ox	5	**oxen**
3.	wolf	4	**wolves**	12.	pony	3	**ponies**
4.	goose	5	**geese**	13.	fish	9 or 1	**fish or fishes**
5.	livery	3	**liveries**	14.	ally	3	**allies**
6.	potato	8	**potatoes**	15.	alley	2	**alleys**
7.	deer	9	**deer**	16.	child	5	**children**
8.	wife	4	**wives**	17.	moose	9	**moose**
9.	roof	6	**roofs**	18.	fox	1	**foxes**

Exercise 5: Underline each subject and fill in each column according to the title.

	List each Verb	Write PrN, PA, or None	Write L or A
1. Wild <u>onions</u> are poisonous.	are	PA	L
2. <u>Honesty</u> is a virtue.	is	PrN	L
3. <u>Virgil</u> won the race.	won	None	A
4. <u>Milk</u> is rich in Vitamin D.	is	PA	L
5. <u>Grandma</u> is the family matriarch.	is	PrN	L

Exercise 6: On another sheet of paper, make a list of twelve contractions, then write the words from which the contractions come. (*Answers will vary.*) (*Use the contraction chart to check students' work.*)

Exercise 7: In your journal, write a paragraph summarizing what you have learned this week.

CHAPTER 22 LESSON 4 CONTINUED

TEACHER INSTRUCTIONS

Use the Question and Answer Flows below for the sentences on Chapter 22 Tests.

Question and Answer Flow for Sentence 1: Diet and exercise are the central focus of wellness.

1. What are the central focus of wellness?
   diet and exercise - CSN, CSN
2. What is being said about diet and exercise?
   diet and exercise are - V
3. Diet and exercise are what?
   focus - verify the noun
4. Does focus mean the same thing as diet and exercise?
   Yes.
5. Focus - PrN
6. Are - LV
7. What kind of focus? central - Adj
8. The - A
9. Of - P

10. Of what? wellness - OP
11. And - C
12. SN LV PrN P4 Check
13. Linking verb - Check again.
14. (Of wellness) - Prepositional phrase
15. Period, statement, declarative sentence
16. Go back to the verb - divide the complete subject
    from the complete predicate.
17. Is there an adverb exception? No.
18. Is this sentence in a natural or inverted order?
    Natural - no change.

Classified Sentence:

		CSN	C	CSN	LV	A	Adj	PrN	P	OP

SN LV   Diet and exercise / are the central focus (of wellness). **D**

PrN P4

Question and Answer Flow for Sentence 2: The president of our organization went to South America and talked about peace.

1. Who went to South America and talked about peace?
   president - SN
2. What is being said about president? president went and
   talked - CV, CV
3. About - P
4. About what? peace - OP
5. And - C
6. To - P
7. To what? South America - OP
8. Of - P
9. Of what? organization - OP
10. Whose organization? our - PPA

11. The - A
12. SN V P1 Check
13. (Of our organization) - Prepositional phrase
14. (To South America) - Prepositional phrase
15. (About peace) - Prepositional phrase
16. Period, statement, declarative sentence
17. Go back to the verb - divide the complete subject
    from the complete predicate.
18. Is there an adverb exception? No.
19. Is this sentence in a natural or inverted order?
    Natural - no change.

Classified Sentence:

	A	SN	P	PPA	OP	CV	P	OP	C	CV	P	OP

SN V   The president (of our organization) / went (to South America) and talked (about peace). **D**

P1

Question and Answer Flow for Sentence 3: The sirens gave us a warning about the approaching tornado!

1. What gave us a warning about the approaching
   tornado? sirens - SN
2. What is being said about sirens? sirens gave - V
3. Sirens gave what? warning - verify the noun
4. Does warning mean the same thing as sirens? No.
5. Warning - DO
6. Gave - V-t
7. Sirens gave warning to whom? us - IO
8. A - A
9. About - P
10. About what? tornado - OP
11. What kind of tornado? approaching - Adj

12. The - A
13. The - A
14. SN V-t IO DO P3 Check
15. Verb-transitive - Check again.
16. (About the approaching tornado) - Prepositional phrase
17. Exclamation point, strong feeling, exclamatory
    sentence
18. Go back to the verb - divide the complete subject
    from the complete predicate.
19. Is there an adverb exception? No.
20. Is this sentence in a natural or inverted order?
    Natural - no change.

Classified Sentence:

	A	SN	V-t	IO	A	DO	P	A	Adj	OP

SN V-t   The sirens / gave us a warning (about the approaching tornado)! **E**

IO DO P3

CHAPTER 22   LESSON 5

New objectives: Writing Assignments #33 and #34.

 **WRITING TIME**

WRITING WITH DIALOGUE AND WITHOUT DIALOGUE

You will do two narrative writing assignments. The first narrative writing assignment will be a story without dialogue. The second narrative writing assignment will be the same story with dialogue. Both rough drafts will go through the revision and editing stages. (*Read the boxes below for more information about students' writing assignment.*) You will choose the point of view for each assignment.

Select one of your favorite Biblical stories to write about. Instead of conversation between and among the characters, you—the writer—will tell the story completely in your own words.

Writing Assignment Box #1

Writing Assignment #33: A Narrative without dialogue (First or Third Person)
(Remember, first person pronouns are *I, we, me, us, my, our, mine, and ours.*)
Remind students to make a Story Elements outline.

**Writing topic: Choose a story from the Bible and write it without dialogue, or choose your favorite story and
write it without dialogue.**

Use that same Biblical story as the basis for your second paper. In this narrative, use dialogue and let the characters speak with one another.

Writing Assignment Box #2

Writing Assignment #34: A Narrative with dialogue (First or Third Person)
(Remember, first person pronouns are *I, we, me, us, my, our, mine, and ours.*)
Remind students to make a Story Elements outline.

Writing topic: Write the same story from the Bible with dialogue, or write the same favorite story with dialogue.

Read, check, and discuss Writing Assignments #33 and #34 after students have finished their final papers. Use the checklists as you check and discuss students' papers. Make sure students are using the regular editing checklist and quotations rules correctly.

(End of lesson.)

CHAPTER 23   LESSON 1

New objectives: Grammar (Practice Sentences), Skills (parts of a friendly letter, parts of an envelope), Practice activity, and Vocabulary #1.

JINGLE TIME

Have students turn to the Jingle Section of their books. The teacher will lead the students in reciting the previously-taught jingles.

GRAMMAR TIME

First-Year Option: Put the Practice Sentences from the box below on the board or notebook paper. Use these sentences as you practice the concepts that have been taught. For the greatest benefit, students must participate orally with the teacher. **Second-Year Option:** Have students classify the Practice Sentences independently on paper. Check students' sentences with the answers provided below. (*If you have the CDs for Practice Sentences, have students check their sentences with the CDs.*)

Chapter 23, Practice Sentences for Lesson 1
1. _____ Does your father's store open at noon today?
2. _____ Two members of my family recently became dentists.

TEACHING SCRIPT FOR PRACTICING MIXED PATTERNS

We will practice classifying Mixed Patterns. We will classify the sentences together. Begin. (*You might have your students write the labels above the sentences at this time.*)

Question and Answer Flow for Sentence 1: Does your father's store open at noon today?
1. What does open at noon today? store - SN	9. SN V P1 Check
2. What is being said about store? store does open - V	10. (At noon) - Prepositional phrase
3. Does - HV	11. Question mark, question, interrogative sentence
4. At - P	12. Go back to the verb - divide the complete subject
5. At what? noon - OP	from the complete predicate.
6. Does open when? today - Adv	13. Is there an adverb exception? No.
7. Whose store? father's - PNA	14. Is this sentence in a natural or inverted order?
8. Whose father? your - PPA	Inverted - underline the subject parts once and
	the predicate parts twice.

Classified Sentence:

                 HV   PPA PNA   SN   V   P OP Adv

     SN V   Does your father's store / open (at noon) today? **Int**

     P1

CHAPTER 23 LESSON 1 CONTINUED

Question and Answer Flow for Sentence 2: Two members of my family recently became dentists.

1. Who became dentists? members - SN
2. What is being said about members? members became - V
3. Members became who? dentists - verify the noun
4. Do dentists mean the same thing as members? Yes.
5. Dentists - PrN
6. Became - LV
7. Became when? recently - Adv
8. Of - P
9. Of whom? family - OP
10. Whose family? my - PPA
11. How many members? two - Adj
12. SN LV PrN P4 Check
13. Linking verb - Check again.
14. (Of my family) - Prepositional phrase
15. Period, statement, declarative sentence
16. Go back to the verb - divide the complete subject from the complete predicate.
17. Is there an adverb exception? Yes - change the line.
18. Is this sentence in a natural or inverted order? Natural - no change.

Classified Sentence:

			Adj	SN	P PPA OP	Adv	LV	PrN

SN LV
PrN P4   Two members (of my family) / recently became dentists. **D**

SKILL TIME

TEACHING SCRIPT FOR THE PARTS OF A FRIENDLY LETTER

Close your eyes. Picture a good friend or favorite relative that you really like but don't get to see very often. Open your eyes. The memory of that favorite person in your life brought a smile to your face, didn't it? Remember that keeping in touch with favorite people brings smiles to their faces, too. Writing a letter is a great way to stay in touch with people you care about and who care about you.

A letter written to or received from friends or relatives is called a **friendly letter**. Listen carefully to some tips that will make your friendly letter interesting and enjoyable to read. (*Read and discuss the tips below. Option: You might choose to dictate the writing tips to your students to enhance their listening skills.*)

Tips for Writing Friendly Letters

Tip #1: Write as if you were talking to the person face-to-face. Share information about yourself and mutual friends. Tell stories, conversations, or jokes. Share photographs, articles, drawings, poems, etc. Avoid saying something about someone else that you'll be sorry for later.

Tip #2: If you are writing a return letter, be sure to answer any questions that were asked. Repeat the question so that your reader will know what you are writing about. (You asked about . . .)

Tip #3: End your letter in a positive way so that your reader will want to write a return letter.

CHAPTER 23 LESSON 1 CONTINUED

Now that you know what things to write about, you must learn to put your friendly letter in correct friendly-letter form. The friendly letter has five parts: the heading; the friendly greeting, which is also called the salutation; the body; the closing; and the signature.

Each part of a friendly letter has a specific place where it should be written in order for your letter to have correct friendly-letter form. Look at the five parts of a friendly letter and the friendly letter example in Reference 67 on page 45 in your book. We will now go over each of the five parts, what information is contained in each part, and where each part is placed in a friendly-letter form. (*Go over the letter parts and the letter example reproduced below with your students.*)

Reference 67: The Five Parts of a Friendly Letter

1. Heading
1. Box or street address of writer
2. City, state, zip code of writer
3. Date letter was written
4. Placement: upper right-hand corner

2. Friendly Greeting or Salutation
1. Begins with *Dear*
2. Names person receiving the letter
3. Has comma after person's name
4. Placement: at left margin, two lines below heading

3. Body
1. Tells reason the letter was written
2. Can have one or more paragraphs
3. Has indented paragraphs
4. Is placed one line after the greeting
5. Skips one line between each paragraph

4. Closing
1. Closes letter with a personal phrase-(Your friend, With love,)
2. Capitalizes only first word
3. Is followed by a comma
4. Is placed two lines below the body
5. Begins just to the right of the middle of the letter

5. Signature
1. Tells who wrote the letter
2. Is usually signed in cursive
3. Uses first name only unless there is a question as to which friend or relative you are
4. Is placed beneath the closing

Friendly Letter Example

1. **Heading**
P.O. Box 372
Akron, IN 18043
August 19, 20___

2. **Friendly Greeting, (or Salutation)**
Dear Mary Jo,

3. **Body (Indent Paragraphs)**

　　How wonderful that you are coming to spend the holidays with us. I can hardly wait. Mom plans to make your favorite dessert while you are here.

4. **Closing,**
Your cousin,

5. **Signature**

CHAPTER 23 LESSON 1 CONTINUED

TEACHING SCRIPT FOR THE PARTS OF AN ENVELOPE

In order to address the envelope of your friendly letter correctly, you must know the parts that go on the envelope and where to write them. Look at Reference 68 on page 45 and follow along as I read the information about the parts of an envelope. Notice what information is contained in the two parts, and where each part is placed on the envelope. (*Go over the information below with your students.*)

Reference 68: Envelope Parts	Friendly Envelope Example	
The return address: 1. Name of the person writing the letter 2. Box or street address of the writer 3. City, state, zip code of the writer **The mailing address:** 1. Name of the person receiving the letter 2. Street address of the person receiving the letter 3. City, state, zip of the person receiving the letter	Return Address Lydia Martin 468 Pickwick Road Stanton, IA 92434 Mailing Address Mary Jo Faulkner P.O. Box 372 Akron, IN 18043	Stamp

 PRACTICE TIME

Have students turn to page 75 in the Practice Section of their book and find Chapter 23, Lesson 1, Practice. Go over the directions to make sure they understand what to do. Check and discuss the Practice after students have finished. (*Chapter 23, Lesson 1, Practice instructions are given below.*)

Chapter 23, Lesson 1, Practice: Use butcher paper, large pieces of construction paper, or poster board to make a colorful wall poster, identifying the five parts of a friendly letter and the parts of an envelope. Write the title and an example for each of the five parts. Illustrate your work. Then, give an oral presentation about the friendly letter and the envelope when you have finished. (*This project may take several days.*)

 WRITING TIME

Have students make an entry in their journals.

 VOCABULARY TIME

Assign Chapter 23, Vocabulary Words #1 on page 8 in the Reference Section for students to define in their Vocabulary notebooks. After they write each word and its meaning, students are to write a sentence using the vocabulary word.

Chapter 23, Vocabulary Words #1
(reconcile, sever, reimburse, refund)

(End of lesson.)

CHAPTER 23   LESSON 2

New objectives: Grammar (Practice Sentences) and a Practice activity.

JINGLE TIME

Have students turn to the Jingle Section of their books. The teacher will lead the students in reciting the previously-taught jingles.

GRAMMAR TIME

First-Year Option: Put the Practice Sentences from the box below on the board or notebook paper. Use these sentences as you practice the concepts that have been taught. For the greatest benefit, students must participate orally with the teacher. **Second-Year Option:** Have students classify the Practice Sentences independently on paper. Check students' sentences with the answers provided below. (*If you have the CDs for Practice Sentences, have students check their sentences with the CDs.*)

Chapter 23, Practice Sentences for Lesson 2
1. _____ The store's manager organized a food drive for the needy in our neighborhood.
2. _____ Our Spanish friends gave us a map to their town.

TEACHING SCRIPT FOR PRACTICING MIXED PATTERNS

We will practice classifying Mixed Patterns. We will classify the sentences together. Begin. (*You might have your students write the labels above the sentences at this time.*)

Question and Answer Flow for Sentence 1: The store's manager organized a food drive for the needy in our neighborhood.

1. Who organized a food drive for the needy in our neighborhood? manager – SN
2. What is being said about manager? manager organized – V
3. Manager organized what? drive - verify the noun
4. Does drive mean the same thing as manager? No.
5. Drive - DO
6. Organized - V-t
7. What kind of drive? food – Adj
8. A – A
9. For - P
10. For whom? needy - OP
11. The - A
12. In - P
13. In what? neighborhood – OP
14. Whose neighborhood? our - PPA
15. Whose manager? store's - PNA
16. The - A
17. SN V-t DO P2 Check
18. Verb-transitive - Check again.
19. (For the needy) - Prepositional phrase
20. (In our neighborhood) - Prepositional phrase
21. Period, statement, declarative sentence
22. Go back to the verb - divide the complete subject from the complete predicate.
23. Is there an adverb exception? No.
24. Is this sentence in a natural or inverted order? Natural - no change.

Classified Sentence:

$$\begin{array}{llllllllll} & A & PNA & SN & V\text{-}t & A\ Adj\ DO & P\ A\ OP & P\ PPA & OP \end{array}$$

<u>SN V-t</u>   The store's manager / organized a food drive (for the needy) (in our neighborhood). **D**
DO P2

CHAPTER 23 LESSON 2 CONTINUED

Question and Answer Flow for Sentence 2: Our Spanish friends gave us a map to their town.

1. Who gave us a map to their town? friends – SN
2. What is being said about friends? friends gave – V
3. Friends gave what? map - verify the noun
4. Does map mean the same thing as friends? No.
5. Map - DO
6. Gave - V-t
7. Friends gave map to whom? us - IO
8. A - A
9. To – P
10. To what? town – OP
11. Whose town? their – PPA

12. What kind of friends? Spanish - Adj
13. Whose friends? Our - PPA
14. SN V-t IO DO P3 Check
15. Verb-transitive - Check again.
16. (To their town) - Prepositional phrase
17. Period, statement, declarative sentence
18. Go back to the verb - divide the complete subject from the complete predicate.
19. Is there an adverb exception? No.
20. Is this sentence in a natural or inverted order? Natural - no change.

Classified Sentence:

```
                          PPA  Adj     SN      V-t  IO A DO    P  PPA OP
     SN V-t     Our Spanish friends / gave us a map (to their town).  D
     IO DO P3
```

TEACHER INSTRUCTIONS FOR A PRACTICE SENTENCE

Tell students that their sentence writing assignment today is to write a sentence pattern of their choice. They may choose any Pattern, 1-4, for a Practice Sentence. They are to follow the same procedure used in the previous lessons. They should decide on their labels, arrange them in a selected order, write their sentence, and edit the sentence for improved word choices. (*Students do not have to write an Improved Sentence at this point unless you feel they need more one-on-one word choice writing practice.*) Check and discuss the sentence pattern chosen after students have finished.

 PRACTICE TIME

Students will continue letter-writing activities. Have students turn to page 75 in the Practice Section of their book and find Chapter 23, Lesson 2, Practice. Go over the directions to make sure they understand what to do. Check and discuss the Practice after students have finished. (*Chapter 23, Lesson 2, Practice instructions are given below.*)

Chapter 23, Lesson 2, Practice : Write a friendly letter to a special friend or relative. Before you start, review the references and tips for writing friendly letters. After your letter has been edited, fold the letter and put it in an envelope. Address the envelope properly and mail it. Don't forget the stamp. (*E-mail does not take the place of this assignment.*)

 WRITING TIME

Have students make an entry in their journals.

(End of lesson.)

CHAPTER 23   LESSON 3

New objectives: Grammar (Practice Sentences), a Practice activity, and Vocabulary #2.

JINGLE TIME

Have students turn to the Jingle Section of their books. The teacher will lead the students in reciting the previously-taught jingles.

GRAMMAR TIME

First-Year Option: Put the Practice Sentences from the box below on the board or notebook paper. Use these sentences as you practice the concepts that have been taught. For the greatest benefit, students must participate orally with the teacher. **Second-Year Option:** Have students classify the Practice Sentences independently on paper. Check students' sentences with the answers provided below. (*If you have the CDs for Practice Sentences, have students check their sentences with the CDs.*)

Chapter 23, Practice Sentences for Lesson 3
1. _____ My sister is a gospel singer with the choir from Memphis.
2. _____ I have taught Mitchell seven scriptures in the past month.

TEACHING SCRIPT FOR PRACTICING MIXED PATTERNS

We will practice classifying Mixed Patterns. We will classify the sentences together. Begin. (*You might have your students write the labels above the sentences at this time.*)

Question and Answer Flow for Sentence 1: My sister is a gospel singer with the choir from Memphis.	
1. Who is a gospel singer with the choir from Memphis? sister - SN	13. From what? Memphis - OP
2. What is being said about sister? sister is - V	14. Whose sister? my - PPA
3. Sister is what? singer - verify the noun	15. SN LV PrN P4 Check
4. Does singer mean the same thing as sister? Yes.	16. Linking verb - Check again.
5. Singer - PrN	17. (With the choir) - Prepositional phrase
6. Is - LV	18. (From Memphis) - Prepositional phrase
7. What kind of singer? gospel - Adj	19. Period, statement, declarative sentence
8. A - A	20. Go back to the verb - divide the complete subject from the complete predicate.
9. With - P	21. Is there an adverb exception? No.
10. With what? choir - OP	22. Is this sentence in a natural or inverted order? Natural - no change.
11. The - A	
12. From - P	

Classified Sentence:

```
                        PPA  SN  LV  A  Adj  PrN     P   A   OP     P     OP
        SN  LV          My sister / is a gospel singer (with the choir) (from Memphis).  D
        PrN  P4
```

Level 5 Homeschool Teacher's Manual

CHAPTER 23 LESSON 3 CONTINUED

Question and Answer Flow for Sentence 2: I have taught Mitchell seven scriptures in the past month.

1. Who have taught Mitchell seven scriptures in the past month? I - SP
2. What is being said about I? I have taught - V
3. Have - HV
4. I have taught what? scriptures - verify the noun
5. Do scriptures mean the same thing as I? No.
6. Scriptures - DO
7. Taught - V-t
8. I have taught scriptures to whom? Mitchell - IO
9. How many scriptures? seven - Adj
10. In - P
11. In what? month - OP
12. Which month? past - Adj
13. The - A
14. SN V-t IO DO P3 Check
15. Verb transitive - Check again.
16. (In the past month) - Prepositional phrase
17. Period, statement, declarative sentence
18. Go back to the verb - divide the complete subject from the complete predicate.
19. Is there an adverb exception? No.
20. Is this sentence in a natural or inverted order? Natural - no change.

Classified Sentence:

```
                    SP  HV   V-t   IO   Adj   DO    P  A  Adj  OP
        SN V-t       I / have taught Mitchell seven scriptures (in the past month).  D
        IO  DO  P3
```

PRACTICE TIME

Students will continue letter-writing activities. Have students turn to page 75 in the Practice Section of their books and find Chapter 23, Lesson 3, Practice (*1-2*). Go over the directions to make sure they understand what to do. If students need a review, have them study the information and examples in the Reference Section of their books. Check and discuss the Practice after students have finished. (*Chapter 23, Lesson 3, Practice instructions are given below.*)

Chapter 23, Lesson 3, Practice 1: On a sheet of paper, identify the parts of a friendly letter and envelope by writing the titles and an example for each title. (Use References 67 and 68 to check the parts of a friendly letter and envelope.)

Chapter 23, Lesson 3, Practice 2: Write a friendly letter to a neighbor, nursing home resident, or relative. This person must be someone that is different from the person chosen in the previous lesson. Before you start, review the references and tips for writing friendly letters. After your letter has been edited, fold the letter and put it in an envelope. Address the envelope properly and mail it. Don't forget the stamp.

VOCABULARY TIME

Assign Chapter 23, Vocabulary Words **#2** on page 8 in the Reference Section for students to define in their Vocabulary notebooks. They should write each word, its meaning, and a sentence using the word.

Chapter 23, Vocabulary Words #2
(provoke, pacify, reputable, honest)

(End of lesson.)

CHAPTER 23   LESSON 4

New objectives: Test and an Activity (concluded).

 JINGLE TIME

Have students turn to the Jingle Section of their books. The teacher will lead the students in reciting the previously-taught jingles.

 STUDY TIME

Have students study the vocabulary words in their vocabulary notebooks. Remind students that any vocabulary word in their notebooks could be on their test. Also, have students study any of the skills in the Practice Section that they need to review.

 TEST TIME

Have students turn to page 106 in the Test Section of their books and find Chapter 23 Test. Remind them to pay attention and think about what they are doing. Go over the directions to make sure they understand what to do. (*Chapter 23 Test key is on the next page.*)

 CHECK TIME

After students have finished, check and discuss their test papers. Make sure they understand why their answers are right or wrong. (*For total points, count each required answer as a point.*)

 ACTIVITY / ASSIGNMENT TIME

Have students present the projects they developed in Chapter 22. Reminder: They must include a written description of the project, an illustration of the project, and a cost estimate of the project. Students may present their projects several times to different family members and friends.

(End of lesson.)

Chapter 23 Test
(Student Page 106)

Exercise 1: Classify each sentence.

```
            A     Adj   Adj   SN    V      Adv          P    A    Adj    OP
1. SN V     The  giant white bell / rang continuously (from the large steeple).  D
   P1
```

```
            CSN   C  CSP   HV    V-t    Adj    DO      P   PPA   Adj    OP
2. SN V-t   Rachel and I / have preached many sermons (during our missionary trip).  D
   DO  P2
```

Exercise 2: Identify each pair of words as synonyms or antonyms by putting parentheses ( ) around *syn* or *ant*.

1. provoke, pacify	syn **(ant)**	4. superficial, genuine	syn **(ant)**	7. mandatory, required	**(syn)** ant
2. reconcile, sever	syn **(ant)**	5. reimburse, refund	**(syn)** ant	8. amateur, beginner	**(syn)** ant
3. reputable, honest	**(syn)** ant	6. conceited, humble	syn **(ant)**	9. precarious, stable	syn **(ant)**

Exercise 3: Choose an answer from the choices in parentheses. Then, fill in the rest of the columns according to the titles. (S or P stands for singular or plural.)

Pronoun-antecedent agreement

1. The turtles in the woods are burying (its, <u>their</u>) eggs.
2. The stewardess lost (<u>her</u>, their) oxygen mask.
3. A letter in the mailbox lost (<u>its</u>, their) stamp.
4. My cousins misplaced (its, <u>their</u>) shoes.
5. The ice cream lost (<u>its</u>, their) flavor.
6. The immigrants gained (its, <u>their</u>) citizenship last week.
7. Everything in the files is in (<u>its</u>, their) place.
8. The mayor handed the gavel to (<u>his</u>, their) successor.

Pronoun Choice	S or P	Antecedent	S or P
their	P	turtles	P
her	S	stewardess	S
its	S	letter	S
their	P	cousins	P
its	S	ice cream	S
their	P	immigrants	P
its	S	everything	S
his	S	mayor	S

Exercise 4: Underline each subject and fill in each column according to the title.

1. <u>Viruses</u> are contagious.
2. <u>Kyle</u> is this year's winner.
3. <u>Accidents</u> are unavoidable.
4. <u>Flags</u> fly from the capitol dome.
5. Her <u>umbrella</u> was a lifesaver.

List each Verb	Write PrN, PA, or None	Write L or A
are	PA	L
is	PrN	L
are	PA	L
fly	None	A
was	PrN	L

Exercise 5: Write the seven present tense helping verbs, the five past tense helping verbs, and the two future tense helping verbs. *The order of the answers may vary.* (*Present*: am, is, are, has, have, do, does; *Past*: was, were, had, did, been; *Future*: will, shall)

Exercise 6: On a sheet of paper, write three sentences, demonstrating each of the three degrees of adjectives. Identify the form you used by writing **simple, comparative,** or **superlative** at the end of each sentence. (*Answers will vary.*)

Exercise 7: On a sheet of paper, identify the parts of a friendly letter and envelope by writing the titles and an example for each title. Use References 67 and 68 to help you. (*Use References 67 and 68 to check the parts of a friendly letter and envelope.*)

Exercise 8: In your journal, write a paragraph summarizing what you have learned this week.

CHAPTER 23 LESSON 4 CONTINUED

TEACHER INSTRUCTIONS

Use the Question and Answer Flows below for the sentences on Chapter 23 Tests.

Question and Answer Flow for Sentence 1: The giant white bell rang continuously from the large steeple.

1. What rang continuously from the large steeple? bell - SN
2. What is being said about bell? bell rang - V
3. Rang how? continuously - Adv
4. From - P
5. From what? steeple - OP
6. What kind of steeple? large - Adj
7. The - A
8. What kind of bell? white - Adj
9. What kind of bell? giant - Adj
10. The - A
11. SN V P1 Check
12. (From the large steeple) - Prepositional phrase
13. Period, statement, declarative sentence
14. Go back to the verb - divide the complete subject from the complete predicate.
15. Is there an adverb exception? No.
16. Is this sentence in a natural or inverted order? Natural - no change.

Classified Sentence:

                     A Adj Adj SN   V   Adv   P   A Adj   OP

   SN V   The giant white bell / rang continuously (from the large steeple). **D**

    P1

Question and Answer Flow for Sentence 2: Rachel and I have preached many sermons during our missionary trip.

1. Who have preached many sermons during our missionary trip? Rachel and I - CSN, CSP
2. What is being said about Rachel and I? Rachel and I have preached - V
3. Have - HV
4. Rachel and I have preached what? sermons - verify the noun
5. Do sermons mean the same thing as Rachel and I? No.
6. Sermons - DO
7. Preached - V-t
8. How many sermons? many - Adj
9. During - P
10. During what? trip - OP
11. What kind of trip? missionary - Adj
12. Whose trip? our - PPA
13. And - C
14. SN V-t DO P2 Check
15. Verb-transitive - Check again.
16. (During our missionary trip) - Prepositional phrase
17. Period, statement, declarative sentence
18. Go back to the verb - divide the complete subject from the complete predicate.
19. Is there an adverb exception? No.
20. Is this sentence in a natural or inverted order? Natural - no change.

Classified Sentence:

                  CSN   C CSP HV   V-t   Adj   DO   P   PPA Adj   OP

   SN V-t   Rachel and I / have preached many sermons (during our missionary trip). **D**

   DO P2

CHAPTER 23   LESSON 5

New objectives: Writing Assignments #35 and #36.

 **WRITING TIME**

TEACHING SCRIPT FOR WRITING ASSIGNMENTS

Today, you are assigned two different kinds of writing. You will write a five-paragraph expository essay and a friendly letter. <u>You will revise and edit both writing assignments</u>. (*Read the box below for more information about students' writing assignment.*) As you edit, make sure you use the checkpoints in the editing checklist provided in Reference 35. For the essay, remember to read through the whole essay, starting with the title, and then edit, sentence-by-sentence, using the five sentence checkpoints for each sentence. Use the paragraph checkpoints to check each paragraph. You should use the Beginning Checklists for all other instructions. Remember, your editing is now more detailed and more comprehensive, so take your time.

Writing Assignment Box #1

Writing Assignment #35: Three-Paragraph Expository Essay (First or Third Person)
(Remember, first person pronouns are *I, we, me, us, my, our, mine, and ours.*)
Remind students that the 3-paragraph essay has three parts: 1. Introduction 2. Body 3. Conclusion. The body has one paragraph instead of three. Have students use their regular editing checklist to edit this assignment.

Writing topic: Things the President of the United States Should Do or **Things Needed to Change a Flat Tire in the Dark** or **Choose your own topic.**

Your second writing assignment is to write a friendly letter. (*Read the box below for more information about students' writing assignment.*)

Writing Assignment Box #2

Writing Assignment #36: Write a friendly letter to a person of your choice. Before you start, review the references and tips for writing friendly letters. After your letter has been edited, fold the letter and put it in an envelope. Address the envelope properly and mail it. Don't forget the stamp.

Read, check, and discuss Writing Assignment #35 after students have finished their final papers. Use the checklists as you check and discuss students' papers. Make sure students are using the regular editing checklist correctly. Read and discuss Writing Assignment #36 for fun and enrichment.

(End of lesson.)

CHAPTER 24   LESSON 1

New objectives: Grammar (Practice Sentences), Skills (parts of a business letter, parts of a business envelope), Practice activity, and Vocabulary #1.

 JINGLE TIME

Have students turn to the Jingle Section of their books. The teacher will lead the students in reciting the previously-taught jingles.

 GRAMMAR TIME

First-Year Option: Put the Practice Sentences from the box below on the board or notebook paper. Use these sentences as you practice the concepts that have been taught. For the greatest benefit, students must participate orally with the teacher. **Second-Year Option:** Have students classify the Practice Sentences independently on paper. Check students' sentences with the answers provided below. (*If you have the CDs for Practice Sentences, have students check their sentences with the CDs.*)

Chapter 24, Practice Sentences for Lesson 1
1. _____ Did you give your mother a free tape of the sermon?
2. _____ During the prom, Ms. King was the chaperon until midnight.

TEACHING SCRIPT FOR PRACTICING MIXED PATTERNS

We will practice classifying Mixed Patterns. We will classify the sentences together. Begin. (*You might have your students write the labels above the sentences at this time.*)

Question and Answer Flow for Sentence 1: Did you give your mother a free tape of the sermon?	
1. Who did give your mother a free tape of the sermon? you - SP	13. The - A
2. What is being said about you? you did give - V	14. Whose mother? your - PPA
3. Did - HV	15. SN V-t IO DO P3 Check
4. You did give what? tape – verify the noun	16. Verb-transitive - Check again.
5. Does tape mean the same thing as you? No.	17. (Of the sermon) - Prepositional phrase
6. Tape - DO	18. Question mark, question, interrogative sentence
7. Give - V-t	19. Go back to the verb - divide the complete subject from the complete predicate.
8. You did give tape to whom? mother - IO	20. Is there an adverb exception? No.
9. What kind of tape? free - Adj	21. Is this sentence in a natural or inverted order? Inverted - underline the subject parts once and the predicate parts twice.
10. A - A	
11. Of - P	
12. Of what? sermon - OP	

Classified Sentence:

```
                           HV  SP   V-t  PPA IO    A Adj  DO    P  A    OP
            SN V-t      Did you / give your mother a free tape (of the sermon)? Int
            IO DO P3
```

CHAPTER 24 LESSON 1 CONTINUED

Question and Answer Flow for Sentence 2: During the prom, Ms. King was the chaperon until midnight.	
1. Who was the chaperon until midnight? Ms. King - SN	12. The - A
2. What is being said about Ms. King? Ms. King was - V	13. SN LV PrN P4 Check
3. Ms. King was who? chaperon - verify the noun	14. Linking verb - Check again.
4. Does chaperon mean the same thing as Ms. King? Yes.	15. (During the prom) - Prepositional phrase
5. Chaperon - PrN	16. (Until midnight) - Prepositional phrase
6. Was - LV	17. Period, statement, declarative sentence
7. The - A	18. Go back to the verb - divide the complete subject from the complete predicate.
8. Until - P	19. Is there an adverb exception? No.
9. Until what? midnight - OP	20. Is this sentence in a natural or inverted order? Inverted - underline the subject parts once and the predicate parts twice.
10. During - P	
11. During what? prom - OP	

Classified Sentence:

```
                            P    A   OP     SN    LV  A   PrN     P    OP
     SN LV        (During the prom), Ms. King / was the chaperon (until midnight).  D
     PrN P4
```

Use Sentences 1-2 that you just classified with your students to do an Oral Skill Builder Check. Use the guidelines below.

Oral Skill Builder Check	
1. Noun check. (Say the job and then say the noun. Circle each noun.)	**5. Identify the complete subject and the complete predicate.** (Underline the complete subject once and the complete predicate twice.)
2. Identify the nouns as singular or plural. (Write S or P above each noun.)	**6. Identify the simple subject and simple predicate.** (Underline the simple subject once and the simple predicate twice. Bold, or highlight, the lines.)
3. Identify the nouns as common or proper. (Follow established procedure for oral identification.)	**7. Recite the irregular verb chart.** (Located on student page 17 and teacher page 143.)
4. Do a vocabulary check. (Follow established procedure for oral identification.)	

SKILL TIME

TEACHING SCRIPT FOR THE PARTS OF A BUSINESS LETTER

Sharing information with a friend or relative is not the only reason to write a letter. Sometimes, you may need to write a letter to someone you do not know about something that is not personal in nature. This kind of letter is called a **business letter**. Even if you are not in business, there are several reasons why you may need to write a business letter. We will discuss four reasons for writing business letters, and then we will study the four types of business letters and what type of information should be included in each one. Look at Reference 69 on page 46 and follow along as I read the information about business letters. (*Reference 69 is reproduced for you on the next page.*)

CHAPTER 24 LESSON 1 CONTINUED

Reference 69: Four Types of Business Letters	
Four common reasons to write business letters and information about the four types:	

1. If you need to send for information - letter of inquiry.
2. If you want to order a product - letter of request or order.
3. If you want to express an opinion - letter to an editor or official.
4. If you want to complain about a product - letter of complaint.

Letter of Inquiry	Letter of Request or Order
1. Ask for information or answers to your questions. 2. Keep the letter short and to the point. 3. Word the letter so that there can be no question as to what it is you need to know.	1. Carefully and clearly describe the product. 2. Keep the letter short and to the point. 3. Include information on how and where the product should be shipped. 4. Include information on how you will pay for the product.
Letter to an Editor or Official	Letter of Complaint About a Product
1. Clearly explain the problem or situation. 2. Offer your opinion of the cause and possible solutions. 3. Support your opinions with facts and examples. 4. Suggest ways to change or improve the situation.	1. Carefully and clearly describe the product. 2. Describe the problem and what may have caused it. (Don't spend too much time explaining how unhappy you are.) 3. Explain any action you have already taken to solve the problem. 4. End your letter with the action you would like the company to take to solve the problem.

The form of a business letter is like the friendly letter except that a business letter uses language that is more formal. A business letter also has an inside address above the greeting that tells who is receiving the letter. The inside address saves companies or business people time because they do not have to read the entire letter in order to know which person in the company receives the letter.

TEACHING SCRIPT FOR THE SIX PARTS OF A BUSINESS LETTER

Now that you know the different reasons to write business letters, you must learn to put your business letter into correct business letter form. The business letter has six parts: the heading; the inside address; the formal greeting; which is also called the salutation; the body; the closing, and the signature. I will briefly tell you some extra information about the new things that you will find in a business letter.

First, how you write the inside address will depend on what you know about the business or company that will receive the letter. If you know the name of a person in the company who can help you, you will use that name as part of the inside address. If you do not know the name of a person in the company who can help you, you will just use the name of the company.

Second, greetings in business letters are formal. This means that you use the title and last name of the person who is receiving the letter, followed by a colon. If you do not know the name of the person receiving the letter, you should use **sir** or **madam**.

Third, when writing the signature of a business letter, you should always sign your first and last name.

CHAPTER 24 LESSON 1 CONTINUED

Each of the parts of a business letter has a specific place it should be written in order for your letter to have correct business letter form. Look at the business letter example in Reference 70 on page 46 in your book. We will now go over each of the six parts, what information is contained in each part, and where each part is placed in the business letter. (*Go over the example reproduced below with your students.*)

Reference 70: Business Letter Example

1. HEADING

615 Calumet Drive
Arlington, VT 49122
March 16, 20___

2. INSIDE ADDRESS

Dr. Forrest Garner
Garner Dental Clinic
363 Fulton Manor
Brighton, TN 82821

3. FORMAL GREETING, (OR SALUTATION)

Dear Dr. Garner:

4. BODY (INDENT PARAGRAPHS)

    My uncle broke his lower denture in half while eating popcorn last night. If you will send me a tube of your famous adhesive, I will gladly send you a money order to pay for it.

5. FORMAL CLOSING,

Most sincerely,

6. SIGNATURE

Fulton Asher

TEACHING SCRIPT FOR THE PARTS OF A BUSINESS ENVELOPE

In order to address the envelope of your business letter correctly, you must know the parts that go on the envelope and where to write them. The parts of a business envelope are similar to the parts of an envelope for a friendly letter. There are two differences in the mailing address for the business envelope that you should remember.

(1) You must put the name of the person within the company to whom you are writing and his/her title (if you know it) on the first line of the mailing address.

(2) You must put the name of the company on the second line of the mailing address. If you do not know the name of a particular person in the company who would handle your request or problem, you can just choose a department within the company (for example, SALES, SHIPPING, ACCOUNTING, etc.) to write on the first line of your mailing address, or you can leave the first line blank.

Look at Reference 71 on page 47 for an example of the parts of a business envelope. (*Go over the information and example reproduced on the next page with your students.*)

CHAPTER 24 LESSON 1 CONTINUED

Reference 71: Envelope Parts	Business Envelope Example

The return address:
1. Name of the person writing the letter
2. Box or street address of the writer
3. City, state, zip code of the writer
 	
The mailing address:
1. Name of the person receiving the letter
2. Name of the company receiving the letter
3. Street address of the person receiving the letter
4. City, state, zip of the person receiving the letter
	Return Address
	Fulton Asher
	615 Calumet Drive
	Arlington, VT 49122
	
	          Mailing Address
	          Dr. Forrest Garner
	          Garner Dental Clinic
	          363 Fulton Manor
	          Brighton, TN 82821

PRACTICE TIME

Have students turn to page 76 in the Practice Section of their book and find Chapter 24, Lesson 1, Practice. Go over the directions to make sure they understand what to do. Check and discuss the Practice after students have finished. (*Chapter 24, Lesson 1, Practice instructions are given below.*)

Chapter 24, Lesson 1, Practice: Using butcher paper, large pieces of construction paper, or poster board, make a colorful wall poster identifying the six parts of a business letter and the parts of a business envelope. Write the title and an example for each of the parts of the business letter and envelope. Illustrate your work. Then, give an oral presentation about the business letter and the envelope when you have finished. (*This project may take several days.*)

WRITING TIME

Have students make an entry in their journals.

VOCABULARY TIME

Assign Chapter 24, Vocabulary Words **#1** on page 8 in the Reference Section for students to define in their Vocabulary notebooks. Tell students they are to use a dictionary or thesaurus to look up the meanings of the vocabulary words. After they write each word and its meaning, students are to write a sentence using the vocabulary word.

Chapter 24, Vocabulary Words #1
(noble, paltry, repulsive, vile)

(End of lesson.)

CHAPTER 24 LESSON 2

New objectives: Grammar (Practice Sentences) and a Practice activity.

JINGLE TIME

Have students turn to the Jingle Section of their books. The teacher will lead the students in reciting the previously-taught jingles.

GRAMMAR TIME

First-Year Option: Put the Practice Sentences from the box below on the board or notebook paper. Use these sentences as you practice the concepts that have been taught. For the greatest benefit, students must participate orally with the teacher. **Second-Year Option:** Have students classify the Practice Sentences independently on paper. Check students' sentences with the answers provided below. (*If you have the CDs for Practice Sentences, have students check their sentences with the CDs.*)

Chapter 24, Practice Sentences for Lesson 2
1. _____ Amazing! I saw the awesome miracle clearly during the revival!
2. _____ Go to your pastor's office today after services.

TEACHING SCRIPT FOR PRACTICING MIXED PATTERNS

We will practice classifying Mixed Patterns. We will classify the sentences together. Begin. (*You might have your students write the labels above the sentences at this time.*)

Question and Answer Flow for Sentence 1: Amazing! I saw the awesome miracle clearly during the revival!

1. Who saw the awesome miracle clearly during the revival? I - SP
2. What is being said about I? I saw - V
3. I saw what? miracle – verify the noun
4. Does miracle mean the same thing as I? No.
5. Miracle - DO
6. Saw - V-t
7. What kind of miracle? awesome - Adj
8. The - A
9. Saw how? clearly - Adv
10. During - P
11. During what? revival - OP
12. The - A
13. Amazing - I
14. SN V-t DO P2 Check
15. Verb-transitive - Check again.
16. (During the revival) - Prepositional phrase
17. Exclamation point, strong feeling, exclamatory sentence
18. Go back to the verb - divide the complete subject from the complete predicate.
19. Is there an adverb exception? No.
20. Is this sentence in a natural or inverted order? Natural - no change.

Classified Sentence:

                                I   SP V-t A   Adj   DO   Adv   P   A   OP

          <u>SN   V-t</u>   Amazing! I / saw the awesome miracle clearly (during the revival)! **E**
           DO P2

CHAPTER 24 LESSON 2 CONTINUED

Question and Answer Flow for Sentence 2: Go to your pastor's office today after services.

1. Who go to your pastor's office today after services? (you) - SP (understood subject pronoun)
2. What is being said about you? you go - V
3. To - P
4. To what? office - OP
5. Whose office? pastor's - PNA
6. Whose pastor? your - PPA
7. Go when? today - Adv
8. After - P
9. After what? services - OP

10. SN V P1 Check
11. (To your pastor's office) - Prepositional phrase
12. (After services) - Prepositional phrase
13. Period, command, imperative sentence
14. Go back to the verb - divide the complete subject from the complete predicate.
15. Is there an adverb exception? No.
16. Is this sentence in a natural or inverted order? Natural - no change.

Classified Sentence:

```
                (You) SP   V   P  PPA  PNA   OP   Adv   P    OP
                SN  V    / Go (to your pastor's office) today (after services).  Imp
                P1
```

TEACHER INSTRUCTIONS FOR A PRACTICE SENTENCE

Tell students that their sentence writing assignment today is to write a sentence pattern of their choice. They may choose any Pattern, 1-4, for a Practice Sentence. They are to follow the same procedure used in the previous lessons. They should decide on their labels, arrange them in a selected order, write their sentence, and edit the sentence for improved word choices. (*Students do not have to write an Improved Sentence at this point unless you feel they need more one-on-one word choice writing practice.*) Check and discuss the sentence pattern chosen after students have finished.

 PRACTICE TIME

Students will continue letter-writing activities. Have students turn to page 76 in the Practice Section of their book and find Chapter 24, Lesson 2, Practice. Go over the directions to make sure they understand what to do. Check and discuss the Practice after students have finished. (*Chapter 24, Lesson 2, Practice instructions are given below.*)

Chapter 24, Lesson 2, Practice: Write a friendly letter to a special friend or relative. Before you start, review the references and tips for writing friendly letters. After your letter has been edited, fold the letter and put it in an envelope. Address the envelope properly and mail it. Don't forget the stamp.

(End of lesson.)

CHAPTER 24   LESSON 3

New objectives: Grammar (Practice Sentences), Practice activity, and Vocabulary #2.

 JINGLE TIME

Have students turn to the Jingle Section of their books. The teacher will lead the students in reciting the previously-taught jingles.

 GRAMMAR TIME

First-Year Option: Put the Practice Sentences from the box below on the board or notebook paper. Use these sentences as you practice the concepts that have been taught. For the greatest benefit, students must participate orally with the teacher. **Second-Year Option:** Have students classify the Practice Sentences independently on paper. Check students' sentences with the answers provided below. (*If you have the CDs for Practice Sentences, have students check their sentences with the CDs.*)

Chapter 24, Practice Sentences for Lesson 3
1. _____ The mischievous little boy ran quickly to his mother's room!
2. _____ Keith gave Jan a necklace of pearls for their anniversary.

TEACHING SCRIPT FOR PRACTICING MIXED PATTERNS

We will practice classifying Mixed Patterns. We will classify the sentences together. Begin. (*You might have your students write the labels above the sentences at this time.*)

Question and Answer Flow for Sentence 1: The mischievous little boy ran quickly to his mother's room!

1. Who ran quickly to his mother's room? boy - SN
2. What is being said about boy? boy ran - V
3. Boy ran how? quickly - Adv
4. To - P
5. To what? room - OP
6. Whose room? mother's - PNA
7. Whose mother? his - PPA
8. What kind of boy? little - Adj
9. What kind of boy? mischievous - Adj
10. The - A

11. SN V P1 Check
12. (To his mother's room) - Prepositional phrase
13. Exclamation point, strong feeling, exclamatory sentence
14. Go back to the verb - divide the complete subject from the complete predicate.
15. Is there an adverb exception? No.
16. Is this sentence in a natural or inverted order? Natural - no change.

Classified Sentence:

```
                         A    Adj        Adj SN    V    Adv    P PPA PNA    OP
              SN V      The mischievous little boy / ran quickly (to his mother's room)! E
              P1
```

CHAPTER 24 LESSON 3 CONTINUED

Question and Answer Flow for Sentence 2: Keith gave Jan a necklace of pearls for their anniversary.

1. Who gave Jan a necklace of pearls for their anniversary? Keith - SN
2. What is being said about Keith? Keith gave - V
3. Keith gave what? necklace - verify the noun
4. Does necklace mean the same thing as Keith? No.
5. Necklace - DO
6. Gave - V-t
7. Keith gave necklace to whom? Jan - IO
8. A - A
9. Of - P
10. Of what? pearls - OP
11. For - P

12. For what? anniversary - OP
13. Whose anniversary? their - PPA
14. SN V-t IO DO P3 Check
15. Verb-transitive - Check again.
16. (Of pearls) - Prepositional phrase
17. (For their anniversary) - Prepositional phrase
18. Period, statement, declarative sentence
19. Go back to the verb - divide the complete subject from the complete predicate.
20. Is there an adverb exception? No.
21. Is this sentence in a natural or inverted order? Natural - no change.

Classified Sentence:

SN   V-t   IO   A   DO   P   OP   P   PPA   OP

SN V-t
_____   Keith / gave Jan a necklace (of pearls) (for their anniversary). D
IO DO P3

PRACTICE TIME

Students will continue letter-writing activities. Have students turn to page 76 in the Practice Section of their books and find the instructions under Chapter 24, Lesson 3, Practice (*1-2*). Go over the directions to make sure they understand what to do. Check and discuss the Practice after students have finished. (*Chapter 24, Lesson 3, Practice instructions are given below.*)

Chapter 24, Lesson 3, Practice 1: On a sheet of paper, identify the parts of a business letter and envelope by writing the titles and an example for each title. Use References 70 and 71 to help you. (*Use References 70 and 71 to check the parts of a business letter and envelope.*)

Chapter 24, Lesson 3, Practice 2: Write a business letter. You may invent the company and the situation for which you are writing. Before you begin, review the reasons for writing business letters and the four types of business letters (*Reference 69 on page 46*). After your letter has been edited, fold the letter and put it in an envelope. Address the envelope properly.

VOCABULARY TIME

Assign Chapter 24, Vocabulary Words **#2** on page 8 in the Reference Section for students to define in their Vocabulary notebooks. They should write each word, its meaning, and a sentence using the word.

Chapter 24, Vocabulary Words #2
(notorious, reputed, solitary, alone)

(End of lesson.)

CHAPTER 24   LESSON 4

New objectives: Test and an Activity.

JINGLE TIME

Have students turn to the Jingle Section of their books. The teacher will lead the students in reciting the previously-taught jingles.

STUDY TIME

Have students study the vocabulary words in their vocabulary notebooks. Remind students that any vocabulary word in their notebooks could be on their test. Also, have students study any of the skills in the Practice Section that they need to review.

TEST TIME

Have students turn to page 107 in the Test Section of their books and find Chapter 24 Test. Remind them to pay attention and think about what they are doing. Go over the directions to make sure they understand what to do. (*Chapter 24 Test key is on the next page.*)

CHECK TIME

After students have finished, check and discuss their test papers. Make sure they understand why their answers are right or wrong. (*For total points, count each required answer as a point.*)

ACTIVITY / ASSIGNMENT TIME

Have students choose a country or continent that they would like to visit. Have students write several letters requesting information about the country. (*Have them research the different places to send the letters.*) Next, have students research encyclopedias, newspapers, magazines, and even the Internet about the places they would like to visit in their chosen country. They will continue different aspects of this project for several weeks. Make sure students finish this part of the assignment by Lesson 4 in Chapter 25 because they will be given new things to do as they continue learning about the country they have chosen.

(End of lesson.)

Chapter 24 Test
(Student Page 107)

Exercise 1: Classify each sentence.

	A	SN	P	A	Adj	OP	LV	A	CAdj	C	CAdj	PrN

1. **SN LV**   The pies (from the pastry shop) **/** are a tasty and delightful dessert. **D**
   PA P5

	A	Adj	Adj	SN	V-t	DO	P	A	Adj	OP

2. **SN LV**   A strong, young guide **/** took us (down the wild rapids). **D**
   PA P5

Exercise 2: Identify each pair of words as synonyms or antonyms by putting parentheses ( ) around *syn* or *ant*.

1. noble, paltry	syn **(ant)**	4. provoke, pacify	syn **(ant)**	7. reputable, honest	**(syn)** ant
2. reconcile, sever	syn **(ant)**	5. abscond, escape	**(syn)** ant	8. reimburse, refund	**(syn)** ant
3. vile, repulsive	**(syn)** ant	6. notorious, reputed	syn **(ant)**	9. candid, sly	syn **(ant)**

Exercise 3: Underline each subject and fill in each column according to the title.

1. <u>Popsicles</u> are refreshing.
2. This <u>address</u> is incorrect.
3. <u>Sandi</u> ate her orange outdoors.
4. <u>Novels</u> are lengthy stories.

List each Verb	Write PrN, PA, or None	Write L or A
are	PA	L
is	PA	L
ate	None	A
are	PrN	L

Exercise 4: Choose an answer from the choices in parentheses. Then, fill in the rest of the columns according to the titles. (S or P stands for singular or plural.)

Pronoun-antecedent agreement

1. The lions in the cage are venting (its, <u>their</u>) anger.
2. The president of the group lost (<u>her</u>, their) notes.
3. Wyoming lost (<u>its</u>, their) claim to copper.
4. Clifton gave (<u>his</u>, their) approval to the purchase.

Pronoun Choice	S or P	Antecedent	S or P
their	P	lions	P
her	S	president	S
its	S	Wyoming	S
his	S	Clifton	S

Exercise 5: On a sheet of paper, identify the parts of a business letter and envelope by writing the titles and an example for each title. Use References 70 and 71 to help you. (**Use References 70 and 71 to check the parts of a business letter and envelope.**)

Exercise 6: On a sheet of paper, write three sentences, demonstrating each of the three degrees of adjectives. Identify the form you used by writing **simple, comparative,** or **superlative** at the end of each sentence. (Answers will vary.)

Exercise 7: On a sheet of paper, write one sentence for each of these labels: ① (S) ② (SCS) ③ (SCV) ④ (CD) ⑤ (CX). (Answers will vary.)

Exercise 8: On a sheet of paper, write three sentences in which you demonstrate each of the double negative rules. Underline the negative word in each sentence. (Use your book for the double negative rules.) (Answers will vary.)

Exercise 9: In your journal, write a paragraph summarizing what you have learned this week.

CHAPTER 24 LESSON 4 CONTINUED

TEACHER INSTRUCTIONS

Use the Question and Answer Flows below for the sentences on Chapter 24 Tests.

Question and Answer Flow for Sentence 1: The pies from the pastry shop are a tasty and delightful dessert.

1. What are a tasty and delightful dessert? pies - SN
2. What is being said about pies? pies are - V
3. Pies are what? dessert - verify the noun
4. Does dessert mean the same thing as pies? Yes.
5. Dessert - PrN
6. Are - LV
7. What kind of dessert? tasty and delightful - CAdj, CAdj
8. And - C
9. A - A
10. From - P
11. From what? shop - OP
12. What kind of shop? pastry - Adj
13. The - A
14. The - A
15. SN LV PrN P4 Check
16. Linking verb - Check again.
17. (From the pastry shop) - Prepositional phrase
18. Period, statement, declarative sentence
19. Go back to the verb - divide the complete subject from the complete predicate.
20. Is there an adverb exception? No.
21. Is this sentence in a natural or inverted order? Natural - no change.

Classified Sentence:

     A SN   P A   Adj   OP   LV A CAdj C CAdj   PrN
SN LV The pies (from the pastry shop) / are a tasty and delightful dessert. D
PrN P4

Question and Answer Flow for Sentence 2: A strong, young guide took us down the wild rapids.

1. Who took us down the wild rapids? guide - SN
2. What is being said about guide? guide took - V
3. Guide took whom? us - verify the pronoun
4. Does us mean the same thing as guide? No.
5. Us - DO
6. Took - V-t
7. Down - P
8. Down what? rapids - OP
9. What kind of rapids? wild - Adj
10. The - A
11. What kind of guide? young - Adj
12. What kind of guide? strong - Adj
13. A - A
14. SN V-t DO P2 Check
15. Verb-transitive - Check again.
16. (Down the wild rapids) - Prepositional phrase
17. Period, statement, declarative sentence
18. Go back to the verb - divide the complete subject from the complete predicate.
19. Is there an adverb exception? No.
20. Is this sentence in a natural or inverted order? Natural - no change.

Classified Sentence:

     A Adj   Adj SN   V-t DO P   A Adj   OP
SN V-t A strong, young guide / took us (down the wild rapids). D
DO P2

CHAPTER 24   LESSON 5

New objectives: Writing Assignments #37 and #38.

 WRITING TIME

TEACHING SCRIPT FOR WRITING ASSIGNMENTS

Today, you are assigned two different kinds of writing. You will write a descriptive paragraph and a business letter. <u>You will revise and edit both writing assignments.</u> (*Read the box below for more information about the students' writing assignment.*) As you edit, make sure you use the checkpoints in the editing checklist provided in Reference 35. Remember to read through the whole essay, starting with the title, and then edit, sentence-by-sentence, using the five-sentence checkpoints for each sentence. Use the paragraph checkpoints to check each paragraph. Remember, your editing is now more detailed and more comprehensive, so take your time.

Writing Assignment Box #1

Writing Assignment #37: Descriptive paragraph (First or Third Person)

**Writing topic choices: My Favorite Bible Character or A Treasured Pet or An Unforgettable Dream
                          or Choose your own topic.**

Your second writing assignment is to write a business letter. (*Read the box below for more information about students' writing assignment.*)

Writing Assignment Box #2

Writing Assignment #38: Write a business letter. You may invent a company and a situation for which you are writing. Before you begin, review the reasons for writing business letters and the four types of business letters (Reference 69 on page 46). This business must be different from the businesses chosen in the previous lessons. After your letter has been edited, fold the letter and put it in an envelope. Address the envelope properly.

Read, check, and discuss Writing Assignments #37 and #38 after students have finished their final papers. Use the editing checklist as you check and discuss students' papers. Make sure students are using the editing checklist correctly.

(End of lesson.)

CHAPTER 25 LESSON 1

New objectives: Grammar (Practice Sentences), Skills (thank-you notes), and a Practice activity.

JINGLE TIME

Have students turn to the Jingle Section of their books. The teacher will lead the students in reciting the previously-taught jingles.

GRAMMAR TIME

First-Year Option: Put the Practice Sentences from the box below on the board or notebook paper. Use these sentences as you practice the concepts that have been taught. For the greatest benefit, students must participate orally with the teacher. **Second-Year Option:** Have students classify the Practice Sentences independently on paper. Check students' sentences with the answers provided below. (*If you have the CDs for Practice Sentences, have students check their sentences with the CDs.*)

Chapter 25, Practice Sentences for Lesson 1

1. _____ My friend sold Sherry a pretty red bicycle for her daughter.
2. _____ Indeed! Candles are a source of light during a blackout!

TEACHING SCRIPT FOR PRACTICING MIXED PATTERNS

We will practice classifying Mixed Patterns. We will classify the sentences together. Begin. (*You might have your students write the labels above the sentences at this time.*)

Question and Answer Flow for Sentence 1: My friend sold Sherry a pretty red bicycle for her daughter.

1. Who sold Sherry a pretty red bicycle for her daughter?
   friend - SN
2. What is being said about friend? friend sold - V
3. Friend sold what? bicycle - verify the noun
4. Does bicycle mean the same thing as friend? No.
5. Bicycle - DO
6. Sold - V-t
7. Friend sold bicycle to whom? Sherry - IO
8. What kind of bicycle? red - Adj
9. What kind of bicycle? pretty - Adj
10. A - A
11. For - P

12. For whom? daughter - OP
13. Whose daughter? her - PPA
14. Whose friend? my - PPA
15. SN V-t IO DO P3 Check
16. Verb-transitive - Check again.
17. (For her daughter) - prepositional phrase
18. Period, statement, declarative sentence
19. Go back to the verb - divide the complete subject from the complete predicate.
20. Is there an adverb exception? No.
21. Is this sentence in a natural or inverted order?
    Natural - no change.

Classified Sentence:

	PPA	SN	V-t	IO	A	Adj	Adj	DO	P	PPA	OP	
SN V-t	My friend / sold Sherry a pretty red bicycle (for her daughter). D
IO DO P3

CHAPTER 25 LESSON 1 CONTINUED

Question and Answer Flow for Sentence 2: Indeed! Candles are a source of light during a blackout!

1. What are a source of light during a blackout? candles - SN
2. What is being said about candles? candles are - V
3. Candles are what? source - verify the noun
4. Does source mean the same thing as candles? Yes.
5. Source - PrN
6. Are - LV
7. A - A
8. Of - P
9. Of what? light - OP
10. During - P
11. During what? blackout - OP

12. A - A
13. Indeed - I
14. SN LV PrN P4 Check
15. Linking verb - Check again.
16. (Of light) - Prepositional phrase
17. (During a blackout) - Prepositional phrase
18. Exclamation point, strong feeling, exclamatory sentence
19. Go back to the verb - divide the complete subject from the complete predicate.
20. Is there an adverb exception? No.
21. Is this sentence in a natural or inverted order? Natural - no change.

Classified Sentence:

```
                            I       SN     LV A PrN   P  OP    P  A  OP
              SN  LV     Indeed!  Candles / are a source (of light) (during a blackout)!  E
              PrN P4
```

SKILL TIME

TEACHING SCRIPT FOR THANK-YOU NOTES

Close your eyes again. Relax and clear your mind of clutter. Now, think of a person who has done something nice for you or has given you a gift. Sometimes, a person even gives a gift of time, so a gift does not always mean a "physical" gift. After you have thought of someone, open your eyes. That person deserves a thank-you note from you after such a nice gesture. Therefore, it is time we learn about thank-you notes.

You usually write thank-you notes to thank someone for a gift or for doing something nice. In either case, a thank-you note should include at least three statements.

1. You should tell the person <u>what</u> you are thanking him/her for.
2. You should tell the person <u>how the gift was used</u> or <u>how it helped</u>.
3. You should tell the person <u>how much you appreciated the gift or action</u>.

A thank-you note should follow the same form as a friendly letter: heading, greeting, body, closing, and signature. Look at Reference 72 on page 47 and follow along as I read the information about thank-you notes. (*Go over the information and examples reproduced on the next page with your students.*)

CHAPTER 25 LESSON 1 CONTINUED

Reference 72: Thank-You Notes	
For a Gift	**For an Action**
What - Thank you for... (tell color, kind, and item) **Use -** Tell how the gift is used. **Thanks -** I appreciate your remembering me with this special gift.	**What -** Thank you for... (tell action) **Helped -** Tell how the action helped. **Thanks -** I appreciate your thinking of me at this time.

Example 1: Gift	4142 Dogwood Trail Austin, NV 21676 June 27, 20__

Dear Lois,

   How could I ever thank you enough for the autographed copy of Jesse Stuart's book? It is a treasure, and I will add it to my collection of rare books.

Most sincerely,
Wanda

Example 2: Action	46401 Bursley Road Grafton, OH 65703 July 21, 20__

Dear Brandon,

   Thanks for helping me change the flat tire on Dad's truck last night. I doubt that I could have done it without your help. You are a true friend!

Appreciatively,
Lance

 PRACTICE TIME

Have students turn to page 76 in the Practice Section of their book and find Chapter 25, Lesson 1, Practice. Go over the directions to make sure they understand what to do. Guide students closely as they do the practice exercises for the first time. (*Students may use the Reference section in their books to help them remember the new information.* Check and discuss the Practice after students have finished. (*Chapter 25, Lesson 1, Practice instructions are given below*.)

Chapter 25, Lesson 1, Practice: Write your own thank-you note. First, think of a person who has done something nice for you or has given you a gift *(even the gift of time)*. Next, write that person a thank-you note using the information in the Reference section as a guide. (*Check and discuss students' thank-you notes after they are finished. Note: Give students who cannot think of anyone the option of making up someone of their choice.*)

 VOCABULARY TIME

Students will no longer have assigned Vocabulary Words. As they find new or interesting words, have students add them to their list in their Vocabulary notebook.

(End of lesson.)

CHAPTER 25 LESSON 2

New objectives: Grammar (Practice Sentences), Skills (invitations), and a Practice activity.

JINGLE TIME

Have students turn to the Jingle Section of their books. The teacher will lead the students in reciting the previously-taught jingles.

GRAMMAR TIME

First-Year Option: Put the Practice Sentences from the box below on the board or notebook paper. Use these sentences as you practice the concepts that have been taught. For the greatest benefit, students must participate orally with the teacher. **Second-Year Option:** Have students classify the Practice Sentences independently on paper. Check students' sentences with the answers provided below. (*If you have the CDs for Practice Sentences, have students check their sentences with the CDs.*)

Chapter 25, Practice Sentences for Lesson 2

1. _____ Parishioners of all religions worshiped the Lord at the community church.
2. _____ Sit at the far end of the bleachers with Larry's family.

TEACHING SCRIPT FOR PRACTICING MIXED PATTERNS

We will practice classifying Mixed Patterns. We will classify the sentences together. Begin. (*You might have your students write the labels above the sentences at this time.*)

Question and Answer Flow for Sentence 1: Parishioners of all religions worshiped the Lord at the community church.

1. Who worshiped the Lord at the community church? parishioners - SN
2. What is being said about parishioners? parishioners worshiped - V
3. Parishioners worshiped whom? Lord - verify the noun
4. Does Lord mean the same thing as parishioners? No.
5. Lord - DO
6. Worshiped - V-t
7. The - A
8. At - P
9. At what? church - OP
10. What kind of church? community - Adj
11. The - A
12. Of - P
13. Of what? religions - OP
14. How many religions? all - Adj
15. SN V-t DO P2 Check
16. Verb-transitive - Check again.
17. (Of all religions) - Prepositional phrase
18. (At the community church) - Prepositional phrase
19. Period, statement, declarative sentence
20. Go back to the verb - divide the complete subject from the complete predicate.
21. Is there an adverb exception? No.
22. Is this sentence in a natural or inverted order? Natural - no change.

Classified Sentence:

```
                          SN     P Adj  OP      V-t   A  DO  P A    Adj     OP
        SN V-t        Parishioners (of all religions) / worshiped the Lord (at the community church). D
        DO P2
```

CHAPTER 25 LESSON 2 CONTINUED

Question and Answer Flow for Sentence 2: Sit at the far end of the bleachers with Larry's family.

1. Who sit at the far end of the bleachers with Larry's family?
   You - SP (understood subject pronoun)
2. What is being said about you? you sit - V
3. At - P
4. At what? end - OP
5. Which end? far - Adj
6. The - A
7. Of - P
8. Of what? bleachers - OP
9. The - A
10. With - P
11. With whom? family - OP
12. Whose family? Larry's -PNA
13. SN V P1 Check
14. (At the far end) - Prepositional phrase
15. (Of the bleachers) - Prepositional phrase
16. (With Larry's family) - Prepositional phrase
17. Period, command, imperative sentence
18. Go back to the verb - divide the complete subject from the complete predicate.
19. Is there an adverb exception? No.
20. Is this sentence in a natural or inverted order? Natural - no change.

Classified Sentence:

<pre>
                 (You) SP   V   P A Adj OP   P A   OP   P PNA   OP
                 SN V   / Sit (at the far end) (of the bleachers) (with Larry's family). Imp
                 ‾‾‾‾‾‾
                 P1
</pre>

TEACHER INSTRUCTIONS FOR A PRACTICE SENTENCE

Tell students that their sentence writing assignment today is to write a sentence pattern of their choice. They may choose any Pattern, 1-4, for a Practice Sentence. They are to follow the same procedure used in the previous lessons. They should decide on their labels, arrange them in a selected order, write their sentence, and edit the sentence for improved word choices. (*Students do not have to write an Improved Sentence at this point unless you feel they need more one-on-one word choice writing practice.*) Check and discuss the sentence pattern chosen after students have finished.

SKILL TIME

TEACHING SCRIPT FOR INVITATIONS

With all the commercial cards today, the art of personal, unique, and individual invitations is almost obsolete. And whether you ever have occasion to write personal invitations or not, as an astute student of English, it is your responsibility to learn how, especially since it is so easy. Today, you will plan a special event or occasion and make an invitation to send out. It is time we learn about writing invitations. It is always best to make an outline for an invitation. Your invitation outline should include the following information in any logical order.

1. What - Tell what the event or special occasion is.
2. Who - Tell whom the event is for.
3. Where - Tell where the event will take place.
4. When - Tell the date and time of the event.
5. Whipped-cream statement: A polite statement written to make the person feel welcome.

An invitation will sometimes have an RSVP. This is a French expression that means, "please respond," and a reply is needed. If a phone number is included, reply by phone. Otherwise, a written reply is expected. An invitation should follow the same form as a friendly letter: **heading, greeting, body, closing, and signature**. Now, we will go over the five outline parts of an invitation again and see how they are used in a sample invitation.

CHAPTER 25 LESSON 2 CONTINUED

Look at Reference 73 on page 48 and follow along as I read the information about invitations. *(Go over the information and examples reproduced below with your students.)*

Reference 73: Invitations		
1.	What	– a surprise birthday party
2.	Who	– for Hunter Davis
3.	Where	– at Barton Community Center
4.	When	– on Saturday, August 7, at 7:00 p.m.
5.	Whipped Cream	– hope you can join us!

238 Virginia Cove
Upton, Florida 44602
July 30, 20__

Dear Lonnie,
    We are having a <u>surprise birthday party</u> for <u>Hunter Davis</u> on <u>Saturday evening, August 7, at 7:00</u> and <u>hope</u> that <u>you can join us</u>. It will be held at <u>Barton Community Center</u> on Merrill Drive. There will be all kinds of good things to eat. Be there!

Your friends,
Jerry and Jared Wagner

Notice that the five parts of an invitation are underlined in the example; however, you would not underline them in an actual invitation.

 PRACTICE TIME

Students will continue letter-writing activities. Have students turn to page 76 in the Practice Section of their book and find Chapter 25, Lesson 2, Practice. Go over the directions to make sure they understand what to do. If students need a review, have them study the information and examples in the Reference Section of their books. Check and discuss the Practice after students have finished. *(Chapter 25, Lesson 2, Practice instructions are given below.)*

Chapter 25, Lesson 2, Practice: Make your own invitation card. First, think of a special event or occasion and who will be invited. Next, make an invitation to send out using the information in the Reference section as a guide. Illustrate your card appropriately. *(Check and discuss students' invitation cards after they are finished.)*

 WRITING TIME

Have students make an entry in their journals.

(End of lesson.)

CHAPTER 25   LESSON 3

New objectives: Grammar (Practice Sentences) and a Practice activity.

JINGLE TIME

Have students turn to the Jingle Section of their books. The teacher will lead the students in reciting the previously-taught jingles.

GRAMMAR TIME

First-Year Option: Put the Practice Sentences from the box below on the board or notebook paper. Use these sentences as you practice the concepts that have been taught. For the greatest benefit, students must participate orally with the teacher. **Second-Year Option:** Have students classify the Practice Sentences independently on paper. Check students' sentences with the answers provided below. (*If you have the CDs for Practice Sentences, have students check their sentences with the CDs.*)

Chapter 25, Practice Sentences for Lesson 3
1. _____ Kelly showed the class the exciting pictures from their trip.
2. _____ My mother and I visited a city hospital for children.

TEACHING SCRIPT FOR PRACTICING MIXED PATTERNS

We will practice classifying Mixed Patterns. We will classify the sentences together. Begin. (*You might have your students write the labels above the sentences at this time.*)

Question and Answer Flow for Sentence 1: Kelly showed the class the exciting pictures from their trip.

1. Who showed the class the exciting pictures from their trip? Kelly - SN
2. What is being said about Kelly? Kelly showed - V
3. Kelly showed what? pictures - verify the noun
4. Do pictures mean the same thing as Kelly? No.
5. Pictures - DO
6. Showed - V-t
7. Kelly showed pictures to whom? class - IO
8. What kind of pictures? exciting - Adj
9. The - A
10. From - P
11. From what? trip - OP
12. Whose trip? their - PPA
13. The - A
14. SN V-t IO DO P3 Check
15. Verb-transitive Check again.
16. (From their trip) - Prepositional phrase
17. Period, statement, declarative sentence
18. Go back to the verb - divide the complete subject from the complete predicate.
19. Is there an adverb exception? No.
20. Is this sentence in a natural or inverted order? Natural - no change.

Classified Sentence:

```
                   SN   V-t   A   IO   A   Adj    DO      P  PPA OP
        SN  V-t    Kelly / showed the class the exciting pictures (from their trip).  D
        IO DO P3
```

CHAPTER 25 LESSON 3 CONTINUED

Question and Answer Flow for Sentence 2: My mother and I visited a city hospital for children.

1. Who visited a city hospital for children?
   mother and I - CSN, CSP
2. What is being said about mother and I?
   mother and I visited - V
3. Mother and I visited what? hospital - verify the noun
4. Does hospital mean the same thing as mother and I?
   No.
5. Hospital - DO
6. Visited - V-t
7. What kind of hospital? city - Adj
8. A - A
9. For - P

10. For whom? children - OP
11. And - C
12. Whose mother? my - PPA
13. SN V-t DO P2 Check
14. Verb-transitive - Check again.
15. (For children) - Prepositional phrase
16. Period, statement, declarative sentence
17. Go back to the verb - divide the complete subject from the complete predicate.
18. Is there an adverb exception? No.
19. Is this sentence in a natural or inverted order?
   Natural - no change.

Classified Sentence:

         PPA CSN   C CSP V-t   A Adj   DO   P   OP
SN V-t My mother and I / visited a city hospital (for children). **D**
DO P2

 PRACTICE TIME

Students will continue thank-you note and invitation activities. Have students turn to page 76 in the Practice Section of their books and find the instructions under Chapter 25, Lesson 3, Practice *(1-2)*. Go over the directions to make sure they understand what to do. Check and discuss the Practice after students have finished. *(Chapter 25, Lesson 3, Practice instructions are given below.)*

Chapter 25, Lesson 3, Practice 1: Write another thank-you note. First, think of a person who has done something nice for you or has given you a gift *(even the gift of time)*. Next, write that person a thank-you note using the information in the Reference section as a guide. *(Check and discuss students' thank-you notes after they are finished.)*

Chapter 25, Lesson 3, Practice 2: Make another invitation card. First, think of a special event or occasion and who will be invited. Next, make an invitation to send out using the information in the Reference section as a guide. Illustrate your card appropriately. *(Check and discuss students' invitation cards after they are finished.)*

(End of lesson.)

CHAPTER 25   LESSON 4

New objectives: Test and an Activity (continued).

JINGLE TIME

Have students turn to the Jingle Section of their books. The teacher will lead the students in reciting the previously-taught jingles.

STUDY TIME

Have students study any of the skills in the Practice Section that they need to review.

TEST TIME

Have students turn to page 108 in the Test Section of their books and find the Chapter 25 Test. Remind them to pay attention and think about what they are doing. Go over the directions to make sure they understand what to do. (*Chapter 25 Test key is on the next page.*)

CHECK TIME

After students have finished, check and discuss the test sentences they created. Make sure they understand why their test questions and answers are right or wrong. (*For total points, count each required answer as a point.*)

ACTIVITY / ASSIGNMENT TIME

In the last activity, students wrote letters for information about the country that they want to visit. They also researched reference materials and the Internet for more information about the places that they would like to visit in their chosen country.

For this portion of the project, have students study different maps of their country. Have them write an outline of all the things they could find out about their country from maps. (*Mountains, rivers, cities, roads, etc.*) Have them develop a travel schedule that shows where they want to go, what they would see, and the time they will allow for each place. It can be as detailed as the teacher wants it to be. Finally, they should chart their route on a map of their country. Have them figure the miles they will have traveled during their trip.

(End of lesson.)

Chapter 25 Test
(Student Page 108)

Exercise 1: Classify each sentence.

```
            Adj    SN    HV    Adv            V-t      Adj   DO
1.  SN V-t   Bible scholars / are constantly documenting new research.  D
    DO P2

            SN   HV Adv  V    P  A  Adj   OP       Adv
2.  SN V     Cindy / is not going (to the golf tournament) today.  D
    P1
```

Exercise 2: Write a thank-you note. First, think of a person who has done something nice for you or has given you a gift (even the gift of time). Next, write that person a thank-you note using the information in the Reference section as a guide. (*Answers will vary.*)

Exercise 3: Make an invitation card. First, think of a special event or occasion and who will be invited. Next, make an invitation to send out, using the information in the Reference section as a guide. Illustrate your card appropriately. (*Answers will vary.*)

Exercise 4: Write the seven present tense helping verbs, the five past tense helping verbs, and the two future tense helping verbs. (*The order of the answers will vary.*) (<u>Present</u>: am, is, are, has, have, do, does; <u>Past</u>: was, were, had, did, been; <u>Future</u>: will, shall)

Exercise 5: On a sheet of paper, write three sentences, demonstrating each of the three degrees of adjectives. Identify the form you used by writing **simple, comparative,** or **superlative** at the end of each sentence. (Answers will vary.)

Exercise 6: On a sheet of paper, write three sentences in which you demonstrate each of the double negative rules. Underline the negative word in each sentence. (Use your book for the double negative rules.) (Answers will vary.)

Exercise 7: In your journal, write a paragraph summarizing what you have learned this week.

CHAPTER 25 LESSON 4 CONTINUED

TEACHER INSTRUCTIONS

Use the Question and Answer Flows below for the sentences on Chapter 25 Tests.

Question and Answer Flow for Sentence 1: Bible scholars are constantly documenting new research.

1. Who are constantly documenting new research?
   scholars - SN
2. What is being said about scholars?
   scholars are documenting - V
3. Are - HV
4. Scholars are documenting what?
   research - verify the noun.
5. Does research mean the same thing as scholars? No.
6. Research - DO
7. Documenting - V-t
8. What kind of research? new - Adj

9. Are documenting how? constantly - Adv
10. What kind of scholars? Bible - Adj
11. SN V-t DO P2 Check
12. Verb-transitive - Check again.
13. No prepositional phrases.
14. Period, statement, declarative sentence
15. Go back to the verb - divide the complete subject from the complete predicate.
16. Is there an adverb exception? No.
17. Is this sentence in a natural or inverted order?
    Natural - no change.

Classified Sentence:

	Adj	SN	HV	Adv	V-t	Adj	DO

SN V-t   Bible scholars / are constantly documenting new research. **D**
DO P2

Question and Answer Flow for Sentence 2: Cindy is not going to the golf tournament today.

1. Who is not going to the golf tournament today? Cindy - SN
2. What is being said about Cindy? Cindy is going - V
3. Is - HV
4. Is going how? not - Adv
5. To - P
6. To what? tournament - OP
7. What kind of tournament? golf - Adj
8. The - A
9. Is going when? today - Adv

10. SN V P1 Check
11. (To the golf tournament) - Prepositional phrase
12. Period, statement, declarative sentence
13. Go back to the verb - divide the complete subject from the complete predicate.
14. Is there an adverb exception? No.
15. Is this sentence in a natural or inverted order?
    Natural - no change.

Classified Sentence:

	SN	HV	Adv	V	P	A	Adj	OP	Adv

SN V   Cindy / is not going (to the golf tournament) today. **D**
P1

CHAPTER 25   LESSON 5

New objectives: Writing Assignments #39 and #40, Bonus Option.

  WRITING TIME

TEACHING SCRIPT FOR WRITING ASSIGNMENTS

Today, you are assigned two different kinds of writing. You will write a business letter for the first writing assignment. For the second writing assignment, you will have a choice of topics. This assignment will require a title that will accurately reflect the content of your paragraph/essay. <u>You will revise and edit both writing assignments.</u> (*Read the box below for more information about students' writing assignment.*) As you edit, make sure you use the checkpoints in the editing checklist provided in Reference 35.

Writing Assignment Box #1

Writing Assignment #39: Write a business letter. You may invent a company and a situation for which you are writing. Before you begin, review the reasons for writing business letters and the four types of business letters (Reference 69 on page 46). This business must be different from the businesses chosen in the previous lessons. After your letter has been edited, fold the letter and put it in an envelope. Address the envelope properly.

Writing Assignment Box #2

Writing Assignment #40: Your choice (First or Third Person)

Writing choices: (1) **Expository**   (2) **Persuasive**   (3) **Narrative**   (4) **Descriptive**

Bonus Option: You will again write a story with hidden names. As you write this story, use at least 30 different names of books of the Bible. Remember to weave the names into the story so they do not seem out of place. Apostrophes and other slight changes can be made when necessary.

Example: <u>Esther</u> *called and said that* <u>Joshua</u> *and Joel will* <u>judge</u> *the science fair in Lake* <u>Proverb</u> *next week.*

Create your story and edit it carefully for mistakes. Be sure to edit the story for meaning. Do all the sentences flow together and make sense? Then, give your story to several family members to see if they can find all the books of the Bible that you incorporated in your story. (*Don't forget to make a key that shows the books you used in your story so you can check it quickly.*)

Read, check, and discuss Writing Assignments #39 and #40 after students have finished their final papers. Use the editing checklist as you check and discuss students' papers. Make sure students are using the editing checklist correctly.

(End of lesson.)

CHAPTER 26   LESSON 1

New objectives: Grammar (Practice Sentences).

GRAMMAR TIME

First-Year Option: Put the Practice Sentences from the box below on the board or notebook paper. Use these sentences as you practice the concepts that have been taught. For the greatest benefit, students must participate orally with the teacher. **Second-Year Option:** Have students classify the Practice Sentences independently on paper. Check students' sentences with the answers provided below. (*If you have the CDs for Practice Sentences, have students check their sentences with the CDs.*)

Chapter 26, Practice Sentences for Lesson 1
1. _____ Have the children walked to the park today?
2. _____ Several tadpoles in our pond recently became frogs.

Question and Answer Flow for Sentence 1: Have the children walked to the park today?

1. Who have walked to the park today? children - SN
2. What is being said about children?
   children have walked - V
3. Have - HV
4. To - P
5. To what? park - OP
6. The - A
7. Walked when? today - Adv
8. The - A

9. SN V P1 Check
10. (To the park) - Prepositional phrase
11. Question mark, question, interrogative sentence
12. Go back to the verb - divide the complete subject from the complete predicate.
13. Is there an adverb exception? No.
14. Is this sentence in a natural or inverted order? Inverted - underline the subject parts once and the predicate parts twice.

Classified Sentence:

```
                    HV    A    SN      V     P   A   OP    Adv
        SN  V      Have the children / walked (to the park) today?  Int
        P1
```

Question and Answer Flow for Sentence 2: Several tadpoles in our pond recently became frogs.

1. What recently became frogs? tadpoles - SN
2. What is being said about tadpoles? tadpoles became - V
3. Tadpoles became what? frogs - verify the noun
4. Do frogs mean the same thing as tadpoles? Yes.
5. Frogs - PrN
6. Became - LV
7. Became when? recently - Adv
8. In - P
9. In what? pond - OP
10. Whose pond? our – PPA
11. How many tadpoles? several - Adj

12. SN LV PrN P4 Check
13. Linking verb - Check again.
14. (In our pond) - Prepositional phrase
15. Period, statement, declarative sentence
16. Go back to the verb - divide the complete subject from the complete predicate.
17. Is there an adverb exception? Yes – change the line.
18. Is this sentence in a natural or inverted order? Natural - no change.

Classified Sentence:

```
                    Adj     SN     P PPA  OP     Adv       LV    PrN
        SN  LV     Several tadpoles (in our pond) / recently became frogs.  D
        PrN P4
```

CHAPTER 26   LESSON 2

New objectives: Grammar (Independent Sentences), Skills (parts of a book), and a Practice sheet.

GRAMMAR TIME

Have students make up four sentences, one for each sentence pattern, 1-4. They should decide on their labels, arrange them in a selected order, write their sentences, and edit the sentences for improved word choices, if necessary. Check and discuss the sentence patterns after students have finished.

SKILL TIME

TEACHING SCRIPT FOR INTRODUCING PARTS OF A BOOK

Do you know the parts of a book? Let's see how many we can name. (*Call on different students to name the parts they know. See the parts below.*) Actually, the parts of a book can be divided into the front part and back part. We will learn the front parts of a book, and then we will learn the back parts. Anytime you use a nonfiction book to help you with an assignment, it is necessary to understand how to use that book efficiently.

Knowing the parts of a book will help you make full use of the special features that are sometimes found in nonfiction books. I will now give you a brief description of each of the features that could appear in a book. We will start with the front parts of a book. Look at Reference 74 on page 48 in the reference section of your book. (*Read and discuss the parts of a book below and on the next page with your students.*)

Reference 74: Parts of a Book

AT THE FRONT:

1. **Title Page.** This page has the full title of the book, the author's name, the illustrator's name, the name of the publishing company, and the city where the book was published.

2. **Copyright Page.** This page is right after the title page and tells the year in which the book was published, and who owns the copyright. If the book has an ISBN number (International Standard Book Number), it is listed here.

3. **Preface** (also called **introduction**). If a book has this page, it will come before the table of contents and will usually tell you briefly why the book was written and what it is about.

4. **Table of Contents.** This section lists the major divisions of the book by units or chapters and tells their page numbers.

5. **Body.** This is the main section, or text, of the book.

CHAPTER 26 LESSON 2 CONTINUED

Reference 74: Parts of a Book, Continued

AT THE BACK:

6. **Appendix.** This section includes extra informative material such as maps, charts, tables, diagrams, letters, etc. It is always wise to find out what is in the appendix, since it may contain supplementary material that you could otherwise find only by going to the library.

7. **Glossary.** This section is like a dictionary and gives the meanings of some of the important words in the book.

8. **Bibliography.** This section includes a list of books used by the author. It could serve as a guide for further reading on a topic.

9. **Index.** This will probably be your most useful section. The purpose of the index is to help you quickly locate information about the topics in the book. It has an alphabetical list of specific topics and tells on which page that information can be found. It is similar to the table of contents, but it is much more detailed.

 PRACTICE TIME

Have students turn to page 77 in the Practice Section of their books and find Chapter 26, Lesson 2, Practices (*1-3*). Go over the directions to make sure they understand what to do. If students need a review, have them study the information and examples in the Reference Section of their books. Check and discuss the Practices after students have finished. (*Chapter 26, Lesson 2, Practice keys are below.*)

Chapter 26, Lesson 2, Practice 1: Match each part of a book listed below with the type of information it may give you. Write the appropriate letter in the blank. You may use a letter only once.

A. Title page	B. Copyright page	C. Index	D. Bibliography	E. Appendix	F. Glossary

1. __D__ A list of books used by the author as references

2. __B__ ISBN number

3. __C__ Used to locate topics quickly

Chapter 26, Lesson 2, Practice 2: Match each part of a book listed below with the type of information it may give you. Write the appropriate letter in the blank. You may use a letter only once.

A. Title page	B. Table of contents	C. Copyright page	D. Index	E. Bibliography
F. Preface	G. Body			

1. __D__ Exact page numbers for a particular topic

2. __G__ Text of the book

3. __F__ Reason the book was written

4. __E__ Books listed for finding more information

Chapter 26, Lesson 2, Practice 3: On a separate sheet of paper, write the nine parts of a book and label them front or back. **(Front: Title Page, Copyright Page, Preface, Table of Contents, Body) (Back: Appendix, Glossary, Bibliography, Index)** *(Answers can be in any order.)*

(End of lesson.)

CHAPTER 26   LESSON 3

New objectives: Grammar (Independent Sentences) and a Practice sheet.

GRAMMAR TIME

Have students make up four sentences, one for each sentence pattern, 1-4. Students are to follow the same procedure used in the previous lessons. They should decide on their labels, arrange them in a selected order, write their sentences, and edit the sentences for improved word choices, if necessary. Check and discuss the sentence patterns after students have finished.

PRACTICE TIME

Have students turn to pages 77 and 78 in the Practice Section of their books and find Chapter 26, Lesson 3, Practice (*1-2*). Go over the directions to make sure they understand what to do. If students need a review, have them study the information and examples in the Reference Section of their books. Check and discuss the Practice after students have finished. (*Chapter 26, Lesson 3, Practice instructions are given below.*)

Chapter 26, Lesson 3, Practice 1: Write the nine parts of a book on a poster and write a description beside each part. Illustrate and color the nine parts. **(Title page, Copyright page, Preface, Table of contents, Body, Appendix, Glossary, Bibliography, Index)** (*Check and discuss students' definitions and illustrations after they have finished. Note: Students may use their reference pages to help them.*)

Chapter 26, Lesson 3, Practice 2: Underline each subject and fill in each column according to the title.

	List each Verb	Write PrN, PA, or None	Write L or A
1. <u>Grapefruits</u> are healthy.	are	PA	L
2. His <u>decision</u> was final.	was	PA	L
3. My <u>cousin</u> paid the bill.	paid	None	A
4. <u>Greenland</u> is a remote island.	is	PrN	L
5. Most <u>parents</u> are wise.	are	PA	L
6. <u>She</u> sometimes sleeps in church.	sleeps	None	A
7. The <u>platypus</u> is a shrewd hunter.	is	PrN	L
8. The <u>interstate</u> is a dangerous road.	is	PrN	L
9. <u>Spelunkers</u> are modern-day explorers.	are	PrN	L
10. <u>Plagiarism</u> is a violation of the law.	is	PrN	L

(End of lesson.)

CHAPTER 26   LESSON 4

New objectives: Test and an Activity (continued).

JINGLE TIME

Have students turn to the Jingle Section of their books. The teacher will lead the students in reciting the previously-taught jingles.

STUDY TIME

Have students study the vocabulary words in their vocabulary notebooks. Remind students that any vocabulary word in their notebooks could be on their test. Also, have students study any of the skills in the Practice Section that they need to review.

TEST TIME

Have students turn to page 109 in the Test Section of their books and find Chapter 26 Test. Remind them to pay attention and think about what they are doing. Go over the directions to make sure they understand what to do. (*Chapter 26 Test key is on the next page.*)

CHECK TIME

After students have finished, check and discuss the test sentences they created. Make sure they understand why their test questions and answers are right or wrong. (*For total points, count each required answer as a point.*)

ACTIVITY / ASSIGNMENT TIME

In the last activity, students used maps to help them learn about their country. They also developed a schedule of the places they wanted to go and how long to allow for each stop. Finally, they used their maps to figure the number of miles they would travel.

For this portion of the project, have students cut out pictures of favorite places and make a traveling picture album. If they have not received any information that they requested in their letters, they can use brochures and maps from travel agencies and the Internet.

(End of lesson.)

Chapter 26 Test
(Student Page 109)

Exercise 1: Classify each sentence.

```
              HV    SN          V-t  IO  A   Adj   DO
1. SN  V-t    Will Mrs. Green / give you a music lesson?  D
   IO  DO  P3
```

```
                   A   Adj    SN      V-t   DO    P PPA  OP
2. SN  V-t    The band conductor / lost money (on his trip).  D
   DO  P2
```

Exercise 2: Match each part of a book listed below with the type of information it may give you. Write the appropriate letter in the blank. You may use a letter only once.

A. Title page	B. Copyright page	C. Index	D. Bibliography	E. Appendix	F. Glossary

1. __D__ A list of books used by the author as references

2. __F__ Meanings of important words in the book

3. __A__ Publisher's name and city where the book was published

4. __B__ ISBN number

5. __C__ Used to locate topics quickly

6. __E__ Extra maps in a book

Exercise 3: Match each part of a book listed below with the type of information it may give you. Write the appropriate letter in the blank. You may use a letter only once.

A. Title page	B. Table of contents	C. Copyright page	D. Index	E. Bibliography
F. Preface	G. Body			

1. __D__ Exact page numbers for a particular topic

2. __A__ Author's name, title of book, and illustrator's name

3. __E__ Books listed for finding more information

4. __G__ Text of the book

5. __F__ Reason the book was written

6. __B__ Titles of units and chapters

7. __C__ Copyright date

Exercise 4: Write the five parts found at the front of a book. **(Title page, Copyright page, Preface, Table of contents, Body)** **(Answers can be in any order.)**

Exercise 5: Write the four parts found at the back of a book. **(Appendix, Glossary, Bibliography, Index)** **(Answers can be in any order.)**

Exercise 6: Underline each subject and fill in each column according to the title.

	List each Verb	Write PrN, PA, or None	Write L or A
1. The <u>iris</u> is a beautiful flower.	is	PrN	L
2. The <u>venison</u> was delicious.	was	PA	L
3. Leah's <u>mom</u> called for help.	called	None	A
4. <u>Maine</u> is a fishing state.	is	PrN	L
5. Harp <u>music</u> is very soothing.	is	PA	L

Exercise 7: In your journal, write a paragraph summarizing what you have learned this week.

CHAPTER 26 LESSON 4 CONTINUED

TEACHER INSTRUCTIONS

Use the Question and Answer Flows below for the sentences on Chapter 26 Tests.

Question and Answer Flow for Sentence 1: Will Mrs. Green give you a music lesson?

1. Who will give you a music lesson? Mrs. Green - SN
2. What is being said about Mrs. Green?
   Mrs. Green will give - V
3. Will - HV
4. Mrs. Green will give what? lesson - verify the noun
5. Does lesson mean the same thing as Mrs. Green? No.
6. Lesson - DO
7. Give - V-t
8. Mrs. Green will give lesson to whom? you - IO
9. What kind of lesson? music - Adj
10. A - A

11. SN V-t IO DO P3 Check
12. Verb-transitive - Check again.
13. No prepositional phrases.
14. Question mark, question, interrogative sentence
15. Go back to the verb - divide the complete subject from the complete predicate.
16. Is there an adverb exception? No.
17. Is this sentence in a natural or inverted order?
    Inverted - underline the subject parts once and the predicate parts twice.

Classified Sentence:

```
                        HV       SN        V-t  IO  A  Adj    DO
        SN V-t       Will Mrs. Green / give you a music lesson?  Int
        IO  DO  P3
```

Question and Answer Flow for Sentence 2: The band conductor lost money on his trip.

1. Who lost money on his trip? conductor - SN
2. What is being said about conductor? conductor lost - V
3. Conductor lost what? money - verify the noun
4. Does money mean the same thing as conductor? No.
5. Money - DO
6. Lost - V-t
7. On - P
8. On what? trip - OP
9. Whose trip? his - PPA
10. What kind of conductor? band - Adj

11. The - A
12. SN V-t DO P2 Check
13. Verb-transitive - Check again.
14. (On his trip) - Prepositional phrase
15. Period, statement, declarative sentence
16. Go back to the verb - divide the complete subject from the complete predicate.
17. Is there an adverb exception? No.
18. Is this sentence in a natural or inverted order?
    Natural - no change.

Classified Sentence:

```
                        A   Adj     SN       V-t   DO    P  PPA  OP
        SN V-t       The band conductor / lost money (on his trip).  D
        DO  P2
```

CHAPTER 26   LESSON 5

New objectives: Writing Assignments #41 and #42, Bonus Option.

 **WRITING TIME**

TEACHING SCRIPT FOR WRITING ASSIGNMENTS

Today, you will be given two writing assignments. With each, you will have a choice of topics. Once you have drafted your writings, you will then revise and edit both assignments. The second assignment will require a title that will accurately reflect the content of your paragraph/essay.

Writing Assignment Box #1

Writing Assignment #41: Your choice

Writing choices: (1) **Friendly Letter**   (2) **Business Letter**   (3) **Thank You Note**

Writing Assignment Box #2

Writing Assignment #42: Your choice (First or Third Person)

Writing choices: (1) **Expository**   (2) **Persuasive**   (3) **Narrative**   (4) **Descriptive**

Bonus Option: Research churches from at least six countries, using the Internet, travel agents, travel magazines, and the library. From each country, choose a church that impresses you the most. Then, write an article, summarizing the interesting things that you discovered about each church. Don't forget to draw or locate a picture of each church to illustrate your article. You may type the articles on the computer or write them in ink. Interview preachers or church members of several local churches and write an article about their unique history. Include pictures to personalize your research. Finally, put all your information in a booklet with the title, *Churches Around the World*. Illustrate the cover of your booklet. Share the booklet with friends, family, and members of the community. (*This project will take several weeks to complete; therefore, this assignment will be repeated for the next several lessons.*)

Read, check, and discuss Writing Assignments #41 and #42 after students have finished their final papers. Use the editing checklist as you check and discuss students' papers. Make sure students are using the editing checklist correctly.

(End of lesson.)

CHAPTER 27 LESSON 1

New objectives: Grammar (Independent Sentences), Skills (main parts of the library), and a Practice sheet.

GRAMMAR TIME

Have students make up four sentences, one for each sentence pattern, 1-4. Students are to follow the same procedure used in the previous lessons. They should decide on their labels, arrange them in a selected order, write their sentences, and edit the sentences for improved word choices, if necessary. Check and discuss the sentence patterns after students have finished.

SKILL TIME

TEACHING SCRIPT FOR INTRODUCING MAIN PARTS OF THE LIBRARY

A library is a good place to find information. In order to make the library an easy and fun experience, you need to know about some of the major sections in the library and the most common materials found in the library. As we study the different sections, we can put the information on different-colored construction paper.

Teacher's Notes: Make cards from large sheets of different-colored construction paper. Write these titles on them: *Fiction Section, Nonfiction Section, Reference Section, Dictionary, Encyclopedia, Atlas, Almanac, The Readers' Guide to Periodical Literature*, and *The Card Catalog*. Under each title, write the information provided below. You and your students might also illustrate and laminate the cards.

Fiction Section
Fiction books contain stories about people, places, or things that are not true. Fiction books are arranged on the shelves in alphabetical order according to the authors' last names. Since fiction stories are made-up, they cannot be used when you research a report topic.

Non-Fiction Section
Non-Fiction books contain information and stories that are true.

Reference Section
The Reference Section is designed to help you find information on many topics. The Reference Section contains many different kinds of reference books and materials. Some of the ones that you need to know about will now be discussed.

Dictionary (Reference Book)
The dictionary gives the definition, spelling, and pronunciation of words and tells briefly about famous people and places.

Encyclopedia (Reference Book)
The encyclopedia gives concise, accurate information about persons, places, and events of worldwide interest.

CHAPTER 27 LESSON 1 CONTINUED

Atlas (Reference Book)
The atlas is primarily a book of maps, but it often contains facts about oceans, lakes, mountains, areas, population, products, and climates of every part of the world.

Almanac (Reference Book)
The World Almanac and *Information Please Almanac* are published once a year and contain brief, up-to-date information on a variety of topics.

The Readers' Guide to Periodical Literature (Reference Book)
The Readers' Guide to Periodical Literature is an index for magazines. It is a monthly booklet that lists the titles of articles, stories, and poems published in all leading magazines. These titles are listed under topics that are arranged alphabetically. The monthly issues of *The Readers' Guide to Periodical Literature* are bound together in a single volume once a year and filed in the library. By using the *Readers' Guide*, a person researching a topic can know which back issues of magazines might be helpful.

Card Catalog (Reference File)
The card catalog is a file of cards, arranged alphabetically, and usually placed in the drawers of a cabinet called the card catalog. It is an index to the library. Some libraries now have computer terminals that show the same information as the card catalog, but the information is stored in a computer. Often, the computer listing will also tell whether or not the book is currently on loan from the library.

In a card catalog, the cards inside the drawers are arranged in alphabetical order. The labels on the drawers tell which cards are in each drawer. The cards inside the card catalog contain information about every book and nearly all the other materials located in the library. Sometimes this information is listed in files in a computerized card catalog. (*A sample card catalog is provided below for you to demonstrate what the card catalog looks like.*)

Sample Card Catalog

A-Az	Fed-Gus	La-Mz	S	W
=	=	=	=	=
B-Cam	Gut-Iz	N-Pz	T	X-Y
=	=	=	=	=
Can-Fec	J-Kz	Q-Rz	U-V	Z
=	=	=	=	=

A book is listed in the library in three ways--by author, by title, and by subject. The card catalog has three kinds of cards: the **author card**, the **title card**, and the **subject card**. All three kinds of cards are arranged alphabetically by the words on the top line.

Look at Reference 75 on page 49 in your Reference Section. This gives you an example of the three cards as we talk about them. All three kinds of cards -- the author card, the title card, and the subject card -- give the name of the book, the name of the author, and the call number of the book. They also give the place and date of publication, the publisher, the number of pages in the book, and other important information.

CHAPTER 27 LESSON 1 CONTINUED

Reference 75: Card Catalog Cards		
Author Card	**Title Card**	**Subject Card**

812.83
Author-Jensen, R. K.
Title   <u>Looking for Limericks</u>
       Ill. by Meg Brady
       Sumpter Press Albany
       (c1999) 182p.
	812.83
	Title <u>Looking for Limericks</u>
	Author-Jensen, R. K.
	       Ill. by Meg Brady
	       Sumpter Press Albany
	       (c1999) 182p.
		812.83
		Topic Types of Poems
		Author-Jensen, R. K.
		Title <u>Looking for Limericks</u>
		       Ill. by Meg Brady
		       Sumpter Press Albany
		       (c1999) 182p.

Author cards have the name of the author of the book on the top line, and author cards are filed alphabetically by the author's last name. **Title cards** have the title of the book on the top line, and title cards are filed alphabetically by the first word of the title (except *A, An,* or *The*). **Subject cards** will have the subject of the book on the top line, and subject cards are filed alphabetically by the first word of the subject (except *A, An,* or *The*).

We are going to discuss how to find nonfiction books in the card catalog and on the library shelves. To find out if your library has a certain nonfiction book, look in the card catalog for the title card of that book. If you don't know the title, but do know the author, look for the author card. If you don't know the title or the author, look under the subject of the book. Also, look under the subject if you are interested in finding several books about your topic.

After you find the card for the book you want in the card catalog, you must know how to find the book on the library shelves. Nonfiction books are arranged on the shelves in **numerical order**, which is number order, according to a **call number**. A call number is the number located on the spine of nonfiction books.

The *Dewey Decimal System* is a way of identifying books by numbers, and a **call number** is part of that system. Since the Dewey Decimal System is a number system for locating nonfiction books, all nonfiction books are given a call number, which will identify where they are located on the shelf. Be sure to write the call number down on paper before you look for the book on the shelves.

When you go to the library shelf, look at the call numbers printed on the spines of the books until you find the same number on the book that you copied from the catalog card. All three catalog cards for a book will have the same call number in the top left corner of the cards. It is important to note that individual biographies and autobiographies are arranged on a separate shelf by the last name of the person about whom they are written.

We are going to discuss how to find fiction books in the card catalog and on the library shelves. To find out if your library has a certain fiction book, look in the card catalog for the title card of that book. If you don't know the title, but do know the author, look for the author card. If you don't know the title or the author, look under the subject of the book. Also, look under the subject if you are interested in finding several books about your topic. Sometimes, fiction books are not classified by subject like other books. You must then look for the title or author of the book.

After you find the card for the book you want in the card catalog, you must know how to find the book on the library shelves. Fiction books are arranged on the shelves in **alphabetical order** according to the **authors' last names**; therefore, a fiction book is located not by title but by the author's last name.

If you look on the spine of a fiction book, you will see only a letter(s). This is the first letter in the author's last name, and all three catalog cards will have the first letter of the author's last name in the top left corner of each card. Be sure to write the author's last name and the book title down on paper before you look for the book on the shelves.

CHAPTER 27 LESSON 1 CONTINUED

When you go to the library shelf, look at the letter printed on the spines of the books until you find the same letter(s) on the book that you copied from the catalog card. If two authors have the same last name, their books are arranged in alphabetical order according to the authors' first names. If there are two or more books by the same author, they are arranged in alphabetical order by titles. (*You might want to take your students to the library for a demonstration of what they have just learned.*)

 PRACTICE TIME

Have students turn to pages 78 and 79 in the Practice Section of their book and find Chapter 27, Lesson 1, Practice (*1-4*). Go over the directions to make sure they understand what to do. If students need a review, have them study the information and examples in the Reference Section of their books. Check and discuss the Practice after students have finished. (*Chapter 2, Lesson 1, Practice instructions are given below.*)

Chapter 27, Lesson 1, Practice 1: Underline the correct answer.
1. The type of reference book that is published annually is the (atlas, dictionary, <u>almanac</u>, encyclopedia).
2. Maps of rivers, lakes, oceans, and continents are the principal contents of (a dictionary, <u>an atlas</u>, an encyclopedia, an almanac).
3. The type of catalog card one should check if he/she does not know an author's name or the title of a book is (a wild card, <u>a subject card</u>, a trump card, a fragment card).
4. The number in the upper left-hand corner of a catalog card is called the (press number, copyright number, page number, <u>call number</u>).
5. Nonfiction books are arranged on the shelves in (<u>numerical</u>, alphabetical) order.

Chapter 27, Lesson 1, Practice 2: Write True or False after each statement.
1. The first line of information on a title card and subject card is the same. **False**
2. Biographies are arranged on the shelves by authors' last names. **False**
3. The <u>Readers' Guide to Periodical Literature</u> is an index to biographies of contemporary Americans. **False**
4. Pronunciations and origins of words are contained in dictionary entries. **True**
5. Fiction books are arranged alphabetically by authors' last names. **True**

Chapter 27, Lesson 1, Practice 3: Select eight of your favorite fiction books and alphabetize them by the authors' last names.

Chapter 27, Lesson 1, Practice 4: Draw and label the three catalog cards for this book on a sheet of notebook paper:
850.6 *Lyrics and Lyres* by Jill Criswell, Bluffton Press, Erie, 1997, 262 p.

1. Author Card

850.6
Author   Criswell, Jill
Title   <u>Lyrics and Lyres</u>
            Bluffton Press, Erie
            (c 1997) 262p.

2. Title Card

850.6
Title   <u>Lyrics and Lyres</u>
Author   Criswell, Jill
            Bluffton Press, Erie
            (c 1997) 262p.

3. Subject Card

850.6
Topic   Poetry
Author   Criswell, Jill
Title   <u>Lyrics and Lyres</u>
            Bluffton Press, Erie
            (c 1997) 262p.

(End of lesson.)

CHAPTER 27   LESSON 2

New objectives: Skills (index), Practice activity, and an Activity.

SKILL TIME

TEACHING SCRIPT FOR INTRODUCING THE INDEX

When you are looking for information about a specific topic in a book, you can use the index to help you find the information quickly. The index is located in the back of the book. It has an alphabetical list of specific topics and tells on which page that information can be found. It is similar to the table of contents, but it is much more detailed. There are three main reasons to use an index:

1. When you want to find an answer quickly.
2. When you want to know the answer to a specific question.
3. When you want to know more about a subject.

There are **six features of an index** that you should know. Look at Reference 76 on page 49 in your Reference Section. Look at the sample index while I go over the six features of an index. Listen carefully. (*You might also want to put the six features on the board to give your students a visual while you teach.*)

1. An index is located at the back of the book.
2. An index lists information alphabetically.
3. When an index lists key ideas in a book, they are called topics.
4. When an index lists specific information under the topic, it is called a subtopic.
5. The numbers following topics and subtopics tell on which pages the information is found.
6. Punctuation of page numbers in subtopics:
   •When you see a **dash** between numbers, say **"through."** (*23–25 means page 23 through page 25*)
   •When you see a **comma** between numbers, say **"and."** (*23–25, 44 means page 23 through page 25 and page 44*)
   •When you see a **semicolon**, it means **stop**. Go no further for pages on this subtopic.

Reference 76: Sample Index		
L	**S**	**T**
Layovers, 36–39, 102	Sleep,	Time off, 57
	at rest areas, 104–107, 109; daytime, 40–41;	Travel schedules, 86
	nighttime, 42–43; at truck stops, 111–115	

I will walk you through the different parts of the sample index in your reference box. Look under the letter *S*. What is the index topic? (*Sleep.*) Notice that *Sleep* is the only word that is capitalized and the subtopics under it are indented. Each subtopic tells about the main topic *Sleep*.

Page numbers are listed after each subtopic. Look at the page number listed after the subtopic *at rest areas*. What do the dash between the 104 and 107 and the comma between the 107 and 109 mean? (*It means that information about rest areas for sleeping is found on pages 104 through 107 and on page 109.*)

CHAPTER 27 LESSON 2 CONTINUED

 PRACTICE TIME

Have students turn to page 79 in the Practice Section of their book and find Chapter 27, Lesson 2, Practice. Go over the directions to make sure they understand what to do. If students need a review, have them study the information and examples in the Reference Section of their books. Check and discuss the Practice after students have finished. (*Chapter 27, Lesson 2, Practice instructions are given below.*)

Chapter 27, Lesson 2, Practice: Using the index of a science *(or other subject)* book, write ten things that the index could help you answer quickly and the pages where the answers are found.

 **WRITING TIME**

Have students make an entry in their journals.

 ACTIVITY / ASSIGNMENT TIME

Take students on a field trip to visit their local library. Have them take pencils and notebooks to take notes and draw a diagram of the library. After they return home, have students design a library and put it on poster board. They are to label and illustrate as many areas in the library as possible. Finally, have students write a report about their study of the library. They will finish their library project during the next lesson.

(End of lesson.)

| CHAPTER 27   LESSON 3 |
| New objectives: Skills (table of contents), Practice sheet, and an Activity (concluded). |

SKILL TIME

<u>*TEACHING SCRIPT FOR INTRODUCING THE TABLE OF CONTENTS*</u>

Make your study time count. Learn to use the shortcuts already available in a book. When you are looking for general information in a book, you can use a table of contents to help you find the information quickly. A table of contents tells you four things:

     1. What the book is about.
     2. How many chapters a book has.
     3. The title of each chapter.
     4. The first page of each chapter.

Look at Reference 77 on page 49 in your Reference section. This is a sample table of contents, and you will use it while I am teaching and also during your test.

Reference 77: Sample Table of Contents		
CONTENTS		
CHAPTER **TITLE**		**PAGE**
1 *What It Takes to be a Trucker*....................................		1
2 *Life on the Road*		24
3 *A Few Days Off the Road*		46
4 *Scheduling Long-Distance Trips*		58
5 *Daily Recovery: Where to Stop*		90

Look under the main heading *Contents*. Read the first title "What It Takes to be a Trucker." This is the title of the first chapter. Read over the rest of the chapter titles. (*Read over the titles with your students.*) What is this book about? (*trucking*)

Look at the chapter numbers. The chapter numbers are the numbers on the left under the heading *Chapter*. How many chapters are in this book? (*five*)

Look at the page numbers. The page numbers are the numbers on the right under the heading *Page*. The page number listed to the right of each title tells the **first** page of the chapter. Look at Chapter 1, *What It Takes to be a Trucker*. On what page does Chapter 1 begin? (*page 1*) To find the last page of Chapter 1, go to the page where Chapter 2 begins and back up one page number. Chapter 2 begins on page 24. Back up one number, and you will be on page 23. So, Chapter 1 ends on page 23.

CHAPTER 27 LESSON 3 CONTINUED

 PRACTICE TIME

Have students turn to page 79 in the Practice Section of their books and find Chapter 27, Lesson 3, Practice. Go over the directions to make sure they understand what to do. If students need a review, have them study the information and examples in the Reference Section of their books. Check and discuss the Practice after students have finished. (*Chapter 27, Lesson 3, Practice instructions are given below.*)

Chapter 27, Lesson 3, Practice: Use the Table of Contents example in Reference 77 to answer the questions below.

  1. What is the title of the chapter that would tell you how a trucker recovers at the end of a long day on the road? (*Daily Recovery*)
  2. On what page does chapter 2 end? (*page 45*)
  3. In what chapter would you find information about the qualities needed to be a trucker? (*Chapter 1*)
  4. On what page does chapter 4 start? (*page 58*)

 ACTIVITY / ASSIGNMENT TIME

Have students finish their library illustrations and report. Students will read and discuss their library project and library reports with family members, friends, or relatives.

(End of lesson.)

CHAPTER 27   LESSON 4

New objectives: Test and an Activity (concluded).

 JINGLE TIME

Have students turn to the Jingle Section of their books. The teacher will lead the students in reciting the previously-taught jingles.

 STUDY TIME

Have students study any of the skills in the Reference Section and the Practice Section that they need to review.

 TEST TIME

Have students turn to pages 110 and 111 in the Test Section of their books and find Chapter 27A and 27B Tests. Go over the directions to make sure they understand what to do. Remind them to pay attention and think about what they are doing. (*Chapter 27A and 27B Test keys are on the next two pages.*)

 CHECK TIME

After students have finished, check and discuss the test sentences they created. Make sure they understand why their test questions and answers are right or wrong. (*For total points, count each required answer as a point.*)

 ACTIVITY / ASSIGNMENT TIME

In the last chapter, students made a traveling picture album of their country.

For this final portion of the project, have students write an essay about everything they learned in the research about their country. Have them outline the major areas and list the most important details they want to cover. This will help narrow the topic enough to cover the major points. Students will read and discuss their essays with family members, friends, or relatives.

(End of lesson.)

Chapter 27A Test
(Student Page 110)

Exercise 1: Classify each sentence.

               SN   V-t   A   DO   P   A   OP   P   A   OP

1. <u>**SN V-t**</u>   Fred / opened the door (to the cellar) (with a crowbar). **D**
   <u>**DO P2**</u>

               PNA   SN   LV A   PrN   P A   OP

2. <u>**SN LV**</u>   Dorothy's costume / was the highlight (of the evening). **D**
   <u>**PrN P4**</u>

Exercise 2: Underline each subject and fill in each column according to the title.

	List each Verb	Write PrN, PA, or None	Write L or A
1. <u>Jerky</u> is very chewy.	is	PA	L
2. The <u>siren</u> startled the pedestrians.	startled	None	A
3. <u>Waycross</u> is a small town.	is	PrN	L
4. Motel <u>rooms</u> are expensive.	are	PA	L

Exercise 3: Use the Table of Contents example in Reference 77 to answer the following questions.
1. Look over the chapter titles. What is this book about? **Trucking**
2. How many chapters are in this book? **5**
3. What is the last page of Chapter 1? **Page 23**
4. You are considering becoming a trucker, just like your dad. What two chapters might give you the best insight into what you might need to know to make a career choice? **Chapter 1 (What It Takes to Be a Trucker) and Chapter 2 (Life on the Road)**
5. Your dad will be home next week. You want to know what life will be like for him during his break. What chapter would you look in for insights? **Chapter 3 (A Few Days Off the Road)**
6. Your dad wants to be sure he is in a safe place when he parks his truck at night. In which chapter would you look for sound advice? **Chapter 5 (Daily Recovery: Where to Stop)**
   On which page does that chapter begin? **Page 90**
7. Which chapter would you look at to see how companies schedule long-distance trips for their drivers? **Chapter 4 (Scheduling Long-Distance Trips)**
8. Your dad wants to talk to his boss about getting next week off for your birthday. This would involve delaying his trip to Ohio. Which chapter would have information about how he would do this? **Chapter 4 (Scheduling Long-Distance Trips)**
9. A roadside rest near Phoenix is the most logical place for your dad to stop on his trip to California. He needs to know whether or not it is advisable to spend the night there. On what page would you begin looking? **Page 90**
10. When your dad gets a week off next month, you'd like to do a few things with him. Which chapter might offer you some suggestions? **Chapter 3 (A Few Days Off the Road)**
11. Bonus: 1. How many pages are in Chapter 3? **11**

Exercise 4: Answer the following questions about an index on another sheet of paper.
1. What are three main reasons to use an index?
   (1.) **When you want to find an answer quickly.**
   (2.) **When you want to know the answer to a specific question.**
   (3.) **When you want to know more about a subject.**

2. Where is an index located? (**At the back of the book**.)
3. How does an index list information? (**alphabetically**)
4. When an index lists key ideas in a book, what are the key ideas called? (**topics**)
5. When an index lists specific information under the topic, what is it called? (**a subtopic**)
6. What do the numbers following topics and subtopics tell? (**on what pages the information is found**)

Chapter 27B Test
(Student Page 111)

Exercise 5: Write the correct answers for numbers 1-6. Underline the correct answer for numbers 7-8.

1. The type of reference one would check for articles on the recent presidential election is what? (**The Readers' Guide to Periodical Literature**)
2. If you don't have the title of a book or an author's name to check, what type of catalog card would you check? (**subject card**)
3. To plan a safari, one would do well to research the terrain of the country where you're going. What type of reference would provide maps of various countries and continents? (**Atlas**)
4. To find the spellings of homonyms, one would go to what type of reference? (**dictionary**)
5. The type of books arranged numerically on the shelves is what? (**nonfiction**)
6. Published annually, this reference provides updates on facts and figures about such things as moon phases, tides, populations, and so on. (**Almanac**)
7. Biographies are arranged on the shelves by (**the name of the author, <u>the person written about</u>**).
8. Fiction books are arranged on the shelves in (**numerical order, <u>alphabetical order</u>**).

Exercise 6: Put the fiction books below in the correct order to go on the shelves. Write numbers 1-7 in the blanks to show the correct order. *(Alphabetize fiction books by authors' last names.)*

1. *The Scarlet Letter* by Nathaniel Hawthorne   2
2. *A Farewell to Arms* by Ernest Hemingway   3
3. *Now in November* by Josephine Johnson   4
4. *The Pathfinder* by James Fenimore Cooper   1
5. *Moby Dick* by Herman Melville   6
6. *The Grapes of Wrath* by John Steinbeck   7
7. *Ulysses* by James Joyce   5

Exercise 7: Write True or False for each statement.
1. Biographies are arranged on the shelf by the author's last name. **False**
2. The call number for books is located in the upper right-hand corner of a catalog card. **False**
3. Nonfiction books are arranged on the shelves numerically. **True**
4. An almanac is a reference containing maps. **False**
5. The title of a book is located on the top line of subject cards and title cards in the card catalog. **False**
6. The <u>Reader's Guide to Periodical Literature</u> is an index to magazine articles. **True**
7. Books of fiction are arranged alphabetically by the author's last name. **True**
8. Encyclopedias are references that provide brief information about people and places and events of worldwide interest. **True**

Exercise 8: Draw and label the three catalog cards for this book on a sheet of notebook paper: 843.7 *Poetry's Well-Traveled Roads* by Dan Lindsay, Phoenix Press, Sacramento, 2001, 358 p. *(Use the catalog card examples in Reference 75.)*

1. Author Card

813.14
Author   **Bryant, Jerome**
Title   <u>**In Search of Stories**</u>
      Bayside Press, Duluth
      (c 1999) 246p.

2. Title Card

813.14
Title   <u>**In Search of Stories**</u>
Author   **Bryant, Jerome**
      Bayside Press, Duluth
      (c 1999) 246p.

3. Subject Card

813.14
Topic   **Things to Write About**
Author   **Bryant, Jerome**
Title   <u>**In Search of Stories**</u>
      Bayside Press, Duluth
      (c 1999) 246p.

Exercise 9: In your journal, write a paragraph summarizing what you have learned this week.

CHAPTER 27 LESSON 4 CONTINUED

TEACHER INSTRUCTIONS

Use the Question and Answer Flows below for the sentences on Chapter 27A Tests.

Question and Answer Flow for Sentence 1: Fred opened the door to the cellar with a crowbar.

1. Who opened the door to the cellar with a crowbar?
   Fred - SN
2. What is being said about Fred? Fred opened - V
3. Fred opened what? door - verify the noun
4. Does door mean the same thing as Fred? No.
5. Door - DO
6. Opened - V-t
7. The - A
8. To - P
9. To what? cellar - OP
10. The - A
11. With - P

12. With what? crowbar - OP
13. A - A
14. SN V-t DO P2 Check
15. Verb-transitive - Check again.
16. (To the cellar) - Prepositional phrase
17. (With a crowbar) - Prepositional phrase
18. Period, statement, declarative sentence
19. Go back to the verb - divide the complete subject from the complete predicate.
20. Is there an adverb exception? No.
21. Is this sentence in a natural or inverted order?
    Natural - no change.

Classified Sentence:

$$\frac{\text{SN V-t}}{\text{DO P2}}$$

SN   V-t   A DO P A OP   P   A OP
Fred / opened the door (to the cellar) (with a crowbar). **D**

Question and Answer Flow for Sentence 2: Dorothy's costume was the highlight of the evening.

1. What was the highlight of the evening? costume - SN
2. What is being said about costume? costume was - V
3. Costume was what? highlight - verify the noun
4. Does highlight mean the same thing as costume? Yes.
5. Highlight - PrN
6. Was - LV
7. The - A
8. Of - P
9. Of what? evening - OP
10. The - A

11. Whose costume? Dorothy's - PNA
12. SN LV PrN P4 Check
13. Linking verb - Check again.
14. (Of the evening) - Prepositional phrase
15. Period, statement, declarative sentence
16. Go back to the verb - divide the complete subject from the complete predicate.
17. Is there an adverb exception? No.
18. Is this sentence in a natural or inverted order?
    Natural - no change.

Classified Sentence:

$$\frac{\text{SN LV}}{\text{PrN P4}}$$

PNA   SN   LV A   PrN   P A OP
Dorothy's costume / was the highlight (of the evening). **D**

CHAPTER 27   LESSON 5

New objectives: Writing Assignments #43 and #44, Bonus Option continued.

 WRITING TIME

TEACHING SCRIPT FOR WRITING ASSIGNMENTS

Today, you will be given two writing assignments. With each, you will have a choice of topics. Once you have drafted your writings, you will then revise and edit both assignments. The second assignment will require a title that will accurately reflect the content of your paragraph/essay. Rather than choose the type of writing you used in a previous assignment, select a different one for this second writing assignment.

Writing Assignment Box #1

Writing Assignment #43: Your choice

Writing choices: (1) **Friendly Letter**   (2) **Business Letter**   (3) **Thank You Note**

Writing Assignment Box #2

Writing Assignment #44: Your choice (First or Third Person)

Writing choices: (1) **Expository**   (2) **Persuasive**   (3) **Narrative**   (4) **Descriptive**

Bonus Option: Research churches from at least six countries, using the Internet, travel agents, travel magazines, and the library. From each country, choose a church that impresses you the most. Then, write an article, summarizing the interesting things that you discovered about each church. Don't forget to draw or locate a picture of each church to illustrate your article. You may type the articles on the computer or write them in ink. Interview preachers or church members of several local churches and write an article about their unique history. Include pictures to personalize your research. Finally, put all your information in a booklet with the title, *Churches Around the World*. Illustrate the cover of your booklet. Share the booklet with friends, family, and members of the community. (*This project will take several weeks to complete; therefore, this assignment will be repeated for the next several lessons.*)

Read, check, and discuss Writing Assignments #43 and #44 after students have finished their final papers. Use the editing checklist as you check and discuss students' papers. Make sure students are using the editing checklist correctly.

(End of lesson.)

CHAPTER 28 LESSON 1

New objectives: Skills (outlining) and a Practice sheet.

 SKILL TIME

TEACHING SCRIPT FOR INTRODUCING THE OUTLINE

In order to develop good report writing techniques, you must learn to make and use an outline effectively. Making an outline will give you a visual map of your report. Today, you will learn the vocabulary of outlines and how outlines are organized. There are two reasons to use an outline when you plan to write. First, outlining helps to put ideas and information in the correct order for writing. Second, outlining helps you remember information more easily.

There are two kinds of outlines: the **topic outline** and the **sentence outline**. In a topic outline, information is written in single words or phrases. In a *sentence* outline, information is written in complete sentences. Outlines have very rigid rules about how they are organized and formatted. Even though the *topic* outline and the sentence outline are formatted the same, you cannot mix the two styles by using both phrases and complete sentences in the same outline.

Outlines have a vocabulary and set of rules that are unique to outlining. All outlines follow the same basic plan. Since the *topic* outline is the easiest and most commonly used outline, you will learn about outline format by studying the topic outline. Look at References78A and 78B on pages 49 and 50 as we study the information about outlines. (*References 78A and 78B are reproduced below and on the next page. Read and discuss the information with your students.*)

Reference 78 A: Outline Information

Outline Guide	Sample Outline
Title	Seasonal Tasks Outdoors
I. Introduction	I. Introduction
II. Main Topic (First main point)	II. Spring tasks
A. Subtopic (Supports first main point)	A. Rake fallen leaves
1. Details (Supports subtopic)	1. Mulch shrubs
2. Details (Supports subtopic)	2. Create compost pile
B. Subtopic (Supports first main point)	B. Weed yard
C. Subtopic (Supports first main point)	C. Plant garden
III. Main Topic (Second main point)	III. Summer tasks
A. Subtopic (Supports second main point)	A. Tend garden crops
B. Subtopic (Supports second main point)	B. Mow grass
IV. Main Topic (Third main point)	IV. Autumn tasks
A. Subtopic (Supports third main point)	A. Harvest produce
B. Subtopic (Supports third main point)	B. Plant spring bulbs
V. Conclusion	V. Conclusion

CHAPTER 28 LESSON 1 CONTINUED

Reference 78 B: Outline Information

First, an outline has a **TITLE**. *(Direct students' attention to the title at the top of the Outline Guide above.)*
- At first, your outline title should be the same or similar to your narrowed topic. This will help you stay focused on the main idea of your report. If you decide to change the title for your final paper, you must remember to change your outline title.

- Capitalizing rules for titles are the same for outlines as for final papers: Capitalize the first word, the last word, and all the important words in between them. Conjunctions, articles, and prepositions with fewer than five letters are not usually capitalized unless they are the first or last word. Titles for reports are not underlined or placed in quotation marks unless the title is a quotation.

Second, an outline has Roman numerals denoting MAIN TOPICS. *(Explain Roman numerals if necessary— I, II, III, IV—and direct students' attention to the main topics beside each Roman numeral.)*
- There must always be two or more Roman numerals. There can never be just one. For each Roman numeral, there is a paragraph. *(Three Roman numerals - three paragraphs.)*

- The information following a Roman numeral is called the main topic and gives the main idea, or main point, of each paragraph. It will be used to form the topic sentence of the paragraph.

- Every first word in a main topic is always capitalized.

- The periods after the Roman numerals must be lined up under each other.

Third, an outline has capital letters denoting SUBTOPICS. *(Direct students' attention to the subtopics beside each capital letter.)*
- There must always be two or more capital letters. If you only have one, do not put it in the outline. Each capital letter is indented under the first word of the main topic.

- The information beside a capital letter is called the subtopic and gives details that support the main topic, or main point of the paragraph.

- Every first word in a subtopic is always capitalized.

- The periods after the capital letters must be lined up under each other.

Fourth, an outline sometimes has Arabic numerals denoting DETAILS. *(Explain Arabic numerals if necessary—1, 2, 3—and direct students' attention to the details beside each Arabic numeral.)*
- There must always be two or more Arabic numerals. If you only have one, do not put it on the outline. Each Arabic numeral is indented under the first word of the subtopic.

- The information beside an Arabic numeral is called a detail and tells specific information about the subtopic of the paragraph.

- Every first word in a detail is always capitalized.

- The periods after the Arabic numerals must be lined up under each other.

Now, I will summarize the basic rules you have just learned. See if you can find these rules in your reference box as I summarize the *rules for outlining*. **(1)** Put periods after Roman numerals, capital letters, Arabic numerals, and any word that would require a period in a sentence. **(2)** Capitalize the first word of each line and any word that would be capitalized in a sentence. **(3)** You cannot have a Roman numeral I. without a Roman numeral II., an A. without a B., or a 1. without a 2. Remember, you can always utilize the information in this Reference box if you forget how to structure an outline.

CHAPTER 28 LESSON 1 CONTINUED

TEACHER INSTRUCTIONS

Compare the <u>Outline Guide</u> with the <u>Sample Outline</u> in Reference 78A with your students. Show students how the titles (topics, subtopics, and details) in the Outline Guide explain how to organize the Sample Outline.

Read and discuss the parallel form for outlines in Reference 79. (*This information is reproduced below.*) Then, go over the discussion points for the parallel form that are given to you under the reference box. Make sure your students understand how to select words that will keep their outline in parallel form because they will be tested on their ability to add or change words to make their outline parallel.

Reference 79: Parallel Form for Outlines

Parallel Form

1. All the main topics in an outline should be in parallel form. This means that all the main topics should begin in the same way: all nouns, all verbs, all noun phrases, all verb phrases, all prepositional phrases, etc. If necessary, change or rearrange the words of your outline so they are parallel.

    (I. Spring tasks II. Summer tasks III. Autumn tasks) or **(I. A farmer's spring tasks II. A farmer's summer tasks III. A farmer's autumn tasks)**

2. All the subtopics under Roman numeral II must be in the same form. The subtopics under Roman numeral III must be in the same form, but Roman numeral II subtopics do not have to be in the same form as Roman numeral III subtopics, etc.

    (A. **Rake** fallen leaves B. **Weed** yard C. **Plant** garden) (A. **Tend** garden crops B. **Mow** grass)

3. All the details under Subtopic A must be in the same form. The details under Subtopic B must be in the same form, but Subtopic A details do not have to be in the same form as Subtopic B details.

    (1. **Mulch** shrubs 2. **Create** compost pile)

Discussion Points for Parallel Forms

1. Parallel form means using the same type of words to start each division of your outline. You can start each section with all nouns, all verbs, all prepositions, adjectives in front of nouns, etc.

2. Discuss how the first examples in number 1 are written (adjectives in front of nouns).

3. Discuss how the second examples in number 1 are written (phrases beginning with *my.*)

4. Discuss how the examples in number 2 begin with verbs.

5. Discuss how the details under Subtopic A also begin with verbs.

6. Stress that it doesn't matter how each section begins, it is just important to make sure each section has the same parallel form (begins the same way). If it is a new section, it can have a different parallel form.

CHAPTER 28 LESSON 1 CONTINUED

 PRACTICE TIME

Have students turn to page 80 in the Practice Section of their book and find Chapter 28, Lesson 1, Practice. Go over the directions to make sure they understand what to do. Check and discuss the Practice after students have finished. (*Chapter 28, Lesson 1, Practice instructions are given below.*)

Chapter 28, Lesson 1, Practice: Give an oral report on parallel forms for outlines. Make an outline as a visual aid to help in your presentation. Include different parallel forms in your outline. You may use the discussion points on parallel forms that are listed below. (*You may also use Reference 79 as your guide.*)

1. Explain that parallel form means using the same type of words to start each division of your outline.
2. Discuss how you can start each section with all nouns, all verbs, all prepositions, adjectives in front of nouns, etc.
3. Discuss how you used parallel form in each section of your outline.
4. Each new section can have a different parallel form. Explain that it doesn't matter how each section begins, it is just important to make sure each section has the same parallel form.

(End of lesson.)

CHAPTER 28   LESSON 2

New objectives: Practice sheet.

 PRACTICE TIME

Have students turn to page 80 in the Practice Section of their book and find Chapter 28, Lesson 2, Practice. Go over the directions to make sure they understand what to do. Check and discuss the Practice after students have finished. (*Chapter 28, Lesson 2, Practice instructions are given below.*)

Chapter 28, Lesson 2, Practice: Copy the notes below into a two-point outline. Change wording to put notes into correct parallel form.

Notes	Outline
types of camping-out	**Types of Camping-Out**
in a tent	I. In a tent
magic of night sounds	A. Magical night sounds
starry nights	B. Starry nights
motel	II. At a motel
voices in adjacent rooms	A. Unfamiliar voices in adjacent rooms
ceiling lights	B. Ceiling lights

 WRITING TIME

Have students make an entry in their journals.

(End of lesson.)

CHAPTER 28   LESSON 3

New objectives: Practice sheet.

 PRACTICE TIME

Have students turn to page 81 in the Practice Section of their book and find Chapter 28, Lesson 3, Practice. Go over the directions to make sure they understand what to do. If students need a review, have them study the information and examples in the Reference Section of their books. Check and discuss the Practice after students have finished. (*Chapter 28, Lesson 3, Practice instructions are given below.*)

Chapter 28, Lesson 3, Practice: Copy the notes below into a three-point outline. Change wording to put notes into correct parallel form.

Notes	Outline
kinds of gardens	**Kinds of Gardens**
vegetable gardens	I. Vegetable gardens
that grow above ground	A. Above ground
underground	B. Below ground
flowers	II. Flower gardens
perennial varieties	A. Perennials
annuals	B. Annuals
herbs	III. Herb gardens
from seeds	A. From seeds
root sprouts	B. From sprouts

 STUDY TIME

Have students study any of the skills in the Reference Section or the Practice Section that they need to review.

(End of lesson.)

CHAPTER 28   LESSON 4

New objectives: Test.

JINGLE TIME

Have students turn to the Jingle Section of their books. The teacher will lead the students in reciting the previously-taught jingles.

STUDY TIME

Have students study any of the skills in the Reference Section or the Practice Section that they need to review.

TEST TIME

Have students turn to page 112 in the Test Section of their books and find the Chapter 28 Test. Go over the directions to make sure they understand what to do. Remind them to pay attention and think about what they are doing. (*Chapter 28 Test key is on the next page.*)

CHECK TIME

After students have finished, check and discuss the test sentences they created. Make sure they understand why their test questions and answers are right or wrong. (*For total points, count each required answer as a point.*)

(End of lesson.)

Chapter 28 Test
(Student Page 112)

Exercise 1: Classify each sentence.

           Adj   SN   HV   Adv   V   P   COP C COP

1. **SN V**   Most fans / were enthusiastically cheering (for Travis and me). **D**
   P1

           Adj   Adj   SN   V-t Adj   DO   P A   Adj   OP

2. **SN V-t**   Four French tourists / gave stern lectures (to the inconsiderate teens). **D**
   DO P2

          HV SP V-t IO Adj DO   P   OP   Adv

3. **SN V-t**   Will you / serve us fried okra (for lunch) tomorrow? **Int**
   IO DO P3

Exercise 2: Copy the notes below into a three-point outline. Change wording to put notes into correct parallel form.

Notes	Outline
types of poems	**Types of Poems**
lyrical poems	**I. Lyrical**
highly musical	**A. Highly musical**
sensory	**B. Very sensory**
narratives	**II. Narrative**
built on action	**A. Typically built on action**
dialogue, usually	**B. Usually contains dialogue**
dramatic poems	**III. Dramatic**
to be read aloud	**A. To be read aloud**
performed on stage	**B. To be performed on stage**

Exercise 3: On a sheet of paper, write all the jingles that you can recall from memory. There is a total of 19 jingles. (*Check students' jingles from the Jingle Section in their books.*)

Exercise 4: In your journal, write a paragraph summarizing what you have learned this week.

CHAPTER 28 LESSON 4 CONTINUED

TEACHER INSTRUCTIONS

Use the Question and Answer Flows below for the sentences on Chapter 28 Tests.

Question and Answer Flow for Sentence 1: Most fans were enthusiastically cheering for Travis and me.

1. Who were enthusiastically cheering for Travis and me? fans - SN
2. What is being said about fans? fans were cheering - V
3. Were - HV
4. Were cheering how? enthusiastically - Adv
5. For - P
6. For whom? Travis and me - COP, COP
7. And - C
8. How many fans? most - Adj

9. SN V P1 Check
10. (For Travis and me) - Prepositional phrase
11. Period, statement, declarative sentence
12. Go back to the verb divide the complete subject from the complete predicate.
13. Is there an adverb exception? No.
14. Is this sentence in a natural or inverted order? Natural - no change.

Classified Sentence:

                       Adj   SN   HV   Adv   V   P COP C COP

       SN V   Most fans **/** were enthusiastically cheering (for Travis and me). **D**

         P1

Question and Answer Flow for Sentence 2: Four French tourists gave stern lectures to the inconsiderate teens.

1. Who gave stern lectures to the inconsiderate teens? tourists - SN
2. What is being said about tourists? tourists gave - V
3. Tourists gave what? lectures - verify the noun
4. Does lectures mean the same thing as tourists? No.
5. Lectures - DO
6. Gave - V-t
7. What kind of lectures? stern - Adj
8. To - P
9. To whom? teens - OP
10. What kind of teens? inconsiderate - Adj
11. The - A

12. Which tourists? French - Adj
13. How many tourists? four - Adj
14. SN V-t DO P2 Check
15. Verb-transitive - Check again.
16. (To the inconsiderate teens) - Prepositional phrase
17. Period, statement, declarative sentence
18. Go back to the verb - divide the complete subject from the complete predicate.
19. Is there an adverb exception? No.
20. Is this sentence in a natural or inverted order? Natural - no change.

Classified Sentence:

                       Adj   Adj   SN   V-t   Adj   DO   P A   Adj   OP

       SN V-t   Four French tourists **/** gave stern lectures (to the inconsiderate teens). **D**

        DO P2

Question and Answer Flow for Sentence 3: Will you serve us fried okra for lunch tomorrow?

1. Who will serve us fried okra for lunch tomorrow? you - SP
2. What is being said about you? you will serve - V
3. Will - HV
4. You will serve what? okra - verify the noun
5. Does okra mean the same thing as you? No.
6. Okra - DO
7. Serve - V-t
8. You will serve okra to whom? us - IO
9. What kind of okra? fried - Adj
10. For - P
11. For what? lunch - OP

12. Will serve when? tomorrow - Adv
13. SN V-t IO DO P3 Check
14. Verb-transitive - Check again.
15. (For lunch) - Prepositional phrase
16. Question mark, question, interrogative sentence
17. Go back to the verb - divide the complete subject from the complete predicate.
18. Is there an adverb exception? No.
19. Is this sentence in a natural or inverted order? Inverted - underline the subject parts once and the predicate parts twice.

Classified Sentence:

                       HV   SP   V-t IO Adj DO   P OP   Adv

       SN V-t   Will you **/** serve us fried okra (for lunch) tomorrow? **Int**

        IO DO P3

CHAPTER 28   LESSON 5

New objectives: Writing Assignments #45 and #46, Bonus Option continued.

 WRITING TIME

TEACHING SCRIPT FOR WRITING ASSIGNMENTS

Today, you will be given two writing assignments. With each, you will have a choice of topics. Once you have drafted your writings, you will then revise and edit both assignments. The second assignment will require a title that will accurately reflect the content of your paragraph/essay.

Writing Assignment Box #1

Writing Assignment #45: Your choice

Writing choices: (1) **Friendly Letter**   (2) **Business Letter**   (3) **Thank You Note**

Rather than choose the type of writing you used in your last assignment, select a different one for this second writing assignment.

Writing Assignment Box #2

Writing Assignment #46: Your choice (First or Third Person)

Writing choices: (1) **Expository**   (2) **Persuasive**   (3) **Narrative**   (4) **Descriptive**

Bonus Option: Research churches from at least six countries, using the Internet, travel agents, travel magazines, and the library. From each country, choose a church that impresses you the most. Then, write an article, summarizing the interesting things that you discovered about each church. Don't forget to draw or locate a picture of each church to illustrate your article. You may type the articles on the computer or write them in ink. Interview preachers or church members of several local churches and write an article about their unique history. Include pictures to personalize your research. Finally, put all your information in a booklet with the title, *Churches Around the World*. Illustrate the cover of your booklet. Share the booklet with friends, family, and members of the community. (*This project will take several weeks to complete; therefore, this assignment will be repeated for the next several lessons.*)

Read, check, and discuss Writing Assignments #45 and #46 after students have finished their final papers. Use the editing checklist as you check and discuss students' papers. Make sure students are using the editing checklist correctly.

(End of lesson.)

CHAPTER 29 LESSON 1

New objectives: Writing (A Fascinating Person "Me Booklet").

 WRITING TIME

I. A Fascinating Person – Me

This activity produces a booklet about you. The instructions on how to make this booklet are given below. You will also be given directions on how to add artwork for each topic. Remember, this is a unique opportunity to express who you are at this stage of your life. This booklet would also make a wonderful gift to your parents, or you may save it and read it at different times as you grow older. You will certainly enjoy remembering what you were like as a fifth grader.

1. Have two sheets of construction paper. Use one sheet for the title page of your booklet and one sheet for the back cover.

2. Make a title page and illustrate it (or put a picture of yourself on it).

3. Make a separate page for each topic. Make each page special by doing some artwork for each topic. (Example: Draw a big football and put "Goals for My Life" inside the football, and write your paragraph inside the football. You might want to add goal posts at the top and bottom of the page. Draw weights for "My Strengths," etc. Use creativity to match each topic with different kinds of artwork.)

4. Do neat work.

5. Put the back cover on and staple your booklet on the left-hand side when you are finished. You can be proud of this booklet. No one else has one quite like it. It is an original, just like you!

(Title Page) A Booklet About a Fascinating Person ME! Written by (put your name here) Illustrated by (put your name here)	(Page 1) Things I Like to Do: with a friend... with my family... by myself... that cost money... that are different... that are special...

(End of lesson.)

CHAPTER 29   LESSON 2

New objectives: Writing ("A Fascinating Person Me Booklet" continued).

 WRITING TIME

I. A Fascinating Person – Me Booklet   Continued

(Page 2) Goals for My Life	(Page 3) Goals for the Rest of This School Year

(Page 4) My Strengths	(Page 5) My Weaknesses

(Page 6) My Special Feelings I am happy when... I am angry when... I hope that... I finally... I am good at... I admire... I want to be like... I get excited when... I need... I feel safe when... I am thankful for... I am afraid of... I feel sorry for... I am proud of... I am really good at...	(Page 7) My Family Other Special People

(End of lesson.)

CHAPTER 29   LESSON 3

New objectives: Writing (autobiographies).

 WRITING TIME

VIII. Autobiography

An autobiography is an account of a writer's life. Write an autobiography of your life. Use the outline below to help you write each paragraph.

Title: My Autobiography   Introductory sentence: My name is ___ ____ , and I am ____ years old.

I. Family
   A. Birth
   B. Parents
   C. Brothers and sisters
   D. Grandparents

II. Family life
   A. Chores and responsibilities
   B. How we celebrate special holidays
   C. Family vacations
   D. Special things about my family

III. School days
   A. Friends
   B. Teachers
   C. Best/worst subjects
   D. Special things about school

IV. Special interests
   A. Hobbies
   B. My achievements
   C. My likes and dislikes
   D. Other

(End of lesson.)

CHAPTER 29   LESSON 4

New objectives: Writing ("Me Booklets" and autobiographies concluded).

 CHECK TIME

Read, discuss, and enjoy students' "Me Booklets" and autobiographies.

(End of lesson.)

CHAPTER 29   LESSON 5

New objectives: Bonus Option concluded.

 CHECK TIME

If the project "Churches Around the World" is finished, share it with friends, family, and members of the community. If it is not finished, make it a summer project.

(End of lesson.)

Level 5
Jingles & Introductory Sentences

Track	Description
1	Introduction
2	Noun Jingle
3	Verb Jingle
4	Sentence Jingle
5	Adverb Jingle
6	Adjective Jingle
7	Article Adjective Jingle
8	The Preposition Jingle
9	Object of the Preposition Jingle
10	Preposition Flow
11	Pronoun Jingle
12	Subject Pronoun Jingle
13	Possessive Pronoun Jingle
14	Object Pronoun Jingle
15	The 23 Helping Verbs of the Mean, Lean Verb Machine
16	The 8 Parts of Speech
17	The Direct Object Jingle
18	The Indirect Object Jingle
19	The Predicate Noun Jingle
20	Another Predicate Noun Jingle
21	Chapter 2, Lesson 2 Introductory Sentences
22	Chapter 2, Lesson 3 Introductory Sentences
23	Chapter 2, Lesson 5 Introductory Sentences
24	Chapter 3, Lesson 2 Introductory Sentences
25	Chapter 4, Lesson 1 Introductory Sentences
26	Chapter 5, Lesson 1 Introductory Sentences
27	Chapter 5, Lesson 2 Introductory Sentences
28	Chapter 6, Lesson 2 Introductory Sentences
29	Chapter 6, Lesson 3 Introductory Sentences
30	Chapter 7, Lesson 1 Introductory Sentences
31	Chapter 8, Lesson 1 Introductory Sentences
32	Chapter 9, Lesson 1 Introductory Sentences
33	Chapter 12, Lesson 1 Introductory Sentences
34	Chapter 16, Lesson 1 Introductory Sentences
35	Chapter 19, Lesson 1 Introductory Sentences
36	Chapter 22, Lesson 1 Introductory Sentences

Shurley Instructional Materials, Inc.
366 SIM Drive
Cabot, AR 72023